MOGUL INDIA
1653–1708
OR
STORIA DO MOGOR

Volume 3

Translated with Introduction and Notes
WILLIAM IRVINE

NICCOLAO MANUCCI

ATLANTIC
PUBLISHERS & DISTRIBUTORS (P) LTD

ATLANTIC
PUBLISHERS & DISTRIBUTORS (P) LTD

7/22, Ansari Road, Darya Ganj, New Delhi
Tel.: +91-11-4077 5252, 2327 3880
E-mail: orders@atlanticbooks.com
Web: www.atlanticbooks.com

This edition published in 2025 by Atlantic Publishers & Distributors (P) Ltd.
Reprint 2022, 2025

Printed & bound in India by Atlantic Print Services

CONTENTS

PART III. (*Continued*)

PART IV

ILLUSTRATIONS TO VOL. III.

HISTORY OF THE MOGUL

THIRD PART—Continued

NOTICE [90].[1]

I have thought it desirable, before beginning what I have to say on the Hindu religion, to give the reader a short notice on that subject, for he may be surprised that, so many books having appeared about it already, I should design to add my remarks. To this I reply that what ought to have made me refrain is the very thing that induces me to take up my pen. For, although I knew that several persons had written on this matter, I have been told that their accounts are defective; and I believe this short account could not be otherwise than agreeable to the public. In those hitherto laid before it, some have wished to suggest that these poor idolaters had received some slight knowledge of Christian mysteries, upon which they had built their show of a religion. Others have concerned themselves with nothing beyond some of the principal customs and ceremonies.

My account has nothing in common with all that. I have set myself to know the foundations of their belief, of their politics and their government, on which I have drawn up the memoirs here presented. It will be seen that their religion is nothing but a confused mixture of absurdities and coarse imaginings, unworthy even of the rational man; much less has it the least trace of Divinity as its author. I cannot refrain from admiring the goodness of our Creator in having illuminated us with the light of His Gospel; for, from the example of these poor idolaters, it is possible to note the unruliness of the human mind when abandoned to its own devices.

As to their government, it will have been seen that there could be nothing more tyrannical, and that there are slaves in Turkey whose condition is preferable to that of the free people of this country. I have in addition gathered together their chief

1. Mr. R. W. Frazer, late of the Madras Civil Service, has done me the great service of reading through this, section, to which he has added some most valuable notes.

ceremonies and customs, as much regarding marriage as their disposal of the dead, their way of eating, *et cetera*. I am able to make the declaration that in all I say there is nothing but the truest things, to which absolute faith can be accorded, and of which I have myself been a witness during many years, and am so still.

However strange and extraordinary what I advance may appear to our Europe, it is none the less veritable. I will not farther here on these things, beyond wishing that those who read these words may make the same reflections in reading as I have made in beholding them. Let us all unite in giving God the glory that He has called us from the kingdom of darkness into that of light. This ought to impose on us eternal gratitude, and make us pray that He will give light to so many miserable beings groaning in the [91] darkness of error and idolatry—a supplication to which, I doubt not, every Christain will assent with all his strength [92].[1]

1. I have looked at P. Baldaeus's account of Hinduism (see vol. iii. of A. and J. Churchill's 'A Collection of Voyages and Travels . . .,' folio, 1744-46. Baldaeus is earlier than Manucci, his work having been first published in 1672, while our author wrote in 1699. Both accounts are of the same popular, superficial character; but the details differ, and I think Manucci did not copy from his predecessor. B. Ziegenbalg, of Tranquebar, who wrote later, in 1713, is more scientific in his 'Genealogie der Malabarischen Götter.' Of Ziegenbalg's book there is a german edition and an English translation, both published at Madras in 1867; the pictures of the gods which he sent to Europe are in the Franckeschen Museum at Halle.

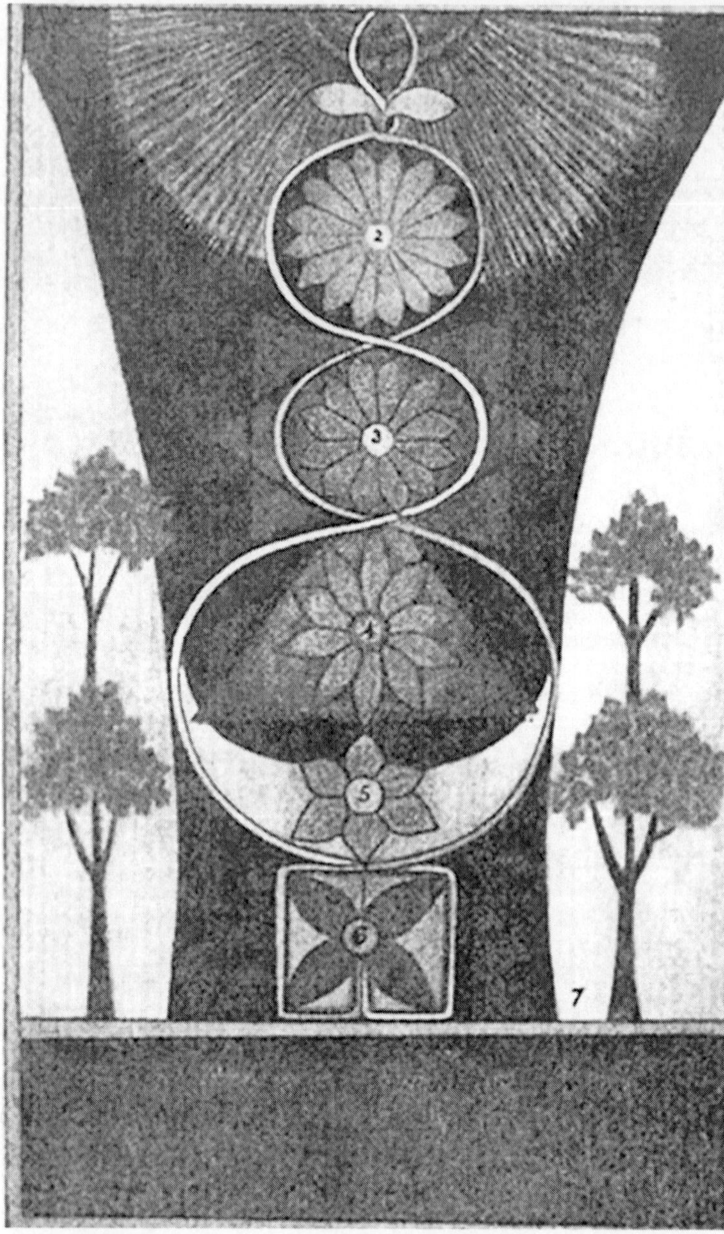
2
3
5
7

SHORT ACCOUNT OF WHAT THE HINDUS BELIEVE ABOUT GOD, AND THEIR IDEAS ABOUT HIS ESSENCE.

I undertake to write this essay for the satisfaction of the inquiring reader, having no doubt of his contentment in reading about the errors or stupidities of these poor people, feeling sure that it will of itself inspire him with compassion for them to see they hold ideas so misshapen and so contrary to reason itself.

CHAPTER I

WHAT THE HINDUS SAY AND BELIEVE ABOUT GOD AND HIS ESSENCE

There is not an individual among them who denies that there is a God; still, they have so many different views in what they say of God that they are incompetent to find the truth. Some say that water is God, and they style this 'the infallible science'; others, that God is a spiritual substance widely diffused. Then shortly afterwards, with hardly any discussion, they will tell you that it is the air which is God, and there is none other. But as they have no fixity in their belief, they will next tell you briefly, after setting forth the above statements as infallible, that the sun is God; that it has created, and still creates—that it preserves and destroys all things in this world.

It is in this last belief that the greater number of the heathen, of India live, never failing on the rise of that luminary to prostrate themselves before it, and to yield it homage and adoration; and this they do once more when they go to bed.

There are those who think more of their stomach than of anything else. They worship cooked rice as their god, and as a sign of their veneration never fail before eating it to offer to it their humblest homage. These are the people who have made the definition that there is but the one God, who is called Parama Bruma (Parama Brahma), which means 'Superior Knowledge,' or 'Most Excellent.' They say of Parama Brahma that he is the letter O; and they believe that when they breathe and pronounce the letter O they fail not at that juncture to enter into glory.[1] For it is then, they say, that the soul of such a person comes out by the crown of his head and passes with the velocity of an arrow into the centre of the sun, where it takes its position amidst heavenly glory. They hold that anyone who dies while doing this act is a true martyr.[2]

In addition to this Parama Brahma there are, they say, three hundred and thirty millions of gods. The king of them they call Vendyrem (Devendram)[3]—that is, 'Lord of the Gods'—of whom [93] I will say something hereafter. At present I wish to speak of the belief that these Hindus have in a sort of false Trinity. They say very dreadful things of this pretended Trinity, such as are not only unworthy of God, but even of man. Since, in such an essay as this, there arise many things which are undesirable or even contrary to good manners, I shall not say anything not permissible for a historian to write, and, so far as I may, will keep within the bounds of modesty set to a Catholic believer.

But before beginning I think it desirable to give an explanation of the figures[4] here inserted, which represent their false

1. On the mystic syllable *om* (composed of the three letters, *a, u,* and *m*), see Monier Williams, 'Brahmanism and Hinduism,' p. 45, and his 'Indian Wisdom,' p. 103.
2. The skull is supposed to bear a suture, through which the soul escapes on death. At the funeral rites the skull should be cracked by a piece of sacred wood to facilitate the passing of the soul. A Yogi, on death, has his skull cracked by a blow from a coco-nut, and he is buried, not burned (R. W. F.).
3. Ziegenbalg, English edition, 7, 177, 183. Mr. Frazer quotes the following from Arnold's 'Vedic Metre,' 1905: 'The drink ceremony is associated with a god or hero Indra, well described by Oldenberg as a "barbaric god," a great feeder, swiller, and fighter; he stands out as the type of the Aryan adventurer prince in Vedic times.' As to the Hindu Triad, see M. Williams, 'Brahmanism and Hinduism,' 44.
4. There are no drawings, as here referred to, in the Phillipps MS., 1945, at Berlin; but I insert copies of two coloured pictures found between fols. 365 and 366 of Codex XLIV. (Zanetti) at San Marco in Venice, kindly procured for me by Dr. Cóggiola. There are drawings of gods and goddess in Codex CXXXVI., Class VI., of the Same library, of which I have noted the subjects in the Introduction. I have not thought it worth while now to have these drawings reproduced, so much fuller information having become accessible in the 200 years since Manucci wrote.

The God Agastya

Vol. III *To face page 5*

gods. I have had them drawn with all possible exactness, in order to instruct the reader.

No. I. is a god of which the Hindus themselves do not know the name.

No. II. is the air, which, as I said, they place among the gods.

No. III. is the wind, which they distinguish from the air.

No. IV. is fire, also put among the gods.

No. V. is water, also according to them a divinity.

No. VI. is the earth, which they also deify.

No. VII. is the tower which encloses all the other figures and signifies Parachety (Para Sakti), mother of the other gods. The picture of a man seated on a tiger-skin is that of the author of all the brutalities believed by the Hindus. He is esteemed among them as much as Aristotle was of old. They have him represented in their temples just as he is seen here. The name of this worthy person is Agastian (Agastyan).[1]

EXPLANATION OF THE SECOND SET OF FIGURES.[2]

No. I. is the principal door in the porch of a great courtyard in the midst of which the Hindus build their temples as can be seen in this drawing.

No. II. are the smaller gates through the said porch, which is all faced with stone. Round this porch are trees, but inside there is another portico, with its gateways as shown in the drawing.

No. III. Within the said portico at a few paces' distance is the stone socket of a flagstaff, shaped as in the drawing.

---

1. Ziegenbalg, 7, 56, 182. Mr. Frazer says: 'Agastya is another name for Siva. The temple described is one to the worship of Siva, where the bull, *linga*, etc., are indications of his productive power, for his main characteristic of Destroyer is always associated with reproduction.'
2. There is no such drawing either in Phillipps, 1945, or Codex XLIV. (Zanetti). I have substituted No. 33 from the volume i of gods and goddesses, Venice Codex, No. CXXXVI., Class VI. It is called the Plan of Kanjivaran (Conjeveram) Pagoda. The numbers on it, I regret to say, do not agree with those in the text, but everything is shown except the altar with the bull. Thus, I (text) = 1 and 6 (drawing), II. = 2 and 5, III. and IV. = 8, V. = 3 and 4, VII. (wanting), VIII. = 9.

No. IV. Upon the said stone is a mast with a sort of flag on it; it is used for attaching yourself to with iron hooks as a penance.

No. V. is the gate of the other porch, where are the images of their temples.

No. VI. are four stones on which the offerings given in the temple are placed.

No. VII. is a small house in front of the temple in which stands the image of a bull bearing a saddle; this is the mount which they say Rutrim (Rudram) rides on.

No. VIII. is an image placed in the middle of the temple in the way shown in the drawing It is called (*lingam*). The outline and buildings of the temple are shown in blue and in red[94].

WHAT THEY SAY OF THEIR FALSE TRINITY CALLED BRAHMA, VISHNU, AND RUTRIN (RUDRA)

There was a woman called Paracceti (Parasakti)—that is, 'Superior Power' and 'Most Excellent.' This woman had three children. The first, so they say, had five heads and is called Brahma—that is, 'Knowledge.' To him she granted power over all things visible and invisible. The name of the second is Vishnu; to him she gave the power of preserving all that his brother created. The third is called Rutrim (Rudram);[1] of him, too, it is said that he has five heads, and that his mother granted him power of destroying and dispelling all that his brother should do or create. They follow this up by saying the woman married her own sons. But as they are never clear in their beliefs, they split off here into five different opinions.

Some say that the mother of these three, she who is called Parachety (Parasakti), is the First Cause and the Veritable God; others that it is the eldest son, Brahma, who is First Cause; others—and these are the most numerous—that it is the second son, Vishnu, who is alone God and the First Cause; others assert it is the third son who is God. Finally, the last group, to reconcile

1. An epithet of Siva, 'The Roarer,' the name of one of his faces (Ziegenbalg, 1, 30, 34). Mr. Frazer writes: 'The Vedic Rudra, the bearer of the thunderbolt, and father of the "Maruts," or storm gods, has become the Destroyer of the Universe, or Siva (see Macdonell's "Sanskrit Literature," and Oldenberg, "Religion des Vedas," p. 223).'

Plan of a Hindu Temple

this diversity of opinions, say that all three jointly are the First Cause and Veritable God. They also assert that none of them by himself nor the three jointly can be God, for whatever is human like other men could never be God. What they say to this effect seems reasonable enough; but they hardly ever adhere long to these views. For, through the number of changes made by them in their discourse, they are unable to carry on an argument in form. It now remains to give the life of each of these separately.

THE LIFE OF BRAHMA

These Hindus state in their fables that Brahma, the eldest son and husband of Paraxcety (Parasakti) was born in the navel of his younger brother.[1] They have no shame at thus placing the effect before the cause, which is obviously contrary to the very nature of things. Making no reflection on all these contradictions, they pass on to tell you the virtues residing in Brahma's countenance. From it, as they assert, the Brahmans were produced. This class of men is among them the most considered and the noblest. Being themselves the authors of all these fables, they accept without any hesitation the origin I have just stated, and thus call themselves, so to speak, the god Brahma. From his shoulders, they say, came the rajahs,[2] who hold the second rank of nobility. From his thighs came the Catharis (Khatris, Kshatriyas), or traders and shopkeepers, who are the third group. Lastly, the fourth grade issued from his feet, and are called Chutre (Shudra), the lowest caste, the most abject of all.

They say that this same Brahma writes in the head of every

1. 'So far as I was able to ascertain, I could only hear of two temples dedicated directly and primarily to Brahma' (M. Williams, 'Brahmanism and Hinduism,' 557). Images of Vishnu, with Brahma in the act of being evolved out of his navel, are common enough' (*ibid*).
2. Manucci—at any rate, in this section of his work—seems to use the word 'Rajah' as synonymous with 'Rajput or Kshatriya.' Mr. Frazer writes: The author has been misinformed. "Manu," i. 31 ("Sacred Books of the East," xxv.), states that the Creator, "caused the Brahmana, the Kshatriya, the Vaisya, and the Sudra to proceed from his mouth, his arms, his thighs, and his feet." The Kshatriya has a duty "to protect the people," the Vaisya "to trade" (see "Manu," i. 88, 90).

man what he will do throughout his life.[1] After this writing has been made neither he, nor his brothers, nor the three together [95] can efface it or withdraw it. But what he has written in the heads of others he has to undergo in his own person. They recount that, wishing to take his own daughter to wife, and conscious that this was not the conduct of a man, he took the shape of a stag. He then gave his daughter to the stag. When they had celebrated the ceremonies of marriage, they retired into the woods. But the gods Vishnu and Rudra and the other three hundred thousand millions of gods, seeing the infamous act of Brahma, and the disgrace reflected on them thereby, resolved to punish him. Rudra was selected to execute the decree they had made. This god was directed to behead Brahma, and this he did with his finger-nail. Nevertheless, Brahma did not thereby die. For he had four heads left, one only of the five having been removed.[2]

This Brahma, in addition to finding himself without a head, found himself also without a temple, without followers, and without molten image, the reason of which I will here state. The Brahmans say that they are themselves the god Brahma, and their dwellings are places appointed for worship—that is to say, where this god ought to be prayed to, and the adoration and homage rendered which are his due; that it is to them that other men should deliver all that they possess in order to secure the happiness, the wealth, and the enjoyment they desire. All that these Brahmans say is believed by the other Hindus to be infallible. Yet are they such deceivers that they keep faith with no one.

Lastly, they say that Brahma married a woman called

---

1. Mr. Frazer says: 'A common proverb in Southern India is that, "According to the writing on a man's forehead, so it must happen." ' He adds that the legend that follows in the text is from the 'Matsya Purana' (quoted in Wilkins's 'Hindu Mythology,' p. 86; see also the 'Aranyaka Upanishad,' and the 'Satapatha Brahmana,' xiv. 4, 24). Dubois, 'People of India,' p. 371, speaks of Brahma being the father and husband of Sarasvati.
2. The story of the loss of Brahma's fifth head is detailed in Kennedy's 'Hindu Mythology,' p. 276. One account is that 'Siva, seeing Brahma's fifth head inflicting distress on the Universe by its effulgent beams, brighter than a thousand suns, approached him and said, "Oh, this head shines with too much splendour !" and immediately cut it off with the nail of his left thumb, with as much ease as a man cuts off the stem of a plantain-tree' (R. W. F.).

Sarasvadi (Saraswati), who was very learned.[1] For this reason he always carries her about on his tongue in order to be correct in all his answers. He suffers patiently for that reason the annoyance and the pain that such a continuous lodgment must necessarily bring upon him. Others say the god Brahma is the generative power of men, that being the sole god Brahma. Here, then, is what is said and believed by one or the other; by the last class he is called 'potter,' a very derogatory name in this country.

THE LIFE OF VISHNU

They say of Vishnu that he is the second son and the husband of Parachety (Parasakti); and notwithstanding this, they say elsewhere that he is the First Cause, and was married to a woman called Lachime (Lachhmi or Lakshmi). The latter they assert to be ox, horse, house, mountain, money—in short, everything in the world that can be wished for.[2] This wife is always carried under his arm, so that she may not take to flight.

Vishnu has, they say, been incarnated nine times.[3] The first time was as a fish, for which they assign no reason. The second was as a tortoise; and listen to what followed—to what, as they declare, was its motive. There are in this world, according to them, seven seas. Of these one is of milk, and to obtain the butter the gods brought a mountain of gold [96], weighing

1. Sarasvati, wife of Brahma, is often known as Vac, or Speech, and as such is the Goddess of Learning (see Macdonell, 'Sanskrit Literature,' p. 93) (R. W. F.).
2. Lakshmi, or Sri, the wife of Vishnu, appeared in various forms, celestial or mortal, in the various incarnations of Vishnu (see Wilkins, 'Hindu Mythology,' p. 108, quoting from the 'Vishnu Purana'). 'In a world of gods, animals, and men, Hari (Vishnu) is all that is called male; Lakshmi is all that is termed female; there is nothing else than they' (R. W. F.).
3. J. Garrett, 'Classical Dictionary of India' (Madras, 1871), 717, gives ten incarnations—*viz.*: (1) Matsya (Fish), (2) Kurma (Tortoise), (3) Varaha (Boar), (4) Narasinha (Man-lion), (5) Vamana (Dwarf), (6) Parasurama (Ram of the Axe), (7) Ramchandra, (8) Krishna, (9) Buddha, (10) Kalki (White Horse) But the authorities differ as to the number. Mr. Frazer quotes from M. Williams, 'Brahmanism and Hinduism,' 107: 'In some of the "Puranas," Vishnu's ten incarnations, are multiplied to twenty-two, twenty-four, and twenty-eight.'

two hundred and eighty carats.[1] In this mountain are contained fourteen worlds; it is called Magammero Paravadam (Maha-meru-parvatam); around it lies a serpent with a thousand heads called Sextera (Sesha), within which, as they say, this world subsists. This serpent the gods used as a rope. Then the giants, always the enemies of the gods, pulled in one direction and the gods in another. Such force did they exert that the whole world shook, and would assuredly have fallen to pieces had not Vishnu noticed this disturbance and turned himself into a tortoise, putting himself beneath the world to sustain it. The serpent, unable to endure the vigour with which they were pulling, vomited on the giants a great quantity of poison, killing many of them. But Vishnu was not content with doing this much damage. After the gods had collected the butter, which they call ambrosia, the giants, who had been deprived of their share, became their deadly enemies, and overcame them several times. To remedy this trouble, Vishnu took the form of a lovely and pleasing courtesan, by a vision of whom he much embarrassed the giants, until such time as the gods had consumed the ambrosia, after which he (Vishnu) disappeared.[2]

The third incarnation was as a boar, and his object was equally ridiculous. Here is their story: One day there arose a great dispute among the gods as to who was greatest among them. Thereupon Rudra said to Brahma and Vishnu that he would go and hide; whoever found his feet and head would be greatest among the gods.[3]

---

1. The word is *quilates*, which has the meaning given; but the quantity seems very meagre for such a mountain.
2. This well-known account of the churning of the ocean is from the 'Vishnu Parana.' Here Vasuki is the name of the serpent coiled round the mountain. Sometimes in this 'Purana' Sesha is king of the Nagas, or snakes, in Patala; sometimes Vasuki is king. 'The thousandheaded Sesha is sometimes represented as forming the couch and canopy of Vishnu whilst sleeping during the intervals of creation' (Monier Williams, 'Sanskrit Dictionary,' s.v. 'Sesha') (R.W.F.).
3. This account of the boar incarnation differs in detail from that of the 'Vishnu Purana' and 'Vayu Purana.' The detail concerning the thistle lower is of interest, and it would be well to ascertain if it is excluded from Saivite temples (R.W.F.).

To find this head Brahma transformed himself into a swan and flew away into mid-sky. When in despair of success in his search, he found in his course a thistle flower, and going to it, it told him where Rudra's head was. Brahma in the form of a swan heard this, and without a word made off in haste to find it. It is impossible to describe or imagine the resentment felt by Rudra at being thus discovered by Brahma. He had thought it an impossibility. Aware that it was the flower that had revealed the secret, he bestowed his curse upon it. This is why the Yogis never put this flower in the temples of Rudra. Instead of acknowledging Brahma for the greatest of the gods, as agreed on, Rudra imposed on him as a curse that he should never be worshipped, should have no temples, no sacrifices, and no followers.

Thus arose, as they say, the condition Brahma finds himself in due to having discovered the head of Rudra. To find his feet, of which I spoke, Vishnu turned himself into a boar, and went off to grub in the earth with his tusks; he dug so deep that he reached the bottomless abyss without ever finding the feet he sought for. Thus he had to return as stupid a beast as he had set out. This is why nowadays there is not in these regions anyone who reverences the boar.

The fourth incarnation was that of a man and lion jointly. The reason alleged for this is as follows: There was a giant called Hiranie (Hiranya-Kasipu),[1] to whom Rudra accorded [97] the privilege of immunity from being killed by anyone, whether by night or day, at home or abroad. The giant grew so high and mighty at this privilege that he promulgated an ordinance that none other name than his should be pronounced throughout the world. If anyone brought to mind the gods or invoked them, he should suffer no lesser penalty than death.

At the time when this giant was the most puffed up, imagining to himself that no one in the world remembered the gods, a son of his, called Paragaladam (Prahladam), was a schoolboy. When his teacher told him to read and pronounce the name of his father, Hiranya, he brought forth that of Vishnu. Upon this

1. Ziegenbalg, 3, 75. Mr. Frazer writes: 'The account is from the "Vishnu Purana." It says that Hiranya Kasipu had obtained as a boon from Brahma that he should not be slain by any created being, but the "Kurma Purana" excepts Vishnu (see Wilkins, "Hindu Mythology," p. 124).'

the teacher, afraid of the father's anger, made an accusation to him against his son. Hiranya menaced his son with death by snakes, bears, tigers, and elephants; but the boy, through his devotion to Vishnu, was delivered from all without difficulty.

Then Vishnu, having tired of the devices and evil deeds of the giant Hiranya, menaced him with death to obtain the deliverance of his adherent, Prahlada. This menace was followed a moment afterwards by his issuing from a pillar turned into a man-lion. Then, when the sun was sinking, when it cannot be called day because that planet is no longer above the earth, and it cannot be called night because the light still peeps through the half-shut door, which cannot be said to be either inside or out-side of the house—in this time, and at this place, I say, Vishnu came forth against the giant, and tearing open his chest with his claws, dragged out his entrails. Then he lacerated his throat, and as a proof of victory drank all his blood.[1] But this draught produced such violent frenzy that the god became thereby mad for the rest of his life. In my judgment, those, too, are not less mad who worship him as God.

The fifth incarnation was as a dwarf, and here is the description they give: Once upon a time there reigned in this world a single king, called Magapelly Chacarvartey (Mahabali Chakravarti)[2] To seize and destroy this king, Vishnu took upon himself the form of a Brahman dwarf, extremely small. Then, coming to visit the king, he asked from him as a grace the grant of a plot of ground, three feet long, to build a house for himself. At the time the king had at his side as counsellor the Morning Star, who perceived that this demand was from an enemy, and

1. The 'Bhagavata Purana' says that Vishnu, in the form of a being half man and half lion, came forth from the pillar, laid hold of Hiranya Kasipu by the thighs, with his teeth, and tore him up the middle. Brahma's boon was that no common animal should kill him; that he should die neither in the day nor in the night, in earth or in heaven, by fire, by water, or by the sword. This promise was kept in the letter, for it was evening when Vishnu slew him, and this is neither day nor night, It was done under the droppings of the thatch, and this, according to a Hindu proverb, is out of the earth, and he was not killed by a man or any common animal ('View of History... of Hindus,' Ward, ii. 78) (R.W.F.).
2. Chakra-vartin (nominative, Chakra-varti) is a ruler who possesses the chakra, or magic disc, which accompanies him in all his campaigns.

to prevent acquiescence it placed itself by magic arts in the king's elbow. The king, to signify that he had granted the Brahman's request, had, according to the custom of the country, to pour water into his right hand. But the magic was no great success. The king finding that the movement of his elbow was impeded, without his knowing the cause, decided out of pique to have it opened with a lancet. In so doing one eye of Morning Star, who was hindering him, was destroyed. Then he poured the water into the right hand of the Brahman dwarf in proof of his granting the three feet of ground asked for.

But when the dwarf went to take possession he grew so enormous that the whole of earth and air were not big enough to hold one of his feet. He was forced to go back to the king, Mahabali Chakravarti, and say to him: 'You have promised me three feet of ground,[1] but on what you own there is not room to place one foot. Where am I to put the other?' Upon hearing this, the king became aware that it was nothing but a deception by the god Vishnu. Thus he was obliged to worship him, adding: 'Lord, here is my head, and on it you may place the other foot.' On hearing this answer, Vishnu accepted the offer, and put [98] his other foot on the king's head and thrust him down into hell. When the wretched king found himself there, he asked Vishnu what his end would be. To this the god replied that he would dwell for ever in hell; only once in the year, in the month of November, he would return to earth. At that time, in every year, would be observed a solemn festival in his honour. This the Hindus never fail to carry out.[2]

The sixth, the seventh, and the eighth incarnations took place in a man called Rame (Rama). The reason on the first occasion was as follows: A class of men called Rajputs became so

1. The 'three feet' are the three steps of Vishnu. 'Vishnu seems originally to have been conceived of as the sun—as the personified, swiftly-moving luminary which, with vast strides, traverses the three worlds. He is in several passages (Vedic) said to have taken his three steps for the benefit of mankind' (Macdonell, 'Sanskrit Literature,' p. 80) (R.W.F.).
2. Mahabali Chakravarti, sent to Patala by Vishnu, is the most popular legendary king in South India. His greatest festival falls on the full moon in Katik (Karttika), or October. In Maisur popular songs in his praise are sung on the last day of the Nauratri ('Madras Manual of Administration,' iii. 68).

haughty that they allowed no one to live in peace on the earth, nor would they permit a king of penitent monks, called Mongis (Muni), to perform his penances. In brief, they inflicted pain on everybody in general. Noticing this, Vishnu incarnated himself as Rama, and for a space of twenty-one generations he was busy in slaying all the Rajputs, and bathed himself in their blood. Thus by this means the barbarous tribe of Rajputs came to an end.

The second time of his incarnation as Rama was to kill a giant called Catavari Argune (Kartavirya Arjuna), who had not less than a thousand arms. He was destroying the world, and no one able to resist him. On perceiving this, Vishnu incarnated himself a second time as Rama, and taking as weapon a ploughshare, he broke with it all the giant's bones and cut off his arms, though not without a great deal of labour, and slaying him, made his bones into a mountain.

The third incarnation as Rama was to kill the giant Rachanem (Ravanam) and his brothers Bacarnem (Kumbhakar nam) and Vibichinem (Vibhishana) and their armies, made up of innumerable giants, who were always in opposition to the gods, and often derided Vishnu when in the form of Rama. Furthermore, they had deprived him of his wife, and he was unable to find out where she had gone. After many contests and combats, with varying results, Vishnu found he could neither vanquish them nor trace his wife, Sidy (Sita); he therefore called on the monkeys to help him against the giants. With their aid he conquered, and found once more his wife after twelve years' captivity. Afterwards, having overheard a washerman say that he was not quite such a fool as the god Vishnu, who had made himself into Rama, and taken back his wife after she had been twelve years in the power of the Lord knows who, he led her back to his home in much dejection, and, leaving her there, he turned pilgrim and wandered the world over.

The ninth incarnation was in the shape of a man called Chrisne (Krishna)—that is, 'Black man,' one of the lowest of the people. Here is the story told on this subject. Reigning over the whole sublunary world was a king called Caprassem (Kansa), 'the' persecutor and enemy of every virtue. The king had a sister called Echzudy (Yasoda).[1] After she had been married, he obtained absolute knowledge through diviners that the eighth child born by his sister would cause his death. This fact inspired him with the most irreconcilable hatred of the children of the said sister, so much so that as soon as they were born he slew them. The time came when Vishnu [99] became incarnated to take the life of his uncle, for he was the eighth son born to Echzudy (Yasoda).

When Kansa was told of the birth, he resolved to take the child's life with still greater precautions than observed with its brothers. But the mother had learnt by experience through the death of her other children, and feared that this one, too, would be made away with by her brother. She handed the child to her husband, and told him to flee with it. It was not an easy order to put into execution, for this brother-in-law had posted sentries all over the town. Nevertheless, by subterfuges he escaped, and gave his son to some cowherds to be brought up. His brother-in-law was kept in ignorance.

Yet the boy was not so well hidden that the king did not find it out, and he went himself in search, hoping to kill him. When he thought he had caught his nephew, and to get rid of him wanted to beat his head against a stone, he found he held a little female infant. It had been brought there by Krishna through magic arts, and he thus got the means of escaping. Then the little girl, who had been substituted by magic art in the hands of his uncle, did not come to an end forthwith. But she gave a vigorous kick in the stomach to Kansa, and laid him low, thereby evading the fate of becoming a victim of his hatred. She told him, 'He whom you seek is elsewhere.'

It would be difficult to describe the king's displeasure at finding himself thwarted, and that the nephew he sought had escaped his rage. Nevertheless, he did not desist from his endeavours, but sent to all his vassals, ordering them to kill Krishna. Then, finding they could not carry out this command, he told the giants to take the boy's life. As they were equally unsuccessful, he gave his orders to the devils, but they were as powerless as the others. For Krishna was so keen that he found out for himself that his uncle wished to kill him by means of an apparition

1. Yasoda is pronounced in Tamil Esodai; she was the wife of the herdsman Nanda, and foster-mother of Krishna.

that he had appointed to be his nurse. To circumvent her he drank her life from her along with her milk, and in that way escaped.

When Krishna had grown bigger he stole from his cowherd foster-parents a large quantity of butter. He had decided on flight with the proceeds of this theft in order to escape from the hands of his cowherd brothers, just as he had done from those of the king, his uncle. But this time he was not so fortunate, and having been made a prisoner by the cowherds, he was tied to a post and well beaten. On growing older, he went out to fight in person against the king, his uncle, and, after many battles, put him to death. When he found himself delivered from this powerful enemy, he longed to take some rest.

After having married two wives, he took to frequenting houses of ill fame along with sixteen thousand cowherds. But as he had not forgotten the whipping given him in their house, he was unwilling to incur the danger of another, and one night multiplied himself into several like himself. At one and the same time he visited all the courtesans, and sold to each his favours, so that through the love they cherished for him they forsook all the others. After all these tricks he played one still more audacious.

For, seeing a number of modest women bathing in a pond, as is the custom of the country, he carried off their clothes, placed by them near at hand on the edge of the pond. When the women emerged, covered by leaves they had found in the water, he declined to return their clothes unless they worshipped him by raising the hand to their head, by which mode of adoration they were forced to uncover themselves. When they had complied he gave them their things [100]. Thus can you see what little shame such divinities possess! Still less of it have those who admit them to be gods; and such are the false tales they relate of their false god Vishnu, or, rather, as much as Christian modesty allows me to repeat.

THE LIFE OF RUDRAM

Rudram is the third and last son of Parachety (Parasakti) and her first husband. Rudra was a *jogi* by calling, and one of the wickedest men then in the world. He was atanary (*ardhanari*)—that is to say, a hermaphrodite; he espoused Paravady

(Parvati), daughter of the king of the mountains, and lived a thousand years with her. . . . Seeing this, the gods Brahma, Vishnu, and the other three hundred and thirty thousand millions of gods concluded that Rudra was mad. Thus, they all joined and separated him by force from Paravady (Parvati); but she was so angry that she cursed all the gods with the imprecation that they should never have children nor any wife of their own, but only concubines. This malediction, as our authors say, produced its effect. Rudra became, as it were, mad, and impregnated the four elements beyond the capacity of air, fire, and sea. The earth alone received it at one spot, where it gaped in six places; and forthwith was born a little child with six heads.

But as in this world there was no nurse who could suckle him, the seven stars, styled ordinarily David's Wain, were called down to give him suck, and they named him Camaro Svami (*Kumara Swami*)—that is, 'Lord Son.' These wretched people are so devoted to him that on all their writings, obligations, contracts, and correspondence they insert Arumugam Tumca (Arumugam tumika)—that is, 'Thou with the six faces, be with us.'[1]

Subsequent to this miracle, they imagine that Paravadi (Parvati) was born a second time to a king called Dacha Pariadi (Daksha Prajapati), and that Rudra was a second time married to her. One day, as she was bathing in the garden, she had an intense longing for a son, who forthwith appeared in her hand out of the sweat wiped from her breast. She gave him the name of Vinaigem (Vinayakam)[2]—that is, 'He who is not God.' Rudra came home, and, ignorant of this event, was much dejected when he saw Vinayaka talking to Parvati. On this account he resolved to renounce her. But she knew whence his anger arose, and calmed him by describing how the thing had come to pass. When he learnt the truth, his sadness changed into joy; what had been a source of sorrow became a subject of rejoicing.

But he was not left long in this condition, for the king, his father-in-law, had to offer up a sacrifice, which they call *echiam*

1. *Arumugam* (Tamil), an epithet of Subrahmanya, youngest son of Iswara; from *aru*, 'six' + *mukham* (Sanskrit), 'face' (Ziegenbalg, 63, 64). The whole phrase gives the common formula *Arumugam-tunai*, 'help of A,' equivalent to the Mahomedam *bismillah*.
2. Ziegenbalg, 56, 60, another name for Vighneswara or Ganesa.

(*yajna*),and to it he invited all the gods [101]. But whether by forgetfulness, or through ill-will to the god, his son-in-law, caused by the tricks he played, he did not invite him. That very moment Rudra, aflame with rage, presented himself where his father-in-law was sacrificing to the gods and feasting them. As soon as he arrived, he in his rage drew forth a horse-whip and struck it on the ground with all his strength, and by force of this blow there was born instantly a giant, who breathed vengeance for the slight done to and suffered by Rudra. Among the other violent things he did, he gave such a smack to the Sun that it knocked out all his teeth. This is why all the things now offered by the Hindus to this planet are soft, such as milk, butter, flour, and very ripe fruit. After this assault, he trod the Moon's face underfoot, and made the scars still to be seen on it to this day. After he had slain the king, Daksha Prajapati, and many more, some among the survivors cut off the head of Vinayaka.

When the choler had evaporated and the dispute blown over, Rudra sought for his son. He had fallen before the giant's violence. He found only a headless body, and was thus forced to cut off an elephant's head, which he so made to adhere that his son came to life.[1] The father then told his son he must never marry until he found a woman as lovely as his mother. This is why in this country this idol is always turned with its face to the east, looking for a woman equal to his mother. But up to this time the resuscitated Vinayaka, also called by them Polyar (Pillaiyar),[2] has not found her.

By order of the gods Rudra went to cut off the head of Brahma, who had turned himself into a stag and seduced his own daughter. In doing such an act, as they assert, Rudra was guilty of a heinous sin. To expiate it he divested himself of clothing, increasing his penance by wearing nothing and dwelling in graveyards. There, smeared with ashes and holding Brahma's head in his hand, he passed his days and nights with grievous groans, until he thereby lost his senses. However, in the end he grew weary of such heavy penance, and decided to obtain some solace.

1. There are many accounts of the origin of Ganesa and his elephant head. The story here given is similar to that in the 'Siva Purana' (see Wilkins, 'Hindu Mythology,' p. 269) (R. W. F.).
2. Pillaiyar, the son *par excellence*, another name for Vighneswara or Ganesa (Ziegenbalg, 60).

He knew that in a neighbouring desert there dwelt many ascetic Brahmans, and by magic arts he filled their wives with concupiscence; then, appearing at that spot all naked, he asked for alms. The Brahman women quitted their husbands in pursuit of the god, and followed him. Here, where he hoped for the greatest transports, he encountered a still worse cause of chagrin; for the ascetic Brahmans, revolting at such treachery, uttered a malediction upon the god. Forthwith he was turned into a eunuch. Unable to remedy his misfortune otherwise, he announced a grant of heavenly glory to whosoever for his love became a eunuch. This several men did forthwith; and not [102] stopping short at the sacrifice thus made, they converted it into an idol, which some hang from their neck, some place on their head, others on their arms. This is called *linguon* (*lingam*).[1] Thus does the great god made of stone, besides filling all the temples and all the streets, go about hung to the necks of a sect of men and women called yogueys (*yogis*). These are the fiercest enemies of God's Law that can be found, extremely degraded and haughty, also the most cowardly people in the world.

There is still another sect which imitates the disgraceful penance of Rudra. They call them Larres (Illar),[2] or filthy *yogis*. They go about naked, covered all over with ashes, and demand alms everywhere; they are held to be holy men. Many carry the *lingam* idol tied on their hands, and those hands extended above the head; they are never lowered, but always raised at full length and motionless. From this cause someone else is required to put food into their mouths, and those who do this believe they are performing a great work of charity.

After the malediction, Rudra married the river Ganges, described by the Hindus as a very handsome woman; but with her he was impotent, and had no children. He had to content himself with carrying her always on his head. But she was not

1. *Linga* = a mark or sign. Siva worshipped in the form of a phallus (R. W. F.).
2. In regard to *Larres,* Mr. Frazer writes: 'No pure Tamil word can begin with *L;* it must be preceded by *I* or *U*. If it be *I,* we get *illares* or *illar*; for, *ar* being the plural, we can drop the French plural *es. Il* is the negative 'not'; so *illar* are those who possess not, those without anything, the destitute. It is here evidently, applied to the fact that they "are without [clothes or possessions]." Dr. Barnett suggests *uralar,* 'dirty men'.

satisfied, and without the knowledge of the god, her husband, she sought someone else, devoid of the defect of Rudra as above stated. Thus, in the course of several adventures, Vishnu delivered Rudra from the greatest peril he had yet undergone; for a giant, called Pasmevram (Bhasmasura)[1]—that is, 'Lord of Ashes'—after having done penance for several years in honour of Rudra, came to him one day to ask reward for so many hardships. Rudra conferred on him the power of reducing to ashes anyone on whose head he placed his hand. As the giant was eager to know if the gift were a veritable one, he wanted to test it upon Rudra himself. The latter became conscious of his mistake, and seeing himself in greater straits than ever before, he resorted to magic, and became invisible within a fruit. It was the size of a filbert or hazel.

Vishnu learnt of this difficulty, and taking the form of a courtesan, appeared to the giant, who was taken with her beauty, and asked leave to put up in her house. Vishnu's answer was that, having lived as an ascetic for so many years, his head had been fouled by the crows, rooks,[2] and other birds to such an extent that it was very dirty. He must go to the river to wash it; after that she would take him into her house. Thereupon off went the giant to the river in great glee; but he met with destruction where he had looked for the highest delight; for, in rubbing his head with his hands, he touched himself, and was thus reduced to ashes, to the great satisfaction of Vishnu.

Having quitted that shape, Vishnu resorted to Rudra to tell him it was time to quit the fruit, the giant being now destroyed; and warned him not to be such a fool again as to enter into such agreements. Then Rudra, anxious to know the device, asked Vishnu to show him the form in which he had appeared. But he refused [103], telling Rudra over and over again that if he saw the figure in which he appeared before the giant, his mind would lose its balance. In spite of this, Rudra reiterated his demand, and prayed for his desire to be satisfied. Touched by this, Vishnu consented; when Rudra, beholding so much beauty, went out of his senses, and by mere force of passion produced a son, which

1. Platts, 'Dictionary,' a demon who reduced to ashes all that he placed his hand upon. *Bhasma* = 'ashes.'
2. '*Graille, s.f.*, nom vulgaire de la corbine, dite aussi *graillaut* ou *graillot*' (Littré, 'Dictionary'). Compare Portuguese '*gralha,*' *s.f.*, a rook.

through that apparition came to life in the hand of Vishnu. They named it Arigara Putrim—that is, 'Son of Vishnu and Rudra.'[1]

These two imaginary persons are the most revered of all by those barbarians, and they have the most worshippers. These Indian people are so naturally ignorant that they are unable to philosophize, or convince themselves by light of Reason, that all these stupidities and improprieties are unworthy, to say the least of it, of the Divine Essence.

Another error of these Hindus is that they hold God to be whatever thing can exist. Moreover, they hold that God is the author of sin, and as they have not the science for distinguishing between permitting and willing, it is very difficult to convince them that they are unblushingly admitting the existence of two contraries. That remark means that they say God forbids sin and is most just, and at the same time they say He desires sin, and yet chastens mankind for their sins.

CHAPTER II

WHAT THE HINDUS SAY OF PARADISE AND OF HELL

They imagine that we enter into glory in five different places. The first they call Zoarcan (Swargam). It is here that in their opinion dwells the king of the gods, called Devydyrey (Devendra), with his two wives Yzachy (Sachi)[2] and Indariny (Indrani), and five mistresses famous for their excessive beauty. There the three hundred and thirty thousand million gods keep him company, and with several millions of mistresses taste and enjoy delight of every sort. They, too, share in the glory of Swarga. They add that forty-eight thousand ascetics participate in this felicity, and without their advice the gods can order nothing in this world or the other.

As for this heavenly glory and their esteem for it, they cannot be great, because they hold that several pleasures of this world

1. Hari-Hara (Vishnu-Rudra), spelt according to Tamil phonetics.
2. Sachi, Garrett, 266, says, is the second name of Indrani. For 'Indra,' see Ziegenbalg, 7, 179, 191, 195, and for 'Indrani,' *ibid.*, 180; also Muir's 'Original Sanskrit Texts,' v. 12.

rise above and surpass those of the other; for their king of the gods was not content with the delights there, and quitting what they imagine to be his glory there, came to enjoy those of this world. To confirm this fantastic belief, they relate a fable. To the river Ganges came an ascetic called Gaudamé (Gautama),[1] who lived there with his wife Gaudalay (Ahalya), and she was, according to them, very beautiful, so much so that the king of the gods resolved to consort with the ascetic, and share this part of his mortification.

In order to gain more time for his wiles, and knowing that the ascetic went every morning at cock-crow to bathe in the Ganges, he crowed two or three times at midnight in imitation of a cock, quite close to the ascetic's house. Not to break his good habits, the ascetic rose promptly and went away to the river. But finding her (the river) still asleep, he concluded from this [104] that the cock had not crowed, but he had imagined it in a dream. Returning to his home, he found the king of the gods with his wife, and at this he was so angered that he cursed the king, saying, 'May all the members of your body be transformed into the likeness of that wherewith you committed adultery and accomplished your desires.' Without delay, so they say, the malediction did its work. The poor god, ashamed at finding himself in a condition unfit for view, threw himself at the feet of the ascetic, supplicating him to do away with such a degrading penance. The ascetic complied at once in part, and ordained that his sight should always make him see things in one way, while to others he should appear to be full of eyes. In this pitiable state the king of the gods found himself. If such be the state of the king, you can easily conjecture the obscene condition of his subjects. As for the adulteress, she expired on the spot under the curse of her husband. But being taken by Vishnu, she was revived, and peace was made with her husband. By this fable it can be seen that Deviderey (Devendra) is not less than a god.

The second place is styled Vaycondam (Vaikuntham). They say that Vishnu dwells here with his two wives and a bird used by him to ride upon. For this reason all Hindus worship this very bird with such veneration that kings and princes when they come forth, if they see it fly by, descend from their palanquins or other

1. Garrett, 225. Gautama, a *rishi*, married Ahalya, daughter of Brahma (Ziegenbalg, 7, 179, 182).

vehicle, and prostrate themselves on the ground and pay it adoration.[1] The followers of Vishnu say that after death they go to this heaven, and just as fire converts into its own substance whatever is put upon it to feed it, so also Vishnu converts into part of himself all those who have the felicity of beholding him in his glory.

The third place of glory is called, according to our authors, Caylachaon (Kailasam), which is, they say, a mountain of silver situated towards the north, and there (as they say) dwells Rudra with his wives. There, too, is found his bull upon which he rides. It is here that, according to their legend, all those go who belong to the sect of Rudra—that is, those with the *lingams*, and several other groups. When you ask them the nature of the heavenly felicity enjoyed in this place, they answer you that it lies in the enjoyment shared in by the gods as well as by men, their followers, of every sort of delight and grandeur. Besides dwelling in the presence of the god, some serve to fan him and prevent his feeling the heat; others hold a spittoon for him, so that His Mightiness may not demean himself by spitting on the ground; others hold lighted torches to prevent his being inconvenienced by darkness—in short, all wait on him for one purpose or another, and all make themselves useful. In addition, as they assert, he has numerous mistresses. From all the things these poor creatures say, it can be clearly seen that he is not God, nor is such a region worthy the name of heaven.

The fourth region of glory, according to the authors, is named Brama Logaon (*Brahma-lokam*), which means 'Brahma's world'; they also call it *Satia Logaon* (*Satyalokam*), which means 'World of Truth.' In this region of glory there dwell, so they say, Brahma and his wife Sarasvady (*Saraswati*), and a swan, the bird on which, as they say, he rides, and this bird is found in no other place. They give few details about this heaven, for the truth is that they know nothing beyond the name, and are ignorant of its properties [105].

The fifth region of glory is called Melaonpadar (Mel-ampadam), which is, 'Place superior to all others.' In it is to be found, as they say, the First Cause, whom they call Parubravastu (Parama-vastu), which means 'Most excellent essence.' They

1. *Garuda,* the vehicle of Vishnu, a mythical bird; also a name for several large birds of the crane or vulture species.

say that the felicity here enjoyed consists in five things, called by them *sunitiam* (*santiyam*), *samippiam* (*samipyam*), *sanchiam* (*sayujyam*), *sarrupiam* (*sarupyam*), *salochiam* (*salokyam*), which mean 'presence,' 'proximity,' 'mingling,' 'corruption,' and 'vision.'[1] At this point they divide in opinion, for some say it needs only some of these things to make a man exceedingly happy; the others that all five are needed. They assert that their religious orders, named *Sanyasis,* acquire them, and when they die enjoy fruition of them all.

As for hell, they say it is not only underneath this world, but also below six others, which they describe as following one after the other beneath our world. In this spot, as my authors say, there exists as president and executioner of sentences a minister of Chivem (Sivam) called Yamadar Maharaige (Yamadhar, Maharaj), with a scribe they call Chistranguptam (Chitraguptam), who keeps an account of all the sins and all the good deeds of mankind. When a man dies they believe he is led before the president of hell, who asks him whether he prefers first to enjoy the reward of his good deeds, or undergo the due punishment of his sins. According to the choice and the reply of the dead man, the said president pronounces sentence. If he wishes first to obtain the reward of his virtues either in the Zoarcan (Swargam), or other region which he prefers, orders are given that afterwards he must return to hell to expiate his faults. But after he has given satisfaction in this said hell for his evil deeds, he is born again, each one according as he has done good or evil. For he who has worked evil, and belonged to a poverty-stricken family, comes to life again in one still more miserable. They say, for example, that a Brahman who during life should have served and lived one month with Chutres (*Shudras*), the lowest and most despised of all the castes, will not fail to be chastened in hell for this sin. He will either re-enter life in the Shudra caste or in some other ten million times lower and more degraded. Upon this subject they say that it is part of their faith to believe that even if the Brahman had not served that class of people, but only

1. *Santa* (*junction*), *samipya* (proximity), *sankshipa* (union), *sarup* (similarity), *salochana* (seeing) ('Madras Manual of Administration,' iii. 771). 'The heaven of Vishnu gives four states: *Salokya* (same world), *samipya* (nearness), *sarupya* (same form), and *sayujya* (complete union)' (M. Williams, 'Hinduism,' p. 51).

conversed with them, he could not avoid having the same punishment. As for the penalties endured by men in hell, they say that in that place are all imaginable torments and sufferings. In it are to be found all kinds of venomous animals for torturing men. If at the moment of death a man takes hold of a cow's tail, and receives a little water from a Brahman's hand and spills it upon the ground, giving some money in alms to the Brahman who brought the cow, he who does all this is assured, they believe, that by these good deeds the cow will go to wait for him in the other world close to a river of fire, adjoining the town where dwells the president of hell. The river is called Vaicarany (Vaikarni). At that spot the cow holds out its tail, the defunct seizes it, and crosses over tranquilly to the farther side of the river of fire.

Not only does Eyamen (Yama) preside over all these things and everything else that goes on in hell, but he is also the god of death. According to them, their belief is that he died and came to life again, and here is the story that they tell about it.

There was an ascetic named Maruganda Magarecchi (Maharshi Mrikanda), who sorrowed for the want of children. He asked for them from Echivem (Sivam) with many prayers. Siva inquired if he wished many sons or one; if he wished for several, they would live for a long time [106], but would be wicked men. If he would be satisfied with one, he would be good, but would not survive beyond sixteen years of age. The ascetic elected to have one son only, although he objected greatly to losing him at so tender an age. The son, then, was born to him, and he named him Mercadem (Markandeya). When the boy grew up, he devoted himself ardently to the service of Siva, and offered up to him *arquineis* (arghyam), which is a sort of sacrifice of flowers, at Turrcadau (Tiruvengada),[1] a place celebrated among the Hindus, However, when the sixteen years were passed,

1. Tiruvenkada, or Tirupati (Ziegenbalg, 51). Tiru-vengadam (Holy White Mountain), a name of Tirumala (Holy Hill), a place of pilgrimage in the Northern Arkat district. It is called Upper Tirupati, and is close to Lower Tirupati, the village ('Madras Manual of Administration,' iii. 896). Mr. Frazer writes: '*Tiru* is the Tamil pronunciation of the Sanskrit *sri*, holy. *Tiru-ven-kadu*, a Saiva shrine=Holy+White+ Forest., Dr. Barnett doubts this identification, as Tirupati is a place of Vishnu, and not of Siva, worship, and suggests Tirukadavur in Tanjor, where there is a Saiva sanctuary.

the minions of Yama, God of Death, came for him. The youth declared absolutely that he did not mean to die, and the King of Death's underlings beat a retreat. Sad and shame-faced they returned to report to their master that Markandeya would not die, and had no reasons leading him to wish an end of his life. On hearing that he was defied, the King of Death flew into a passion, hastily bestrode his buffalo, and hied to Markendeya. He talked to him and tried to persuade him by many a reasoning that he had no right to wish for longer life, for Siva had accorded no more than sixteen years of life in the promise made to the ascetic, his father. But Markandeya turned a deaf ear to all his persuasions, replying persistently and boldly to the King of Death that he need not worry himself so much; he absolutely had no intention of dying. Then, to escape the wrath of the God of Death, he threw his arms around the idol of the *lingam*. Seeing this, the grisly monarch, supporting himself on his buffalo, threw a rope round the neck of Markandeya and the *lingam* which he was hugging. When he attempted to carry away the whole into hell, Siva jumped out of the *lingam* and planted a mighty kick upon his infernal and mortuary Majesty, whereby he was deprived of life. Thus the god delivered his worshipper Markandeya.

When the God of Death had passed from the number of the living, no one was left as slayer of mankind. Thus they multiplied so exceedingly that the earth groaned beneath the burden of their multitude. In fact, the world was driven to demand relief from the gods, who went in a body to Siva to ask his reason for killing the King of Death. Siva answered that when he granted sixteen years of life to Markandeya, his meaning was that, whatever his true age, he should always look like sixteen. Yama, misinterpreting his meaning and paying no respect to his (Siva's) *lingam*, round which Markandeya had put his arms, wanted to kill the youth, and by this act of contempt to show his own power and carry Markandeya off into hell. This was the reason for which he (Siva) had taken the god's life.

The gods, having listened to these reasons, decided that they were not acceptable, nor of sufficient weight to allow the world to be inconvenienced, as it was, by the innumerable inhabitants then upon it, which it could no longer carry or provide with sustenance. By this and such-like arguments they forced Siva to resuscitate the King of Death, that he might diminish the excessive population of the earth. Siva, who had overlooked these consequences, was convinced by their strong arguments, and changing his opinion, brought back to life [107] Yama, King of Death, conferring on him the same powers as before. By virtue thereof he sent out a proclamation through the public crier, ordaining that all the old must die and no respite would be given. But before the crier had made this ordinance public, he got drunk, mounted an elephant, set the cymbals beating, and announced to all the world the following declaration:

'Yama, King of Death and ruler of Hell, ordains that every fruit, raw or ripe, every flower, and every leaf, shall fall from the trees.'

They state that after the publication of this ordinance old people and young, youths and infants, began to die—a strange thing, for up to that tragic occurrence none but the old fell a prey to the King of Death, executioner of the pains of hell, though, according to their false belief, these are endured by no one eternally; and owing to this error, as it would seem, the poor creatures find it so much the less difficult to give way to their sins.

CHAPTER III

DEALING WITH HINDU OPINIONS IN REGARD TO THE SOUL

The Hindus say that man has a soul, that this soul is a vital power of the physical and material body; but the soul of man being a thing spiritual, none among them knows its true essence, and they divide themselves in respect to it into several conflicting schools of opinion. Some of them place two souls in man—one visible, the other intellectual.[1] The first, they say, is of the same species as, or

1. The two souls here mean the *Atman*, the Self or Soul of Man, and the *Parama Atman*, the Self or Soul of the Universe. This is the doctrine of the Vedanta philosophy held by nearly all thinkers in South India, and expressed by Max Müller in 'India: What it can Teach Us,' p. 254, as follows: 'Behind all the mythology of Nature, the ancient sages of India had discovered the *Atman*—let us call it the Objective Self; they perceived also behind the veil of the body, behind the senses, behind the mind, and behind our

identical with, all animate or inanimate objects. The second they style Paramatumaon (*Paramatman*), and this they hold to be God Himself. It is composed of one essence only, and is the same in all men; others add, also the same as in all animals. These last in their theology say in substance that the difference between a reasoning soul and that of an animals is that the latter has not reason, while the other is endowed with understanding. Just to show how they never agree in anything, and are always in error, there are some who say that our Lord God is the soul, not only of all the elements, but of all the elementary bodies.

Some say that the soul is not really God, but only a part of God; others, that God, our Lord, is not the soul, neither in whole nor in part, but he created all souls at one moment of time, and they pass into one body after another. Finally, there are others who assert that it is not alone God, our Lord, who is the creator of the soul and their author, but that the earthly father and mother really contribute to the production of the soul, just as much as they do to that of the body. The latter being mortal and corruptible, so also must man's soul be the same.

CHAPTER IV

WHAT THE HINDUS SAY ABOUT THIS WORLD

The Hindus suppose there are fourteen worlds—that is, seven above and six below this earth; the one in which we live makes the fourteenth. They state their position in the following manner [108].

The lowest of all is, they say, Hell; the next above is another world called Magadalam (Mahatala); the next is Saladaland (*Sutala*); then Backchadaland (? *Gabhastimat*), which is a world of quicksilver, and they also assert it to be the world of snakes. The one which comes next is Chuduland (? *Nitala*), and above it is Vedeland (*Vitala*); then between it and our earth is Adaland

reason (in fact, behind the mythology of the Soul, which we often call Psychology), another *Atman*, or the Subjective Self.' The schools of complete specific and pantheistic nonduality, qualified duality, and duality, are next described by the author (R. W. F.).

(*Atala*).[1] Next comes our terrestrial world, within which, they say, are seven seas, one of salt water, one of melted sugar, one of toddy-spirit, one of butter, one of curds, and one of milk. In this last, according to them, dwells their Vishnu, and there a very beautiful serpent with five heads forms his bed. Finally, they say there is one more sea, the last of all, which is of very pure and crystal-like water.[2]

Below the terrestrial world is Air, then Zoarcan (Swargam), where all those who in this world have sacrificed to the gods enjoy every sort of delight. Not to be deprived of what they consider the greatest of all delights, they have there a great number of courtesans. Yet they overlook the fact that they have already said that in this region dwells the king of the gods, called Vendirem (Devendram). Above *Swarga* lies Magalogan (Mahalokam)— that is, 'Great World'—where Vendirem (Devendra) and the other three hundred and thirty millions of gods dwell divided into two kinds, one called gods and the other giants; and these wage perpetual war against each other.

Above the world just spoken of there is, they say, Genelogam (Jana-lokam),[3] which signifies 'World of Giants,' in which place there are many such, of all degrees. After this comes Tabalagam (Tapa-lokam),[4] which means in effect 'World of Penitents,' where dwell all those who have been ascetics in this world. The last of the fourteen worlds is called Satia logaon (Satyaloka), signifying the 'World of Verity.' There, as they say, are to be found Brahma and his devotees, all of whom change into or

1. Garrett, 451, s.v. 'Patala': (1) Atala, (2) Vitala, (3) Nitala, (4) Gabhastimat, (5) Mahatala, (6) Sutala, (7) Patala (the lowest region in the interior of the earth). In M. Williams, 'Brahmanism and Hinduism,' p. 102, they are: Atala, Vitala, Sutala, Rasatala, Talatala, Mahatala, and Patala.
2. Garrett, 199, s.v. 'Dwipa': (1) Jambu-Dwipa, surrounded by a sea of salt; (2) Plaksha, by a sea of sugar-cane juice; (3) Salmali, by a sea of wine (*sura*); (4) Kusa, by a sea of clarified butter (*sarpi*); (5) Krauncha, by a sea of curds (*dugdha*); (6), omitted; (7) Pushkara, by a sea of fresh water.
3. Janaloka (Garrett, 285), the heaven of saints; Tapaloka (*ibid.*, 635), the world of the seven *rishis* (sages); Tapas=penance, self-mortification.
4. Garrett, 567: Satyaloka, the world of infinite wisdom and truth. For the four higher heavens, see also M. Williams, 'Brahmanism and Hinduism,' p. 403.

become absorbed into him, and become, as it may be said, the god Brahma himself. If you ask the time fixed for this transubstantiation, they tell you it is in this terrestrial world, when the Brahman who turns monk cuts in two the thread they all wear round the body, and removes the long lock of hair usually worn at the back of the head as proof of their high caste. When by the removal of this sign of rank they have denoted their adoption of an ascetic life, they take in the right hand a bambū staff as tall as themselves, either of eight, nine, ten, or fourteen knots, and in the left hand a kind of pot, copper or earthen. Then they tie round their waist a piece of yellow cloth, pronouncing the words 'Agam Brahma'—that is, 'I am the very god Brahma.'[1] The Brahmans present at this ceremonial prostrate themselves and worship the man as God. The Brahman women bring a kind of tart or cake which they lay before the new-made god. The latter, as a proof of asceticism, must not during that night eat of any other food. These men are the haughtiest of all the people in this country. At death they say they go to Brahma's world.

Here is their account of their fourteen imaginary worlds, said by them to be placed one upon the other in a mountain of very fine gold of twenty-four carats. They call this mountain Magameru Paravadam (Maha Meru Parvatam)—that is, 'Very Great Mountain.' They hold that it is sustained by an elephant, which rests in turn on a tortoise, and it, again, upon a snake, called Sexen (Sesham). If you ask them how that snake keeps its place with such a great weight upon it, they reply that they do not know, because [109], up to the present, their books make no mention of that, referring only to what is above it. In the books it is, however, stated as an unquestionable fact that, when an earthquake visits us, it is nothing but the snake moving the world off one shoulder on to the other to rest himself of his burden. They also say that the same snake causes eclipses.

1. The 'Aham Brahma' is an expression of Vedanta belief in spiritualistic pantheism. The 'Brahman' here is clearly the same as Spinoza's 'Substantia' (Max Muller, 'Vedanta Philosophy,' p. 123). The author (Manucci) misunderstands the meaning of the word 'Brahman' here used, which is a neuter noun expressing essence, not the personal god Brahma, the Creator (R.W.F.).

CHAPTER V

BELIEFS OF THE HINDUS ABOUT THE PLANETS

These people accept the twelve celestial signs, and with them the twenty-seven fixed stars, to which they give proper names in their language.

They assert in their astronomical treatises that the sun moves above the earth at a distance of six hundred and twenty-five thousand leagues, and the moon is raised above the sun a similar distance. This is the reason, so they say, that eclipses are not caused by the interposition of the moon between the earth and the sun. But here follows what they declare to be the cause.

When the gods and the giants were removing the butter from the milky occean, Vishnu, when he interfered with the giants, gave a feast at which this nectar was served out to all the gods invited by him. But the snake Sesham. whom they call one of the principal gods, was not present at this banquet. Sun and Moon, whom they style the most luminous of the gods, were most greedy, and ate the snake's portion. On his subsequent arrival the snake missed his share. The other gods informed him that the Sun and Moon had eaten it, when the snake, filled with rage and wrath, swore to make them find it a bitter morsel; when he found it convenient, he meant to swallow them and punish them for their greediness.[1]

If he spoke well, he acted still better. When he swallows the sun, that planet is in eclipse; and when it is the moon he swallows, the moon is relipsed. But in order that the world be not left in an unending night, the gods, the Brahmans, and others, never fail to bathe at these conjunctures, and offer up prayers, not only with fasting, but with the shedding of many tears. They ardently implore the snake that he be pleased to release the sun or the moon, according to which of them is in eclipse.

1. Rahu, with four arms and ending in a tail, disguised himself as a *Daitya*, and drank a portion of the *Amrita*, or nectar, produced at the churning of the ocean; but the Sun and Moon detected the fraud, and in Tevenge he occasionally swallows them and produces eclipses, while his tail, known as *Ketu*, produces comets and meteors (see the 'Sanskrit Dictionary* under 'Rahu,' and Ward, ii. 81) (R.W.F.).

Such is their persistence in these prayers, that for one day before the completion of the eclipse they neither eat nor drink, they cook nothing, and allow no food to be in their houses. They declare that the eclipse only ends because the snake Sesham, being effected by so many prayers, releases those two great planets that he had already swallowed.

With regard to time, they divide it into four parts, which they call Nerutavigam (Krita-yugam), Duabraingam (Dwaparayugam), Terridasugam (Treta-yugam), and Calvigam (Kaliyugam).[1] Their belief is that the first three ages of the world have passed, and that those were true golden ages, not only in length, but in their nature, owing to the good fortune and the pleasant lives which all the world had and enjoyed. In the third age lived a king, the father of Rama, of whom I spoke in the life of Vishnu. This man lived sixty thousand years without having issue. Then in his old age and decrepitude he had a son. This *vingano* (yugam), or age of the world, has not had, according to my authors, any beginning or end, nor do they state any principle of its age or being.

As for the fourth age, the one now in existence [110], it is, they say, an iron age, both for the misfortunes and hindrances men undergo in it, and for the short duration of their lives. They suppose that this age began four hundred thousand four hundred and forty-eight years ago. In spite of the lapse of such a long period, there are still many more years to come than the number already past before it will come to an end. They say that what has passed is in comparison with what is to come, as is a mustard- seed to a pumpkin. In this fabulous account the Hindus are divided into two contrary opinions. Some say that at the end of this fourth age of the world there will be no subsequent age. The others assert that the world is to endure for ever, and on the conclusion of this iron age, the vanished golden ages will arise anew and begin their course once more.'[2]

---

1. 'There are properly four *Yugas*, or ages, in every *Maha Yuga*— *viz.*: *Krita, Treta, Dwapara,* and *Kali*, named from the marks on dice, the *krita* being the best throw, of four points, and the *kali* the worst, of one point' (R.W.F.).
2. At the termination of the *Kali* age, according to the 'Vishnu Purana,' 'Vishnu is expected to come again, bearing the name of Kalki, to put an end to wickedness, and establish a kingdom of righteousness similar to the first or *Krita* age' (Wilkins, 'Hindu Mythology,' p. 205) (R.W.F.).

Although the four ages spoken of above are celebrated among these idolaters, they relate also, in a book they call the 'Chronicles of the World,' that preceding these four ages there had been fourteen others.[1] The first of these, they say, lasted one hundred and forty millions of years; the second, one hundred and thirty; the third, one hundred and twenty; the fourth, one hundred and ten; the fifth, one hundred million years; the sixth, ninety millions; the seventh, eighty millions; the eighth, seventy millions; the ninth, sixty millions; the tenth, fifty millions; the eleventh, forty; the twelfth, thirty; the thirteenth, twenty; the fourteenth, ten millions of years; the fifteenth, nine millions and sixty thousand years; the sixteenth, seven millions five hundred thousand and three hundred years; the seventeenth, five millions and nine hundred thousand years; the eighteenth, four millions five hundred thousand and three hundred years. To this fable of the age of the world, which by computation comes to 1,076,960,600 years, they add the total length of the planets' existence, which they consider to be animated by a reasoning soul. Nay, they insist that they are gods, that they are married, and have many children.

CHAPTER VI

OPINIONS HELD BY THE HINDUS IN RESPECT TO MAN

I said at the beginning that the Hindus divided all mankind into four kinds or classes. Some men they make out to be born Brahma's face, and these people are called Brahmans, who are divided into several branches. The second kind of men they make out to have been bom from the shoulders of the said Brahma, and these they call Rajahs,[2] also divided into several branches. The third kind are said to be born from the thighs of the said Brahma, and these are the merchants or shopkeepers, of whom

1. *Sic* in text. The enumeration below gives eighteen. Mr. Frazer writes: Within each *Kalpa*, or age, there reigned 14 Manus. A *Maha Yuga* is equal to 4 *Yugas*, and 1,000 *Maha Yugas* are equal to one day of Brahma, or a *Kalpa*, which is equal to 4,320,000,000 mortal years' (see 'Vishnu Purana,' vi. I (R.W.F.).
2. *Raja* for *Rajanya*, as sometimes in classical Sanskrit.

also there are many varieties. Finally, there is the fourth or last kind, born, as they say, from the feet of Brahma; these are the Chutres (Sudra), who, just like the others, have many subdivisions, and it is difficult even to count them.

To these four kinds or classes they add one more, which is not counted along with the above, but is held by them to be separated from the general body of men. These people are called in their language Chandalon (*chandalam*), or blacks. These are divided into four kinds, named Achivanatar (? Vettiyar), Palis (Palli), Parias (Paria), and Alparqueros (shoemakers).[1] All these people that they call blacks are, and pass among the natives of the country as, so low and infamous that it is [111] an irremediable contamination and disgrace, not only to eat with them, but even to behold them drink or eat. Thus other castes never do one or the other, happen what may. Nor can any one of the other castes live in the house of any of these blacks, or take from their hand anything to eat or drink. They would much rather be left to die unheeded than touch, or allow themselves to be touched by, one of those blacks, or take from their hands anything to eat or drink. For if that happens, in addition to the penalty of death attached thereto, if the fact comes to the knowledge of the magistrate, all the family and descendants are marked with infamy, and become on a level with the blacks themselves, and have no hope of ever being able to re-enter their caste.

These blacks, then, live outside the inhabited places and towns occupied by all the other castes, including the learned, whom

1. The Pariahs (3,223,938) and Pallis (1,295,049), taken together, are the most numerous caste in the Madras presidency. The common subdivisions of the Pariahs are: (1) Pariah; (2) Pullar, or, in Malayalam, Pulyar; (3) Chucklers, or Shakkiliyar (workers in leather, evidently Manucci's *al parqueiros*); (4) Toti ('Madras Manual of Administration,' ii. 232, 234). Mr. Frazer says that in all these words the termination *or* is the sign of the plural. Pariah comes from *parai,* a drum used at funerals. They are a class originally employed as drummers at funerals. They' are the chief fighting supporters of the 'right hand,' and the Pallis of the 'left hand' caste, a division of the populace (Caldwell, 'Dravidian Grammar,' edition 1875, p. 546). For *achivanatar,* all I can suggest is the Vettiyaur Pariah of p. 655, vol. iii., of the 'Manual.' Mr. Ferguson says that *vanniyar is* an alternative name for the Palli caste. Chandaliya is in Hindi the name of a caste of scavengers, the supposed issue of a Brahmani and a Sudra father.

they call chares (*acharya*),[1] and the monks, whom they call Saniares (*Sannyasi*);[2] and all these better classes may not even speak to the outcasts. Should by accident one of these low fellows touch any pots or vessels used by any of the other castes for cooking or holding water, the owners can no longer touch them or use them. But they must throw them away, or make them over to people of the caste which had touched them, be the vessel empty or full of food. What is to be wondered at is that they are not allowed either to enter the temples, where their false gods are worshipped, or to draw water from the wells used by the other castes. If while on a voyage one of the other classes should fall ill where there was no one else than some of these blacks, they would sooner die than take water or any other thing from their hands. To give some conception of the infamy attached by the Hindus to these blacks, I will say that there are no words to express the vileness of the esteem in which they are held.

Of these five castes, or different kinds of people, some say that the first only—that is, the Brahmans—have a soul; others, in direct contradiction to the above, assert that all men have one and the same soul, or that all their souls are of one and the same substance.

CHAPTER VII

OF THE MANNERS, GOVERNMENT, AND CUSTOMS OF THE HINDUS AMONG THEMSELVES

The first error of these Hindus is to believe that they are the only people in the world who have any polite manners; and the

1. *Acharya* affixed to a name is now a mark of learning. It was originally the title of the spiritual guide ('Manu,' 2, 140), who invests with the sacred thread, instructs in the Vedas and ritual (R.W.F.).
2. The rule in Vedic times was that the fourth stage of a Brahman's life should be spent as a Sannyasi, when he discards the sacred thread, shaves his top-knot, and begs food ('Manu,' vi. 54-56). 'Now the chief *Gurus* (superiors) of the three great sects who follow respectively the *Dvaita* (duality), *Advaita* (non-duality), *Visishtadvaita* (qualified duality) schools of philosophy must be *Saniyasi* (*sic*), only, instead of leading a wandering life, they reside at the chief seats of theological power, and, though they subsist by the alms of the faithful, their revenues are in reality very large indeed' (Padfield, 'The Hindu at Home,' p. 221) (R.W.F.).

same is the case with cleanliness and orderliness in business. They think all other nations, and above all Europeans, are barbarous, despicable, filthy, and devoid of order.

The civilities they pay to each other are as follows, divisible into five categories. In the first they raise the hands to the head and prostrate themselves on the ground; this is the form in which they adore God, and salute their spiritual leaders, the *Sannyasis*, who are their monks, and they also employ it for kings, princes, and the great. Although this is practised by nearly every caste, it is not observed by the Brahmans; they prostrate themselves only before God, their teachers, who are always Brahmans, and their monks, also invariably of their own caste.

The second manner of salutation is to lift the hands to the head. It is in this fashion that they salute ordinary persons [112], governors, generals, and ministers of kings and princes. The third manner is to raise the hands only as high as the stomach; and this is the course adopted by equals and friends, followed by an embrace. The fourth manner is to display the two hands with the palms joined. This is done by the learned and by monks before princes and the great, when those persons make use to them of one of the three methods above described. Finally, the fifth and last mode of salutation is to display the palm of the right hand raised on high; this is how superiors act to inferiors.

Brahmans salute kings in the second manner only; and to it the latter respond in the same form. But what is delightful is to see a Brahman on a visit to another man, for without the slightest salutation he seats himself, and in the conversation the host accords him the title of lordship or excellency, and often that of highness. When he takes his leave he goes off most solemnly without being any more polite on going away than on entering.

There are also among these Hindus some families in the east called Sudra, the least noble of the four castes I have spoken of (and to this caste belong nowaways the kings and princes of this Country), who are called Vanangamory (Vananga-mori).[1] These people pay no civility either to princes or kings, not even to their own false gods; they appear neither in the palaces nor the temples.

1. Mori = 'word' in Tamil, and is used at the end of compounds for 'those who say.' *Vananga* (from *vanangu, a* reverence, a bow), 'bows not the head' (see 'Kurral,' Book I., 9, for *vananga-talai*, 'he who bows not the head'). So *vananga-mori* = 'those who say they bow not the head' (R. W. F.).

XXVI. Bahadur Khan. foster-brother of Aurangzeb

If you ask them the reason why, recognising as they do the king for their lord, and confessing the idol to be their god, they do not pay them homage like other men, they tell you that the greatness of their sect consists in this; and with that answer, being content with it themselves, they imagine you ought also to be satisfied.

With respect to their fashions of dress, I may say that the great nobles wear nothing more than the following: They bind their hair with a scarf of very fine gold stuff that they call *romals* (*rumali*). Then they tie round their waist a piece of white cloth (as is the usual practice in India); it is about four cubits in length, and has a red border. It comes down to their knees. Above this they wear a white wrapper; but it is to be noted that the manner of putting this on varies in each caste. Some among them wear gold or silver rings on the toes. The children of these last carry from birth to seven years of age little bells on their legs, either of gold or silver, and a little chain of the same metal round the waist. As for the rest, they are no more covered than when they were brought into the world.

Some great lords wear a sort of turban on their heads, and put on a gown of white cloth that they call a *cabaye* (*qaba*), and underneath it very tight drawers; on their feet they have shoes of velvet or of red leather. These they remove when they enter a house or speak to a person of quality, for it is a great piece of bad manners in this country to speak to such a person with your shoes on and your head uncovered. The monks, called *Sannyasis*, are excepted, also ascetics, called Tavagi (*tapasa*),[1] and Brahmans, and all castes up to about the age of eighteen.[2] This last exception is because up to that age they neither allow their hair to grow nor bind on the scarf of gold, of which I spoke above; they only leave on the middle of the head a little tail of hair [113].[3]

---

1. *Tapasa*, a performer of penances.
2. The sentence is elliptic; it evidently means that the classes enumerated do *not* cover their heads.
3. According to 'Manu,' the *Kesanta*, cutting off the hair, is in the sixteenth year for a Brahman, twenty-second, year for a Kshatriya, and twenty-fourth year for a Vaisya (see 'Manu,' 11, 21*a*, for the two rites of tonsure and cutting the hair) (R. W. F.).

The above is the apparel of the princes and the richest nobility. As for the soldiers, labourers, and other ordinary people, they have no more than a cloth bound round their head, and a little string round their middle, attached to which is a morsel of cloth, a span wide and a cubit in length, about the size of one of our ordinary napkins. With this cloth they cover the parts of the body that natural modesty requires to be concealed. Lastly, they have another cloth, somewhat of the same size, bound round the body, which serves in the day-time as a garment and at night as a bed, their mattress being identical with the damp earth. A stone or a piece of wood serves as bolster. Thus what would be looked on in Europe as a severe penance is in this country the ordinary habit. There are some so badly provided that they content themselves with the piece of cloth spoken of above as used to cover the private parts. In this equipment they hold themselves fully dressed and fit to talk to anyone, wherever it might be.

Having spoken of men's dress, the next thing is to say a little about that of women. It is very indifferent, and little can be said about it. From the age of twelve and upwards almost all of them allow their hair to grow long; up to that age they wear only a small tail of hair on the top of the head, like that of the little boys. They do not bind anything on, nor do they make the hair into tresses, but make it into a roll on one side of the head. All have their ears pierced, but not in the European way, for the holes are so large that the ears droop almost to the shoulders. In these holes they wear their ornaments, each according to her degree or her wealth. The custom of having the ears pierced is in this country common to men and women.

Women, when they are not widows, also wear ornaments on the neck, according to the diversity of their castes or of their wealth. Up to the age of nine or ten years they have no more clothing than, as I described above, is worn by boys up to the same age. After that time they wear a piece of white or red cotton cloth that they bind on like a petticoat. Sometimes the *pane* (*punjam*)[1]—for so they call this cloth—is

1. I suggest for *pane* of the text *punjam* ('Madras Manual of Administration,' iii. 707), a cloth 18 yards long by 38 to 44 inches wide, what in Northern India is called a *sari*. The Word *pane* is used again farther on in this part (iii. 133). Mr. Frazer proposes the Portuguese *panno*, 'cloth' (Latin,

striped in two colours. One half of the said *pane* (*punjam*) is thrown over the shoulders or the head when speaking to a person of any position; but when they go to the well or a spring to fetch water, and when at work in their houses, they keep the whole *pane* (*punjam*) bound round the waist, and thence upwards are naked. They wear nothing on the feet, not even princesses and queens; but the latter wear on their legs jewels of great value, and any other women who are able to afford it do the same.

This is briefly the clothing of these people. Their dwellings also are very small. Excluding the temples of their false gods, some of which cost great sums, and the palaces of a few kings, princes, *et cetera,* which are built of brick and mortar, and even then have no architectural style, all other houses are constructed of earth and pieces of wood bound together with ropes, without much regard to appearances. These wooden posts serve as supporting pillars, and the roof is of thatch. In this way they build a house without using a single nail. The floors of the houses are not stone-paved, nor covered with the sort of cement they make in this country of lime, eggs, and other ingredients mixed together. The floors are of pounded earth only, spread over with a wash of cow's dung. This is the bed of the great majority of humble people in this country, who have no other mattress to lie on. However, rich people have a mat or a quilt on which they sleep; and those that possess this much believe themselves in possession of one of the greatest luxuries in the world [114].

The ordinary dwelling of these Hindus being as poverty-stricken as I have described it, their mode of life is no better. For in this land there are no tables or chairs; everybody sits upon the ground. They do not use table-napkins, table-cloths, knives, spoons, or forks, salt-cellars, dishes, or plates; they eat no bread, they drink no wine, and all eat seated upon the ground.

Princes and kings eat in the following manner: They are seated on the ground on a piece of fine cloth. Then the house or the room in which they are to eat is rubbed over with a solution of cow-dung. As the palaces of kings have floors made

---

pannus), and La Loubere ('Royaume de Siam,' 1691, i. 91), in describing the dhoti, or loin-cloth, says it is called by the Portuguese *pagne*, from the Latin *pannus*.

of a cement which looks like fine marble, there they do nothing more than throw down some cow-dung mixed in water, and then wipe the floor with a piece of cloth. The floor then looks like a looking-glass. Without all this ceremonial of cleansing with the dung of this animal, as above described, no person of quality sits down to eat. These preparations finished, they bring a great platter of enamelled gold, which is placed on the ground in front of the diners, but without allowing it to touch the cloth on which they are seated. After this some small gold dishes are placed around, and the food is brought from the kitchen in bowls or vessels of silver, fashioned in the shape of cooking-pots. First of all, from these bowls they place rice cooked without salt or other condiment in the large dish, and on this they put some stew. If the whole cannot be contained in the large dish, they put the remainder in the small dishes round about it.

Then the rajah takes whatever pleases him, throwing it with his hand into a plate of rice, where he mixes it and rolls it into balls, which he throws into his mouth with the right hand. The left hand is not allowed to touch any food. All is swallowed without mastication. This fashion they consider very cleanly, and that there is no better way of satisfying oneself; and they say that Europeans eat rice like pigs. Then, before finishing the meal, they send as much as they think sufficient to their wives. For in this country these never eat with their husbands, even though those waiting on the king be eunuchs, children, or women.

The way of eating among the other castes who are not kings is as follows: Monks, ascetics, Brahmans, and the learned before eating wash their hands and bodies. Then they put upon their foreheads, stomach, shoulders,' knees and sides a little ashes mixed in water. This ash is either of a white earth they call *naman* (*namam*),[1] or of sandal, according to their caste or the faith they follow. Next they enter the house, finding its floors all rubbed over with cow-dung, in the way I have spoken of. They bind round their body a piece of cloth, and sit down with their legs crossed, or upon a small mat of about one cubit in

1. The upright white Vaishnava line, or the centre line of the trident mark; also the earth, or pipe-clay, with which it is made. If there are three lines, like a trident, the central one is red or yellow. (R. W. F.).

length. Before them is placed the large leaf of certain trees, or smaller leaves of other trees stitched together, not with needle and thread, but with rushes. Upon this leaf is put First of all a pinch of salt and two drops of butter, with which they anoint or rub the leaf. This ceremony completed, they deposit on this platter some rice cooked in water without salt, followed by a little vegetables and some green stuff. When this is eaten, they throw upon the rice left on the said leaf a little sour curds or some whey. When all this food has been swallowed, they rise from the place and move to a courtyard or garden, if [115] there is one in the house where they live. If there is not, they go into the street, and there bathe their hands, mouth, and feet. They do not return to their dwellings till the leaves they have eaten from have been removed, and the ground has been rubbed over afresh in the way already mentioned. For they say that if they did so their bodies would be as polluted as the house.

Since neither Brahmans, ascetics, monks, nor the learned eat any meat or fish in this country (eggs, being here included under the head of meat, are also avoided),[1] I think it as well here to state the food and manner of eating of the other castes. None of those I have hitherto spoken of ever eat cow's flesh. To do so is a very low thing, a defilement, and sinful beyond all imagination. But they eat all the other meats consumed in Europe, and, in addition thereto, rats and lizards. As for shellfish, these also are classed among the most impure of things, and are not used except by the pariahs. However, almost all the castes eat of the other kinds of meat, and judge it to be most delicious fare.

The food of these people is usually placed on a little cooked rice, and it consists generally of a portion of dry and salted fish. For goats, sheep, chicken, rats, and lizards, are only for the nobility, and if other men eat of these, it is solely at their

1. 'Meat can never be obtained without injury to living creatures, and injury to sentient beings is detrimental to the attainment of heavenly bliss: let him, therefore, eschew the use of meat' ('Manu,' v. 48). 'There are, it is said, tribes of Brahmans who may eat fish, and we know that many of the manifold divisions of the fourth caste eat fish and mutton or goat's flesh freely. There is, however, among all classes, the lowest outcastes excepted, the greatest repugnance to eating the flesh of cows or oxen' (Padfield, 'Hindu at Home,' p. 159) (R. W. F.).

festivals and at marriages. Their plate is a leaf, as described above, or a small plate of copper, out of which the whole family eats, one after the other.

Although these people hold it an abomination to eat of the cow, they believe, however, that it is a venerable thing, and one worthy of all praise, to drink that animal's urine, and to smother their faces with it.[1] It is in pursuance of this opinion that the most noble and the most gallant among them rise betimes in the morning, and holding a cow's tail, worship the spot covered thereby. The reason they give is that this is Lakshmi, mother of their god, Vishnu, and goddess of prosperity. Their worship over, they hold out their two hands and receive the cow's urine, of which they take a drink. Then, turning the tail into a sort of holy-water sprinkler, they immerse it in the said liquid, and with it they daub their faces. When this ceremonial is over, they declare they have been made holy.

To obtain plenary indulgence for all their sins, they say it is necessary to obtain a beverage composed of milk, butter, cow-dung and cow's urine. With this medicament not only is all sin driven away, but all infamy. In this the Brahmans intervene, for it is they alone who can secure this 'jubilee.' It is obligatory when marrying for the first time, when women arrive at puberty, and on unlucky day. Even the cleverest men, those who look down on the rest of the world, have their houses rubbed with cow-dung before they eat, and then, without other ceremony, have their food brought, and eat it.

There is another class of persons called Nostiguer (? Nastika),[2] who not only may not be looked upon when

1. The *pancha-gavya* are the five products of the cow—milk, sour milk, butter, urine, and dung. The three horizontal lines on the fore-head of Siva's followers are made with the ashes of burnt cow-dung (Padfield's 'Hindu at Home,' p. 89). (R. W. F.).
2. An atheist; anyone who doubts the divine authority of the Vedas or the legends of the 'Puranas' ('Madras Manual of Administration,' iii. 539). This doubtful identification of Nostiguer is given in default of a better; if Nastika is correct, it may be here an abusive term for the Jains. I am told that one sect of them entirely remove the hair of the head, and the Madras Jains will not eat with Hindus. Mr. Frazer writes: ' "Manu," ii, 11, declares that Nastikas, or Atheists, should be treated with contempt; but it is not known that they had, or have, any peculiar habits of eating or wearing their hair.'

eating, but may not hear the sound of any human voice while so occupied. So far is this carried [116] that, when eating, they cause a copper vessel to be beaten hard at their door. Men of this caste do not allow their beard to be touched, either by the razor or by scissors, but it is dragged out, hair by hair, with a small pincers. The first time that the pulling out of the hair of the head and beard is begun, if the patient betrays no sign of pain, he is accepted as a firm disciple; if, on the contrary, he weeps, cries, or makes faces, they say he is too tender, and thereby unworthy to be admitted into the confraternity.

These men are not the only ones who may not be seen, eating, for other castes may not look at Brahmans who are eating. In regard to this these Hindus have a rather amusing habit. The Brahmans, according to their view, are the noblest family of all mankind, and the one most venerated, not merely as superiors, but as gods. Other castes cannot wait on them or fetch them water, nor cook for them. They must wait upon each other for these two purposes, or do it each for himself. With all that, however, they may carry water and cook for the other castes, which appears a moral contradiction, for if it dishonours them to be served by others, how can they be servants to others?

When Brahmans cook for another caste they act as follows: after having cooked the food, they bring it in brass or copper vessels to the house where it is to be eaten—that is, of the man who have given the order. Not being a Brahman, he cannot enter the kitchen, nor inspect the pots in which the food is being cooked. The food having been brought, it is laid out upon leaves, or on copper or brass vessels made like dishes. Having helped the food, the Brahmans do the waiting until the end of the repast. Then they and the master and his guests, if any, come out, and the Brahmans throw water over the eaters' hands and feet; but they do not clear away what has not been eaten, for that would be a dishonour and a disgrace beyond repair. To remove the unused food it is necessary to have another man who is not a Brahman, and if there is none such, he who has eaten must himself remove the leavings, along with the leaf or dish from which he has eaten, and afterwards cleanse the house in the way already described.

As to their mode of eating, it is as follows: they all eat with the right hand, and may not touch anything with the left, not even the plate or leaf from which they have eaten, nor the spoon with which they sup a concoction by way of wine, which is some water boiled with pepper. But a vessel of cold water they lift with the left hand, at the same time never putting the vessel to the mouth. They hold their mouth open and raised to catch the liquid they pour into it. In fine, the greatest piece of refinement in this country is considered to be eating in a clean and orderly way, but this is carried out in no other manner than that described above. Yet, being so very different from that practised by Europeans and Mahomedans, it forms the ground for their strong contempt for these latter [117].

ON THEIR MODE OF GOVERNMENT AMONG THEMSELVES

The Hindu government is the most tyranniç and barbarous imaginable, because, all the rajahs or kings being foreigners, they treat their subjects worse than if they were slaves. All land belongs to the crown; no individual has as his own a field, or estate, or any property whatever, that he can bequeath to his children. The method in which the rajahs let out their lands is as follows:

At the beginning of their year, which is in June, the officials come from the court to the villages and compel the peasants to take up the land at a certain rate. This bargain made, they must give notice at harvest-time to the king's officers, for without their permission the peasants may not harvest the grain. As soon as notice is received the officials proceed to the spot, and before allowing the crop to be cut, they ask the cultivators whether they are willing to give a half or a third more than they have contracted for at the beginning of the year. Should the cultivators agree to this, writings are drawn up and security taken; but after having made the bargain, they usually find that what they gather in does not suffice to meet the king's rent. It thus happens, more often than not, that they find themselves ruined by this revenue payment.

It is for this reason that many of them, when the royal officials try to increase the demand, reply that they can pay no more than they agreed to before signing the papers. But this way, too, they find themselves equally ruined, for the officials then remain present during the harvest, and inspect the cutting of all the crops, the cultivator also being present. When all is ready, they first place on one side the cultivator's share; next they compel him, then and there, to buy the king's share. When in the countryside one measure is selling for six *sols*, they force the peasants to give them nine. In this way, whatever be the method employed, the poor cultivator finds himself ruined. Nothing is left to him to maintain his family, seeing that they are obliged to enter every year into new engagements in order to get a subsistence for their family and obtain fresh supplies.

Nor is it particularly easy to take to flight, for wherever they go they find the same tyrannies. It may be said of them what Martial sang of Phauno:

> 'Et mortem fugeret se Phaunius ipse peremit.
> Die mihi non furor este ne memoriam mori.[1]

Besides, all the cultivators give sureties to the king. These sureties are usually given by one village for another. Thus the poor cultivators live on in hope. For, ordinarily, the rajahs or kings appoint fresh officials every year to lease out the village lands. These men, in order to get them taken again by the cultivators, make fresh promises, including that of governing justly and rationally. Then they advance the cultivators something to induce them to cultivate the land carefully. After the man has ploughed and sown, and is engaged in working the land, he is no longer free to remove elsewhere [118]. In this way they recover from the peasantry by consent or by force whatever they have lent them.

1. 'Ut mortem fugeret se Phaunius ipse peremit.
Die mihi non furor iste ne memoriam mori.
(To escape death Phaunius killed himself.
Tell me, what madness is that to have no thought
or memory of death ?)

The correct text is:
'Hostem cum fugeret, se Faunius ipse peremit.
Hie, rogo, non furor est, ne moriare, mori?'
(Himself he slew, when he the foe would fly.
What madness this, for fear of death to die !)
'M. Val. Martialis Epigrammata,' edition W. M. Lindsay (Clarendon Press), Lib. II., Epig. LXXX., and 'The Epigrams of Martial translated into English Prose' (G. Bell and Sons, 1877).

This is the tyrannical system with which the rajahs or kings of these countries rule over the country people. These well deserve such treatment from their pride and their contrariness, for, if they were treated otherwise, it would be their entire ruin; they would all kill each other, as is demonstrated by experience among those of them who have anything to lose.

The rajahs deal thus tyrannically with the agricultural population, that being the occupation of the greater number of the inhabitants of the country, without distinction of descent or caste, for everyone may follow it. At the same time, they behave no less cruelly to their creatures and officials. For, having sent them into the provinces to collect the rents, the only business confided to them, and having allowed them to pass several years in that employment, the rajah, on the simple supposition that they must have embezzled (as to which there need be no doubt), causes them to be seized, has them whipped and exposed to other cruel tortures. All that the officials have is taken from them, and he who yesterday was a great lord is to-day the most abject of mendicants; he who yesterday was rolling in wealth wanders to-day from house to house and door to door begging an alms.

All the collectors of the crown rents are, during the time they are in office, absolute masters of the province made over to them, and can take cognizance of all disputes, whether regarding civil or criminal questions, even matters relating to religion. In everything they can pass final sentence without appeal, even when the death penalty is involved. Since there is not throughout this empire any written law or ordinance, each one acts as it best pleases him, and puts to death anyone as he thinks fit. He can do this, since there is no one to demand an account of his acts, above all when he is a receiver of the crown rents.

When any hungry wretch takes it into his head to ruin the kingdom, he goes to the king and says to him: 'Sire! If your Majesty will give me the permission to raise money and a certain number of armed men, I will pay so many millions.' The king then asks how it is intended to raise the money. It is by nothing else than the seizure of everybody in the kingdom, men and women, and by dint of torture compelling them to pay what is demanded. Such financiers are hateful and avaricious men. The king generally consents to their unjust proposals, as he thereby satisfies his own greed; he accords the asked-for permission, and demands security bonds.

The men, armed with the order, and impelled by their desire to gain an overplus on the sum contracted for, go about seizing everybody and putting them to torture. For, without such pressure, no one would pay anything, experience in time past having proved to the subjects that, should any of them, through fear of punishment, make no difficulties about paying what is demanded, he does not thereby evade torture. For the financier and his agents always accept on account what the poor fellow has offered; but they infer that he who pays so readily, thinking more of torture than of his money, must have a deal more than he can give. This is why they demand from such a man as much again; and, if he refuses, he is subjected to torture to enforce payment. He is not released till he has paid all that has been demanded the second time.

The tortures to which they subject these men are very severe. The first is made by water, and is very cruel. They place two pieces of wood at the bottom of a pond or a river bound to four posts driven into the ground. They lay the poor sufferer on [119] the two pieces of wood with his arms bound, either behind, at his side, or in front. Then two or three men are seated upon him, and after leaving him like that for a time, he is extricated. They then ask him to agree to what they want. If he refuses, they resume the above treatment until he makes the required promise.

If they do not succeed in this way, they expose him to fire by making him tread on red-hot iron bars, and brand him on the ribs with iron axes heated in a fire. Others are drawn with red-hot pincers, others are tortured with cold pincers, which hurt even more. Some have their arms tied with ropes up to such a point and so tightly that the blood comes in drops from their finger-ends; and thus tightly bound they are suspended from two iron rings placed abreast and flogged with all imaginable cruelty with the whips that are used to horses. Others are stretched on the ground tied to four posts, and there they rub the man's face with *criques* (bricks)[1] so violently and forcibly that it is made as flat as a board. Others are thrown naked upon sharp thorns, and on the top of the man is placed a board, on which three or four men walk up and down.

1. *Criques*: Thus in the French text. I substitute *briques*.

In other cases they tie thick cords steeped in oil to all the fingers of the hands and throw the cords over a beam, suspending the fingers in the air, without any power of movement. They then set light to the ends of the cords and let them burn to the last, unless the sufferer before that time promises what is asked. If he makes a promise it is reduced to writing, and the poor wretch has to procure a surety.

It is by these means and others like them, which I omit in order not to be too lengthy, that they find out and lay hold of all that these poor wretches may possess, not even allowing one of them to escape, not even the priests serving their own idols. Indeed, they often begin with the children and the nearest relations of the rajah, so that no one can excuse himself from meeting their demands, if not in one way, then in another. If through, affection they do pass anyone over, even though he may not be worthy of any punishment, they think that they are doing a very great favour, and that they would be avoiding their duty if they did not act upon the orders of their tyrannical government.

When the financier has satisfied the prince by paying the money agreed upon, the latter orders him into arrest, and applies to him what he has done to others, and deprives him of all he has acquired. It often happens that, by a just judgment of God, such persons, either from want of fortitude or fear of being so wanting, and disinclination to paying the money asked for, give up their lives under such tortures. All that is stated above is ordinary and settled custom throughout India, and it may be said, in a general way, that all, great and small, are little else but thieves. He who is the most adroit and the keenest in this trade passes as the most agreeable comrade. As I speak of the Malabaris, I think it judicious, for the reader's satisfaction, to append some reflections on what I have said.

I know that those who read this account will not be able either to understand or imagine what sort of people those of this country are who are subjected to such tyranny, and yet continue to dwell in a country where such things are practised. To this objection I reply that all the neighbouring princes are the same sort of tyrants. To leave the dominions of this one and seek refuge in those of that one would be to seek repose by exposing one's self to greater hardships. In addition to that, I say, it must be remembered [120] that these regions are extremely populous. Everybody of both sexes marries, and a considerable number of men take more wives than one. In this way it is practically impossible for one of these kingdoms to provide room and means of subsistence for the population of a second kingdom.

Although this is the fact, there are some who, like men suffering from fever, imagine that by changing their abode from one place to another they will find some relief. For this reason they are always removing from one province to another, though it be within the same kingdom. But they encounter throughout the same treatment that they sought to avoid, and often encounter greater hardships, for, without house or covering, they find themselves strangers in the land, and yet that fact does not give them any immunity from punishments.

In addition to these tyrannies and ways of robbing people, there are other practices more continuous and more inevitable. There are certain noblemen who have under them people they call guardians of the realm. These persons, in their turn, place subordinate officials in every village as guards. These subaltern officials are like little sovereigns in those places, where they issue their commands in civil as well as in criminal business. If this be not by right, they do it by force. The cultivators and the other persons belonging to the body forming the community entertain them, and pay punctually certain annual contributions. They are under obligation to prevent thefts within the bounds committed to their charge. If there is a theft, they must pay compensation; but they are themselves the greatest thieves ever heard of, and they take away the best of the things to be found in the houses under their protection. Their assertion is that they are not bound to compensate for what is stolen in the daytime.

As for thefts happening at night, they ask to be shown the thief, and forthwith he shall be made to pay. If anyone ventures to open his mouth, and asserts that everything he had has been taken, that he shall go to the superior officer to complain, these same watchmen seek him out at night, and, if they do not kill him, give him a sound beating. They strip him of all he has, and warn him that if he opens his month on the matter they will kill him and all his relations. The guardians of the realm, let alone their being the most ambitious and the most inhuman of human beings, kill or procure the killing of anybody and everybody for a mere nothing, and carry on such a disastrous warfare against each other that it is rare to see one of them die of disease.

The cruelties perpetrated in some other of the kingdoms are not less severe, principally in the lands subject to certain rajahs. Here is one sample. If, for instance, there be born a son to a rajah or to one of his relations on a day held by them of evil augury, adopting the advice of Brahmans, they endeavour to avert the day's malignant influence by sending men out on that and the following nights to burn down one or two villages, or sometimes more. Since almost all the houses are thatched with straw or grass, many poor persons lose their lives as well as all their property.

These rajahs have still another measure of policy—the keeping as prisoners of those who will succeed them. This they do as long as they live; no sooner do the rulers die than the chief men of the country release those prisoners, proclaim them, and crown them as rajah. However, it is noticeable that, though the rajahs take all this trouble to suppress treason or alteration in the government, such things are continually happening, from an absence of justice, which can never be well exercised [121] where there is a want of experience.

Having set forth the cruelty and bad usage meted out by the Hindus to the natives of the country, their natural-born subjects, it is easy to picture their dealings with foreigners. It is impossible to live among people so barbarous, such enemies of all kinds of justice and sound reason.

I come now to their mode of making war. When two rajahs are at war, they retain ambassadors not only at the court, but often in the army which is opposed to them. Since secrecy is the soul of government, a rule which these barbarians ignore, I do not consider that I am wronging them when I say that their political condition is that of a body without a soul; for every intention and every design of an enemy is known to his opponent and to everyone else—so much so, that when an ambassador dispatches a letter to his rajah, it is read out by him in public. Ordinarily in the council where the letter is read there is present an envoy of the enemy, or some dependent of his. It is a common practice among these rajahs to end up a war by a payment made from the weaker to the stronger, for money is their only passion. As regards the men, not a native of this country has any loyalty, or gratitude, or power to keep a secret.

Armies never march in formed bodies, but always in long files. Almost every soldier has with him in camp his wife and children. Thus a soldier may be seen carrying under his arm an unweaned infant, and on his head a basket of cooking-pots and pans. Behind him marches his wife with his spears, or else his matchlock, upon her back. In place of a bayonet they stick into the muzzle of the gun a spoon, which, being long, is more conveniently carried there than in the basket borne by the husband upon his head. The want of order being so great, the desertions are very numerous, for to-day a soldier will be serving in one army and to-morrow in an opposing force; then, when it so pleases him, he will rejoin his first service without any hesitation, and as often as not may even be promoted. These soldiers being so brave and agile, one need not be astonished at my saying that even when a battle is very bloody, the number of killed and wounded never exceeds one hundred; because, as soon as the battle has begun, flight is resorted to on one side or the other. So great is their fear of cavalry, that forty thousand infantry will not stand against two thousand horsemen. As soon as these come in sight, the men on foot begin to run nearly as fast as the horses can gallop, even should the riders not be carrying any kind of firearm.

CHAPTER VIII

CUSTOMS FOLLOWED BY HINDUS AT THEIR MARRIAGES

To their idea, there is not in this world anything to compare in importance with getting married. It is in marriage, as they understand things, that consists one of the [122] greatest felicities of human life. Imbued with that opinion, children, as soon as they can talk and know how to say 'father' and 'mother,' are taught to say that they want to marry. Often their daughters are married even before they have learnt to talk; and as in this country there are so many different kinds of castes and tribes, there are equally many different manners and customs. First of all, then, I will state what practices are common to everybody, and, secondly, what is peculiar to each caste.

It is ordinarily the case among the Hindus that the husband is some years older than the wife, but both are of one caste. Almost all of them hold the essence of the marriage rites to consist in binding on a little piece of gold called a taly (*tali*),[1] which the husband must attach to the bride's neck, just as in Europe rings are exchanged. The parents on both sides agree to the conditions of the contract, and fix the day of the marriage. This is carried out in front of the house door in a species of arbour constructed expressly, and quite new. This arbour is erected for everybody, from the king down to the shepherd. Although all the conditions have been settled, should, on this occasion of attaching the piece of gold, someone else, through envy or hatred or some family reason, step in front of the bridegroom and tie the piece of gold to the bride's neck, this man is held to be her true husband and the bride his real wife, although she may not want him—may, indeed, have resisted and opposed it with all her strength.

After this the bridegroom and his relations come out into the open to search for signs favourable to their purpose. If they meet with such, they go to the girl's father's house, and ask for her as their daughter-in-law. After the father and mother have entertained those who have come to ask for their daughter's hand, they, as a rule, raise objections to the demand, saying that they will consult the omens and then give an answer. In this way they send off the demanders, asking them to return in a few days. In conformity to this request, they come back, and the omens are examined. If favourable, the contract is completed. It is not uncommon for a husband to buy his wife.[2]

---

1. From *tala*, Sanskrit, the palmyra-tree; from the original practice of wearing for this purpose the palmyra-leaf dipped in saffron-water. It is now a piece of gold, forming either the centre or the sole ornament of a necklace, which is tied on the neck of the bride by the bridegroom at the time of marriage, a practice common to all the people of Southern. India. The *tali* is worn till the woman becomes a widow, when it is removed by the husband's relations. Many *talis* are made of two pieces which separate; some are cup-shaped, some are flat and oval. Some have the figures of Vigneswaram, Lachhmi, a *lingam*, the sun, or the moon engraved on them. The *tali* is fastened round the neck by a string dyed yellow with saffron ('Madras Manual of Administration,' iii. 882; see also Winslow's 'Tamil Dictionary,' and Padfield's 'Hindu at Home,' p. 126).
2. 'Manu,' iii. 51, prohibits the receiving a gratuity for giving a daughter in marriage; nevertheless, 'it is by no means uncommon for the bride's parents to demand a sum of money' (Padfield, 'Hindu at Home,' p. 115) (R. W. F.).

When the price has been fixed, the man's parents procure a part of the money, and carry it to the girl's father. That done, they bring a bunch of flowers, a cono-nut, and a branch of figs (bananas),[1] to be presented to the bride. After this ceremony, if the bridegroom repents and declines to marry the girl, he loses the money he had advanced as a sort of earnest-money. If it is the woman who breaks the agreement, the parents must return double the money they have received.

CHAPTER IX

CEREMONIES OBSERVED BY BRAHMANS AT THEIR WEDDINGS

After a Brahman who wishes to marry has applied to his future father-in-law for his daughter's hand, he quits the place where his future wife resides and enters another house, where he is awaited by the relations of the girl. Then, after conversing [123] some time, the bridegroom pretends he is angry, and rising in a great hurry, he puts on a pair of old clogs, takes a staff in his hand, puts a book under his arm, and says to the assembly that he is off for a pilgrimage through the world. He does really go away, but not very far, for the nearest relations of the woman hinder him by their implorations, and promise, for the purpose of appeasing his feigned anger, that he shall be married without delay.

As proof that what they say is not a mockery, but the unalloyed truth, they take hold of him and place him on a table and carry him to the bride's door, where the girl's mother is waiting. After she has bathed his feet with cow's milk, and he has wiped them on the clothes he is wearing, they make him sit a little time on a new mat. Then the parents raise him by the hand, and seat him beside the bride on a swing made of boards tied to a beam with ropes. Then while some propel the swing, others break forth into laudatory songs.

When the bridegroom gets down and the music is over (all this taking place at the street-door), they bring him into the

1. The *banana* was called by the Portuguese the Indian fig (Yule, 56, quoting Pyrard de Laval).

courtyard of the house, where they offer sacrifices and worship fire, which they hold also to be God.[1] They offer also a coconut to an idol. When this is completed, the brother of the bride brings her forth in his arms. He seats her on a *scuderis*.[2] Then, before the bridegroom can bind on the piece of gold (*i.e.*, the *tali*), the bride's father and her other relations put themselves in front of him and demand for the girl more money than agreed on in the beginning. On this point there is always a grand dispute, which does not always end without the interchange of abusive words, the least of which would in Europe make a man kill himself, or in any other land where there was the least feeling of shame and modesty. To end up with, the bridegroom is called upon to pay the extra money that the father-in-law continues to ask for—that is, unless he prefers to give up the alliance. After this dispute is over, he ties the piece of gold to the neck of the bride, whereby the marriage is concluded. The bridegroom finishes with a profound bow to his mother-in-law that is to be, throwing himself at her feet. She raises him, and gives him a coco-nut However, she is not allowed to speak to him again for many a year. This obeisance over, the bridegroom takes hold of the bride's foot, and before everybody puts it three times on a stone which they use to crush their pepper and similar articles of food. Then they resume once more their sacrifices.

All that concerns the contract being accomplished, the banquet ceremonial follows, which is carried out thus: First of all, the ground beneath the arbour, surrounded by branches of trees, is carefully rubbed over with cow-dung. Then the guests seat themselves on the ground, and before each is placed the leaf of a tree, or several leaves sewn together, as already spoken of (III. 114). On each is then placed a little salt and a small morsel of fruit preserved in vinegar. Next come the viands, carried by

1. The *homam*, or sacred fire, 'is made and kept up in the centre of a prepared place during the whole of the marriage festival days' (Padfield, 'Hindu at Home,' p. 129) (R. W. F.)
2. The French text has *scuderis*, which I take to be = *sudarium*, an old French word borrowed direct from the Latin (see Bescherelle, 'Nouv. Dict. Nat.,' 1631: 'Sorte de mouchoir, le plus souvent en lin, dont on se servait pour essuyer la sueur qui couvrait le visage.' I have seen *sudaris* used in Scotch for a handkerchief; but, quoting Padfield, "Hindu at Home,': p. 123, Mr. Frazer points out that 'the bride is brought out seated in a kind of wicker basket,' not on a Handkerchief.

the attendants in baskets. They consist of cooked rice, of which each receives on his leaf as much as can be eaten, for nothing ought to be left. After this, as second *plât,* they bring cooked grain, over which they pour a little butter, and add various kinds of green-stuff A second time they ladle out cooked rice on the top, and last of all some broth made of water and pepper, and a little curds.

Then, as the bride may not eat at table with her spouse, the latter pays her a delicate compliment: he goes up behind her with a ball made of rice and grain from his leaf-plate, and thrusts it into her hand. Holding her face averted, she takes it, and then flees with the swiftness of a deer.

The feast ended, the Brahmans rise, and carrying off the leaf from which they have eaten, throw it outside. After washing their hands and feet, they thoroughly anoint their forehead, breast, and arms, with dissolved sandal. In these matters so bad are their manners, that if anything is deficient, they give the greatest abuse to the master of the house, in the hearing of everybody.

On the third and fourth days the relations of the bride and bridegroom place them upon a platform, and raising it on their shoulders, carry the pair all over the town, halting from time to time; and then the relations or other friends present them with some fruit or other eatables. This visitation over, they carry the bride and bridegroom to their swing, and begin once more to sing their praises. The next day they rub oil on the head of the bride. The girl in sport throws some of it into the eyes of the bridegroom and the other bystanders. Then the same oil with which her head has been anointed is offered up by the married pair as a sacrifice.

When all the ceremonies have been performed, the newly-married man allows his wife to go back to her father's house, and he returns to his own abode accompanied by his relations. But the father and mother-in-law do not deliver their daughter to their son-in-law until she has attained puberty. This event is celebrated with all possible solemnity and even greater obscenity. Without offending Christian modesty, it is impossible to state what they say and do on such occasions. This is why I shall pass over in silence their conduct on such a day. I will merely say that the bride is shut up for twelve days in a little room outside the house, where no one may enter. There her food is pushed in at the room door. I will not repeat all the gross and coarse things said by the Brahman women and girls who collect there during the twelve days. These they utter not only in the house, but in the street, and that not only to each other, but to anybody passing along the road, whether known to them or unknown. No reproof or direction to hold their tongues comes from the fathers or husbands, in spite of their disapproving it. Yet no one stops the women, for their say it is the (custom of their caste, which no one has the power to alter.

On the day that the girl arrives at puberty the father announces the fact to all his relations and friends, and calls upon them to rejoice with him. The first to be informed is the son-in-law, to whom notice is given, as to all the other relations, by writing letters on palm-leaves dyed with saffron, a sign instituted by these people for these great solemnities. After the twelve days have elapsed the woman goes to her father-in-law's, where are assembled all the relations, and almost the same ceremonies are performed as at the wedding, sacrifices and adoration of fire being offered anew. A second feats is given, and this day is called the day of second marriage, of the wedding feast of puberty. It is after this second celebration that the woman is given over to her husband, and not before.

After she has been made over to her husband, and he has taken her home, she may not [125] speak to him before anyone. Nor may she do so to her mother-in-law or her sisters-in-law, or any other of the male or female relations of her husband. Furthermore, she is compelled to do the lowliest duties of the household, such as going to fetch water and so forth. If she wants anything she has to ask for it by signs, which seems very ridiculous.

If she becomes *enciente*, similar ceremonies to those gone through at the two festivities are performed at the end of the eighth month. This is called the third wedding feast, or the Feast of First Child-bearing. And then are finished, as they reckon, the Brahman wedding ceremonies.

If the Brahman in question dies after binding the piece of gold on the woman's neck, which is the sign denoting the essential part of the marriage, the woman can never marry again, even should she be only four or five years of age. This is the usual age for fathers to marry off their daughters. There are, however, some who postpone it to the tenth year, but never beyond that age. After a husband's death, a widow adopts one of four courses. Those most sprightly and vigorous burn alive with the corpse of the defunct husband. This is carried out as follows:

Wood is heaped up to a height of eight or nine feet, and about the same length and breadth. Upon the top the corpse of the dead Brahman is laid, dressed as when alive, the head to the south and the feet to the north. After he has been laid thus on the bonfire, there comes the wise man of the village and pronounces certain magic words at the five organs of sense, and anoints them with butter. The anointing done, the parents and the nearest relations throw four or five grains of uncooked rice into his mouth.

When these ceremonies are finished, they turn the body over on its side. As they do so the widow without tears—nay, on the contrary, all radiant and joyous—mounts to the top of the pyre, and lying down on her side, closely embraces her dead husband. At once the relations bind her feet strongly by two ropes to two posts driven into the ground for the purpose. Next they throw some more wood and dried cow-dung on the two bodies; the quantity is almost as much as that beneath them. The woman is then spoken to by her name, and three times distinctly she is called on to say whether she consents to go to heaven. To this she replies in the affirmative. Her answers having been received, they apply a light, and when the bodies have been consumed, each man returns home envying the firmness and constancy which the woman has been granted the felicity of displaying.

Widows who on their husband's death lose their modesty, depart as soon as he expires to one of the large towns, and become public courtesans. Some pursue the same course in their husband's lifetime, for which crime there is no legal punishment inflicted in this country. Others who are not filled like the first set with the spirit of honour, nor like the second give themselves over to an abandoned life, remove upon their husband's death to their parents' house, and wait on them like servants. But this condition is not easy to put up with, while, on the other hand, they are keen to preserve their characters. Thus they often make complaint to those who might rescue them from this sad condition, a malady all the heavier for having no possible relief unless the Brahmans chose to relax their rules. But they are a people who cannot be reasoned with in that direction.

Other women, when the husband dies, since it would be disgraceful in their caste to marry again, and they cannot remain [126] as they are, go from door to door selling rice. They think nothing of this dishonour, which would be counted among Europeans as the depth of misfortune. Yet it may be said that those who adopt this plan are generally the wisest, for the work occupies them and frees them from the evils which follow in the train of laziness and idleness. Fod it may be said that Idleness is the mother of all the vices.

The conduct of the Brahmans being such as I have described, I may assert that their pride is equal to their silliness, and many be justly styled that of Lucifer, for without subterfuge they claim to be gods, and as such they require all the other castes to honour and adore them. But their pretension is not justified, for in everybody else there are some evil traits, while all the rest is good; whereas in the Brahman caste, where there ought doubtless to be something good, one meets with nothing that is not entirely evil.

OF THE CEREMONIES FOLLOWED BY THE RAJAHS[1] AT THEIR WEDDINGS

When the conditions have been agreed on, and the price to be paid to the father-in-law for his daughter has been fixed, on the day before the wedding they throw a string over the bridegroom's head. It is made of three strings of three threads each. In each of these three threads, again, there are three cotton threads. The string is passed over one shoulder and under the other armpit. It is a sign or mark of nobility, and this is called the Marriage of the Thread.

After this has been done, the future husband declares that he will enter into no farther bonds, and departs in simulated anger. But the parents follow him, call him back, by arguments

1. The word 'Rajah' seems to be used throughout this section as the equivalent of 'Rajput' or 'Kshatriya.' The author probably means the 'Rauz' or 'Radzu' caste of the 'Madras Manual of Administration,' iii. 754, a Telugu-speaking caste who claim a Kshatriya descent.

and smooth words persuade him he must marry. Since no one is more desirous to do so than he is, no long discourses are needed to convince him.

The following day the omen-readers, who have been called in, fix the marriage day. A sort of awning is made of white cloth, and this is carried aloft by four men. Then four women, related to the bridegroom, bring four water-pots, which they carry with the awning held over them, as far as the street-door [of the bride's house], where there is a sort of high arbour erected on purpose. It is here that the wedding ceremony has to be performed. The water is placed in this arbour along with the awning. Then there is a certain tree in this country that they class as a Brahman, and style the Marriage God. A branch of this tree is brought, and also one of another tree with bitter leaves, which they call Parechi (Parisa),[1] meaning that it is the wife of the other tree, according to them. The two branches are then interwoven round a post put in the centre of the arbour. There is also some sugar-cane which they tie on. At the foot of all this are placed some leaves of a certain herb which is used to make powder. At the foot of the other pillars they place a quantity of little dishes of earth, in each a sort of hot cake made of rice-flour, and these are eaten by the women guests before the feast begins.

On this ceremony having been completed, the bridegroom appears loaded with gold jewelry, generally borrowed, his body thoroughly rubbed with powdered *sandal*-wood, and covered with flower necklaces sprinkled [127] with little leaves of gold. In this array he is placed in a palanquin, carried on the shoulders of six or eight men. Before him go all the relations and friends on foot, escorting him, while a great number of trumpets, flutes, and drums are played. When the bridegroom with all this pomp reaches the door of the house where the wedding is to be celebrated, he gets out of the palanquin. His future mother-in-law comes to bathe his feet with cow's milk, wiping them with a piece of silk cloth.

1. *Thespesia populnea* or *Hibiscus populneoides*, the flowering *pipal*, *palas pipal*, or tulip-tree. 'Materia Medica of the Hindus,' by Udoy Chand Dutt, with a glossary by Sir George King (Calcutta, 1900) p. 312 ('Madras Manual of Administration,' iii. 712; s.v. 'Portia').

As he who is clean does not want even his feet washed he objects, but the other side maintain that he has not been purified. They must wash the whole of his body. By this means the bridegroom has to remove the whole of the jewelry with which he has come adorned. Binding round himself a morsel of cloth, he allows his body and head to be washed by the relations of the bride with a certain drug made from green-peas.[1] This has been prepared on purpose. At the same time the parents deal similarly with the bride. Then both proceed to some river or pond to bathe, but at different places.

The bathing finished, the future husband arrays himself as before, and, escorted by his relations to the sound of music, they make for the arbour above mentioned, there to have the business concluded. The bride arrives escorted by her relations, but by a different way from the bridegroom's route. The parents of the bride await him, and throw over him and his following a basketful of uncooked rice mixed with other things. The other side retort by throwing some similar mixture. The same is done to the bride by the relations of both parties.

Having arrived at the arbour and performed the sacrifice of worshipping fire, a Brahman appears, who begins by blessing the piece of gold called *taily* (*tali*), which the bridegroom has to tie to the bride's neck. He hands it round to be touched by all the respectable persons present. Next he makes it over to the bridegroom, who is by this time seated with his lady-love on a sort of camp-bed covered by a carpet. Then to the sound of trumpets and flutes, the letting-off of matchlocks, and the throwing of squibs into the air, the relations and friends attach the *taily* (*tali*) to the bride. In this, as they hold, consists the essential rite of the marriage.

Subsequently, having first sung two very pretty songs in praise of the newly-married couple, they go back a second time to their sacrifices. During this they worship an idol they call Polcar (Pillaiyar), of whom I spoke in the first chapter (III. 101). They say that this god has such control over marriages that his own father when he married worshipped him in the manner practised at this day. It is for this reason that they

1. Probably *besan*, the flour made from *channa*, or gram, is intended.

style him 'the son born before his father.' The sacrificing and worship ended, they throw at once into a large vessel, placed there in readiness and full of water, an imitation fish made of a substance resembling flour. One of the relations of the newly-married pair holds it by a string, and moves it to and fro in the water. Then the bridegroom, as a proof of his skill, shoots a small arrow from his bow at this fish. If he hits, everybody breaks forth in his praise, saying he is very skilful in the use of arms, most valiant, most fortunate. If he misses, they say her is unlucky and maladroit. But hit or miss, the game ends.

The father-in-law regales all the guests in the same way as the Brahmans do. Next day they carry the newly-married couple in palanquin, which is followed by the relations and all the guests, to the strains of the orchestra above described (III. 127). It may be [128] here remarked that all the courtesans of the place form one of the leading attractions of the festival, these women of no character bearing the title of 'Servants of God' (a somewhat curious name). These women walk close to the palanquin, and are decked out with silver and with gold. In this order the procession passes through all the streets of the town, stopping *en route* at the door of any friend or relation, from whom presents are received, consisting of fruit or some pieces of cloth. At last they disperse, and everybody goes home.

On the third day the wife rubs oil on the husband's head, and in the same way the husband on the wife's. Then the two together, sheltered under one cloth, which is carried above their heads, go to some river or pond and bathe. The cleansing over, they return home with the same ceremony displayed in going round the town.

When the bridegroom has spend some days in the house of his father-in-law, he leaves for his own house, whether it be in the same locality or at a distance. After the lapse of fifteen- days his parents go back to the bride's home, when, which much ceremony and a large retinue, they convey her to her husband's house. After a stay of eight to ten days she is reconducted to her father's. There she usually remains until the age of puberty, on which occasion there is a feast like that observed by the Brahmans, except that no coarse or obscene language is used. The custom of the other castes is the same.

Among the caste of Rajahs it is imperative that on the husband's death the wife be burnt alive with his body, for should regard for her own honour even not force her to this act, the relations will force her to it, it being an inviolate custom of their caste. It is so whether the husband die at home of disease or of wounds upon the field of battle. The latter death is common among Rajahs (Rajputs), for all who are not princes are soldiers. In war they carry nothing but a sword or a short spear. It would be an insult if they were forced in an army to make use of bows and arrows or fire-arms, or anything taking effect at a distance. Since it is one of the fundamental rules of their caste never to give way, but either to die or conquer, those with a high sense of honour are usually compelled to die in battle. The only reward they gain by their efforts is the fame of not having turned the back on an enemy. In spite of all that, those who disregard what may be said against them, seek whatever means of saving their lives they think most appropriate.

Be this as it may, no sooner has news of a Rajah's death arrived in his country, and the wife is satisfied that he no longer lives, than she is accorded three days of grace. During those days she is permitted to adorn herself as magnificently as she can; and thus arrayed she goes about the streets with lemons tied round her head like a crown;[1] her body is uncovered from the waist upwards, and rubbed over with saffron, as also is her face. In this state she takes leave of all those she meets in the streets with a smiling face and free manners, and speeches repugnant to her sex and her claim to nobility.

When the three days have passed, they prepare in an open field a circular pit, deep and wide, which is filled with wood and cow-dung. Fire is then applied. On beholding this pyre, she who is to be the victim of her honour, issues, clad in new attire, covered with divers coloured flowers, some arranged like crowns, others like necklaces. Escorted by all her friends, male and

1. For the symbolical meaning of the bearing of lemons by the widow as a luck-bringing fruit, see Theodor Zachariae in his articles Zur Indischen Witwenverbrennung' in the *Zeitschrift des Vereins für Volkskunde* (Berlin, 1904-5), and J. M. Campbell, Indian Antiquary, vols. xxix., xxx., who explains the lemon as used to keep off evil spirits (W. I.). On festival days in India lemons are always given as auspicious presents (R. W. F.).

female, she approaches the fire. Before it stands a small screen about five feet high. Over its top they throw into the fire a little saffron and some butter and other spices. After prayers have been recited the heroine withdraws about forty paces and returns two times, one after the other, to the place she started from, and each time performs the same ceremonial. At length she retires for the third time some forty paces farther than before; at that moment the screen before the fire is withdrawn. Then, with a rush, she bounds into the pit, and in a short time there is nothing left her ashes to furnish an epitaph on her constancy.

The Hindus think so highly of those who are burnt in this way that they assert their reincarnation as goddesses in the heaven of Vishnu; and in that quality there are erected to them statues as soon as they are dead. This is done equally for the husband.[1] They assume that men blessed with wives of such great virtue as to sacrifice life for their honour, must without fail be placed among the gods.

But if any wife is found to have greater love of life than of honour, her relations do not leave her to enjoy it for very long, for they throw her into the fire by force, where she ends by undergoing the same suffering without acquiring the same laudations. Thus it is much better for them to endure this hard penalty with firmness and equanimity than to be subjected to it by the violence of others.

OF THE CEREMONIES OBSERVED BY MERCHANTS AND SHOPKEEPERS AT THEIR WEDDINGS

The people of this caste observe in their marriages no other ceremonies than those performed by Brahmans and Rajahs, with the exception that no marriage can take place without informing the shoemaker of the locality.[2] These are the lowest and the most despised among men. When the shoemaker has consented, they make earthen[3] figures of his two-edged scraper, his awl,

1. The man's cenotaph is called a *chhatri*, that of the wife a *sati*.
2. 'The Comaty shopkeepers of Madras, before contracting marriage, send an offering of *betel* to the *Chucklers*, or shoemakers' ('Madras Manual of Administration,' iii, 654).
3. The French text uses the word *passe*, which I hold to be the same as a word used by Manucci in, Portuguese in the various forms of *pauso, pausado, posso, poco passo*, From a comparison of all the passages, I conclude that he means by it—(1) a pond or marsh, (2) mud or clay.

his paring-knife, and his other tools. These are made over to the man about to marry as proof positive that they have leave of the shoemaker. The reason some assign for this base practice is that in olden times that caste originated from a Brahman and a shoemaker's wife. This man, as they say, looked on the woman, disregarding the restrictions of his caste, by the maxims of which not only should he not have spoken to her, but not approached within eighty or more paces of her. In spite of this, he went near enough to be able to ask her if she would marry him. Her persistent reply was that without the permission of her husband she would grant nothing to satisfy his wishes. But this answer was not powerful enough to make the Brahman desist [130] from his pursuit. On the contrary, he became only the more inflamed, and each time he saw her he sought means to win her. On seeing this the shoemaker's wife said to her husband: 'You who have done so many virtuous actions in your life and given so much away in alms, give me as an alms to this Brahman, and it will form, I assure you, one of the most meritorious works you have either done or could do. For' (she wound up with saying) 'this Brahman is our god, and to do his will is like sacrificing to God, for which you will be recompensed some day without fail.'

The poor shoemaker, overcome by this reasoning so opposed to honour, and also by the poverty of his condition, gave his wife to the Brahman. The children born of this union follow in many respects the customs of their ancestor. Anxious to regain the honour they have lost, they still follow their forefather's habits, such as to twist thread,[1] not to eat flesh or fish, not to cook nor eat where other castes can see them. For if anyone went and touched, or even drew near to, the place where they prepare their food or where they eat it, they would consider themselves polluted and defiled. On such occasions what they have already eaten they artificially vomit, and break the pots in which it has been cooked. They go off at once to bathe themselves so as to recover their purity. Furthermore, by the marriage above referred to, they have lost the honour of belonging to the Brahman caste, and equally so the right to study religion and

1. I presume this means they wear the *janeo*, or Brahminical thread.

sciences, a thing allowed to the Brahmans alone in this country. From this cause these others, knowing not what else to do, have been obliged to turn into merchants. This is why all the other castes, even those of the Sudras, who know the constitution of this caste, will not eat or drink in their houses.

It would seem that those who assign this origin to the caste of shopkeepers are more regardful of truth than those telling the fable I gave in my fifth chapter (III. 110), where they say that this caste is the third in the country because it was born from the thigh of Brahma. For, if this fable were held to be true, it is quite certain that the Sudra castes, who assume that they came forth from the feet of Brahma, would raise no difficulty about eating and drinking in the houses of shopkeepers, nor would they hold that class in such low esteem as they do. All the same, the business caste has a high conception of itself. So high do they esteem themselves that they will not allow their women to marry again after the husband's death, even, when they are very young. They either burn alive with the corpse of their husband or remain widows until they die. But they observe much more restraint than the Brahman widows. If the men come to know that any widow of their caste has misbehaved, they kill her without fail. They endeavour in all their acts to prove themselves of high descent, superior to the Sudras, of whose marriages I now proceed to say a few words.

OF THE CEREMONIES OBSERVED BY SUDRAS AT THEIR WEDDINGS

Owing to the Sudra caste being divided into several branches, I cannot state the customs practised by each one in particular at their weddings. That would be to sin [131] against the brevity that I promised at the opening of this account. , Still less need I do so because the more important castes among the Sudras, in spite of their differing in many things, are very much alike in regard to the ceremonies and practices at their marriages. Thus to distinguish between what are the more essential differences among them, I shall confine myself to a few remarks on the customs of the caste of Thieves.[1] It is

1. The Thief caste must be meant for the Kallar caste ('Madras Manual of Administration,' ii. 236, and Bernouilli, 'Recherches,' ii. 47). They were formerly the terror of the community owing to their thieving.

looked on by the Sudras as the lowest of their order. But the ground-work for their manners corresponds very well with their caste name; for living almost entirely in the open country and paying no heed to magistrates, they come forth nightly and rob at will, even in the towns and at the courts of kings and princes. As for the helpless traveller, he is not only robbed but murdered, or else he receives so many blows on his legs that he is almost always left for dead.

Among these thieves, all the conditions of a marriage having been arranged, as in the other castes, all the relations and friends assemble under the arbour where the wedding ritual is to be performed. There they encounter the brother of the bridegroom with a stick, thin but at the same time strong, held in his right hand. At this moment the bride comes out of the house carrying in her right hand a ball of cow-dung and mud. When the brother-in-law sees her, he asks her with what object she is going out. To this she relies that it is to get married to him who seeks her, and to offer him what she has in her hand to eat. Forthwith she hurls the ball at the brother-in-law's nose. He, not to have the worst of it and to give her something for her dose to him, falls upon her with the stick he has in his hand, and lays on most valiantly till she seeks shelter in the house.

Then as a reward for the courage and dexterity with which he has comported himself in this encounter, the parents give him a present. The poor bride, having received a good beating, is taken by her parents and seated upon a mat, and the bridegroom's sister ties on the piece of gold called *taly* (*tali*), which is also among these people the essential part of marriage. After that is done, the bride and all the relations feast together, and drink mostly joyously. When this feast is over, they proceed with another outside the house under the arbour already mentioned. This is for the bridegroom, his relations, and invited guests. The other ceremonies that follow are almost identical with those that I have mentioned for the caste of Rajahs.

However, there is in this caste of the thieves, as well as in some other castes of the Sudras and black men, a barbarous

---

propensities. They were employed as watchmen, but their profession was plunder.

practice. When the husband is tired of his wife he gives her a straw called turumbo (*turumbu*).[1] By the giving of this straw the marriage is broken, so that without any offence against the woman the man can remarry; and equally, without any offence to the man, the wife can take another husband. What is remarkable is that it is not only the husband who may repudiate his wife by that ceremony, but she, too, if she is weary of him, can force him to give her the turumbo (*turumbu*), the special sign by which he repudiates her and entirely dissolves the marriage. But this practice is not known anywhere [132] in the Brahman or Rajah caste, nor in those of the shopkeepers, nor among Sudras of decent standing; for, although these may divorce their wives and marry others, the divorced wives, either in the husband's lifetime or afterwards, are not able to marry again. In all these better castes, after the husband has attached to the neck of the woman the piece of gold called a *tali*, the marriage becomes indissoluble. It results that the man may marry again several wives, either successively or simultaneously; for among the Hindus there is no probitition against having several wives. There have been kings in these days who have had as many as five thousand at once. But, as to the woman, she can marry only one husband.

Having set forth the way in which all the castes conduct their marriages, it remains now to speak of the blacks and *pariahs*, who are people of one and the same sort. These men at their weddings dress like the Brahmans do, and perform the same ceremonies, but no one can attend but those of the same caste.

Now I come to funeral ceremonies for the dead; and as all have the same practice—namely, that the wife removes her *tali* on the death of her husband—I shall say little, and that only briefly, about the ceremonies with which they cremate a dead body and carry out the details connected therewith. It is after these are completed that the woman must cut off her *tali*, and therein consists her act of widowhood; and it is for

1. *Turumbu*=a straw, rush; a token of divorce. 'Paille, fétu, un rien, paille ou chose semblable donnée en signe de divorce' ('Pondicherry Dictionary') (R. W. F.).

this reason that in their language the name given to a widow means 'the woman who has cut off the *tali*.[1]

FUNERAL CEREMONIES OF THE HINDUS FOR THEIR DEAD

All Hindus bum their dead, except the infamous sect of the Lingam. These bury the bodies, not in their temples—for that, in this country, would be the most abominable sacrilege that could be committed—but in a field distant from their dwellings. As to all other castes, they also burn them in a field distant from the town or village, which each locality has set apart expressly for this purpose.

The mode of burning the body is as follows: First of all, no Brahman, however rich he may be, is allowed to die within his house, for in their belief all within it would be thereby defiled. This is the reason that before he expires they carry him into a courtyard, and there place him under a Sort of gallery, which every house has for the purpose. Should it happen that the Brahman dies a sudden death within the house, they carry the body at once, with all imaginable haste, and place it under the gallery alluded to. Then, breaking all the earthen vessels in the house, all the inmates quit it, and do not re-enter it until it has been well rubbed over with cow-dung, and until, as one may say, the interdict has been removed by a number of ceremonies, used by them for this purpose.

When a Brahman dies, all his female relations and female friends stand in a circle, and with their stomachs bared beat themselves severely with their two hands, weeping for the dead; and, moving round, they sing a song learnt for the purpose. It is extremely well suited to the conditions of the time and place in which they find themselves. After [133] they have been round three times in this fashion, they bathe the body, dress it in new clothes, put some ground *sandal*-wood on the forehead, and then deposit it in a sort of coffin which is quite open. It may be interjected here that this coffin is made just as our hand-barrows for manure, constructed like them from pieces of wood tied together with straw. Then four Brahmans carry the body

1. Mr. Frazer writes: 'There is no special word; the Dravidian construction, by use of relative particles, forms relative clauses of the nature referred to, there being no relative pronouns in Dravidian. Thus a widow would be ''*Tali*-whorhas-cut-off-woman," the "who-has-cut-off" being a relative participle.'

XXVII. Daler Khan, Pathan

Vol. III *To face page 68*

to the burning-ground. They are preceded by a sort of shrine, highly ornamented and covered with flowers. Having arrived at the cemetery, they perform for him all the usual ceremonial, and burn him with all the solemnities that I have remarked upon in regard to their marriages.

After the body has been burnt, the Brahmans bathe their bodies, and wash the pieces of cloth which they used for clothing themselves. All dripping as they are, they put these on again and return home. Thence they proceed to the house of the deceased, where a feast is given. On that day it is served under some palm-trees, which they say represent the deceased. There for the space of ten days all the friends and relations weep for the deceased; each of the nearest relations gives a sort of petticoat they call a *panes*[1] (*punjam*) to the deceased's widow, and his brothers subscribe and give her a half-moon of silver.

On the tenth day, after loud lamentation, the deceased's widow flings her arms round the neck of another widow, weeping and displaying all imaginable signs of grief. Meanwhile, all the other widows present cut off the piece of gold attached to her neck, which they call a *tali*. It should be noted that no married women may take part in this act, which constitutes the woman a widow.

Every year upon the anniversary of her husband's death a young widow performs a holocaust, feeds four or five Brahmans, and if she is rich she also gives them clothes. She does the same every month at the new moon, but with less expense and formality. Whatever is essential in funerals of the Brahman caste is also common to the other castes. This is the reason that I shall not say anything special about them, and I pass on to the opinions held about Europeans, known to them under the name of Farangis.

OF THE OPINIONS HELD BY THE HINDUS ABOUT EUROPEANS AND MAHOMEDANS (MAURES)

The Hindus call all the Europeans and Mahomedans[2] in India by the name of *Farangis*, a designation so low, so disgraceful

1. See *ante*, note 58, III. 113.
2. This inclusion of Mahomedans among Farangis is an exceedingly disputable statement. 'Farangi' seems to have had a more contemptuous connotation in Southern than in Northern India.

in their tongue, that there is nothing in ours which could reproduce it. At they hold the Farangis to be vile and abominable they have persuaded themselves that people have no polite manners, that they are ignorant, wanting in ordered life, and very dirty. For these things they would sooner die unaided than drink a cup of water from the hand of a *Farangi*; nor would they eat anything that he has prepared. They believe such an act to be an irremediable disgrace, and a sin for which there is no remission.

The reason is, as I imagine, this. When the Europeans began to make use of the mode of speech used in this country, they were entirely ignorant of oriental languages [134]. At the very commencement, when they had discovered India, they were forced to use its language. Either intentionally, or from ignorance, they made use of the phrases adopted by the Mahomedans, who when they wished to persuade a Hindu to turn Mahomedan, asked him to join their caste. By this they meant, besides the necessity of becoming a Mahomedan like the speaker, that the convert would also be required to follow all the Mahomedan's other habits, and abandon all those in which he had been brought up himself, including the purity maintained by those of his caste, to which they attach more importance than to matters more strictly religious.

In addition, the Hindus suppose that when a man is above others in nobility of race, he also surpasses them in understanding. They assert, relying on this unsound prejudice, that only those who are as high-born as Brahmans can know religion and true science; and that all those who are low by birth (which they believe to be the matter most essential) are ignorant, and consequently incapable of being superiors. They state openly that a man of low birth is as despicable as is a Farangi;[1] in spite of being rich and brave, he can never be wise. For this' paradox they assign as a reason that the highest nobility lies in wisdom; and as no one can be both lowly and noble at once, it is clear that he who is not of abject condition must be wise.

But, just as all that the Brahmans say is chimerical and fantastical, so is it with their nobility and their science. For

1. For confirmation of the hostile or depreciatory use of 'Farangi' (a European), see Yule, 353, s.v. 'Firinghee.'

they have no hesitation in carrying loads on their backs day and night in public places, nor in working with an axe and doing other acts which among Europeans would pass for very humble. To all this I need only add that more often than not they cannot read or write.

I have stated in my history that the Hindus know no higher delight in the world than consorting with women. To that I think it appropriate to add what they say about that sex. They hold that in this world there are four kinds of women. The first they call Padmani (*Padmini*), the second Chaterni (*Chitrini*), the third Asteni (*Hastini*), the fourth Sengueni (*Sankhini*).[1] The first means 'Perfection,' as much in body as in mind; for, so they say, such women are liberal, love their husbands, and are invincibly faithful to them. They have much wit, are of a sweet and peaceable disposition; in short, they possess all the perfections that God and Nature can bestow upon a mortal. Those of the second class are also most beneficent and have lovable qualities, but do not approach the perfection of the first class. Those of the third class are of a very bad disposition, and do not maintain the fidelity they owe to their husbands; and when they get their five fingers into any place, they never fail to clear it of everything to be found there. The women of the fourth class are of such a nature that they do not keep their word, they love noise, they sow discord wherever they can, and are very ill-bred [135] in their mode of life.

About these four kinds of women the Hindus have a number of curious statements, and they possess a book four fingers thick from which these details may be learnt. They are distinguished by the different signs they bear upon their bodies. According to the position of these, their humours and dispositions may be recognised.

In my preface to this section (see III. 90), I have said that several persons have written upon the manners and customs of the Hindus. To this I have to add that the reader must remember

1. Monier Williams, 'Brahmanism and Hinduism,' p. 389, follows the 'Kama Sutras' in describing the four well-known divisions of women as—(1) The *Padmini*,or lotus-like woman; (2) the *Citrini*, or woman of varied accomplishments; (3) the *Sankhini*, or conch-like woman; and (4) the *Hastini*, or elephant-like woman. In his 'Sanskrit Dictionary' there is a full description of the four classes.

that any difference found between what is said by me and by others is due to the difference in the places we have visited and the peoples we have come across. For the East is an extremely large region divided into many provinces widely separated from each other, divided also by many mountain ranges. The inhabitants of these places differ in their customs, as well as in their mode of life, the ceremonial at their temples, and the doctrines of their religion. It should be remembered that what I have recorded refers to the manners and customs of the Hindu subjects of the Great Mogul and the Malabaris,[1] these being the countries I have seen and through which I have travelled.[2]

[Pages 136-143 of the Text are blank; on page 144 the narrative is resumed in Portuguese instead of French.]

[144] ABOUT ELEPHANTS

As I have promised to speak about elephants, I will give a brief account of them, but it will not be what some of the ancients wrote. What I am to relate is founded on true information obtained from various hunters of these animals, and also from what I have seen. I shall speak of their manner of engendering, their birth, and the means by which they are captured in various places; how to domesticate them with ease, desirous of owning them, simply to be able to say that they are and other matters. All the grandees in the Mogul country are lords of such-and-such a number of elephants.

These animals, when they desire to approach the female, show it by certain signs. They discharge from holes near the ears a black and very fetid oil. [The author enters into further details which I do not reproduce.] Ordinarily, elephants live in herds, where there are one hundred and fifty, two hundred, and up to three hundred. All accompany the female, while the elephants of other neighbouring herds withdraw on hearing the cries of the female about to bring forth. Should any of them remain, the male elephants belonging to the herd of the said female attack them and kill them. After delivery, they

1. In the usage of the seventeenth and eighteenth centuries Malabar meant chiefly the Choromandal coast (see Yule, 541).
2. The above section on the Hindu religion has been read in proof by Dr. L. D. Barnett, and I am indebted to him for many valuable suggestions.

remain in that jungle for some days until the young one can travel; at its birth it is the size of a calf three months old. The mother runs her trunk over it until it is cleansed and quite dry, then she helps it up with her trunk. It feeds by passing between the legs of its mother to her teats, stretches out its little trunk along the mother's stomach, and Sucks the milk with its mouth. In this way it is reared for two years, and the third year the mother becomes pregnant again. The infant elephant [145] grows four inches every year, but it grows no more when it gets to twelve feet (*covados*,literally 'cubits'?); and usually they reach one hundred years of age.

The mode of hunting the elephant is in Cochin as follows: They make large pits on the paths over which the animal pass, as recognised by their footmarks. Then they put sticks, straw, and earth over these pits, so that the elephant cannot discover them. Passing from one place to another, they fall into the pit, and there they are left for some days, giving them very little food. On finding that from hunger the animal is more gentle, they begin little by little to fill up the pit to a height which enables a man to mount on the elephant. Its feet are bound by heavy iron chains; then, in company of domesticated elephants, it is removed somewhere else, after which it readily becomes submissive.

In Ceylon elephants are hunted in another way. In the forests where the elephants go to and fro they clear some ground of the large trees standing on it, making a sort of half-moon, which is palisaded everywhere, leaving in the middle a very narrow entrance. On both sides of this they plant strong stakes close together in form of a stockade. This is covered over with leafy branches, as also the end of the stockade, all well fixed on.

These preparations made, they let loose a domesticated female elephant anointed with a certain oil. She goes to find the elephants. These, attracted by the scent of the oil, follow in her wake until she reaches the half-moon. There she pauses and waits for the arrival of all the elephants dwelling in that wood. Finally, the female moves very slowly into the passage, and all the assembled elephants follow her. Thus, when they are once inside, they are driven in so that they can neither advance nor turn their bodies round.

This effected, the hunters go to the farther door, and the domesticated female follows. The wild elephants are stopped by heavy beams, so that the femall is let go free and they are prisoners. Jumping into the enclosure, the elephant-drivers mount the captives and tame them, which is ordinarily done by force of hunger and blows. Heavy iron chains and ropes are put upon their feet. One by one they are withdrawn from their prison, and a few little ones are released as being useless, all but one here or there that they see by its points will turn out well. Such a one is sold along with the full-grown animals. The very old ones are killed for their tusks. The natives eat the flesh of the trunk, which is held to be dainty food, having the flavour (so they assert) of pork. By the same method they take elephants in the kingdoms of Aracao (? Arakan), Pegu, and Gueda (Quedda).[1]

Usually there are some superstitions involved in these hunts [146]. It happened in Cochin that an elephant fell into one of the pits described, but was able somehow to get out. To preserve himself and not fall in another time, he began to carry a stake in his trunk, with which he probed the earth where he wanted to go. Thus these animals have great discernment, as I have seen and experienced.

There was a youth who was a great hunter. Leaving his companions, he penetrated far into the forest, and close to a river he met an elephant. Seeing the danger to his life if he were pursued, he climbed on to a large tree. Coming after the youth, the elephant, in the hope of seizing him, broke off branches and tried hard to knock the tree down. Finding this impossible, it trumpeted loudly, whereupon there came up a female elephant blind of one eye. The two together recommenced pushing at the tree to uproot it. Seeing that the tree did not move, they began to strike at the roots with their feet. But the earth was too hard, and the female was left on guard at the foot of the tree while the male went to the river as fast as he could go to fetch water in his trunk. He emptied it at the foot of the tree and began to strike, so that the tree shook. The poor youth was in a great fright, realizing his danger; but noticing that the female was one-eyed, when the male elephant went for

1. Quedda or Kedah, on the west coast of the Malay Peninsula, a tributary of Siam (Yule, 750).

more water the youth hastily descended from the tree on the side of her blind eye and scrambled up a larger tree, whence he watched what they were doing, still somewhat perturbed. The two elephants worked at the tree till they had uprooted it. When they failed to find the youth, the male broke off a branch and gave the female a sound beating, and pursuing her, they disappeared. The elephant had continued its efforts from eight o'clock in the morning until two in the afternoon. The youth awaited nightfall, and then set out to find his companions. From that time forth he never attempted again to follow the chase.

In Africa they hunt elephants in different ways, but only to obtain their tusks. Anyone who wishes may go in their pursuit. Two natives of the country go out, each carrying three *asseguais* in his hand. These are a Sort of small spear about five palms in length, with a very sharp head four fingers in breadth. Coming across some elephant with large tusks, one man quickly gets in front, while the other remains in its rear. The man in front comes out in sight of the elephant and cries out. Perceiving him, the elephant attacks, but the hunter flees and hides. At the same moment the man behind flings an *asseguai* at the beast's belly and gives a cry. The elephant turns and pursues, taking him for the man first seen. The man in front comes out, and does as the other did. They continue doing thus until the elephant falls. The lower portion of the tusk belongs to the lord of the country, and that nearer the head is the hunter's. This was recounted to me by a mulatto called Joao Pereira, who was long at Mozambique, where he' saw the Kaffirs entice elephants by magic arts, preventing them from quitting the forest until they had left their tusks behind them. Through the power of magic they struck their tusks on the trees until they fell to the ground, and then the spell was broken and they were able to escape.

It is also said that there was a man whose only livelihood was the sale of wood, which he brought in person [147] from the forest. Going one day on this business, he found a great stack of wood. He was quite astonished at the quantity collected between one day and the next, yet no one else went to collect wood at that spot. When he arrived opposite the woodpile to bind his bundle, there suddenly came out an elephant who had been hiding behind it, and had collected all the wood.

It seized him without hurting him, and lying down on the ground, it showed him one of its feet, in which a great thorn had stuck. The wood-cutter understood that it wanted help, and plucked out the thorn for him. The elephant rose and moved a pace or two, and tried if his foot still hurt him; then, going to the heap, laid hold with his trunk of a quantity of wood, and went off along the road to the man's home. Seeing that the elephant was doing him service, he followed. It went with him to a certain point and deposited the wood on the ground; then, raising its trunk, it stood before the man a moment or two in sign of gratitude, and departed. The wood-cutter went home with his bundle. Next day he went out to his work as usual, and at the same place where he had parted from the elephant he found a large quantity of wood placed there by it. Ever afterwards it left wood at the same spot, and the man was saved the trouble of a long journey for it.

These animals are most grateful, and recognise any benefit done them; they also feel an injury, and when the opportunity arises take a cruel revenge. This have I seen suffered by many an elephant-driver for the ill-treatment he had been guilty of, some because of stealing their food and not giving them their full rations, others for having without cause struck and abused them. It happened to me once that I was attending a princess, entering and issuing by a great courtyard, where I saw collected together her horses and elephants. On my leaving, the princess presented me with some *betel* leaf. I passed near an elephant, and holding out my hand, offered it the *betel* leaf. It put out its trunk, took it, placed it in its mouth, and ate it. Every time I came out of the palace it recognised me, and put out its trunk, and I made over to it all the *betel* I had received. In a short time the princess recovered, and I went no more to the house. A year afterwards I was passing through the city with some horsemen in my train, when an elephant approached me with its trunk raised, and followed me. I cried out angrily to the driver to keep his elephant under control. He answered that the elephant knew me again and wanted *betel* leaf, to which he had become accustomed on my visits to the princess's house.

One day, coming from the palace, I passed through a street, where I saw many elephants collected before the door of Mamencan (Mumin Khan), the official in charge of them. He was seated at the door of his mansion, and seeing me, called to me. I got down from my horse and walked between the elephants, which stood very close to each other. Near the door the space was very narrow, and I could hardly pass. I put my hand on the trunk of a small female elephant to make it give way. It could not move aside, and without my imagining such a thing, it suddenly put its trunk between my legs and deposited me lightly in a shop close by, which was full of *gurguris* (pottery pipe-heads), from which the Mahomedans smoke tobacco, and as I subsided I heard-a great disturbance of cooking-pots, *gurguris*, and other crockery; though put out at finding myself in such a state, without any turban on my head, I was not hurt in any way. The female elephant put her trunk into her mouth and trumpeted loudly. This was to show she was in fault, but that the crowded position in which she found herself had forced her to take such a course [148].

When Mahabat Khan was governor of Gujarat, he kept many elephants. Among them were some very choice, large, and handsome. The driver in charge of the chief of these elephants (its name was *Zalzalah*—that is, 'Earthquake') bore a grudge against a greengrocer. To revenge himself, he went past the man's shop, and, halting the elephant, gave it a sign. It set to work with its trunk and scattered the whole of the goods in all directions—radishes, turnips, garlic, onions, lemons, and so forth.

In the confusion, a bull belonging to the vegetable-seller, which had been tied up close by, broke its rope and pursued the elephant, prodding it between the legs from behind with its horns. The elephant, not accustomed to such unusual attentions, was terrorized, and without waiting for more, broke into flight, the bull after him. The driver, looking on it as a point of honour, made the elephant pull up and face the foe. Upon this, the bull also halted, and began to paw the ground with his fore-feet, raising a great dust, and bellowing at the same time. This caused the elephant to be still more frightened. It turned and fled; the bull, overtaking it, renewed the attack with its horns. In this way it pursued, until it had ejected the elephant from the city, to the great admiration of the people, who ran to see this singular sight.

Informed of the facts, Mahabat Khan ordered into his presence the bull and the elephant to see this curious thing himself. As soon as the bull saw the elephant, it did as before. Mahabat Khan, too, feeling his honour at stake, wanted the elephant to kill the bull. He ordered other elephants to be called in. One after another made the attempt, but still the bull remained victor. The reader must understand that when the bull saw the elephant approach, he went to attack him, and raising a great deal of dust with his feet, deceived the elephant. In this cloud of dust the bull suddenly got behind the elephant and used its horns. In this way it overcame the elephant. Finding the bull so violent, Mahabat Khan kept it, and gave a present to its owner of two hundred rupees, and he used it to punish any mad elephants that had broken their chains and caused injuries. I saw once, as I was passing along in the city of Lahor, an elephant break its chain, and the elephant-men could not catch it. They let the bull loose, and it, by its cleverness and the use of its horns, drove the elephant back to its place. Mahabat Khan was so pleased with this bull that he gave it the name of 'Chastiser of Elephants.'

They say that formerly there died a King of Arakan without leaving a successor, at a time when the nobles were in discord and each one wished himself to become king. In the end they decided to let the chief royal elephant loose outside the city, and he who should return mounted on it would be made king. After three days the elephant appeared in front of the royal palace with a boy upon his back. The lad was the son of a shepherd; but he was accepted as king.

Among the many elephants owned by the King of Gulkandah, he had one very lofty and superb animal, which the king valued most highly. This elephant formed a great affection for a young girl who lived close to its stable; and every time the elephant was fed with various kinds of grain, cooked food, and sugarcane, it threw a portion with its trunk to the girl. She, being used to the elephant, would go up to him fearlessly, and would walk beneath him and between his legs without being hurt. The older she grew, the greater was the elephant's affection.

Aurangzeb heard that the King of Gulkandah had this fine elephant; and as he was accustomed to demand all that was best in that kingdom, he directed the king to send it. Unable to make denial, the king ordered the elephant to be sent. When it saw itself outside the city, and knew it was going a long journey, it got out of hand and would not obey the drivers, but returned to its stable. Whenever they began the journey, the same thing occurred [149]. In time they recognised that he would not start, through the affection he bore to the child. On being assured of this, they reported to the king. Orders were given to send the girl with him, also her parents, and then he proceeded on his way without any difficulty. On reaching the Mogul's court the king was told of the affair, and he granted pay for the girl and her parents. The girl when she grew up drove this elephant, and it obeyed her without hesitation.

[150, 151][1] I could extend my remarks to greater length on the instinct of these animals, but that would carry me too far, and therefore I will conclude my account with an unusual event occurring in the island of Ceylon. The king of that island was angry with one of his nephews for some trick he had played. He ordered him to be put to death in his own presence by a mad elephant. The elephant advanced towards the victim. The latter cried out at once to the animal, and told it not to kill him. The elephant recognised the voice, because the man had formerly ridden on it, and drew back, raising its trunk as a mark of politeness and respect.

At this the king grew angry with the driver, and commanded him to drive the beast forward once more. The victim began to cry out again, saying he relied upon him not to kill him. On seeing that the elephant did not mean to obey, the king stood up and shouted to it; all the same, it did not obey his orders. 'Kill,' said he, 'this traitor forthwith, for such is my will.' At this the elephant, finding itself forced by the king's orders, put his trunk into his mouth, and shutting his eyes, rushed as quickly as possible at the unfortunate being without touching him with his trunk or his tusks. These are the members with which they are accustomed to kill anyone. But in spite of that it did not fail to take the man's life by crushing him under its feet.

The Siamese assert that in old days, in the great forests of that kingdom, there appeared a multitude of elephants. Among

1. Here the text begins again in French. This leaf (pp. 150-151) is interpolated.

them there was one of great stature which was quite white in the body, but had orange-coloured tusks and nails. When the king was informed of this, he used all possible exertions for its capture. But all was in vain; and because he could not be caught, the Siamese called him the 'King of Elephants.' For this reason the King of Siam takes the title of 'Lord of the White Elephant.' Because some other princes dared to assume this title—that is, the Kings of Pegu and Arakan—the King of Siam has fought some cruel wars against them.

[149 resumed.][1] Since I have spoken of these huge animals, it gives me the opening to speak also of small ones. In the Mogul country is a kind of animal, very finely formed, of about the size of a goat, cinnamon in colour. They are wild, and when over twelve years old the lower half of the body becomes white, and from the horns to the tail the upper half of the body is black. The horns are three palms in length, and twisted like a rope, the points being very sharp. They run with such velocity that no horse can overtake them. The changes of colour referred to occur in the male; the female remains all her life the same colour. They are called in India *haran* [*i.e.*, 'deer']. Usually these animals pass their nights in the woods, and during the day come to graze in the fields. Each male is followed by fifteen to twenty females. When the young male grows up and begins to disquiet the females, the father ejects him from the herd by using his *horns*; and the young male lives solitary, as none of the other haran [deer] will allow him to approach. His life is thus passed until he finds himself in full force and vigour. Then he goes in search of the gazelles; the master of the herd comes out to meet him, and they fight vigorously, the one in defence of his females, the other to acquire them. During the fight, which usually lasts more than an hour, the females draw up in a fright, and do not stir from the spot, looking on at the struggle until it is finished. The victor purses his opponent till he gets near some similar herd, and there he leaves him, and goes back to find the females. These gather round him, and indulge in springs and jumps to betoken their delight. The same is done by them to the stranger if he wins.

In the Mogul country all the great lords keep these animals

1. Here the narrative returns to Portuguese.

in domestication; they are used for fighting, and also to hunt others of the same sort. When used for this purpose, they fix ropes on their horns, and let them loose where there are a considerable number of the wild herds. The male of the herd advances in a rage to repel the intruder, and they begin to fight. In this fight the wild deer gets entangled by the rope, and the hunters capture him and tame him, so that he may serve in the same way to catch others. The females are also used to capture others. When the hunter finds that he cannot reach such animals with his matchlock, he hides himself, and lets loose one of these females in the plain with a slender string attached to its neck. This is done in sight of other deer, who come at once in search of her. At this time the hunter pulls the cord, and the male follows the captured female at the will of the hunter, who then kills with an easy shot. The hunters are so dexterous in this process that when the king goes to the chase they draw the animals under this coercion to the very muzzle of the matchlock. To this intent they raise a shelter of green branches in which are some little holes. This is planted into the ground at the most convenient place. In this way the great men amuse themselves with shooting without undergoing much labour, as I have myself experienced many times.

OF THE DOGS OF HINDUSTAN

As I have spoken of these animals [the deer], I do not wish to omit some remarks on the thefts committed by the dogs of India. As a rule, they live on thefts made in the villages and *saraes*, where there are a number of them, and they look in a miserable condition. Usually cooking is done in sight of the passers-by. Seeing [152] anyone a little inattentive, the dog takes what there is in the man's very presence. If the pot is on the fire, and he gets a moment's chance, he knocks it on to the ground with his nose and carries off the contents.

At night they work hard at their tricks, wandering among the travellers when they are asleep, and finding the place by scent, they pull from under the pillows the food made ready for the next day's breakfast. This is done with more dexterity than can be imagined. If perchance a traveller hits the dog, he suppresses any cry for fear that the other people in the enclosure may collect and beat him still more. But when he finds himself outside the enclosure and quite safe, he then begins to howl.

I have seen that many Europeans newly arrived in India, and thus without experience, have lost knives, forks, and spoons of silver tied up in cloths along with cheese, meat, or bread, a dog having carried them off. It is experience that turns a man into a master-hand. Yet for all my experience of these thieves, I did not fail myself to be taken in. Carrying with me a bag of sugar to refresh myself during the season of great heat, I hung it up in the middle of the room, which, as usual in *saraes*, had no door. I fancied it was secure there, the place being somewhat lofty. My artfulness was of no avail, for when day dawned I found the bag torn and empty, and the ground showed signs of having been licked by dogs. When these animals find themselves at such feasts and occasions, you may be certain there is no fighting, so as not to be heard.

Another case happened to me in a village. To make my food secure, I placed it within a basket fastened by a lock, which I had placed quite close to me. In all confidence I went to sleep and took my rest, but when morning came the basket was not to be seen. I supposed some thief had been there and carried it off. On making a diligent search, I found the basket outside the village all torn to pieces. There was no food, but the other contents were intact.

The inquiring reader will wonder, and ask how a dog could carry off a basket. But on such occasions many unite together, and, without leaving a trace, raise the load into the air, and getting it to a place of security, eat amicably all that is to be found. A similar case happened to some Armenian merchants. They were in a village on Easter Eve, and at night were cooking some mutton and some fowls in a large cauldron, which they left upon the fire. Then they went to sleep, and next morning they could not find the cauldron. By diligent search they found the cauldron in an orchard outside the village, where it had been carried by dogs.

The dogs of a place called Burjamguel (? Bhagwan-golah), in the neighbourhood of Bengal, and near the river Ganges, are very famous in this respect. When Hindu travellers arrive at the place, they go to the interbank, they draw a circle on the ground, and within it with their own hands cook their food.

While they are busy with this process, a number of dogs collect, placing themselves at a distance one from the other, seated on the ground as if waiting for some food to be thrown to them. When all is ready, and the food placed in the dishes, the Hindu waits for it to cool. The dogs know by the smell that the table is laid. Two of them rise from their post and simulate a flight, while the other dogs that had been scattered about fun up to take part, and raise a great noise. During this fictitious fight they draw nearer and nearer until they can reach the food. On reaching the spot the fight is dropped, and they consume the food most amicably, while the Hindu has to get out of the way for fear of being bitten. Thus his labour is entirely thrown away, seeing that the dogs have trodden within the circle already referred to.[1] For if a stranger touches that place or the man's body, any food present there becomes impure, according to the precepts of his religion. If the dogs fail to get hold of food, and there be any lighted lamp, they blow it out and lick it until it is empty. If this cannot be got, they carry off the traveller's shoes. Ordinarily it is found that they take that of the left foot. It is impossible to know the attraction they have in this matter.

I will finish with these thieves by recounting an instance that happened in the Mogul country at a village near [153] a mountain. It is not far from the jungles of Manddo (Mandu). A traveller arrived at this place, and rested in the village. Next morning he missed a bundle containing the best of what he had. He noticed before the door where he had slept some footprints of dogs. He took up the trace, and, following these marks, went on till he got to the foot of the mountain. He noticed that caught in the thorns were pieces of torn cloth, and he continued by this route, and with great difficulty guiding himself by the marks left, he arrived at the highest point, where he found a large and very ancient temple partly in ruins. He saw there some dogs and many destroyed bundles.[2] Along with his own things lay torn silk cloth, calico all in pieces, much coin in gold and silver, chains, jewels, rings, pearls, and precious stones. The complainant saw

1. The *chauka*, or spot prepared and cleansed for cooking and eating on.
2. The words in the text are at *atados aruinados*, Mr. D. Ferguson writes: 'Fibres or threads *tied* (*atados*) together to form a ligature; hence *bundles* (generally of faggots).'

that they had been stolen by the dogs, and that no one knew it. Profiting by the occasion, in complete silence he gathered up the best of the valuables, and set out for his home. Thus things go in this world; one man collects with the sweat of his brow, and others eat without having laboured, and he to whom God wishes to give never fails in resources.

A traveller left a *sarae*, and a dog followed for a journey of three days, showing himself most faithful. On arriving at the other *sarae*, where he meant to rest, he noticed that the dogs of that place did not interfere with the dog that had followed him. It was well received by them, and they approached with their accustomed marks of politeness, smelling it and wagging their tails just as if they were old friends. The traveller went off to sleep, and below his pillow he put some food, relying upon his faithful dog, who was on sentry at the door. In the midst of his deepest sleep a dog caught him by the foot, and he hurriedly raised his head to drive it away. His faithful companion, already posted at his bed-head, laid hold of the bundle containing the food, and in all haste carried it off. Next morning he found his companion had disappeared, and the politeness displayed to him by the other dogs on entering the *sarae* had not been done in vain. Many times such dogs have followed me, and took their leave by carrying something off.

Equally I do not like to pass on without a mention of the cunning of certain birds, that in the Mogul country are called *colong* (kuling).[1] They arrive in the month of September from the lands of Tartary and the mountains of Kashmir to feed in the regions of Hindustan. Then in the month of March, when the hot season begins in the Mogul country, they return whence they came. They are of the size of a turkey-cock or cock of India, of ashen colour, legs two spans in length, the neck of three spans, the beak 5 inches long. Usually they arrive in flocks of over five hundred, and they descend upon the fields or marshes. They live upon grain, and not upon shell-fish. When in repose they stand all close together, the head under the wing, and one foot raised. Four of them at some little distance from the resting place march back and fore as sentinels, equally by day as by night.

---

1. The coolen, or crane, *Ardea sibirica* (Platts, 'Dictionary,' 844).

The hunter gets near with great difficulty, the sentinels being very vigilant. On the least suspicion, one of them, stretching out its neck, cries in a low voice, while the other sentries reply in the same way. By great care the hunter arrives closer, when, suspicion being further aroused, they cry again, a little louder than the first time. In the same manner the others reply, and increase their efforts to discover what is wrong. When they perceive there is some danger they cry aloud, so that all the flock awakes, and with a long run they make off with loud cries.

The Mogul kings have issued decrees that no one may hunt them [the *kuling*] for a distance of twelve leagues from the cities of Agrah, Dihli, and Lahor, the only places excepted being gardens in which pigeons and turtle-doves may be caught. To carry out this decree there are watchmen. For the distance named the *kuling* is preserved for the royal person, that he may with ease hunt these cranes by birds of prey; and although they are so large, they [? the *kuling*] are yet very tasty.

Also [154] in the Mogul country they hunt them in another way. There is a kind of animal like a large cat called *xagox* (*Shagosh*)[1]—that is, 'Royal Ear.' Their colour is grey, and their ears larger than those of the cat, having at the tips some rather long hairs, black in colour. This animal is released a long way off, where it can see these birds. It then works its way rapidly, crouching first here, then there, as a cat does, and hiding its body until it is within the distance required for its spring. It then makes a rush, and the frightened bird makes an attempt to fly. In the meanwhile the lynx has made its bound and seizes its prey. When the huntsmen see the other birds take to flight, they know that their prey is safely caught. In this way they take them alive. It seems to me that these birds [the *kuling*] are cranes (*gros*), because they cry in the same manner.

In the year one thousand six hundred and eighty-six, seven days after my arrival at. Madras, Governor William Guiford (Gyfford)[2] sent for me, and informed me that the governors and

1. A mistake for *Siyah-gosh*, 'black ear,' an animal of the panther kind, a lynx.
2. William Gyfford, Governor from 1681 to July 25, 1687 (J. T. Wheeler, 'Madras in the Olden Time,' i. 124-172; see also Mrs. Penny's Fort St. George,' pp. 82, 107). An account of the Company's troubles

officials of the Mogul king in the Bengal province had been illtreating his [the English] factors. They hindered them from exercising the privileges conceded to them by the Mogul kings. For two years he had made efforts to bring his grievances before the king, and had spent much money, yet had been unable to impart to the king in person the damage they were doing to him. On this account they had begun a war against the governor of Hugli.

He prayed me to find some means by which King Aurangzeb should take notice of the oppression inflicted on them by his officials. I wrote a letter to one of the king's eunuchs, a very familiar friend of mine, called Necruz (Nekroz)—that is, 'Fortunate Day.' In it I informed him with great politeness of the troubles suffered by the English nation within His Majesty's dominions, including many necessary particulars. I prayed him as a favour to deliver this letter to the king, and he, out of his great friendship for me, and aware also that His Majesty himself knew who I was, delivered the letter with confidence when the king was among his women. Having read it, the king put it in his pocket, then went out into the '*Am-Khass* '(the audience-hall) and began to hold audience. After hearing several complaints brought before him by his officials, he drew the letter from his pocket and began to read it again, shaking his head meanwhile. Then he said aloud: 'It is true that the English are in the right, and the fault lies with my officials.' The persons present were much agitated.

He turned his face in the direction of Mahabat Khan,[1] and asked him if there was at the court any agent of the English. He answered that there was not. The king ordered him to write to the governor of Madras that he forgave the temerity displayed by the English in plundering the town of Hugli,[2] and on their

---

in Bengal, which was then sub-ordinate to Madras, will be found in Stewart's 'History of Bengal,' 311-323; Yule's 'Diary of W. Hedges,' ii., liii-lxxxvi, s.v. 'Job Charnock'; and Orme's 'Historical Fragments,' edition of 1805, p. 281.

1. This Mahabat Khan f'M.-ul-U.,' iii. 627) is identical with the Muhammad Ibrahim who helped N. M. to escape from Shah 'Alam's camp (See Part II, fols. 228, 231).
2. Hugli town was attacked by the English on September 28, 1686 (Yule, 'Diary of W. Hedges,' ii., liv).

side they must excuse the troubles caused to them by his officials. The governor should send to court persons properly empowered, and he might be assured of acquiring new favour. During this going to and fro the war in Bengal went on.

By the time the answer arrived Governor Gyfford was already out of office, and there governed in his place Alexandre Hayel.[1] The latter, on seeing the good-will shown by the king, was very pleased, but was unable to send off any representative at once, because he had to report to the general, who lived in the island of Bombajm (Bombay), at a great distance from Madras. The officials at the court, finding that no agent appeared in time, and being aggrieved at what the king had said in audience, so managed affairs that they forced the king into investing the fortress of Bombahim (Bombay). That place was so closely pressed that it very nearly fell into the hands of the Mogul. Finally, the [English] general was obliged to send an envoy to the court. Great expenditure was incurred before he obtained entry in the manner that everybody obtains; and he received his leave to depart when an order to raise the investment of Bombay had been issued. The English undertook to send orders to withdraw their fleet Bengal.[2] If these efforts had only been made at the proper time, there would not have been so much expense or damage, for from a single neglect flow many evils [155].

NOTE ON GOVERNORS GYFFORD AND YALE'S NEGOTIATIONS WITH THE GREAT MOGUL, 1686-1688.

We find confirmation of pany's records now at the India Office. On May 13, 1686 ('Factory Records,' Fort St. George, No. 4, p. 49), it was found that the agent (*wakil*) at Court had not stated the English grievances; he was therefore directed to conclude matters within

1. Correctly, 'Elihu Yale,' who succeeded Gyfford, and remained Governor until October 23, 1692 (Wheeler, 'Madras in the olden Time,' i. 173-258).
2. Hunter, 'History of British India,' ii, 265. Surat factory was seized, and Bombay invested by the Sidi fleet. The disputes were not settled till the *farman* of February 27, 1690, was issued, and Job Charnock did not land again at Calcutta until August 24, 1690.

a month, or return to the coast (Madras). On February 17, 1687 (*ibid.*, No. 20, pp. 70-71), Gyfford wrote to the Great Mogul excusing delay in sending an envoy, as the French and Dutch had done, but he had feared displeasure about events in Bengal. Muhammad Sharif, their *wakil*, had been at Court two years, and a hearing for him is asked and redress prayed for. A complaining letter of the same date was addressed to the who was in the camp of Bahramand Khan, the *wazir's* son-in-law, together with a petition to the *wazir's* Asad Khan, entreating his mediation. The *wakil* could not be found, and all three letters were brought back on April 11, 1687 (*ibid.*, No. 4, Part II., p. 53). Another letter was addressed to the Mogul on March 10, 1687 (No. 20, p. 71), reiterating the complaints, and enclosing a claim of 64,75,000 rupees for damages forwarded from Bengal.

Next, on March 17, 1687 (No. 20, p. 94), Gyfford addresses Thomas Goodlad and Richard Cogan at the Mogul's camp, saying that Senhor Nickola Manuche had recommended them. The Council's object was to obtain the delivery of a letter into the Mogul's own hands and the securing of an answer. This letter and the enclosure went by the hand of Manucci's servant, Hasan. Next Masulipatam was informed (June 9, 1687, No. 20, p. 1861) that no Englishman could be sent on account of the danger and expense, but that communications had been opened with their 'old friend' Mirza Ibrahim (*i.e.*, Mahabat Khan).[1]

On July 25, 1687, Elihu Yale succeeded Gyfford. On August 11 the new governor wrote to Job Charnock, agent in Bengal (No. 4, Part II., p. 124), announcing the arrival of letters dated July 9 from the Mogul's camp—one from Mahabat Khan, stating that he had informed the Mogul of the English complaints,

1. This man Muhammad Ibrahim, known as the *Qumar-baz* (gambler), was a native of Central Asia. He is described as a crafty, smooth-spoken man. Under the two Brahman ministers of Abu,l Hasan, of Gulkandah, he rose to be Generalissimo by soft words and flattery. He was ennobled as Khalilullah Khan, Tiger-slayer (*sher-hamlah*). When Aurangzeb's wrath was kindled against Abu,l Hasan, the 'Sugar-seller,' the 'Monkey-showman,' he sent an invading army, and Khalilullah Khan marched out to oppose its approach, but was defeated. He surrendered to Prince Shah 'Alam, and Aurangzeb gave him the new title of Mahabat Khan. In 1686-87 he was appointed Governor of Barar, and a year afterwards was transferred to the Panjab. There he died in 1100 H. (between October, 1688, and June, 1689), The chronogram is 'Mahabat Khan,' 1099 H. ('Ma,asir-ul-Umara,' iii. 627).

and the other a long report from Khwajah Abnus, the Armenian agent employed at Gulkandah.

The report is to the following effect: The letters sent by Manucci's servant were made over by Senhor Thomas [Goodlad] to Bastian Weale [? Sebastian Velho], They spoke to Ihtimam Khan, who kept them waiting three months uselessly. News of the trouble in Bengal arrived, the Mogul was angry, and they durst not deliver the letters..Abnus then applied to Mirza Ibrahim, now Mahabat Khan, but he hesitated. Manucci's servant was asked for the governor's letter; he referred them to Velho, and Velho said the letter was given already to Eetinon ghan [? Ihtimam Khan]. Then the servant informed Abnus that his master (Manucci) had also written to Nukzood (? Nekroz). This letter was recovered, and given to Mahabat Khan. The Khan delivered it to the Mogul. Aurangzeb complained bitterly of the English. The Khan rejoined that the Mogul officials at Surat and Hughi had begun the quarrel, and he recommended me (Abnus) as a good agent to treat with the English. A present of oil of nutmeg and of clove was got ready; and the letter and the claim for damages were recovered from Manucci's servant. Abnus added to the bottle of oil a 'crystal gurglet,' and a plate mounted in gold and stones. The letter and account were presented by Mahabat Khan. No answer as yet had been vouchsafed. From the conversation with Mahabat Khan, it seemed he thought he could get a *farman* settling disputes at Surat and the Bay (Bengal), and (1) that the English would be excused the poll-tax; (2) that they should pay no duty on saltpetre; (3) that all goods forcibly taken at the Bay or Surat would be restored; (4) that they might also settle new factories wherever they pleased; (5) that the *farman* would be sent by a responsible person to Bengal, and there proclaimed. The agent enjoins on the Council to write at once to Mahabat Khan, and insert something for the protection of the fort and town of Madras; for Gulkandah could not long hold out, and that kingdom would soon fall to the Moguls.

Bribes are all-powerful, and Mahabat Khan must be 'remembered.' Three more bottles of the oil would be acceptable. Abnus puts in a plea for his brother, Joseph de Marcoss, and their personal losses. He did not write in Portuguese, but in his own language (Armenian), as more secure. The governor's answer must be in Persian, but without mention of gifts or presents, as it would be shown to the Mogul.

Yale's comments to Charnock on this report are dated August 24, 1687 ('Factory Records,' No. 21, p. 24). He dwells on the evil results of the hostilities in the Bay: for four months the Mogul would not receive their letters; his only answer was that when he had finished with Gulkandah he would call Madras to account. At last Aurangzeb took the letters, but gave no answer. But through a third person they were advised to write a smooth, flattering letter, setting forth truly the affronts and injuries received, asking compensation and the restoration of their ancient privileges. They believe this suggestion was written with the Mogul's cognizance.

On September 15, 1687 (No. 21, p. 67), Yale replied to Abnus. He recounts how Gyfford selected Abnus and Senor Manuche, 'late surgeon to Sultan Shah 'Alam,' to present their letters about Surat and Bengal. It is now found that Abnus by himself is competent: 'We shall [not] hereafter apply ourselves, nor trouble any other therein.' On October 12, 1687 (No. 30, p. 101), Mahabat Khan advises the English to gain 'Alamgir's favour, and complaints of their violence, which 'will ruin your house'; he recommends Abnus to them. Next Yale writes to Mahabat Khan on November 15, 1687 (No. 21, p. 199), begging him to procure a 'cowl' (*qaul*, or agreement) for a good reception at Court, and they would send up a principal person of the Council. On the same day he wrote (p. 129 *ff.*) to Senhor Joan de Marke, alias Khwajah Abnus, at Gulkandah, much to the same effect, asking who is to be Mahabat Khan's successor, he having been transferred 'to these parts.' Peace had been made in Bengal. Mahabat Khan's *parwanah* of October, 1687, was acknowledged on December 2 (p. 140 *ff.*) No letter having come from Abnus, he is written to on December 8 (p. 145 ff.), and the privileges to be asked for are detailed. Monsieur Daniel Chardin and Salvadore Rodriguez receive charge on December 9 (p. 148) of 10,000 *pagodas* for Senhor Joseph de Marke (*i.e.*, Abnus). Another letter to Abnus left on December 12 (p. 154 *ff.*), saying they heard their friend Mahabat Khan was removed [that is, he had been appointed to Lahor]. Progress was reported to Surat on December 19, 1687 (pp. 159-163).

In February, 1688, the desired *qaul* arrived from Gulkandah, sent by Ruhullah Khan,[1] the new governor. It is dated December 6, 1687, and invites them to send a trustworthy person. At the same time I'tibar Khan reports that the letters addressed to Mahabat Khan had been made over to Ruhullah Khan, who had delivered them to 'Alamgir. A *dastak*, or safe conduct, for the 'Captain from Madras' was enclosed. Then follows a letter from Abnus reporting that the letters of September 7 and 9, 1687, were delivered to Mahabat Khan, and he handed them to the Mogul. A few days afterwards the Khan was transferred to Lahor. Asad Khan, the *wazir*, took possession of the papers. Abnus said an Englishman must be sent up, a wise and understanding man. If he (Abnus) had only had a power of Attorney in Mahabat Khan's time, he could have settled the business.

Yale wrote to Ruhullah Khan on February 7, 1688 (No. 21, p. 191), thanking him. A person of the Council would have been sent had not Shiva Ji's people prevented it by their plundering and seizing the letter-carriers. They cannot travel two leagues out of this town [Madras] without danger to life. Abnus will act for them. Chardin and Rodriguez report, on January 24, 1688, their safe arrival at Bhagnagar (Haidarabad). Abnus and left for Court; what were they to do with the money? Ruhullah Khan is, they hear, honest but greedy, both in eating and in getting. Five days later they make many complaints of Abnus, after having seen him. They hear he visits the Court more for his own affairs than the Company's, and uses their money for his own purposes. The Mogul was about to leave [? for Bijapur], and Abnus would never carry through the negotiation. On his side, Abnus makes bitter complaint that the Frenchman (Chardin) withholds the money, and the Armenian boasts that he will pledge his own jewels to put the English business through. He did not think an Englishman now required, and great expense would be saved by not sending one.

Yale wrote on February 7, 1688 (No. 2, pp. 191-194), blaming Chardin and his companion for distrusting Abnus: the money was to be handed over, and they were to help him. They are

1. Ruhullah Khan was the second son of Khalilullah Khan, Yazdi (Manucci's 'traitor' of 1658), In the thirty-first year (1687-88), when Aurangzeb set out for Bijapur, he left Haidarabad, *Dar-ul-jihad*, in charge of Ruhullah Khan. He died at the end of the thirty-sixth year, 1103 H. (April, 1692, to April, 1693) ('Ma,asir-ul-Umara,' ii. 309).

prayed to write in French or Portuguese, as more intelligible than 'broken English.' Abnus was told that the Council still confided in him. On April 12, 1688, in another letter to Abnus (No. 21, Part II., p. 16), Yale complaints that the articles of the proposed *farman* are not as liberal as he had hoped. At the Council on May 24, 1688 (No. 5, p. 93), it was announced that Abnus had nearly settled terms with Ruhullah Khan about the general *farman*. He hoped to proceed to the Court to get it confirmed. But they (the Council) had letters that the General (Sir John Child) had made a general peace at Surat, and the *farman* had gone there. They assumed that Madras and Bengal were included. Their attempts at Gulkandah were to be suspended till they heard farther. Finally, on July 9, 1688 (No. 5, p. 139), Abnus writes from Gulkandah, enclosing a letter of Nawab I 'tibar Khan from Bijapur, advising that the *farman* had gone to Surat, and he (Abnus) need not proceed to Bijapur.

Not more than sixty years ago this Madras was a sandy beach in the territory of Gulkandah, where the English began by erecting straw huts.[1] In time, by slow degrees, through prudence and good government they came to building a fortress, castles, and spacious suburbs. By the freedom given to merchants of all nations, it has now become very populous. Great profits are earned there, it is very famous, and larger than any place on the Choromandal coast. Merchants throng to it from all parts, it having whatever they are in want of.

The founder of this place was an Englishman called Ricardo Coguem (Richard Cogan),[2] whom I knew in the year one thousand

1. The site of Madras was obtained by a grant dated March 1, 1639 ('Madras Manual of Administration,' ii. 271). As N. M. was writing in 1699, this was exactly sixty years before.
2. The founder of Madras was *Andrew* Cogan (see W. Foster's 'Founding of Fort St. George,' p. 24). Mr. Foster tells me that Richard was the son of Andrew Cogan, and quotes a diary of Puckle, 1675-76 (India Office, 'Masulipatam Records,' vol. xii.), where several Englishmen are spoken of as being then in 'Moor service at Golconda.' Among them 'One Coggins (whose father built Fort St. George) is now chief gunner in the Roome of Mr. Mingham, decd., 500 pagodas and Sallary. 'Mr. Foster considers Richard was the offspring of some irregular union, probably with a native woman; otherwise, he would have become Sir Richard Cogan on his father's death. Andrew Cogan married (about 1630-33) a daughter of

six hundred and eighty-six at the city of Gulkandah. He ended his life in poverty. The ruin of the city of Sao Thome was of great benefit to Madras, for its materials were used to extend it.

[Pages 156-165 of the text are blank.]

[166] Now that I have finished the Third Part of my book, I fill up the time meanwhile with informing the reader of various matters that I have seen and encountered in India. For I desire, if God grant me life, to recount the dealings of Aurangzeb with Shiva Ji [*i.e.*, the Mahrattahs].

It seems to me that the reader will be pleased if I insert some account of the empire of Narsinga (Nar Singh),[1] of the Hindu race, whose court was in the Karnatik. More than two hundred years ago there reigned an emperor called Ramrajo (Ram Rajah),[1] who was so generous that it is remarked in the chronicles that he never refused any favour asked. He confirmed any grant he made by a record on golden plates. Up to this day the Portuguese preserve one of these plates for a gift to them by the said Ram Rajah of the city of Sao Thome. Owing to the liberality of this emperor his fame spread, and many men of different nations resorted to him and entered his service, principally foreigners. He gave them pay, and confided to them offices of profit. His empire was so extensive that it reached to the river Narbada, which divides the lands of Hindustan from those of the Dakhin, as I have already said. This was the northern frontier; that on the north-east was Jagarnate (Jagannath), on the coast of Gergelim (Jinjili).[2]

In addition, he was lord over all the coast of Choromandal and the Pescaria coast (Fishery coast) as far as Cape Comeris (Comorin), including the said cape, of all the coast of Travamcor (Travancore) and Canara as far as Surat. Thus, out of all these lands he formed one great monarchy, very prosperous and rich in seed-pearls, pearls, and diamonds. It was very productive in

---

Sir Hugh Hammersley, and had two daughters, but no recognised male offspring. Richard Cogan is mentioned in Governor Gyfford's letter of March 17, 1687 (see Note, *ante*).

1. The kingdom is that of Vijayanagar, founded in 1366. Nar Singh succeeded in 1479, and reigned until 1490. Ram Rajah, a minister, founded a new dynasty shortly after 1509. Ram Rajah was killed in battle in 1564 ('Madras Manual of Administration,' i. 150-153).
2. Jinjili coast (see Sir R. C. Temple's 'T.` Bowrey,' 120-128). It lies between Orissa and Masulipatam.

food-stuffs, wheat, rice, and all kinds of grain. Throughout his dominions were many great cities and fortresses, full of inhabitants and rich merchants, and also great harbours on the sea. By reason of all this there flocked to this country much people of many nations to do business, in particular men from China and Achem (Achin), bringing much gold, whereby the country was still farther enriched.

This emperor, in his great generosity, gave his principal provinces to his servants and slaves. Thus the province of Bijapur was given to one of his slaves called Issof (Yusuf), carver at his table, a Georgian by race. The province of Gulkandah he gave to Abrahim Maly (Ibrahim Malik), of the same race, who was the emperor's chief huntsman. The province of Daltabad (Daulatabad) went to another slave of Abexim (Habshi or Abyssinian) race, his chamber-servant; and the province of Burhanpur to the head carpet-spreader,[1] of the same race. In this way he distributed all the provinces in his kingdom. All the above men were Mahomedans, but over the country in the direction of the Karnatik he placed one of his Hindu [167] servants.

After this division he led a happy life, without attending to government or taking any notice of what went on. From this cause the governors grew very rich and powerful; and at his death every one of them rebelled and proclaimed himself king and independent ruler, refusing to recognise or obey those who belonged to the royal blood, and claiming the succession as of right. In the course of time they grew more and more powerful. The princes of the blood royal, seeing that they were not acknowledged as such, remained in Karnatik territory, and the rebel governors gave them something in charity for their support, and on this they lived in poverty. Their descendants survive to this day.

The rebel governors continued to rule their lands in great prosperity. Then came the Mogul king called Akbar and seized Brampur (Burhanpur), Amadanaguer (Ahmadnagar) and Doltabad (Daulatabad). One of these rebels, even the prince of Madorey (? Madura), who grew in the course of time very powerful, forgetting what his ancestors had done to their emperor, fell

1. The text has *estrausiro,* or *estraueiro,* which I take as meant for *farrash* (carpet-spreader), from *estradar,* 'to cover with carpets'; or it might be 'scavenger' (from *estravo,* 'dung, manure'). Mr. Dames prefers estancero, keeper of a *sarae—i.e,* a *bhattiyara.*

into the same error. He divided his territory among eighteen of his captains on condition that they should hold them, they and their descendants, as his vassals. When occasion or necessity arose, these people would have to assemble and render assistance.

One of these captains, named Tevere (Tevara),[1] obtained the lands of Marava,[2] the island of Utiar (? Udayar) or Raman-varao (Rameshwaram),[3] where there is a temple highly venerated by the Hindus. People throughout India hold the belief that by entering it their needs will be satisfied. In it there was much buried treasure.

---

1. 106. Tevere, Tevarem = Tevar, a local form for Deva, and is the caste name of the Maravas ('Madras Manual of Administration,' iii. 475, line 29). For the Marava tribe, see vol. i. of same work, p. (124) note 7.

WODEYA TEVAR, of Ramnad.
d. 1623
[made Setupati, or Lord of the Bridge, about 1590; a vassal of Madura].

- Cootam, Setupati, d. 1637 *s.p.*
- Delavoy [S. 1637; taken prisoner to Ramnad; released 1640; recovered one-third of his country; put to death by Tamby 1649].
  - Daughter [m. Tanalka], one-third share
  - Vijaya Raghunath Tevar, one-third share [adopted son; reunited all the shares 1659]; d. 1685.
    - Son [few months old].
    - Son [three months] old].
    - Kizhava or Kilava, Setupati. s. 1686; d. 1723 [John de Brito martyred by him 1693].
- Bettana Naik (*alias* Tamby) [supported by Tirumal naik of Madura], s. 1623 to one-third share: d. soon after 1649.

2. Marava (warrior), a race found in Madura, Tinnivelly, Ramnad, and Shivaganga. Deva (*tevar*) is the caste name of all Maravas ('Madras Manual of Administration, iii. 474).
3. See a description of the temple in Thornton's 'Gazetteer, 818, and 'Madras Manual of Administration, iii. 741. Thornton says there is a splendid view of this temple by Daniell. For 'Utiar' Mr. R. W. Frazer suggests 'Udayar,' the sun, the rising sun; but I have found no authority for the application of this epithet to Rameshwaram Island.

It happened more than sixty years ago that this Tevara withdrew his obedience from his superior lord, believing himself to be gifted with some supernatural powers, and also prompted by the possession of great wealth. Upon becoming aware of this revolt, the prince of Madura was much disturbed, and sent him various orders to appear and do homage. In case of disobedience he would resort to force, and chastise him as a rebel. Tevera paid no heed to these threats; and with an army of sixty thousand men, infantry and cavalry together, took the field against Madura.

This Tevara was a huge-limbed and gigantic man, of great strength and great courage. The strongest horse could not bear him farther than two leagues. At one meal he ate as much as twenty ordinary men, and drank much wine.[1] But he never entered on eating or drinking without going through superstitious performances with the wine. Angered at the revolt of Tevara, the prince of Madura sent out an army
of eighty thousand combatants under a general, China Tamby Modely (Chinna Tambi Mudeliyar),[2] a man astute, sagacious and valorous.

Tevara took several towns and fortresses of Madura, leaving in them a sufficient garrison for defence. In this style he went on weakening his force, and when he met China Tamby Modely, there remained under his command no more than twenty-five thousand combatants. With this small force he imagined (misled by his great courage) that he would overcome his enemies. Both sides gave battle, and for three hours the fight was in the balance. After that he (Tevara) began to perceive that his opponent had the advantage. In this crisis he tried to bring into action twelve [168] pieces of artillery that he had left behind in the charge of seventy Europeans, not supposing them to be required by a man of his calibre. But the enemy gave him no time to avail himself of these cannon.

Finding his army lost and routed, Tevara left the field, descended from his elephant, and hid himself in an adjacent

1. He ate only once a day (Venice Codex, fol. 430).
2. According to the 'Madras Manual of Administration,' i. 124 note, Tambi was a relation and rival claimant to the throne, backed by Madura. *Chinna*, term of affection; *tambi*, younger brother; *mudeliyar*, a headman, a ruler. Perhaps the last word is *Mudali*, 'a chief (Yule. 569).

wood.[1] China Tamby Modely, in the rage of conquest, spared no one; hardly anyone escaped alive. They found Tevara in the wood, but to make him surrender cost many a life. He was brought before the prince of Madura, who was highly delighted to see as his prisoner a man of such stature and courage. As a recreation, he directed him to be attached by two thick fetters in the hall where audiences were held. The imprisoned Tevara for two days refused to eat. The prince asked him why he did not eat. He answered that he could not eat unless he had wine to drink, and could carry through his usual ceremonial. The prince asked what he would have done if he (the prince) had fallen into his hands, and the indomitable Tevara replied that if Fate had made him victor, he would have pounded his enemy in a mortar, and then, well mixed with clay, would have made of him pellets for his boys to shoot birds with.

On hearing this answer, the prince laughed and said: 'For this speech I want to give you your liberty; what have you to give me?' Tevara replied: 'If you release me, I will give you forty thousand *pagodas'* worth of precious stones.' 'What security shall I have?' responded the prince. 'My chief wife shall be left as hostage,' replied the other; 'but you will have to swear not to touch her.' The prince was satisfied, but just then the general came in, made over his staff to the prince, and said that if he liberated Tevara he would turn *jogi*, or wanderer. As for the forty millions[2] promised, he undertook to give double on condition that in his presence the prisoner were ordered to be killed.

The prince asked Tevara how he wished to die. He replied that he should like to die at the hands of the Madura general. But first let them cut off one leg and one arm; let a sword be made over to him, and another put in the hands of the general. Thus fighting, his life could be taken. The prince ordered the prisoner to be mutilated in his presence. To this he retorted by abusive language. In this manner they went on removing one

1. 'Or, to speak more correctly, he was carried away and placed in the wood; for he could not walk, owing to the armour he wore' (Venice Codex XLIV., fol. 430).
2. The Venice Codex XLIV. (Zanetti), fol. 431, has 'millions' in both places, and this second passage has been overlooked, and not made to agree with the revised text. In the Venice text the details of Tevara's. execution are much more brutally given.

limb after another. But he had such endurance that he uttered much abuse both of the prince and of his general. Finally he was decapitated.

After his death, they went on conquering his territory and chastising the rebels until they reached his capital, into which the general entered with a large force, and the whole kingdom was brought into subjection. The Marava women pledged their word to each other that they would deny their husbands all marital rights, and not allow them near them until [169] they had taken vengeance for their sons and their Tevara. Thus put to shame, the men killed in one night the general and all the soldiers in the town. They raised to the throne a nephew of Tevara, who made a brave defence until he came to terms with the Prince of Madura, conceding the government to that prince more by force than by free will.

These Marava women are very brave and faithful to their husbands. There was once a woman of this race who lived in a house outside the village. Her husband was away, and she had an unweaned infant. By chance a *faqir* arrived and asked for alms. Seeing her beauty, and that the house stood at a distance from the village, he formed designs against her, and shut the garden-gate from inside. The woman became aware of the faqir's evil thoughts and ran for her room, fastening the door on the inside. In her hurry she had left her child outside. On reaching the door the *faqir* prayed her to open, saying thousands of amorous words, to which the woman did not reply. On finding that she did not answer, the *faqir* threatened her that if she did not open the door he would kill the infant. She uttered not a sound.

In a rage the *faqir* cut off one of the infant's arms, and through a hole there was threw it inside. In spite of this she did not open her mouth. The *faqir* went on severing the child's limbs, and threw the pieces in as he had done the first. Finally he decided to get into the room by mining under the threshold enough to let his body through. Seeing the *faqir's* deliberate attack, and the danger to her honour, the woman placed herself close to the hole with a large stick in her hand, so that when the *faqir's* head emerged she applied the stick with such energy that his brains came out. Thus did she inflict justice for the death of her son. Towards evening the husband returned. Finding the door fastened inside, he called to his wife. As she gave no

Vol. III

To face page 98

answer, he climbed over the garden wall. On drawing near the door of the room, he saw the entrails of the infant and the dead *faqir* with half his body outside. He shouted for his wife, and she from inside, without opening the door, gave an account of the event. The husband went at once to report to the ruler. On hearing the story, the latter praised the woman highly, and, going to the spot, made her mount his elephant, and took her all round the town as a token of great honour. When the prince of that land heard of the case, he gave orders that all *faqirs* found in his territories should be killed. In this way more than three thousand *faqirs* were destroyed—men who, under the cloak of sanctity, are the greatest villains in the world. Up to this day no *faqirs* wander into those parts.

The Prince of Tanjor had a daughter of rare beauty. Inflamed by reports about her, the Prince of Madura asked her in marriage, saying he was anxious to become his (Tanjor's) son-in-law, and they two united would be able to resist the armies [170] of the whole world. The Prince of Tanjor was much offended at this embassy, and replied that his daughter could not be given to him, seeing his great inferiority in blood and rank. He should remember how humble his forefathers were (referring to the emperor Ram Rajah having raised his ancestors from a lowly condition). He must not entertain such lofty ideas.

By this answer the Prince of Madura was thrown into a great rage, and gathering all his forces, he started in person to devastate the lands of Tanjor.[1] The latter also made ready his whole army, and sent his general in advance to impede the pro.' gress of the Madura ruler. But such Was the sagacity and astuteness of that prince that he brought the Tanjor general over to his side with all his troops. When the Tanjor prince heard of his general's treason, he was greatly concerned, and took the field himself with a strong army, and awaited the arrival of the Madura prince. In a few days the two forces were in sight of each other. But the Tanjor leaders, already tampered with by the Madura prince or the traitorous general, gradually deserted

1. The Madura prince referred to must be Chakka-nath, Nayak, who succeeded in 1670. He defeated and slew Vijaya Raghava, King of Tanjor ('Madras Manual of Administration,' i. 121 note). His own death took place in 1674 (*ibid.*, ii. 126).

their prince and sovereign; by daybreak be found himself entirely abandoned, and was forced to retire into the city.

He made efforts to collect the people to defend the place, but through the great confusion that existed could not succeed; and in desperation he loaded his cannon with all his great store of precious stones, and scattered them over the country. When this had been done, he went to his magnificent palace, where, shutting up seven hundred wives that he had, together with his daughter and all his wealth, he blew them up by a powder-mine, reserving only his most cherished wife, who was anxious to die in his company. He liberated fifteen thousand and three hundred concubines, who had been picked from the most lovely women in his kingdom.

Let not the reader start at the prince having this number of women. For in this so great was his haughtiness and vainglory that he wanted to imitate one of his gods called Quisina (Krishna), of whom it is said in their Scriptures, that he had this number of wives. While these things were happening, the enemy came and attacked the city. In order not to be made prisoner and be disgraced, the king decided to die bravely. He came out with three sons and eighteen horsemen, his relations, bearing on his horse's hindquarters his beloved queen. She, at the approach of the enemy's mighty force, felt afraid, and spoke tender words to her husband, saying that as evil Chance was so great a tyrant as to rob her of further delight in his society, she prayed him to end her life with his own hand, so that she might not fall into the enemy's power; nor should they ever obtain that delight he had enjoyed, while she would escape the horror of further afflictions. She repeated several times supplications to the same effect, but the prince was unable to steel him self to such cruelty, seeing the great love he bore her. Still, the arguments of the afflicted and determined princess were so strong that, finding the enemy already close upon them, he was forced at length to yield to her entreaties. Seizing his sword, he cut off her head, and, his blade all bare and crimson, galloped into the enemy's ranks, followed by his companions, and in a brief space ended his life.

Thus did the Madura prince become lord of [171] Tanjor. The cause of the ruin of that prince (Tanjor) was his want of capacity and his ambition to be like the god Krishna in regard to the daughters and wives of others, mostly his captains and generals. Being thus aggrieved, these men perpetrated the treason referred to.

This prince if Tanjor was the first to give permission to Father Ruberto Nobre (Roberto de' Nobili),[1] a Jesuit and Italian by race, to build churches and preach our holy Faith and argue with the Brahmans. He held this father in much respect. Nobili was the first to begin that mission which at present, by God's grace, finds itself with more than one hundred churches. Continually it increases in the number of its Christians, to the greater glory of its founder. But at this moment, for the Christian communities in these provinces there is a great lack of missionaries.

In the year one thousand six hundred and eighty-two (1682) the Dutch commissary with a fleet of thirty vessels tried to destroy the temple of Ramanavarao (Rameshwaram), and remove the great treasures buried within it. While this work was in progress he received a letter from the principal Hindus, wherein they wrote that if he determined to do any damage, or if his people got as far as within the shadow of the temple, they were prepared to set on fire and destroy all the cities, fortresses, and factories upon this coast, and the name of the Dutch would be blotted out for ever. Upon reading the letter, he made sail at Once in the direction of Turuchorim (Tuticorin),[2] and thus abandoned his intention in order not to lose the great wealth they drew from that coast.

Since I am speaking of that coast, I will state how they obtain seed-pearls on the shores of Tutochorim (Tuticorin) and in Manar. The inhabitants know the time of year for removing the pearls. It is in the months of March and April. The Dutch, as lords of the sea-shore on the coast of Tuticorin, and of the coast of Manar in the island of Ceylon, give licenses to fish for twenty-one

1. Roberto de' Nobili, of a noble Florentine family, born at Monte Pulciano in Tuscany in 1577, entered the Society of Jesus in 1597, and went to India in 1605. He began his mission on the Malabar (Choromandal) coast in 1606, gave himself out as a Roman Catholic *rajah* or *sanyasi*, kept only Brahman servants, lived like a Brahman, and addressed himself only to Brahmans. He left the mission in 1648, and died at Mailapur, close to Madras, on January 16, 1656, at the age of nearly eighty years (M. Müllbauer, 'Geschichte der Katholischen Missionen in Ost-Indien,' pp., 171, 207; Freiburg, 1852). There is a portrait of Nobili in 'Mémoires 'Historiques' by Pere Norbert, Capuchin (Besancon, 1747), vol. i, p. 14, of which we insert a copy.
2. The word is correctly 'Tuticorin' in the Venice Codex XLIV.

different days. In this way they begin at the end of March, and spread the fishing out to May 20 or thereabouts. In this fishery participate six hundred *toni* (Tamil, *toni*),[1] which are vessels sufficient for the purpose. Every vessel has a crew of thirty men, who pay the Dutch six *patacas*[2] a head if they are Christians, nine if Hindu, twelve if Manomedans, The Christian boats are three hundred, those of the Hindus one hundred, and of the Mahomedans two hundred. Added together, these come to eighteen thousand men. These are the divers. Many more people collect as traders, carriers, including women and children. Ordinarily, during the fishing season there are forty thousand people. Each vessel pays one *pataca* for a *cartajo* (a license or permit). All this money together amounts to one hundred and forty-four thousand three hundred *patacas*.[3] Besides this, the Dutch provide supplies of rice, pulses, salted fish, and flour, *et cetera*, for sale to all [172] this crowd. From this they derive great profit, for they sell at whatever prices they like.

The way of obtaining the seed-pearls is as follows; These vessels anchor in ten, twelve, or even sixteen fathoms. The divers are naked and oiled all over. In entering the water they lay hold of a rope, at the end of which a stone is attached, and this helps them to get nearer the bottom,[4] Another separate rope is tied round the man's waist. He has a basket hung across his shoulder, and holds in his hand a *coita* (? rod)[5] which he uses to detach any shells which may be stuck to stones. Thus he rapidly fills the basket, and this done, he shakes the rope round his waist. His companions in the vessel, on

1. Yule, 323 (s.v. *Doney* or *Dhony*), who quotes the form *tony* from Baldaeus, 'Ceylon,' Dutch edition, 1672.
2. See I. 113, where one *pataca* is made equal to two rupees; also, see Yule, 683, a dollar or piece of eight.
3. I make the total come to 143,600 *patacas*.
4. The Venice Codex XLIV. adds that a weight is fastened to the diver's feet.
5. There can be no doubt that a stick or rod, probably of iron, must be meant. For *coita* I propose to read *cetro* (or *sceptro*), a *sceptre*, which is, after all, a short rod or stick. Mr. Dames objects to sceptro, and proposes *cota* (*de facd*), the back of a knife, but agrees that 'an iron instrument with a stout blade' must be meant. Mr. D. Ferguson writes: 'I cannot find that the divers carried anything but the basket or net in which to put the oysters. The word must be an error if a stick is intended. If right (*i.e.*, *coita*), I can only suggest Tamil *katti*, knife; Sinhalese *katta*, a bill-hook.'

getting tins signal, haul him up as fast as they can to the surface, and take the shells. The diver who went down first takes a rest, and another man takes his place. Thus they continue the whole day, taking it in turns, and in the evening they withdraw, and from every boat they collect the shells and put them in a place set apart for them.

Some merchants take the chance of buying unopened oysters, the highest price given being one *pataca* per thousand. If the oysters turn out not to be rich in pearls, they do not lose their money; while some have such good fortune as to enrich themselves at the cost of one *pataca*. The fishing being over, they leave the oysters to rot, and the smell makes anyone ill who is present. They leave the oysters to decay, because in this way the pearls turn out of a better colour, and the Dutch as over-lords of the site purchase the best, and at the cheapest rates. Every year at this fishery there die without fail a considerable number of the divers while diving.

There is also another fishery of a shell-fish they call *chanchos* (*sankh*),[1] which is a business carried on by the Dutch only; they carry them to Bengal and earn large profits. For the Hindus make from them bracelets, rings, and other curiosities for their women. They are always at a good price, for when any man dies all the female relations of the defunct break their bracelets and rings in sign of grief, when new ones have to be made. In this same way they fish, but at all seasons, for seed-pearls in the Persian Gulf, whence are derived a larger quantity and of higher value.

While I was in Madrastapatao (Madras) there came a barque from Macao, and among other news they told of an extraordinary case that had lately happened. A vessel sailed from Siao (Siam) for Manila. In the latitude of Paragoa it met a [173] typhoon, by which it was driven on a rocky shore and perished. The greater number of the crew got into a boat in the hope of reaching some port, but to this day nothing has been heard of them. Fourteen men, however, took refuge on a peak of land, where they dwelt for nine years. They lived for six months on birds and for six months on turtle, according to the

1. *Chank, chunk, chanco, chanquo*, a large kind of shell (*Turbinella rapa*), prized by the Hindus. It is found especially in the Gulf of Manaar (Yule, 184).

seasons, together with roots that served to sustain them, also on shell-fish. They suffered much for want of water, and forced by necessity, they searched diligently throughout the isle, until at one spot, digging a hole among the stones, it ended in a very sweet water springing up sufficient for their necessities. They lived on in this manner till there was a quarrel, when they divided into two settlements, each with its own chief. This continued for some time, and then they reunited.

In the said isle they often held council how to get out of it. To effect this, they decided to make a boat ready for the time when Fortune should favour them. All the timber and the trees driven to the island by the currents were collected, and the best kept for the above purpose, and the rest served for cooking. They kept the nails and pieces of iron found in the timber, and with these prepared the necessary iron and wood-work in the best way they could; only files and hand-saws they could not procure. With the skins and feathers of birds they clothed themselves, and of the gut they made string. The coverings of the turtles served as bowls and plates.

As soon as they had timber enough, they began to build their boat, which looked like a box. They made in it a tank to carry water, and put on a deck. The mast alone delayed them six months, shaving and paring it; it was twelve cubits long. With the skins and feathers of birds they manufactured sails. The boat having been completed in the best way they could they provisioned it with flesh of birds salted with salt they had made, and other flesh fried in tortoise fat, and of their shells they made water-jars and vessels. Dried yams served instead of biscuit. During their stay in the island two of the company died.

Having worked at their preparations for fifty days, they embarked and set sail, abandoning themselves to the will of Fate, and leaving behind one of their companions who had lost the use of his limbs. After the lapse of some days they came in sight of an island and made for it, and, beaching their boat, enjoyed themselves for two months. They caught a large number of birds, which they easily seized with their hands, they captured turtles, dug yams, and collected other wild productions. After two months they revictualled the boat, and once more set sail, navigating without knowing where they were going.

After thirty days they perceived an island straight ahead of the boat, whereat they greatly rejoiced, for [174] they were suffering much from the want of water. Keeping on the same course there appeared a number of islands, which they recognised as the islands of Aisnaos,[1] inhabited by Chinese. They were thus reassured, and made every effort to reach land search for water, for they were dying of thirst. The natives, seeing such a boat and such figures, fled in fright, carrying off with them their children and all that they could carry, those who caused all this confusion not knowing what was the matter.

The Chinese governor, on being informed, sent soldiers to inquire into this novel affair. These men, seeing the feathered sailors, became alarmed and halted at a distance. On the fugitives perceiving the fear the soldiers had of them, one of them divested himself of his plumage, and from afar began saluting and telling them in Chinese that they were shipwrecked mariners. They were conveyed to the presence of the governor, and he, taking them to be pirates, ordered them to be seized, while men went to search the boat and see if things were as the sailors said. Finding in the end that they were shipwrecked men, he treated them honourably, gave them food to eat and clothes to wear, for they smelt of the feathers in which they were clothed. After some days he sent them off, accompanied by some soldiers, who carried them to terra firma, and produced them before the chief governor with a letter which reported the facts.

After having been examined a fresh, they were well treated. In this way they passed through the land of China with a guide provided by each governor of a fortress. They traversed many forests full of wild beasts. At the end of a long journey they reached the city of Macao. There at that time the wife of one of the band was about to marry again; she broke the marriage off when her husband arrived, and took back her husband, although he was very emaciated and much battered by long travel.

As they were of different countries and different places, each one from this port took his road for his own home. One of them set out for Siam, and there found his wife already married again, and with sons. The *curé* had married her

1. This may be intended for the Island of Hainan, of China.

obliged the woman to return to her first husband, although this was against her will.

The story I have told was confirmed to me by a Portuguese, one of the band named Bento Marques. He told me many details of this shipwreck, and I have only reproduced the principal events; I will leave it to the reader to reflect on all that must have passed to satisfy the reader's wish, I give the names of the men who were in this shipwreck: Bento Marques, Portuguese; Manoel Machado, of the same race; Paulo Dono, Agostinho de Moraes, Paulo de Siqueras, Urbano da Silva, Joao Gomes. These formed one settlement when they mutinied; and they had as chief Bento Marques, who was possessor of a knife. Those in the other settlement were Manoel da Costa, a native of India, selected as chief, and he had a nail for his only weapon; Antonio de Matos, Joao da Silva, Antonio da Costa. The three who [175] died were called Joao de Rozario, Joao da Costa, Luiz Pexoto da Silva. These seven were of the other settlement at the time of mutiny, and when they reunited, the majority of votes decided. This affair is well known in the greater part of India.

In the village of Trivambur (Tiruvottiyur),[1] a league and a half from San Thome, there was a wall enclosing a temple, and on the stones of this an inscription stating and pointing out the road or highway for reaching the sea, for the benefit of those coming from inland. At the present time that village is quite close to the sea. In the year one thousand six hundred and fifty-one (1651), it happened at San Thome that a fisherman went there to fish. His hook caught at the bottom, so that he was unable to pull it up. He dived to see what his hook had caught in, and found it was an anchor. He put a buoy to his line to mark the place, and went off to tell the governor of the place nearest the sea. Divers were sent to haul up the anchor. When they got it out they saw the fluke had been embedded in

1. Probably intended for Trivettore (Tirvvottiyur); from *Tir* ('holy') + *atti* ('Shiva, the first one') + *ūr* ('village'), a' place of pilgrim in the Chingleput district, Sydapett talook, three-quarters of a mile west of the sea. There is an old Shiva temple with inscriptions. The place visited by Fryer in 1673, and mentioned (edition of 1873, p. 203) under the name of Triblitor, seems to be different, as it was four miles north of Madras ('Madras Manual of Administration,' iii. 900).

clay, a sign that in olden times the sea was distant, and the place was the site of a village. The hooks (*barba*) of the anchor had already disappeared from the saltness of the sea, and it was without a stock.

The learned men of Hindustan are in the habit of writing on metal plates. This is from the habit they have of preserving the memory of antiquity. On one of these plates it is written that from the port of Surat, and Dyo (Diu) in Hindustan, caravans started for Mecca by land. Nowadays all is sea: Surat, Barocha (Bharoch), Cambaja (Kambayat), Dyo (Diu), Syndi (Sind)—all these are at present on the shore of the sea. In my time the Mahomedans destroyed the temple [at Trivambur] and the enclosure referred to in order to erect new buildings, for they abominate the antiquities of the Hindus.

I will tell you of a terrible affair that happened in the Portuguese territory. There was a man married to a rich and influential lady of good connections. He misbehaved with a girl servant of the house; but from the hate the lady thereby conceived for him, she dissembled until she found the occasion she needed. She killed the negress, and after mutilating the body, ordered it to be buried in the garden behind the house. The flesh removed from the body was taken by the lady into the kitchen, and in her own presence a dish was prepared with it. When her husband came home she presented the dish to him herself, and told him she had made it. The husband ate and praised it for its exquisite taste. Then the woman lifted the dish and flung the contents in his face, saying it was not enough to have enjoyed her while she was alive; even in death she was of good savour. Her anger overflowing, she gave her husband plentiful abuse, and, quitting the house, went to live with her relations, nor for the rest of her life would she consent to meet her husband.

Here is another case which happened at San Thome in the year ninety-five (1695). There was a Portuguese called Antonio Pinto, married to a woman whose name was Izabel Rapoza, and he went the evil way with a married woman called Antonia de Torres, who allowed this Portuguese to enter her house publicly. The wife heard of this, and not being able to cool down her passion, found an opportunity one day about noon, and came out of her house followed by four strong and stout slaves. She attacked the house of her adversary, and dragged her out by her hair into the street, there to have her bones broken by a good thumping and her face disfigured by shoebeating. The aggrieved wife then retired with ail dignity to her own house, and the wretched Antonia de Torres went off to Madras to be healed. Thus were she and Antonio Pinto branded with infamy all over the country. By way of restoring his credit, he assigned as a reason for his leaving his wife that she was impotent, and this rumour was generally current among the Portuguese.

Another such thing happened in San Thome. There was a lady married to Cosmo Lourenço Madeira, a Portuguese; her name was Dona Escolastica, the daughter of Joao Pereira de Faria. She imprisoned in her house one of her slaves for having stolen something. By reason of severe punishment and deprivation of food he died, and was buried in the dunghill. No one dared to ask any questions, for if the Mahomedans had known they would have chastised the gentleman, Cosmo Lourenço, as he had done to his slave. This murder of slaves and slave girls is common among the Portuguese, and few are the houses in which the skeletons of their bodies would not be found.

Near the town of Bassaim (Bassein) dwelt a well-born gentlewoman on her estate. She was called Dona Luiza de Abello, and was a rich and influential woman. When she left her house for recreation, she was escorted by fifty sturdy, well-armed Kaffirs[1] with their quarter-staves. When the woman saw any Portuguese youth who pleased her, she carried him off to her house and toyed with him till she was tired of him. As his reward, she would order him to be killed and buried in her orchard. In this way she passed her life, while the hand-somest youths in the country disappeared.

Her cruelties became known, and the youths, thus warned, kept out of her way. The lady referred to, on her way to church, saw a boy whom she fancied, and on coming out took him home with her against his will, and he was never seen again. The lady was related to the highest-placed gentlemen to be found in Bassein. These men, recognising her disorders and misdeeds, made overtures to certain negro women of her household that, if they would destroy her in her sleep, their lives would be protected.

1. Caffre was then the Portuguese (and English) name for Africans (Yule, 140).

Listening to the proposal, the slave women killed her by hitting her on the head [177] with a big stone and crushing her brains. The magistrate arrested the negresses, who were sentenced to death. On their way to execution they passed in front of the church of the Jesuit Fathers, who came out with the flag of Mercy, and they were liberated. This affair happened while I was in India, and many affirmed to me that it was true. When I passed through Bassein I merely addressed a question to some well-born gentlemen who were her relations, and they replied that it was worse than what I had heard said, and therefore God had punished her.

I will relate a ridiculous affair that happened in the town of Cochin when it was held by the Portuguese.[1] There was a Portuguese merchant, married and very rich, who started on a voyage to China. After the lapse of three years he arrived again in the port with much wealth, and in possession of a slave to whom he meant to give his liberty. At the same time he wished to puzzle his wife, and test the depth of her love for him. He sent the man to her house with instructions as to what he was to say to the lady. On his reaching home all were rejoiced—above all, the lady. She asked the slave how her husband was. He replied joyfully that his master was hearty and well: God had brought him back in safety with much wealth. On hearing this, all of them grew happier and still more pleased. The lady gave orders to deck the bed with rich curtains and adorn the whole house. They were to set to work in the kitchen, and prepare all that was required.

After these orders had been given she called the slave apart, and asked him quietly what sort of life his master led, and how many lady acquaintances he had made (for it is a usual thing for wives to spy on their husbands, and find out what they have been doing). The slave simulated sorrow, and told her that when his master reached the house she would be able to see. The wife fell into a state of mind and renewed her questions, urging him to state the truth, and she would keep his secret. The slave declined and showed fear of telling. His mistress, still more confused, asked again more urgently, and became more eager than ever to find out. Finally, the slave told her quietly

1. Cochin was taken by the Portuguese in 1507, and conquered from them by the Dutch in 1663 ('Madras manual of Administration,' iii. 194).

that his master was afflicted with a complaint which made him impotent. He then left the house.

On hearing this the lady withdrew into her room and wept, and sadly bewailed her miserable fate. The women servants in the house ran to her, and asked the cause of her tears and complaining. She replied impatiently that God desired to chastise her youthful follies, and she repeated what the slave had told her. On hearing this, each began to express her ideas: some said it were better their master did not return, but stopped in China; others said he ought to be ashamed of himself to come home in that condition, having a young wife at home; others asked of what use were riches, when one was unable to enjoy them; others expressed other opinions. All were up in arms for their mistress. She took to her bed and shut herself up in her room, and countermanded all her former orders. She instructed her women that, should the husband arrive, they were to say to him that their mistress was unwell [178]. From joy the whole household was turned to mourning.

In the afternoon the husband came ashore, and reaching his house, found that no one came out to greet him; all was silence. The joker, though he knew the cause, pretended he did not, and rushed off to the room where his wife was, and going in, embraced her and asked her the cause of her keeping her room thus. Pretending to be ill, she answered softly and slowly that she was troubled with pains in the head, and could not bear loud talking. The cunning fellow came out hurriedly from the room and went after the servant girls, shouting to them and enjoining some of them to go within and look after their mistress. He ordered the cooks to prepare some dishes for their mistress to eat; others he sent to heat water to bathe his body. Then he took up position in the middle of the house, and complained that if his wife were only well, the house would not be in such disorder, nor would the negro women be thus careless. The women pretended not to hear, and neglected to carry out his orders. He affected anger, and ran about with a stick to oblige them by force to bring the hot water. Then, tying on a cloth round his waist, he bathed his body, the negro women attending on him. While washing he negligently allowed the cloth to drop.... The negresses reported to the wife. She rose up, and all the sad sentiments that afflicted her were dissipated. She ordered that as quickly as possible they should return to wait on him. She got up hastily and peeped through a window, and observed that there was nothing wrong, and the negresses were right. Undeceived about the falsehoods reported by the slave, she came out in a great rage with the negro women, wanting to know why they had not looked better after their master. She ordered clean, perfumed sheets and linen to be brought, that the bed be made ready at once, that the cooks without delay prepare to cook everything that was necessary.

The husband, on seeing his wife's energy, was satisfied, and joined in her diatribes at the neglect of the negro women during her illness. The lady was pleased at her husband's return, and made great complaint of the slave, who by this time had disappeared. She thought the mis-statement was due to malice on the slave's part, and made secret efforts to catch him in order to punish him.

Thus, as I would wish to show, before anyone marries it is well for him to reflect deeply whether marriage is suitable for him. For I have seen many in India who no sooner were settled than they repented themselves, and were obliged to give up their wives. They became the mock of many. Just as happened once when I was in Goa, it was the rumour that seven of the principal inhabitants were impotent [179]. In the case of one of these, whose name I will not mention, his wife left his house and published the matter all through the city. Then she laid a complaint before the Lord Archbishop that her husband was totally impotent. His Lordship's order to the lady was that she must retire for three years to a respectable household. Meanwhile all possible remedies would be tried, and if the doctors did not succeed, she might marry again. His Illustriousness sent for the chief physician, and confided the young man to him. He was to make a minute examination, and do all he possibly could to restore him fit to resume cohabitation. Instead of prescribing some drug to give him vigour, the physician directed him to be placed in a tub of cold, then into one of hot water. His object was to see if any change was effected, and he administered no other ingredients, but pronounced him impotent.

Ten days before the term at which the woman was to receive liberty to marry again I arrived in Goa. The Theatine fathers[1] informed me of the case, and begged of me to try some remedy.

1. The Goa mission of the Theatine Order was founded in October, 1640 (Müllbauer,' 'Geschichte,' p. 351).

I sent for the young man, and found him suffering from obstruction of the spleen, and his body swollen. Having put the necessary questions, I found that if freed from this complaint he would be capable of matrimony. I advised him to go to the Lord Archbishop and ask him for forty days more for treatment, after which, if he was not restored, the said lady might take another husband. His Illustriousness gave permission. I set to work at once to get rid of the obstruction, and gave him sustaining and fortifying medicine. In this way the youth became capable of marrying, and going before the Lord Archbishop, demanded his wife. The Archbishop called for the chief physician and the chief surgeon to test his statements. . . . They admitted that he was entitled to be married, and reported truthfully to the Lord Archbishop; and the latter told the man to take his wife to his house. This was against her will, for she had taken a dislike to him, fancying he would be as heretofore. Afterwards she found out he was as she wanted, and they lived happily.

In Negopatao (Negapatam) there was a man called Joao Soares Cove, married to a beautiful woman. He went on a journey, and left his wife at home. There was another man named Christovao Pexoto, married, rich, and influential. I saw his wife at Madras when she was very old. This man fell in love with the wife of Joao Soares Cove, sending her a message that he wished to be her friend. As an honourable woman she declined to accept, stopped at home, and never came out for fear of this Christovao Pexoto. Paying neither respect nor heed to the citizens, he entered the woman's house in open day and used force. In this way he began to go and come as if it were his own house [180]. He carried off the woman in his palanquin, and traversed the town. He mocked the magistrate and the inhabitants, and showed that he was afraid of no one.

Joao Soares Cove returned from his journey. When he landed on the beach, his friends told him of what had passed. Seeing that he had neither strength nor force to obtain satisfaction for the affront, he never entered the house, but started at once for Goa. He presented himself before Dom Phelipe Mascarenha, then viceroy.[1] He put on his head a large bonnet covered with horns, and he made complaint of the injury done to him by Christovao Pexoto. On becoming aware of that man's

1. No. 49, Filippe Mascarenhas, 'Viceroy,' 1646-51. Danvers,. ii. 488.

insolent conduct, the viceroy gave complainant a letter enjoining on the magistrate and the married men of Negapatam that in one way or the other they must deprive the disturber of his life. The man, when he knew of this, withdrew from the town, and settled in the country of a Hindu prince not far from that place.

Finding that they could not carry out their orders, the magistrate and residents sent a present to the prince, and a letter requesting him to make over Christovao Pexoto to them alive. This money, a thing which can effect much among the Indians, caused the prince to make over the insolent fellow in chains into the hands of the citizens. These ordered his delivery to Joao Soares Cove. On reaching his presence. Pexoto, instead of showing repentance and asking pardon, called Cove over and over again a cuckold and other unseemly names. His wrath rising higher and higher, the injured man flung himself on his enemy with a pointed knife and stabbed him to the heart. Instead of commending his soul to God in these his last throes, Pexoto continued his abuse until he expired. Cove filled his two hands with the blood flowing from the wound and drank it, then smeared his whole body, face and head, with the blood, finally mutilating the dead man. After this was over, he hastened home to kill his wife. But, warned in time, she had fled to Trangabar (Tranquebar) in the company of a servant-boy she took to show her the way. On reaching his house Cove found his wife gone, and that the servant had removed her. He left the town and hid near the road, and as the servant was returning he killed him. For several days he went about all bloody, solely to prove that he had wreaked vengeance for his wrongs.

I will recount an extraordinary case which happened in the town of Bassaim (Bassein), when the rector in office was Father da Costa, of the Society of Jesus, a virtuous priest, who was himself my informant. [Story of a child brought up as a girl, who on marriage turned out to be a boy. On the author's passing through Bassein, the priest pointed out the supposed girl to him, and told him the story.] [181]

It seems to me also desirable that I should praise certain ladies who gave evidence of their good conduct and patience. It happened in the same town of Bassein that a young and wellborn man was desirous of marrying a lady of equal rank. The more efforts he made the less inclined she showed herself, and in the end he sent to say that if she did not marry him, he would not all his life long marry anyone else. This woman married a young man whom she loved, and with him she lived happily for twelve years.

The night of the wedding the young man whom she had refused came beneath her window with his friends carrying a number of instruments, and began to sing a doleful ditty which at last came to an end, when he drew a profound sigh, and exclaimed, 'Ah, tyrant! thou knowest not the laws of love.' At the end of the music the instruments were flung on the ground and smashed to bits. The serenaded pair were much put out, and took it as an affront.

After twelve years the husband died, and the serenading young man once more made his proposal of marriage to the widow. She had not forgotten what he had done, and sent word that he should call to mind the affront he had practised when he broke the musical instruments beneath her window. At this final repulse he lost all hope. The widow married another young man whom I knew, but he turned out different from what she expected, for he was a young woman. It was a remarkable fact for a woman of India to endure this patiently, yet she kept it a profound secret for the sake of her husband's honour. This shows how different she was from those others whose story I have told.

It happened in Bassein that a well-born lady of good station, and married, was delivered of a girl after a pregnancy of three years. When the child was twelve, she, too, married, and also was with child three years before being delivered. I have noted the fact that in Hindustan some have brought forth after fifteen months or two years, or there abouts, and the medical men, being inexperienced, thought it was due to some disease or to some accumulated humours. They administered drugs, which brought on premature confinement, and a perfect child was born, although they had not allowed the time fixed by nature to be completed.

When I left the court of the prince Shah 'Alam for Goa, I went via the town of Damao (Daman)[1] in the year eighty-one (1681), and I rested there some forty days. In that interval it happened that the magistrate, who had not long arrived from

1. Daman, 101 miles north of Bombay, lat. 20° 24,' long. 72° 53'. The year can hardly have been, 1681, but it might be 1683.

Goa, fell in love with a widow woman, rich and honoured. She declined his advances, and felt so insulted that she sent word to him not to be overbold, else it would cost him his life. The impatient gentleman [182] continued to trouble her, and, blinded by the purpose he had formed, ignored the answer she had sent. Finding he could not win her by smooth words, he sent her threats. The honoured lady not only had these wrongs inflicted on her, but he also tried to get hold of the farms from which she supported herself.

Being a widow, she was at home about ten at night. The official, not foreseeing the evil fate in store for him, clad himself sumptuously, and boldly entered the woman's house. Men were lying in wait for him, and, wringing his neck, put an end to him. Aided by some relations, these men silently dragged the body by a rope to the foot of the city wall, on the outside, towards the sea. Placing the body in a sitting posture, they propped it against the wall, as if seated for a necessary purpose. They covered him with his cape, removed the rope, and cocked his hat on one side, so that he looked as if come to fish.

When morning came, the *ouvidor's* friends turned up at his house as usual to pay their court, but did not find him, nor could they get any news of him. Making inquiries, they discovered some fishermen who said the *ouvidor* (they recognising his cloak) was on the seashore attending to his necessities before going to fish. The crowd ran to the spot, and saw him as the fishermen had said. Not aware that he was dead, they made their bow to him. Finding he made no response, they asked him the reason of his coming alone without attendants. Remarking that still there was no reply, they removed the cloak, and found him dead with his tongue hanging out.

Upon the unlocking of the city gates the woman moved out to her country house, and thus in a short time got rid of the crime. They told me that three magistrates had died from similar causes in the same town. At the auction of the deceased's effects I bought some cupboards, among them an escritoire. In it was a paper with a heart painted on it pierced by an arrow, which survived him as a mark that he had died for love. But it would have been more correct to paint his portrait with his neck broken, because from scoundrels in office noble deeds cannot be looked for.

Another case was that of a man married to a virtuous woman. The wife took no notice of the misdeeds of the husband with a slave girl, while the latter was eager to make away with her mistress and take her place. She made false accusations, and told her master that his wife had taken to evil ways, receiving a paramour in the house at fixed hours every night. She described the place at which he entered. In saying this, she failed to reflect on what might happen to herself. She imagined that, on seeing this verified, he would return and kill the lady. But it did not turn out as she desired. To carry the thing out [183] she disguised herself as a man, and went at the appointed hour to the place she had mentioned. The master came to find out if it was true, and ascertained that the negress spoke truly. In his anger he let off his matchlock, so that she fell from the wall to the ground, and as she fell she gave a cry. This saved the husband from killing his wife, for he recognised at once both the voice and the maliciousness of the negro woman.

There was a married man whose wife boasted that she could keep a secret. To test her whether it was so or not, one night he came home carrying beneath his cloak a wrapped-up napkin covered with blood, and told his wife that in it was the head of an enemy whom he had decapitated. It was desirable to bury it without anyone knowing. He prayed her to keep his secret, for if it came to be discovered it would cost him his life. They went together to the garden and secretly buried it. Some time elapsed when the wife, anxious to domineer over her husband, gave him some sharp answers, and did not show him the usual respect. Feigning apprehension, he caressed his wife and did as she wanted. The ungrateful creature admitted she was satisfied, but with her little sense went on aggravating her husband. Getting into a rage, he ignored his wife, and, imposing his authority, thrust her into a room and bolting the door, left the house. The servant-girl intimated to her mistress that master was gone out, and the door was bolted. The lady from inside gave an order to open, and as soon as she was out unlocked her boxes, drew out the best of her belongings, and carried herself and them off to the house of her mother. Next she went straight to the magistrate, and informed him how her husband had killed a man, had brought the dead man's head home and interred it. She described the spot, and protested she was innocent of the homicide. She was compelled to report it, for if the authorities learnt it through her she would escape punishment. The judge, supposing it to be true, went to the man's house along with the wife. She pointed out the spot, and he ordered it to be dug up. They found a sheep's head! Thus was brought to light the woman's disloyalty, and the husband had made a fool of her. I give the advice that no one disclose matters of importance to women, and thus be able to live without anxiety.

[Pages 184 and 185 are blank.]

[186] A fearful thing once happened. A well-born damsel married a youth of her own rank. At night, after they had withdrawn to their room, the people of the house heard great cries from the young lady calling for help. The people pretended not to hear, it being the general custom in India that young women on such occasions, be it veritable or pretence, should show that they are hurt. In the morning, when the bridegroom did not appear, they opened the door, and they beheld him pacing restlessly up and down the place, his eyes staring unnaturally; he was foaming at the mouth and mad. He fell upon the people, and they were obliged to secure him. They sought the bride, and found her in the room cut to pieces, her breasts gnawed, her eyes plucked out her face and her whole body bitten. Within twenty-four hours the bridegroom died in agony, barking like an angry dog. The cause of this disaster was that nearly three months before the marriage a mad dog had bitten him on the leg. He did not have this attended to properly, and the night he was with his wife the poison overcame him, and he acted as described. From what I have experienced in India many times, to heal a man who has been bitten by a mad dog it is necessary to apply at once the actual cautery to the bite, and without any other treatment he recovers. Equally I have seen and tested that anyone bitten by such an animal, if he goes on a sea voyage is not affected by the poison.[1]

1. Manucci also advocates elsewhere the use of the actual cautery for obstruction (III. 49) and cholera (II. 128). Professor Zachariae, of Halle, has kindly pointed out to me a reference to Manucci's advocacy of this treatment to be found in 'Lettres Edifiantes et Curieuses,' nouvelle ed. (Paris, 1781), xi. 159 note (letter from Père Martin). N. M. is spoken of as 'un médecin habile venu d'Europe, qui s'est fait une grande reputation k la cour du Grand Mogol, òu il a demeuré quarante ans.' Its use in those days is also referred to in Fryer, edition 1873, p. 315, and in 'Traité des Maladies,' at the end of Luillier's 'Nouveau Voyage,' p. 220, 16mo., Rotterdam, 1726.

Since I have spoken of the town of Sao Thome, I will relate some things that happened there. I was told these stories by various old inhabitants, natives of the place. Formerly it was richer than all the other towns held by the Portuguese in India, owing to its great trade with China, Java, Malacca, *et cetera*. The merchants gained more than a thousand per cent.; but this was before the Dutch came out to India. They received goods and paid for them by the *para*, which is a measure used us *Europe*[1] to measure corn and vegetable. Nowadays they measure in those measures rice, lime,[2] and other products. The coins for which these goods were exchanged are called *pagodas*, which are still current. These coins, which are of gold and weigh a drachm, are small and circular, stamped only on one side with the symbol of some idol.[3] The ancients must have thought little of gold from the way they used it in painting and adorning various unnecessary places, such as beams, doorways, windows in their houses; and for various purposes, such as on chests, escritoires, chests of drawers, benches, chairs, *et cetera*, adding nails and fastenings of gold and silver, or putting gold feet and other ornaments to their bedsteads of aloes-wood[4] or of sandal-wood, also to the chairs and benches of the same woods.

There was a lady called Justa Padrao who slept in a bed of which the head [187] was adorned with little bells of gold and silver, and these served at times to amuse her. She was so rich that she had her own room swept with brooms of gold, and other places with brooms of silver. Brooms in India have handles of fine twigs (*ydes*),[5] and are not like those of Europe. When this lady left the house, either to go church or pay a visit, two women servants preceded her with two golden censers to incense her. She had other special censers of silver to lend to the church on solemn occasions. From the little that I have said the reader

1. *Sic* in text; I propose to read 'India,' and take *para* as meaning the *pari* or *padi* measure. Approximately, it is of 100 cubic inches, and holds 3 pounds 1-26/76 ounces of rice ('Madras Manual of Administration,' iii. 721, *puddy*).
2. The word is *cal* (lime), but it may be meant for *çal, sal* (salt).
3. The 'Madras Manual of Administration,' iii. 643, confirms this account substantially.
4. *Pao de aguila*, or eagle-wood (Yule, 16). It has a fragrant scent.
5. I cannot trace the word *yde* (elsewhere, in Part I., 36, 'hide'), but have guessed at the sense.

can conceive in what grandeur the greater part of these people lived. The woman spoken of above when she came to die was so miserably off that she had not even a piece of cloth to make a shroud, and at her burial she was wrapped in a reed-mat. This is the fate of him who so far forgets his Creator.

It is patent to everybody that when the Portuguese were masters of this town (S. Thome) there were in it many oppressions and much injustice. They slew one another; they dug and fortified trenches in the streets, furnishing them with cannon. Both sides had their rendezvous, and spent much money in maintaining soldiers. If anyone passed carelessly down the street, they shot at him with their matchlocks. They obtained reward for their evil deeds, paying no respect even to the Holy of Holies, shooting down men during religious processions. Owing to the risings in the town the convents and churches were barricaded. The friars were forced to go in person to fetch water, and, out of charity, carried into their house men of the weaker party, and from the other side at various times wrested matchlocks, of which they broke off the pans.[1]

Besides this, merely to see the laming of an innocent person who was passing in the street, he[2] ordered his servant to fire his gun. This order he gave when praying, rosary in hand. The servant fired, and reported to his master that the passer-by was lamed. He took his station at the window, repeating "Our Father in heaven." He saw the injured man was wounded, and was making off on all fours in hopes of saving his life. He stopped saying the Lord's Prayer, and gave a second order to fire another bullet to finish killing the man.

Among them was a man called Antonio de Viveros, who lived by the sale of poisons, raising false accusations against married women in the hope that the husbands might buy poison from him, and he draw profit from the money. If the husband had no money with which to pay, he would give the poison on credit. It was noted that twenty-nine married women had died of poison sold by this man to their husbands, among whom were friars and secular priests.[3] A few days before the Mahomedans

1. As Mr. Dames points out, the powder-pan of the matchlock projects on one side, and could easily be broken off. The word used is *panella* (a little pot).
2. What is the antecedent of 'he' is not clear.
3. The sentence is doubtful.

took the town, which was in the year one thousand six hundred and sixty-four (1664),[1] the above fellow died, and as he had many relations, these all assembled. There were many neighbours and acquaintances, who came to see if it were true. They were afraid he might be shamming to be dead, and they all rejoiced that he was really dead.

Such a crowd filled his public room that, through their weight, the house being an old one, the whole of it collapsed [188], with the corpse and most of those present around it. Some of the men were killed, some had their legs or arms broken or injured. Others died smothered, for the *godown* (warehouse) beneath the sitting-room was full of lime; and this *chunambo* (*chunam*, lime) did great damage, blinding some and stifling others. Great uproar and lamentation ensued; and the greater part of the town said with tears: 'It was not enough for Antonio de Viveros to kill so many as he did in life, but he must needs destroy as many more at his death.' Instead of commending his soul to God, they wished it at the devil.

I will also recount what happened to me, and what I have seen and undergone. I have already told you in my book (Part II., p. 235) how, upon my arrival in these regions, the chief personages of San Thome did me the honour to receive me with civility, and offered to put themselves at my service. Among them were Manoel Texeyra Pinto, chief captain (*capitao mor*), Joao da Costa de Sua, Cosmo Lourenço Madeyra, Antonio Palha de Lima, and Manoel da Silva de Menezes. I had treated them and their families gratis.

A year afterwards there came to me from Goa a sum of three thousand and seven hundred *patacas* (= Rs. 7,400), which I had deposited with Father Salvador Gallo,[2] prefect of the Theatines. The said father handed the money to my attorney Joao Lopes de Figueredo, a Portuguese born in India, to be delivered to me. When this man arrived at the port of San Thome the above named were at that time governing, and were also the magistrates. Thus,

1. It is generally asserted that St. Thome was taken by the King of Gulkandah in 1662; according to the 'Fort St. George Records,' vol. xiv., it fell on May 1 or 2, 1662.
2. Salvator Gallo, a native of Milan, appointed Prefect in 1672 He left Europe in August, 1673. with four other Theatines. He died somewhere about 1693, and is described as 'the soul of the Theatine mission in India' (Müllbauer, 'Geschichte,' 355, 357).

when the said Joao landed, they seized him and confiscated everything he brought with him, taking possession also of his ship, under the false declaration that he was the debtor of certain Jews called Bertolameo Rodrigues, Domingos do Porto, and Alvaro da Fonçequa. These magistrates called upon him to pay a debt due from a man of his (Figueredo's) faction, called Francisco de Lima, owed to the above Jews. These latter were much delighted at the benefit thus done them.

Finding this great wrong being done, and that I should also lose my money, I had recourse to these same magistrates. I laid before them the receipt of Joao Lopes [de Figueredo], the letters of Father Salvador Gallo, and attestations by Dom Rodrigo da Costa,[1] Governor of India, who had also written a separate letter to the leading men of San Thome recommending me to their favour, because their Indian dominions were under great obligations to me. He certified that Joao Lopes conveyed this money to be delivered to me. Thus he had done his very best to carry through my business [189].

None of these efforts did me any good. Once more I presented fresh testimony received from Goa, from Agustinho Ribeyro and Pascoal Gomes, also the Letters Patent with which the King of Portugal had honoured me. These men had been present when the said Father (Gallo) delivered the said money to Joao Lopes de Figueredo. He was under obligation to pay me in current coin, and to take seals [sealed receipts]. Joao Lopes also demanded leave to pay me. He only owed money to me and nothing to anyone else; as was the truth, for no statement was produced to show how he was a debtor. In the end the said Joao Lopes was ruined and destroyed. As for my claim, which they could not deny, after much worthless argumentation, they resolved to pay me two thousand *patacas* [Rs. 4,000]. This they declared was a favour they were doing me. The balance they would not pay. One man so decided because I would not marry one of his relations; others said if I settled among them in San Thome I should not lose my money; another said that there was no ground to complain, that the two thousand *patacas* sufficed, as I had a sufficient income to live upon all my life; the rest uttered similar irrelevant opinions, and I was sent about my business.

1. Dom Rodrigo da Costa, Governor, 1686-90 (Danvers, ii. 489, No. 63).

With regard to the wrong done to Joao Lopes, let the reader understand that there were two reasons for it. The first was envy at seeing him, a man born in India, with some fortune and the owner of a ship, a thing they did not possess. The second reason was because three of the said magistrates had asked the wife of Joao Lopes in marriage, she being a rich woman, and, as she had refused them all, this produced the hate and envy which impelled them to ruin the man.

When twelve years from this dispute had passed by, in the year one thousand seven hundred (1700), there came as Governor of San Thome, on behalf of King Aurangzeb, a friend of mine called Xefican (Shafi' Khan). He was told of the injustice and robbery done to me by the Portuguese of San Thome, and revived the suit. The men were summoned to his presence. He asked them about the debt due to me, when they answered boldly that they knew of no such thing, nor did they owe me anything, and they offered to swear upon the Holy Evangelists.

As the governor did not know the European languages, he applied to Mr. Thomas Pitt, Governor of Madrasta (Madras), sending him my papers and affidavits for inspection, and asked him to decide according to right. The said governor sent the papers to be translated into English. There was a delay of two months in getting this done. At the end of this time he sent for the Portuguese, and asked them in a friendly way to give me some satisfaction, because it seemed to him that Nicolas Manuchy (*sic*) was a most reasonable man, and they ought to come to an agreement with me. In a most haughty and contumacious manner they replied they owed me naught, nor would they pay me anything.

A few days afterwards he (Mr. Pitt) assembled the whole council; the magistrates, and the learned men of different nations. They all sat together and deliberated [190]. The Portuguese were called in, and in their presence in a loud voice he (the governor) read my documents, when those present decided unanimously that I had been wronged. It was decreed that the debtors must pay me. They were thus unmasked before all the Europeans and Mahomedans; yet not for this would they reform and turn from their evil ways.

I will add another case which happened to me in the same San Thome with the aforesaid Manoel da Silva de Menezes in the year ninety (1690), in the month of March. I had advanced five hundred *patacas* to a Genoese merchant called Jorge Bianco for trading in Pegu. He sent the principal with the agreed profit to be paid to me in San Thome. The said Manoel da Silva de Mendezes was then judge. He took possession of my money, and wanted to pay with his usual arguments; and in spite of all my efforts I could not obtain payment of what was mine. In the end I made use of certain friars who interceded for me with Thomas de Maya, the chief captain then holding office, and he did what he could out of friendship for me. He ordered me to be paid; but behold the way Manoel da Silva wanted to satisfy me! He had bought some *koris* (scores or twenties) of cloth for thirty patacas the score. He wanted to pay me in this cloth, entering every score in my account at eighty *patacas*. Since I declined to accept, I only received a little cash, losing part of my principal and all the profit.

It seems to me that readers will approve, also those intending to come to India, of having this information by which they can guide themselves, making use of my experience. They can also refer, in the opening of my book, to the warning that I have given (Part I., p. 1).

At the time those men governed there arrived a Portuguese 'priest from Manila, a good theologian; his name was Luis Pereyra. He brought with him some money for the purpose of helping his parents, who lived in Daman. About the same time there was a newly-arrived Portuguese, Martim de Lemos by name, who had quitted Portugal because of his being a lawbreaker and highway robber (the greater number of the Portuguese who come to India are of the same sort). He had no resources, and begged help from those who governed. The reply they gave was that he might search for his expenses wherever they were to be found.

Finding that he could carry out his plot easily and securely, one Sunday at seven in the morning he (Lemos) went into the house of Father Luis Pereyra, pointed a pistol at his breast, and ordered four Kaffirs to bind him. Breaking open the boxes, he robbed all that was in them and started for Madras [191]. At the time I was in the churchyard of the church Madre de Deos[1]

1. See Constable's "Hand Atlas of India,' Plate XLI, plan of Madras andenvirons. 'Mai de Deos' is a church on the south side of San Thome.

on my way to Mass, and conversing with those who governed and with some foreigners. Then the urgent report was brought that Martin de Lemos was robbing the priest. Some of the foreigners wanted to run to the spot, but Antonio Palha, one of those who governed, said: 'Your Honours are excused from taking that trouble, for I will see to it.' He and the rest went leisurely to their houses, giving time for the robber to carry out his attempt and get away in safety.

He (Palha) sent first to see if the thief had already gone, and a report was brought that he was now a long way off. On obtaining this report, out Palha came fully armed, shouting along the street for everybody to come and help Father Luis Pereyra. They went to him, and found him tied to a pillar. They undid him, and tried to console him by saying they had made all possible haste to succour him, but to come sooner was impossible, they being at Mass. Next day Martin de Lemos went off to Monte Grande (St. Thomas's Mount) with four Kaffirs at his heels, armed with staves, and interviewed the canon, Custantino Sardinha Rangel, and in a most dictatorial tone said to him: 'Your Honour must absolve me forthwith, for I have business I must attend to.' The canon, in fear of the staves, asked not a single question, and gave absolution.

I have seen in India that many vicars pronounce unmerited excommunications: this comes from their being illiterate, ignorant, and without the experience that befits the priestly office. I have no wish to speak of cases which have happened; I simply leave it to their prelates to see to it.

I will tell of a matter which happened in Gulkandah during the reign of the seventh king, Abdulau (Abu-l-Hasan),[1] when his great minister, Madana, was in power. It chanced in his time that a Persian was washing his face on the banks of the river. While he was there a Hindu came, and close to him began to wash a cloth with such rashness and inattention that the water splashed over the Mahomedan. Anxious to keep himself clean—

1. Abu-I-Hasan, the seventh king, reigned from 1672 to 1687 (S. Lane Poole, 'Mohammadan Dynasties,' 321). For Madana, Brahman, see 'Ma,asir-i-'Alamgiri,' 227, 272. The head of Madana, Brahman, who had been decapitated by Abu,l Hasan as proof of his submission, was sent to Shah 'Alam, who forwarded it on by the hand of Bahadur 'Ali Khan to the Emperor Anrangzeb (p. 272), twenty-ninth year, 1097 H. (1685-86).

for the water sent over him by the Hindu was dirtying him—he asked the man civilly to find another place. The rude Hindu, instead of paying heed, replied with abuse, and made as if to strike him. The Persian lost patience and gave him a slap, whereby arose a great tumult. Many Hindus arrived, seized him, gave him many blows, bound him, and carried him to the presence of the minister Madana.

The minister's sentence was that the hand of the Persian with which the blow had been given should be cut off. The order was forthwith executed. Finding that neither the government nor the courts were in the hands of the Mahomedans, but in those of the Hindus, the Persian said nothing, but, frying the severed hand in oil, he took it, and, quitting the kingdom of Gulkandah, resorted to the court of Aurangzeb. There he showed the hand and the mutilated arm, and in a loud voice ejaculated [192] that God had made him (Aurangzeb) king to redress injustice, such as this done to a Sayyid, a descendant of the Prophet. Repeatedly he made the same complaint, and in the end Aurangzeb ordered some money to be disbursed to him for his support. He was told to be patient, and in due time punishment would be inflicted for the little respect paid by the tyrant to the chosen of God. When Aurangzeb tried conclusions with the King of Gulkandah, the crimes he alleged were these: high handedness, oppression, permitting public drinking-shops, women of evil life, and gambling-houses, choosing Hindu governors, maintaining temples, and not allowing to Mahomedans that free liberty which they are entitled to. Therefore God had made him (Aurangzeb) king for the suppression of all these disorders allowed by Abu-l-Hasan.

This king of Gulkandah, Abu-l-Hasan, was descended from, and was of the blood royal of the kings of that line; but he was poor and despised, passing his life in taverns and shops, looking on at dancing and listening to music. At the death of the king Cotobxaa[1] (Qutb Shah) they made him king, seeing that the

1. The sixth king of the Qutb Shahi line was 'Abdullah, Qutb Shah. He died in 1672 (S. Lane Poole, 'Moharamadan Dynasties,' p. 321). Beale, p. 8, has Rabi', 1085 H. (June, 1674), and says Abu,l Hasan was his predecessor's son-in-law. So also does Jag Jivan Das, a contemporary ('Muntakhab-ut-tawarikh,' British Museum Additional MS., 26,253, fol. *76b*, completed in 1719), who further says the man was a Mughal from Hamadan. This writer bears out Manucci's details about Abu,l Hasan's

deceased monarch had no son, and he (Abu-l-Hasan) was of the royal blood. Thus he received the crown, never having imagined that he would come to reign. Finding himself thus elevated, and being devoid of experience of the world, he asked the Dutch factor if there were horses in Europe. The answer was that there were horses and also valiant warriors, who fought without their aid. The king replied that he had always heard that the Europeans fought nowhere but on the sea. 'If it is as you say, said he, 'show me some picture representing a battle on horseback.' The Dutch factor imparted the king's desire to the governor of Negapatao (Negapatnam).[1] A large painting was sent by him, in which a battle was depicted, fought by the Dutch against the Spaniards. It showed squadrons of cavalry and infantry contending most fiercely one with another; also various bloody and dying figures and objects. The picture referred to was given to the king, and he was much astonished. Next day, sending for the factor, he told him to carry away his painting to his own house; that it was of no use to him (the king); that all night long he had been unable to sleep merely thinking of it. The painting hangs to this very day in the Dutch Factory in the town of Gulkandah, where I have seen it. Such fears have those who have never been in a battle and have no experience of the world. It was from this cause that he lost his kingdom in the year one thousand six hundred and eighty-six, as I pointed out in the Second Part of my book (II. 242).

When Da,ud Khan was in charge of Patnah, as I have already said (II. 61), there was found one morning in the Ganges river, near the English Factory adjoining the city gate, a rock crystal eight palms in length and thirty palms in circumference. As it was a rarity, it was sent to the king in a boat. I saw it myself, and measured it in the year one thousand six hundred and sixty-three (1663).

From what I have been able to gather about the ancient Portuguese, they were, as shown by their conquests and the strong fortified places they took, religious men, just, disinterested,

---

profligacy and bad government. Fryer, edition 1873, p. 176, says he was a man of low fortune.

1. Nagpatanam, on the coast in the Tanjor district, long. 79° 53′, lat. 10° 46′, 160 miles south-south-west of Madras, taken by the Dutch from the Portuguese in 1660 ('Madras Manual of Administration,' iii 580).

valorous, void of fear, men of their word, and modest withal. For this reason God was their helper. At the present day, from what I have seen and experienced, I find that, instead of faithful men, they are unbelievers and pretenders. The cause I know not—whether it be because they are a mixture of Jews, Mahomedans, and Hindus, either having an admixture of their blood, or having drunk it in with their nurse's milk—but in place of just, they have become unjust; [193] robbers and oppressors instead of disinterested men. They are avaricious, forgers, envious; from brave men they have turned into cowards, who by ambushes and treacheries slay simple folk. Instead of men of their word, they are liars and deceivers; in place of being modest, they are shameless, miserable wretches, filled with a pride which they maintain as if they were upholding the First Commandment.

For these reasons they are in these days ruined, reduced, and poverty-stricken, despoiled of their famous conquests, their treasures, delights, and pleasures having been appropriated by the Dutch or annexed by the Arabs, and they themselves are oppressed by the Moguls. The few who survive are respected only from the fame of the ancient Portuguese, but such men are not even the shadows of their predecessors. I speak not of the Lusitanians who dwell in Europe. Yet even those Portuguese, on arriving in India, change in character and in name; each man claims to be of gentle birth, and a man of quality. Arrived in Goa, and on the point of dying of hunger, they retire into a convent, and hardly have two years elapsed before they are sent forth somewhere or other as vicars and become missionaries, and while quite young wield the great powers conferred on them by their prelates, which they make use of to the discredit of Christianity.

The reader will have seen in my Second Part (II. 205-224) the efforts I had made and the services. I had rendered in Goa when the Portuguese found themselves in such great peril. Thome de Azevedo, the chief physician, a priest of Jewish birth, ordered the bailiffs to seize me and thrust me into prison. The bailiff had compassion on me and sent me secret word of these orders, and advised me to get out of the way. At that moment I was entering the house of the Secretary of State, called Luis Gonsalves Cota, to translate the reply to a letter from Sambha Ji, which the viceroy was about to send. After the letter was translated,

I mentioned to the Secretary the orders that had been given by the physician. The Secretary answered very frigidly that the physician could acs thus, as he had the leave of His Excellency. If he had me arrested he had cause, for I had no permission to treat the poor. He reprehended me, and said I was acting ill; he had also heard it stated that I had some little pills with which I made an easy cure of wounds and buboes. I answered that I treated none but mendicants and the indigent, and that without fee. It was my habit wherever I travelled to help the necessitous, and for such good deeds I was esteemed throughout the Maho medan country, where I was held in much respect. Thus I would seek some other place so as not to give annoyance, and preserve my liberty. The secretary was very stiff, and gave me not a word of reply, instead of paying some attention to or remedying my grievance.

I concealed my feelings, though disappointed in him, and lost no time in placing myself [in sanctuary] within the church of the Theatines.[1] Thence I sent information to Dom Rodrigo da Costa, who at the time was in command of the fleet, and on hearing from me he went to see the viceroy, Count Francisco de Tavora. The latter was annoyed with the chief physician [196] for wishing, in that dangerous time, to interfere with me. The physician was sent for, and also the chief surgeon, Francisco da Silva, and they were told by the viceroy in an angry voice that if they touched me, he would have satisfaction from them. I was let alone and in freedom.

[194, an interpolated leaf.] *A propos* of what I have said, I will relate two cases which happened in my presence in connection with this chief physician. There was an Augustinian friar who fell ill of pains in the testicles combined with swelling. The pain he suffered was insupportable, and he had arrived almost at the point of death. The chief physician and the other proficients were unable to cure him. There was an old woman who lived close to the convent, who, hearing of the illness, came and offered to cure it. She applied some stewed leaves to the painful place, and took away the pain together with the swelling, and the good friar was completely restored to health. When the chief physician was told of this, he sent orders to imprison

1. The Theatine missionaries at Goa were from Milan, and, as fellow-Italians, probably friendly to Manucci.

the charitable old woman, and to obtain her release she was forced to sell everything she had in her house, and thus buy off the chief physician's demands. From that time the poor old woman wandered through the streets in search of alms.

There was a Hindu practitioner who knew a perfect cure for scrofula. The chief physician wanted to learn his secret, and sent the poor fellow to prison. He was informed that he would not recover his liberty until he had taught his secret to the physician. The timid Hindu resolved rather to die in prison than to divulge his secret. Such-like effects spring from the grant of power to ungrateful villains.

[Page 195 is blank.]

[196, resumed.] I believe the reader will not be astonished at my writing with so much liberty, for I profess to declare the truth, which, as it seems to me, is the only thing likely to be of use as a warning to any curious person undertaking any long voyage, or in especial one coming to these parts of India. Many is the time I have wished to do good to and help necessitous persons; but afterwards, instead of being thanked, I issued from the matter under sentence of crime as a misdoer and a rogue. Thus was it with what happened to me in the year one thousand six hundred and eighty-two (1682).

Taking with me the ambassador from Goa, Joao Antonio Portugal, I set out for the army of Shah 'Alam, then lying near Goa territory.[1] In our company were twenty men of rank, one Jesuit called Antonio de Barro, a Theatine called Dom Joseph Tedesqui,[2] and a priest known by the name of Gonsallo Lopes. The whole party was put up by me in a large tent which the prince had assigned as my quarters, and there I entertained them as befitted them.

The next day I brought them to the court of Shah 'Alam, and there with the greatest difficulty I obtained leave for the entry three persons only; but out of respect for me they were relieved of the heavy expenditure which has to be incurred by custom at all such courts. The prince Shah 'Alam desired me to remain with him, and in order to compel or induce me sent

1. This visit to Shah 'Alam has been already treated (see *ante*, Part II., p. 218). The year was more probably 1683 than 1682.
2. Joseph Tiveschi, a native of Ferrara, one of the priests who left Europe in 1673 with Father Gallo (Müllbauer, 'Geschichte,' 355).

his confidant, Mirza Muhammad Riza, officer of his table and a great friend of mine, to make over to me two thousand rupees, which I was to accept, giving as a reason that I had spent considerable sums on His Highness's service. He had express orders that he must make me accept the money. I brought forward some objections to receiving it, but he embraced me, and, encouraging me, earnestly besought me to accept. The supplicant, finding I did not want to accept, left the money, beat a hasty retreat, and I gave orders to lock up the cash.

The ambassador and some others were present. They began to talk softly to each other, and then angrily asked me in a loud tone who the rupees were meant for. I replied that the prince had sent them to me for my expenses. In their anger they answered me with misplaced words and such-like talk, so that I held it better not to answer ignorant men who did not speak to me in a proper manner. It was reported among them that the prince had sent the two thousand rupees to the ambassador, and that I had usurped them [197].

This matter was not such a secret that it did not come to the prince's ears, and he was annoyed, saying he could not have supposed that such people could be so ignorant, and the higher he had thought of them the more aggrieved he felt. To restore my honour, he ordered one of the principal officials of his court, Mir Muhammad Sadiq, to send for the ambassador to his tent with all his retinue, and apply a remedy for the above false statement. With me standing near him and the others round him, he asked me if I had received the above-mentioned money. I replied in the affirmative. Then in a loud voice, with his hand raised, he said it had been heard that there was someone rash enough to assert that Manuchy had stolen the said money. If he could only find out who were these slanderers, he would unfailingly cram their mouths; full (be it said with all respect) ....of dirt. Most of them hung their heads, and said not a word; they had imagined they were sent for to receive some present.

When I had finished the negotiations in favour of the viceroy, Shah Alam ordered that in his presence the three persons should receive each a *sarapa* (set of robes). At that moment appeared two men with two thousand rupees in two bags, and from behind the ambassadors shouted in loud voices these words: 'Here are the two thousand rupees that Your Majesty confers on the Portuguese ambassadors.' They recited these words three times. Joao Antunes Portugal was alarmed at such shouting, as he did not know the language, and asked me the reason. I told him it was about the two thousand rupees that the prince had ordered to be given, and that it was in this manner the gift was made, instead of sending the money to his tent. He cast down his eyes, recognising the reason why the prince acted thus. It was solely that no doubt might be thrown on my good faith. Joao Antunes Portugal was incensed at this affair, and in place of being sorry sought means to take my life. If he did not succeed, it was because I did not remain in Goa, but returned to the Mogul prince's service.

I will insert a small affair that happened to me on the same occasion. In Goa there was a well-born man called Lourenço da Cunha, who pretended to be my friend. On my taking leave of the viceroy, at the time when I was about to start for the Mogul army to undertake negotiations for the State, this man carried me to his house, where I stopped all night. He asked me to convey in my [198] boat a box containing various Chinese curiosities, which might be worth fifty rupees, hoping to sell them in the army. I excused myself for two reasons. The first was that the goods were not suitable for Mahomedans, being images of tigers, cats, cocks, *et cetera*. The second was because the things could not be carried safely, owing to the difficult marches we were to make. On hearing these objections he said nothing, but at midnight while I was asleep he made over the said box to the boatman with an order to inform me after I had reached the army. When I arrived at the army the boatman told me about this box, but at the time I passed the matter over in silence. The next day my friend Lourenço da Cunha turned up and demanded from me four hundred and fifty rupees for the goods he had put into my boat. My arguments were of no avail, he talking preposterously. Finding all this trouble, and being careless about money, I ordered the payment of the amount he claimed, and before his face caused all the contents of the box to be distributed to common people. He declared he was doing me a favour in letting me have the things so cheap. These fellows glory in cheating foreigners without scruple.

This incident brings to mind that in seventy-six (1676). I left the Mogul territory and stopped a few days at Damao (Daman).[1] At that time a Portuguese fleet arrived as convoy to the ships going to Surat and Kambaya. The principal men in this fleet begged me to open my boxes, as they wanted to see some of my curiosities. I could not refuse, and holding them to be gentlemen of position, I allowed them an inspection; but it was not long before some of the articles had disappeared. I suppressed any remark, for if I had taken any action they would have assassinated me without fail, as is customary among them.

In the year ninety-two (1692) there came a Hindu officer from the army in the Karnatik, a commander over five thousand horse, recommended to me by the Nababo (Nawab) Julfacarcan (Zu,lfiqar Khan), Mirza Mahdi, the captain of Cavalry, and other friends. He wanted to be treated, and promised me four thousand rupees. The Portuguese of San Thome now interfered, including the head of the bishopric, a priest, then in charge also of the civil government, who was under obligation to me for having cured him of an obstruction. All these men, hearing of the above Hindu, took to him a physician, who offered to effect a speedy cure at a less price. They arranged matters so that the said officer believed them, and sent me a message that I need not trouble, and if he wanted me would let me know.

After the lapse of a few days he sent a message to me, because he had not recovered his health as he desired, but I declined to attend him. I replied to those who had written to me that the said captain had declined to listen to my advice; and he went back as he had come, lamenting his evil fate, for thus do the people of India talk when things do not succeed with them as they would wish. This captain was a rajah [199]; his name was Dalpat Rao, son of Champat Bundelah,[2] he whom Aurangzeb sacrificed after crossing the river of Dholpur [*i.e.*, the Chambal] to give battle to Dara, as described in my First Part (I. 185).

1. This visit to Damao has been referred to (*ante*, Part II., p. 178).
2. Dalpat Rao, Rajah of Datiya (killed at Jajau, 1707), was the son of R. Subhkaran (died 1683), who had succeeded his brother, R. Pirthi Singh (died 1658). Dalpat Rao was not the son of Champat Rae. He was a protégé of Zu,lfiqar Khan. Champat Rae was not executed in 1658, as suggested here, but was killed in October, 1661, and his head sent to Dihli

XXVIII. Shahab-ud-din Khan, afterwards Ghazi-ud-din Khan Firuz Jang

In San Thome there was a Portuguese called Joao Carvalho, who had been endowed by Nature with such length of arm that his hands reached below his knees.[1] Owing to this gift of Nature, Hindus when they met him prostrated themselves, worshipping him as they do their idols. For it is written in the Hindu prophecies that a person with long arms should be venerated like an idol. This man was called before the Inquisition, but after giving sound reasons, he was liberated. The condition of release was, however, that when any Hindu prostrated himself on the ground, he should at once prostrate himself likewise. Thus poor Joao Carvalho did not often leave his house during the day, for fear of undergoing this penance.

There was another similar case when a long-armed Portuguese went to stay at Jagarnath, adjoining Bengal, where there is a very large and ancient temple, greatly renowned in India and very wealthy. On this man's arrival, the Hindu priests and the people of the town heard of him. They all came to meet him and conducted him straight to the temple with great respect and veneration. They made over to him the idols and all the wealth of the temple.

Having become master, and receiving their obedience, he led a joyous life, regaling himself with delicate dishes and requisitioning young girls whenever he pleased, they imagining he did them a great honour, whereby they were much satisfied. The great man lived for some years in this way, when, disgusted at leading such an unbridled and luxurious life, he resolved to employ the wealth of the temple in another way. To this intent he wrote to Goa to one of his brothers, with instructions how to act. The brother, turned into a merchant, appeared at the temple, where the would-be holy man recognised him, displaying great astonishment and telling him he was a great sinner, rash in his-undertakings, and if he did not amend he would be heavily punished.

The sagacious brother fell at his feet, saying he hoped to receive the means of salvation by the passing of an order to admit

1. I am indebted to Mr. W. Crooke for the following note: 'To have long arms was always regarded as an attribute of divine personages. Ward ("Hindoos," i. 122) specially quotes from the "Siva Purana" the account of the ideal beauty, Sarada, daughter of Brahma, in which she is described as having arms reaching to her knees. The same feature occurs in Buddhist statues, and has thence come down to modern Hindu idols.'

him for several days into the temple to be catechized and put in the right way. Both brothers feasted at night within the temple, and took counsel together how they could carry off the wealth. The consultations were so secret that they were able to remove all the wealth from the pagoda without being found out. At their secret departure they gouged out the eyes of the idols, they being valuable diamonds; then they disappeared after fastening the temple doors. The Brahmans and other devout persons who came to perform their ceremonials imagined that the false saint was at his orisons. When three days had passed they entered and found out the trick, and were undeceived. From that time they allow no Christian to enter. Aurangzeb made great efforts [200] to destroy this temple; but he did not find it possible, owing to difficulties from the great jungles and the mighty rajahs, who were prepared resolutely to defend it. Seeing them so resolved and the consequent danger, he abandoned his idea. Until this day the said temple rears its head, and to all the ships that sail from Goa along the coast, or from other places, for Bengal, this temple serves as a landmark. Frequently these temples are adorned with obscene figures.

Usually at these temples the Brahmans rear a number of monkeys, which live on the offerings brought by the devout, and they are well fed through the care that the Brahmans take of them. They are at liberty, and wander through the village and the bazaars asking for alms. The Hindus never refuse to give them what is necessary as a matter of charity. At nightfall they retire to the temple, where they take up quarters in the storehouses, the window-sills, and the rooms, some attending to their family affairs, others picking lice from each other. Each one has a female, and no one else may approach her. If perchance any other of them has the temerity to touch another's female, the whole body join and bite him to death. When the Brahman gives them their food, the largest and oldest approach first, and when their belly is full they withdraw and allow room for the others to eat. Should any of the small ones come up while the big ones are feeding, they are fallen upon, and given a lesson in politeness.

All the devout who visit the temples carry with them in their hands some food or fruit, and as they pass near the monkeys throw it down before them. Once as I was inspecting the decorations of the Mathura temple there came a woman wrapped in a sheet on her way to pray. Passing the monkeys without throwing them anything, they took it as an insult, and attacked her, tearing her sheet and leaving her absolutely naked. There she stood, afraid to move a single step, the monkeys surrounding and menacing her, until the Brahmans came to her aid. They gave her a good scolding for coming to the temple with empty hands. When Aurangzeb sent orders to destroy this temple, as I have stated (II. 116), the monkeys there withdrew into the Rana's country, the number exceeding three thousand.

In some of these temples they also rear cobras, for whom they have a special house with various hiding-places and holes, *et cetera*. The Brahmans see that they are fed, calling them by striking a rod on the ground. The food is rice cooked in milk and sweetened. Usual foods are also eggs, butter, curds, *et cetera*. I have also seen in some of these temples, engraved on stone, the sun and a cobra, and the cobra in the act of swallowing the sun. The Hindus do this to show that, as they say, an eclipse of the sun proceeds from a great serpent attempting to swallow it. Thus, to rescue it, it is the custom in India during an eclipse to make a great noise with gongs, drums, and other instruments, added to shouts and cries [201]. They also distribute alms. All this they do, so they say, for two reasons. The first, as to the noise, is to disturb the cobra so that he shall be unable to swallow the sun; the second reason for the alms they give, is that their charity may make the snake compassionate. All the Hindus and many Mahomedans have faith in these superstitions.

In the Karnatik, inland six leagues from Madras, is a famous and ancient temple called Tripiti (Tirupati).[1] Here assemble many people from all parts of India. The shrine is very wealthy from the large and frequent offerings presented, and owing to

1. From *Tiru* (Tamil for *shri*) 'holy,' + *pathi* (Tamil), 'village,' a town seventy miles west-north-west from Madras. It is extremely old, with ruined temples, some fifteen in number, many insignificant. In September the town is full, and in April or May there is a ten-day festival. 'A waterfall descends from a hill north of the town, and enters corridors of stone supported upon carved pillars. It is the duty of every pilgrim to bathe in this waterfall before ascending the hill, and if he can swim, to go and sit upon a figure of Hanuman over which the water falls' ('Madras Manual of Administration,' iii. 899).

the large revenue derived from it, Aurangzeb has to this time postponed its destruction. But it seems to me the reason for not doing so was his fear of renewed rebellions difficult of suppression.

This temple is on a rather high hill, the ascent of which occupies two hours.[1] There are various shelters in which there are many hermits, and hollows occupied by Brahman priests, who live just like that Portuguese man lived at Jagarnath (*ante*, III. 199). Impelled by their barbarous religion, all the devout go there, and every year there is a festival for fifteen days. A large number of people assemble, and take up their' quarters in a village at the foot of the hill. Others shelter themselves in tents or camp under trees. At those season if any man approaches a woman at night she does not refuse I the idea being that it is the idol come down in the form of limit in search of them. The Brahmans have old devout woman who serve them in these matters. If a Brahman sees any woman that pleases him, he seeks a way of mastering her. To this end the old woman, under the cloak of sanctity, goes and questions the woman that the Brahmin desires, asks her age, her race, whose daughter she is, and other similar questions.

The Brahman having been thus well posted up, comes in a great hurry, one day before their departure, crying out the name of her who is to be his victim. Reaching her, he says in a loud and pompous voice that the idol the night before had become enamoured of her beauty. Then, in order to confirm the truth of this, he recites the particulars given him by the old woman. Finding these statements true, the neighbours and parents believe the rest of his story; and thus he takes away the woman, who is detained under the name of a servant of the temple, and she is seduced by the Brahmans. In this manner every year they acquire five or six of the most beautiful women.

On this pilgrimage people must shave their heads and faces in order to be cleansed of their sins. These innocent folk give credit to all that the deceiving priests assert, and, in addition offer them presents. Many also do penance [202] by climbing

---

1. In the Venice Codex XLIV. (Zanetti), fol. 444, the idol is styled Vengatta Ispra Permal (Venkata Ishwar Perumal). The 'Madras Manual of Administration,' iii. 973, has *Venkata-achala-parumal* (Tiru pati) + hill + great god (Vishnu).

the hill on all fours, or on their knees, others at full length, rolling their body over and over. Others carry up water to wash the temple, *et cetera*.

Generally at all the temples, in the middle of the room where the idol stands, or near it, is a large circular stone like those for grinding wheat, and in its centre is stuck a small stone representing the male organ. It serves as an excuse to the Brahmans to conceal their knaveries. The facts of which I speak are very well known throughout India, and many mothers, by reason of some danger or necessity, or difficult delivery, offer to the temple the virginity of their female infant. When the girl is twelve years old they make her over to a Brahman, who carries her away to the room spoken of. . . . Opening the door, he announces that the idol is satisfied with the offering. Some mothers do the same on the advice of the Brahmans. Many of those dedicated to the idols bear its mark on their arms and head, pricked in by a thorn and filled in with ink, becoming thus set apart; and these must live their whole life long in the service of the temples. The Brahmans profit by the money they earn.[1]

In addition to the above, there are public women, dancers, who are required to appear several times a week to sing and dance before the idol. For this purpose they have some allowances, from which they are under obligation not to be absent. I have seen Hindus who, on festival days, through religious fervour, climbed up a mast where there was a wheel bearing two iron hooks, and fixing these into their loins at the back, hung down, and praising the idol, swung round three times, making various gestures with their hands and feet. Such persons are held by Hindus in great esteem.

In India there is a sect which is called Emperumalvedam[2] that is, 'the Multipliers.' When I was on my journey as

1. Owing to their significance in a comparative survey of religions, the above-given description, and several of the same nature, have been reproduced, after the suppression of the grosser details.
2. This strange word has baffled even Dr. Grierson, who has looked through Wilson, Raghunath's 'Bombay Beggars' (*Indian Antiquary*, vols. x., xi.), and Ward's 'View.' The sect referred to is probably *Saiva-Sakta*, and not *Vaishnava*,Trimbak being one of the great *Saiva* centres. The name might be *Nirmala*, a sect which worships at Trimbak. No such word as *amba-*

envoy, having been sent by Rajah Jai Singh as related in my Second Part (II. 99), I arrived at a village called Termec (Trimbak),[1] where I rested for several days while waiting an answer to some proposals in which I was interested. The said village is between Aurangabad and Bassein, in the Grand Mogul's territories, and not far from die source of the river Quixina (Kishna),[2] which is the name of a Hindu god.

At the time I was there it chanced that one of the chief Brahmans of the temple fell in love with a beautiful woman in the village, who was a married woman. To secure her he entered her house and told her that during the previous night his god had given orders that the following night he required her society. If she did not obey, the god would of a certainty ruin her house and family, destroy her wealth and her many gardens. She knew the manner in which she had to submit herself. She obeyed at once, and went to the pagoda.

There she found a large hall made for such purposes, with several doors opening into the temple. Into the hall in question came at night many men and women of this sect, and the temple Brahman. They sat eating and drinking until nine o'clock at night, when everyone was forced to help in clearing away the table. On this being done, they returned to the same place, and the principal door was shut. At the end of the hall were two lighted lamps [203]. The Brahman took the woman to the end of the room, where, in the full light, he removed the fine clothes and ornaments she wore, and with hair unbound and totally naked, she stood facing the rest of the company. This done, he sat down in front of her with a tray full of flowers. The Brahman referred to placed the flowers upon the woman, begining at the top, on her head, eyebows, nostrils, lips, muttering certain words meanwhile. In this way he placed them all over her body till he got to her toe-nails, the last flower applied being thrown between her legs.

---

parimala exists in Sanskrit; but if it be lawful to concoct one, he would suggest it as the explanation—viz.: *Amba* (Durga) + *parimala* (coition)+ *vedam* (religion).

1. Trimbak, in the Nasik district, lat. 19° 58′, long. 73° 32′.
2. The Kistna, or Krishna, River does not rise near Trimbak, N. M. is confounding it with the Godaveri, which rises to the west of Nasik.

At this point the lights were quickly extinguished, for which two Brahmans were kept in readiness, and those present laid hold of the women, without sparing mother or daughter or sister. The Brahman seized the naked woman and took her into the temple to a handsome and highly-decorated chamber, where stood a bed smothered in flowers. He ordered her to take her repose, and her god would visit her. Putting out the candle and fastening the door, he came out. The company in the hall, having ended their obscene revels, left the place and went home. The love-sick Brahman closed the temple gate and went to seek his beloved. He spent the night with her, and as day dawned he quitted her, leaving her inside and fastening the door upon her. When the sun had arisen he opened the door, returned her clothes, and ordered her to go and give thanks to the idol for the favour done to her. Having gone through this ceremony, she returned to her house, where the husband and relations received her as one sanctified, and all held her in great respect.

A similar case also happened in Tirupati, of which village I have already spoken. In that territory there was a youth who had a very beautiful sister, and they were invited to be of this filthy company. The girl, finding herself in such a place, became suspicious and kept close to her brother, of whom she was very fond. On the lights being extinguished, she embraced him, and they kept on their feet with their backs to the wall until the doors were opened. After that they returned home, and consulting together, resolved to abandon the country and change their religion, being much disgusted with such swinish habits. These two persons came to Pudicherry (Pondicherry),[1] which lies on the sea and is governed by the French. Here they turned Christians, and the brother, becoming a soldier of the [French] Company, supported himself; while the sister married a man of her own rank in life. This event occurred in the time when Monsieur Pedro Dileter[2] was governor.

Near the territories of the Rana is an ancient city called

1. In Hindi *pulchari*, but really (Tamil) *puthuççeri;* from *puthu*, 'new,' + *sheri*, 'village.' It lies 105 to 106 miles south of Madras ('Madras Manual of Administration,' iii. 694).
2. Deltor in Codex XLIV. (Zanetti), fol. 446, which is correct,. He was chief of Pondicherry from 1680 to 1686, F. Martin being then in charge of Surat (see Jules Sottas, 'Histoire de la Compagnie Royale des Indes Orientales,' p. 104, Paris, 1905).

Ugem (Ujjain), which was in old days the principal capital of the Hindu kings. In it were many lofty temples, and it was esteemed [204] by the Hindus as their chief holy place, and unto this day the Hindus display to it much respect and devotion. But now it is in ruins, and according to what they assert, it is now very many years since it was overthrown. Nor can there be any doubt that this is so, for I have seen the place several times. Where at present there are rows of houses and small temples, and heaps and hollows of ruins, if you dig up the earth you find copper cooking-cauldrons and other things. I remarked that at this spot there are still some very large bricks, two and a half palms long and two wide, also pillars and various images.

In this city a woman, young, beautiful, seventeen years old, made a religious vow to her idol to do penance by standing for nine years and never lying on the ground. At the time when I saw her two years remained for the accomplishment of her vow. She performed this penance solely in order that when she had finished it she might enjoy the pleasures of this world at her will. This woman's mode of existence involved eating and drinking standing, together with relieving nature in the same position. For this she had persons who attended on her. When she was tired and wanted to rest or sleep, she leant her body upon a stick hung from two ropes. Her legs were swollen. Many Hindu people resorted to her out of piety, offering her ample alms.

I made considerable effort among the learned to discover the year and time when this city was overthrown. These men told me that it was about seventeen hundred years ago. The city is close to a river which has many hollows, and on its banks Aurangzeb and Murad Bakhsh fought a severe battle with Jaswant Singh and Qasim Khan (Part I., 178).

Aurangzeb having resolved on war with the Rana, a Hindu king, as I have related (II. 186), recalled Shah 'Alam, ordering him to march to Ujjain, and halt there until the rainy season had passed and further orders should be issued. We acted accordingly. I noted during our stay at that city that a Brahman dwelt in a house adjacent to a ruined temple. To that house resorted in any women, not from piety, but for evil purposes. But they were foiled, for the Brahman was a chaste man. Seeing they could not gain his affections, they resolved to ruin his father. To do this they came to Shah 'Alam's court, saying they wished to make him a present of treasure, as they knew the place where it was buried.

On hearing this good news Shah 'Alam invested her with robes of honour and mounted her on a fine horse, surrounded with officials, well-armed soldiers, pipes, and instruments of music. When they came close to the house of the merchant, he (Shah 'Alam) ordered them to dig. They found some stones [205] of an ancient temple, but nothing of what the Brahman woman said. But the latter told them to break down the wall of the merchant's house, and there they discovered much money. Then the officials suspended operations, not thinking it advisable to knock down other houses; for they perceived the Brahmani's ill-will, and they took her back to the prince. On receiving their report, he ordered them to tear in pieces the robes that had been conferred. Then, mounting her on an ass with her face to its tail, she was taken round the city, and after a flogging, was released.

The river Kishna is thus called because the Hindus say that their god Kishna, shooting an arrow into the mountain-side opened a way for it. For this reason they gave it his name; and in the Hindu books it is said he was of marvellous strength, hurling mountains about the world. At the distance of one league from the village is a high mountain ridge, on the top of which stand great rocks like pyramids at a little distance from each other. The Hindus believe that there came here a god opposed to the god Kishna, and, scoffing at him in his mother's presence, said he did not possess the strength he boasted of. In a passion his mother exclaimed: 'I will show you his strength, so that you may believe.' Seizing the nipple of her breast, she squirted the milk in the direction of the mountain. It came forth with such force that it rent and tore away that mountain-top. Thus, as a sign, those stones like pyramids still stand there. She said: 'Behold the milk that my son drinks, what power it has; you can judge then what is his strength.'

I believe the reader will not weary in his enjoyment of the many stories I bring up about the people of India. It happened that I was on my way from the court to Lahor when I came up with a Hindu, well attired, accompanied by some of his friends, and taking with him several bearers carrying trays of sweet fruit, rose-water, goats, and hens. All these were followed by players on pipes and cymbals,[1] as I have already described (III. 127). Curious to find out the cause of all this joy, I learnt how the said man was a trader who had come home after six years and found his wife had brought forth four sons. Delighted at finding his house thus favoured, he invited his relations and neighbours to a feast [206]. Some readers will protest at what I have said, because they have no experience of the artfulness of Indian women. The husband asked his wife how she got these sons. She answered that while asleep she dreamt of him, and from that moment was with child. The Brahmans upheld her in this asseveration, one of them being her lover. They appealed to the example of their false gods, of whom it is said that they were born, one from perspiration, another from the dew of the nostrils, and another from making water on the ground, from which a figure proceeded. The woman's husband, accepting these explanations, was entirely satisfied.

I will give a brief account of the feasts and practices in Hindustan at births and marriages.[2] In the case of any great man having a male child born to him, the feasting and banqueting are prolonged, with much music and sounding of instruments, and the relations assemble to present congratulations to the new-born child. These people send their presents called *quichydi* (? *kishti,* a tray). They consist in a great assortment of different trays full of fruit, fresh and dried, a quantity of sugar, camels laden with sugar-cane, sweetmeats of various colours, rose-water, all kinds of food-supplies, butter, oil, pieces of silk and fine cotton cloth, together with some gold and silver coin. The whole of these things are brought out of the house at night escorted by a number of torches and lanterns of various colours, flags, dancing-women, musicians with drums [*tabales* = *tabl* (?), Urdu] and other instruments, cavalry and elephants. In the midst moves the lady with her damsels in palanquins and carriages, surrounded by many armed men on foot. Thus they traverse the principal streets of the city that all may see their grandeur and the expense they are at. All this grandeur, profuseness, and almsgiving usual

1. Or 'drums,' *tabales*. Query the Urdu word *tabl,* or Portuguese *tambor,* a drum.
2. These are the Mahomedan usages; those previously given were those of Hindus (III. 121-131).

among the Mahomedans are meant to leave a memory of them in the world. There is no intention to be charitable. Six days after the birth the final feast is given; it lasts all night with great illuminations, music, dancing, and fireworks.

At a wedding the feasting lasts fifteen days, and the friends and relations send their *kishti* in the way already stated. At seven o'clock at night the bridegroom sallies forth on horseback, finely clad, with a gold network fixed to his head and falling down to his chest, being also decorated with various flowers according to the season. Thus accoutered, he passes through the principal streets very slowly with a number of torches, women dancing and men playing upon elephants and camels, making a great noise, and the musical instruments sounding. As they proceed along the route they let off bombs and fire-works. A large cavalry escort follows.

Thus they proceed until they arrive at the bride's door. Here there appears and stops the way a numerous body of men with rods [207] in their hands, shouting to them not to come any nearer. The people with the bridegroom draw up when they see the way is barred. They demand that it may be opened to them, the bridegroom having business within. Making believe to be adversaries, some of the others begin to resist with oranges, lemons, egg-plants,[1] turnips, radishes, and similar things. This being ended, they grasp their canes and make a great tumult and outcry, being all in disorder, the turbans of one set falling off, while another group tear each other's clothes. But they do not touch the bride-groom.

At this moment of their efforts to enter, there appears some person on behalf of the bride, who shouts that there must be a truce. All becomes quiet, and they listen to his statements. He says that before the doors are opened for the bridegroom's entrance it is necessary for him to pay some money to be allowed a passage. Thereupon the quarrel is partially resumed. At this time a man of some position advances from the bridegroom's retinue and says the bridegroom ought to have nothing to pay, but on his behalf he will give a present. He distributes some rupees, and the gate is opened.

1. *Biniales*, for *brinjal*. Query the Portuguese name for the *baingan*, or egg-plant.

The bridegroom enters, followed by his relations, servants, and slaves, and the rest of the men remain without. The bridegroom, with the above-named following, goes on till he encounters another troop of wormers, who act as the men did outside, holding rods, garlanded with flowers. When the fray is over, they all join and conduct the bridegroom to a great hall. In the midst the bride is sitting on a highly decorated throne, clad in costly raiment and adorned with precious jewels. Round her stand many matrons with many instruments of music.

On the bridegroom's arrival opposite to her, never having seen her before this moment, he salutes her and makes the customary bows; and the singers, raising their voices, proclaim a welco me to the bridegroom, with wishes for the happiness of the marriage. At this point an aged Mulla (man of religious learning) appears; he is the priest. He holds his head low and keeps his eyes down, in a very modest attitude. He makes them husband and wife on condition that if there is any divorce the bridegroom will have to pay the bride so many millions.

Once more the singers begin their song, saying these words: 'May the marriage be blessed a hundredfold.' They divide into two choirs, one singing the bridegroom's and the other the bride's praises. At the end of an hour they present the bridegroom with a box containing a paste that they call *mendi* (*menhdi—i.e.*, henna). With this he anoints his hands and nails so that they turn red. After another hour they wash his hands with rose-water and offer the water for him to drink, in sign of confirmation of the marriage, as is the custom.

Some bridegrooms, warned of the tricks played by women in India, refuse to drink. The reader should be aware that the dislike of the bridegroom [208] to drinking the water is that in the syrup above referred to there is mixed a liquid, in virtue of which the bridegroom becomes frantically enamoured of her (the bride). The matrons, on seeing the difficulties made by the bridegroom, force him by such strong arguments and oaths that he believes and drinks. The singing women once more resume their song, saying. 'May it profit you.' The whole night is passed in this mirth, and before daybreak the bridegroom takes the woman to his house, carrying the dowry along with him, making the pretext for with drawl of needing repose.

Among the Mahomedans it is the practice not to see their bride beforehand, but to marry upon reports, interests, or respect. First cousins are allowed to marry. Poor people conduct their marriages in the same way, to the extent of each man's resources. The Hindus also give a similar feast, but it is accompanied by other ceremonies and sacrifices. Among these latter when the husband dies they shave the widow's head, and she never marries again. This can be seen in more detail in my remarks upon the Hindu religion (III. 122-132).

When a Mahomedan dies, there are special persons who come to wash the corpse. These people make their living by this office; they are abhorred, and no one eats with them. They put the body in its shroud and place it in a coffin covered with rich pieces of stuff; the turban bound with gold is laid upon the outside, as a token that inside is a dead body. It is carried to the grave accompanied by all the deceased's insignia of rank, flags, elephants, cavalry, with a large following, and many perfumes. On the way they commend the departed in loud voices to Muhammad. Until the burying is completed, passers-by who meet the body halt and pray for his soul.

The wives of these great men do not marry again, though in no way prohibited. When those who followed the corpse return home, they bathe their bodies and put on clean clothes. The widow and all in the household equally bathe their bodies and remain in mourning for forty days. The relations of the deceased distribute alms of bread, cloth, and money. After forty days are over they go to the grave, where they prepare many dishes and distribute them among the poor. When these great ladies come out, as a sign of their being widows, they cover their palanquins with green cloth. Similarly, when any one of the wives of these nobles dies, there are special women for washing: the body, which is placed in its grave-clothes with much special ceremony; it is carried to the grave, followed by women and eunuchs. In the case of women they do not call out the commendations to Muhammad as is done for men, for they declare that women have no entry into heaven.

When a Hindu dies, they carry him to be burnt at once with a great noise of drums and trumpets. Those who follow go bareheaded, with no shoes on their feet.

Being resident in the city of Agrah, I went out for pastime, impelled by curiosity, to shoot peahens, doves, and pigeons, of which there are quantities in the gardens round that place. It happened once that, passing close to the place where Hindus are burned. I saw a man who removed from the pyre a portion of the burnt flesh of some corpse and ate it. It served him as sustenance, and he ate nothing else. I sent someone to call him, and I asked him the reason why he did not allow the body to be thoroughly consumed. He replied to me that the savour of human flesh was such that it forced him to dwell in that deserted place. I noticed that the man was tall, lean, harsh-looking, of a dejected countenance and taciturn, and reluctant to answer the few questions I put to him.

When Hindus burn a dead body, they place it on the top of a heap of wood, and over the body they pile as much wood again. A light is then applied. The relations who had followed the body leave for their homes with the exception of four men. These had carried the body, and are called *bettiao* (*battiyan*),[1] which means 'burners.' These men place themselves round the pyre at some little distance, each holding a long, thick stick in his hand. As it burns, the corpse makes movements through the relaxing of the muscles, the face is scorched, and the hands and feet shrivel up, and it looks as if it wanted to sit up. On these occasions the bettioens (burners) exert themselves to extend the body by thrusts with their sticks. Finally, after bathing in the river close by, they go away.

The following day the relations go to the burning-place, and collecting the bones, place them in an earthen pot and throw some milk upon them, by which they are wetted. They are then thrown into the river with the necessary ceremonial. They state that the putting on of milk is to cool the soul of the defunct, and they throw the ashes into water in order that there be no doubt of his salvation. They distribute cooked food of vegetables with rice, giving to eat even to the crows, of whom there are enormous numbers throughout India. Then they bathe themselves in the river and return home.

These Hindus have many superstitions, of which should I begin to speak I should occupy a very long time, and I should

1. Probably from *batti*, a lighted taper; *batti* dikhana, to set a light to anything (Platts, 'Dictionary,' 132).

be wearisome. Among them it is the habit, when carrying water home, if they should encounter a corpse, to throw away the whole of that water, going back to refill the vessel. Coming out of the house, if anyone sneezes, or if a cat crosses in front of them, they turn back and relinquish the business for that day.

When a marriage is in prospect, the boy's parents go to see the girl intended as his bride, examine her all over, and if she has any mark that they hold to be inauspicious, or if she does not take their fancy, they will on no account accept a marriage with her. If she possesses marks that they approve of, they send some money as a token that they accept the girl. It is the custom of the Hindus that when the bride comes to her husband's house she acts as servant to all [210] the house—sweeps, cleans, cooks, and performs all the other work. She never opens her mouth, keeps her head down, enduring the importunate demands of her mother-in-law. When she is in child-bed she has a little liberty, and during her periods she has to retire to a separate room kept for this special purpose, where no one speaks to her. Her food is left at a distance; no one approaches her. Ordinarily the marriage is between a little child and a grown man. When there is a miscarriage the fetus is buried within the house; the same is done if the first child dies, for, being an infant, it is not cremated. Nor do they bury it outside for fear that witches may disinter it, to employ it in doing sorcery. When a female child dies who has reached twelve years of age or upwards, she is burnt, and for boys the age is fourteen years. The reason is that in India at those ages they are capable of sinning against the Sixth Commandment. Of these customs I spoke more amply under the head of the 'Hindu Religion' (III. 92-135).

It is wonderful to see what is done when any Hindu rajah or prince expires. Before he is taken away to be burnt they shave his head, his beard, and his whole body, anointing it with essence of roses, binding it up in fine cloth all smeared with different jasmine oils mixed with saffron. The body is laid upon laths of sandal and aloes wood, bound together in the shape of an open bier. The women who are to be burnt with him follow; they are women with whom the rajah had lived. The principal wife who has sons is preserved, with the idea of maintaining the family line. The women sacrificed are commonly fifteen, twenty, or even thirty in number, as I have seen at various times.

It is a memorable thing to see these women on horseback surrounding the corpse, and calling out thousands of praises of their husband, the good life he led, and the pleasures he enjoyed here below. Feeling under an obligation for so many favours received, they look forward in the next life to receive still greater delight in his society there. All this is carried out with much joy and animation, they being richly clad, oiled, and perfumed.

Reaching the place of death, they descend gracefully from their steeds, and assist in lifting the bier on to the heap of wood. This stands in a pit. The principal wife among them places herself on one side, embracing the corpse and uttering innumerable praises; the others range themselves round the body in the same way. The burners set fire to the wood all round, and dexterously empty on it pots of oil and butter to increase the rapidity of the cremation. When the fire has taken they throw on more oil, and when the heat reaches them the women naturally move and begin to shriek. They are soon choked by the smoke [211], while the men surrounding the pyre raise a great noise with drums and gongs and loud shouts, while the burners skilfully force them to lie down by thrusting at them with poles. Thus are they burnt both for this life and the next.

The next day the Brahmans and many relations go to the spot and collect the bones, and send them to be thrown into the Ganges river, whatever the distance may be. Some people out of piety send them to be thrown in the river at the *Tirt*h (place of pilgrimage), of which I have spoken (II. 58), flowing below the fortress of Allahabad. If such princes die in battle, the women immolate themselves with still greater alacrity on receiving the turban sent them as a sign of their husband's death. With it in their hands they are cremated. I have seen some die with their husband's body in their arms without making a sign of movement. The reason is that the Brahmans provide them with certain beverages—*bhang* (hemp), opium, and such like, which entirely stupefy them.

Others, by use of sorcery, become eager, ardent, mad, demanding that the authorities put no hindrance in their way when in search of their beloved, alleging as a reason that they are suffering acutely from deprivation of their loved one. This happened at Vizagapatao (= *visakha* + *patanam*)[1] at the time

1. So named from a temple to Visakha (a sage, one of the sons of Kumara) which once stood there.

when Mestre Olca (Mr. Holcombe)[1] governed it. He refused permission for the burning of some woman of this sort. She appeared in his presence, and with great anxiety prayed him to set no impediment to what was her desire. Mr. Holcombe and the rest of those present noticed that she seemed to have abandoned her feminine nature. He entreated her in the cause of humanity, and offered her the good advice not to give herself up to die by burning. He undertook to support her for the rest of her life. This talk caused her pain, and she persisted in demanding permission. Mr. Holcombe, seeing he could not stop her, spoke secretly to a Brahman who was with her, promising him a sum of money if he removed the apprehensions that possessed the woman. If he did not effect this he would have to burn alongside of her, and also the rest of the Brahmans who had come with her. Saying this, he sent orders to close the factory gates as if quite ready to act. The Brahmans, not to lose the money, and not to put their own lives in danger, went behind the woman without her being aware of it, and gently touched her clothes at the back with their fingers. She totally changed colour, and, raising her hands to her face, and drooping her head in a shamefaced way, went back to her house.

When I was in Goa in the year one thousand six hundred and sixty-six (1666), at the time when Antonio de Mello de Castro[2] governed, there happened to be a Portuguese named Antonio de Azevedo, not long arrived [212] from Portugal. He was Secretary of State. He wanted to marry a widow lady who was very rich, and he therefore sent her a message that he wanted to espouse her. She sent word back briefly that he might save himself taking that trouble, as she did not mean to marry him. This rumour went about in the city till some gentleman asked the secretary if what was spoken of were true. Magnifying his own merits, he replied that it was just the contrary, for the widow had sent him an offer of marriage, to which he had replied that he had no desire to espouse her. The widow heard of this, and to wipe out the affront sent a Kaffir to him with a note. The man had orders, when the secretary should

1. Wheeler, 'Madras in the Olden Time,' ii. 132. Mr. Holcombe was Deputy-Governor of Vizagapatam from 1698 to 1705. He died shortly after May, 1705.
2. Antonio de Mello e Castro, Governor and then Viceroy from 1662 to 1666 (Danvers, ii. 488, No. 56).

be reading it, to give him a cut across the face. It was so-effectually done that it went from ear to ear. When his wound had healed, he left for Europe, for fear his life might be taken. When he set out on this voyage, he invited me to accompany him. I made my excuses to him, as it was my intention to go back to the Mogul country. Thus does it happen often to boasters, who, in their desire to exalt themselves to the discredit of others, for reward earn some such chastisement, as will be seen from the following case.

There was another case in the same city in the same year. One day at early dawn they found a dead body lying near the arch of Misericordia,[1] with the tongue rooted out, and in the mouth a note which read thus: 'For mixing in and speaking of things which did not concern you, you lost your life and your tongue as well.' These two cases will serve as examples to some people not to interfere in matters with which they have nothing to do.

In the same city there happened to be a well-born man, left well off by his parents. His name was Lourenço da Cunha, and he was married. He had a differençe in words exchanged with a trader of the same city, and this sufficed to deprive the poor merchant of his life. Lourenco da Cunha wrote a note, in which he placed a small awl, and made it over to one of his Kaffirs with instructions what to do. Off went the Kaffir to find his man, whom he met going by in a palanquin. The Kaffir went up to him and presented the note, suddenly striking him with it on the breast. Letting go of the awl and the note, he made a rush and got inside the church of Sao Paulo, where he obtained sanctuary. Lourenço da Cunha escaped and lived for some months in Bombaym (Bombay) [213] until he had arranged with the opposite parties and the magistrates. He remained unmolested, as was most often the case.

In the city of Goa there was a well-born man, well known among the nobles; his name was Ignacio Sarmento de Carvalho.[2]

1. The Santa Casa and the Church of the Misericordia are mentioned in 'Pyrard de Laval' (edition Gray), ii. 10, 351, but no Arch of that name. See also J. N. da Fonseca, 'Sketch of the City of Goa' (Bombay, 1878), p. 244.
2. This is probably the Ignatio Sarmento mentioned in Danvers, ii. 327, The surrender of Cochin was signed on January 7, 1663 (*ibid.*, 328). Manucci-also refers to him in Part II., 110.

He was governor of Cochim (Cochin)[1] when the Dutch took that place, of whom I have already spoken (II. 110). This man married one of his daughters to a well-born Portuguese—I will not give his name—who claimed to be of high quality. At the end of some years he became a widower, but was all the same well treated and housed by his father-in-law. The confidence accorded him was such that he was guilty of something dishonest in the house, which involved discredit to the person of Ignacio Sarmento. The son-in-law, fearing that it might come to Sarmento's ears, plotted to take his life. To this intent, he selected and equipped twenty soldiers to carry out his plot at an opportune moment. He waited until his victim had confessed and taken the sacrament, which took place on Palm Sunday. At seven o'clock in the evening the soldiers entered the house all of a sudden, ten taking post at the door, while the other ten made haste to mount the stairs, drawn sword in hand. Ignacio Sarmento was seated with some accounts in his hands. Seeing the men, he perceived that treachery was to the fore, and endeavoured to seize his arms. He was unable to do so, and was forthwith dispatched by sword-thrusts.

This event occurred in the year one thousand six hundred and seventy-six (1676). The soldiers crossed the river, and went in search of a livelihood, having received a considerable sum of money from the noble gentleman. The latter was seized and sent to Portugal. He asserted that he had shown great consideration to his victim in not slaying him until he had confessed and received the sacrament, whereas he might have had it done before. As it seems to me, Ignacio Sarmento had just reason not to be astonished at dying in that way, for in his day he, too, had done similar deeds more than once.

Another case was what happened to a Portuguese, judge of the Orphans, a neighbour of mine, who lived near the Arch of the Conception close to Pelorinho.[2] He had married a good-

1. Cochin, from *Kochhi* (Malayalam), a 'small place' ('Madras Manual of Administration,' iii. 192). The final *n* was added by the Portuguese.
2. Judging from p. 193 of J. N. da Fonseca's 'Sketch of the City of Goa (Bombay, 1878), this must have been another name for the Arco dos Vice-reys, or principal gate, on which there is an inscription dedicated to the Immaculate Conception, and dated 1656. The Pelourinho Velho (Old Pillory) was not far off (*ibid.*, p. 247, see also 'Pyrard de Laval,' edition Gray, ii. 47, 55, 69).

looking half-caste named Anna Lestoa. This woman had been sought by several men of birth, and not having been able to secure her, they sent men to murder the husband. But God preserved his life; he escaped with wounds all over his body, one ear gone and without one arm. The wretched man was forced to seek shelter in the convent of the barefooted Carmelites to recover from his injuries. In spite of their coming in search of him, he was kept a [214] whole year, until the arrival of a new viceroy, Joao Nunis da Cunha,[1] Count of Sao Vicente. He it was who sent out a fleet against the Arabs; but it was a failure, as I have related (II 129). I was a friend of the Carmelites, and my leisure time was passed in their convent,[2] where I had long talks with the said Portuguese, and he confirmed to me the case of witchcraft at Mascate (Masqat), he being then a soldier in that garrison.

In the same city (Goa) there was another well-born man among the principal inhabitants called Manoel Corte Real, who brought great wealth from Mozambique. He married one of his daughters to a well-born youth called Dom Vasco de Gama, related to the family of that famous Gama who conquered India, he whose statue stands as a memorial to this day over the gate entering into the city, near the viceroy's palace.[3] To her the father gave as a dowry the sum of two hundred thousand *patacas* [Rs. 400,000]. The youth, a person of small understanding, finding himself so rich, began to spend inordinately in an ostentatious way.

There was an honourable lady who lived at her country house outside the city, and she had one lovely daughter. The

1. Joab Nunes da Cunha, Conde de S. Vicente (Viceroy, 1666-68). He arrived at Goa on October 11, 1666, and took over the government on the 17th (Danvers, ii. 488, No. 57). He died in India on November 6, 1668 (*ibid.*, 363, 364).
2. J. N. Da Fonseca, 'Goa' (Bombay, 1878), p. 256. This convent, with its church, was on a height to the east of the town. It was healthy, and had a fine view. As the Fathers were not of Portuguese nationality, Manucci would naturally be friendly with them.
3. Danvers (ii. 121) says this marble statue over the principal gate of the city was thrown down by the people and broken in 1600. They hung the pieces in public places (see also Stevens, 'Faria y Souza,' iii. 123). Mr. Albert Gray, 'Pyrard de Laval,' ii., Introduction, xxxviii, says 'the statue now in the niche was substituted a year or two later,' and thus could have been seen by Manucci in 1666-67 and 1683-84.

youth heard of this girl's beauty, sent to interview her, and promised her a great deal of money. As she was prudent and honourable, she declined to accede to the young man's proposals. Finding that money was of no avail, he resolved to carry out his design by violence. With this intent he made preparations along with other gentlemen of his kidney. Going one night to the place, they broke in the door, entered, and violating mother and daughter, went home again.

When the lady found they did not return, she sent a friendly message that he might visit her house without apprehension. The simple Dom Vasco, never supposing that this amorousness was fictious, called together his chief friends, who had been his companions on that other night, and off they went to the widow's house. She received them with feigned joy, and entertained them with a feast where the dishes were poisoned. Of such refined power was this poison that at the first mouthful three fell down then and there, while the fourth with the morsel in his mouth, seeing Dom Vasco and the others succumb, spat out the mouthful and fled in terror. Three days afterwards he, too, expired, the flesh falling off his body in small pieces. The well-born lady and her daughter retired to the nunnery of Santa Monica.

In Europe there is no idea about whether people in India are punctual or not in satisfying their debts to their creditors, because when they are in need they ask with much modesty, making a thousand bows, promising to pay the debt according to the obligations of a written bond. They show themselves as being very much obliged, and offer with humility to be [215] of service in any way. But, the money once in their hands, they remember no more about it and make no effort to pay. When the term of payment arrives they invent pretexts, making moan that the voyage they had just made ended in a loss because their goods had not sold. As they have no intention of paying, they invent such-like excuses. Thus to secure payment is a laborious business, and often one must have recourse to the law courts, wearing one's self out with fatigue, and all the while spending money. Over and over again the principal sum is lost, and from being friends you and your debtor turn into enemies. I have often seen this. Some men, in place of recovering their due, lose their lives by a blow on the head, or lose an arm, or some other similar mishap befalls them. This can be seen by the following case:

On my journey from Surat to Daman. I met on the road a Portuguese who was quitting the territory through fear of the law; for this man had taken some money on loan, and the creditor being in need of money, sent to ask for the debt. The Portuguese sent back word that it was only in person that the creditor would be paid. In the hope of payment, he went to see his debtor. Instead of paying, the debtor had the creditor bound and his ears cut off, saying that he might thank his stars for getting off alive with only the loss of his ears, which were cut off because of his temerity in asking a gentleman to pay a debt.

Once in Goa, being in my house, there suddenly appeared a gentleman of birth, who with much assurance took a seat without uttering any words of politeness. At his back stood four Kaffirs with staves in their hands. He said he was a gentleman of high rank, and occupied an important position in His Majesty's service, but fortune had not been kind to him. He had been wealthy, the lord of many plantations, but to pass the time he had gambled and lost all. Then, raising his eyes, he looked at me and said: 'I have heard that your honour is a merchant, a person of position, and the reputation you enjoy has induced me to visit you.' But he could not stay long, because the viceroy was waiting for his appearance to begin his dinner; and since he was in want of pocket-money, he would borrow a sum from me. I replied that I was a poor soldier, and not a merchant; he had been misinformed. Raising his voice, he said: 'These arguments will not do for me; either lend me or give me what I need.' At these words the Kaffirs raised their staves. On seeing this I fell into a quandary, and began to reflect on what might be the result. I tried to retire into my room, when he said to me roughly, raising his voice, that I was not to stir from my place. Then, dissimulating [216] as to the pressure put on me. I told my boy to bring me my writing-desk. I opened it in front of him and showed what it contained—namely, thirty *ashrafis* (gold coins). I handed him this amount with the greatest politeness, saying that, had there been more. I should most willingly have offered it to him. He felt so honoured that he took twenty-five coins, saying that would suffice for his wants during that day. He put his good services at my disposal, instructing his Kaffirs that when I needed them for giving anyone a beating with bamboos, or stabbing anyone, they must carry out my orders. He then departed. Conceiving that I had got rid of him very cheaply, I gave thanks to God, and at once changed my quarters, going to live close to the convent of the Carmelites; and there I lived with my doors barred, for I had seen many houses robbed by bodies of masked men entering them.

It is the custom to close the shops at six o'clock, as soon as the sun sets, for if this were not done they would be plundered. This is because the soldiers and Kaffirs, dying of hunger, are forced into such conduct. The *Baniya* shopkeepers, in order to sell their goods—such as garlic, pepper, butter, and the rest—have a hole in the shop-door through which they receive the money and hand out what is wanted. Even this precaution did not avail them always, for some thieves pretending they wanted to buy something, a shopkeeper put his hand through the hole to take the money; they seized his hand and pricked it with a knife and asked for the goods required, saying if he did not give them they would cut off his hand. The shopkeeper, seeing himself in this fix, could think of nothing but making the best bargain he could. So, calling to his wife to bring all he had, he offered the amount to the thieves. As soon as they had the money they released his hand. Let the reader just think of that *Baniya's* affliction, they being a very timid and avaricious class. When reports of this case reached the other *Baniya* shopkeepers, to circumvent the thieves they adopted a long wooden spoon to take the money and deliver the goods, and on no account would they put their hand through the hole. Experience had been their teacher.

Long ago, when the Portuguese were still great and rich, citizens kept many Kaffir[1] slaves in their houses. Each householder had fifty, seventy, and up to a hundred, or thereabouts. At night these men were masters [217] of the city, moving in all directions, robbing, murdering, and committing many excesses. They paid no heed to the Portuguese soldiers, and in the morning these guards would be found lying dead in the streets. At Goa,

1. The old spellings were Caffer, Caffre, Coffree, from Arabic *Kafir*, 'an infidel,' a term applied by the Portuguese to pagan negroes; Yule, 140.

in the time of the viceroy Dom Phelipe Mascarenha,[1] there were every morning dead soldiers, plundered houses, and robbed individuals. The viceroy found that the patrols could not overcome the great number of Kaffirs, and therefore ordered the citizens to keep all their Kaffirs within doors from eight o'clock at night. He then gave secret orders to the captains of infantry to post soldiers at night, with orders to kill every Kaffir they came across. On receiving such orders, the Portuguese soldiers were delighted to take vengeance on the Kaffirs for their misdeeds, at the same time acquiring liberty for themselves to wander about at night. In executing the viceroy's orders, owing to their ill-feeling towards the Kaffirs, they collected one morning two hundred and fifty dead bodies, not reckoning wounded who had got away. Continuing this process for several days, the Kaffirs were intimidated, and did not venture on so much violence. In spite of this, there continues to this day to be some of this disorder.

In addition, the soldiers were the perpetrators of much oppression. When I was present once at the house of the lord archbishop[2] there came a woman there, her hair streaming, and cried aloud for help, because a soldier had carried off from her house a maiden daughter; and she prayed for speedy succour, before the soldier could dishonour the captive. A domestic took a message inside to the archbishop, who sent word for the woman to go to a public scribe and reduce her petition to writing, stating therein what were her grievances. On perusing this, he would dispose of the case. On hearing such an answer, the old, woman raised her hands to her head and went home weeping. I was amazed to see such inattention; and I was revolted, for, in all the lands I have lived in, never have I beheld, in similar circumstances, the same want of energy.

I will say something more about this city of Goa, which, as it seems to me, is dominated by some disquieting planet, or by demons who throw it into confusion, filling it with murder, disunion, and oppression, as I have tested by experience. Seeing

1. Dom Filippe Mascarenhas, Viceroy, 1646-1651 (Danvers, ii. 488, No. 49).
2. From 1678 to 1681 the government was in commission, Dom F. Antonio Brandao, Archbishop, Antonio Paes de Sande, and Francisco Cabral de Almada being the commissioners (Danvers, ii. 489, No. 61). Or it may refer to the time in 1683 when Archbishop Manoel de Sousa e Menezes was in temporary charge (see II. 207).

that what I have said of the lay inhabitants is not the whole truth, I must add that it is the same thing in the convents of men dedicated to the religious life. In them there is also discord, as I have myself witnessed. There are opposing factions in the same convent, one virulent against the other, carrying [218] cutlasses and fire-arms hidden beneath their gowns. Walking through the city, should they encounter the other side, there is a fight. In the end they threw the prior out of a window, and he died from the injuries. This case happened at the convent of the Augustinians.[1]

This discord lasts up to this day without anyone succeeding, in stopping it. The friars wander outside their convents, do not obey their priors; they scatter themselves over the kingdoms of the Mahomedans, live as they please, and are bound by no scruples. There was a similar quarrel in the convent of the Carmelites, but in the course of time they were reconciled'. During the viceroyalty of Antonio de Mello de Castro,[2] in sixty-five (1665), the Dominicans also began a disturbance of the same sort. The viceroy was desirous of putting a stop to it, but they paid no heed to him. He ordered out pieces of artillery to knock down the convent. To pacify him and avert this damage the lord archbishop and the inquisitors acted as mediators, and they quickly brought the parties to terms.

On the part of the Jesuits no such behaviour occurred, for they ruled their concerns with more prudence. If among them any difference arises, it is kept such a secret that no one hears of it. All the same, a notable case happened among them, during the time that the government was held by the viceroy Dom Bras de Castor.[3] It was this: there came to Goa a favourite of Sultan Muhammad 'Adil Shah, King of Bijapur,[4]

1. The convent and church of the Augustinians formed the finest group of buildings in Goa ('Pyrard de Laval,' edition Gray, ii. 57, 58,. and J. N. da Fonseca, 'Goa,' p. 311). The site was to the west of the town (see the latter author's map, Nos. 35-37).
2. Antonio de Mello e Castro, Governor and then Viceroy, 1662-66 (Danvers, ii. 488, No. 56). The Dominicans had been in Goa since 1548; their convent was to the east of the town, rather near the river (Fonseca, 'Goa,' 250; 'Pyrard de Laval,' edition Gray, ii. 49, 71).
3. Dom Braz de Castro, a usurper, 1653-55 (Danvers, ii. 488, No. 52).
4. Muhammad 'Adil Shah reigned 1035-70 H. (1626-60 A.D.). S. L. Poole, 'Mohammadan Dynasties,' 321.

to be treated medically. He was in charge of the royal jewels, and he brought from the royal treasury a precious stone of great price. On it he borrowed twenty thousand *asharfis* (gold coins) from Father Gonsallo Martins, Jesuit, known widely as a great money-dealer. When some time had passed the favourite went to redeem his stone, and offered the interest that he owed. Gonsallo Martins, impelled by his grand ambitions, denied everything—had never heard of the man, knew nothing of such a stone. The owner, finding that his efforts produced no effect, made the matter known to his king. The latter, in order to find out the truth, sent other officials, who pretended to be jewel merchants. Arriving in the city of Goa, they purchased a number of stones, and paid a good price. They announced their desire to buy some larger stones of high value. Gonsallo Martins, fancying he would now make the profit he wanted, showed the disputed stone to the merchants. They identified it as the same, said nothing, and disagreed as to the price. Then they reported to their king, Sultan Muhammad 'Adil Shah, who employed the following device to recover his stone.

He wrote several letters to the provincial of the Jesuit convent at Goa, in which he said that God had made him a man of learning, he knew that the true faith was that of the Messiah, and to save his soul he wanted to become a Christian, he, his family, and the nobles of the kingdom. For this reason he begged the prior to send him his most learned priests, specifying each by name, and including Gonsallo Martins [219]. On this news reaching Goa, great joy spread over the whole city, the bells were set pealing, and there was much rejoicing.

The priests referred to started for Bijapur; they were well treated on their road, and on reaching the king's court he gave them a civil reception, and entertained them at a splendid banquet. When this was over, the treasurer and the pretended merchants appeared, and the king, in place of entering on religious discussion, asked him (Martins) if he had brought the stone pledged to him by the treasurer. On hearing these words the priests were upset, especially Gonsallo Martins. The latter denied absolutely, and would not give way to the arguments of the witnesses. Seeing this persistence in denial, the king ordered them all to be seized, dealing with Gonsallo Martins more rigorously, by flogging, torture, and starvation. The king threatened to kill then if they did not return his stone.

Finding themselves in this predicament, they wrote to their provincial of the Jesuit house at Goa, asserting that through his fault they were suffering innocently, while Gonsallo Martins, unable to endure his sufferings, wrote separately, asking him to send the stone, so that he and the other prisoners might regain their liberty. At Goa no heed was paid to their supplications, and the question was evaded. On finding out this evasive conduct, the king wrote the details to the viceroy, sending the witnesses at the same time. The viceroy took steps to obtain satisfaction for the said king, but was unable to convince the Jesuits.

When the king saw that he could not obtain his rights pacifically, he dispatched an army against Goa, destroying the country in Salsette and Bardes. Finding himself in this danger, and the contumacious Jesuits declining to hand over the stone, the viceroy was obliged to post sentries round the Jesuit college, and stop all supplies. Finally he made preparation by posting artillery round the college to knock down its walls if they did not yield up the stone. Most assuredly he would have done it. But at last, being in this extremity, they surrendered the stone, though very much against the grain. The viceroy sent it to the King of Bijapur, and thereby the investment was raised and the priests released.

The story of this affair spread through the city, creating great astonishment everywhere, and there were many murmurings. As a diversion to these murmurs they invented colouring a donkey they had in use a green colour, and then tying some thorns beneath its tail. They let it loose at the gate of the bull-ring. Hurt by the thorns, the donkey went plunging and lashing out through the city. Thus in those days talk about the stone ceased, and nothing was heard of except the green donkey. This affair was notorious throughout India, and I knew Father Gansallo Martins in the year one thousand six hundred and sixty-six (1666), when he was procurator for the Queen of Portugal.[1]

In the palace of the viceroys is a large hall, which is called the *salla real* (royal hall). At its end on the wall is a large picture,

1. 'Adil Shah did invade Portuguese territory on August 12, 1654, after eighty-seven years of peace. He returned in October (Danvers, ii. 308). But there is nothing about the Jesuits, the precious stone, or the green donkey. Peace was made with Bijapur on March 7, 1655 (*ibid.*,309).

the portrait of the King of Portugal; beneath it the seat of the viceroy with a canopy. It is here that he receives ambassadors. Round the hall hang the portraits of all the viceroys, who have ruled in India, with their names and their period of office.[1] The Bijapur ambassador was received in audience in this hall. As he advanced very slowly he inspected minutely the features of the viceroys, and asked who they were. They replied that these were the conquerors and governors of India. On hearing this he shook his head, and said: 'I see none with their heads off; it is impossible they all ruled well, and a king who decapitates no one secures neither good decisions nor quiet government.' He instanced his own king, who beheaded anyone who governed badly.

There was in Goa an archbishop, a man of virtue, who made attempts to put an end to so much disorder and evil practices. So they resolved to kill him; and he being informed of their purpose, lived most cautiously. But all his efforts were of no avail, because they took his life through poison put into the sacred elements.

It is sixty years ago, or thereabouts, that a viceroy named Conde Dovido ruled in India, and as he endeavoured to suppress the disorders existing in India, the gentry seized him, put him in chains, and sent him back to Europe.[2] The accusations against him included many falsehoods. The complaints were rejected, and to punish such a rebellion they sent to Goa as viceroy the Conde de Sargides.[3] He tried to reduce the rebel gentry (*fidalgos*), but in a few months he was poisoned. It is also related of another viceroy who wanted to decide uprightly that the insolent gentry, accustomed to disobey, took counsel together to have him assassinated. The viceroy knew of this plot, to be executed when he passed in his boat a place called 'Beco de

1. Compare Fryer, 375, reprint of 1873. 'Pyrard de Laval,' edition Gray, ii. 51, and Fonseca, 'Goa,' 194, speak of this hall and the collection of portraits, which seem to be still in existence.
2. Evidently meant for No. 51, Dom Vasco Mascarenhas, Conde de Obidos, Viceroy, 1652-53 (Danvers, ii. 488). He was deposed during a revolt on October 22, 1653 (*ibid.*, ii. 304).
3. Dom Rodrigo Lobo da Silveira, Conde de Sarzedas, Viceroy. He assumed the government on August 23, 1655 (Danvers, ii. 488, No. 53). 'He died at Goa on January 3, 1656, and a strong suspicion prevailed that he had been poisoned' (*ibid.*, ii. 319).

bacharel, (Bachelors' Alley). It is near the river bank, where they collect materials for ships. He knew that at this spot the traitors meant to carry out their plot, therefore he told off a servant to take his place in the boat. As the boat passed close to that landing the blunderbuss men slew the servant, fancying he was [221] the viceroy. They were delighted, and rumour reported throughout the city that the viceroy was dead. Hence throughout that night confusion prevailed; but at dawn the viceroy came forth, and ordered the traitors to be arrested. During the execution of these orders some were found, but the rest escaped. The well-born among them were sent back to Portugal in custody. For such men could not be beheaded in India, and those who were not well-born were put to death by hanging.

In the year ninety-six (1696), at the same place (Goa), they killed the commander of the fleet, named Antonio Machado Supico, by firing a blunderbuss through a window, breaking his sword. Seeing that he was not totally dead, a gentleman called Tristao de Mello, the doer of this deed, went into the house with some companions and finished him (Supico) off with sword-thrusts. In spite of this, in the midst of the pain, Supico failed not to plant his mark on Tristao de Mello, giving him a cut on the head with his broken sword. Among the conspirators was a man expelled from the convent of the Order of St. Dominic, who a few months before had held the post of Secretary of State. The reason for killing Antonio Machado Supico was his unbridled tongue, which spared neither priests, householders, nor widow women. He abused everybody in disgraceful language, and for this he was done to death by treachery. He is the same Antonio Machado who travelled with me to Agrah, of whom I spoke in the Second Part of my book (II 178).

Further, I noticed in this city (Goa), and in all its districts, much injustice done by the officials. They studied only their own convenience, interests, and consideration, without regard to the fear of God. I could recount many things under this head, but: I have no wish to let myself go, and will confine myself to the following instance.

In that city dwelt a rich merchant, a widower, who had one son. At the time of the father's death the son was away from home. As there was no other heir, the defunct entrusted all he had to the hands of a Hindu clerk (in India everybody employs such men). When the son arrived, the clerk made over to him everything that was in the house, but, as the deceased [222] had made no will, he retained the best of the jewels. The youth who knew what the house had contained, demanded from the said clerk the retraining articles. The man declined most decisively to do so. The dispute went into court, and it was a long time before any finding could be secured, putting the youth to considerable expense. Finally the Hindu, who had bribed highest, was favoured by the court, and obtained a decree in his favour.

The young man, perceiving the wrong, and the little effort they made [at Goa], had recourse in secret to the Mahomedan governor of Bicholim,[1] near the island of Goa, where was the home of the said Hindu clerk. The governor held his appointment from the King of Bijapur. The young man explained the case to him, and stated what had happened. The Mahomedan governor reassured him, and said he should get back his jewels. Meanwhile he might take a rest, and in due time he would send him word. To get at the truth the governor had recourse to the following plan.

It was as follows: He allowed it to be noised abroad that a captain from Bijapur was coming to him on a visit. He set on foot fictitious preparations, and prayed the Hindu merchants to give him the loan of jewels for the decoration of his dancing-girls. As a security to them he gave the sums they asked, and promised that he would return the jewels with the interest for the time they should be in his possession. Seeing that the jewels would be quite safe, the merchants came in numbers, attracted by the interest to be earned. Among them appeared also the Hindu clerk to lend the jewels that he had embezzled along with those that he had of his own.

When all this had been carried out, the governor sent for the young man, and showed him the whole stock of jewellery, telling him to pick out those articles that were his. As he knew them all, he forthwith pointed them out. The governor was convinced that the youth spoke the truth, for he never touched any of the other jewels, claiming solely those he had been deprived of by the said Hindu clerk. When certified of this fact, the governor returned to each man his jewels, and took back

1. A town in Portuguese territory, about four miles north-east of Old Goa (see map in Danvers, vol. ii., and Thornton, p. 119). It does not seem to have belonged to the Portuguese before 1705 (Danvers, ii. 375).

his security money, paying to them the promised interest. But the young man's jewels he kept back. Finally he sent for the Hindu clerk, and asked him whose jewels these were, and how he had obtained possession of them. The Hindu was terrified, and could give no sufficient account of them. Then the youth entered, throwing the clerk into still greater confusion, and, apprehensive of some severe punishment, he Confessed the truth. Thus did the young man recover his jewels, and the governor sent to inform the Goa law-court that, whenever it found itself in a difficulty about the decision of any case, they should make it over to him, and he would willingly dispose of it.

The first time I was in the city of Goa (II. 128). I lived in the street called Santo Aleixo,[1] opposite some large houses. In one of these lived a widow called Dona Christiana; she was rich and led a quiet life [223]. She wanted to marry me, a thing I never dreamt of. Seeing that I made no approaches and made no effort, she resorted to a trick. This consisted in sending for the prior of the Carmes, Friar Pheliciano de Santa Teresa, a native of Milan and a great friend of mine. To him she complained that I had been pursuing her, sending her offers of marriage, to which she had replied that she had no thought of such a thing. The father believed her words, being unaware of Indian women's trickish ways; and coming to pay me a visit, as he constantly did, he prayed me with the greatest gentleness not to persecute Dona Christiana with such proposals as I had sent her, saying I wanted to marry her. When I heard the padre talk like this, I was plunged in thought, trying to remember if on any day I had given the widow occasion for such a complaint about me. Examining my mind thoroughly, I found I had not the least remembrance of her, and said so to the father. He smiled, and said he hoped there would be no more complaints against me. As a satisfaction to him I left the neighbourhood and lived elsewhere.

Eight days afterwards the same priest came straight from the widow's house to find me, and directly he saw me began once more to complain harshly, saying I should be the cause of that woman losing her reputation. He begged me, for the love of God, to abandon any such thoughts. Feeling myeslf quite

1. Probably near the church of St. Alexius. No. 26 in Fonseca's map, towards the east end of the town, not far from the Carmelite convent.

innocent in the matter. I replied to the padre that never had. I dreamt either of stopping or of marrying in Goa. As it seemed to me, it was *she* who wanted to marry me, and had thus called in the padre as intermediary and made use of this artifice. I laid before him many similar affairs that had happened in India. But the priest was not a practical man, and had not been long in India; so he believed what the woman said, and made me out the culprit. He told me I was not speaking the truth; and finding my arguments did not prevail, I gave my word to the priest that in a short time. I would quit Goa, if he would only give me the time to prepare, and this he *did*.

At that time there was in the city of Goa an old friend of mine, a French merchant, named Clodio Menolhao.[1] He had a dispute with a shoemaker, a native of the country, over the price of a pair of shoes. The shoemaker was called a shameless cheat, but said nothing at the time, and went [224] away. Clodio had spoken thus without imagining what would happen to him. Two days had passed when, at eleven o'clock in the forenoon, the merchant shut up business and went off to get his breakfast. Passing down a narrow street, all of a sudden he beheld the shoemaker holding a small pot in his hand, with him one of his comrades holding a loaded blunderbuss. The Shoemaker inquired whether he preferred a shot from the blunderbuss or a potful of excrement. Clodio found himself in a scrape, and though it best, since he did not want to lose his life, to respond most humbly that he liked better to get a potful of filth than a shot from the blunderbuss. Abusing him right and left, the shoemaker threw the contents of the pot over him, and he, hastening his steps so as not to be seen, came into my house smelling most vilely, and in a great rage told me the story. I consoled him by saying that it was better to wash a live body than a dead one.

Thus the natives who live in the territory of the Portuguese are also troubled by the point of honour, and foreigners are not welcomed in those parts. If they do resort there, they should obey the precept of the three statues cut in stone, which stand in a wall close to the church of Sao Paulo, nowadays styled the

1. Probably identical with Claude Maillé, of Bourges, in Tavernier, i. 116, 117 (Gandikot, year 1652), and i. 286, 289 (Allahahad, year 1665), and the man of that name who befriended N. M. at Dihli in 1656 (see Part I., p. 48).

XXIX. Asad Khan, the Wazir

Vol. III *To face page 164*

'Bom Jesus.'[1] These three statues are of this sort: one has a finger touching its eyes; the second has the fingers on its ears; the third stands with the finger pressed to the lips. There is an inscription saying: 'He who sees, hears, and says nothing, lives a life devoid of care.' Let those be warned who want to pass through that country.

Another similar affair occurred when some well-born men were playing high and one of them lost. Upon the chair of the loser there leant another gentleman who had been governor of Mozambique. Inadvertently he jogged the chair. The gentleman sitting on it, put out at losing, turned his face and said: 'It seems your Honour learnt these courteous manners at Mozambique?' The ex-governor of Mozambique suppressed his feelings and went home, but ordered his Kaffirs to kill the gambler when he came out. This they did as he issued forth.

In the same city there was a Portuguese merchant, a rich widower, whose only daughter was very lovely. This girl suffered from a sore on the leg which no physician had been able to heal. Desponding at the state of his daughter's health, the father had recourse to a sturdy young Frenchman who was an able surgeon. This man he told [225] that if he could cure his daughter he would give her to him to wife along with an excellent dowry. The young man pledged himself and accepted the terms. In the short space of two months she was perfectly well. The girl, being now in good health, desired to marry the young man, both out of affection and for the obligation she was under to him. But the father, now his daughter was all right, gave orders that she was never to appear in the young man's presence, who by this time was not very cordially received when he came to the house.

Relying upon the promise made to him, the young main saw the father of the young girl and set forth his wishes. He was prayed to be seated, and his request would be at once complied with. The father went inside and brought out five hundred

1. No. 23 in Dutch map of Goa reproduced in Danvers, i. 259. It was at the south-east corner of the town. See also Fonseca, 'Goa,' p. 279, where there is a picture of the church. It is No. 31 on his map. It is mentioned in 'Pyrard de Laval,' edition Gray, ii. 54, 59, 97. These writers do not mention the three statues referred to Manucci.

Venetians (coins).[1] These were offered as a present, accompanied by a little speech. 'Your Honour has little knowledge of the Portuguese in India: a Portuguese who has to maintain his daughter would never consent to her marrying a foreigner. In this he spoke truth, for I have come across cases in India where they married their daughters to poverty-stricken Portuguese soldiers rather than give them to a rich and well-placed foreigner. The young man declined to accept the money, and departed for Europe without waiting to get anything more in India. This case happened in the year one thousand six hundred and seventy-eight (1678).

I could tell other stories about the men born m Portugal who came out to India, but I have no wish to expand. All I will say is that in the town of Macao there was a rich merchant who wrote to Goa to one of his representatives, enjoining him to send a Portuguese-born youth to be married to his daughter. This agent chose out of a number a well-built young fellow and sent him off to Macao. On reaching that place he was well received, and in a short time the marriage came off. At the end of the feast the newly-married pair retired, and instead of conciliating the wife, the bridegroom struck her till her face swelled. Never having expected such injuries, the wife passed the night in affliction. When morning came the bridegroom called for his breakfast, as if he deserved it. The girl's mother, seeing his confident manner, assumed that he had behaved well to her daughter. But the girl made great complaints to her mother of the way she had been treated. The mother imagined it was all right [226], and consoled her.

For two nights in succession he acted in the same way, and the bride, disheartened, fled from her husband. The parents, finding out he was a brute and unfit to be married, said to him that as he had illtreated his wife, they would for a time send him to Goa with some merchandise to trade with. A recommendation was sent that as soon as he reached that place he should be assassinated. To meet the required expenditure, five thousand *asharfis* were sent. On his arrival these orders were executed.

1. *Venetians*, a word used for *sequin* (Yule and Burnell, 964). See *Chick* (*ibid.*, 193), die short for *chickeen* (meaning *zecchino*, or *sequin*), a gold coin worth four rupees.

In his place they sent another man from Portugal, named Antonio Galvao. He was wisher, and marrying with a good dower, lived in peace with his wife. After some years he left Macao with his family, and came to live in the city of Goa. The viceroy, Antonio de Mello de Castro,[1] made him governor of the fortress at Chaul. On my passing through that place. I received from him good help on my way and great urbanity; he was very fond of foreigners. In the year one thousand six hundred and eighty-two (1682), when I came back to Goa, he was then dead; but I came across his son called Francisco Galvao, when we were neighbours. During the fighting with Shiva Ji [i.e., Sambha Ji, son of Shiva Ji] on the island of Santo Estave (Estevao),[2] he was hit by a ball from the enemy's cannon which took off his head.

There was another ridiculous business at Macao. A peasant fellow, born in Portugal, married a rich wife. Before entering the bridal chamber there came four young Chinese women-servants, well made and light-coloured, to wash their feet, carrying a ewer and basin of silver. Others bore delicate curled-up towels. The bridegroom, who was not accustomed to—in fact, had never seen—any grandeur, rose from his chair on seeing these girls, and made them a profound bow, and would not let them wash his feet. The reason he gave was that they were white as he was, and he was not worthy of so much honour. These answers disconcerted his father and mother-in-law. After a great deal of trouble, they managed to wash his feet, he helping and begging their pardon all the while, saying he was prodigiously obliged.

After this was over he was taken to a room decorated with rich stuffs. Seated on the bed was the bride, and, seeing her, he flung himself on his knees in the middle of the room, beating his breast and saying: 'I am your most devoted, O Santa Catherina mine !? The wife, seeing at once what a savage he was, rose to her feet and said: 'I am your wife; I am no Santa Catherina. This room is made ready for your honour to go to bed in.' By this time he understood that there was no turning back. Making a compliment to his wife, he begged her to occupy the bed, and he would sleep on the floor, not being worthy of

1. Governor, 1662-66 (Danvers, ii. 488, No. 56).
2. Santo Estevao, about two miles north-east of Old Goa. The fight was on November 25, 1683 (see *ante*, ii. 213).

any other place. The bride, finding herself thus embarrassed, after immense trouble got him to understand.

When the Portuguese were masters of India they were rich and powerful, living in pomp and magnificence. Owing to this fact the natives [227] of Portugal who came thence to India, never having seen or been accustomed to such grandeur, looked with awe on their Indian fellow-subjects. But this is no longer the case nowadays, for in India they have barely enough for food, and when they marry any girl they obtain on loan almost everything that is wanted for the wedding. The day after the wedding feast everybody comes and carries off whatever has been lent. The greater part of the house stands empty, the bride without jewels, the negro servants without ornaments, or other small things which I do not specify. As for the dower which the bridegroom received at a high valuation, there is not really the half of what was promised him.

It happened that a native of Portugal came to India with recommendatory letters to a citizen of Negapatao (Negapatam), who had a daughter he wanted to get married. He stated to this man the dowry he intended to give, and the young man agreed to it. When a few days had elapsed, a married man told him he should not marry anyone from that house. He offered his own daughter instead with a larger dowry. The ungrateful man from Portugal accepted the proposal, and spoke no more to his first friend. The latter on learning the facts was much annoyed.

The girl, seeing that the new arrival was governed by his interests, fond of her money and not of her, advised her father to promise him the double of what the other had offered. The self-seeker, being an ambitious fellow, came to the old man's house, and in a few days they went to church for the wedding ceremony. The priest asked the groom if he was willing to marry this lady. He replied most confidently in the affirmative. The same question was put to the bride, and she, in place of saying 'Yes,' lifted her hand and gave him a smart smack on the face, and said: 'With this big rogue I have no intention of marrying; he wants the money, find is not worthy of being my husband.' The man, put to shame, hurried out of the church, and was obliged to leave the district, for everyone in the city cracked jokes about him.

At the time this affair happened there was present at the same wedding a rich youth. Seeing this noble action of the damsel, he took a fancy to her, and asked if she would marry him. He would accept her without any money benefit. The bride lifted her eyes and had a look at him, then accepted him as husband, and the feast was held for him. This was conduct that had entered into no one's imagination. They lived pleasantly and honourably, for in this nation on the least jealousy or suspicion they kill a wife without hesitation, and I have seen many die thus [228].

Since I have promised to say something about the province of Kashmir I will insert here some notices of it according to what I have read. For further information you may refer to the book of Monsieur Bernier, who has written at length on this province. It is fertile, and abounds in fruit which is all very cheap, so that ten persons can regale themselves in eating it daily for one *pataca*, while moving about in a handsome boat through a great lake listening to music and other amusements, and also shooting different kinds of birds which are found with great ease.

My informant was Maria de Taides, one of the sisters living in the palace of King Shahjahan, who had been brought prisoners from Bengal, as spoken of under the reign of Shahjahan (I. 121). She told me that when Shahjahan went to that province for recreation, he desired to plant a garden by way of memorial, as is done by all kings and governors who proceed there. On digging the ground they unearthed an ancient dome, in which a light was beheld. Suspending work, they reported to the king. He ordered them to cover the place up. The physician, Muqarrab Khan,[1] asked the king's permission, as he wished to remove and inspect the lamp, and if it got broken he undertook, by his own ingenuity, to make another. Much against the king's will, he gave his consent, and Muqarrab Khan entered the dome "and tried to remove the light, but when he touched it, it fell and disappeared. The dome was covered in again, and the new

1. Muqarrab Khan, Shekh Hasan (*alias* Hasu), of Kairanah, now in the Muzaffarnagar district. He was Governor of Gujarat when Sir Thomas Roe reached India. He died on December 18, 1646, aged about ninety ('Ma,asir-ul-Umara,' iii. 379, and 'Tarikh-i-Muhammadi,' 1056 H.).

buildings were erected elsewhere. Muqarrab Khan was unable to replace the lamp by another.

After the lapse of some years 'Ali Mardan Khan came from Persia, the man who surrendered Qandahar to Shahjahan. The above-mentioned Maria de Taides was given to him in marriage, and he was made viceroy of Kashmir. He started the building of a palace, and in digging the ground to put in the foundations they came across an ancient building, and in it found a large hall. In the midst was a skeleton lying at full length. The diggers, on seeing this object, were afraid and began to run. The foreman wanted to force them to enter and break it up. They refused, for they would not venture inside. To give them courage the foreman entered first. On his coming to the extended figure it rose up with effort and gave him a heavy blow, so that he fell on the ground as if dead, and the workmen fled. On hearing of this matter, 'Ali Mardan Khan ordered them to remove the foreman, to leave the dead man untouched, and build up the place as it had been before. They administered remedies to the man who had been struck and he recovered, but had his mouth awry for the rest of his life. What I have said was recounted to me by Maria de Taides when she had become a widow and lived in Lahor, during the years I dwelt there, and by her I was treated with much urbanity and confidence.[1]

As I have promised to speak of the fruits of India, chiefly of the mango and jack-fruit. I may mention that the best mangoes grow in the island of Goa. They have special names,[2] which are as follows: mangoes of *Niculao Affonso, Malaiasses* (? of Malacca), *Carreira branca* (white Carreira), *Carreira vermehla* (red Carreira) of *Conde*, of *Joani Parreira, Babia* [229] (large and round), of *Araup, of Porta, of Secreta*, of *Mainato*, of *Our*

1. 'Ali Mardan Khan came to India in 1047 H. (1637), and was made at once Governor of Kashmir. He died on his way to Kashmir on the 12th Rajab, 1067 H. (April 27, 1657), and was buried at Lahor (Beale, 57; 'Ma,asir-ul-Umara,' ii. 798).
2. As we were told in Part II., 128, these names are derived from the first growers. According to Watt, 'Dictionary of Economic Products,' v. 150, mangoes are now divided into four classes: (1) Bombay; (2) Kharbuza; (3) Budayas, late varieties; (4) Barah-masa. The only name given by Watt corresponding to Manucci's list is the Affonso, or Afooz, which is still known all over India.

Lady, of *Agua de Lupe*. These are again divided into varieties, with special colour, scent, and flavour. I have eaten many that had the taste of the peaches, plums, pears, and apples of Europe. The mango is a little bit heating and laxative, and however many you eat of them, with or without bread, you still desire to eat more, and they do you no harm. While still unripe they are added to dishes, to pasties, et *cetera*. The juice of the ripe fruit mixed with milk is drunk, and is sustaining. They also make the fruit into preserves, which are exported to various places; various kinds of pickles are also made, which keep good for two years, and the stones are employed in medicine. The tree on which the mango is grown is the size of a walnut-tree; the fruit grows in clusters, like plums in Europe.

Nor must I neglect to mention a kind of mango that a Portuguese had in his house in the town of Goa; those mangoes were the best and the finest of those I have named. Through the fame of their having a flavour different from others, it came to pass that the Lord Inquisitor heard of this delicious fruit, and being desirous of tasting it, he sent a message to the Portuguese requesting him to send some. The servant boy of the Portuguese informed his master that a message had come from the Lord Inquisitor. On hearing this the owner was terrified and grew pale. Still, he managed to get to the door to hear the message. The messenger told him the Lord Inquisitor had heard that in the gentleman's garden was a tree producing a kind of mango most excellent, of which he would like to have a few, and therefore, the messenger added, he had come to ask for them. The Portuguese, on hearing this speech, came to himself and took heart, for he now knew that the messenger had not come to carry him off. Quite pleased, he pulled all the fruit from the tree and sent it off to the Lord Inquisitor with the greatest willingness. When the messenger had departed he set to work at once and uprooted the tree, for fear that another time a similar message should reach him. It had caused him great fear and tremor, for the Holy Office of the Inquisition requires to be held in great respect.

A propose of this case, I may mention that, on arriving in the town of Bassaim (Bassein) in one thousand six hundred and sixty-six (1666).[1] I was sent for by the commissary of the

1. More probably the year was 1667.

Inquisition. He was the prior of the Franciscan convent and three times over he examined me to find out about me and my life. Discovering nothing suspicious by his interrogatory, he made me swear upon a holy crucifix. Then, finding that there was nothing wrong in my replies, he embraced me, and treating me as an educated man with a clear conscience, he sent me away, saying that now, I was free and he would not send for me any more. I came to discover [230], in the course of time that my accuser was the father Damiao Vieira, a man expelled from the Jesuit order. This is the man who came as an envoy to Rajah Jai-Singh, and promised to reduce the city of Bijapur by miracle (see *ante*, Part II., 107).

Owing to the hatred in which he held me, he denounced me, and I was sent for by the commissary as I have just said. I was innocent, and could not make out why I had been sent for. As the friar found he could not harm me in this way, he came to Goa while I was living there, and urged a well-born man called Antonio de Souza Coutinho,[1] who had once been governor of India, to put an affront on me. But, like a wise man. he would not consent; he invited me to his house, and in his conversation told me to live very cautiously, for the father in question was not fond of me. Thus I was far from secure, and for these and other reasons I quitted Goa.

The jack-fruit I spoke of is of three kinds—*barca, papa,* and *pacheri* jack-fruit.[2] These fruits are very large; some weigh eighty pounds or thereabouts. The tree is of the size of a walnut-tree. The fruit referred to grows on the trunk and on the larger branches; some grow from the roots, and these are discovered by the earth being pushed up, also by the smell which the spot emits. This fruit has a green rind an inch in thickness with projections in the nature of thorns. It is known to be ripe by the smell it emits. Inside it is full of seeds, somewhat about the size of pears; these are very sweet, and on opening them, a juice issues sweet as honey, and in the

1. Antonio de Sousa Coutinho, one of three commissioners who held he government in 1651-52 (Dangers, ii. 488, No. 50).
2. Yule, 443, quotes P. Vincenzo Maria, 1672, for two kinds—*barca* and *papa* ('II viaggio all' Indie Orientali del P . . . Procuratore-Generale de' Carmelitani

middle are stones like the chestnuts of Europe. In these jack-fruit the seeds are sometimes white and sometimes red; some are hard, some are soft, and each variety has its special flavour.

Of these seeds mixed with rice-flour they make a kind of fritters, which in India are called *paniara*.[1] These, too, have their own flavour. When this fruit (the jack) is cut, a white liquid like bird-lime oozes from the rind, and sticking to the hand, it cannot be removed till it is anointed with oil. I will tell you a story of what I saw in the Carmelite convent. I was-walking up and down in the courtyard of the convent with the father prior, Frey Salvador de Nossa Senhora, when, as one of his servant boys passed below a jack-tree, one of the fruit fell and hit him on the forehead, flaying his whole face; it swelled like a pot and he could not see, and even after the wounds were healed he remained disfigured.

I must mention another fruit found in India called *ananas* (the pine-apple), which looks like a large pine-cone of Europe, and it has a corrugated rind. It is necessary to slice off this rind somewhat thickly to get rid of some natural depressions it has in it. The centre, when eaten, has a sweet, slightly acid, but very pleasant flavour. This fruit is heating, and if you leave a knife in it all night, the next day you will find it bitten into as if it had remained in aqua fortis. The distilled juice of this fruit is useful for dissolving stones in the kidneys and bladder, as I have found by experiment. The plant on which the fruit forms is a cubit in height; it grows up like an ear of corn, each plant yielding no more than one fruit. The leaves are a cubit in length and two fingers in breadth, with prickly edges. In no part of India have I seen them in such quantities as in Bengal, where they were large and fine. The reason for this is that it is a low-lying and humid country.

In the Mogul kingdom at different places, such as in the province of Gujarat, the mountains of Srinagar (? Garhwal), and of Butando (? Bhutan), grows a wild fruit exported from India to Europe. They are called *Mirobolanos quebulos* (Chebulic Myrobalan),[2] and are used in medicine. Among them, through

1. Possibly meant for *piuni*, a kind of sweetmeat—balls of rice-flour and sugar (Platts, 275).
2. *Terminalia Chebula* (Roxb.), in Persian *Halila-i-Kabuli* (Yule, 186, s.v. *Chevuli*, and 607-610, *Myrobalan*).

rarely, are found some of greater size than the others; these, if attached to the hand, are mildly purgative. They are valued for having this virtue, and great nobles give large sums to obtain them.

In Hindustan they also sow a grain that in Italian is called *cheche* (? *cece*)[1] and in French *pueê* (? *pois*). Of this grain I have seen large quantities used in Europe, chiefly on ship-board. Upon this plant when it is green there collects a dew which is very acid. The great nobles use this liquid instead of vinegar; and to gather it men go out before sunrise and run a sheet over the plants until it is thoroughly steeped. The liquid is then wrung out and kept in well-closed bottles. I state this because in Europe. I have neither seen nor heard of such a thing.

At the actual moment of writing I have received a letter from a monk of the Franciscan order called Friar Boa Ventura de Roma, and another from his companion. Friar Antonio de Castro Ocaro, and three others of his company named Ludovico Antonio Apiani, Joao Donato Meza Falche, and Joao Muliner. These men travelled from Rome through Turkey and Persia, and came to anchor in the port of Madras. Here they meant to take ship for China to carry on their mission. As they could not find a ship, they put up with me in my house [232].

After a year had elapsed there were some vessels sailing for Manila, and they embarked in these, meaning to continue thence the journey to their destination. On their arrival in Manila they encountered some other fellow-friars who had also left Rome for the same object. From that place (Manila) each went on his way as opportunity offered. The two friars above-named, together with Father Estevao Delicato, Antonio de Bareinome, and the illustrious lord Dom Alvaro de Benevento, of the order of St. Augustine, nominated as bishop for China, embarked in a Spanish ship of which the captain was Dom Joao Antonio Fernim de Andaya, nephew of the Maitre-de-Camp of Manila. Their destination was China, and setting sail, they made the harbour of Macao. The captain wished to land, and desired to take with him the lord bishop and the rest of the fathers. But they had been forewarned that if they went ashore on Portuguese territory they would be made prisoners

1. This must be the Italian *cece*, 'chick-pea,' 'vetch.'

and carried away to Portugal. They were thus unwilling to land, and made their excuses. The captain assured them that he would first sacrifice his life rather than that they should be touched. Confiding in him, but against their own desire, they disembarked. As soon as the Portuguese of Macao were informed, they made ready to apprehend them. On hearing this report, the captain had recourse to the Mandarin, who is the Emperor of China's magistrate. This official reassured him, and said he might keep his mind at rest, pledging his word that no one in his government would dare to interfere with them. After the lapse of some days the captain with the rest of the priests returned to the ship escorted by a company of soldiers sent by the Chinese governor, and in this way they escaped. The Portuguese had tried to do the same at Sao Thome, under an order received from Goa, but they could not carry it out, that country and its government belonging to the Mogul king.

There can be no about that something curious can be written about a tree which generally grows in India near the sea. It is called palm-tree or coco-tree. This tree has many roots about the thickness of the little finger, and it grows to a great height but increases very slowly. When seven years have passed it begins to yield fruit; ordinarily it occupies a circumference of two cubits and three-quarters, there or thereabouts, and it lives for a hundred years. At that age it grows to as much as ten arms' length; the stem is straight like the mast of a ship, with the branches [233] or palm-leaves at the summit about two arms in length. The leaves are two cubits long, lying close to one another like organ-pipes, three inches in breadth. In the middle of the leaf is a rib, of which they make brooms, *et cetera*. They also make mats from the branches, and these serve as carpets to the native of the country. They thatch houses with the leaves, mid they are also used as decorations at festivals. Every month a new branch appears in the middle of the palm-tree, and the oldest one falls off. Each tree has about thirty branches, and amidst them comes out the flower, enclosed by nature in a shield about a cubit long, nearly ten inches in circumference, and coming to a sharp point. When it has reached its proper size, the covering opens and the flower shows in the shape of brooms. On each branch of the flower you see its fruit stuck on like buttons, and these, swelling until they are like nuts, are then called *coquinhos* (little coco-nuts); they are used for many infantile complaints, such as diarrhoea and mouth-sores. When grown to the size of twenty-eight up to thirty inches round, and as much in length, they are called *lanha*.[1] The nut is then full of a sweet water, a drink of which is very refreshing. It is used in inflammation of the liver, the kidneys, and the bladder, and increases urination. It is also good for excessive heat of the liver, pains in the bowels, or discharges of mucus or of blood; it also refreshes in the season of great heat.

When the nuts have become ripe, the rind hardens outside and the water inside changes into a pulp called *coco*, which lies inside a hard shell that is called *chereta* (*chiratta*)[2] and is like a nut. When the rind has been drawn off, they use it to make ropes and cables. The *coco*, when out of its husk, has sixteen to twenty thumbs (*pollegadas*), which European physicians call *Nos Indica* (Indian nut). From the shells (*chereta* or *chiratta*) of these *cocos* are made dishes (*porzulanos*), vessels, spoons, handles, rings, rosaries, buckets to draw water, and many curiosities. The substance inside, which has about this thickness of an inch, is used for many dainties, being added to dishes in cooking. An oil is also made and usually applied by the women to their hair, which is their greatest delight. This oil is also employed for many medicinal purposes, such as in burns and ulcers, and an ointment is made with it. It serves for a purge to the lean and irascible, expels bile, and reduces adipose tissue.

Usually these trees [234] yield four or five flowers, and in each flower are contained fifteen to twenty *cocos*. Every year it produces fruit three or four times, according to the strength of the soil; in Goa I have seen it yield four crops.

Having finished talking of the palm-tree's fruit. I will now speak of its juice, called by the Indians *sura*.[3] When they want to draw the liquid, it is first necessary to open the flower, it being then in its rind; the end is cut, and then they begin to depress the whole flower in order to collect the juice, and fixing it, they attach

1. *Lanha, s.f.*, the fruit of the coco-tree when it is tender and green (H. Michaelis, 'A New Dictionary').
2. *Chiratta*, the Malayalam for the shell of the coco-nut ('Madras Manual of Administration,' iii. 197). For *Nos Indica*, or Indian nut applied to the coco-nut, see Yule, 228.
3. *Sura* (Yule, 874), the same as *toddy*, or the fermented sap of several kinds of palm. It is a Hindi word (see Platts, 'Dictionary,' 650).

to the end an earthen cup into which the substance drips. This is done twice a day, and each flower yields each time twenty ounces, more or less, of the distillation. When drunk fresh it is sweet and suave, but kept for twelve hours, it tastes like beer and goes to the head. It is used by the Indians in place of wine. From this liquid are manufactured *agua ardente*, vinegar, and sugar. The Indians ascend and descend these trees by clinging to the trunk and putting round it a rope of fibre, and into its ends they place their feet.

There is another class of palm-tree which is called *Palmeira brava* (the wild palm),[1] which takes many years to grow. This tree produces fruit in the month of March, and the yield lasts up to August. Inside each fruit there are ordinarily three lumps of soft pulp which are very refreshing. Eating them is useful in clearing the sight of those unable to see at night. In the same season it yields a liquid called *sura*, and it has the same effects as, and some resemblance to, the palm-tree juice already described. The spirits distilled from this palm-juice are the best. From the leaves they make fans, mats, sunshades, small baskets, and other curiosities. After the fruit has ripened the pulp hardens, and the juice is drawn from the shell; leaving this for a few days in the sun, it becomes a sort of marmalade, eaten by many of the natives in place of bread. From all these palm-trees good returns are obtained.

[Pages 235 and 236: I omit here a Japanese story of true-love, it being neither Indian nor historical.]

[237] In the year one thousand six hundred and ninety-four, eight years after my arrival in Madras, there was a love-story in which I am sure the reader cannot fail to be interested, so I will give a resume of it in a few words. There was in Madras a young man, born in the country, of humble parentage but lofty thoughts; his name was Joao da Cunha. He became enamoured of a young lady, and, as it seemed to him. Fortune could not favour him better than by making her his wife. As the father never gave it a thought nor could the young lady imagine such a thing, he had not the courage to declare his concealed feeling. He came to the house every day, nursing a mystic passion, and anything required to be done at the house was carried out by him with exactitude. But now and again he would say that many marriage

1. See Yule, 111, under *Brab*, the palmyra-tree, or *Borassus flabelliformis*; from the Portuguese *P. brava*, or 'wild' palm. In Hindi *Tar*. See also *ibid.*, 664, under *Palmyra*.

proposals were made to him, though he would not accept any one of these proposed brides, save one whom he strongly desired.

Seeing the little progress he was making, he went one day to the old father of the damsel, saying: 'This morning they bribed me to make a marriage by offering a dowry of one thousand *patacas* (2,000 Rs.). The person is of some position and of good fame; she is called Catharina da Silva. What advice does your Honour give me?' Well might it be said of him what is sung in an Italian comedy:

'Ardo e languisco in un cotinuo foco
Celato amante, e paleçato amico.
Le parlo, le discorro, burlo e gioco,
E delle pene mie nulla glie dico.
Cost amando e temendo, a pouco a pouco
Procuro di scubrirmi e mi disdico,
Procuro desiamar, e piu me infoco.'

(I bum and languish in continuous fire,
A secret lover, an avowed friend.
I speak to her, I discuss, joke and banter,
And of my sufferings not a word I say.
Thus loving and dreading, little by little
I try to declare myself, but do the reverse;
I try to forget my love, and only burn the more) [238].

The old man replied that it was quite certain that God had come to his aid; he must accept the proposal. They talked with such secrecy that the whole household heard what they said. Everybody congratulated him. He went on to say that he never meant to marry, if the woman were not to his liking. Some days elapsed, and they were continually asking him, by way of joke, when the wedding was to be. The man was put out, and not wishing to be counted a liar, made out a paper for the banns, showed it to them, and said he was going to the vicar to have the banns published. He delivered the paper to the vicar, who published the banns on two Sundays, the bridegroom, his sisters, and all his parents receiving everybody's congratulations. Everybody asked about the bride, and he said she was away from Madras and lying ill at Sao Thome, which is one league from Madras. Under this pretext he borrowed jewels from his relations and from the young lady's parents.

The following Saturday he went to confession, and during the mass, when about to receive the host, he fell to the earth in a swoon just as if he were dead, and thus remained nearly two hours before recovering his senses (a just chastisement for his evil deeds). It was thus that God hindered him from receiving the sacrament.

At night he left secretly, and made off to Sao Thome, and thence sent word to his relations that he was now married, that his wife was ill, and growing always worse. A few more days passed, and he removed to Monte Grande,[1] (Big Mount), a distance of two leagues from Sao Thome. There he hired a house, and with the greatest secrecy shut up one room, and said that in it was his suffering wife, whom he had brought to the Mount to recover health. From Madras his relations sent to ask whether they might come and see his wife. He sent back word not to trouble; he would send conveyances when the proper time arrived, for his wife was delirious, and it was not good for them to see her in that state. The inhabitants of the Mount, with the two hermits from Boa Vida, all went to visit him and give him a welcome, to which he in a very despondent tone answered: 'Cursed be the hour when I married, and cursed be the dowry paid me, for greed of money made me take a wife troubled with a thousand ailments, so that I was forced to transport her to this Mount to get her well, and I expect that here she will find a sepulchre.' They asked him what was the matter with her, to which he said not a word, but burst into tears and lamentation.

At this time a woman servant arrived; he had brought her with him on purpose, and she said the lady was very weak; it was two days since she had eaten anything. He told the maid to see if the sufferer could not take some broth or medicated drink. The woman went inside before everybody with the bowl of food, and said such words from within that those outside imagined the wife to be really very ill.

On the third day he made a figure of straw and enshrouded it so that it looked like a real corpse, and set up many candles which he had brought for the purpose. Then he sent a message

1. Monte Grande (Big Mount), what is now called St. Thomas's Mount, as contradistinguished from Little Mount (Monte Pequeno) (see 'Madras Manual of Administration,' iii. 435, 778). Monte Grande is eight miles south-west of Fort St. George (Madras), while Little Mount is only six miles *south*-south-west from that place, and two miles east of Monte Grande.

to the vicar to have the bell tolled for his wife [239]. Catharina da Silva, she being dead; and in great haste dispatched an advice to his relations at Madras that his wife had died, and they must all come to attend her funeral. The vicar descended to the plain, very angry that they had not sent word to him, so that he might have confessed her and administered extreme unction. The would-be husband answered that she had already been confessed at Sao Thome.

You should only have seen the excess of grief he displayed over the bundle of straw! Everybody was much affected, and the whole night long the two hermits sat in vigil over the body, in company with all the poor of the Mount and some other devout persons who were there. From time to time an old woman, whose name was Bernarda, bribed beforehand with a small sum, asked Joao da Cunha, 'What of the lady Catharina da Silva? The day before yesterday I saw her with these very eyes alive, and to-day she is already dead! How much better for your Honour not to have married her, for you would not to-day have been styled a widower.' During this time the servant-woman cried: 'O my mistress! How could you yield yourself to this wretch who had so long followed you? When I supposed that I was to see you happy, you were going to your death.' Joao da Cunha fell upon the corpse of straw, and emitted such cries that all present were moved to compassion. Fearing a fit, the Hermits and the other guests present wanted to carry him away and place him on a bed.

The cheat, suspecting that those surrounding him might go and inspect the pretended corpse, wrested himself out of the arms of the Hermits, and once more threw Himself upon the sack of straw and renewed his exclamations. Very early next morning his relations arrived, and they wailed greatly. With a considerable number following the cortège, the burial took place at the foot of the Mount, and each man retired to his own home. On that day he distributed much alms, and ordered many masses to be said.

But as the secret lay among some poor women, it soon began to be said that what had been interred was a straw figure. The rumour spread, and it came to the ears of the lord bishop. He sent orders to open the tomb, and they lighted upon the straw figure, buried there eight days before. The sorcerer then made himself scarce, but a month afterwards came to pray pardon for his offences, and he was then given absolution. The story was known all over Madras and Sao Thome, and everybody was greatly amazed at Joao da Cunha's trick and his temerity.

All this he had done to embezzle a few ornaments and a little cash because he could not get the old man's daughter in marriage, as stated at the beginning. The Hermits Pascoal de Quintal and Manoel da Cunha, when they knew of the fraud, complained bitterly of their neighbour, Bernarda. They said by her weeping she had admitted that the straw figure caused her great grief. I may add that for many a year they ceased to believe in any old women, having found in them much deception. I ask pardon of the gentlemen who read this, for there are many old women of this kind full of gall; from such old women, who live by similar deceptions, I counsel them to flee as from the very devil [240].

Since I have spoken of the *bezoar* stones of the kingdom of Gulkandah (III. 59). I will also mention something that I have heard from monks who have been in Borneo. They told me that in that country was an island where there were many baboons. The natives inflict wounds on them with a small poisoned arrow shot from a *zarvatana* (blow-tube).[1] The baboon, aware that the wound is poisoned, takes to flight at once, and goes to find a certain herb which is an antidote. The blood is then stanched and the wound closes, but at the spot, instead of flesh, the blood congeals into a stone which possesses the virtue of the plant that was eaten. The natives recognise these baboons by their height, and killing them, withdraw the stone which has greater potency than any others. In this country of Borneo there are also produced diamonds, and much gold and pepper.

Good fortune still continues to wait on Aurangzeb. It happened that in the year seventeen hundred (1700) a piece of the wall fell at the fortress of Serpali,[2] in the Karnatik, and in the space disclosed was a found a treasure, for the disinterment of which my friend Sefi can (Safi Khan) was deputed. This

1. *Sarbatani, Sarbacane,* a form from the Spanish, Portuguese, and Italian, going back to the Arabic *zabatana* (Yule, 795). Yule's only instance is of 1516; here we have one of 1700.
2. Possibly meant for Shiyali, a town in the Tanjor district, 131 miles south-south-west of Madras ('Madras Manual of Administration,' iii. 827).

was in the month of November in the year seventeen hundred (1700).

Though Aurangzeb holds himself to be very intelligent and a grand plotter, none the less does Shiva Ji (*i.e.*, the Mahrattahs) employ against him his own artifices, as I have demonstrated on many occasions. One of these plots happened in the year one thousand six hundred and ninety-eight. Shiva Ji announced that the King of Gulkandah had escaped from prison at Daulata bad, that he (Shiva Ji) had carried him off, and that he was in Mahrattah territory. His army, it was announced, was getting ready to restore him to his kingdom. They wrote fictitious letters to a number of the Gulkandah officers who had taken service with Aurangzeb inviting them to join this enterprise.

This report was the cause of many desertions of soldiers to the side of Shiva Ji, among them being a leader called Purdil Khan, who governed a province containing seven forts. Confident that the story was true, he made these forts over to Shiva Ji, and deserted to him in person with all his men, fully persuaded that he should find his king there. When he discovered that he had been deceived, there was nothing else for him but to take service with the Mahrattahs, and plunder the territories of the Mogul.

The report caused great anxiety to Aurangzeb, for it spread in all directions, and to prove that there was nothing in it, he was forced to withdraw Abu,l Hasan from the fortress of Daulatabad, and transfer him to that of Balier (? Gwaliyar). He was hidden in an *ambari* (high-sided elephant howdah), or a closed litter, so that no one should know, and there went with him a large guard. Aurangzeb was forced into this demonstration entirely with the object of disabusing the people's mind, and it seems to me that years ago he must have sent orders to have him killed at that fort, Balier (? Gwaliyar), because no one has heard of him again since he was put in that prison[1] [241].

Finding that after nineteen years of warfare he was still unable to prevent the raids made into his territories by the Mahrattah armies, Aurangzeb decided in the month of November, one thousand six hundred and ninety-nine (1699),[2] to take the

1. Native historians say nothing about any removal from Daulatabad, but say that Abu,l Hasan died there in 1114 or 1115 H. (1702-3).
2. Aurangzeb camped outside Satarah on the 25th Jamda II., forty-third year, 1111 H. (December 18, 1699) (Ma,asir-i-'Alamgiri,' 413).

field in person. He invested a fort called Sataraguer (Sataragarh). While he was making this effort and fighting with rocks, the armies just referred to (the Mahrattahs), acting more vigorously than before, sacked and plundered cities, towns, and villages. They seized and carried off whatever was to be found, stopping supplies of treasure and food on their way to the royal army. The king's troops, owing to the officers' sloth, timidity, or prudence, did nothing to hinder them. Thus it was that the royal army suffered as much from hunger as from fighting, and other evils arose from the drinking of noxious water.

But good luck was still on the side of Aurangzeb, for it happened that Rama Raia (Ram Raj),[1] the Shiva Ji, fell ill and died of his complaint in the month of March of the year one thousand seven hundred (1700). The commanders of fortresses, finding themselves without a prince, and encouraged by gifts and promises from Aurangzeb, made over some of their strong places. The chief one so surrendered was Sataragarh, and five others of little value.[2] But the raiding armies never desisted from their free action, still continuing their accustomed efforts. In order to carry on the government, Ramchant Pundit (Ram Chandar, the Pant Amat),[3] a man of good judgment, first counsellor and minister to Shiva Ji, took action. Upon the death of his master, he gave the title of prince to a minor son of the deceased. This child bore his grandfather's name, Shiva Ji, and at this moment of writing the usual warfare is being continued under him.

During this march (of Aurangzeb) it happened that the son of a rajah called Quexanchin (Kishn Singh) had some sort of dispute with his father, and going to the king, offered to become a Mahomedan on condition that his father's territories were made over to him. The king agreed, and allotted him some

1. Raja Ram had spitting of blood and inflammation of the lungs (Grant-Duff, 175). After lingering for thirty days, he died at Singarh about the middle of March, 1700.
2. The author of the 'Ma,asir-ul-Umara,' i. 293, says: 'It is notorious that in the closing years of Aurangzeb's reign many of Shiva Ji's forts that were recovered from his officers were obtained by money expended by the Mughal nobles, who hoped thereby to secure the Emperor's favour for their apparently successful fighting and exertions.' The remark is made with regard to the year 1704.
3. The 'Pant Amat' was the second official in Shiva Ji's council of eight ministers (Grant-Duff, 118).

troops to depose the father and obtain the country for himself. After this rajah had reached his home country, his mother was clever enough to poison his father. When the son knew this, he left the royal camp very early in the morning after cutting the throats of all the Mahomedans in it, and made for his own territories. The viceroy of Ugein (Ujjain), called Moctiar Can (Mukhtar Khan), father-in-law of Bedar Bakht, attempted by the king's order to suppress the rising, but was killed in battle along with his son, while his army was annihilated. On finding himself victorious the rajah plundered the city of Ujjain, and continued to ravage the royal territories at the head of forty thousand horsemen. The king was obliged to send another army with fresh orders.[1]

It is usual to have such occurrences in this empire, and war never ceases. In the month of September of the same year (1699) Aurangzeb withdrew from his undertaking with great loss in troops and heavy expenditure. The war still goes on, and is becoming more severe. Aurangzeb is in the kingdom of Bijapur, encamped near a village called Barrampur (Brahmanpuri),[2] and today it is December of one thousand seven hundred (1700).

During this retreat, made by Aurangzeb after having taken the fortresses of Shiva Ji as above stated, he resolved to remove by poison Sultan Sikandar, King of Bijapur, who was a prisoner in his camp. He was now thirty years of age, and the deed was done for fear of his taking to flight and causing a fresh rebellion. The cause of this captive king being put to death was the flight from prison of Sambha Ji's son,[3] who made his escape into his

1. Bedar Bakht was the eldest son of A'zam Shah, second son of Aurangzeb 'Alamgir. He was married to Mukhtar Khan's daughter on the 15th Muharram, 1098 H. (December 1,1686) ('Ma,asir-i-'Alamgiri,' p. 284). Mukhtar Khan was appointed to Malwah (in which Ujjain is situated) in the forty-first year of Aurangzeb 'Alamgir (March 24, 1697, to March 2, 1698). He was not killed there, but in the forty-fifth year was transferred to Agrah ('Ma,asir-ul-Umara,' iii. 656). He died in 1121 H. (March, 1709) ('Tarikh-i-Muhammadi').

2. 'Alamgir's camp arrived from Bijapur at the village of Brahmanpuri (renamed Islampuri), on the Bhimra River, on the 17th Shawwal of the thirty-ninth year, 1106 H. (May 31, 1695). He left it after four years ('Ma,asir-i-'Alamgiri,' 375, 408).

3. I can trace no escape of a son of Sambha Ji's; all his sons were) prisoners at Aurangzeb's death in 1707. Can the reference be to Ram Raja's escape

own territories, and raised fresh armies to wreck vengeance upon Aurangzeb [242].

I have now satisfied in substance the reader's curiosity, and given him all I had promised at the beginning of this work. I say 'in substance,' for I have not placed in my work any but the matters of greatest importance, holding it to be superfluous to choke the volume with petty details. Still, as I can assure the reader, so many are the things that have occurred to me since I left my native land, that I should never get to the end if I began to tell them all; and as I am an aged man. I should never be able to give satisfaction to my friends in the object with which I undertook this labour. What I intreat of the inquiring reader who by chance comes to this part of the world is that he do not assume anything of all I say to be of little account. My purpose is that he may not afterwards have to repent himself when there is no longer any remedy. This is the design I have followed in this work. If perchance (as is the ordinary habit). he does not care to take my advice. I shall live consoled by the fact that he will be able to blame none but himself. All he can do is to repeat what is said in my country: 'Chi he cauza del suo mal, pianga se stesso' [The causer of evil to himself has to weep for himself]. If he attentively considers my instructions, it is certainty that he will pass his time well, and every day will thank me for my advice.

During the time that I have been composing this book I have acquired a secret which from its rarity seems to me fit to be imparted to the reader. It is a thing that might benefit many, and it has been tested by me and seen by many of my friends. I have found the bone of an animal which, when added to certain medicaments, has the greatest virtue against every kind of poison and venom. The following is the mode of application:

If any person should be bitten by a viper or other snake (*cobra*), even if it be a hooded one (*de capello*), a mad dog, a scorpion, a tarantula, or other venomous animal, a small cut is made at the site of the wound, if it is not already sufficiently open. Over this is tied the liver of a cock, and the remedy against poison, in a quantity equal to one or two grains of pepper,

---

from Jinji in 1697? (see Grant-Duff, 170). Sikandar 'Adil Shah died in Aurangzeb's camp in 1112 H. (June, 1700, to June, 1701).

is ground on a stone. Mixed with water, this is given to the person poisoned, and the bone referred to is applied at the place to which the poison has risen, causing it to flow back to the bite. By doing this the patient is entirely restored [243]. This remedy may be applied although the patient appears beyond recovery. For the bite of a scorpion or other small animal, it is not necessary to administer it internally; after attaching the liver for a little, it suffices to apply the bone in the way I have said above. I have often made trial of this in these lands. For those who have drunk poison or eaten it, it is enough to give a potion of half the quantity that I have named above. I give the reader this information, because there are found to be in this India many animals that may be used with much profit to mankind.

As I have given many general warnings about the rules by which everyone should live in the Mogul kingdom and throughout this country, by referring to which men may govern their conduct and evade evil encounters, it seems to me appropriate to place at the end of this book a warning for the reverend father missionaries who, moved by holy zeal, desire to come here and work for the salvation of souls.

First of all it is necessary for a missionary desirous of coming here to bring with him some money, to meet the initial expenses which are necessary to start this holy work, for to hope to acquire here any alms for such necessary expenses is a mistake. For want of these I have seen many a friar deprived of the power of carrying out his intentions, and thereby much dejected. The Christians living here in these territories are mostly poor, while those who have money, all of whom give themselves out to be Portuguese, never afford any aid to non-Portuguese missionaries. Most of them hold the opinion that it is solely by being a Portuguese that you can be of the Catholic and Roman faith. Everybody else they designate by the name of 'foreigner.' They do not allow the name of Catholic to all those who have received holy baptism. To say a man is a 'foreigner' is the same as saying he is not a Roman Catholic. Solely by the means they have up to this time acquired are the fathers of the Society (*i.e.*, the Jesuits) free of this hindrance, and therefore, although suffering the same persecutions as others, can yet do much far the service of God. For they have money, enabling [244] them to incur the necessary expenses, which I will detail below. Every friar should arrive provided with all that is necessary, and then he can do service for God in conformity to his befitting zeal.

Throughout the territories of the Mogul missionaries do much for the service of God by baptizing many infants (for in regard to grown persons that is an impossibility), and to be able to confer on infants this benefit it is necessary that they know the aft of medicine. They must be able to cure ulcers and to bleed. They will then be in demand at many places; and when they see that the infants are at the point of death, they can sprinkle them with the water of baptism. In this way not a day would pass that they would not gain for heaven some soul or other.

Thus it happened with me at Lahor: When I became a physician I baptized in eight years more that fifteen thousand [? infants], besides those I found on the roadsides moribund, and whom I baptized. It became so well known that whenever medicine was asked for water would be sprinkled; that many women, both Mahomedans and Hindus, imagined that if their infants were sprinkled with water before they fell ill they would never suffer from any complaint. Thus they would entreat me to sprinkle the child. But I baptized none except those infants who, as I could clearly see, were bound to die. By this means I have baptized sons of persons in very good positions, princes, and even some of the blood royal. With this profession of doctor it is possible to do some service for God.[1]

The way in which missionaries ought to live is as follows: It is necessary to have a useful horse and one camel. On the latter are carried the requisite supplies, both of drugs and other instruments. In this country it is incumbent on a doctor to prepare medicines, ointments, and distillations—in fact, all things that appertain to the apothecary's office. Many a time it is also necessary to instruct as to the fashion of preparing the patient's food. It would be a good thing to bring from Europe antidotes to poisons, for frequently it happens, especially among the nobles, that poison has been given, as may have been seen in my narrative, I also give warning that it is a necessary thing to travel accompanied by some person of confidence, and never to trust absolutely to

1. Many instances of the baptism of the unconscious moribund will be found in the Jesuits' reports in 'Lettres Edifiantes et Curieuses.'

the natives of the country. There should also be some rarities for giving to great persons to preserve their good-will.

After they have got used to the country and have obtained the repute of good doctors, the fathers will never be in want of occupation to fill their lives and sustain themselves [245] reputably. To do this it is not necessary to look miserable, but they must show themselves of a generous and charitable spirit.

The greater part of the persecutions suffered by the missionaries who do not come from Portugal is caused by the Portuguese and the local Christians, who admit no other arguments but what the Portuguese tell them. The Portuguese in this India here, under cloak and in the name of their king, do such things against missionaries that it is impossible a king so pious and so Catholic, eager for the extension of the holy faith, could be aware of all the persecutions suffered by the missionaries and done to them under his name. For I have seen such things, and have had very certain knowledge that the king does not consent to them. But nowadays the Portuguese are in such a condition that they use their king's name to vent their own passions, and on seeing anything to be gained, they interfere and say at once it is according to the king's order. If they do not see any convenience to themselves they say, on the contrary, that they make no account of their king. Thus it is a sorrow fit to make one weep tears of blood to behold such improper methods, so widely divergent from those they followed in the days of old.

The Portuguese, in any negotiations they have with the Moguls or the rajahs in India, are accustomed to send priests as ambassadors. It appears to them that by so doing they make certain of success; but by the experience I have had, and from what I have heard from the leading men at the court, there could not be a greater error committed. For it causes everybody to think of and estimate the King of Portugal as an impecunious king, who is unable to provide the requisite expenses for an ambassador, and therefore sends *faqirs*; for such is their conception of the position of these fathers. They have veneration and consideration for these whenever they see them exempt from worldly business. On the contrary, directly they mix in temporal concerns they think slightingly of them and of the princes who send them; for they hold it as true that states governed by the counsels of *faqirs* must he badly ruled, because the profession of a *faqir* is to live far apart from all the affairs of this world, and to consider nothing but things of God. Hence proceeds the little estimation in which the natives- of India hold the King of Portugal. They see on the one side that in Goa and in all its provinces nothing is done without the advice of priests; on the other hand, they see that the Portuguese do not have in their territories abundance of commerce, which is also* one of the grounds from which they infer the greatness of a king. The reason for their having these opinions is that the Mahomedan *faqirs* never mix themselves up in any matter of government or politics; on the contrary, they flee from them. It is the same for the Hindus with their *jogis*, who hold the character of priests, as I have stated in my history.

[Pages 246 and 247 are blank.]

[248] There are to be seen commonly in this country a want of the fear of God and of love to one's neighbour. I will relate here some cases which happened in my sight of a diabolic nature. It is a practice very common among the Hindus and others, which does not fail also to lay hold of the Christians living in this country, who from want of true faith allow themselves to be persuaded into such-like errors.

A woman wished to become with child, and not succeeding with drugs, had recourse to a magician. His orders were that at midnight she should go and stand below a large forest tree which in India is called *badd* (*bad*, *bar*)[1] It produces a small red fruit. Here she was to perform the sacrifice as to which he had instructed her. She then became pregnant, and the tree referred to became sterile, and never yielded fruit so long as it lived.

In Bassahim (Bassein), a town of the Portuguese, there was a well-born woman—I will not mention her name—who wished to have a son to whom to leave her wealth. Secretly she had recourse to a magician, who by diabolic arts made it so appear that she was really pregnant, with all the signs that women have who are about to bring forth. When the time came she was seized with pains, and several ladies came to assist, and she brought forth a tray full of sand; thereupon the delivery was complete. She lost all the great expenses she had gone to in preparing a feast for the occasion.

---

1. The *Ficus Indica*, or Indian fig-tree.

There was another case in Sao Thome about the same time. A young friar had a woman-servant who cooked for him. This woman threw such a spell over him that he could not exist without her for one moment. Anyone who went to visit the friar was an annoyance; he sent them away as soon as possible, and the few words he uttered would all be in praise of the serving-woman. This friar fell ill of diarrhoea, and was already almost at the point of death. In place of fixing his mind on God to secure salvation for his soul, his whole concern was for the servant. At this time there arrived some friars from Goa, and seeing him thus forsaken, knew that he was bewitched. They seized the negro woman, and by force of torture made her relieve the friar of the spell she had thrown over him. After this happened he could not bear to see her or hear her name. It did not take long to cure him of his disease (? the diarrhoea).

I will tell you another instance. There was a Portuguese called Thome Borges de Villalobo, an inhabitant of Sao Thome. To recover after an illness he moved with his family to the foot of the four hills,[1] which are three leagues from Sao Thome. After some days had passed he felt relieved of his illness. But one night, failing to get to sleep, he went out to walk about the town by moonlight. Hearing in a house the sound of dancing and the tinkling of bells, his curiosity led him to look through a peep-hole in the door. There he saw two small boys, well clothed, with bells on their feet, wearing jewels, and holding bows and arrows in their hands. Opposite them was a magician seated on the floor, holding a rod with which he struck the ground. To the sound of these strokes the children danced. From time to time the magician uttered a cry, and by reason of the gyrations made by the boys in dancing, their eyes became as flaming coals of fire, their faces heavy and fearful to behold. When this condition arrived, they swooned and fell to the ground as if dead.

The man's wife, awaking, saw the door open and her husband absent from the room. She went to look for him, and found him lying senseless at the magician's door. Hastening home, she

1. The Rev. F. Penny suggests that the place intended is most probably Vandalore or Vendalur, nine miles (three leagues) south-west of San Thome. An alternative identification he puts forward is Pundmulli (now pronounced Punamalli), west-north-west of the same place at the same distance.

brought her brothers and servants, and in dead silence they removed him to his house. There they began to lament. The lady [249] who owned the house, hearing the weeping, came to them. She was told what had happened to the husband, found lying in front of such-and-such a door. The old lady showed amazement, so that all present were more disturbed than before. Upon seeing this the old lady consoled them, saying that she knew a cure. Leaving home, she had recourse to the magician, who appeared in about an hour. Entering the house, he said there had been too great temerity in seeking to see things which did not concern one. All the relations entreated him to tell them some cure. He gave the man certain fumigations, and placed medicine upon his eyes. After one hour had passed the patient began to move, and when morning came he was able to tell his story, as I have above recounted it. After that he went back to Sao Thome. At the present time the widow of that Portuguese, being now seventy years of ago, lives in my house, and the poverty in which she was left has forced her to do this.

In the days when I was at Agrah I went to pay my respects to the brother of Shaistah Khan, who was called Faracfal (Falak-fal),[1] which means 'The Diviner.' He was a very ugly man, and never appeared at court for fear the people would joke at his odd physiognomy. This gentleman had a magician who gave him much information about what was going on. In my presence the magician raised his head and voice, saying that apples, pears, peaches, and several other fruits would fall. Accordingly, in the sight of all there present, they began at once to fall. This was a thing to be remarked on, for at that season there were no such fruits in that country. He offered me some to eat, but I declined to take them, knowing them to be a product of magic, so I thanked him for his kindness. This thing he could do whenever he liked.

As it happened, there came to Sao Thome on the loss of Malacca[2] a widow woman with two unmarried daughters, and took up her abode in the street called Galeras. This woman was

1. The histories do not speak of any son of Asaf Jah under this name. It may be either Farrukhfal (Happy Omen) or Falak-fal (Heaven Augury).
2. Malacca surrendered to the Dutch on January 14, 1641 (Danvers, ii. 281).

poor and without protectors, but of a noble family, of good behaviour, respected, and of a retired life. In the same town dwelt a youth called Joao Coelho, who was very rich. He did not know how much he had, and at that time did not count his money, but measured it by bushels as if it were grain. Relying upon his wealth, and seeing that the above woman was poor, he sent people to intrigue with the elder daughter, asking her to become his mistress. This insulting message she imparted to her mother, and it caused great indignation in the family.

The widow had a servant girl of Rajava[1] race, who noticed the anger there was in the household, and made bold to ask her mistress the cause of so much indignation. They told her what was going on. Thereupon the Rajava woman asked leave from her mistress to live out of the house for some days, till she could plan a remedy for such impertinence. The widow, who was aggrieved by the young man's overture, willingly gave leave of absence to the servant girl.

The reader should know that these Rajava people are for the most part magicians, and have a compact with the devil. After five days had passed, the servant girl returned to the house of her mistress with other three of the same race. She consoled the lady, saying that in a few days she would secure a remedy, and would obtain satisfaction of her desire. She asked for a separate room for these others to live in, into which no one must enter. The mistress consented. After three days they rubbed a medicine on the eyes of the girl that the youth was in pursuit of, and directed her that when he was passing she should take post at the window.

Not many hours had elapsed when the youth, as was his practice every day, passed as anticipated in sight of the window to show himself off. The girl appeared at once, and then withdrew. When Joao Coelho saw his beloved, in place of going on his way, he came forthwith straight to the door [250] of the widow, and began to knock, most humbly asking leave to enter and speak to the lady of the house. The Rajava servant advised them not to be in any hurry to open. The youth, growing impatient, began to knock vigorously, and shouted for them to open. They answered him from the window by abuse, ordering him to go away. To such an insolent fellow they would not open. On hearing

1. Rajava may be intended for Rakshasa, a demon, a goblin.

this answer, he prostrated himself on the ground, and said he had come for a proposal of marriage to her whom he had seen at the window.

They allowed him to enter. Then he sent off his servant-man to fetch a priest to marry them. This was carried out at once without delay, and the bride became lord over the husband and all his wealth, which turned out to be the cause of his undoing. Thus does it frequently happen that money in the hands of persons like this causes their perdition. After the lapse of some time, she found that her husband loved her passionately, and she had not the liberty of action that she wanted. She asked the servant-girl to find a device by which she might be able to live more according to her own fancy. The sorceress made an oil with which they anointed the soles of the husband's feet when asleep. He never more paid any heed to his wife, and noticed nothing that went on in the house. Next she resorted again to the servant-woman for means of getting hold of a young man for whom she longed.

The cunning sorceress by her arts fulfilled the desire of her mistress, and the youth came and went when she so required. The younger sister, seeing the delights her sister enjoyed, became desirous also of passing her days according to her pleasure. She informed the Rajava servant of her intention. As the magician was practised in curing such complaints, she made over to the young lady the youth that she affected, and he, too, came and went like the other one.

The Rajava woman warned the two sisters never to take betel from the hands of their lovers, for if they acted to the contrary, never again would the young men leave the house. Paying no heed to the warning of the sorceress, they took betel from the hands of their lovers, who never quitted the house again, but ruled over their mistresses as they pleased. The elder sister became enceinte. Her lover told her that when the procession of Corpus Christi passed, as it was to do the next day, she must not go to the window to lock out.

On the day of the procession, many ladies came from different parts of the town to the house of the aforenamed lady. When the procession was passing, the lady visitors noticed the absence of the lady of the house. They sought for her, and partly by force, partly by entreaty, dragged her to the window. On beholding the pyx of the most holy sacrament, she fainted and fell, getting a great wound on the head, and thereby arose great outcry and disturbance.

The younger sister, who was in a room apart, hearing the noise, came out hastily to see. As she was coming her lover appeared and gave her a blow which knocked out one of her eyes. Upon this the confusion and the uproar were redoubled. The people in the procession, observing the disorder in the house, entered in numbers to accommodate matters. The three companions of the Rajava woman, seeing succour entering the house, disappeared at once in a little boat of dough made of fine flour, which they had prepared for the purpose. Along with them went the two lovers, and the two sisters were left wounded in the house. The Rajava woman, wanting to make off like the others, could not reach either the boat or the other fugitives. She was tortured, and confessed that what has been told above was done by her diabolical arts. She was hanged and quartered. The elder sister brought forth a son, to whom she gave the same name as the father, and all the town called [251] him 'Son of the Devil.'

This family came to be in such a state that they went round asking for alms, and the race continued until the loss of the city. These (? their houses) were so badly haunted that no stranger could dwell there with safety to his progeny. It chanced that there came three strangers, and finding no place to shelter themselves, they took these houses, and hardly was it seven o'clock at night when there came a dead man with chains on his legs, and walked round the room where the said men were. On seeing this figure, they fled in great haste to the door, and came out tumbling over each other, and hurting their hands and feet. When the skeleton reached the window, it said: 'You were lucky to run away so quickly; if you had delayed at all. I should have had to take notice of your temerity.' Upon hearing this, they turned and ran until they were placed in safety.

To these same houses there came to live a captain and his company of soldiers. He was called Pe-de-patta (? Flat-foot)—a very valiant man; and where he planted his foot, there he stood fast. Then at six o'clock in the evening of the first day they saw a soldier come from outside, and pass through the midst of the soldiery without making any salute. He made his way to one of the rooms. Again oh the second night the same thing happened;

on the third day they made ready to find out who the intruder was. When he entered the house, they ran after him, their bared swords in their hands. Those pursuing were fourteen men, who went into the room he had entered. Within they measured swords, but the aforesaid man had vanished, and the fourteen men wounded each other, and all came forth in evil case. Then next day they gave up the house, and Joao Coelho came to it and lived in peace.

In Madras I knew a Portuguese, of good position, honoured, and wealthy. His name was Joao Pereira de Faria, and he was married to Donna Maria de Souza. He was a great friend of mine, and had great confidence in me, he and all his family. He came and settled in Madras upon the loss of Negapatao (Negapatam).[1] His wife told me of what happened to her, and her story was confirmed by many.

One of her slave-girls was much favoured by her husband. This lady's-maid wanted to kill her mistress by magic arts. For this purpose she stole some money from her master and resorted to a young Hindu servant of the house to get him to take measures to put an end to her mistress's life. When the lady was dead she would become head of the house, and would reward him. The youth accepted the task (for such persons when there is anything to gain have neither religion nor conscience). He tried to do what the slave-girl wanted, and not succeeding, had recourse to a magician. This man directed him to bring some hair, nail-clippings, and a piece of defiled cloth belonging to the lady. The youth reported to the slave-girl, and she sent what was required. When some days had passed, the youth made over to her a doll into the head of which had been thrust one pin, the point of which reached nearly to the stomach, and another pin was stuck into the naval coming half-way down the legs.

She was told that at midnight she must go entirely naked into the middle of the house-garden, holding up in one hand the doll, and in the other a piece of burning wood. Orders as to what she was to do were added. She was warned that while acting as above there would appear a black cat, but she must not be

1. Naga-patanam, 'Snake-town,' in the Tanjor (Tanjam + ur, 'Shelter + place') district, lat. 10° 46′, long. 79° 53′, 160 miles south-southwest from Madras; taken by the Dutch from the Portuguese in 1660, and conquered by the English in 1781. ('Madras Manual of Administration,' iii. 580). For Negapatam, see also III. 179.

afraid. The wretched woman did as instructed. Going to the centre of the courtyard, she set fire to the ends of the doll's feet and hands' At that moment there appeared to her the aweinspiring cat, with eyes which looked like two flames of fire. On seeing such an apparition the slave-girl was in terror.

At this time [252] there arose in the house loud cries and commotion. Being frightened, the girl went into her mistress's chamber as if she wanted to help, carrying with her the doll, which she hid in the sacking of the lady's bedstead. In her hurry and agitation she did not thrust it well in, so that it remained half hanging out. The lady of the house was in mortal anguish, complaining that she felt on fire from her head to her stomach, and from the navel down to her lower limbs, her hands and feet burning with insufferable heat and agony.

They called in the doctors, who could not determine what ailment it was, and the remedies given her did not take effect. For several days the lady suffered in the same way. Then it chanced that a child of three years, playing about, went under the bed and saw a doll half projecting. It pulled it out with a cry of delight, and, playing with it, showed it to its nurse. When the woman saw it she recognised at once what it was, and showed it on the spot to her mistress and the rest of those present, saying that it was a piece of magic and through it she had suffered.

Upon making sure of this, they called in a Hindu magician, who as soon as he entered the house went to Joao Pereira de Faria, and told him he was the cause of his wife's sufferings. He was ashamed, and hung his head. Upon seeing the image the magician told the wife that in a short time she would be restored to health, but the people of the house must not be alarmed if they saw her lie without sense or movement. For his purposes the magician retired into a room and very slowly drew out the pins, unstitching the image bit by bit in each separate member. Finally he opened up the abdomen, where were found the nail-clipping, the hair and the cloth spoken of above, with Other mixed items put in by the magician. When the image had been entirely pulled to pieces, he threw it into a vessel of milk, and after making his incantations, he threw that vessel into the sea.

At the expiration of twelve hours Donna Maria came back to her senses and lost her pains: but she was so weak that it took her three months to recover her strength. The magician fixed upon the slave-girl who had done the mischief, and the negress, on confessing it, was punished and banished for the rest of her life. The originator of the trouble was the master of the house, who had given such authority to a slave in order to gratify his own desires in an illicit direction. The slave thus thought she could become lady of the home upon the death of the wife. I have seen some lose their lives or ruin their families by the commission of such insults and discords in their own houses.

Be it known to the reader that slave-girls in India are generally thieves, evaders of work, and self-indulgent, and ladies endure much from their disrespectful manners. The men slaves and servants are very troublesome, insolent thieves, with no object but their own interests. It is necessary to be on your guard with them. How much do soldiers suffer on the march, and have to put up with their servants' impertinence, owing to the necessity they are under on such occasions! Servants are ordinarily slothful and shameless, and reply publicly with irrelevant arguments, as may be seen in my Third Part (III. 70).

As a reward for curiosity I will give some account to the reader of the Christian [253] women in India. They are very eager to read futurity and know hidden things. For these ends they support certain old women who are practised in this art. I knew an old woman of Bengal called Anna Vas, who lived in Lahor, and was very devout. She told me that in her young days there were several women of her race, from whom you could acquire or know whatever you desired. She told me several instances, of which I will insert one that happened to her.

The relations of a Senhor de Souza, a renegade, then deceased, applied to this old woman to find out by her prayers if the defunct were in Purgatory or Paradise. The old woman prepared herself for the ordeal by fasting seven days. On the eighth day at midnight she bathed and went naked into a room containing an oratory where she was accustomed to pray. Lighting six candles, she fell on her knees and began to pray. While thus occupied she felt a pebble fall in her presence; then she continued her prayer. In a short while another fell. When a few minutes had gone by, another stone came down. Lifting her head, she looked to the ceiling of the room, where there appeared a man clothed in black, who asked her three times in haste wherefore she had summoned him.

Anna Ves replied that she wanted to know from him what he had done with the deceased, Francisco de Souza. His answer was that she might spare herself the trouble of praying for his soul, since he was in Hell; and at that moment the figure disappeared. Next morning she told the deceased's relations what she had heard, and they gave up praying for him. When I heard this story form the old woman. I gave her a good scolding, telling her it was a sin, prohibited by the church, and that she must not renew such practices. She answered in her simplicity that she thought she was doing a good work, but, listening to my advice, told me she would never again engage in such acts.

Something the same happened with a rich woman of Madras who had a married daughter. When the daughter was with child, the mother wanted to know whether it would be an easy delivery or not. To this intent she sent to a similar old woman to get her to pray. The woman placed herself for prayer near the door to the street at nine o'clock at night. This she did on two nights. The third night while praying she heard a voice say: 'We shall die and leave no remembrance.' On hearing this much, the old woman was disconsolate, and said nothing to the widow, so as not to lose the payment promised to her. She produced other reasons to pacify her, and the old woman, to maintain her own credit, went about saying what would happen to the pregnant woman. The latter died in child-bed.

In Madras was a woman married to a merchant who was away from home. Being delayed in his voyage, and no news coming of him, she wanted to know about him, so she went to one of these old women directing her to pray, and ask that in a dream she might see what had become of her husband. While asleep she saw the ship wrecked, when several died of drowning, including the husband. The news was disclosed to the wife, who mourned and was unable to keep the secret (ordinarily there are few secrets kept by women). She communicated it to her neighbours, and thus the story passed through the whole town. At length it came to the ears of the Father Vicar, who made [254] efforts to abolish such an abuse by preaching and admonishment. None the less did the practice persist, and faith was still placed in the old women, the advice of the priests being disregarded.

XXX. Qazi 'Abd-ul-Wahhab

Some months had passed, and news came of the husband's death; he had been drowned. Thus was borne out what the old woman had said, and she earned much money through her renown as a diviner, and there was no lack of well-placed ladies who had recourse to her to find out their objects.

In Madras was a rich widow who became anxious to know whom she would marry; so she sent for one of these old women, gave her a reward, and commanded her to perform her rites in her presence. For this purpose the old woman sent to fetch for her a clear glass phial, and breaking some eggs, poured them into it. The old woman prayed into the mouth of this bottle, and the eggs formed into a human shape with some letters showing the name of the person who was to become the widow's spouse. In those regions there was none who bore such a name. After some months there appeared a man who bore the name announced by the phial, and when the widow saw him, she declared he resembled him that she had seen, and she married him. I knew this man, and had many a talk with him.

At Sao Thome there was another lady who sent for one of these old women diviners, and requested her to pray in her house in favour of a certain intention which she recommended to her. For the purpose a special chamber was set aside. After ten o'clock at night the old woman took her seat at a window, and engaged in prayer. Fancying she would hear a voice, according to her intention, there appeared instead in the middle of the room a face surrounded by white. On seeing it the old woman became speechless and was in a state of terror, sitting motionless, while the face remained stationary for some time. Finding that no question was put, it went out again by the same window. The old woman then fell down.

The people of the house, hearing the fall, ran into the room, where they found the woman extended on the ground in a swoon. They raised her up, and with the help of medicines she came to herself by the morning; but she was unable to move one of her legs. Asking her what had happened, she explained that as the face passed out of the window, she felt it touch her on that leg. On inspection, they found the leg withered into a mere stick, and its flesh all shrivelled. Remedies were applied, but were not effective, and for the few years she survived it remained in the same condition. She ever repented herself of her deeds, for no one can fully understand an evil who has not actually experienced it.

Not to put the reader out of humour. I will wind up, noting only four more instances very briefly. If I tried to state all those I have seen, It would take up much time to explain the differences and minutiae of all the similar doing of these old witches, who ruin women and young servant-girls.

At the present time there is in Madras an old blind woman called Androza. She lived with the reputation of a saint, many women resorting to her to discover matters similar to those already stated. They bestowed liberal alms on her, by which she lived comfortably [255]. Through her fame for holiness, a whole village of fisher-folk had recourse to her, presenting to her good fish and some money. They enjoyed hearing her conversation, and did not come to church as usual. The vicar noticed their absence, while the alms that they usually brought to church at the time of mass and their other offerings were also missing. On his taking up the question, he discovered the pretensions of the blind Androza, who had imposed this superstition upon the whole fisher village. She was admonished, expelled from Madras, and her deceptions were unmasked. After these events Androza removed to Monte Grande,[1] to the foot of a hermitage called Nossa Senhora [da] Comseiçao (Our Lady of the Conception), where she lived on the alms given her by the devout. There she went on with her accustomed practices.

In Sao Thome there was a lady who asked an old woman of a confraternity to inform her on some questions she wanted answered. In the depth of night, when the old woman was performing her ritual in the lady's house, there appeared an aweinspiring monster, who seized the old woman by the hair and forced her out of the house, leaving her in the street half dead from the blows it applied. At the same time a ball of fire fell upon the house and all it contained was burnt, the inhabitants escaping with the greatest difficulty. The old woman found herself in the street, and on recovering her senses she repented herself, and decided never again to perform such rites. It took her a considerable time to recover health, and for the few years she lived she seemed to be in a state of fright, and trembled at the recol-

1. For St. Thomas's Mount, see note, *ante*, III. 238.

lection of what had happened to her. It was a merited punishment for meddling in things that did not concern her. Not even by this example have they mended their ways, for they continue to act as before without any compunction and many of these old women have I seen die in misery.

A young man had gone to buy fish from an old woman of this sort, and disagreeing about the price, he took it by force. After he had eaten it his stomach swelled, and he had acute pain which medicine did not cure. While he was in this condition they remarked that his breath smelt of stale fish, and his bowels discharged rotten fish. By these signs they recognised that it was some sorcery. Finding no cure for this, he died, and on opening his bowels they found a live fish.

Many a time I have seen in cities and in camps, when there has been a robbery, that to recover what had been lost they went to sorcerers. These men take a brass bowl, and put into it some grains of uncooked rice and some flowers over which an incantation has been recited. Then they take another bowl of the same metal, and beating with a short stick, they say some words softly, and the first bowl with the flowers begins to move of itself very slowly. At last it arrives at the place where the thing lost is lying. The thief, seeing the crowd and hearing the sound of the basin, runs off, abandoning everything. The owner, after detailing the marks of his property, carries it away, while the rest of the fugitive's goods are seized by the police.

There happened to be in Sao Thome a Portuguese called Manoel Maçedo de Azevedo. This man dreamt several nights running that inside his house, in a *godown* (storehouse), was buried a treasure, close [256] to a pillar on which the house rested. To find out if the dream were true, he called in a sorcerer, to whom he set forth what he had dreamed. The sorcerer asked for three days to inquire and see if things were as he had dreamt.

To find out by experiment whether the sorcerer knew how to divine what had been buried, the Portuguese placed some money and jewels in the earth at four places in his garden. When the three days had passed, the sorcerer came, and going into the garden, drew forth a small paper from his pocket, and took from it a certain black [powder] and anointed his eyes. Then the Portuguese led the sorcerer to the places where he had buried the things already referred to. The sorcerer halted, and described minutely what had been interred.

The Portuguese now believed in the sorcerer through the proof that he had put him to, and took him to the middle of the *godown* of which he had dreamt. The sorcerer came and stood there, and displayed great astonishment, saying that in that spot was a large caldron full of gold; but it was down seven cubits deep near the water-level. The caldron had two rings, and each ring was placed on the horn of an ox which upheld the caldron. On hearing this the Portuguese was delighted, and wanted to order the pot to be excavated and withdrawn. The sorcerer advised him it was inexpedient to touch it without having performed a sacrifice. In obedience to his counsel, goats and cocks were sacrificed; then men were set to work to dig while the master stood by. As soon as they had dug down about four cubits and the work was still in progress, an announcement was made that the governor of the place had come to call on him (the Portuguese).

The work was suspended, the labourers were turned out, and the door locked. Then the master went to greet the governor at his gate, and conducted him to the garden. While they were in conversation the house fell down, owing to the removal of the foundations of the pillar. Thereby the man saw how good God had been to him, and the net which the Devil had tried to spread for him. Repenting himself, he abandoned his attempt. All the city heard of the case, and of the unholy rites the man had performed. He was compelled to appear at Goa to defend himself before the Inquisition, from which he came out free.

I am not yet satisfied with the accounts I have given of the superstitions and sorceries of the Indian people, for there still remains something for me to say, and thereby to give satisfaction to inquiring readers. In my time there was at Agrah a man called Hortencio Bronzony (Ortencio Bronzoni),[1] a native of Venice, married to one of his slaves, a Hindu by birth. Her name was Suzana Borges, and she had a son by her [first] husband, called Nicolao Borges, a young man of twenty, married to a daughter of Francisco de Souza.

This Suzana Borges, without her husband's knowledge, paid money every month to a diviner or sorcerer to obtain information

1. Ortencio Bronzoni, a lapidary, already referred to in Part I., 164.

on any subject she wanted, and give her such advice as was necessary. Ordinarily all women in Agrah and Dihli more or less make use of the same art, and are of much the same sort. The mother of the young man wanted to know how many years her son's wife would live, so she asked the sorcerer. He replied that if some treatment were not speedily applied, she had not long to live. The mother asked him what was the course to be taken, when he pledged his word that he would so act that the daughter would survive for many years. But the condition was that the necessary expenses were provided for the rites that must be performed. To meet these she sent an ornament of gold, weighing fifty Venetians,[1] to be melted. She also gave a band of silver, her gold rings, a bow and a small arrow of silver [257], a gold chain, various kinds of silk and white cotton cloth, with fifty rupees for expenses. All this was given as a present to the sorcerer, who carried off the whole to his house.

After three days he returned, and placed in the hands of Suzana Borges a well-dressed doll, which he ordered her to place in a room upon a bed. Four times every day she must enter the room slowly and inquire from the said doll in a low voice what it would like to eat, how it felt, how it had slept, and whether it wanted anything. His orders were that she should put these questions for ten days. Meanwhile at his own house he would make the necessary sacrifices. At the end of ten days the sorcerer appeared and instructed her afresh. She was to ask the doll if anyone owed it money, or if it had buried jewels anywhere, or if anyone had promised it a reward. Let it tell the truth; for it could see the efforts they were making for its health, so that it might be cured. She was to continue thus for five days, doing these acts each day four times. His further orders were that the wife of Nicolao Borges should not sleep upon her bed, that she must diet herself, not washing her body or putting on fresh clothes.

Suzana Borges did as she was told, obeying the sorcerer in every particular. He came back after five days, and told her to send for her acquaintances and friends. Of these twelve

1. The word used is *vaquinha*, a young cow or heifer (?); perhaps an ornament shaped like a cow. *Venetian* is another word for the *sequin* (see Yule, 964).

assembled, the chief among them being Isabel Bocara and Isabel Correa, Catherina Correa and Maria Toscana. He ordered all these and the bride to enter the room, and, standing round the couch, to make lamentation over the doll, as if weeping over some dead body. After an hour the doll was to be wrapped in a shroud and put into a little coffin. They were to follow it in a body, carrying it as far as a certain garden, where it must be buried. They were then to renew their lamentation and undo their hair. All this accomplished, they consoled each other and exchanged condolences, and, having carried out the sorcerer's directions, they returned home. There, according to his instructions, they all bathed and put on their richest clothes and finest jewels. The bride did the same, decking herself as if it were her wedding-day.

At this point a banquet was made ready, which lasted all night, with music, dancing, and feasting. Everybody congratulated the bride on the long life she was to have, while at the street-door they sacrificed four goats and eight cocks. In this way were the orders of the sorcerer carried out. He received what they had to give him; he was dismissed with additional presents and profuse thanks. He was mocking at them all.

The inquisitive reader will ask how the master of the house could give consent t to such goings on. I say that this sort of men who take wandering negro women as wives, or keep them in their houses, are persons of small capacity and little judgment. They let these women do as they like, and if one of them attempts to reform his household, he stands a good chance of losing his life; and usually they bind these men to them with such witcheries that they are in their hands tender as a ewe-lamb.

Such a case happened to a man I knew, called Thomas Gudellett,[1] an Englishman. On arriving in the Mogul country he took into his house a public woman of evil life called Leanora Nunes Pereira de Mello, a native of India. Three days afterwards, being accustomed to full liberty, she took up with a Mohamedan servant without any disguise. At that time

1. No doubt the same as T. Goodlad, one of the persons at Gulkandah to whom Governor Gyfford, of Madras, wrote on March 17, 1686-87, having been recommended to them by 'Snor. Nickola Manu choha' (*sic*) (see Factory Fecords, Fort St. George, No. 20, p. 94, now in the India Office).

Gudellett returned home, and beheld this perverted inclination [258] and uncontrolled lust. Driven out of himself with passion, he rushed to find some staff or weapon. Just then the woman shut the door, and, opening the window, cried loudly to the neighbours for help. The 'Farangi' who lived in her house was drunk and wanted to murder her, and had cursed Muhammad. The servant who was in her society went to the other window; and also shouted to the same effect. The man's own servants came and attacked their master with sticks and stones. The neighbours and passers-by aided in binding him, giving him a thorough beating. He was taken before the magistrate on the charge of having cursed Muhammad. There he received many affronts and was punished. When word was brought to me, I had great labour in getting him released, expending money from. my own purse. Thomas Gudellett said to me that had he listened to my advice, such calamities would not have overtaken him. God, who is our Lord, punished the woman. She did not have long enjoyment of the boy, for within a year they killed him.

I will recount a few more similar cases. In Dihli there was an English renegade named Joao Witt (? John White),[1] who had married a Mahomedan woman. She was addicted to vicious practices. As the Englishman suspected his wife, he decided to reform matters in the house. When she saw this, she disappeared, taking with her the best of their belongings. The young man at this result was very sorrowful and anxious; he made every effort to discover her retreat. In the end he came to know that she was in the house of some people whom she declared to be her relations.

On obtaining this information he sent a message, not daring to go himself for fear of a beating. He told her that she might return without any hesitation. She did not respond to the young man's overtures, but sent him many menaces and much abuse. The man persevered with all possible diligence, in the hope of winning her over. In the end the wife made the concession that she would return home, the condition imposed being that he should come to see her where she was, and, falling at her feet in the presence of everybody, beg her pardon. He was to state

1. This might be the John White, artilleryman, of the Sloane MS., No. 811 (R. Bell's Travels').

as his excuse that his suspicions arose from his having been drunk, and that long ago he had withdrawn them.

He agreed to all these conditions, and, going to the house where his wife was living, fell at her feet. The woman spurned him and overwhelmed him with abuse, while those present did nothing but try to add fuel to the wrath of the aggrieved wife. In this way the husband was led to agree to another condition—that he would deliver a signed paper, attested by witnesses, to the effect that she should be absolute mistress in the house; that he must yield her obedience, and must seek her advice, doing nothing without her consent. The money he received as pay must be made over untouched to her, and other similar articles.

All this he executed, and these preliminaries ended, the infatuated youth ordered a carriage to be brought to carry her home. Once more she flew into a rage and tossed the paper at him, saying that it did not satisfy her, and that only when he did as she demanded would she accompany him. What she required was that the fool should give a feast to her relations, and that when she left their house he should precede her carriage on horseback. Round it were to be carried a number of trays of flowers and fruit, attended by dancers, pipes, kettle-drums, and trumpets, until they reached their own house.

As I was passing along the street I saw the renegade [259] in high delight, his chest covered half-way down with flowers. He was also elevated by a glass or two he had drunk, and he was chewing betel. Altogether he looked like a bridegroom conveying home a newly-married wife. I pulled up, and sent to inquire who it was that he had married now, and they brought back an answer to the effect of what I have above related.

There was another case of a woman named Luiza Barboza. She was excessively corpulent, and therefore asked a sorcerer for some cure for this excess of fat. His orders were that she should take the stoutest slave-girl she had in her house, should bind her hand and foot, and place her on the ground flat, so that she could not move. Then she was to sit over the negress, and bathe herself, and not to rise up until the slave expired. This was done by Luiza Barboza. Next the sorcerer ordered that within eight days the corpse must be carried to the river. He handed to her some ointment to be applied to the soles of the feet; and while carrying away the body she fell into a quagmire and disappeared, a merited chastisement for her cruelty.

It would take me a great deal of space to detail all the wiles of sorcerers that I have seen and heard, for they are infinite and quite common in Indian countries. I will tell one small instance that happened at Agrah to a Portuguese named Pero Gomes de Oliveira. He was friends with a sorcerer, whom he entreated to show him something of the art. To gratify him, the sorcerer took him with him at midnight outside the citadel, and advised him not to breathe a word, whatever he might see during that night, nor ask him any questions, until the sun had risen. If he disobeyed it would cost him his life. The inquisitive Portuguese accepted this condition, and in the company of the sorcerer left the city.

They travelled half a league, and then took a rest beneath a large tree. The sorcerer lighted a candle, and made a sign to Pero Gomes to stay where he was. The sorcerer, with the lighted candle, went off to search under the tree for a man who had been hung on it. When he reached the body, he put the light below the soles of the corpse's feet. When four minutes had elapsed, the body turned gently three times and gave forth a most affrighting yell, at which Pero Gomes fell flat on the earth and covered his eyes with his two hands. Thus did the corpse move three times in twelve minutes.

At the completion of this the sorcerer scraped from the soles of the executed man's feet the lamp-black made by his candle, and carried it off to employ in his spells. When these were finished, Pero Gomes up, took the candle and carried it, and both men re-entered the city before daybreak. Pero Gomes himself told me of this case that had happened to him, and he swore an oath that he would never again have any intercourse with a sorcerer, owing to what he had undergone during the terrors of that night.

During the time when Masqat was governed by the famous Ruj Freori de Andradi,[1] Portuguese, many complaints were brought to him of a Mahomedan sorcerer whose name was Cafata. It was said that he could by a simple look kill people whenever he pleased. As there was no proof of this power the

1. Ruy Freire de Andrada commanded at Ormuz in 1622, when it was taken by the English. In 1617 he had been sent to cruise in the Persian Gulf with a fleet of five galleons (Danvers, ii. 209, 212).

governor declined to believe it. Then it happened that a woman had a child two years old, stout and in perfect health. Suddenly it died. The mother carried it to the presence of Ruy Freire, and with lamentations [260] and complaints said the sorcerer had looked on the child and killed it.

Ruy Freire caused the child to be dissected, when it was found that its heart and liver had gone entirely. Fie recognised the evil deed of the sorcerer, but, pretending to be angry, he ordered the woman to be turned out, and assuming the side of the sorcerer, he said it was false that the man had taken the child's life. When the sorcerer heard the result he lost the fear he had that Ruy Freire would do him an injury. Therefore, taking some trays of fruit, he offered them as a mark of gratitude, and made offers of service. Ruy Freire received him affectionately, and begged him to frequent the house, for his conversion and talk pleased him. The Mahomedan was gratified, and, being entirely reassured, came back and fore to the house.

Some days afterwards the said Ruy Freire feigned anger and depression about a man of rank with whom he had some difference. He was in search of revenge, and pretended that he wanted to slay his opponent. He took the Mahomedan into his counsels as to how this could be effected. The man replied that if orders were issued he would find a way to execute them. Ruy Freire made out he was satisfied with what the sorcerer said, but expressed some doubts, and asked how he would set to work. The man answered that he would employ a sorcerer who would teach him certain words, and through these he could effect the business, should the person not be clad in scarlet; should that be the case, the words would have no effect.

The following day the Mahomedan came and said that he was now prepared. Ruy Freire answered that he would never be satisfied till he had first afforded some proof. With this object, he placed a melon on the table, and told him to consume it by those words he knew. Gazing intently at the melon, he moved his lips as if reciting words, and then stopped. Ruy Freire cut the melon open, and found it void of seeds and pith, with nothing left but the rind. He was satisfied, and said to the man; 'Now I am certain you have the power to do what I want. Tomorrow I will point out the man concerned.

As he had already knowledge from the sorcerer that, should the person be dressed in scarlet, the magic would not work, Ruy

Freire made use of the fact. Next day when the sorcerer appeared there fell on him four men clad in scarlet cloth. He was bound hand and foot, and thrown into the sea with an anchor attached to his neck. Ruy Freire assumed that, having been plunged into the sea, the sorcerer had died. Five days or so afterwards the man's mother and wife came to the [governor's] gate and complained that the guards on the beach would not allow them to carry away and eat what was at the bottom of the sea. Ruy Freire ordered that they should be allowed to draw out the food. When they began to pull it up, he [the sorcerer] came out. The governor sent the four men in scarlet with orders to apprehend him once more. They were to place him at the mouth of a cannon and fire it off. This was the end of the sorcerer. If he could with his eyes consume the entrails of living beings, the cannon consumed him bones and all. They say that, to this day, similar sorcerers are found in the regions of Masqat and Arabia. I was assured of the truth of this story by an ancient Portuguese called Joao Carvalho, who was very intimate with me, and he had actually been a soldier in Masqat, in addition to which the matter is notorious in India [261].

This Ruy Freire was a leader of much valour, and fortunate in war. I have heard this from persons who served with him, and I have seen in his chronicles many marvels, principally done against the Arabs, a warlike race, among whom the name of this captain roused great terror. To pacify any restless or crying child, it sufficed to pronounce Ruy Freire's name to suppress and subdue the noise. The Arabs, finding themselves thus oppressed by this governor, concerted with the neighbouring princes to eject the famous Ruy Freire, so that they might enjoy more liberty. With this object they made ready a great fleet, and came out with great resolution to attack the hero. They met near Masqat. He brought out only a small force, leaving the rest in port, in reliance upon his own valour, as he was used to do

On this occasion fortune did not smile upon him. After many deaths and the spilling of much blood, he was defeated and taken prisoner.[1] The Arab general received him with a great show of affection, doing him much honour, as his bravery

1. I suppose this is a garbled and traditionary account of Ruy Freire's surrender to the English at Ormuz on February 1, 1622 (Danvers, ii. 211).

deserved. His only object in flattering him was that through this means he might become master of the fortress of Masqat, a very strong place—nay, impregnable. Ruy Freire pretended that he wished to cede him the fortress, hoping to gain his own liberty. During the days that this negotiation lasted Ruy Freire seemed much cast down and full of melancholy. The Arab general asked the reason of this depression. The deceiver replied that he was sorrowful because, being a prisoner, he was unable to celebrate the festival of his birthday, as he had hitherto been used to do. The Arab general replied that he would provide all the supplies that were required, and he might do what he wished. The trickster remarked that without wine there was no gladness. He was then permitted to send for some, boats being provided which brought a large supply of wine. Then the general and other Arab officers joined him, and they sat all night drinking deeply. In this way they all became intoxicated. The astute prisoner fell on the ground and made out he had drunk too much, rolling about and vomiting. The Arabs, who were also drunk, returned to the island without any one of them taking possession of his boat.

In the depth of night the make-believe drunkard, seeing that most of them were senseless and the rest had gone, rose up gently, followed by two men of his own faction, whom he had already warned to this end. These men were slaves of the Arab general, who for some injury done them wanted to take vengeance upon him. The three entered a boat and landed at Masqat, where the escaped captive set to work to fit out the rest of his fleet. Next morning he fell on the enemy's ships unawares, cannonading them, setting them on fire and destroying all that was in them; then, disembarking on the mainland, he seized the general and the rest of the officers who had got drunk, not being accustomed to wine. Thus did Ruy Freire obtain a signal victory by his own skill and genius. He took his prisoners to Masqat, and instead of making that place over to the general, as had been demanded, he forced the Arab to deliver to him much booty. Thus the Arabs lived during his government in great fear and trembling.

During the time I was in Hindustan (Northern India) there was a woman who dwelt near the city [262] of Cochin, in the territory of a Hindu prince. Her name was Lunna; she was an Indian, and a great magician or sorcerer. This woman made her living by the sale of devil-dolls in the shape of rats, rings, jewels, buttons, flowers, *et cetera*. Within them were enclosed the demons, who did as she told them. There was a young man who wanted to obtain illicit possession of an honourable woman. Not having money enough to buy one of these troubling demon-dolls, he had recourse to Lunna to acquire something from her. She directed him to bring a hair from the head of the woman that he coveted. The youth took steps through a servant girl of the woman, who made a fool of him by giving him the hair out of a sieve.

The amorous swain carried off the hair to Lunna, who ordered him to remain in his house at night, when the woman would come to his room in search of him. At night, when the youth was in his room waiting for the woman, behold suddenly a sieve appeared and began to mount on him and worry him, without his being able to get rid of it. The youth, on finding himself thus pursued, had recourse to Lunna, the sieve following him. She acted so that he was delivered, and he thereby discovered the trick played on him by the negress.

I have heard it said that the famous Mir Jumlah, of whom I have spoken, had bought from the said Lunna one of these devil-dolls, with which he did extraordinary things and could learn what was going on. This may be so, as may be seen from the events of his life as related by me (I. 161-164; II. 72-74).

There was a Portuguese youth who lived on friendly terms with Lunna. This man had a wife in Lisbon, and he pressed the witch to give him news of his wife. The witch told him his wife was already engaged to be married; if he wanted to go home before his wife married, she would give him the means. Unable to suffer this slight, the young man accepted Lunna's advice. She bound up his eyes, and put a staff into his hands with its end on the ground. Then she ordered him to turn his body three times, and after that let go of the stick and open his eyes. Doing as he had been told by Lunna, he found himself in his house at Lisbon, and by his arrival he stopped the marriage. Confessing himself to the Holy Office (the Inquisition), he was absolved.

It happened that a married woman lived in Cochin, while her husband was in Portugal. She desired to see her husband, and enlisted the services of Lunna, the magician. The latter sent her to Portugal to visit her husband, the condition being that she should act so as to bring him back a second time to India. She gave the requisite spell for going, and taught her what to do in Portugal to succeed in her efforts. In one night the woman reached Portugal and visited her husband; without being recognised, she drew a ring from his finger, and the same night returned to Cochin. After the lapse of some months the husband arrived at the same port, and disembarking, went to his house. His wife came out to greet him, made over his ring to him, and declared she was pregnant. Then she told him the facts, detailing particulars of the year, month, day, and hour. The husband, having ascertained it was the truth, said nothing, for if he had, he would have lost his life. On making confession to the Inquisition, she was not interfered with. This woman (Lunna) was much renowned in India, and it may be forty years since she died, leaving [263] the house where she dwelt so haunted that no one could live in it.

In this same land of Cochin, where a Hindu prince ruled, there was an alligator or crocodile in the river which the Hindus called the 'Crocodile of the Oath.' When they wanted to asseverate the truth of any plea, they would appeal to the crocodile. All would go to the river bank, and there he who was to swear placed himself on the crocodile and said these words: 'If I swear falsely, you must throw me into the middle of the river; and if I swear the truth, you must bring me back again and deposit me in this same place.' Thus many times did it happen that the truthful were brought back and released on the river-side, and the liars were pitched into the middle of the river and drowned.

It happened once that a youth, the son of a rich man, after his father's death appropriated the whole estate, and refused to share with his brother. They appealed to the Oath of the Crocodile. This youth, finding himself pledged to make an oath, took a staff and put into it half of the property he had appropriated, having converted it all into precious stones. They were really the property of his brother. With this staff in his hand, and quite easy in his mind, he came to the river-side and called the crocodile. He then proposed to his brother to take the oath in this form; ' "I owe you nothing; what was mine I took, and what was yours I made over to you. I speak the truth." Meanwhile, until I come back, hold this staff.' He placed the staff in his brother's hand. When he had done speaking these words, he mounted on the top of the crocodile, which carried him round in the river without harming him, and brought him back to the same place in safety. The magistrate and those present shouted out great abuse to the man who had the staff in his hand. The latter, enraged at the injustice done him by the crocodile, and put out at the abuse poured on him, struck the staff angrily on the ground, and broke it by the blow. The precious stones in it fell out, and thereby everyone perceived the deceit and trick of the first brother, the correct conduct of the crocodile, and the plaintiff's innocence. All that was in the staff was made over to the claimant, and thus he obtained his inheritance which the other had embezzled.

It looks as if I had said enough touching sorcerers, and I will finish with telling one small instance. There was a man called Antonio Gonçalves, who was married and had a sickly daughter three years old. In order to search for remedies to restore her to health, he left the city and went to a village to obtain the services of a Hindu physician, who was renowned as a great doctor. This physician gave him medicine, and in a few days the daughter grew well. The physician gave him a written note, bound with threads of different colours, and said this paper was of use against the evil eye, malignant winds, the ghosts of birds, and such-like superstitions. The said paper was tied to the child's waist, and they put her to sleep. Then during the night the child began to cry, wanting her father and mother. They ran and saw that on the bed were two awful-looking monkeys, and when they wanted to come close [264] the wild monkeys menaced them.

The father made off in all haste to inform the physician as to what had happened after tying on the paper. The doctor calmly gave him another inscribed paper, telling him to carry it in his hand and show it to the monkeys. They would be forced to leave the place, and then they could remove the paper that was attached to the child's waist. That paper was to be brought back to him, and they were not to be frightened. When Antonio Gonçalves went into the house with the paper in his hand the monkeys disappeared. Taking the paper that the doctor wanted back, he set out again. On the way he had need to urinate, and hardly had he undone his drawers, when he saw himself surrounded by a host of monkeys, who seemed as if about to attack him. Seeing this, he laid hold of his drawers with one hand, and of the paper with the other; and thus equipped, he went to the doctor's house, followed by the monkeys. He made over the paper, and recounted what had happened on the road. The doctor replied that the reason of the attack was the little respect he had paid to the letter in wanting to make water with it in his hand.

From what I have observed, Hindu doctors do not exercise their profession or prescribe without having given offerings to the devil. These men imagine that the drugs will not operate if these incantations I have described are omitted. From such doctors and such drugs *libera nos, Domine*!

In order that everyone who visits this country may guard himself against entering into certain kinds of friendship, which the young mostly count mere civility and pastime. I will relate what happened to me in the year one thousand six hundred and fifty-five (1655)[1] at the city of Dihli. There was a woman of eighteen years of age (the same age as myself), who was the daughter of a European, and her name was Maria Veronea. She was very desirous of forming a close friendship with me. As I found she did not suit me. I drew back.

Desirous of satisfying her inclinations, she pursued me to my very house. Aware that an intimacy such as she desired was unsuitable to me. I ordered my servants to say when she came that I was not at home. A few days afterwards she turned up, and my servants, in obedience to my orders, gave her the above message. They stopped her entry into the house. She was put out at this message, and went off to a sorcerer called Dolang (whose name remains in my memory from the experience I had of him). The magician performed his spells, and assured the woman that it would not be long before I was in her presence.

Thus it came to pass, for before an hour had elapsed the woman in question came to my mind, and caused me the very greatest uneasiness for not having allowed her to enter. Added to this uneasiness were regrets, afflictions, and various imaginations. Leaving no time for reason to ponder the question. I ordered my horse to be fetched at once; and not waiting for him to be saddled. I jumped on his back and went off. My servants in consternation asked where I was going. But my

1. Properly, it should be 1657 (see *ante,* Introduction, p. Liv on N.M.'s chronology).

movements were guided by imagination only, and in reality I knew not the place [265], for I had not seen it; nor did I know the name of the quarter, the street, the house, or its landlord. Thus I cried to my servants to follow me, and then I would show where I wanted to go. This was done. Going through various streets, and turning various corners, all by myself, I finally appeared in front of a house. Behind the door stood the said woman, and opening it, she began to laugh and to make complaint at one and the same time, only to be by a few words from me delivered from the passion under which she had hitherto suffered.

When I was in Bandora,[1] near the island of Bombaim (Bombay), in the year one thousand six hundred and seventy-seven, there was a Portuguese there called Antonio de Deixas, who wanted me to marry his daughter. His hope was that he would be supported by me, as I had a quantity of money. He made many efforts through priests and friars, who are ordinarily in this land of India the marriage-brokers; but finding that no effort prevailed over me, and that I had already penetrated his true purpose, he went to a sorcerer to ask for a potion to make me love his daughter. The sorcerer gave the drug. The Portuguese wanted to test whether the mixture was efficacious, and took a little. Forthwith he fell into such miserable condition that, leaving the rightful paths of Nature, he became mad and pursued his daughter, committing such acts as to force his relations to separate them, and put him in another dwelling. Nor by this did he get rid of his trouble; it was requisite to put chains on his legs, and in this miserable condition he soon after died, and I had a lucky escape.

Now I have come to the finale of my History, an object by me so ardently desired. As I have had the good fortune to finish these three Books, and narrate the things that happened to me in these eight-and-forty years, may it also please God that this work, which I present to Europeans, may succeed in the object on which I have set my heart. Meanwhile I am making my preparations for a much longer journey, and am in search of the true route and the safest that can be hoped for.

1. See *ante*, Part II., 177.

The veritable terminus of our desire being what the Lord All-Powerful wishes, may He grant assurance to my search for it. The reader must meanwhile content himself with accepting these my labours, without pointing out in them the absence of flowers. For how can one produce flowers when for ever dwelling in the midst of thorns?

END OF PART III.

APPENDIX

PASSAGES IN VENICE CODEX XLIV. (ZANETTI), FOLS. 417-455, NOT FOUND IN MS. PHILLIPPS, 1945

[As the above-named two manuscripts diverge a good deal. I have procured a copy from Venice of fols. 417-455, and insert here whatever does not appear in the Berlin MS.]

[417] It seems to me that the inquiring reader will be pleased if I inform him how these Mogul kings are accustomed to write in a contemptuous tone to other powerful kings, princes, and rulers, demanding surrender of any strong place they want to usurp. This was done by King Aurangzeb after he had taken the kingdoms of Bijapur and Gulkandah.

AURANGZEB'S HAUGHTY LETTER TO THE QILA'HDAR OF ADUNI

Holding the fortress of Aduni,[1] a place belonging to the kingdom of Bijapur, there was a governor called Xidi Maxaud (Sidi Mas'ud) Abaxi (Habshi), or African, born in India. This man declined to hand over the place to the said king (Aurang zeb). To force a surrender, the latter sent his valiant general Guiazudin Can[1] (Ghazi-ud-din Khan), in the belief that he would speedily compel a capitulation by an investment and attacks in various directions. The brave African held out vigorously, killing many of the king's men. On this being reported to him, the king caused a letter to be written to him, of which the following is a copy:

'Mas'ud, I warn you to repent before those evil days overtake you which you are preparing for yourself; and in addition you have delayed with the keys of the fortress of Aduni, and

1. A town now in the Ballari district, lat. 15° 55′, long. 77° 19′, 261 miles north-west of Madras ('Madras Manual of Administration,' iii. 8). Firuz Jang (Ghazi-ud-din Khan) was sent in the thirty-first year, 1099 H. (1687-88), to take Aduni from Mas'ud, a Habshi slave Sikandar 'Adil Shah's father, who had become almost independent of 'Mas'ud' surrendered on the 18th Shawwal thirty-second year, 1099 H. (August 10, 1688) ('Ma,asir-i-'Alamgiri,' 308, 316).

did not hand them over to the great Ghazi-ud-din Khan, whose-arms are strengthened by my wealth. You have overlooked the gloomy repose made ready for you on the black bed [the grave]. I imagine you must be asleep, and your eyes shut. Have you forgotten that the councillors of Bijapur for a time held their heads high, but in the end were bound in heavy chains; while their ineffective power was trodden to dust beneath the horse-hoofs of the mighty armies led by my generals, and they were consumed. Dost thou remember Abdula Assen (Abu,l Hasan), of Gulkandah, who for twenty years, buffoon as he was, feigned to wear a crown and imagined he was governing? He likewise [418] fell a victim to the claws of wrath and valour of the eagles in my overwhelmingly powerful armies. His marrow was carried off as sustenance to the nests of the falcons in the other world, and he too slept covered with a black pall. I tell you what is to be your fate, so that you may know beforehand. At sight of this order, which is inexorable as death, your business is to obey, and deliver over the keys of the fortress to Ghazi-ud-din Khan, the victorious in war,[1] and he will become your advocate in my presence concerning your misdeeds.'

As an attestation, they attach to these formal orders a seal and the impression of their palm in saffron. These are as follows;

[A circular seal is here inserted as already produced at III. 32 of the Berlin text.]

[419] This is the royal seal with the name of Taimur-i-lang the Great and other kings, his descendants, as you will see by the words. Below it is the impression of the hand in saffron. [Here comes the reproduction of the palm of a very small hand.]

[420] The African, finding his master taken and his kingdom destroyed, and being thus deprived of all hope of succour, was obliged to submit and have recourse to the intercessions of the said general, Ghazi-ud-din Khan, and in the end we shall see what reward he was to receive.

ACCOUNT OF FARMANS

[421] These *formaoens* (*farmans*), which bear the royal seal with the impression of the hand in saffron colour, are sent by the king to the kings, princes, rajahs, and other potentates for

1. 'Vitoriozo da Guerra'; this is a translation of his title—*viz.*: Firuz Jang.

an assurance of peace or other binding promises. By them he makes a gift of a province or lands. Others submit themselves, and become vassals and subjects, at the same time accepting the pay that the Mogul king promises them. But I have seen that many of them, after having submitted, come to the end of their life in a very short time, while others die miserably of hunger; This happened to Sidi Mas'ud, the intercessions of Ghazi-ud-din Khan being of no avail. For a whole year he was shunted from pillar to post without getting any relief; finally he was paid off with a mouthful of poison. The kings of Bijapur and Gulkan-dah had boxes full of these *farmans*, and at last it happened to them as will be seen in my history.

There is another kind of *farman*, which is attested by the above seal only, with the countermark of the chief *wazir*. These serve as evidence for any villages, lands, houses, and so forth, of which the king makes a grant. But these orders are of little use, because the governors and *faujdars* (military magistrates) turn out the grantees unless a present is made to them.

European nations also hold these *farmans*; but they are not left to live in peace, nor have they any security under them. For within their jurisdictions these same officials never desist from squeezing from them what they can. Thus no reliance can be placed on this tribe in their oaths, their friendships, or their speeches—all of them are deceivers.

[Page 422 is blank.]

BIJAPUR KINGS

The kingdom of Bijapur was given by Ram Raja two hundred years before 1699 to one of his slaves, a Georgian by race, a renegade called Isoff (Yusuf), who was in charge of the royal treasury. For this reason he is depicted with the golden key in his hand. Upon the death of the emperor [424] Ram Raja[1] he crowned himself, and took the title of—

1. Sultan Yusuf 'Adil Shah, and he reigned 20 years 1 month and 9 days. His descendants are:
2. Sultan Ashraf 'Adil Shah, reigned 26 years and 19 days.

---

1. Ram Rajah, of Bijayanagar, was killed in battle, 1564 ('Madras Manual of Administration,' iii. 788). Fryer, edition 1873, p. 399, gives a traditional account of the rise of the Dakhin kingdoms something similar to Manucci's.

3. Sultan Ibrahim 'Adil Shah, reigned 24 years 7 months and 25 days.

4. Sultan Muhammad 'Adil Shah, reigned 30 years 6 months and 27 days.

5. Sultan 'Ali 'Adil Shah, reigned 25 years 11 months and 13 days.

6. Sultan Mahmud 'Adil Shah, reigned 44 years 11 months and 9 days.

7. Sultan 'Ali 'Adil Shah, reigned 16 years and 25 days.

8. Sultan Sikandar 'Adil Shah, reigned 15 years.[1]

This last king lost the kingdom, being then fifteen years of age; he became the prisoner of King Aurangzeb, who preserved his life (as it seemed to me) in order to carry out some sacrificial rite. 'Sultan' means 'king'; "*Adil Shah* '—that is, 'Just King.'

GULKANDAH KINGS.

The kingdom of Gulkandah was given to another slave of the same race, also a renegade. He had charge of the hawks, falcons, and the royal hunting establishments. For this reason he is painted with a falcon on his hand of the kind called Baram.[2] Upon the death of the emperor (Ram Raja) he, too, adopted a title, and called himself—

1. Baram 'Ali Qutb Shah, and reigned 38 years 5 months and 7 days. His descendants are:

2. Sultan Jamshid Qutb Shah, reigned 7 years 9 months and 11 days. [At this point are interpolated two pages, 425 and 426, which belong to No. 7, Sultan Abu,l Hasan.]

3. [427] Sultan Ibrahim Qutb Shah, reigned 31 years, 4 months and 13 days.

4. Sultan Muhammad Qutb Shah, reigned 31 years 3 months and 29 days.

5. Sultan Mahmud Qutab Shah, reigned 14 years 1 month and 15 days.

6. Sultan 'Abdullah Qutb Shah, who gave his daughter in marriage to Sultan Muhammad, son of Aurangzeb, as I have

1. The length of the reigns and the order of succession in this list are erroneous, but I give it as explaining the illustration which shows these rulers' portraits.
2. Possibly meant for *bahri*, a falcon; but I know of no other authority for giving this epithet to 'Ali Qutb Shah.

already stated (I. 163). He reigned 48 years 11 months and 29 days.

7. Sultan Abu,l Hasan Qutb Shah, reigned 16 years 3 months and 29 days. This king was the last of this dynasty, and Aurangzeb deprived him of his throne in the year 1686,[1] and sent him a prisoner to the fortress of Daulatabad, with an allowance of ten rupees a day for his support. These kings were styled *Qutb Shah*—that is, 'Star of the North.'[2]

[425] A few years before this last king was deprived of his kingdom, it happened that he lost from his room a dagger worth half a million of rupees. It was covered all over with valuable jewels, and to get it back he made many efforts. The thief was afraid he would be found out; he was a favourite of the king's, a doctor of the law. This man, therefore, produced the dagger before the king and made excuses, saying he had taken possession of it for the sake of safety. The king was aware that he must be the thief and was deserving of death. But he did not punish him, since he passed as a virtuous man, and one learned in the Muhammadan law. The king ordered him to be paraded throughout the city, while a drum was beaten, and proclamation made in the streets that anyone declaring that this man stole His Majesty's dagger would lose his life. In this way the king proved both his wisdom and his sense of justice.

This king was very fond of listening to music and the playing of instruments. Without these sounds he could not sleep. The greater part of his time was passed among his women, neglecting the necessary attention to the government of his kingdom. But from motives of policy he made an inspection twice a year of his cavalry. These great men in India have a notion that we have no cavalry in Europe, and do not know how to use them. They say that Europeans are great navigators, and only skilful at sea.

DAULATABAD [NIZAM SHAHIS]

The kingdom of Daulatabad was given to another of his (Ram Raja's) slaves, named Nizam Shah, an African or Habshi. After he had been crowned, it happened that a woman came to

1. Or more correctly, 1687.
2. The same remark applies to the Gulkandah as to the Bijapur list.

complain that she was not satisfied with her husband. [428] She said he was old and incapable of satisfying her pleasures. The new king ordered her to turn the man out of the house and take another who could content her. She acted accordingly. He then ordered that as many wives as were not satisfied with their husbands might seek for others. As a matter of fact, many women did this. His queen hearing of these orders (for she had more sense than her husband) observed that such an order was unjust, and to prove to His Majesty that he had given a wrong decision, she placed herself at a window and sat there within sight of her husband.

When she saw a young and well-built horseman pass by, she said to the king: 'I want you to give me the right to eject you and take this cavalier, in order that my desires may be satisfied.' The king, in consternation at such talk, and quite forgetting the orders he had given, said to her in anger and amazement: 'O Queen! you were always wiser in your utterances! and you prove you are gone out of your mind.' The careful queen responded: 'Your Majesty gives me an opening to demonstrate to Your Majesty the feelings of the husbands at seeing their wives choose other husbands.' She gave him a long talking to about the error he had made. Finally, she said to him that if women had the privilege of changing husbands, they would be sure to do so often, necessarily giving rise to many disorders in families. All that she said was solely with the object of getting the matter remedied. The king then issued orders that wives must live with their husbands, and remain under an obligation to serve them for the whole of their lives.

This line of kings did not last long, because the Moguls conquered their country.

THE KARNATIK

The remaining lands of the Karnatik were divided [by Ram Raja] among his Hindu pages, while he retained some territory and a few fortresses scattered here and there in the middle of the said Karnatik [429]. This splitting up of his realm and giving it away was the cause of this emperor's ruin, for not many years passed before the princes, called Naiks, rebelled. One of these took possession of Madurey (Madura), another of Taniaur (Tanjor), another of Maxur (Maisur), another of Cholomangalao

(? Choromandal). They ceased to send in their tribute, giving him (the emperor) nothing but a small sum just sufficient for his support.

Upon his (Ram Raja's) death they crowned themselves and announced themselves as kings. Some were Mahomedans, and others were Hindus; but all proclaimed themselves princes of the countries they held. All of them were rich and powerful, taking no notice of nor acknowledging the descendants of the emperor Ram Raja, their former suzerain.

There still survive some of his (Ram Raja's) descendants, but they keep in obscurity in order not to be recognised, otherwise Aurangzeb and his governors would most certainly take their lives. They subsist by begging for alms. One of them discovered himself to the Reverend Father Paul,[1] Carmelite, and held several conversations with him. In one talk he requested him to prevail on one of the kings of Europe to send an army to his assistance. He promised that if such help were afforded he would give a great reward, with much land and many privileges. The said father, I well know, made proposals to several European nations, but his efforts had no result.

ROBERTO DE' NOBILI[2]

The number of Christians is continually increasing, to the greater glory of the founder of that mission. His mind alone could have poured the faith into the hearts of the heathen, for he spoke the Grandonic[3] language, which is their Latin, just as if it were his mother-tongue. At his first visit the Prince of Tanjor asked many questions of the father. The latter replied to every question by a verse in the Grandonic[3] language. The fathers who join this mission suffer great hardships, and all go about clothed like *pandarao* (*pandaram*)[4] who are the same as the Hindu bishops; they eat nothing but vegetables and fruit.

1. This is possibly meant for Father Petrus Paulus a St. Francisco, who in 1696 succeeded to the post of Vicar Apostolic in Bijapur and Gulkandah, with the title of Bishop of Ancyra in *partibus* (Müllbauer, 'Geschichte,' 347); see the note about him in Part IV., fol. 232.
2. For additional details see *ante*, III. 171.
3. From *granthaka*, the language of the holy books (*granth*)—that is, Sanskrit (Yule, 792).
4. A Saiva devotee, an officiating priest at temples of Siva {'Madras Manual of Administration,' iii. 728).

At this time the greater number of Christians are in Madura and Tanjor.

JOHN DE BRITTO AND RAMESHWARAM

Now, not so very long ago, our martyr, Joao de Brito, established Christian congregations in Marava,[1] and when he won the martyr's palm, almost all the nobles were catechumens. All the Hindus who go to purify themselves at the temple of Rameshwaram are obliged to pass close to the place where was executed that martyr for Christ. It is only a few leagues from Utiar (see *ante*, III. 167), which is the passage over the strait, which they so call. This strait lies between the dry land in the island of Jafnapatam and Manar (Mannar),[2] [436] called Costa da Emsiada (? Gulf Coast), a land of about eighty leagues in length, beginning at the point of Coniumeres (Comorin), and reaching as far as Tutucurum (Tuticorin). The narrowest part is the passage of Utiar.

The Hindu princes, thinking that in time a Portuguese fleet might do some damage to their temple, so highly venerated by them, resolved to narrow the passage to two leagues in length and one league in breadth. They obstructed it with blocks[3] of marble, so that even a small boat could not pass, although in any danger they could be succoured. A few small unladen vessels could pass with their crews when they knew the place.

This land of Utiar (? Udayar), where this temple stands, is a rough country without any trees beyond tall thorny bushes with branches and thorns the thickness of a finger. In short, it must be the place that the devil has chosen for himself and his false worshippers..

1. Marava is primarily the name of a race, but they inhabit the Zamindaris of Ramnad and Shivaganga. Father de Britto was beheaded on February 3, 1693 (Müllbauer, 'Geschichte,' 235).
2. *Mann*, 'sand' + *dru*, 'river ('Madras Manual of Administration,' iii.527). For a suggestion as to the meaning and true form of 'Utiar,' see *ante*, III., fol. 167).
3. The text has *pageas*, a word I fail to identify; but the sense is clear. Mr. D. Ferguson suggests *lageas* = 'slabs,' and he adds: 'This confirms Baldaeus ("Malabar and Choromandel," xxii; "Ceylon," 'xli) and R. Van Goens in Valentijn ("Ceylon," 235). Tennent ("Ceylon," ii. 553, note) calls it an "improbable story." I referred to the subject in the *Monthly Literary Register*, iii. 208, 209.'

The lands of that Tavarem (Tevara)[1] end at Tuticorin, where begins the Christian country, that of the Paravas [437], converted by the Portuguese. They display a Christian exterior, were always very loyal to the Portuguese, and by fishing gained much money. Nowadays they are subject to the Dutch and are much oppressed. Already the seas of Tuticorin and of Marar (Manar) no longer yield the quantity of pearls that they anciently did, supposing they were fished for annually. But the best are carried off by the Dutch.

From Tuticorin as far as Cochin[2] there is at every five leagues a church close to the sea. From Cochin another Christian diocese begins, that of the Cassanarios (Kattanar),[3] who call themselves Christians of St. Thomas—that is, converted by St. Thomas. When the Portuguese arrived in India, this diocese was already established. These Christians live in a hilly country, and have over a hundred churches. Their priests say Mass in the *surrjana* (? Syrian) language, and a Cassanario bishop always held the see. In my time the bishop was the son of a Portuguese, but born [438] in India. His name was Dom Raphael Selgado.[4] The country is very fertile and luxuriant, possessing much game—harts, wild-pig, deer, buffaloes; and elephants.

CEYLON AND THE PORTUGUESE

The island of Ceilao (Ceylon) is very fertile, humid, and fresh, by reason of the rain which is always falling. It produces a quantity of fruit, cocos, and areca-palms, and the woods, for the greater part, are formed of fine canes, which the inhabitants use in their cooking. The mountains are full of crystals of

1. That is, the Marava Zamindar of Ramnad. Parava, from *paravai*, 'seaman,' a dark-skinned, almost black, race in the extreme south, living in villages along the sea-coast, and earning their bread as fishermen ('Madras Manual of Administration,' iii. 653).
2. *Kocchi* (the final *n* is from the Portuguese) means 'a small place.' It is the name of a native State, but the town is British, lat. 9° 58', long. 76° 17' ('Madras Manual of Administration,' iii. 193, 194).
3. The word originally meant 'a chief,' and is now applied to a priest of the Malabar Syrian Church (see Yule, 170).
4. In 1677 Raphael de Figueredo Salgado, a native of Cochin, of Portuguese descent, was made Coadjutor Bishop. He was subsequently deposed, and died at Palliporte on October 12, 1695 (Müllbauer, 'Ges chichte,' 309, 310).

many colours; the rivers are full of precious stones—rubies, sapphires, topazes, and other kinds. There are handsome elephants and an infinity of game. Although the Dutch are masters of some of the lands in that island, they enjoy no part of its riches beyond what they can acquire within reach of the sea.

Formerly the Portuguese were masters of most of the places now held by the Dutch, and always maintained a sufficient force, with a view of obtaining possession of the island, an attempt which they made several times. On one occasion they invaded the kingdoms in the interior, climbing mighty mountains and traversing formidable forests. On reaching the capital city, from which the king fled in terror, they sacked the town and the chief temple, removing the great treasures, and with them the tooth of a monkey which was worshipped by the natives of the country. They declare this to be the tooth of that monkey called Anont (Hanmat, Hanuman), who set on fire the enchanted city of Lanca (Lanka). The tooth was forwarded to Goa, and the viceroy kept it for conveyance to Portugal, to be shown to his king as proof that the people of India worshipped such foolishnesses. The King of Candia (Kandy), or Ceilao (Ceylon)—for thus he called himself—was little concerned about the wealth carried off by the Portuguese; but he and his people were deeply grieved at their taking away the holiest relic there was in the kingdom [439], and to recover it the king sent an ambassador to Goa to ransom the imagined relic, offering for it a very large sum of money, with some lands and other privileges.

The viceroy, to demonstrate that he had not been softened, scorned his money and his gifts, but, showing him the tooth, asked if he recognised it as the veritable one. The ambassador and those in his suite said it was the right one, and fell prostrate before it, paying it great veneration, and then rose to their feet and stood with their hands crossed, and showed every mark of devotion.

The viceroy said to them: 'What you offer me as the ransom of this tooth is insufficient.' They said; 'Your Excellency has only to order, and all shall be complied with.' The viceroy took the file tooth in his hand, and said to him: 'Do you imagine my king is? in any want of money, that he has sent me to govern India for monetary considerations? This is not so;

I have come to destroy idols, and prove that the faith of Christ is the only true one.' With these words he cast the tooth into the fire near by. The ambassador and his followers were overcome, beating their faces with their own hands, and left the palace with weeping and wailing, and returned to their own country.

In their desire to conquer this very fertile island, the Portuguese warred continually against this king, while he ever entreated them to leave him alone amidst his mountains. He offered to enter into a treaty of perpetual peace, and concede to them a territory of a considerable extent up to a certain boundary; that he would put up the arms of the King of Portugal in the greatest of his palaces, and recognise him as his suzerain. The Portuguest were not satisfied and entered his country [440].

Finding himself thus attacked, the King of Kandy did what he could to have peace and avoid war. He displayed humility, and erected an altar in the middle of the road by which the Portuguese must pass. Upon it was a crucifix, and he begged them by this venerable sign not to go farther, and he would concede to them all that they had taken if they would leave to him what remained. Otherwise he was determined and prepared for defence, if he saw no other course. This demand was not acceded to.

The Portuguese divided their troops into two forces, giving them orders to enter the mountains, one in one direction, the other in another. The object was that they might advance more quickly and without hindrance, for they could not march all together, the roads not being open; by this division of forces they would also divert the enemy's attention.

It happened that in the same night there fell a thunderbolt, which created a great light. The general in command was called D. Hyeronimo de Azvedo;[1] the next to him was the chief captain, Constantino Sau.[1] This officer imagined that the other force, being superstitious, upon seeing this sign from heaven would never march on that day, but stay where they were. But the general began his march, not to draw back from what he had said. He entered the hilly country, in reliance on the chief

1. Dom Jeronymo de Azevedo, Viceroy, 1612-17 (Danvers, ii. 488, No. 39). Constantino de Saa e Noronha was appointed General of Ceylon in 1618 (*ibid.*, ii. 202, 203).

captain, who also would not fail to advance, as he supposed, and leave the altar in the rear.

The King of Kandy sent to warn the Portuguese that he had already ordered the route to be blocked, and if they insisted on forcing a way, not of one of them would ever escape. The Portuguese force paid no heed to these warnings, whereupon it was attacked and totally destroyed, the general losing his life. The chief captain [441], when this event was reported to him, tried to reinforce his fellow-countrymen, but it was already too late. The victorious enemy came against these reinforcements, and they, too, were routed, not one of them escaping. The king occupied once more the extensive territory of which he had been deprived. The Portuguese were forced to content themselves with the fortresses adjacent to the sea, but they never ceased to attempt the conquest of that island, for which purpose reinforcements came to them from Portugal and Goa.

The king, aware that the Portuguese would come to no terms and meant to continue their attacks, sent secret overtures to the Dutch, who at the time were actually at war with the Portuguese, promising that if they would come and make war he would assist them. In effect, they did come with a fleet of twelve vessels, under a Dutch captain of sea and war called Riclof,[1] manned by six thousand Europeans, mostly of French nationality, commanded by a general named Tuf de Barbon,[2] a Dutchman, and other valiant leaders, such as Arriam Vandermuis Coquinto, and others like him.

With the help of the king [of Ceylon] they took some places and fortresses from the Portuguese. Finally they occupied the town of Colombo, the principal fortified place within the island. But both sides lost heavily before it was reduced. It surrendered in the year 1656, on the 12th May,[3] and to this day [? 1699] it is

1. For Admiral Rijkloff van Goens, see Danvers, ii. 307 (in 1654 he had eleven vessels), 310 (1655), 325 (December, 1661, Quilon). Dubois, 'Vies des Gouverneurs-Generaux,' 188, says Van Goens succeeded Van der Meyden in 1660.
2. Apparently this is meant for Gérard Hulft (see Dubois, 186).
3. Colombo was evacuated on May 12, 1656. The Dutch commander, Hulft, had been killed on April 10 (Danvers, ii. 317). The Portuguese were under Antonio de Souza Coutinho, Francisco de Mello de Castro, and [Antonio, De Souza's son] (*ibid*).

held by the Dutch. A few months before the Portuguese lost these territories there were signs from heaven, for it rained blood in various places. The blood congealed in pieces the size of cowries,[1] and from it came insects with wings, which, if they touched any animal—a buffalo, cow, goat, or human being—it at once fell dead. This plague lasted some days. There were other portents, such as the falling of fire from heaven, which burnt woods, villages, and houses in many directions.

It seems to me all this was God's punishment for the fearful tyranny exercised in those lands. Many times the Portuguese stormed the stockades and villages within the king's boundary [442], sparing no single creature. Other captives they would send out to the road, and put them on spits on both sides of it for the distance of a league. There were other cruelties and oppressions which I have no wish to relate, in order not to anger the reader. Their losses of territory in India itself were due to the same pauses.

THE KARNATIK, BIJAPUR AND GULKANDAH

Let us return once more to our account of the Karnatik. The kings of Bijapur and Gulkandah being powerful and also enemies to the Hindus, made war against the Nayaks[2] before referred to, who belong to the Karnatik, taking their lands and fortresses. The King of Bijapur conquered as far as Porto Novo,[3] which is a harbour on the sea; and the King of Gulkandah equally made himself master of everything as far as Sadrasta,[4] close to the sea. In the middle of this conquered country of the Karnatik is a river near the sea called Marcane (Marakkanam),[5] which is over half a league in width. At this place is the division between the two kingdoms, and thus there are two Karnatiks, one of Bijapur

1. The text has *basrio*, for which Mr. Dames would substitute *buzio* (easily misread as *basrio*), which yields a satisfactory meaning.
2. Nayaks—that is, the rulers of Bijayanagar (1325-1674), and the lords of Madura (1559-1741) (Yule, 614).
3. Porto Novo, on the coast in the South Arcot district, 115 miles south-south-west of Madras ('Madras Manual of Administration,' iii. 712).
4. Sadras, a town in the Chinglepat district, forty miles south of Madras ('Madras Manual of Administration, iii. 775).
5. A town and port in the South Arcot district, Tindivanam *talooka*, sixty-four miles south-south-west of Madras. The village stands on a backwater at the mouth of a short river ('Madras Manual of Administration,' iii. 474). It is between Porto Novo and Sadras.

and one of Gulkandah. The Karnatik was formerly a very powerful kingdom with great cities, fortresses, castles, and ancient edifices. The country was very rich by reason of the great traffic. For gold came there from China, Japan, Aracan, Achin, or Sumatra (visited by many ships), Pegu, Bengal, Queda, Malacca, and the island of Amboyna, whence come nuts, mace, and cloves, Bantam, Camboje, Manila; pepper brought from the coast of Sumatra, and cinnamon from Ceylon—all these came, and were collected in this Karnatik, passing thence to Persia, Turkey, and Europe. Since the Europeans came to India all these spices are taken away by sea [443].

In the Karnatik there was much treasure buried by those of old time; hence Mir Jumlah recovered some coined money, of which the name was not known; and Shiva Ji also discovered some hoards of money, which he spent on increasing his army. So also the common people, when they set to work to build, recover ancient money that has been buried, but are unable to make use of it for fear of discovery. The lord of the country takes possession of it, and gives a good flogging in addition, to try and find out if there is any more.

I knew a poor oilman who lived in a village called Trimanavas (Tirumani).[1] Digging up the soil to bury a vessel of oil, he recovered seven jars full of various coins, all of gold, some weighing two to two and a half drams, but the larger number were small coins, of which four-and-twenty weighed the same as one piece of eight (a dollar). The lettering could not be read; the larger pieces had on one side nothing but an image, and no one knew whose it was. The worthy oilman was sufficiently astute to remove these coins in oil-jars, which he carried for sale into another territory, and kept the money in the hands of his relations, never returning to his own country. With this money he did more or less good, building some great pagodas, or making idols, tanks, ponds, and rest-houses for travellers on the roadside, and other good works.

At a distance of twenty leagues inland from Madras is a village called Canchy (Kanchi),[2] which is as if you said 'Full of

1. Possibly the Tirumani in the Chinglepat district is meant (see 'Madras Manual of Administration,' iii. 172). It is about thirty-seven miles south of Madras.
2. Panchipuram (Conjeeveram), or 'Shining City,' in the Chinglepat district, forty-five miles west-south-west from Madras ('Madras Manual of

Treasures.' In old days this village was a great city, whence the Hindus to this day hold it in great veneration, owing to the existence of large and lofty temples. Each one of these would make an excellent fortress; and inside of them are many buildings [444] with figures of idols and gilded paintings of the lives and infamies of their false gods. In the midst is a large tank, the four sides built of large stones. Behind one of the temples I have seen a square pond without water; it is four cubits in depth, and twenty-four palms across. This pond was once full of coin, but a Brahman, offended by the other Brahmans and unable to avenge himself otherwise, discovered the secret to the general Allis Mardacan ('Ali Mardan Khan),[1] who happened to be passing through. This coin served him once as ransom money, when he had been captured by Shiva Ji.

These temples are in parts destroyed, for when any army passes that way they make efforts to find, if they can, what 'Ali Mardan Khan found. I have not the least doubt that in these temples there is buried money, but it cannot be easily discovered, the edifices being very spacious and paved with large stones. He who knows the place of concealment is the oldest and principal Brahman. Before he dies he informs another who is to take his place. Their idea is that if any Hindu king should gain the kingdom and make war on the Mahomedans, they would then disclose the existence of these hoards, and use the money to support him against the enemy. But in all these fifty-four years I have seen no Hindu prince on the increase, but only ruined; Shiva Ji alone have I seen living and thriving in the manner that I have recounted.

TRIMBAK HILL

This village Trimbak is situated at the foot of a high hill. At the top is a gloomy cavity full of water. In the rains this overflows, and running down the hill, forms a stream twenty feet wide, which passes close to the village. It is walled in on both sides with stone. Lower down it becomes wider, and thence this river continues its course until it joins the sea between Masulipatam and

---

Administration,' iii. 210). N.M. evidently confounds the word with the Persian *ganj*, 'a treasure.

1. This probably refers to 'Ali Mardan Khan, Haidarabadi, who was captured outside Jinji by Santa Ji, Ghorparah, in the thirty-fifth year of Aurangzeb 'Alamgir (1691-92) (see 'Ma,asir-ul-Umara,' ii. 824). He died about 1706.

the island of Diva.[1] It is a rather large stream with very sweet running water. Its name is the Kishna.

In the village is a temple, into which I went from curiosity. I saw various figures of idols, and outside the gate of the temple were two stones, one on the top of the other, like millstones. I noticed next day that men and women came, having some object in their mind, and placed their hand on the stone. They waited for the devil to move it and show them what they wanted to know. If it moved towards the right, they were pleased, and entered the temple to render thanks; if it turned to the left, they were disconsolate, supposing that things [449] would not turn out well with them, and they quitted the spot in dejection. Out of curiosity I resolved to see in what consisted this miracle. I remarked that the under stone was somewhat oval and the upper one concave, smooth, and covered with oil. Thus, hardly had you placed your hand on it when the slightest movement made it turn a little. In this way these simple and stupid folk, not recognising this fact, were bamboozled.

HINDU HOLY PLACES

In this realm of India, although King Aurangzeb destroyed numerous temples, there does not thereby fail to be many left at different places, both in his empire and in the territories subject to the tributary princes. All of them are thronged with worshippers; even those that are destroyed are still venerated by the Hindus and visited for the offering of alms. The Hindus assert that in the world there are seven principal places where it is possible to obtain what one has imagined and desired—that is to say, in cases where a person wishes to become emperor or king, wealthy, powerful, or to attain other positions of the same order. Now they ordinarily hold that on dying a person's soul is transferred according to the deeds he has done; if he has done good, his soul will pass into some one of consideration or of wealth, and should the deceased have done evil, his soul will be sent into some animal—an elephant, camel, buffalo, cow, tiger, wolf, a bird, a snake, a fish, *et cetera*. Now, some great sinner, deserving of hell, may be

1. The Kistna, or Krishna, River, does fall into the sea near these points, but then it does not rise near Trimbak, but at Mahabaleshwar. N.M. confounds the Kistna and the Godavari Rivers; the latter does rise somewhere west of Nasik.

XXXI. Mohammad Amin Khan, son of Mir Jumlah

Vol. III *To face page 232*

noble, or whatever he fancies; it can be done by sacrificing his life by drowning himself in a river or in the tanks found near temples at the foot of the gates.

The principal temples referred to above are these—that is to say:

1. The first, Maya,[1] to be found among the mountains of the north.
2. Matura (Mathura), which is near the city of Agrah.
3. Caxis (Kashi), which is on the Ganges, in the city of Benares.
4. Canchis (Kanji), in the Karnatik.
5. Evantica, in the mountains of Tartary.
6. Puris (Puri), on the borders of Cochin China.
7. Darahotis (? Gangotri), at the source of the Ganges, as they suppose it to be [451].

Bands of interested persons make these lengthy pilgrimages, enduring a thousand hardships on the way, only at the end to drown by their own choice, without considering where they are about to take up their abode.

The chief temples destroyed by King Aurangzeb within his kingdom were the following:

1. Maisa (? Mayapur).
2. Matura (Mathura),
3. Caxis (Kashi).
4. Hajudia (Ajudhya),

and an infinite number of others; but, not to tire the reader. I do not append their names.

1. Maya is probably Mayapur, close to Hardwar. Nos. 2, 3, and 4 are well known. Evantica (5) is unknown to me. Darahoti (7) I take to be Gangotri. No. 6 must be some other Puri than the one in Orissah.

CONTINUATION
OF THE
HISTORY OF THE MOGULS

SIGNOR NICOLAO MANUCCI, VENETIAN[1]

1. From the text in the Biblioteca Nazionale di San' Marco at Venice, Codex Italiano No. XLIV. (Zanetti). In this manuscript Parts I. to HI. occupy 616 pages, and are in Italian; Part IV. begins a new pagination, and is in French.

HISTORY OF THE MOGUL

FOURTH PART

PREFACE

I made some promises in my last book [Part III., p. 79] to continue my history, if it pleased God to preserve me in a little health. Yet it seemed that the advanced age at which I have already arrived, and the serious occupation provided by the prospect of another life, might have dispensed me from writing more about what goes on in the Mogul's empire, wherewith I have entertained you, dear reader, in the first three parts of this history, which I have sent to be printed. Nevertheless, in spite of any inclination I may feel for repose. I am anxious to acquit myself of my promise; and I again take up my pen to tell you of what has happened and is still happening at the court of Aurangzeb. I shall set forth in this Fourth Part any remarkable event that I may have overlooked. I mean to write without passion, but with all possible exactitude and sincerity, just as I have done up to this point, and relate all that has taken place at this renowned court. Here you will find, dear reader, something for your instruction and at the same time for your diversion. The great and generous actions of some will serve as excellent examples to follow, and the faults of others will yield you salutary warnings.

It looks as if everything in India were being made ready for some remarkable revolution. The great age of the emperor, who is more than eighty-six years old,[1] and the ambition to gain the throne continuously displayed by his sons and grandsons, give rise to the apprehension of some catastrophe quite as tragic as that supervening at the close of Shahjahan's reign. In spite of this, the ablest politicians—those who have acquired in the course of many years great experience of, and acquaintance with, the affairs of this crown—assert that all will be peaceful so long

1. Aurangzeb was born on the 15th Zu,l Qa'dah, 1027 H. (November 3, 1618, N.S.), so that early in 1701 he was about eighty-five lunar, and eighty-two solar, years of age.

as the aged monarch is still in this world. In saying this they rely on the admirable conduct and the good [2] government of this prince, who, in spite of his great age and the infirmities inseparable from it, knows how to get himself always obeyed with his former vigour, and to hold every man to his allegiance.

In return for my sitting up at night and all my industry. I hope, my dear reader, to reap the only fruit to which I have ever looked forward, namely, your instruction united with your satisfaction. I shall be more than content if I can succeed to that extent, and for that much will readily give thanks to God, who is the sole Author of all that men can do of good in this world. Farewell.

I begin this Fourth Part of the history with the eighteenth century since the coming of our Saviour. Shiva Ji, the powerful rajah or Hindu king, of whom I have spoken in the previous parts, is the first to present himself for continuing the current of my story. At the beginning of the present year (? 1701) the general Zu,lfiqar Khan besieged the fortress of Parlanaguer [Parnala-garh], a strong place formerly belonging to the kingdom of Bijapur, but now held by Shiva Ji. The Mahomedan general was at the head of an army of fifty thousand foot and thirty thousand cavalry.[1] In the month of February of the same year (1701) this rajah collected his troops and came against his enemy, advancing even to his entrenchments. The fight was bloody, and in the end victory declared itself for Shiva Ji. He defeated Zu,lfiqar Khan's army, and forced that general to retire in disorder from his position before the fortress. All the Mahomedan artillery and baggage fell into the victor's hands, who pursued with all imaginable energy, seizing all the fugitives, and, to sum up, sparing no one who bore arms. As for the others, he was cruel enough to order their right hands and their noses to be cut off; of the latter class there were so many, that they are still to be seen in all the directions to which they have dispersed. Nevertheless, he did not stop short at this one attack, for, finding himself victorious, he has never ceased to disturb the royal army, making new assaults on it from one day to

1. In 1111 H. (June 28, 1699, to June 16, 1700) Bedar Bakht was sent against Parnalah ('Ma,asir-i-'Alamgiri,' 429, last line); Zu,lfiqar Khan's force was also sent (*ibid.*, 430, line 3).

another, engaging it at different points, and stopping the delivery of supplies. From this cause there is nearly always great scarcity in the king's camp, and the price of provisions is very high—so much so that one measure of rice weighing no more than twenty-eight ounces has been at times sold for eighteen rupees.

It was about the same time that a general of Shah 'Alam's cavalry, that prince being then in the province of Kabul, came to him and complained that one 'Aziz Khan, commanding a corps of five hundred horse, had raised a quarrel with him, and had displayed his anger in some sharp and abusive words, his soldiers having backed him up and encouraged him in his insolent attitude. Their reasons were that a great deal of money was owing to them, and that for many a day they had received nothing.

[2A][1] The enquiring reader should recollect that in the Third Part (III. 22, 27) of this history. I spoke of the great pay and allowances that the Mogul gives to the commanders of his armies, the other officers, and, generally speaking, to all his troops; and I have said there that the king gave to those who had a *Hazari* certain lands, from the income of which they were under an obligation to maintain one thousand horse. I ought to add that, in addition to that land, he gives as a favour one rupee a day for each horse. This makes three hundred and sixty-five thousand rupees a year for the thousand horses.[2] Nevertheless, as it is a favour, and the king knows that the *Hazaris*, more often than not, are unable to maintain those horsemen on the pay, he allows them to keep up no more than the quarter of the number. He does not look narrowly into this matter; although, in spite of the deficiency, the said *Hazaris*, the *Mansabdars*, and the other officers of the army never fail to draw their pay as if they had the full number of horse required. In this manner, the name or title is 'of a thousand,' and they receive pay for a thousand men, while the number they entertain is only two hundred and fifty.

Besides the above money which they receive for their

1. Here are interpolated in the original two unnumbered pages, which I mark as 2A and 2B.
2. Rs. 30 6 a. 8 p. per man per month. This must mean the *Tabinan* (troopers') pay (see my 'Moghul Army,' 1903, p. 9).

horsemen, they are also paid for their personal expenses fifty thousand rupees a year. It is just the same with all the other officers, high and low, in proportion. They may be seen from the figures that I have entered in my Third Part (III. 27). Still, in spite of all this [the false musters], the rank, the merit, and the profits of the *Hazaris* and the *Mansabdars* arise chiefly from keeping a large force of cavalry. By acting thus they are more thought of by the king, and more feared by other nobles. From the above springs the fact that there are *Hazaris* and *Mansabdars* drawing identical pay, but not keeping up the same number of horse. There are also several of both classes who have the name and title of two, of three, of four, of five, of six, of seven [*Hazaris*], whose pay is always rising in proportion to the favour they are in.

It is the case with the *Hazaris* that the Mogul does not confer on all of them the same honours; for there are some to whom he accords drums, trumpets, and other instruments of music, which are carried before them, together with hands in silver, as I have stated in my description of a royal march contained in my First Part (I. 50). But this favour is only granted to those towards whom he has a particular inclination, or to those who, as he considers, really merit it by their own, or their father's or grandfather's services.

It must also be mentioned that he does not always give what he promises; for instance, after the conquest of the kingdoms of Bijapur and Gulkandah, he promised numerous privileges and the honours of an Hazari to many men of those countries; but when he had become absolute master of those places, he would only give them Hazari rank carrying four months' pay. This is much inferior to others, as may be seen by referring to my remarks on pay (III. 20). He also treated them less generously than other officers in two ways. First, they were given very few 'cavalry';[1] secondly, he gave them a higher rank than was fitting for *Hazaris* of that pay. Thus, instead of gaining, they were forced to expend their own money to keep up their horsemen.

Not only did he not reward them as he had promised, but he caused several of them to be poisoned, quite light-heartedly, on

1. I interpret this as referring to *suwar* rank, which was in addition to the *zat* rank (see my 'Moghul Army,' p. 9).

mere suspicion, just for fear they might betray him as they had done their former sovereign. He acted in the same way after the conquest of other kingdoms, Hindu and Mahomedan. Several persons belonging to them had blindly confided in him by reason of the promises that he made, and the rewards and honours they hoped to obtain from him. In the end they found themselves looked on as traitors. They had forgotten that the Mogul promises much and gives little. In spite of this being well enough known, he still goes on engaging, and then deceiving, a number of people by such-like false promises. Thus has he always lived, and does still live, like a hypocrite—that is to say, good and holy to look at, but in reality an ill-doer and devil.

Thus have I ever beheld with great astonishment that this prince, from the very beginning of his reign, has never promoted any traitor to his former country, whatever might be the services he had rendered to him. It is true that he has not acted in that way to the children, grand-children, relations, or descendants of such traitors. On the contrary, these he has ever advanced, just like any other of his subjects, according to their merits. In short, this has been all his life long one of his political maxims, to put the fathers, grandfathers, and uncles to death for being traitors to their country, in order not to suffer himself afterwards from similar perfidy; while he has promoted their descendants in the hope of gaming their friendship and affection. He knows, as says Machiavel, that he who desires to obliterate injuries past and done cannot resort to a more effective medicine than the prescribing of silver. Still, some of the first-named men, seeing that their misery and their affliction were increasing day by day, have frequently quitted him and offered their services to Shiva Ji, hoping thereby to improve their lot. In this course they have been imitated by a number of Mahomedans, who daily adopt the same expedient, and subsequently live on nothing but the pillage and brigandage of which they are guilty in the lands of their liege lord and king.

[Here the digression about pay, inserted on the two interpolated pages, comes to an end, and the narrative as to the revolt of Shah 'Alam's troops in Kabul is resumed.]

[3] The prince rose forthwith. As his head was still troubled by the fumes of several bottles of Kabul wine that he had lately

drink, he fell at once into a fury and ordered his cavalry to lose not a moment in massacring 'Aziz Khan and his men. Measures were taken immediately to carry out this barbarous order; but the men composing the attacking force met with more resistance than they had bargained for and they were forced into fighting at close quarters. The contest was not a happy one for 'Aziz Khan; he lost his life, while his five hundred men were cut to pieces. It is true that almost an equal number perished on the other side in executing the prince's order. He had given the order in anger while heated with wine, and did not fail to repent of it as soon as both those incentives had evaporated.

In this same month [? February, 1701] died in that province (Kabul) the well-beloved wife of Shah 'Alam, mother of the Prince Rafi'-ul-qadr. Her name was Nurnicham Begom (Nur-un-nissa Begam);[1] she was in every way a most accomplished princess. Thus, her death was a great affliction to both father and son. All the courtiers offered their condolences; but on this occasion King Aurangzeb took the principal part. He reminded the two mourners that no affliction fell upon man without Divine permission and express decree of Providence, to chastise him for his sins and bring him back to his duty. History afforded many examples of this truth, while our experience taught us the same thing every day. 'Who knows' (as he sent word to Shah 'Alam) 'whether what you are at present suffering has not befallen you in return for the ruin you have brought upon several families, reducing them to misery by killing your captain, 'Aziz Khan, and his troopers, whose throats were cut without mercy in obedience to your orders?'

With regard to Shiva Ji, no sooner had Aurangzeb heard of the rout of the general Zu,lfiqar Khan, and the sad state to which he had been reduced by that rajah, than he made a start in person to succour him. He intended to besiege the fortress, the investment of which the above captain had been obliged to abandon, since the enemy never ceased their attacks on him nor their sorties.

1. Nur-un-nissa was the daughter of Sanjar Khan, Najm Sani, and exercised great influence. over her husband, Her child, Rafi'-ul-qadr, was the third son of Shah 'Alam ('Ma,asir-i-Alamgiri,' 106, 107, and Khafi Khan, ii. 330).

In the month of March of this same year (? 1701) an accident happened to this aged monarch, which displays how he still preserves great discretion, and shows exactly the same character I have before described. While engaged in the siege of this fortress of Parnala-garh, he was returning one day from relieving nature when his strength gave way, so that he fell down and dislocated his right knee. From this accident he has become lame, and can only walk with great difficulty, owing to his hurt having been badly attended to. But to Conceal his infirmity as far as ever he can, before he appears on the throne to hold audience, he causes a curtain to be hung up in front, which is not withdrawn until he has taken his seat. The same practice is followed in the *Ghusl-khanah,* the place where the second audience is held, as I have already stated (III. 77). His passion for reigning is so great, as also his desire that his reign should be long-continued, that he betrays signs of this feeling on all occasions. He displays much firmness and strength of mind. It was with this idea that he said one [4] day publicly that, strictly speaking, kings wanted nothing but sight and speech; God in his mercy had preserved to him both, although eighty-six years of age, 'without counting' (as he added) 'the thirty sound teeth that I still posses.' He wished to insinuate by these words that he had still the same eyes as before to observe everything, the same tongue to issue orders and commands; lastly, thirty teeth to bite with, and punish those guilty of any fault or disobedience to his orders. He added: 'So much is this the case that I think of calling myself from this day "the second Taimur-i-lang" '

That very same day Prince Kam Bakhsh came to announce to the monarch that a son had been born to him, supplicating him in humble terms to confer on it a name and tide, as is the custom. The king replied that he was at liberty to name the child himself; and his (Aurangzeb's) command was that when the son of this infant should be born into the world, he undertook to give it a name. By this he wished them to understand that he looked forward to still living many years—nay, that in a measure he was sure of it. Nor is he the only one holding the opinion that this will come to pass, for they have the simpleness to believe him to be a saint. At this the worthy Nestor is far from displeased; on the contrary, he had hardly contain himself for joy when he hears it said that he is so styled, and that they believe him to be such. Thus he does all that in him lies to persuade men that he is such in reality; and he still displays a patience, proof against the roughest political disturbances, such as he has always exercised.

A few years ago Shah 'Alam, when seated with the king, happened, probably unintentionally, to place his hand on his beard and contemplate it. The king, having noticed this gesture, and being aware of his secret wishes, said to his son that he need not be in such a hurry to look at his beard: his day for reigning was still in the distant future. At these words poor Shah 'Alam sank his head in shame and withdrew. It can be easily understood that such speeches were hardly pleasing to the princes his sons. For each longs to be king, there being in this world nothing sweeter than to be set in authority over others; and it is already sufficient vexation to them to find he has lived so long, without his beginning to boast that he has still a long life before him.

I should never have done were I to recount all the frauds and hypocrisies of this king. But, after all, since I have undertaken to give some stories, as much to entertain my reader as to inform him of the frailties and virtues of mankind, the life of this monarch of Hindustan furnishes me with ample store. Everywhere are seen in it lively pictures of the excesses to which men can be driven by a passion for rule. This is why I shall choose the principal events in it, those that I consider the most appropriate to my design.

We have already seen to what lengths this prince carries the passion for rule. However, feeling himself greatly weakened by age, and consequently unable longer to see to everything himself, he issued an order that Prince Kam Bakhsh should sign on his [5] behalf all papers and dispatches issued by the State. This order was given at a time when several [Hindu] princes seemed to be meditating rebellion, were disobedient to orders, and refused to pay their tribute. They had gone so far in their audacity as to attack his generals and pursue them in divers places. These acts caused much chagrin and disgust to the aged monarch, yet he did not fail to put in force his old precepts, and prescribed to his commanders and generals the methods to be followed for overcoming these enemies and rebels, and misleading the Hindu princes.

When the general Zu,lfiqar Khan appeared to take leave of him preparatory to joining his army, he confided to him several instructions in respect of the above. Among other things he said to him in so many words: 'When you have an enemy to destroy, spare nothing rather than fail, neither deceptions, subterfuges, nor false oaths, for anything is permissible in open war. Invent as many tricks, if possible, as there are grains of purslane[1] on your arm after you withdraw it from a barrel of honey. In one word, make use of every pretext in the world that you judge capable of bringing you success in your projects.'

At the beginning of June in this year, 1701, the fortress of Parnala-garh, finding all its food and other supplies exhausted, was forced to surrender to Aurangzeb.

Learning by reports repeated daily that the rebel Hindu princes had never ceased to ravage and plunder Hindustan still more and more, the monarch issued orders to his son, A'zam Shah, to apply some remedy. Shah 'Alam, as soon as he heard of tins order, lost no time in coming out of the province of Kabul, and made for Multan city. Afraid that A'zam Shah might make common cause with the rebel princes and become master of the castles and cities of Dihli and Agrah, he (Shah 'Alam) directed his son, 'Azim-ud-din, to leave Bengal without delay, and march as quickly as he could to the latter of these cities. He hoped thus to hinder A'zam Shah from carrying out his [supposed] designs.

Here again is a specimen of Aurangzeb's passion for appearing to the minds of his people—above all, to those of his own religion—as a saintly and charitable man. There was a childless woman who had employed all methods, both legitimate and superstitious, to become fruitful, but without success. In the end she took it into her head that she would vow a payment of five rupees to the saintly king. The vow had due effect, and several years afterwards the woman gave birth to a fine, healthy male child. After her recovery she proceeded to the court to

1. 'Pourpier' in the text: an allusion, I suppose, to the minuteness of the seed, and the consequent innumerable drops of honey of that size.

carry out her promise, but she encountered difficulties in approaching the king's person. The fact came to the king's knowledge, and he ordered her to be admitted, desiring to receive in person from her hands the sacrificial offering, which was at once distributed to the poor. This act conquered for him among all those composing his court the reputation of saintliness and great charity. To confirm them in such an opinion, he has never allowed, nor does he ever allow, an occasion to escape which can be used to further this design [6].

Here is one more example which I have selected from a number of others. His wife Depoury (Udepuri Mahal) invited him one day to her apartments, where she wished to treat him to a *ragoût* she had herself prepared. To gratify her the king consented. But as a servant-girl was bringing in the stew, she let the dish drop and broke it. The queen was very dejected at this accident, the more so that she saw herself deprived of the pleasure of offering to her husband a dish that she had prepared with so much trouble. Thus her impulse was to punish the servant-girl at once, but the king interfered, and resorted to every device to appease her wrath, in no way sparing soft and conciliatory words, as is his habit. He reminded her that it was God's good Providence that had thus ordained; It was (he added) a manifestation that a sinner, such as he, was not worthy to eat of so delicate a *plât*. He added order words, which in the end cooled the wrath of the queen.

Moved by this craze of being held a saint, the king got up one night to pray. Before beginning he ordered a eunuch to bring him water to wash his hands and feet, for it is a great sin among the Mahomedans to say your prayers without this ceremony. The eunuch, heavy with sleep, rose in a hurry, and by mischance stumbled against the king and knocked him down. Overcome with fear and dread, the eunuch collapsed at once in the other direction, with all the appearance of a dead man. The king noticed this, and said to him in the mildest of tones: 'Wherefore fearest thou a created being, one like thyself? thou shouldest reserve such fear for God, and thereby hinder thyself from offending Him. Rise and be not afraid.' As soon as this adventure became known among the people, they were confirmed in their previous good opinion of his holiness.

Another time, as the king was on his way to the mosque, one of the officials noticed that the carpet on which he would have to tread had a hole in it, and he therefore attempted to spread a cloth over it. On noticing this action, the king reproved the man most severely, and said that all this cleaning and fussing was well enough for the court, but had no place in God's house, where he was no higher than the least of his subjects. These words were highly prized by the people, and regarded as proceeding from a saint. This is ever the chief end aimed at by this monarch in all his actions and in all his talk. I add another example.

Some years ago there arrived in the Mogul country two Arabs from Mecca, who were differently dressed from Indians. After these men had suffered many privations from inability to get employment in the king's service, they thought of a stratagem which had excellent results. They set to work to study the character of Aurangzeb, and, having done so, they resorted to the mosque one day when the king would appear there. When the king arrived, they began, as agreed on between them, to stand up and make signs to each other [7], expressing extreme astonishment, throwing their glances at the king's person, and making it seem that their wonder was growing greater and greater at each step of his approach to them. The king saw all these grimaces, and asked them what was the cause of their astonishment. 'Your majesty,' they replied, 'it is not without good cause! For only a few months ago we had the felicity of seeing your majesty, clad as a *faqir*, enter into and issue from the dome at Mecca, where our most Holy Prophet is entombed; and here, today, we find you again surrounded by all this state and dignity.' The king, in reply to this speech, said with an air of gravity that entry into the house in question was free only to God's faithful servitors, and that the great could not draw near to it in any other garb.

When prayers were over, he took those two Arabs into his service, and gave them enough for an honourable subsistence. This affair made many people in the Mogul country believe that this king is of a truth a very great saint, that he becomes invisible whenever he pleases, and proceeds to Mecca to hold conversations with Muhammad. From this cause the people revere him, and hold him in the greatest respect. Yet in spite of his being himself imbued with this idea, he assumes always great humility in his attitude. Of this fact here is one example.

For instance, if he sends orders to an officer at a distance in regard to any complaint that has been made of his conduct, and then learns that the said order has passed unheeded, and submission to it has been refused, he betrays no wrath at such insubordination. All he says is (and that in the softest voice) that he is only a miserable sinner, that there is no reason for astonishment if his orders are disregarded, since every day those of God Himself are neglected and repudiated. He does not forget, however, to repeat his orders, and adopt very exact means of getting them executed.

This monarch is also desirous of appearing a great lover of justice. This is why he said one day that it was the bounden duty of kings to apply themselves unweariedly and painstakingly to the dispensing of equal justice to everybody. For, as he said, this duty and that we owe to God for having devoted us to His sole service are the two principal grounds of action on which should rest the conduct of princes. They owe inviolable fidelity to that Supreme Being, and must work without ceasing for the furtherance of His glory and the propagation of religion. The great Taimur-i-lang, my ancestor, that illustrious conqueror and founder of empire, was a rare and magnificent exemplar of these fine qualities. For, as it may well be said, nothing except love of justice and of virtue forced that great prince into the war he undertook against Bayazid, Emperor of the Turks. Everybody knows that it was the cries of the oppressed and innocent that put arms into his hands. He did not drop them until he had enjoyed the pleasing satisfaction of inflicting on this cruel tyrant a punishment proportioned to the heinousness of his crimes. I may well assert without flattering myself overmuch,' he added, 'that they are the [8] same motives which have hitherto impelled me. Yes, the fear of seeing the Mahomedan religion oppressed in Hindustan if my brother Dara had ascended the throne; that of beholding the ruin of the kingdom, which I looked on as inevitable if my father's reign had continued, by reason of his bad government: these are the only causes why I have always opposed myself strongly and without self-seeking to the attempts of everyone to supplant me. In addition, from how many miseries have I not delivered my subjects by the course I have pursued? They are now enabled to enjoy in repose and with delight all the good and pleasant fruits that it has produced. It is by it that my kingdom is now full of noble mosques in place of the hideous temples crowded with idols, which, had I not been here, would undoubtedly have been erected. Instead of taverns and houses of ill-fame, which would have spread their poison all around, we find congregations of devout men, modest and full of wisdom, who proclaim without ceasing the greatness and the virtues of God.' But, in spite of all that this monarch may assert, it is not to be controverted that every day there are committed in Hindustan the most monstrous crimes in the world.

This prince does his utmost to maintain in the eyes of the world the prevailing opinion that he is zealous in the cause of justice. Each day he holds two audiences, where without distinction anyone can gain admission. He listens patiently to complaints, and causes the judgment he pronounces to be executed upon the spot. In spite of all these exertions, his kingdom is overrun with men whose only profession is to act as false witnesses or to forge signatures. These wretches assume a most modest attitude and attire, so that they impose upon people. They wear the clothes of penitents, have long beards, hold a chaplet constantly in their hand, and as they tell their beads are for ever mumbling a prayer. Such men are greatly in fashion, because they seem to be conforming to the king's intentions. Yet the whole country is full of the disorder that these hypocrites have sown in families by their vile false-hoods. For in this vile science they possess all imaginable skill and acuteness. I will lay one example before you.

A Mahomedan I knew had, to oblige a friend, become his surety for some amount of money or other. A little time afterwards the friend died before he had liquidated the debt for which the Mahomedan had stood surety. He to whom the money was due lost no time in taking measures to constrain the guarantor into paying. The latter was informed of the trick that was to be played upon him, and to cover himself he interviewed some of the honest gentlemen of whom I spoke above. In return for a consideration of two thousand five hundred rupees, which he disbursed to them, they were to fabricate for him documents and evidence, by virtue of which he would be entitled to make a still larger counter-claim than the sum his opponent demanded. The suit came before the king, and there the documents of the Mahomedan surety were inspected and accepted as so truly executed that the poor creditor, to whom a great deal of money was owing, was not [9] only defrauded of the money he had demanded but was further condemned to make over to the Mahomedan the total amount of these false bonds. I might bring up an infinite umber of similar cases, for such are newly cropping up every day in Hindustan. But to continue would probably end in wearying my readers. However, I will tell one adventure which not only I, but several other Europeans witnessed; and it will serve as confirmation of the disloyalty of these people and evil conduct.

An Armenian of Madras, having had several unlucky transactions, took flight to the kingdom of Gulkandah. He owed a considerable sum to an English inhabitant of the same town; and this man soon afterwards caused him to be followed, and efforts were made to get payment, or at the least to recover something of what was due. The creditor hoped that on such an occasion the Mahomedans would lend him a helping hand, seeing the rightfulness of his claim. The poor man was sadly deceived! He had also entered on his pursuit in the face of advice to the contrary, given him by a large number of people better informed than he was of the way in which justice dealt out among these peoples. For the debtor collected false witnesses who deposed that the Englishman was largely in debt to the man whose creditor he really was. These wretches swore that in their presence he had admitted the debt, that he had even promised to pay one moiety on the spot. On this evidence he was decreed against, and even thrown into prison. The poor fellow, overwhelmed at this cruel result, wrote to me for advice as to how he should proceed to get out of this awkward fix. I answered as well as I could, giving him such counsels as I thought most useful. Since that time I have had no news of him, and cannot say what has become of him. This affair was an extremely thorny one; for the whole Mahomedan population knows no other influence than that of money. Relations, friends, written recommendations, nothing avails; and besides, they never adjudicate on any dispute, unless they obtain at least one-third of the moneys forming the subject of the suit. This is the most widespread vice of that part of the population; but one must admit that it is so mean a one that it obscures almost all the good qualities that this people might possess.

There was also in the time of Shahjahan a private person who summoned one of his neighbours for the payment of some food-supplies owing to him. He took the case to the *qazi* of the town of Agrah, he being the head judge. The government of the place was at that time in the hands of a eunuch, a man of sense and great judgment. The complainant referred to put in an appearance at the *qazi's* court, and produced his papers and the evidence on which he had instituted his claim. The judge, after examining the documents, said to him that they were not sufficient, and he must in addition produce witnesses. The man was greatly perplexed, and being unable to find any men ready to serve him—for at that time they were not as numerous as they are in these days—he applied to the governor, and [10] laid before him a report of the whole affair.

This officer, a most enlightened man, as I have already said, recognised that the applicant was in the right, and what he asked for was most just. For this reason he advised him to go next morning to the *qazi's* court, and get as close to him as he could, taking every precaution that no one should overhear what he said. Having observed these instructions, he should then pour into the *qazi's* ear all imaginable sorts of abuse, quite regardless of consequences. The man failed not to put this counsel into execution on the following day. On hearing these whispered words, the indignant *qazi* became beside himself with rage at such audacity, and forthwith passed sentence of death upon the man. But as it was necessary for the governor to confirm the order before its execution, the judge was obliged to appear before him to obtain his consent. Having arrived there at the audience-hall, he set forth to the governor the reasons for which he had condemned this man to death. Thereupon the eunuch asked him for witnesses to his assertions. The *qazi* answered that he had none, but he ought to be believed on his word. The governor retorted that this very man whom he had just condemned was thoroughly in the right in the action he had brought, and yet he, the head of the law, had declined to afford him justice, because he had no witnesses. To these remarks he added several words of salutary advice as to the course he should pursue in the exercise of his office, above all, when the matter in hand was the examination and admission of testimony. On hearing this discourse the judge withdrew in confusion, and without delay delivered judgment in that man's case exactly as he himself would have wished.

I think it important to reproduce these stories accurately, so that those who may read my work, and then travel to this part of the world inhabited by Mahomedans, shall be forearmed by reflecting on all that I say. Let them be well on their guard against acting on their own sentiments; if they do, they will be cruelly undeceived, and will tumble into pitfalls from which the best advice in the world will be unable to pull them out; just as it happened to the Englishman whose story I told a little while ago.

To speak in general terms, the Mahomedans are great dissemblers, and of this the ceremonial of their prayers is an incontestable proof. When they acquit themselves of this religious duty, they keep their face turned towards the west, and never omit to deposit before them a stone. During the time of prayer they affect an attitude of abstraction and modesty. Their prayers are addressed to God and their false prophet. First they stand, next they kneel, and while in this position they are a long time striking their forehead against the stone in front of them, so that the mark of it is imprinted on the skin and remains as a sign to everyone that they have just prayed. This gives them great weight among the people, for by this method they are looked on as saints, and acquire such great credit that all they choose to say is held to be absolute verity. Then they employ this good opinion that is held of them as a means of duping and deceiving everybody.[1]

---

1. I never observed myself the use of a stone in this way in India; but my friend Mr. Yusuf Ali, of the Indian Civil Service, tells me that some *Darveshes* (holy men), instead of simply striking the head on the hard ground, place a stone for use in the *sijdah* (prostration). The stone serves also a pillow for sleep. 'With or without a stone, if the floor is hard and the worshipper is constantly engaged in *sijdah*, the ground leaves a hard mark on the forehead, which is looked on as a sign of merit. Many devotees in India bear such a mark. It is supposed that on Judgment Day this mark will render it easier to recognise them as prayerful and pious men.' As Mr. Yusuf Ali truly points out, Mahomedans never address prayer to the Prophet Muhammad. Perhaps we find an instance of this use of a stone in 'Ma,asir-i-'Alamgiri,' p. 346, where we are told that, on his way to the Friday prayer, Aurangzeb carried with him several stones in order to accumulate 'merit' (*sawab*); and an allusion to the practice may, perhaps, be detected in Khushhal Khan, Khattak's, line:

   'Tho' a person dash his head against the ground a thousand times..' (H. G. Raverty, 'Notes on Afghanistan,' part iv., p. 400).

[11] As for the women, in addition to their ordinary devotions, which seem sincere enough, they have a most especial devotion to the Holy Virgin Mary. This seems rather surprising in a country where the Quran is followed; yet none of these women will go to bed without addressing some prayers to the Queen of Heaven. I am fully persuaded that if they were the mistresses, they would embrace the whole religion of our Saviour. They have an infinitude of reasons inclining them to this; but the most touching of all is the precept of our religion forbidding us to have more than one wife. They are much affected by this circumstance, and betray much pleasure and satisfaction when spoken to on the subject.

Here is one story more, one which did more than a little to strengthen people in their belief in the would-be saintliness of Aurangzeb. A woman, the widow of one of the king's generals, finding herself in poverty, presented to him a petition asking for assistance. When the king had read the petition, he ordered three hundred rupees to be given to the lady. She refused the money. When this came to the king's ears, he had her called before him, and asked her why she had not accepted what he had wished to give her. 'The reason is,' she answered, 'that there is no proportion between such a small gift and the great services rendered by my husband to your majesty; and, further, it is in every way far beneath the dignity of so mighty a monarch.' At this retort the king threw her two papers, one bearing an order for one thousand rupees and the other one for three hundred. He told her to pick up whichever she thought fit, when the sum recorded on it would be disbursed to her. Chance ruled that she took up the paper bearing the sum of three hundred rupees. At this the king said to her; 'You see that fortune gives you no more than I had done. Console yourself, then, under God's will, as you have not desired to confide in me.'

Some little time afterwards a trader of Kashmir, a very ingenious man and most skilful workman, made a coat of very rich gold thread, to which he had devoted much time. On this coat he raised in very fine embroidery some words from the Quran. After it was finished and perfected, he laid it before the king, imagining that he would be delighted to buy a coat so richly worked. At first the king was very pleased with it, but on hearing the high price asked for it, he said he had made a vow never to wear costly clothes, nor was he worthy to wear on his body such holy words, miserable sinner as he was. The trader carried away his coat and offered it to Shah 'Alam; but this prince, feeling bound to imitate the king his father, gave him a similar answer. In the end the merchant, seeing all his grand expectations had miscarried, laid the coat before the *wazir* Ja'far Khan. He bought it, although [12] at a much lower price than the owner had asked. The man, not having found anyone else to buy it, left it with Ja'far Khan at the price he offered. During the festival of the Sacrifice Ja'far Khan put on this coat and repaired to court. On seeing him, the king said: 'You seem to be better off than I am.' 'Nay, sire,' was Ja'far Khan's prudent answer, 'I have expended all I possessed in the purchase of this coat; to the end that by clothing myself in such holy words they may wash me clean of my sins and furnish me with all the intelligence and capacity required to serve your majesty efficiently.'

I must allude once more in passing to those wretched pretenders to holiness of whom I have talked so much; and their history is somewhat diverting; for usually they are to be seen chaplet in hand, as I have said, and their habit is to repeat loudly the word 'Alla y alla' (Allah, ya Allah!)—that is, 'O God! O God!' It is their custom to pray in public, but once they get home at night into their houses their tune changes. They take their station at their door, holding their beads in their band, and await the arrival of some of their women devotees. As they tell their beads, they say: 'Let her be between twelve to fifteen years old.' After a time, if no one comes, they change the words and say: 'Between fifteen and twenty.' Another hour having elapsed without an arrival, they change again and say: 'Between twenty and thirty.' Finally, when they are tired out with telling their beads in this guise without catching anything, they make one last attempt by saying: 'Let who may come, even if she be an old woman.' They continue until midnight this odious and ridiculous orison. Then, abandoning all hope of having their desires gratified, they go off to bed, saying: 'Alas! To-day I must have been guilty of some heinous sin, since God has not been gracious to my prayers.'

In 1669 a *faqir* rose one Friday very early in the morning and took it into his head to break with a hammer some of the steps at the great mosque, where Aurangzeb was used to attend and perform his devotions upon that day. The man was caught at work, arrested, and brought before the king when he was on his way to the mosque. The king directed his detention until prayers were over, when he would take cognizance of his crime. The devotions completed, the *faqir* was brought up. Then the king, with a grave and serious air, said to him: 'I am surprised at your professing to serve God, and yet setting to work to destroy a mosque. What profit do you thereby derive, I pray you tell me?' 'What,' said the culprit, without betraying any astonishment, 'you take notice of very minute trifles, and pay no heed to the cruel and barbarous way in which you treated your father and your brothers, nor to the tyrannies and perfidies which are daily carried out under your orders!' The king felt these reproaches most keenly, and asked the *qazi* then in attendance what punishment the *faqir* deserved. The *qazi* answered that he ought to be decapitated [13], for which there were two reasons: First, for wanting to destroy the steps by which the faithful so devoutly mounted to God's house; secondly, for having been so bold as to speak to his majesty as he had done, his offence being intensified by his majesty being the image of God upon earth.

The *faqir*, on hearing this finding, derided it, and said to the *qazi*: 'Those are fine decisions you are in the habit of giving. Are you not aware that the steps can be rebuilt as they were before? but take away my life, and you know not how to restore it. He uttered these words with great firmness, pressing him for a reply to this argument. But as the *qazi* was still deliberating on what he could say upon such a sudden challenge, the king got him out of the difficulty he was in, and said to the *faqir*: 'Withdraw; each man has to render his own account for himself.'

One day the king was anxious to learn from others what he had already known himself for a very long time. He asked the historians who are maintained at his court if they had ever noticed in histories that any of the kings, his predecessors, from Taimur-i-lang until now, had fallen a martyr in the field during a battle against infidels. To this question they answered that they were not aware of such a thing having ever happened. Lifting eyes and hands to heaven, he exclaimed: 'I trust in you, O my God, to favour me so far as to shed my blood and take my life as a sacrifice in your cause against the infidels, so that I may acquire a martyr's crown!' All these words were merely uttered that they might be repeated to Shiva Ji, giving him to understand that the king meant never to desist until his enemy was entirely destroyed. But the latter laughs at the king's hypocritical rhodomontade, the more so that he in turn has just the same designs against the king. Notwithstanding, as has been well noted, Aurangzeb will not easily find the occasion of putting his ideas into execution.

In the year 1689, when Aurangzeb was at the town of Bijapur, Queen Nerongabady (Aurangabadi Mahal)[1] died. The king caused a magnificent tomb to be erected to the princess, provided with a dome of extraordinary height, the whole executed in marble brought expressly from the province of Ajmer, a place full of this fine stone, of which, however, no use may be made without the king's permission. When this superb edifice was completed, he expressed a desire to be buried in the same place. His object was to lead Shiva Ji to understand that he would never leave the Dakhin or stop from pursuing him until he had been forced back into due subjection.

This crafty monarch, finding he was in no position to do any harm to the above rajah, made a pretence of large presents and heavy allowances to those simulated saints of whom I have spoken, in order that they might obtain for him favour from God. Furthermore, he brought to his army a number of *Mullas* and priests, and these busied themselves from morn to eve [14] in reading the Quran in a loud voice. There was a large number of them round the king's tent, also occupied in a similar manner. Over and above these things, he imitated Muhammad by distributing to all his leaders and officers a prodigious number of gold and silver rings set with emeralds, round which he had caused to be engraved words in the Arabic character. When he made these gifts, he said that when Muhammad went forth to war he wore rings like these, and thereby God accorded him the victory.

Nothing can be more surprising than the way things go on in the Mogul Empire. The king, the princes, the governors, and the generals have each their own line of policy, calculated for securing success to their own designs. Under this head I have been witness to the most extraordinary things. Down to the

1. Aurangabadi Mahal died in the Dakhin in 1100 H. (October 25, 1688, to October 13, 1689) ('Tarikh-i-Muhammadi,' on the evidence of a trusty friend's letter, and of the 'Ma,asir-i-'Alamgiri').

very smallest officer there is not one who is not a past master in the art of enriching himself prodigiously. They flinch from nothing in their pursuit of wealth; they ignore even the loyalty due to their sovereign. They maintain a correspondence with the enemy with a view to prolonging the war as much as possible, going so far even as supplying him with all the money he wants. Here is on instance.

Fazil Khan,[1] chief officer of the royal wardrobe, had developed, and had even begun to put into execution, the idea of conveying secretly to Prince Akbar in Persia the sum of five lakhs of gold coin. His attempt was discovered by the governor of Surat, who gave immediate notice to the king. This fact becoming known to Fazil Khan, he saw that his intrigue was unmasked, and at once swallowed some poison, of which he died. He thus avoided the torture which would, no doubt, have been inflicted upon him. However, the king commanded that the cash be removed into his treasury, being extremely annoyed that the man had escaped from his vengeance. It was not owing to any necessity he was in that the money was to have been sent to Prince Akbar, for the traders living in Hindustan never leave him in want of cash. I have reported this affair as proof of what I have just advanced, namely, that no one has the slightest hesitation in violating the fidelity he owes to the king. Here is a second instance.

The general Zu,lfiqar Khan, of whom I spoke at the beginning of this volume (IV. 2), was in charge of the campaign against Shiva Ji (the Mahrattahs). He was the son of Asad Khan, chief minister of Aurangzeb, and in his army was a crowd of Hindu princes serving under him. One of these, named Achep-nar (? Ajai' Punwar),[2] a handsome and wealthy young

1. The man meant is either Burhan-ud-din, entitled Fazil Khan, Tuni, who died in 1113 H. (1701-02) at Burhanpur on his return from his government of Kashmir, or Mir Muhammad Hadi, Faza,il Khan (son of Hazi Muhammad, Wazir Khan), who died in the Dakhin on the 6th Zu,l Qa'dah, 1114 H. (April 6, 1703), while holding the office of *Buyutati* and Deputy Lord Steward, aged sixty-two years. The second is the more probable identification, as his second office corresponds roughly to Manucci's 'Keeper of the Wardrobe.
2. This name might be read Ajai (or Ajit), Punwar, but I can find no mention elsewhere of any such person. An Achla Ji, 'son-in-law of Shiva Ji,' was presented to 'Alamgir in 1097 H. (1680) ('Ma,asir-i-'Alamgiri,' 275); but his further history is not on record.

man, made an offer to the general that in a short space of time he could capture the great fortress of Singy (Jinji),[1] within which Shiva Ji (*i.e.*, Ram Raja, Mahrattah) had taken shelter. The project did not suit Zu,lfiqar Khan's views. Success in it would have ended the war, and with it his own power. Thus he always brushed the proposal aside. The young [15] prince, disgusted at these delays, addressed himself direct to the king, and offered to make him master of the place in eight days by his own troops alone. Unfortunately the letter fell into the hands of the *wazir*, the general's father, who never hesitated to suppress it, foreseeing quite well what would be the consequences to his son. Without any delay he wrote to him about what was going on, and warned him directly on receipt of that letter to kill the 'wolf' for fear he might ruin everything.

As soon as Zu,lfiqar Khan had learnt this news, he sent for Achepnar (? Ajai, Punwar) on the pretext of having something to tell him. Immediately the poor prince appeared he was bound, and orders were given to cut off his head. In spite of all the blows delivered by the executioner, the sword never even grazed the skin. But the prince felt sure that he would never be able to preserve his honour, so he told the executioner to remove from his hair a small writing hidden there, and after so doing he would be able to decapitate him. The man did as he was bid, and after Achepnar had addressed thousands of reproaches to the general, he bowed his head, and it was separated from his body. His corpse was dragged ignominiously round the tents of Zu,lfiqar Khan. Subsequently that captain took possession of all the most valuable articles in the prince's equipage, and the rest he allowed to be pillaged. Then he caused the women to be shut up in a tent close to his own, posting round it a number of sentinels. Among these illustrious sufferers was a son of the defunct, aged about ten years. Along with him were his mother, his sister, and four other of his father's wives. They were convinced that shortly the Mahomedans would proceed to dishonour them. Finding themselves in this extremity, neither the boy nor those afflicted princesses could endure the thought of such an affront. Drawing his sword, he slew them all. Never a word did they utter, but rather felt death to be sweeter far

1. Jinji, in the South Arkat district, eighty-two miles south-west of Madras.

than the condition to which they had been brought. The tragedy was only discovered through the trickling blood issuing from the tent, the only sign to inform the public how these unfortunate princesses had come to their end.

The reader must not be surprised. Devoting themselves to death is common enough among the women of this empire, for I have several times seen a house in a town in flames while the poor women, who might have easily saved their lives, choose rather to be burnt than merely to expose themselves to the view of strangers.

Having performed this dastardly piece of treason, the general wrote to the king that he had caused the Hindu prince Achepnar to be beheaded for rebellion, and the additional crime of being in correspondence with Shiva Ji (= Ram Raja, Mahrattah). The king approved all his acts, and [16] the general proceeded to appropriate the dead man's goods. At the present moment this man (Zu,lfiqar Khan) is the greatest captain in the Mogul service; the king thinks very highly of him, and has conferred on him the title of the 'Valiant.'[1]

The captain, 'Ali Mardan Khan,[2] was subjected to an almost exactly similar piece of treachery. He commanded some troops under the same general, and made a parade of his high valour and great loyalty to the king's service. But the two men could not agree. The general, who hated him, resolved to ruin him, and to secure this he warmly commended him to an officer of Shiva Ji called Santangape (Santa Ape),[3] earnestly entreating him to give the man a thorough good beating the first chance he had. Santa Ji executed this commission without fail a few days afterwards. He inflicted a defeat on 'Ali Mardan Khan, and killed one thousand of his men. The wretched commander was captured and conveyed as a prisoner into the fortress of Singy

1. Probably Manucci is referring to the title *Bahadur* (brave).
2. This 'Ali Mardan Khan was known as the 'Haidarabadi,' having been in the Qutb-Shahi service. His name was Mir Husaini, and he died *circa* 1705 (see 'Ma,asir-ul-Umara,' ii. 824). His first capture was by Santa Ji, Ghorparah, near Jinji, in 1692, and his second by the same commander near Kaveripak, in 1696 (Grant-Duff, 168). He is mentioned again on fols. 118 and 156.
3. Or it may be meant for Santa Ji, Ghorparah, who was very active in the Jinji campaign, and, as already stated, defeated 'Ali Mardan Khan (see Grant-Duff, 168), year 1696.

(Jinji). He could only obtain his release by the payment of three hundred and thirty thousand rupees by way of ransom. This is the conduct of the generals towards those who do not submit implicitly to their wishes; and being great and powerful nobles, they are listened to at the court to the prejudice of everybody else.

It has just come to mind what was said to me by one Kabecales (Kab Kalash),[1] the first minister of Sambha Ji, when I was envoy to that prince on behalf of the Portuguese. I had been submitting to this lord that his excellency the viceroy desired to have matters take such a course as was pleasing to him. He (Kab Kalash) gave me a very good answer. He said princes and the great desire many things, but we do not permit them always to succeed in their designs.

The diversity of government in the nations through which I have passed, as well as their manner of choosing their masters, has often given me occasion to admire the way Providence deals with them. This is so both with regard to the happiness in life which is granted them, and the chastisements dispensed to them. Here are some instances, which I have learnt from persons worthy of belief, as well as some I have seen myself. These may not be unpleasing to the reader.

[17] [Story of the mode in ancient Persia of choosing a king by the alighting of a bird. Omitted as being neither historical nor Indian.]

[18, 19] [Another story of the Champa kingdom in Cochin China, where a he-goat was elevated to the throne. Omitted for the same reasons.]

[19] Some years ago a Hindu prince called 'the Victorious,' whose country is close to Cape Comorin, sought to obtain the privileges of a Brahman, a thing that in that country is absolutely impossible. However, the prince, anxious to carry out this design, called an assembly of all the Brahmans within his dominions. He gave them a great feast, and promised a large sum of money if they would grant him the right to enjoy their privileges. To

1. Kab Kalasha, the celebrated Brahman minister of Sambha Ji (see Grant-Duff, under 'Kuloosha,' pp. 137, 141, 154, 160). He was captured, with his master, by Khan Zaman, Bahadur, and executed on the 21st Jamada I., 1100 H. (January 4, 1689).

this the Brahmans answered that he was asking an impossibility. Nevertheless, he continued to press them with such insistence that to get rid of him they told him that nothing of the sort could be effected until he was born a new in the stomach of a cow.

Not to lose so excellent an opportunity, the prince caused a golden cow to be made secretly such as would suit his purpose. Then he caused the Brahmans to be sent for, and once more renewed his demands. The Brahmans gave the same answer as before. At this the king put on a look of sadness, but retiring, placed himself in the belly of the golden cow, which stood ready in a large hall close by. All the Brahmans were called in, and then the prince issued from the cow and began to bellow like a calf. They performed on him such ceremonies as are observed for a new-born child, in spite of his being then fifty-two years of age.

The Brahmans were much incensed at being thus overreached, and asserted that he was not truly a calf. At these complaints the would-be new-born calf went down on all fours and bellowed louder than ever. In spite of all this they were not satisfied, and they made every effort to evade the claim of this prince. To this intent they set forth divers reasons, to each of which an instant reply was produced. Finally they were reduced to asking that the cow might be sent to the temple where they dwelt. When this had been done, the prince at last obtained what he desired, and enjoyed the privileges of Brahmanhood [20], and after him his posterity likewise.[1]

---

1. The story in the text must be an allusion to the ceremony of *Hiranya garbha* (Golden Womb), of which the best-known instance occurs at Travancore, in which state Cape Comorin lies. It forms part of the rites performed at each king's succession. Anquetil Duperron says the king 'fit faire un veau d'or et entra dedans par le mufle et sortit par dessous la queue.' But the *Padma,* or lotus ceremony, is now substituted. They use for this a gold tub or barrel, 10 feet high and 8 feet in circumference; after it has been partly filled with a liquid containing the *pachgaviya*, or five products of the cow, the rajah ascends by a ladder and enters it, the lid is put on, and he dips five times in the mixture. The object of this act is disputed, but the better opinion is that it raises the ruler to a semi-equality with Brahmans (see on the one side Fra Paolino à San Bartolomeo, 'Voyage,' English edition, 1800, p. 172, and P. Shungoonny Menon, 'History of Travancore,' Madras, 1878, p. 53; and on the other A. Duperron, 'Zendavesta,' I., Discours Préliminaire, cxlix, note, and the Rev. S. Mateer, 'Land of Charity.

[21] [A long story of what is supposed to have lately happened in Tartary. It treats of the adventures of two youths, one of whom becomes a *wazir*, and shares with his friend as agreed on. The friend supplants him, but the first man recovers his position by a subterfuge. Omitted as being neither historical nor Indian.]

[22] In my first three parts I have not spoken of the loss of San Thome, having left that to the authors who have written on it before me. However, as the time and the place lead me to it, it will not be inappropriate to make a few remarks about that siege.[1]

The place was taken in the month of March, 1662, and here is the cause of the King of Gulkandah's making himself master of the town. When he sent Raja Culy (? Riza Quli) to be governor of Karnatik, that official had need of some pieces of artillery for the campaign he was carrying on against the Hindu princes. He begged the inhabitants of San Thome to lend him two cannon, but they refused, letting him know that they declined to recognise him in any way. The King of Portugal, their sovereign, had given them no orders to lend him cannon.

This reply caused much irritation to the governor, who wrote [23] to the King of Gulkandah upon the subject. In his letter he complained of the Portuguese and their ways, and painted them in such colours that the king sent him an order to invest the place and take it out of their possession. As soon as the order arrived, it was put into execution. The first thing done by

---

1871, pp. 169-175, and 'Native Life in Travancore,' 1883, pp. 130, 383, 388). A new rajah reached his majority in 1684, and carried out this ceremony; but I do not find that his name or titles, Revi Varmah, could be interpreted as 'The Victorious.' The next succession did not happen until 1718, after Manucci's time ('History of Travancore,' pp. 106,107).

1. I can find nothing about this defeat and loss in Danvers' 'Portuguese in India. The Fort St. George Records, vol. xiv., state, under March 8, 166$\frac{1}{2}$, that 'St. Thoma is now besieged by king of Golconda to prevent the Dutches surprizing of it.' Compliance with the request for assistance was deferred pending orders from Surat. On April 6, 1662, the siege still continued, and on May 12 we are told that the town had been taken about ten days before, while the Company's fort was also 'much threatened. The Mahomedan general is not named. The taking of San Thome from the Portuguese has been already mentioned in Part III., fol. 188, but the wrong year (1664) is there given.

Raja Culy (Riza Quli) was to Bar the entry into the town of all food-supplies. After forty days it dawned upon the Portuguese that they were dependent upon some one else than their king. At last they were obliged to capitulate in default of provisions, and the Mahomedans became masters of the place. They carried away such artillery as they had need of, and the poor Portuguese found their families dispersed in all directions.

Some time afterwards the King of Gulkandah sent to Mecca two princesses related to him to be married to the Sharif of that place. In the latitude of Sokotra they were captured and carried to Goa by a Portuguese vessel which was on a voyage from Portugal. The viceroy, Antonio de Mello de Castro,[1] confiscated all the property found in the ship which was conveying these ladies. The present sent by the King of Gulkandah to the shrine of the false prophet, and the dowry of the princesses, formed the greater part of it, in addition to all the cargo with which the vessel was laden.

When the vessel arrived at Goa, the ladies were sent to the convent of St. Monica.[2] But the King of Gulkandah, Chapdoula (Shah 'Abdullah),[3] had no sooner learnt the sorrowful news than he ordered the seizure of all the Portuguese scattered about in the outskirts of San Thome, not excepting women and children, nor even the priests. Next he wrote to the viceroy that he must release the princesses and the vessel with all its contents, menacing otherwise to behead his captives. To this the viceroy replied that it rested with the princesses to stay or go as they pleased. But to tell the truth, there was one who could not depart, for she was no longer in this world; as for the other, she did not wish to go, because she was resolved to embrace the faith of Jesus Christ, holding it to be much better than that of Muhammad. In fact, she acted on this intention shortly afterwards, living and dying in the odour of sanctity. The viceroy added that as for the ship and its cargo, they were lawful prize, and for that reason he did

1. Antonio de Mello de Castro, first Governor and then Viceroy, 1662-66 (F. Danvers, ii. 488, No. 56).
2. St. Monica was the only nunnery in Goa. The building was begun in 1606, and finished in 1627. It stood in the north-western part of the town (see Fonseca, 'Historical Sketch of Goa,' 1878).
3. 'Abdullah, Qutb Shah, reigned from 1611 to 1672 (S. L. Poole, 'Mohammadan Dynasties,' p. 321).

not mean to restore them. With regard to the Portuguese captives, the king might cut off their heads, since they were his subjects. This reply led to the release of all the Portuguese prisoners. Some time afterwards the Count of San Vicente[1] succeeded as viceroy. This noble made all possible efforts at the king's court to get back the town of San Thome and its dependencies, but death removed him from the world in the midst of these negotiations. The town remained for some years longer in the occupation of the Mahomedans, but there is little doubt they would have relinquished it had it not been [24] for the count's untimely death. Subsequently the Portuguese did obtain admission to the town; and to secure permission to fly their flag, these gentlemen have expended nearly two thousand *patacas*.[2] But as they are not very well off, they have been obliged, in order to retain this privilege, to become subjects of the Mahomedans. From this cause they endure daily a thousand abusive words and affronts; so much is this the case that often they do not dare to haul the flag up, being forbidden to do it by those infidels.

Further, it must be noted that those two thousand *patacas* were not their own property. They were a deposit made with the government by a poor widow. Afterwards she asked for her money, and they told her that she and her money had been most highly honoured, the one in having expended something in the service of his majesty, and the other in being put to so august a use. Although that answer may cause astonishment in Europe, it is nothing to be wondered at in India among the Portuguese. For it might be truthfully said that all their public buildings are constructed with money derived from the same sources.

In connection with the Portuguese I have before this spoken of Goa, and said a little as to the cause of the mortality among

1. Joao Nunes da Cunha, Conde de San Vicente (Viceroy), 1666-68. He took charge on October 11, 1666, and died in India on November 6, 1668 (Danvers, i. 364, 488).
2. The *pataca* is a coin worth two rupees (see Part I., fol. 113). It was between 1681 and 1686, during the Viceroyalty of Francisco de Tavora, that the King of Gulkandah allowed the Portuguese to return to San Thome (see Francisco de Souza, S. J., 'Oriente Conquistado,' second edition, Bombay, 1881, p. 153, Conquista I., Divisao I., para 34).

its inhabitants (II. 128). To that I must add that, besides the unwholesome air with which the town of Goa is perpetually filled, there is an island situated opposite to it and the mainland which has helped greatly to the depopulation of this Portuguese capital. This island becomes the graveyard of the larger number of its inhabitants. The reason is that it is full of courtesans, Mahomedan and heathen, who bear on them the unhappy poison by which they take the life of so many wretched men, after they have like leeches sucked from them every penny in their purse. It is, above all, the soldiers newly arrived from Portugal who succumb to this sad fate. Having exhausted both their bodily strength and their sanctity-stored purses in the infamous dens allowed to exist there, misery and feebleness overtake them so completely that they are forced to enter the hospital. That is a place from which they hardly ever come forth alive, the number of men dying there being astonishing, every day five to twenty-five dead bodies being carried out, sometimes more, sometimes less, a fact that I have myself observed several times. By this means that island becomes the cemetery of all those newly arrived from Europe, and I honestly believe that at the end of a year not an eighth part survives out of those who landed.

Yet if the reasons are thoroughly investigated, there need be no surprise. For the reverend fathers of the Society of Jesus, being lords of that island, do their utmost to increase its revenue, to be used, as they say (God knows if it is true), 'to the greater glory of God'; and it is with this thought in their minds that their reverences make no scruple of protecting those wretched and abandoned women, together with their infamous trade. Being convinced of the truth of the precept that the end justifies the means, they do not allow the women to be interfered with in the smallest degree. If on some occasions there have been persons so rash as to interfere, they have never failed to meet with prompt and terrible chastisement. For it must be admitted that the criminal law of their reverences is something both frightful and cruel.

Picture to yourself, my dear reader, that they strip the wretched culprit quite naked, bind him to a tree, and there flog him in such a way that the miserable man never undergoes it without having to enter hospital to get the wounds dressed which the scourge has caused. But ordinarily he finds there the cure of all ills, and thus an establishment dedicated to charity and the relief of the poor becomes the shelter of men suffering from disgraceful maladies or of unhappy beings who have felt the rigour of the reverend fathers' sentences. Even these all perish miserably, as [25] I have said.

The King of Portugal, out of his gracious bounty, pays yearly to this hospital fourteen thousand *seraphins* (? *ashrafi*), the money being placed in the hands of their reverences, who come in for the greater part of it. For, as the patients are in the hospital only a short time, the expenses are thereby much diminished. This is profitable to the Society (the Jesuits); nevertheless, they set no great store by it, saying sometimes that they believe there is hardly enough over to pay for lamp-oil in their college. But I should never be at an end if I were to repeat all that might be said on this subject. All the more willingly do I relieve myself of this task because I am persuaded that their reverences are well known to the world, chiefly by all honest and able men. To them I leave it to supplement what I omit. Indeed, were I to continue, there would not be wanting those who would accuse me of hatred or some other passion, in spite of the fact that I have no object but absolute truth and the desire to be useful to those who come to this country. Being informed of the dangers and perils that are met with here, let them avoid them, and take early steps not to fall into the difficulties that others have undergone. In addition to all this. I must say that I have received many and many a civility and favour from their reverences, for which I owe them gratitude. Still, I feel myself under a deeper obligation to speak the truth than to observe any other obligation or friendship in the world.

The wealth possessed by their reverences among the Portuguese in India is immense, and I can assure you that at Goa, Chaul, Thanah, Bassein, Diu, and Daman their income much surpasses the king's. For example, at Goa they have three hundred and sixty thousand *pardos*[1] a year, while the king has only three hundred [thousand]. It is just the same in all the countries in India under that prince's domination, without speaking of the river of Scene (Sena)[2] and of Mozambique,

1. See Yule, second edition, 672-677, s.v. *Pardao*.
2. Mr. D. Ferguson points out that the 'river of Sena' is the Zambesi. Sena is about 150 miles from the sea, and it was founded in 1531. The Jesuit

XXXII. 'Ali Mardan Khan

Vol. III *To face page 266*

from which the king draws nothing or very little, while they get everything. For in the island of Cabaceira[1] alone, which lies in front of Mozambique, they hold fourteen villages, which yield them a rent of one hundred thousand *cruzados*.[2] Besides, it is known for a fact that the property they possess in this country (? India) is worth to them a million of *seraphins*[3] or a little more. This statement is admitted by them themselves at times, without mentioning *le tour du baton,*[4] *et* cetera, uncertain items which amount to three times more than the above.

Thus are they very powerful and extremely rich, through the extensive trade they carry on in all those countries, where they deal in every kind of merchandise and exchange. They govern everything by policy, having unbounded and unmeasured ambition; they arrange for appointments in the ministry of justice and other offices of the kingdom (? Portugal). They set up and depose all sorts of people just as they please. Not only is this so in the case of the police, but also of the militia. In one word, they hold the government and the administration of all strong places and fortresses. To all this they devote very little attention.

That assertion will be proved by what happened in March, 1700, at the fortress of Bandora in the island of Salsette, which is situated to the north.[5] It had to surrender for want of powder and shot, a considerable number of Christians being taken and made slaves by the Arabs. These invaders held the island for thirteen days in their tyrannical grasp, causing great

---

missions in South Africa began in 1560. In 1635 the Jesuits had a large estate given them on Luabo Island, between two mouths of the great river. There was a Jesuit seminary at Sena in 1697, and they were still there in 1751 (Theal, 'Beginnings of South African History,' 1902, pp. 120, 216, 225, 401, 421).

1. Mr. Ferguson writes: 'Cabaceira is not an island; it is the name of the northern shore of the inlet at the back of the Mozambique Island (*op. cit.* 118; see also Linschoten (Hakluyt Society), i. 28, and the map there). The word is Portuguese for a calabash tree.'
2. *Cruzado*: according to the dictionary, a piece of money of which there are very few now in circulation; worth 400 *reis* each.
3. *Seraphins* (Yule, 974) are worth about 1s. 6d. each.
4. *Le tour du baton*, a secret, illicit, or improper profit obtained by a man through his employment (Littré).
5. *I.e.*, the Salsette Island, just north of Bombay, and not that; close to Goa.

injury to and a heavy fall in the revenues of his Portuguese majesty.

In short, their (the Jesuits') power is so great that the governors of fortresses and the lieutenants (heads of police) of the towns dare not fire off one single cannon, be the necessity what it may, without the permission of those reverend fathers, the administrators. The fathers have for this very good allowances which are very regularly paid to them. With this money many needy men of quality might be subventioned, as also the soldiers might be paid who are continually exposing their life in their king's cause.

I insert [26] this detail about the cannon the more willingly that I have been ocular witness of it. For in the year 1666, being in the town of Bassein, I was invited to dinner on Easter Day by Christovaon de Souza Cotinho, governor of the town. He ordered several salvoes to be fired in honour of our Saviour. The order was executed, and, as I recollect, they fired fifteen times. The gentleman was forced to pay on this account forty-five *seraphins*[1] debited to him in the books of account, because he had not asked the permission of the noble administrators. They had been extremely irritated, so much so that the chief Father Administrator, whose name was Father Fortunado Seraphino, reproved him with harsh words, telling him he was astonished at his having dared to fire off cannon without his permission.

It may be recollected that on an earlier page (II. 129) I have spoken of the imprisonment of Antonio de Mello de Castro, Viceroy at Goa; and I may add here that I learnt from Joseph de Castro, his son, that several years afterwards they (? his friends) wrote him some letters, which he showed me, in which they informed him that if he wished to retain the office he held in India, he would need to keep up good relations with the Fathers of the Society (the Jesuits), and he should always more fear the nib of a Jesuit's pen than the point of an Arab's sword.

But what is there that I could not say did I wish to expatiate

1. *Ashrafi,* a gold coin, or, perhaps, the coin worth 1s. 6d. spoken of by Yule (974). Father Fortunato Seraphino went to India in 1646; he was an Italian (see Antonio Franco, S. J., 'Synopsis Annalium Soc. Jesu in Lusitania, 1542-1725' folio, 1726, in the catalogue at the end).

on this subject, and how many are the events that I must pass over in silence, to avoid wearying out my readers! Nevertheless, the way they treat the sick in their hospital, of which I have already spoken, is something so cruel that I cannot resist returning to it. For how many are the sufferers who enter with no more than a simple fever, which there becomes malignant through the little care taken of the patient's health? How many are to be seen there of those young Portuguese newly arrived in India, who on falling ill imagine they will find some relief in that hospital ? But they are deceived in their expectations. For, believing in their simplicity that names have some relation to things, they find instead that these names are very far from possessing the qualities that they denote. In effect, the name that these fathers bear in India and in Portugal denotes the exact contrary to what is their actual conduct. For, as they call themselves Jesuits in India and Apostolic in the other place, people expect to find in them a charity which is veritably Apostolic and Christian. In this those poor men are deceived, for they are waited on in the hospital most carelessly by Konkanis or *Topasses* [native or half-caste Christians], who frequently demand payment for even the water they require. If they have not the means of paying they have to do without. Even then, in the end, those shameless fellows go and complain to the Father Administrator that the unhappy men have declined to obey the rules of diet imposed on them as necessary. Thereupon they are often placed in the cells, which are underground, and so damp that more often than not they die there after a few days.

As a relief to himself the Father Administrator entertains at this hospital a *Topass* chaplain, who looks after the patients, so they say. But if the matter is looked into, he is only there for the better catching of the poor 'renols' [Portuguese fresh from Europe], who, departing this life, leave the chaplain as their testamentary executor. This is why after a death a special auction is held, within the very hospital, of all that belonged to the deceased. All rests in the hands of the Father Administrator or the Father Apothecary; and the things go for much less than they are worth or they could be sold for at public outcry. Such auctions ought to take place [27] at the House of Mercy, in obedience to the orders of his Portuguese majesty. By this device everything becomes a profit to their reverences, who send away these things to the north to other persons, who sell them at a high profit. In this way the poor patients in that hospital are ill-served in life and still worse after death. Thus it is that many who fancy they are falling asleep at night to awake in the morning sleep on with the sleep that knows no waking.

I will not insert here what happened to Monsieur de la Haye,[1] for it can all be seen in the writings of several other inquirers. But I cannot refrain from saying that the French during their stay in India always bear themselves so boldly and valiantly that they gain the respect of everybody, and hold preeminence over all the other nations of Europe. Nevertheless, the King of Gulkandah, through pressure from the Dutch Council, caused that town (San Thome) to be razed to the ground for fear the French might retake it. Not one stone was left upon another.[2] The Portuguese removed thence to Madras, where they lived up to [16]86, when they obtain from the king, Abul Hasan,[3] who had succeeded to Qutb Shah [*i.e.*, 'Abdullah], fresh permission to take up their residence in that town. Since then they have erected buildings and established a sort of government. They hold the land at a rent and pay so much a year. It was there that the affair happened to me of which I have spoken in my Third Part (III. 188, year 1688).

After some time there arrived at the town (San Thome) the

1. The loss of San Thome by the Portuguese has already been touched on (see Part IV., fol. 22).
2. The reference must be to the French occupation of San Thome in 1672, and their subsequent loss of it in 1674. The book meant is probably the account by De la Haye, the French commander, 'Journal du Voyage des Grandes Indes, contenant tout ce que s'y est fait et passé par l'escadre de S.M..' (Orleans, 1697, 12°). There is also a detailed account of the siege in F. Martin's MS. 'M6moires,' Archives Nationales, Paris, Série T*, 1169, fols. 147*a*-212*b*. Martin arrived at San Thome from Masulipatam on January 7, 1673 (De la Haye, 41), was sent to Pondicherry first on April 1, 1673 (*ibid.*, 68), and again on January 13, 1674 (*ibid.*, 150; also see Jules Sottas, 'Histoire de la Compagnie Royale,' Paris, 1905, pp. 43-52). Jacques Blanquet de la Haye left Rochefort March 29, 1670; took San Thome by assault July 25, 1672; capitulated September 6, 1674. Vol. viii. of J. J. Schwabe's 'Allgemeine Histoire der Reisen,' 1747, pp. 597-613, has a very well-divided abstract of De la Haye's book, with good marginal notes.
3. See *ante*, note 21 to Part IV., fol. 23.

most illustrious Lord Dom Gasper Alfonço,[1] Bishop of Meliapur (Mailapur) and other places. This prelate held in his hands both civil and ecclesiastical jurisdiction. Yet he did not meddle much in the former branch. However, as I noticed that he did me the honour to like and esteem me. I begged him to see me righted in the injustice that had been done me. After I had told him my story a few days elapsed. He then gave me his reply,

1. Father Gaspar Affonco Alvares, a Jesuit and Provincial of Malabar, was approved by the Pope as Bishop on November 19, 1691, consecrated on August 31, 1693, in the Professed House of his Society at Goa, usually lived at Madras (read 'San Thome'), and died 1708 (Müllbauer, 'Geschichte,' 372, and F. de Souza, 'Oriente Conquistado,' second edition, Bombay, 1881, p. 154). The Bishop must have reached his diocese before 1695, for my friend Mr. W. R. Philipps tells me that in 1889-90 he noticed in the path outside, and on the seaward side of the cathedral (since rebuilt), a stone with three lines on inscription:

DD. GASPAR ALPHON | SUS. EPISCO.
MELIAPU | RENSIS. ANNO 1695. |

As this Bishop plays an important part in Manucci's pages, and the facts of his career are obscure. I add particulars given me by Mr. Philipps, and furnished to him by Father Van Meurs, S. J., of Limburg, through Father Alexandre Brou, S. J., of Canterbury. They are founded on the 'Synopsis annalium Soc. Jesu in Lusitania' of A. Franco, folio, 1726, and on the Catalogue (MS.) of the Province. Gaspar Affonço was born in 1626, either at the town of Onxira, or the village of Cova de Soavo, in the Diocese of Coimbra. He became a novice on July 14, 1641, and left for Goa in 1647. His studies were finished in 1659, and for a time he was chaplain to a military expedition, He became Superior at Bandora, then Rector of the seminary. Between 1662 and 1664 he was Procurator of the province, Rector of the college at Chaul, and Rector of the probationers' house at Goa. He took his four vows at Goa on September 8, 1663. In 1667 he became Superior of the Canara Mission, a member of the Provincial Council, and visitor of the division called Aquilon (the northern division). He was sent to Rome in 1677 as Procurator. In 1679 he became parish priest of Aquilon, then Rector of the great college of St. Paul at Goa, and *praepositus* of Goa province. In 1688 he was made *praepositus* of the Malabar province, and in 1689 acted as Governor, 'in all of which praise was given to his ability, judgment, experience, and prudence; also to his great talents in all things relating to the affairs of the Society, The dates of his confirmation and consecration are given above. According to Casimiro Christovao de Nazareth, 'Mitras Lusitanas no Oriente' (Bombay, 1888), part iii, p. 96, the Bishop died on November 24, 1708. From 1707 a coadjutor was named in the person of Francisco Laynes, S.J., Bishop of Sozopolis in *partibus*, who succeeded as full Bishop early in 1710 (*ibid.*).

telling me I was in the wrong, that the judges owed me no redress, that it was the Chief Captain who had done the wrong, and it was he who ought to do me amends. 'But,' he added, 'he is no longer in this world, and has left nothing. That is a misfortune for you, but you must bear it, as one must the other ills of this life.'

I resented acutely the inequity of this answer; however, I did not show this for several years. All that time I was reflecting on how I could bring him to feel the injustice of his finding. Finally I determined to take as my model what the prophet Nathan said to David to bring home to him his sin. Full of this thought, off I went to visit the said bishop, putting on a vexed and melancholy air. When we had exchanged compliments I told him I had come to ask him for advice on a thing that had happened to me. To this he replied that with all his heart he would render me such service in all matters as was within his power.

'Monsignor,' said I, 'when I lived with my fellow-countryman, Hortense Bromsoune (Ortenzio Bronzoni), we were both very well known, had good credit, and everybody esteemed us. This induced Juan Dias d'Almeda and Diogo Mendez Botelho to confide to us a chest which contained a quantity of money. My comrade, driven by I know not what necessity, or perhaps by envy, had a false key made, and withdrew one thousand rupees from the chest. This he did in the face of all that I could say to prevent him. Some months afterwards the two Portuguese came and removed their chest. It was not long before they noticed that one thousand rupees were deficient from the total sum. They complained, but as we were well supported we rejected their demand in sharp terms, and ejected them from our house, protesting that they were forgers and rogues.

'Some time afterwards my comrade died, and left me as his testamentary executor. However, as a long time had [28] passed, the affair was no longer spoken of. Now they wish to revive it, and a few days ago I received a letter from the aforesaid Portuguese in which they set forth the distress they are in, that they have a daughter to be married, that I should reflect whether in conscience I do not owe them for that deficiency of one thousand rupees which occurred within my house.'

I added some words praying the bishop to tell me as a matter of conscience whether I was under an obligation to pay that money, with the interest accrued since that time. It was to be remembered that I had not consented to the theft. He answered that I was under an obligation to pay. I took my leave of the prelate and went to see the Jesuits and other regulars and priests, men learned in the law. I told them the same story, and all replied to me in the same terms, but had no idea of the inference I Intended to deduce from their answer. It was my object to make them admit out of their own mouth that what they had decided in my case was unjust, for my case was absolutely identical, changing only the persons. I had been robbed, the inhabitants of San Thome were consenting parties to the theft, and Manoel Texeira was the Ortenzio Bronzoni who had taken my property.

Some of those religious persons read the riddle after I had left, and they told me afterwards I was very clever. But all that was no more than compliments, for that did not hinder the greater number of them from giving certificates in the very teeth of the equity of my demand, clear and evident as that was. Although this business has no interest for the public. I have thought it might serve as a warning to those who travel in these distant parts. It will teach them not to allow their property to be taken from them, for once it has gone, the best arguments in the world will be useless in procuring them redress.

As soon as the Portuguese heard that the Mogul had occupied the kingdom of Gulkandah, they dispatched an embassy to the prince asking for a confirmation of the privileges that the previous (Qutb Shahi) king had granted them. This demand was conceded to them on condition of paying dues in the way the Dutch paid them at Masulipatam. At the end of August, 1702, there arrived at San Thome the deputy-governor of the whole Karnatik. His name was Mahamud Sahid (Muhammad Said).[1] This noble was very ill, and came to me at San Thome in the hope of my treating him for his complaint. I carried this out with such success that in a short time, with God's help, he was restored to his original health. At this he was so satisfied that he paid me largely for my trouble. He gave me two hundred *patacas*, a horse of the same value, some lengths of silk, and the

1. Muhammad Sa'id, Diwan, is mentioned in the Madras instructions to N Manucci and Ramapah, dated January 17, 1702$\frac{1}{2}$ (Wheeler, 'Madras in the Olden Time,' i. 361).

income of two villages and their hamlets, to be held during the whole time he governed the province.

Before he departed for the war he caused an earthen wall to be made all round San Thome,[1] including not only the quarter of the Mahomedans, but that in which the Portuguese dwell. He wrote afterwards to his king that it was good for his interests and an advantage to the crown to make of these places one single village. He added that he had two hundred thousand *patacas* already in hand for the purpose. He awaited only the orders of his majesty to carry out the plan. Just when the walls had been begun an Augustinian friar stepped over them, was taken prisoner, and led ignominiously before the magistrate, and only obtained release by the payment of money.

It was during the years 1678 and 1679 that Aurangzeb decided to impose a new tribute upon all the Hindus.[2] All the high-placed and important men at the court opposed themselves to this measure. They besought the king most humbly to refrain; they represented to him that it would be too heavy a burden upon the people, not only from the novelty [29] of such a tribute, but because the means of his subjects did not suffice for paying such severe demands every year. Of all the other kings, both Pathan and Mogul, not one had engaged in the oppression of his subjects by similar impositions. But all was in vain, and the king stood firm, still more so because it was his purpose to spread the Mahomedan religion among those people (the Hindus). He was of the opinion that he had found in this tax an excellent means of succeeding in converting them, besides thereby replenishing his treasuries greatly, which were daily becoming depleted. The cause of this falling off was either that the revenue was not collected, or that he had been obliged to remit several demands. Therefore he replied to those nobles: 'Think not I am like my grandfather, Jahangir, who spent his time listening to the poet Birbal and his music, or in looking on at plays and other games.

1. The Madras Records of 1696 show traces of a previous attempt to wall in San Thome (see Wheeler, i. 309). Manucci resumes the subject on IV., fol. 32.
2. According to Elphinstone, 'History,' p. 560, the reimposition of the *Jizyah*, or poll-tax, was in 1088 H. (A.D. 1677). But 'Ma,asir-i- 'Alamgiri,' p. 174, twenty-second year, has the 1st Rabi' I., 1090 H. (April 12, 1679). The poll-tax is mentioned again on IV., fol. 236.

No! no! It will never be like that with me. All my thoughts are turned towards the welfare and the development of my kingdom, and towards the propagation of the religion of the great Muhammad.'

These were words worthy of a great sovereign, if he also carried them in his heart. But I have always found, judging by a long experience, that he and all the Mahomedans direct their actions by their own convenience, and for the sole welfare of their own bodies. This is the cause that there are many princes and lords who give alms daily, not from love of God, but merely in the hope that God may grant them good success in their affairs. It is also with this thought that there are many who out of superstition place under their pillow at night what they want to give away in charity. The prince Shah 'Alam was accustomed to thus place aside ten rupees every night with this object.

But let us return to the subject of the new tax. Begam Sahib, eldest sister of the king, a very generous princess, wanted to make a fresh appeal. With this intent she paid her brother a visit, and entreated most humbly that he would not go farther with this affair; and to touch him more deeply she brought forward a comparison. 'Just think, sire,' said she, 'that the lands of Hindustan are like a vast ocean; your majesty and all the other members of our royal family are like ships navigating its waters and ploughing through its waves. Where is there any sovereign prince who would desire to load with imposts the sea on which he sails? Who has ever seen the physician pay the patient? From this reasoning I conclude, with your majesty's permission, that if the sick man has to pay the physician who cures him; if the ships and the sailors must always try to render the seas favourable and pacific towards them in order to navigate with success and arrive happily at port; in the same way your majesty ought to appease and soften the ocean of your subjects. For in what way can you expect them to pay taxes if you overburden them and provoke their waves by this unaccustomed demand? Abandon, then, sire, this purpose, lest there be a rebellion in this kingdom. Let your majesty reflect that violent winds usually raise and disturb the seas, swell high their waves, and transform the whole into a terrifying tempest. By its violence everything is swept to the shore, and the poor and persecuted people are ruined.'

When she had finished this harangue, and impressed on him the force of this comparison [30], she attempted to throw herself at his feet and, as it were, pay him the adoration and homage of a subject to her sovereign. Coming from a sister, this was a thing still more to be prized. But the prince, stiff and unmoved in his ideas, at once dismissed her, saying: 'Madam, forget not that when Muhammad entered the world it was entirely drowned in the idolatry of the unbeliever, but no sooner had that incomparable prophet reached the age of discretion than he busied himself with all his strength in freeing the peoples from so dangerous a condition, by establishing among them his holy doctrines. Of what methods, I beg you to say, did he make use to gain such a happy purpose? Was it not by that of taxation? Thus, as you can see, he had a happy issue of all his undertakings. I have resolved, madam, to imitate so great a man in everything I can, even in the laying on of taxes, and I hope that just as the Lord blessed that great prophet by such means. He will bless me also, me and my designs.' Having finished these words, he bade her good-bye and turned his back upon her, a movement that cut the princess to the very quick.

Not very long afterwards there was an alarming earthquake, by which the great nobles were impelled once more to solicit fresh orders on the subject. With this idea they asked for an audience. When it was granted, they represented to the monarch that Nature, affected at the oppression of his people, gave by this movement a token of its resentment. 'Ah! ' said the king, laughing at their talk, 'is it possible that you have so little wit as to take up things in a contrary sense? It is true that the earth lately trembled, but it is the result of the joy it felt at the course I am adopting. All nature shows marks of this feeling. The skies are darkened, they are covered with clouds, and weep tears of gladness, pouring out their waters upon the earth. In its turn the earth is in no sense ungrateful for these benefits from on high; for, after giving us such startling proof of her extraordinary gratitude by the effort she has recently made, she wishes further to make clear to us that in her heart is joy over our actions. This it is which compels her to be fertile, and give us abundant harvest of fruit and grain. Animals, too, are conscious of my exertions; so much the more that it is from the fertility of the earth that they receive their meat. The birds of the air exult at it in their flight and in their warbling. The horse neighs by reason of it, since he finds wherewithal to appease his hunger.'

'There!' said he, 'that is the way, my lords, to look at things. 'The reason of the people is always selfish, obscured either by passion or by necessity. As for us, we have more good sense, and can well distinguish between things and consider their results.' This was the manner in which this king replied to his nobles. After this he set in motion the collectors of the taxes, and on this head I cannot refrain from remarking that if the tax-contractor pays twenty-five thousand rupees to the crown, he must have at the least recovered one hundred thousand. They always keep back three-fourths for themselves, and pay in one-fourth only to the royal treasury.

I have before this spoken of the poet Birbal,[1] and perhaps inquiring persons will not be displeased to learn who he was. The following is approximately his character. He was loved and favoured by Jahangir, and in consequence much thought of at the court; he was a good poet and a great musician. The man's manners were so pleasant and agreeable that [30] he gained the esteem of everybody. Here is a story which goes not a little way to make known his character.

One day the king asked him why he had been so long in making his appearance at court. 'Sire,' said the poet, 'I was very busy quieting an infant.' 'What!' retorted the king, 'do you want all that time to satisfy a baby? I could do it myself in one instant, for what more is wanted than to give him some fruit, some sweetmeats, or some similar plaything?' 'Ah!' said the facetious poet, 'your majesty, so far as I see, does not understand the acute and importunate nature of infants, and how difficult it is to satisfy them.' The prince, who loved a pleasantry, directed him to imitate an infant, and he would undertake to content him in all that he might demand.

The joke-loving Birbal obeyed forthwith, began to cry, and asked for suck. A woman was sent for at once. No sooner had

1. Mahes Das, Bhat (hereditary bard or panegyrist), entitled Kab Rae (King of the Poets), or Rajah Birbal. He was killed in fighting the Yusufzais on the Peshawar frontier early in Rabi' I., 994 H. (March, 1585). The introduction of Jahangir's name is an anachronism; Akbar it was who was Birbal's patron and friend.

he perceived her than he ran to her with great signs of delight, laid hold of her breast, and began to suck. Making believe that one breast had no milk, he sought the other. From time to time he passed his hand over her face, and to finish with, wetted her and passed wind. But still not satisfied, he began once more to howl, wanted to be taken up and carried, and to be taken into the garden for a walk. This was done; there he asked for fruit and flowers: some he kept, the others he threw away. With all this being still unsatisfied, he demanded several other things, amongst others that they should parade the elephants and horses with all their trappings and standards. He was given in to on every point. Then he asked for gold coins, and distributed them hither and thither—at least, in part, for he took good care to keep back some for himself. All this was carried on with such childish and infantile gestures, just like a little child, that the prince was extremely delighted.

However, the comedy was not yet ended. He asked for cocks, pigeons, other sorts of birds, goats, and other similar animals, the whole with such bright and diverting ways that the king was quite satisfied; not to mention that as an additional joy he forgot not the bottle, which was ever agreeable to him in all his pastimes. Finally, the last scene of this play was a demand for buffaloes and cows. As soon as he saw them, he ordered milk to be drawn from one of them. When the order had been obeyed, he drank a little, and made signs to replace the rest in the cow's udder—a thing obviously impossible. Then the light-hearted Birbal lay down on the ground and roared, thumped and kicked, scratched his face, and used all the gestures of an angry child. No one was able to pacify him by any arguments they could device.

At last the king, as a final remedy, said to him he was an impertinent fellow to ask for impossibilities. 'Such, sire,' replied the poet, 'are all infants, and that is why it is so difficult to satisfy them.' 'Ah!' said the king, 'you are too clever for me. However, here is a question; let us see if you can give a good solution. Tell me, if you please, what is the greatest consolation that man has in this world?' 'Ah, sire!' retorted he without a pause, 'it is when a father finds himself embraced by his [31] son.'

Here is an adventure which happened to King Akbar. I overlooked it in my former volumes; but as it is so strange, it should not fall into oblivion. After he had defeated Baz Bahadur, [1] sovereign of the forests of Mandu, Akbar caused him to be cruelly decapitated, and forthwith proposed marriage to his widow. The affected princess, who was of surpassing beauty, absolutely refused to consent to such a marriage, in spite of all the promises made to her. However, she sent word to him that if he would order a palace to be built for her, and concede to her a year in which to mourn for her beloved spouse and perform the ceremonies due to his memory, she would consent to the marriage.

The amorous prince granted her request, and on the expiration of the year he intimated to her that the time had come for her to carry out her promise. Then the lady dressed herself as magnificently as was possible, putting on her richest jewels, and came to see the king. He received her with all imaginable demonstrations of joy. But when they had engaged in conversation, the beauty drew from her pocket a poisoned betel-leaf, impregnated with a very subtle poison, and ate it. Thus she expired in her lover's arms, repeating frequently the name of her first husband, Baz Bahadur.

This deed showed the king that she could never love one who had sent to his death a person held by her as dear as life itself. Although invariably successful on the field of Mars, Akbar was unfortunate on that of Venus, a fact which can be seen from my First Part (I. 79, 80) in my narrative of the siege laid to the fortress of Chitor. That siege added to his glory but was most fatal to his love for the far-famed Padmini.

As I have said so much about the Portuguese, it will not be useless, I believe, if I tell here the events that happened to two gentlemen of that nation called Mendornaz. Usually the nobles born in India are naturally opposed to people of quality who come from Europe. The two Mendoçaz were from Europe, and they fell into a quarrel with two Indian Portuguese of the

1. Baz Bahadur, King of Malwah, was deposed by Akbar in 1570, but not killed. He was given a command in Akbar's army. He and Rupmati are buried together in the centre of a tank at Ujjain. After Baz Bahadur's flight she committed suicide in order to escape the advances of Adham Khan (Akbar's foster-brother) (Beale, 'Oriental Biography,' 105, 336).

house of the Mellos.[1] These latter procured the assassination of the other two, and then sought refuge in a country-house owned by them. There they collected men, endeavouring to increase their strength sufficiently to enable them to become independent masters of Bassein. However, they did not succeed in this undertaking, for, since they were acting only through the passion of revenge, and not from a desire for justice, God did not permit these two traitors and betrayers to accomplish their design. Shortly afterwards some reinforcements arrived from Goa, not only obliging them to abandon their plot, but to seek safety in flight. In addition to the murder that I have mentioned, these wretches had been guilty of other crimes. They had suborned men to assassinate a Royal Commissary named Carilho, who had been sent to decide the cases against them. During the investigation he allowed them to retire to their houses, there to consider the accusations against them and prepare for their defence. It was precisely this murder which compelled these two traitors to flee into Mogul territory. Upon arriving within it they offered their services to Prince Aurangzeb, and asked from him help in taking the towns [32] of Bassein and Daman, promising that after they had succeeded they would become his subjects. But at that moment Aurangzeb was occupied with his designs upon the crown, and wished to avoid a war with the Portuguese, the more particularly as he had already tested their strength in his campaign against Daman, as described by me in my First Part (I. 123).

For these reasons he advised those two gentlemen to give up their enterprise. He said to them he wanted men for his own purposes, and if they consented to enter his service he would give them a good and honourable position. They declined, and withdrew to Surat. Some years afterwards, when Aurangzeb's objects were attained, these two gentlemen came to see him, and laid before him the same proposal. But the prince declined to listen, harangued them on their rebellion, and said that he held it unfair to make war on a nation for the benefit of two traitors. After this rebuff these two wretches wandered hither and thither in a miserable state until they died.

As I forgot in my Third Part to speak of the virtues of

1. We have heard something of these incidents before in Part II, fol. 109, in the account of Manucci's first visit to Bassein in 1667.

elephant hide and fat, in spite of all I did say about those enormous beasts, I add here that their fat is of use to strengthen weak and shrivelled sinews by rubbing it in on the surface of the skin. Also if you take the hide and the toe-nails, adding some stag's horn, and after mixing place the whole on some live coals, a smoke is produced which is of marvellous effect for haemorrhoids; it also reduces inflammation, relieves pains, and removes hard lumps.

At the end of October, 1701, the sea destroyed about fifteen villages on the coast of Masulipatam (Machhlipatanam).[1] With reference to this catastrophe, I have always noticed in this country that when such disasters occur they are a prelude to war and coming misfortunes. Thus, after the inundations at the above town in 1680, we saw the destruction of the kingdoms of Guikandah and Bijapur, a calamity which reduced the people to extreme misery. At the beginning of this very year of 1701 a comet appeared on the coast of Choromandal; it was about a cubit in length, its head to the east and its tail to the west. All these things foretell nothing but misfortune, for after the earlier floods at Masulipatam above mentioned, a similar comet appeared in the sky. May God deliver us from it! But as I believe that what is about to happen will comprise events worthy of being handed down to posterity. I promise, should God grant me life, to do my very best to satisfy the curiosity of the public by imparting to them all I shall consider worthy of remembrance.

I have mentioned above (IV. 27) that Muhammad Sa'id had written to the court that he proposed to rebuild the town of San Thome, that the money required, or the greater part of it, was ready, and only the king's orders were awaited before commencing. Since then this lord has received an answer to his letter, whereby he is forbidden to begin this work; he is told to think no more of it, for his majesty fears that if the town were rebuilt, the French would again possess themselves of it, like they did once before, as I have told you (IV. 27).

Noticing that all his great strength was incapable of hindering [33] the continual ravages of Shiva Ji (i.e., the Mahrattahs)

1. A search in the Company's Records at the India Office yields no mention of this storm.

in his kingdom, Aurangzeb resolved to advance into the territories belonging to this rajah, with the object of reducing some of his fortresses. The first of these that he had designs against was Quelna (Khelnah),[1] above the high hills that are in the direction of Goa. It is built upon the hillside in such a way that to traverse the roads leading to it is extremely difficult. Moreover the emperor, having entered upon the campaign, soon found himself in trouble from the want of supplies. He was forced to await the help brought to him by one of his generals. Shiva Ji knew of the approach of these reinforcements, and took good care not to let pass unused such an opportunity for advantageous attack. In short, he went out to find this general, delivered battle, and fought with such good fortune that he gained the day, left the general dead upon the field, seized as booty all his goods, and carried off into the fortress the supplies intended for the king's army. Even if this mishap had not occurred, it may be doubted if the prince could have taken the place with the ease that he supposed. Its position is favourable to a defence, while the water-supply and the atmosphere are most pernicious to strangers. Thus they caused many swellings

1. Grant-Duff, 'History of the Mahrattahs,' p. 13, identifies Khelnah with Vishalgarh, a fortress dependent on Kolhapur. It lies in the hilly country of the Ghats, about lat. 16° 52', long. 73° 50' (Thornton, 1006). For this campaign Bedar Bakht, son of A'zam Shah, who had been sent south to pass the rains at Hukeri and Gokak (both now in the Belgaum district), was recalled to headquarters. Aurangzeb's movement from Panchganw began on the 16th Jamada II., 1113 H. (November 13, 1701). Untimely rain made the march difficult. On the 16th Rajah, 1113 H. (December 27, 1701), the imperial camp was pitched some six or seven miles from Khelnah, but from the cramped nature of the position it had to be divided into two or three sections. The fortress was evacuated by the Mahrattahs during the night of the 22nd Muharram, 1114 H. (June 17, 1702, N.S.). A chronogram was found in "*Fath shud qila'h-i-Khelna*,' and Aurangzeb, taking an omen from the Quran, lighted oa '*Al hamdu lilahi az-zi sakhkhara lana haza*' (Surah 43, verse 12). He therefore renamed the place 'Sakhkharlana' 'Ma,asir-i-'Alamgiri,' 445-457; Khafi Khan, ii. 491-502). In a subsequent passage (Part IV., fol. 116) Manucci gives the date of capture as June 28, 1702. If we take this as Old Style, and advance it by eleven days (as is the rule for the eighteenth century), we obtain June 17, N.S., as deduced above from the native historian. Manucci speaks again of Khelnah on fols. 107 and 116.

among the king's troops, who thereby suffered extremely, as also' by the deficiency of food.

To render his march the easier the king divided his force, sending some divisions by one route and some by another, hoping thus to keep the roads unencumbered. The plan has not been a success, for the enemy have not remained idle during the interval, but have inflicted a fresh defeat on the division of Prince Bedar Bakht, son of A'zam Tara. He commands twelve thousand horse under twenty-two officers, all of whom have fallen. The prince himself escaped with difficulty, taking to flight on horseback, accompanied by no more than five troopers.

Near eight o'clock in the evening of December 24, 1701, there was a great noise in the air along with a bright light, which was seen even at Pondicherry, where I then happened to be, although it is distant thirty leagues from this town of Madras.

At the end of my Third Part (III. 30) I have reported that the Chevalier Norris, Ambassador of the New English Company, had left Masulipatam on his way to Surat. He had made magnificent preparations for his journey to the court. Now I must add that he arrived there in the month of March, 1701, exactly at the time when the king was occupied with the campaign against Shiva Ji (the Mahrattahs), as I have just stated (IV. 33). On his (arrival this diplomatist spread the rumour that the pirates who, during seventeen years past, have captured many merchant vessels belonging to Surat, used ships belonging to the old company. This statement having come to the ears of the principal ministers, they demanded proof of what he had asserted. Unable to produce any, he denied the statement, and only got out of it by a considerable payment.

The merchants of Surat had complained to the court several times of the great losses they had suffered by this miserable scum of the ocean. This complaint had compelled the king to imprison the English merchants and the officers of the Old Company who were resident at Surat, and they were released only by dint of argument and the payment of money.

At length, tired out at hearing the complaints renewed every day, the king forced [34] the English, Dutch, and French inhabitants of Surat to protect the ships leaving that port by undertaking to convoy them on all their voyages, and bring them back safe from any insult by pirates;[1] he directed that the English should have the care and direction of all the ships going to and coming from the coast of Bengal, the French of those trading with Persia, and the Dutch of those comprising the fleet of the Mogul (Mecca). But all this was of no avail. The pirates never ceased their robbery, and even took a king's ship returning from Mecca, which had become separated from its convoy. In it there was much valuable property, which became the prey of these thieves, whose brutality was extreme, and they carried it so far as to violate several women of rank who were on board returning from the pilgrimage.

The king, on hearing what had passed in this encounter, felt the insult very bitterly, and ordered the governor of Surat to put the English into prison again, to treat them more harshly than before, and to force from them payment of all losses. When they were thus afflicted the Chevalier Gayer, general of Bombay, moved to their assistance with four ships; but all he could do was to blockade the port, and prevent all entry and exit. The governor, seeing things in this condition—commerce stopped, and merchants nearly ruined—found no other expedient to stop these disorders than to make a peace with the general (Sir John Gayer). This project he worked at. In a few days terms were arrived at between the parties and confirmed by the chiefs on each side. After this the general, Gayer, ignorant of Mogul bad faith, and relying upon the treaty, landed with his wife and a few men. As soon as he was ashore these deceivers seized him at night time and sent him to prison, where he still lies. A demand was made from him for the restoration of all the lost property.[2]

---

1. The terms of the *Muchalkah*, or agreement, taken from the 'Dutch are set forth in full on p. 269, vol. iv., part ii., of F. Valentyn, 'Oud en Nieuw Oost Indien.' It is dated February 4, 1699, and signed by Pr. Ketting, with seven others. It undertook (1) that the Dutch company should pay 24,000 rupees, and (2) should furnish an escort of two or three Dutch vessels to and from Mecca at the expense of the Mahomedan merchants (Dubois, 'Vies,' 263). The second article was carried out for two or three years, but the money payment stipulated in the first article was repudiated at Batavia.
2. See Hunter, 'History of British India,' ii. 342, under date of February, 1701, relying upon G. W. Forrest, 'Selections from State Papers, Bombay, Home Series,' i. 227. Gayer was not released till 1710 (*op. cit.*, 375). On his

The ambassador [W. Norris] reached the court, and a few days afterwards made a public entry, to the admiration of everybody. Never had an ambassador from Europe appeared with such pomp and magnificence. He erected his tents in the open within sight of the royal army, to prove thereby that he had no fear of Shiva Ji (the Mahrattahs). He was armed and provided with good cannon, and had a numerous retinue.

After he had rested for some days, he paid a visit to the chief minister, named Asett Can (Asad Khan),[1] secretary of the king and his counsellor, and prayed him to assist him in the business he had to bring before the court, giving him great presents in order to obtain his support. These were civilly accepted by the minister, who, on the Englishman's taking his leave, paid him many compliments and made him many promises.

This ambassador made a great show, and his expenses were extraordinary. No prince has ever been attended with greater pomp and ostentation, and in addition thereto his liberality was unbounded. He imagined that in this way he could push through his business more quickly. But he was quite ignorant of what the king's intentions were in regard to him. For, after all, the only thing he acquired was the nickname 'King of England,' given him by the common people in the army.

After an interval of some days the king accorded him his first audience, where nothing of any significance passed, beyond his producing several considerable presents, of which, however, the prince accepted only a trifling part. He made great efforts to get his business concluded quickly; but he was not acquainted with the customs of this court, and had no faithful adviser, thus the more he sought to advance the farther off he got. Some months afterwards he went to the court and presented a statement of the things [35] he wished them to grant. In it he asked for factories on the coast of Choromandal, Jinjili,[2] and Bengal.

voyage home he was made a prisoner by a French fleet off Cape Comorin on April 3, 1711, and died of the wounds received in the fight.

1. Muhammad Ibrahim, Qaramanlu, entitled Asaf-ud-daulah, Jamdat-ul-mulk, Asad Khan, became full *wazir* in the twenty-seventh year, 1094 H. (A.D. 1683-84). He died on June 18, 1716, N.S., at a great age.
2. The best account of the Jinjili coast is in T. Bowrey's 'Countries round the Bay of Bengal edited by Sir R. C. Temple, Hakluyt Society, Series II., vol. xii., pp. 120-128. It was the coast from the north end of the Choromandal to the south end of the Orissa coast.

After this the king gave him permission to leave, and sent word he would give him a reply later on.

Some months elapsed and he saw that no answer came, so he abandoned the chief minister and addressed himself to another grandee, by whom he was forced to wait even longer. His expenditure and his exertions were of no avail, except that he was fed on pleasant words which ever renewed his expectations. This is the Mahomedan habit; they always act in this way, with the idea of increasing their gains in the end.

Finally, at the end of nine months, after spending more than six hundred thousand rupees, he was told that his demands were conceded, his majesty would permit his Company to establish factories on the coast of Choromandal, at Machhlipatnam, and in Bengal, but in order to obtain the necessary documents he must present to the king two hundred thousand rupees, and one hundred thousand to the officials.

The ambassador promised to satisfy all these demands. He only did this to be delivered from all the troubles and expenses, and from the overwhelming heat, with all of which he was oppressed. Moreover, a stay in tents extremely inconvenienced him, and had already caused the death of some of his men. In addition, the king was making preparations to march for the country of his enemy, Shiva Ji.

Thus, to obtain from the king his audience of leave-taking, he represented that he had been at his court nearly a year, and he supplicated his majesty for permission to depart. In consideration for this favour, he would pay down the three hundred thousand rupees. The envoy's proposition was laid before the king, but there they spoke of only one hundred thousand rupees as the present, the officials keeping back the other two hundred thousand for themselves. The prince accepted the present, and ordered the speedy preparation of the documents, on condition, however, that the envoy should undertake in writing to be liable for all the losses at sea occasioned to his subjects by the pirates.

The ambassador, who was not expecting any fresh demand, refused to enter into any such obligation. He besought his majesty to think no further of such a thing, because it was on this very account that he had offered to make him a present of other one hundred thousand rupees payable at the port of Surat. Upon hearing this answer the king fell into such a rage that the documents were not delivered, nor was he (Norris) allowed to depart. They kept him amused with soft speeches, extracting from him meanwhile whatever money they could.

At this time the king began his march, and the ambassador, foreseeing nothing but an entry into new troubles, was so chagrined that he broke up his palanquins, set fire to his tents and part of his baggage, and started for Burhanpur on his way to Surat. Upon the king becoming aware of this move, he sent after him an officer called Quefaet Kan (Kifayat Khan), a very great friend of mine, who speaks Portuguese fairly well, and both speaks and writes Latin to perfection. He is son of the astronomer (Qutb Beg, I. 241), who advised Aurangzeb not to ride upon an elephant at the battle that he fought against his brother Dara close to Ajmer.

This official (Kifayat Khan)[1] said to Norris that he had been sent by his majesty solely to let him understand that it was necessary for him to agree to what was asked, since all the European nations at Surat were compelled to do the same. He was also ordered to hinder him from continuing his journey. There were several other things he added, but only by way of advice [36].

Thereupon the ambassador, irritated in the highest degree, and firmly resolved to maintain his purpose, took no heed of all that had been said to him, and went on his way. This fact was reported to the king, and he sent orders to all *faujdars* and all governors to prevent his proceeding any farther, and to block all the routes. However, Norris tried to push on by force, but met with resistance, and the Indian soldiers in his pay were warned that they would be punished if they continued to advance. Thus these people, who were to the number of four hundred, their fear of these menaces being greater than their desire

1. Towards the end of Aurangzeb's reign, Mir Ahmad, son of Mir Baghdadi, held a *mansab* and the title of Kifayat Khan. He had the office of *Diwan* of Bengal, but in the forty-first year (1697-98) was removed, and on the death of Rashid Khan was brought to court and made *Diwan* of the *Khalisah*, or Fisc. He died in the forty-second year, 1109-10 H. (A.D. 1698-99) (Kewal Ram, Tazkirat-ul-Umara,' British Museum Additional MS., No. 16,703, fol. 83*b*). This may be the man intended by Manucci, but the affair with Sir W. Norris did not take place till 1701, two years after that Kifayat Khan's death, nor does the name of his father coincide with Manucci's story.

to do their duty, abandoned him. All these hindrances did not cause him to lose heart' and followed by a few English and Portuguese only, who stuck to him, he made every endeavour to pass, so that eventually they came to blows, and several men were killed. By this means the roads were for a time freed. But when the king received a report of what was going on, he sent orders to Keazudin Can (Ghiyaz-ud-din Khan),[1] governor of Burhanpur, to stop him (Norris), and whatever might be the cost, to prevent his passing until fresh orders had been given. Ghiyaz-ud-din Khan, on receipt of these orders, complied with them. He barred the road, and forbade the furnishing of any supplies. At the same time he made protests of being the ambassador's friend, that on all occasions he would endeavour to prove this fact, that it was his ardent desire to see and converse with him, that he had matters to communicate of the highest importance to his interests. In this way, by polite words, he managed to catch Norris and bring him to the town of Burhanpur, and there he was detained. Ghiyaz-ud-din Khan made his report at once to the king of what had been done, and on this head there is so far no news, and the ambassador is still there awaiting further orders.[2]

I have already said several times, and I cannot resist repeating it, the inhabitants of Hindustan are politic and dissimulators to the highest degree. At the first interview they are able to discover adroitly the intentions of those with whom they have to deal. They are self-seeking even to excess. No promises cost them a moment's hesitation; they are great flatterers, and they always hold out great hopes, in spite of their having not the remotest wish of holding to them. Thus it happens that so many men, when they think they have accomplished their ends, obtain the very contrary of what they had expected.

---

1. This is Ghazi-ud-din Khan, Firuz Jang, father of Asaf Jah, Nizam-ul-mulk. His title is given by some authors as Ghiyaz-ud-din Khan.
2. See Hunter, 'History,' ii. 357, who assigns the Mogul command at Burhanpur to the *wazir*, Asad Khan. Sir W. Norris was detained two and a half months, and he did not reach Surat till March, 1702. N. Manucci's story is otherwise fully corroborated by Hunter's version taken from the English Records. Manucci resumes the subject on fol .38.

Since I am on the chapter of this ambassador [*i.e.*, Norris], there comes to mind three demands put by Aurangzeb to the Persian king's envoy in the early part of his reign. The replies he made were held to be sensible, and worthy of a man of understanding. First he was asked what strength his king disposed of. 'Sire,' replied the ambassador, 'I know not the number of his soldiers, but this I do know: that they are all united.' Secondly, he was asked what might be the extent of his king's treasures. 'Sire,' said he, 'I do not know, but what I do know is that his people are always prosperous.' Finally, in the third and last place, he was asked his king's age. 'Sire,' said he, 'I do not know, but one thing I know well, and that is, he is very prudent.'

Let us come back to Shiva Ji. This rajah has had the temerity to attack the royal army while upon the march, and he pressed forward so boldly that he was within a very short distance of the royal tent [37], and the king was forced to extricate himself as best he could. He took bow and arrow in hand in order to animate and encourage his troops. At this moment a Hindu prince rushed up to his succour at the head of four thousand Rajputs, causing the enemy to retreat. Without this aid, Aurangzeb would have run a great risk of either being made prisoner or of losing his life.

The prince of whom I have just spoken is quite young, not more than twelve years of age, but he is advised by good and experienced commanders. He is the grandson of Jaswant Singh, of whom I spoke many times in the earlier parts of this history.[1] The king, as a recompense and to prove his gratitute for the service just done him, called the youth to his presence, and took him by the hands (an unusual action). Then he told the young man to drag his hands away by force. His object was to see if the young prince would be quick-witted enough to make him an appropriate answer. This he did in the following manner: 'Wherefore, sire, should I withdraw them; the place where they

1. Jaswant Singh, who died in 1678 leaving only posthumous sons, could hardly have had a grandson twelve years of age in 1701. I guess that for 'Jaswant' we should read 'Jai' Singh, and the 'grandson' referred to might be Jai Singh, Sawae, descended in the fourth degree from the elder Jai Singh. He was born circa 1687, and would therefore be about fourteen years of age in 1701.

rest is too highly to be esteemed for that.' The king was highly delighted at such a clever reply from a child, and made a gift to him of two elephants, a very fine horse, and a set of rich robes (*sarapa*). This he did with the greater pleasure that he had need of his services.

In the preceding books it will, no doubt, have been remarked how much persecution and ill-treatment. Aurangzeb had dealt out to a son of Rajah Jaswant Singh. In spite thereof, these [Jaswant Singh's family] have never resented this conduct; on the contrary, they have always served him when the occasion presented itself, as has just been proved once more by the event I reported above.

It must be avowed that things have turned out with this king [Aurangzeb] very differently from what he anticipated when only a prince. For at that time he used to say that if ever God allowed him to mount the throne, he would undertake to rule the empire with an army of no more than twelve thousand horse. Yet at this present moment he has fifty thousand continually in the field, and is nevertheless quite incapable of undertaking anything serious against Shiva Ji [the Mahrattahs]. In addition, he has several other armies posted at various places in his empire, and these are incessantly occupied in recalling to their duty certain rebel Hindu princes. For these men adhere still to their ancient practices, and remain loyal as little as possible. This fact can be seen in my earlier Parts.

Shiva Ji, on his side, was not idle, and allowed no occasion of doing injury to escape him, making continual attacks upon the general, Zu,lfiqar Khan. Seeing this, and suffering from that prince's (the Mahrattah) strength, the general was forced to withdraw and seek for safer quarters. During his retreat he was pursued by the enemy for five days, and lost a number of men. At the end of that time the rajah desisted, seeing that to all appearance he would be unable to inflict a crushing defeat; he then turned off towards the province of Barrar (Barar). On his way he pillaged and plundered everything he could find, as is his custom.

Aurangzeb is well aware that if he does not go in person at the head of his armies, it is impossible to become master of any fortress. To carry on this war he is put to enormous expense, and when all things are reckoned up, many a year he has gained nothing, although he has consumed many men and much money.

Nevertheless [38] he never ceases to push on his purpose, and in this way his conduct of affairs is not without profit to Shiva Ji, who, like an able man, succeeds in making use of this persistence for the advancement of his own interest. At times he is sly enough to let a fort be taken, then, waiting till it is fully provisioned and afterwards fortified, he retakes it with even greater readiness than it had ever fallen before. It is true that his troops are very much better, and more inured to war than those of the Mogul. For they are Dakny[1] soldiers, who pass for the bravest and most enterprising in India. It may also be asserted that if the monarch (Aurangzeb) maintains his design of becoming master of all Shiva Ji's fortresses, he will need, before he succeeds, to live for as many years more as he has already lived. But it is quite clear that he would throw up the war most readily did he not imagine that his reputation is at stake.

He bears himself in such a way as if he were not even aware of all the losses he is suffering. He has lost all the Dakhin, and sacrificed many soldiers and officers without allowing the least sign of chagrin to appear. Nor did he show any at the siege of Bijapur, where he lost twelve thousand sappers by the explosion of the enemy's countermines. On the contrary, this contretemps having been reported to him by one of the principal commanders with evident signs of grief and sorrow, the king answered with a laugh that it was a mere nothing. The reason is that he has a perfect understanding of his empire: he knows It to be thickly peopled; war holds his enemies in fear, while it secures the devotion of his nobles and vassals by providing them with occupation. It keeps their fortunes at the lowest ebb, to which he takes care to add the heavy contributions he obliges them to pay.

At last the king remembered about the Chevalier Norris,[2] and what had happened to him under his orders. He wrote a letter to his own general, Ghiyaz-ud-din Khan, suggesting that he should intercede with his majesty for the said envoy. An extraordinary proceeding this, but often resorted to by these princes when they have made some mistake, or they are in need

1. Spelt 'd'Akny in the text. 'Dakhini' (Southerner) is the Mogul epithet for the Mahrattahs, when they are not styled 'the Accursed Enemy.'
2. The previous events connected with Sir W. Norris were given in Part III., fol. 30, and Part IV., fols. 34-36.

of some one. For in such cases, instead of making overtures to persons involved, they always put them in the wrong, and force them to employ intercessors.

Ghiyaz-ud-din Khan carried out his orders, and bestowed a thousand caresses on the ambassador. In the letter submitted to the king, he represented that the said lord (Norris) had not done wrong in any way, that he had been a long time at the court, where he had been at great expense without obtaining what he wanted, a result sufficiently vexing. 'This is the reason,' he said, 'why I pray your majesty to grant his requests, since he has besought me to intercede with your mightiness on his behalf.'

Upon receipt of this letter the king wrote one to the King of England in which, after the usual compliments, he assured him that he would protect the nation in all things that depended upon him, and would cause justice to be done to the English on all necessary occasions, so far as they were in the right. As a present he sent a sword and a poignard with gold hilts adorned with stones, valued at fifty thousand rupees. These were brought by a *gurzbardar* (mace-bearer) carrying a silver mace. This man's name was Maamad Alibeg (Muhammad 'Ali Beg), and he reached the ambassador on January 22, 1702.

At this time news came to the court that the governor of Surat,[1] named Daniscan (*sic*), had taken by force from the English

1. The Surat letter of October 18, 1701, shows That his name should be Diyanat Khan. There were two groups of complainants—'Husson Ammedan' and 'Abdul Guffore and others'—said to be stirred up by Sir William Norries. The loss by pirates was put at eight lakhs of rupees. On November 24 the Mogul Governor received orders to seize the officials of the old Company, and about December 1 he attempted a surprise. Before December 13 he had seized goods worth nearly Rs. 120,000, which were undervalued by him to the extent of Rs. 50,000. On January 1, 1702, the factory was strictly guarded, and Rs. 13,82,100 demanded. By January 9 'Abd-ul-Ghafur had been satisfied by delivery of Company's goods worth Rs. 182,000, but Rs. 270,000 were still demanded for Husain. The English were still shut up on January 22, 1702, and in October the trouble had not subsided altogether.

   Diyanat Khan had succeeded upon his brother Amanat Khan's death in 1699, but he was removed before Aurangzeb's death in 1707 ('Ma,asir-i-'Alamgiri,' 412, 460; 'Ma,asir-ul-Umara,' ii. 59). The latter authority says he died in 1714 or 1715 while *Diwan* of the Dakhin. 'Abd-ul-Ghafur and his grievances are again prominent in the Dutch correspondence at Surat between September 22, 1703, and March 19, 1704.

merchants there merchandise worth 184,000 rupees or more. These goods he had made over to Abdulgafour ('Abd-ul-Ghafur) by way of recompense [39] for the injury he had suffered from pirates. He had also taken goods from the Dutch, which they estimated at 456,000 rupees and more. These had also been given to the same man on the same account. The person I am speaking of is the most powerful merchant at Surat, and owns over twenty ships of his own. He is a Mahomedan by religion. The king approved of the governor's proceedings.[1] [He sent orders for the release of the general of Bombay and all the other Europeans. He said that for the future those who wished to trade by sea might do so, whether his own subjects or foreigners, provided that they had strength enough to defend themselves against pirates. If any losses accrued from that cause, he did not wish any complaints to be brought to him. He had deliberated on the matter, and held it to be a great injustice to oblige the Europeans to satisfy losses caused at sea by these robbers. This was opposed to the law of nations and prejudicial to the interests of his crown, since all the nations, finding themselves equally ill-treated, would unite and destroy all the ports in his (Aurangzeb's) kingdom. It was for these reasons that he revoked his previous orders. God grant that this may last, and that selfish reasons or false reports may not induce him to reissue those orders.]

But he is not entirely satisfied. For he has issued fresh orders to restrict the European nations at Surat more than ever. These orders have been carried out with extreme rigour. The poor people are now often without bread to eat. The last resource they had has been closed against them. This consisted in certain supplies sent to them from time to time by the Capuchin fathers through a concealed door in their house. The fact was imprudently disclosed to the Mahomedans by an Englishman, who scoffed at their manner of watching them, which did not hinder them from receiving large supplies of provender. Upon this discovery being made, not only did they close the secret

1. The following passage is crossed out in the MS., but it seems required in order to carry on the narrative. The changed views of Aurangzeb are possibly a reference to the *Hasb-ul-hukm* of the 8th Shawwal, forty-eight year (February 14, 1704), extorted by the Dutch blockade of Surat from September, 1703. It cancelled the *Muchalkah* (bond) of February 4, 1699.

door, but hemmed in the Capuchins as they had done to all the other Europeans, so that they also are in the same trouble and are now suffering the pangs of hunger. The object of the Mogul in this matter is to extort from the Europeans an exorbitant sum of money, which he has piled up as the loss suffered by the Mahomedans from pirates during the last seventeen years.

[Folios 41 and 42 of the original are blank.]

[43] The persecutions at Tanjor, of which I am about to speak, have had several causes, divisible into principal and secondary. The latter were, as it may be said, the commencing and far-off predispositions to these calamities; the proximate causes have but served to complete what the remoter began. The earlier or subsidiary causes had merely begun the irritation in the heathens' minds; the later and more important have created this new hatred and this aversion, or at any rate have made them burst forth, not only against the Christian religion, but against all who profess it; not only against ecclesiastics, but against laymen.

Such conduct the heathen had never displayed before during all the sixty or seventy years since the reverend Portuguese fathers arrived and established that mission. The troubles broke out there and in the environs through new ways of preaching the Gospel. Never before had they adopted those lamentable methods, such as I shall note, thereby overturning and destroying by one blow the edifice that had been built up in the course of so many years, not to speak of what the heathen kings threaten to do in the future.

As in all composite results, the original and remote predispositions precede the derived and immediate, and require to be formally adduced first. Thus I have judged it advisable to explain, to start with, as clearly and briefly as I can, the most remote and less influential causes of the persecution of which I am about to speak. Having dealt with these, I shall proceed to the principal and immediate causes which have lighted up and brought into life what has happened, after the other matters had, as it were; prepared the way and predisposed men's minds on the subject.

The first or less important causes are three; the recent and immediate are also three in number. I have learnt this from persons worthy of belief who made inquiries on the spot, and have sent in their report in writing, which I am about to reproduce. I need hardly speak of the general admissions made by Christians in Pondicherry itself, who learnt the facts from their relations and friends just as I did from my correspondents.

But before entering on the facts, it is necessary first to describe the customs followed by the Hindus of these lands, which to them have the force of law. Until this is done it is impossible to conceive how their infraction has contributed to the recent persecutions. The first of these customs [44] is that the idolaters are divided into castes as the Hebrews were into tribes, and this division is observed in the towns by residence in separate streets and wards. Above all others the priests, called Brahmans, insist wherever they are on a very strict observance of this custom; they allow none of the other castes to build houses in their midst or in their streets; above all, they will not tolerate those who eat flesh or fish. They fear either that the odour emitted by these articles when cooking might subject them to temptation, they never eating such things; or, possibly, there are other reasons, which I consider would take too long to set forth, and therefore pass over in silence as outside my subject. Thus it is obvious that to enter upon anything opposed to the above-named custom is likely to upset everything, and to expose oneself at some time or other to a rising not only of the caste affected, but also of others who claim to be upholding their own usages by helping to maintain those of others. Or else there may be a total desertion of their homes by these people, who go where they find themselves better treated, and are allowed to live peacefully in accordance with their customs, without any constraint by force or otherwise.

The reverend Jesuit fathers of Pondicherry were not in ignorance of these Brahman customs, or, at any rate, should not have been ignorant of them—they who know everything; still less should they have overlooked the disagreeables to which those are exposed who infringe these rules. Nevertheless, without regard to the one or the other reason, they undertook about twelve or thirteen months ago to secure their own ends, and for interested reasons (for which they are never at a loss) they resolve to break the rules. They decided to build a house for their Malabar sacristan. This man was of the Mandeli caste,[1]

1. The only identifications that I can suggest are Maravar, who eat flesh ('Madras Manual of Administration,' ii. 230), or Maudigar (*ibid.*, iii. 487), a

which eats flesh and fish. The house was to be erected at the end of the enclosed area of their garden in the middle of Brahmans' houses, which block the view to the north and form one side of a street, where they dwell and follow their customs, as I have said above.

The Hindu priests opposed it at once, and said that it could not be done, being against their customs. But the reverend fathers troubled their heads very little about this opposition, caring nothing about what might be the consequences provided they secured success in their enterprise. Not to be thwarted [45] in it, they went on with the work as commenced. Thus the judge, to whose jurisdiction appertains this class of dispute, was obliged to repair to the spot to investigate the arguments put forward on both sides. In spite of all the arguments from precedent which the objectors could adduce, he decided in favour of the reverend fathers, acting by habit. He declared that they might continue their work in defiance of any opposition. It was carried to completion, and their sacristan lives in the house at this present time.

The Brahmans, finding their claims and requests thrown out, were in no position to do anything more at Pondicherry to obtain redress for the infraction of their customs. For at that place are a strong fortress and a good garrison. Acting the part of wise men, they endured, though, with murmurs, what they could not hinder, neither by argument nor by assertion of customary right, still less by force. They passed it by, hoping to return to it when a favourable opportunity presented itself. This was the opinion at once arrived at by those who know them, and are aware from long experience how acutely these people feel this sort of infringement of their maxims of conduct. Nor have they failed to act as anticipated, as the facts I am about to state will demonstrate. This was the first breach of Brahman customs, as preserved to them by all the nations of Europe who have established themselves on the coast, in order to attract them to settle in their towns and fortresses, with a view to the increase of their trade. The contravention was due to the intrigues of the reverend Jesuit fathers; and this is what I define as the first, more remote,

---

very low caste, equivalent to the Chamar, or leather-dresser, of Northern India.

or secondary cause of the persecution about which I have to speak.

There was a second custom of these Hindus infringed by these same reverend Jesuit fathers, and this infraction was one of the three far-off and less influential of the causes of the persecution. At every temple of their idols (*called pagodas*) there is usually an annexed flower-garden, just as in our parish churches of Europe, without comparing the two, there are grave-yards. This garden is not held less worthy of veneration and respect by these peoples, for every day the officiating priests told off for the purpose gather there the flowers with which they adorn some idols and embellish others. Such gardens are to them what some cemetery is to us where the bodies of saints lie, from which flows some miraculous liquid capable of curing maladies that cannot be benefited by ordinary and natural remedies; or let us say, like some culturable land [46] bequeathed and vowed to any one of our churches, so that the corn produced may be applied for the use of holy men. In this way, just as amongst us a man would be looked upon unfavourably, and be exposed to the fury of an indignant populace, if he began without extreme necessity to cut off a part of the cemetery or the culturable land bequeathed to the church, in order to apply it to other uses, or to destroy it, or to alienate it; so, *caeteris paribus*, you expose yourself here (in India) to some uprising of these Hindu peoples if you attempt to destroy, entirely or in part, these flower-gardens annexed and devoted to the pagodas. These gardens are held in singular veneration, because from them are obtained the flowers used in certain of their ceremonials.

Matters being in the condition above stated, who would ever have dreamt that the reverend Jesuit fathers, above all, French Jesuits—so wise, so foreseeing, men in these days so highly reputed throughout the world as great politicians, that the ablest in the art of politics flock to their schools to learn new views of it—should have wished to attempt the removal or reduction of one of these flower-gardens, annexed and devoted to an idol temple, with no other title than their own convenience, by setting in motion their intrigues, their credit, and their authority? This, too, in a country where the Hindus muster a thousand—nay, ten thousand—to every single Christian; where dependence must be had upon them for all that is necessary to life and commerce.

Nor need we advert to the fact that even their reverences, in the person of the reverend Portuguese fathers of the same society, and all the Christians they have baptized in these regions, dwell under the government and authority of Hindu princes and rajahs or kings of the same Hindu religion. Consequently all these Christian men are exposed to the resentment of those rajahs and the dreadful results that may ensue therefrom.

Nevertheless this is what they undertook some nine months ago, their reasons being, as above recited, their own interest and convenience, also the securing of their ends, their chief and most obvious motive wherever they are to be found. This it is which gives them the various impulses and movements which are displayed in their conduct.

Having got it into their heads that they would build another house in addition to the one I have already spoken of—a house for one of their catechists—they chose a site close to one of the temple gardens. Not finding elbow room enough to make an enclosure of the sort they wished, they let it be announced [47] that they possessed rights over a part of the adjoining garden, or even over the whole of it. But not wishing to give trouble to the worshippers at the temple to which it was consecrated, they were content in their moderation to take no more than one corner, solely to make more commodious the house of their catechist.

The Hindu worshippers at that *pagoda* and their Brahman did not fail to resist; they protested against this encroachment and this unjust claim. Anything given and dedicated to a *pagoda* is no longer under the control of even the donor, nor can he divert it to other uses. But the reverend fathers were in no wise perturbed at all this. Then the complainants gathered themselves together and once more lodged a petition. They prayed the judge to appear once more upon the spot to inquire into the case there, and then come to a decision. This was carried out. After hearing the arguments on both sides, he once more came to a conclusion favourable to the fathers. For he could hardly he expected to do otherwise, having the honour of 'belonging to them as he did, in his capacity of brother of the Third Order of St. Ignatius. What will not one do for one's friends and brethren—above all, when one looks for some return both in this and in the other world! Thus was the dispute decided.

XXXIII. The Qutb Shahi Kings of Gulkandah: (i) Burhan 'Ali; (2) Jamshid; (3) Ibrahim; (4) Muhammad Quli; (5) Muhammad; (6) 'Abdullah; (7) Abu,l Hasan

No one of any sense fails to see and understand, by the condition described by me of the Hindus at Pondicherry and their Brahman priests, that if they were patient on this, as on the first occasion (although inly raging) it was only because they were waiting for their revenge, in which they would have the best of it. These disagreeables, these infringements of their customs, only provoked them to vengeance; it would not be long before they would burst forth with it in the best way they could, and so adroitly that the same measure could not be repaid to them. The Christians were not the strongest, nor could they dispense with the Hindus, as I have already said. For this reason I call this the second remote and indirect cause of the persecution.

The third cause *in illo genere* is a sort of persecution that these same Hindus have suffered at Pondicherry by the hands of the aforesaid reverend fathers. It is due to the indiscreet and ill-regulated zeal of the regent of their school—at least, so the Hindus have considered it when talking about it. He would never let them alone, disturbing them at every turn about the customs and modes of action of this country, which is his own. For this reverend father has been brought up from his youth in the country, donned here the habit of the Society, was ordained priest, learned the Malabar language rather well, and got it into his head that he could convert the whole of this Hindudom. The design is praiseworthy, glorious, fitted for an apostolic missionary, but the means [48] which he adopted were valueless. They were contrary to the customs and the maxims of these peoples, more particularly of those who live at Pondicherry. They are mostly persons who congregated there from the country outside in the hope of earning something after the recent re-establishment of the French Company.[1]

These people are not yet habituated to Europeans as are the persons dwelling in places of older date. For this reason they hold the *Farangis* in most singular aversion, trembling at their approach, more especially the women. Yet the reverend father travelled from house to house every day, sending for some, going himself to seek others, all for the purpose of preaching to them. He mixed himself up with them when they had assembled

1. That is, early in 1699, when, under the Treaty of Ryswick, the French reoccupied Pondicherry.

and were conducting their ceremonies at the gate of their *pagodas*, built partly in the open spaces or in the middle of the streets. Or he appeared when they had collected in the market, and preached to them there. It is quite true that nothing is finer than zeal, especially zeal for the saving of souls. But at the same time it must be granted that it may possibly spoil everything it has secured, even when governed by the dictates of prudence, unless it is continually controlled and directed by one and the same hand.

These Hindus, the objects of the reverend father's zeal, instead of enjoying the teaching that he directed to them in the hope of bringing them to a knowledge of the true faith, felt nauseated, and rejected what he said. His ardour being too vehement, they, instead of listening to him, uttered a thousand silly jokes over his discourses. It is even a question whether they had understood, or had any conception of what he said to them. For, in place of becoming converts, they were only hardened against him. Seeing that he almost forced them to hear what he had to say, they took that as an attempt and an interference meant rather against their liberty than their religion, rather against their persons than their consciences, or, finally, against both. On this account they complained several times, first to such Christians of the country as they knew individually, and these carried it to that good father. They explained to him that what he was doing ought not to be done—at any rate, not in that fashion. Far from winning these unhappy men for Jesus Christ, he was irritating them. They took for persecution what he meant and did for sanctification. That was why the Hindus increased the number of their processions, their ceremonies, and their superstitions, by way of invoking the aid of their gods against such treatment, which counted with them as violence. Their learned men came more [49] frequently to Pondicherry than customary, trying to inspire them with horror for [our] religion.

It would be better to convert annually only a dozen, without frightening the others, rather than end in not converting a single one by attempting to convert the whole of them at one effort. They [the Christians] said, furthermore, that what he was undertaking might have unfortunate results, which would recoil upon lived in those territories where they had the free exercise of our religion, while living under the rule of their own prince. In short, as they told him, the Hindus made a mock of him, taking him for a *jogi*. This is a kind of person in this country who, in order to pick up a few coppers, draws crowds in the market-places to look at certain feats of legerdemain or serpent-dancing, somewhat as done by our conjurers, or marionette-dancers, or hawkers of quack medicines.[1] They added many similar arguments.

But in spite of this excellent and most sensible advice, the reverend father never altered, but went on as he had begun. In the end the Hindus grew tired of his importunities, and stated publicly that they would abandon Pondicherry if they could not be left alone in peace. They would never allow the *Farangis* to enter the enclosures of their houses, where their women live, nor would they permit them (the *Farangis*) to force Christianity upon them.

The matter came to the ears of Monsieur the Governor. He sent warning to the priest's superior to put an end to these disorders, and told the Jesuit himself that he must constrain his zeal within the limits of his church, giving good instruction to the Christians, and receiving there those only who were touched by the Holy Ghost and sought to be baptized, or were brought to him for that purpose by the exertions of the Christians themselves who live in the country. Of these men the Hindus are not frightened. Often by attempting to do everything nothing at all is done—at any rate, nothing of any value; or by wishing to gain all, all is lost. Nothing could be more correct than this advice. But the reverend father, thinking himself more enlightened than other people, or may be upon the instructions of his community, as might be presumed, desisted not at all upon that account. This went on until at last the aforesaid Lord Governor, fearing disastrous consequences for the public welfare, and even for religion itself, such as the flight of the inhabitants of Pondicherry, sent him (the Jesuit) an order prohibiting him from continuing. This order he at length obeyed.

However, the Hindus and their Brahman priests could not avoid feeling resentment for the past, and continued to await a favourable occasion to make the reverend fathers feel in their turn, in the persons of their Portuguese fathers at Tanjor and

1. *Marchands d'orviétan*. This article was an electuary introduced into France by an Italian from Orvieto, who sold it in the public squares, and the name passed from the seller to the drug (Littré).

the Christians there, some portion of what they had suffered from this Jesuit at Pondicherry, This was just [50] what the Malabar Christians had very clearly predicted.

First of all the Hindus complained to their relations and any persons known to them at Tanjor[1] of all the above vexations, and the interference with their customs. These complaints spread among the people and disturbed their minds, and rendered them ill-disposed towards Christians. Then the reverend fathers, impelled by indiscreet zeal, entered upon farther measures, more repulsive than anything yet described. It was these acts that forced the Hindus at length to begin and continue the persecution of which I am speaking. It is for this reason that I call this enterprise 'indiscreet zeal.' Added to this were several abusive speeches and repellent words spoken by the said reverend father to one of the principal Brahmans, who usually lived at Tanjor. His name was Courou Nama Chivaiam (Guru Namas-sivayam). The story may not prove displeasing to the reader. Here it is.

This Brahman was reputed among these people as a holy man and very learned. So great was the veneration paid him that they drank the water in which his feet had been washed. This man came from Tanjor to Pondicherry to visit his disciples with a view to their instruction and consolation, also to fortify them against the outbursts of ill-regulated zeal displayed by the reverend Jesuit fathers. He had vehicles and a retinue in proportion to his dignity and merits, as is the custom with them. The reverend father believed that with one effort he could hit with a sling and fell to earth this Goliath, and put to rout the army of the enemies of God. With this idea he paid the man a visit, and after mutual compliments he started him on the subject of religion. He made every effort to make the Brahman

1. Tanjor, a principality held by the Mahrattahs from about 1678. The capital, of the same name, lies 180 miles south-west of Madras, and about 100 miles south of Pondicherry. The first Mahrattah ruler, a brother of Shiva Ji, died in 1682, and was succeeded by his eldest son, Shah Ji. This was the persecuting rajah of the text; he died September 27, 1711 (see 'Recherches sur l'Inde,' Berlin, 1787, 4to., vol. ii., p. 18; Anquetil Duperron's 'Essay on the Tanjor Rajahs,' founded on 'Der Koniglichen Dänischen Missionarien aus Ost-Indien eingesandte ausführli-chen Berichten,' Halle, 1733, vol. iii., p. 827).

realize his blindness, and how far his spirit had gone astray, in rendering to dumb idols what is due to God alone.

The Brahman answered these words in his own fashion, according to his principles. Since either he did not satisfy the reverend father, or did not succumb to his reasoning, as the father claimed that he ought to do, he (the father) began to use abuse in front of the whole assembly, which was somewhat numerous. He called him a cheat, an ignoramus, a wrong-doer, and worthy of the most exemplary punishment. As for his disciples, not having the same light and knowledge, they were consequently less guilty and more to be excused. We must admit that what he said was true. But who ignores the fact that often many things might be said that should not be said in order to secure some greater good or avoid some still greater evil. 'Truth hurts,' as says the proverb; in short [51], the heart of man is easier gained by gentleness than by abuse, invective, or rage; these Indian peoples esteem above everything else that moral virtue of gentleness and those who possess it. This is the reason of their having an aversion to the opposite quality. In particular they abhor the bilious temperament which takes fire at once, a thing entirely unknown to their phlegmatic temperament, one very difficult to arouse.

However, the Brahman said nothing in reply, his gravity not permitting him to show that he was offended by all that the reverend father had said to him. Yet he felt it all in his mind, as he has demonstrated since. For, together with some of the most prominent men of the same caste, he became one of the instigators of the persecution, helping it with his advice, credit, and authority. He departed from Pondicherry offended and angry, leaving the Hindus, his disciples, irritated and scandalized.

The second of the proximate and principal causes of the persecution was an imprudent act of one of the reverend Jesuit fathers' native (Malabar) catechists. These men always accompany the reverend fathers in all the gatherings they call together in the market-places.[1]

1. For confirmation of the constant employment of catechists, see Father Pierre Martin's letter of December 11, 1700, in J. Bertrand, 'Mission du Maduré,' vol. iv., p. 101. For one reason, the Jesuits feared that their own white faces would betray that they were *Farangis*. Father Martin (same letter, p. 73) describes their denunciation as the deliberate act of three renegade catechists who applied to the King of Tanjor.

The catechist made so bold as to say several times in addressing the Hindu crowd, that the father whom they saw and heard speaking their language was the brother of, and of the same Society as, the Brahman priests of the Christians who dwelt at Tanjor, and consequently those referred to were this one's brothers, members of one and the same body or company. Thus they (the Tanjor fathers) must be Pariahs, for he (the Pondicherry Jesuit), of whom he spoke was reputed such in the minds of these peoples.

But in order to understand fully the importance of the words that this catechist let slip on this occasion, and how imprudent they were, you must know that these Hindus have considerable contempt for Europeans, whom they call Franguis (*Farangi*, a Frank).[1] This contempt is even greater than that of persons of quality in France for night-soil workers and scavengers. For the Hindus account Europeans to be Pariahs, since they eat cow's flesh, or, in other words, are of the very lowest caste or tribe, men with whom they cannot eat without losing their own [caste] —that is, their position in life. Now, to lose your caste and your position among these people is something even more deadly than for a gentleman in France to be degraded and lose his nobility, he and all his [52] posterity. For there a deprived noble can still (above all, if he have any wealth) find respectable men with whom he can form an alliance, such as merchants or others. While, if deprived of his caste, the man of Malabar can no longer find a wife, nor can anyone give him his daughter without incurring the same evils and penalties. He cannot be received in anyone's house, none may eat or drink with him, cannot even serve him or help him in his necessities, even were he at the very point of death. The rule is so strict that he must either renounce marriage or take a Pariah wife. Never to marry at all is the severest punishment that can be inflicted among these people; they hold marriage to be the greatest happiness in life, and, on the contrary, never to marry the greatest of all evils. But for a man to marry a Pariah is to fall from his nobility, to lose his caste, to be rejected by his family and connections; in short, to become himself a Pariah, he and all his posterity *usque in eternum*. That is a most terrible thing. Still, there is a

1. Yule, 353, s.v. *Firinghee*, speaks of the word implying hostility or disparagement; see also his quotations in that article.

method of being rehabilitated and washing away the Pariah stain that has been contracted, and thus re-entering one's lost caste. This method is to drink for forty consecutive days a potion composed of cow's dung and urine. Among this people this compound suffices to cleanse from the most terrible sins.

The reverend Portuguese Jesuit fathers who first established missions in the kingdoms of Tanjor, Madura, another adjacent countries, being aware of the aversion of these people to *Farangis* exerted themselves, when starting their establishment, to persuade the inhabitants that they were not *Farangis,* but Roman Brahmans. The populace retain to this day a great idea of these priests, who call themselves by the elevated and honourable name of Roma-pouri,[1]—that is, 'considerable country or territory of Rome.' By these same means they (the Portuguese Jesuits) had maintained themselves there until the persecution broke out. It is for this reason that to this day it is the practice, when they intend to provide new missionaries for their mission, to send them first to their stations on the coast, where they learn the Malabar tongue, and that of the learned, called *grandaon*.[2] After that they are sent to the distant missions in the interior, where they live after the manner of Brahmans. They dress like them so exactly that they are taken to be Brahmans, and as such revered by all. Of the poor men and Hindus in the kingdom of Tanjor alone they have converted about twenty to thirty thousand [53] since they commenced.

Things being in this position, it was absolutely imperative for the preservation of this mission and those adjoining it, not to unmask to these people the stratagem employed to bring them to Jesus Christ; not to inform them that the missionaries living there disguised as Brahmans were nothing of the sort, but only *Farangis,* consequently Pariahs.[3] To do otherwise was to stake all upon one throw, to bring to the ground in one moment

1. This is an adaptation of *puri,* 'a city,' one of the appellations (or affixes used by the *Dasnami* Order of Ascetics, others being *Tirtha* (shrine), Asrama (an order), *Aranya* (a wood), *Giri* (a hill) (H. H. Wilson, 'Glossary,' s.v. *Gosain*).
2. That is, Sanskrit (Yule, 393, 397); from *grantham,* a book.
3. Great precautions were necessary when any of these missionaries visited a European settlement. In 1701 Father Pierre Martin left Pondicherry at night-time for fear any Hindu might notice that he was a *Farangi* (J. Bertrand, 'Mission du Maduré,' iv. 114). For the same reason the bishops from the west coast had never paid a visit of inspection to these missions.

an edifice erected and upheld for so many years at the cost of many efforts. For who fails to perceive that the Brahmans born in the country having shared the communion with the disguised Brahmans, now known to be *Farangi* Pariahs, a tumult must be excited at once within every family? Lo and behold, consternation everywhere! I must avow, in all simplicity, that I have no expressions strong enough to express the feelings of rage and despair aroused by this discovery of the stratagem practised by the reverend Portuguese Jesuit fathers, which must be the cause to these peoples of a calamity reputed by them to be so great.

Nevertheless, this is what that featherhead of a catechist did, publishing at an open meeting, either by his own impulse or instigated by the reverend French Jesuit fathers, that the father they saw and had heard preach was a brother of and belonged to the same Society as the Brahman priests of the Christians then living at Tanjor, and that consequently these latter were also his brethren.

The Hindus present noticed this remark, and did not allow it to drop. They began to accept as a certainty that the Brahmans of the Tanjor Christians were *Farangis*, a thing that until that time they had only suspected. For the reverend Portuguese Jesuit fathers who live in this disguise have ever made it a point, in order to kill this suspicion, to make more demonstrations of repugnance than even a native of the country would do when anyone called them by this name [*Farangi*]. Both in this mission at Tanjor and in those planted elsewhere among these people, they always avoided being recognised for what they really are.

After this imprudent admission of the catechist so publicly mails, they [the Hindus] communicated the fact repeatedly to their relations and acquaintances, and warned them to be on their guard, and avoid them [the missionaries] as such [*i.e., Farangis.*] There was no longer any doubt of their being Farangis, in spite of their living in all respects [54] disguised as Brahmans, for they had admitted it publicly themselves by the voice of their catechist. Above all was this true of one [Jesuit] then at Tanjor, whom they had themselves seen as one of the

Farangis at Pondicherry. As this news spread it raised excessive perplexity in the minds both of the reverend Portuguese Jesuit fathers and of the Hindus: in those of the reverend fathers, because they foresaw the consequences. For this reason they set in motion all their rhetoric, and invented all they could, both of argument and of effort, to bring back minds from this disastrous apprehension. As for the dismay of the Hindus, its reasons have been already so fully touched upon that I hold it useless to repeat them here.

Take the case of waters which flow from a mountain by various channels, some larger, some smaller, into a valley. There they meet with an embankment in such a manner that they are held back and rise in level. Not being either abundant or impetuous enough, they are unable to overcome the strength of the embankment. But when a storm supervenes and heavy rain falls, the strength of these streams is increased, and uniting, they force a way at some point or another. They overturn the embankment, root out its very foundations, and pile up one upon the other everything that opposes itself to the rage and impetuosity of their course. They spread themselves over the adjacent plains already sown or about to become so, and in one moment the labourer loses the hope of reaping from the one and of sowing the other. In short, the floods ruin him; he loses the fruits of his exertions in the past, the present, and the season to come.

Thus I can say in respect of the subject with which I deal, that all which had been done up to this time, as I have reported it, was probably insufficient to bring on a persecution of the Christians—neither the infractions of Hindu customs made unnecessarily, for mere reasons of convenience or profit, upon the credit or with the authority of the reverend French Jesuit fathers, nor the defects of conduct, the indiscreet and ill-regulated zeal of one particular father, nor the gross imprudence of their catechist. They [the Hindus] would not have proceeded to the extremities since reached, although those things irritated them, made them murmur, grumble, complain, menace even. Their phlegmatic temperament, which is not easily stirred, and loves not bloodshed nor extremes, stood as a strong embankment against the resentments aroused by the past. Besides, they could not display their anger without injuring those of the [55] neighbours who had become Christians. So much did this influence them that they did not overpass due bounds, but bore with what had been done to them up to that time. May be they might have observed this peaceful attitude permanently.

But the reverend Jesuit fathers, always restless, always adventurous, seeking to gain notoriety either for good or for evil, did not act in that way. They did not keep themselves within the bounds of moderation, like those poor blind creatures [the Hindus], but, still insisting on their point, brought to a crisis by a remarkable act what they had to that time no more than laid the train for. By this act all was lost, and thereby their reverences, owing to the harm they have done, have betrayed an unhappy want of foresight. Touching them by it too much on the quick, they have forced the Hindus to reveal their resentment, and once for all avenge themselves for what they had suffered by instalments from these good fathers. Thus the Hindus planned, brought into existence, and set alight the persecution of Tanjor of which I speak. It sped on like a raging torrent, and in a moment overwhelmed and ruined everything. It destroyed the ripe grain ready to be garnered by the evangelical labourers, withered up what was in the stalk and about to produce seed, as well as what was still only springing up and giving rise to hope. Thus fell famine and desolation upon this field of the Lord, ruining the labourer absolutely, and bringing to naught his years of toil.

It is this want of foresight, my dear reader, which I call the proximate, immediate, and principal cause of the persecution at Tanjor. What was this cause, then, but the tragedy, or rather let us style it the farce, that the reverend French Jesuit fathers prepared at Pondicherry in this year of 1701, in the month of February. At that time the Sieur Deslandre (*i.e.*, Deslandes), director of the French Company at their factory in Bengal, was present. It took place before their house, in the presence of the Hindus and of their priests called Brahmans. Its author was the reverend Father Dolu, a member of that same Society (the Jesuits).[1]

1. Dolu, Dolfs, or Dolfus (Charles François), born 1651, left for India in 1688, was made cure of Pondicherry in 1699, returned to Europe in 1710, went to Spain in 1713, retired to La Fléche in 1723, and died there on January 6, 1740. He was the son of Jean Jacques Dolu de

In this farce they represented the most respected and the most venerable gods of the people. Here are their names in the Malabar language and character, also in our alphabet:[1]

பிருமா	*Virouma* [Piruma = Brahma].
விஷ்ணு	*Vistnou* [Vishnu].
ருத்திரன்	*Rutro* [Ruttiran = Rudra].
ரிஷவன்	*Rejaven* [Rishavan = Rishabha].[2]
வேலவர்	*Velaver* [Velavar].[3]

Also a goddess, wife of Brahma, called

பார்வதி.	*Paravadi* [Parvati],
or	
சிவராமி	*Chivalami* [Siva-rami].

after stating some home truths, the actors, who were Malabar Christians, declaimed against these gods and against those men [56] who acknowledge and adore them as such. I admit this was done from zeal, but it was indiscreet and out of place. This can be soon seen, and that easily enough, from the lamentable and unhappy consequences. For they [the Hindus] plucked out the performers' beards and kicked them, following this up, after more ill-treatment and buffeting, by knocking them down and pitching them under the stage into a sort of fire intended to represent hell.

There were Brahmans and other Hindus present at this farce,

Ferrette, Counsellor of State and Commissary-General of Marine. The family was of Alsatian origin (C. Sommervogel, 'Biblliographie de la Compagnie de Jésus,' iii. 123).

1. I am much indebted to Dr. L. D. Barnett, of the British Museum, for so kindly copying the following Tamil words for me, also for much help in the following pages.
2. Rishaha is another name for Nandi, the sacred white bull, the favourite vehicle of Siva (Ziegenbalg, 'Genealogy,' English translation, p. 43).
3. Dr. L. D. Barnett has identified this for me as Kumara—that is, Karttikeya or Skanda (see J. Dowson, 'Classical Dictionary of Hindu Mythology,' p. 152, and Ziegenbalg, English edition, p. 65).

having been invited by the people of the reverend Jesuit fathers and their servants. For several days before the performance they had run about the streets of the town announcing that on such a day there would be a play. Offended and disgusted at this public contempt shown to the majesty of their gods, through their images, the Hindus present reported the facts to the other Hindus and Brahmans of Tanjor. To the existing complaint they annexed all the things done at other times by the same reverend fathers against them and their customs. Their object was to instigate the Tanjor Hindus to take vengeance in their behalf upon the Christians of that kingdom, who were the subjects of the Hindu king there. Thus the Christians of Pondicherry would be made to suffer in the person of those of Tanjor, the Hindus not being able to do anything themselves at Pondicherry, where the Christians live under the French flag and the wise rule of the governor, Monsieur Martin.

One of the principal Hindus, who was a teacher within the palace of the rajah or king, espoused the cause of his outraged gods. Wishing to make the Hindus of Tanjor realize the full horror of the sacrilegious attack—may, the divine high treason —committed upon them by the Christians of Pondicherry, he resolved to repeat that same farce in his fellow-citizens' presence. They were irritated to a degree beyond what can be imagined by this simulated sacrilege, and from that moment dreamt of nothing but the destruction of the Christians, and the prohibition of that free exercise of their religion which up to that day had been permitted to them. Action must be taken before their own temples were destroyed and their idols abased—events they held as certain to happen in the future if the Christians became the more powerful party. This superiority might well be apprehended, since the Christians were growing in numbers from day to day. From this moment the Hindus sought the means of realizing their project.

The Brahman teacher, having succeeded in his first design, which was, as I said, to irritate the Hindus against the Christians, resolved to produce the same impression on the king's mind as he had already produced On those of his subjects. To secure his object and carry out his enterprise successfully he had recourse to- the following stratagem [57].

He prepared a public procession in which was carried, with all the state and pomp of which these people are capable, a representation of the Saviour, and round him stood their five gods already named, in the posture of slaves and servants. One of them presented Jesus with a tray or basket containing betel, a sort of plant that I have before spoken of (I. 39, III. 6), another a platter of areca-nut, another some prepared lime such as is used to spread on the betel, another something else, and so with the rest. But the representative of the Saviour refused their offers and ill-treated them, kicking them after the fashion of the actors in the Jesuit farce at Pondicherry. The procession was made to defile before the king.

Surprised at a thing so unusual, so extraordinary, and from his point of view so sacrilegious, the prince asked with an angry and threatening countenance what it all meant—what was the signification of this unusual ceremonial. Thereupon the Brahman author of the piece—

'. . . In utrumque paratus,
Aut versare dolos, aut certae occumbere morti'
(. . . Ready for either alternative,
To upset their plots, or submit to certain death)—

took up his parable and said to his majesty that he who was seen exalted over venerable gods, repelling them, rejecting them, kicking them, whilst they, in the attitude of slaves and servants, presented betel to him, was the God of the Christians. It was a new god, for they had never heard of him until a few years ago. Certain Brahmans who declared they had come from Rome, though it could no longer be doubted that they were *Farangis,* had come into his country and dominions preaching everywhere and announcing that this God was greater than theirs (the Hindus'), and more powerful. For these Christians dealt with and looked on the Hindu gods as devils, only fit for contempt in every way. This opinion they had shown several times in different plays that they had performed in his majesty's kingdom, in which they had dishonoured and reviled the Hindu gods under the guise of evil spirits. This had happened recently at Pondicherry, as they were informed by several letters from the Brahmans, their brethren, who had been ocular witnesses of what the Christians there had done. Those Christians are of the same religion as those in Tanjor territory. Not being restrained by fear there, as are those in this kingdom, it was at Pondicherry that they had done what the others here have not yet dared to do, except in riddles and allusions.

'For in a tragedy which they have played in one of the public squares, they have represented the gods as we have presented them now before you. After some horseplay, mockery, and contempt, they ordered our gods to be kicked, saying [58] that their would-be god was destined to come and expel and destroy ours, at the same time taking possession of this kingdom. We have acted thus merely to carry our complaints before your majesty, and let you see the importance of the subject. It is concerned with nothing less than the ruin of our pagodas, the destruction of our altars, the upsetting of all that is held most sacred amongst us—in short, the religion of our fathers. To crown it all, there would arise the evil of your losing your kingdom.'

For these reasons they had taken, they said, the liberty of representing before him the pretended god of the Christians kicking the other gods when they stood before him as servants and slaves. In no way had they meant to abandon the respect due to their gods, or to show them contempt. Of this they most humbly prayed his majesty to be assured, and they had full trust that he would apply an early remedy before the evil had grown and become incurable. It had been already long enough overlooked.

Everyone who knows what public affairs are, and how sweet it is to the minds of worldly people to issue orders to others, will easily realize the impression likely to be made on the mind of a jealous and ambitious prince by a discourse of the kind described, including a suggestion that he might lose his kingdom. The king, then, was rendered speechless, and became as it were dazed by the Brahman's words. After a time spent in reflection and complete silence, he came suddenly to himself. 'What!' said he, 'they thus profane, they thus despise the majesty of the gods, who have hitherto deigned to accord us so fortunate a reign! What! does this new sect attack what we hold the most worthy of respect and veneration? do they want to dictate to us, to menace our temples, our gods, and our crown? Put an end—put an end to this procession!' At that moment he issued orders for the assembling of his council, composed for the most part of Brahmans, who are the nobles of the country.

The following decisions were arrived at. First, that they should begin by seizing the goods of all men known to be Christians and avowing themselves such. Their persons were also to be seized; above all, those of their Brahmans, who were at the time only three for all that great congregation of Christians spread abroad in that kingdom.[1] In the year preceding the persecution there had been only two; many times there had only been one.[2]

Secondly, that any man desirous of purchasing his liberty and his release from prison might do so under certain conditions. They must resort again to the pagodas, in no way practise any longer the Christian religion, and must pay a fine proportioned to the nobility of their caste. But their goods [59] would be confiscated in perpetuity for the king's benefit (for what these people have once got hold of it is very difficult to make them return). Finally, all Christians must be marked with a hot iron upon the forehead and on the front portion of the two shoulders.

Thirdly, all churches must be demolished. Fourthly, all person who started by denying they had been Christians, in spite of their having been such, were not to be interfered with, provided that they worshipped at the pagodas or idol-temples, that they remained away from their own Christian festivals, and performed all Hindu rites. This order was carried out.

To begin with, about three thousand persons were arrested; of these, some thousand or thereabouts released themselves by money payments under the conditions above detailed. A still greater number took to flight, and of these the property was confiscated like that of the others, excepting what they managed to carry away with them. There were others of the Pariah caste or tribe. Now these people are distinguished from each other by tribes, something like those of the Hebrews, and these divisions they call *castes*. These Pariahs, then, if once put in prison, were unable to pay a ransom in money, owing to their poverty. On

1. That is, the Jesuit missionaries, the so-called *Romapuris*, or white Brahmans.
2. The missionaries then in Tanjor seem to have been Fathers Joseph Carvalho, Bertholdi, Pierre Martin, and Bouchet (Bertrand, 'Mission du Maduré,' iv. 149, 161, 185). The persecution, when four of Père de Saa's teeth were knocked out and after a term of imprisonment he was expelled the country, seems to have occurred in the previous year (see Father Martin's letter of December 11, 1700, same work, iv. 63). Father Bouchet, in the same volume, pp, 272-302, gives an account of his seizure by the Mahomedan Governor Sexsaeb (? Shekb Sahib) of a place called by him Tarcolan, He gives no dates, so it is impossible to know whether this is part of the events referred to in the text.

the other hand, they had not the courage necessary for abandoning their ancestral hearths or *patrios lares*, still less of suffering aught for God or for the Christian religion that they had professed for years past. To gain exemption, at one stroke, from all inconveniences, they returned all of a sudden to their former vomit, and asserted they were Hindus, denying they had ever been anything else. Of this class there were counted as many as five thousand.

Among this great throng of people arrested for their religion, not one man has had the courage to die in its defence—at least, I have heard of none. Perhaps it may be that resort to torture was forborne, or that they evaded the tortures. The only exception is a young girl, *nigra sed formosa* (black but comely), who was abducted and brought to the king's palace as an addition to the number of his concubines. She made pretext of some necessity to leave the place where she was guarded, and making for the nearest well, threw herself into it, taking with her all the ornaments with which her body had been decked to enhance its beauty.

It is to be feared that this Christian community, the extreme number of them in this kingdom being twenty or thirty thousand, which up to this day flourished under the direction of the reverend fathers, the Portuguese Jesuits, will in a short time entirely return to idolatry. Those priests established it more than sixty or seventy years ago, and have governed it up to this day. It is true we must except from their Christianity certain customs of the Hindus which it is said they have left untouched as matter of indifference, or as even praiseworthy things, though they are rejected by all other missionaries with one accord, being condemned as bad practices, and too much mingled with idolatry.

[All this ruin has sprung) from the indiscreet zeal, to call it nothing worse, of the reverend fathers, the French Jesuits of Pondicherry [60]. They wished to display it [their zeal] in order to distinguish their work from that of the Capuchins, the first missionaries in these parts. These men set to work more simply and more prudently. In the thirty years that they have been settled alongside the Royal Company of France in its commercial settlement. I do not merely say that they have provoked no persecutions, but they have not lost even one of those whom it has pleased God to convert by their means. It is the contrary with the reverend fathers (the Jesuits) at this present date, it being now only two and a half years since they usurped this mission and took it from those poor fathers [the Capuchins]. They have taken from them their cure of souls by intrigues, by the use of influence, and, above all, by a false allegation in regard to the will and pleasure of the Most Christian king [Louis XIV.].[1] They (the Jesuits) have already succeeded in making 6,000 Tanjor Christians into idolaters, and I have no need to speak of those who will become such hereafter.

Only two Christians died in prison, and these of a natural death, and by order of the king their bodies were burnt in the Hindu fashion. Only two reverend fathers, Portuguese Jesuits, were made prisoners in this persecution; of these, one died of dysentery.[2] A third priest, a Frenchman, being quicker and smarter than the others, as soon as he heard of the persecution, made on foot for the nearest place flying his country's flag. Thence he talks and blusters,[3] not about suffering, not being accustomed to it, but of the wars that all the Christian nations, above all, those of the Catholic faith, ought to wage, as he says, against the said King of Tanjor in revenge for the evil and harm he has done to them, and continues to do, in the persons of the Christians, his subjects. A clever embellisher![4] But I am not sure that, be it remarked in passing, he believes in blows, in case the movements of his altogether apostolic zeal should be listened to, and produce them [for himself].

The prison of the reverend fathers, the Portuguese Jesuits, was a house, where they were guarded. All the churches built at

1. This theme is more fully developed in the events of 1706, as given in the Capuchin manifestoes included in Part V., fols. 209-319.
2. The two Jesuit missionaries arrested appear to have been Joseph Carvalho and Father Bertholdi. The former died in prison on November 14, 1701 (J. Bertrand, 'Mission du Maduré,' iv. 185, Father Martin's letter of February 12, 1702). Father Carvalho, a Portuguese, went to India in 1681 (A. Franco, 'Synopsis,' 1726). The Frenchman who escaped must be Father Jean Venant Bouchet, born 1655, died 1732 (see C. Sommervogel, 'Bibliographie,' i. 1864).
3. The word in the text is *ronques*—literally, 'snores; from O. F. *ronchier*, *ronkier*, *ranker*, 'ronfler' (Godefroy, 'Dict. de l'Ancienne Langue Française').
4. 'Emboucheur,' from *emboucher*, which may be taken as meaning either (1) to blow the trumpet, to tell the world, to spread abroad (Littré); or (2) to show off merchandise by putting the best articles at the top (Godefroy).

different places in the [Tanjor] territory were demolished, pillaged, and left in ruins. What excellent results from that Jesuitic farce! Its only object, they said, was the conversion of the Hindus, and from it they expected no less result, after it had been played, than to behold the Brahmans and other chief castes flocking to church in search of baptism. The total ruin of the sheepfolds of Jesus Christ, the desolation of the Lord's house, the dispersion of his sheep who used to gather there to feed on the bread of God's word and to receive that of the angels—are not these things a greater misfortune by a thousandfold than any benefit from the acquisition by the reverend fathers, the French Jesuits, of a wretched corner of ground, of a portion of a flower garden dedicated to a *pagoda*, from its annexation to the house belonging to their catechist, or from the obstinacy they [63][1] displayed in having a house built for their sacristan among those of Brahmans, in opposition to Indian customs? I leave the decision to the judgment of the reader.

In any case, this King of Tanjor, not satisfied with what he had done in his own territories against the Christians, wished still farther to have them persecuted and brought to destruction within the kingdoms of the princes, his neighbours. With this object he wrote, while still impelled by his rage, while the fire of his wrath was still burning, to the Queen of Madura[2] and the King of Aurpaliam (? Udayar-palaiyam),[3] representing to them the danger they incurred for their temples, and even for their thrones, if they did not expel the Christians and the Christian Brahmans—at any rate, if they did not hinder the free exercise of that religion and forbid the baptism of any of their subjects. In this way the numbers of the Christians would not increase. The first of these potentates answered that, just as some were allowed to

1. Here fol, 60 ends, and the sentence is concluded at the top of fol. 63.
2. This queen's name was Mangammal, and she reigned from 1688 to 1704 as regent for her minor grandson ('Recherches sur l'Inde,' Berlin, 1787, vol. ii., pp. 59-62, 85, essay by Anquetil Duperron on Tanjor). Madura lies about 100 miles south-west of Tanjor. The queen is again referred to on fol. 104, where she is called Queen of Trichinopoly; both it and Madura were under her rule.
3. Udayar-palaiyam, about forty miles north of Tanjor, is now in the Trichinopoly district. The town is 144 miles south-south-west of Madras, and forty-seven miles east-north-east of Trichinopoly ('Madras Manual of Administration,'; iii. 609). The place is again referred to on IV., fol. 104. Or Ariyalore in the same district may be intended.

eat rice and others meat, so also was it lawful for each man to practise or' adopt whatever religion seemed to him the best.

As for the King of Udayar-palaiyam, he did not preserve so favourable an attitude towards the Christians as did the Queen of Madura. It is also true that he did not treat them with the rigour and severity that had been exercised in Tanjor. He was content to give orders to arrest four Jesuit missionaries then within his territory, but their reverences were warned and 'preserved themselves for their country' (*servaverunt se patrea*).[1]

The king, having missed arresting their persons, made sure of their property, and of all that was to be found in their house. But the Christians were not touched.

If the account of this persecution is something unheard of, in regard to the causes producing it, the story of the conduct adopted by the reverend Jesuit fathers at Pondicherry as to the ceremonies they allow their Christians to practise will not appear in any degree less strange. Judge for yourself, most judicious reader. Here is a faithful account of what I have seen and learnt, not only about their marriages, but about their burials, *et cetera*. But before commencing I will tell you of a question put to me by some Hindus at Pondicherry which, from its exceptional nature, is worth repeating.

[61] Some Hindus of Pondicherry, having observed the difference between the method of living of the Capuchins and that of the Jesuits, took it into their heads to ask me what religion I was of, what god I adored—whether it was the Capuchins' or that of the Jesuits. They were weak enough to suppose that the Christians had more than one god, just as they have themselves, and that different forms of worship are employed among us. To speak the truth, I was taken aback at this ridiculous question, and put forth all my industry to free them from so gross an error, one at the same time of such prejudice to Christianity. Among other things, I said to them that I worshipped the God of gods; and instructed them that this same God who had given breath to the Romans had also given It to

1. In more familiar language, 'they bolted.' The two fathers were apparently J. V. Bouchet and P. Martin (see the latter's letter of 1701 from Aour—? Udayar—in J. Bertrand, 'Mission du Maduré,' iv. 161). It was at some date subsequent to Easter.

the French and the Mahomedans. This reply astonished them in some degree, and compelled them to the retort: 'But if it be thus, tell us, pray, why it is that the ancient priests and ministers of your religion were led by the same Spirit as the Capuchins, saying and teaching the same thing; whereas the Jesuits, who for a time would not acknowledge our ceremonials, but condemned them as bad and scandalous, now no longer reject them; on the contrary, they approve of them, and hold them pure and holy. Tell us,' said they, 'the reason of this change.'

I was very much concerned that the mode of action adopted by the reverend fathers had raised such feelings in the minds of these idolaters. I replied that the Jesuits did not approve Hindu ceremonial as good or bad in itself, but, living in the midst of Hindus, they believed that these things could be done as matter of indifference and for reasons of policy; governed by this feeling, they permitted some things which looked as if they were Hindu, but were not so in reality. The poor people really believed—for they told me so—that the God of the Jesuits was different altogether from that of the Capuchins, by reason of the great contrast and difference between the ceremonies of the one and of the other; those of the fathers of the Society being remarkably like those of the Hindus, as I have described.

But before ending the narrative of the persecution, it will not be out of place to remark that the weakness of these new-made Christians has been something extraordinary and surprising. Their most famous catechist, Virapavati, was hung up by his hair for a whole night, and by excess of pain was obliged to deny his faith and do what was required of him. After this all the Christians left in the kingdom (Tanjor) went back to their pagodas. It is true that there were a few among this great number who, in spite of their presence at the sacrifice to idols, still did not worship them, but, raising their thoughts to God, gave to him their homage and adoration as if still in church.

It will not be difficult to understand this, if one remembers what is told of the famous astronomer and mandarin of China, the Most Reverend Father Adam, Jesuit.[1] By reason of his

1. Johann Adam Schall von Bell, born at Cologne 1591; entered the Jesuit novitiate at Rome October 21, 1611; arrived in China 1622; called to the

official duties he was forced to be present in the suite of the emperor of that kingdom within the temple of the idol. In order not to be sullied and contaminated by the filthy sacrifices offered up there, he carried, or caused to be carried, a cross hidden in a bunch of flowers. Thus, while present in the Body at a heathen ceremony, he could offer up in the spirit homage to God in sight of this venerable sign of our redemption, and could thus keep both a heart pure and clean and his appointment as a mandarin [62].

This convenient rubric was unknown in the days of St. Cyprian.[1] In that age those Christians were held apostate and renegade who, to evade persecution, the confiscation of property, prison, torture, loss of life, had obtained from the magistrates, either themselves or through their friends, by money payment or otherwise, certain papers or written attestations to the effect that the authorities were satisfied with them, even though they had not gone up to the Capitol nor attended the sacrifices offered there to the false gods, nor, still less, had sacrificed to them themselves.

This rubric,[2] as I call it, may have travelled from China to Tanjor by the intermediary of fathers of the same Society as Father Adam. It would be of use to comfort and lull to sleep the consciences of these poor Malabar Christians. They might hope that, although to avoid persecution they did not confess Jesus Christ in the face of all men at Tanjor, it would suffice for them to do so in their hearts. In this way they could go to a pagoda, but still pray in spirit as at church; they might

---

Chinese Court; thrown into prison, released, rearrested; died October 15, 1669. There is a list of twenty-eight Chinese books by him, in addition to unprinted works in Latin. His portrait is in Kircher's 'China Illustrata' (1667). There are lives of him by Albert Weber (Schaffhausen, 1781, 8vo), and by S. J. Platzweg, 'Lebensbild deutscher Jesuiten' (1882), pp. 220-248, and an Italian essay on him in 'La Civiltà Cattolica' (1873). He is mentioned in Du Halde, 'Description dé la Chine' (1735); also see Moreri, the 'Biographie Universelle,' and De Backer, iii. 588-596; C. Sommervogel, 'Bibliographie,' viii. 706.

1. St. Cyprian was born at Carthage about A.D, 200; suffered martyrdom in A.D. 258.
2. In the sense Manucci is using it, 'rubric' means a formal liturgical rule or direction, usually printed in red in books of devotion.

say that the Lord would never fail to recognise they were his, and to declare them as His before His Father.

It is true that their reverences, seeing the bad effects of their ridiculous play, and finding their conduct blamed by everybody, adopted the course of disguising and excusing their lamentable want of foresight. They started the rumour that it was all untrue, that they had not included the gods of the country in their farce. They had represented the gods of the Romans and others, and the Hindus had unfortunately mistaken them for their own gods. Thus if there had been regrettable consequences, they should be rather imputed to the maliciousness or the wrongheadedness of the Hindus than to their reverences and their indiscreet zeal. But here we must admire the effrontery, not to say more, of the reverend fathers in daring to deny a fact of which there were as many witnesses as there were spectators of their farce. In strict law no more than two witnesses who agree as to a fact alleged against anyone are required to secure his conviction as a criminal. But their reverences declined to be considered criminals, although there are over three hundred persons who could bear identical testimony against them—men who have seen and recognised the images of the Hindu gods made of baked clay and painted by a man, a Hindu himself, called Mouchi,[1] at the house of a Malabar Christian named Vania Peria. Tambi (Vanniya Peria Tambi), son of a certain Cardoso.

From this one case judge the degree of boldness required to contradict so many persons! But what matters it to the reverend fathers whether they lie or tell the truth? they have no more regard for the one than the other; it is their interests alone which make them incline indifferently towards truth or towards falsehood. This may be noticed in the present affair. For if they were to perceive and ingenuously acknowledge their fault, and be in accord with those who stood and saw their farce, they would thereby admit themselves to be the causers of the persecution at Tanjor, and would draw down on themselves most justly the displeasure of the whole church, above all, of their Portuguese fellow-Jesuits. It was these latter who founded and tended for so many years this new Christian community and maintained the mission there. Furthermore, the Jesuit reputation for worldly wisdom would suffer, and

1. Possibly this is a caste name. If so, it represents *Muchiyan* (Tamil), a painter or cabinet-maker.

the credit they have earned would be at stake. The Bishop of San Thome would turn against them, and might withdraw them from the cure of, and mission to, the Malabars of Pondicherry. This charge he has most unjustly, and in opposition to every rule of right and every good reason, taken from the Capuchins. Thus it is not to be thought of that the Jesuits should avow their fault, for they must not become subject to the above-named disagreeables. Still, it is most unjust for them to continue to disguise the facts and deny the truth. But we must go back to our narrative of the reverend fathers' conduct.

In the month of August, 1701, the captain of the *Pions* (armed messengers) at Ariancoupan (Ariyanguppam)[1] was married to the daughter of one Manuel, captain of the *Pions* at Pondicherry, both of them, Christians and Malabaris [that is 'natives of India ']. Here is how the thing was carried out.

Seven days before the marriage the first ceremony took place—one which is also performed by the Hindus in the same man manner [64]. First of all a branch of an *arack* (pipal-tree)[2] was planted in the middle of the courtyard where the wedding was to be celebrated. Before the branch was placed into the earth, the hole was filled with a gallon of cow's milk and a gallon of water. Having been planted, it was next smeared with sandal, red-lead, and saffron, and flowers were hung all round. This ridiculous ceremony is practised by the Hindus from veneration for this tree's connection with Vishnu, one of their false gods, and the goddess Savitri,[3] his wife. For they hold that Vishnu

1. A village in French territory, four miles south-south-west of Pondicherry ('Madras Manual of Administration,' iii. 694).
2. The word used here must be the same as that in Section I. of a parallel drawn up by the Capuchins between Hindu usages and the Christian rites as permitted by the Jesuits (see Norbert, 'Mémoires Historiques,' Besançon, 1747, ii. 232): 'In the middle of the courtyard of the Christian's house they erect a tent adorned with branches of trees, paintings, and chandeliers, and in the middle they plant a bamboo called *Arecani*, or the nail for the *Arachou*. Of this latter, a tree dedicated to Vishnu, several branches are attached to the bamboo.' Vishnu's tree is the *Pipal* (*Ficus religiosa*) ('Madras Manual of Administration,' iii. 987), he having been born among its branches (*ibid*., iii. 673, s.v. 'Peepul'). For its employment at weddlings, see *op. cit*., ii. 236. The name is apparently the Tamil *arasu* (the pipal-tree).
3. See Dowson, 'Mythology,' p. 291, and Garrett, 'Classical Dictionary of India,' p. 378.

dwells in this tree, and that his spouse, changing into wind, came to it as gently as possible in order not to be separated from her beloved. This detestable error plunges them into scandalous and abominable practices, as well as into gross and animal imaginations. For instance, they say that each leaf of that tree represents that portion of woman which modesty forbids us to mention. The red-lead put on it is in the minds of these idolaters something still more unpleasant. The saffron and flowers are offered in sacrifice to the tree so much venerated by them. They hold it a great honour for it to grow in the walls of their houses, and consider it a great crime to pluck it out.

After the completion of this first ceremony, they brought seven small pots full of earth, in which a few days before had been sown some rice and country peas, which have to be taken out on the marriage day. These pots were placed round the foot of the tree. At the same time a stone was placed in position, and on this a coconut is broken on the wedding-day, and the contents spilt.

Seven days afterwards a sort of four-cornered tent was erected, called by these people *ramade*.[1] This was placed so that the tree above mentioned should be kept in the middle. At the four corners mango branches were planted, and all round it leaves were bound on with thread; the meaning of this I will state hereafter. At the foot of the tree an altar was made without either cross or crucifix, its only ornament the image of the Virgin, which the Hindus count to be that of Bengavaty (Bhagavati), mother of their false god, Ram. The altar faced the east, another Hindu custom.

Things being thus made ready, they went in the morning to the church, where the marriage ceremony was celebrated quietly. But in the evening a second ceremony took place in Hindu fashion. At that time the bridegroom left his house to the sound [65] of instruments, riding in a palanquin surrounded by dancers, all of whom are public women, and proceeded to the church door. He went in alone and said a short prayer, then

1. The thing intended must be the usual *pandal*, or temporary shed erected for all marriages. The word used might be *aramanai*, 'royal palace,' or *araimanai*, 'single-room house.' Or can it have any connexion with *Ram-kela*, a name for the plantain-tree? (see 'Madras Manual of Administration,' iii. 687). Plantain-trees are used in erecting the *pandal*.

rejoined his equipage, which waited outside. Getting into his palanquin, and followed by his cortège, he went round the town and returned to the door of his house. Here he was met by three female relations, each carrying a bowl in her two hands. Two of these bowls were filled with saffron water and a small herb resembling couch-grass (*chiendent*), which they assert to be the hair of the idol Polur (Pillaiyar);[1] who has the head of an elephant and a large belly. The third vessel was in the middle; it was full of rice of different colours, and held a ball of cooked rice steeped in butter made from cow's milk, and in this ball was inserted a burning wick fed by cow's butter [? *ghi*] instead of oil. It is true that the women relations, not expecting to be allowed to carry out the usual ceremony themselves, place these bowls into the hands of three dancing-women, who waved them each three times round the bridegroom's head. The intention is to preserve him from evils into which he might otherwise fall, and to hinder the effects of any tricks that might be played off upon him. Then at the end of the third time they emptied the bowls at the bridegroom's feet. After that he entered the tent, where he circumambulated the altar and the things deposited on it.

Next he took his station with his face turned to the altar, and the catechist who acted as a sort of master of the ceremonies, or rather Brahman, took his post beside the altar towards the south, his face to the north, just as laid down in the ritual and usage of the Hindu idolaters. Our man thus posed, they brought to him a large banyan, or fig leaf, on which was spread uncooked rice, and they added two small yellow copper pots, called in the Indian tongue *tambias* (*tambiya*), or *calsia* (*kalsa*),[2] each of them encircled several times with a thread. This last thing is never omitted by the Hindus from their sacrifices, of however insignificant a nature they may be. These *tambiyas* contained nothing beyond pure water, but on the edge of each they placed five mango leaves, and on these a coconut.

---

1. Pillaiyar, or 'the noble child,' the ordinary people's name for the god Vighneswaram, the Ganesa of Northern India, the 'Belly-God' ('Madras Manual of Administration,' iii. 979). The grass referred to is the *darbha* or *kusa* grass, considered especially holy and used in all religious ceremonies (*ibid*., p. 259, and Padfield, 'Hindu at Home,' p. 126).
2. *Tambiya* (Hindi), a copper or brass pot; *kalas* or *kalsa* (Hindi), a water-pot, pitcher, or jar.

Two small stools were next brought and set down in front of our quasi-Brahman, *alias* catechist. On one was a bowl filled with uncooked rice of many colours; on the other a similar bowl holding the *estuli*[1], which is a necklace of gold beads. Next appeared incense and a censer, and they drew out the stone which, as I have told you, lay under the altar at the foot of the tree [66]. Having placed some incense in the censer, and sung the litanies of the Virgin, the catechist took the tambiya (copper-pot) on his right hand, washed the coconut on it with water, and, half breaking it on the stone, allowed the liquid to flow upon it and then separated the nut entirely into two pieces. Next the officiant rose, took the bowl containing the *tali* and placing it (the *tali*) in the centre of the altar, he recited something in the Malabar language, and covered it with the bowl. He incensed the statue of the Virgin and the *tali*, and the latter he presented to the parents and the principal guests, who all touched it with the right hand. Last of all he carried it to the newly-married man, who, to an accompaniment of music, put it round his wife's neck.

The catechist returned then to the altar, drew from the waistbelt a vessel holding some cow-dung, which the Hindus call Tiranourou (*tiruniru*)—that is, 'holy ashes.' This had been blessed and sanctified by the reverend Jesuit fathers.[2] Three times he scattered it on the heads of the newly-married couple, who all this time had remained seated. In this posture they placed their half-opened fists on their knees. Then the catechist ordered a fresh bowl of peas to be brought, took some up in both hands, and showered them three times over the two feet, the two fists, and the heads of the couple. The relations on both sides did the same. Some necklaces of flowers were now produced and placed on the

---

1. *Estuli*: a little lower down this is called the *tali,* which is the medal-like gold charm tied round the bride's neck by the bridegroom in Southern Indian Hindu marriages. As to these emblems, see *ante,* Part III., fol. 122, and *post*. Part V., fol. 307. The string holding it, called the *mangala-sutram* (happy-thread), is tied round the bride's neck by the bridegroom, and this usage still prevails among native Christians (see Padfield, p. 127).
2. In the case of Hindus the ashes are blessed or sanctified by a *muratra* pronounced by a Brahman ('Madras Manual of Administration,' iii 580).

necks of the two, changing them three times. The parents and the principal guests went through the same ceremonies.

All this gone through, the catechist called for a third coconut and another bowl of peas; from the latter he took a small quantity in both hands, and placed both in the hands of the bride. She placed them in the same way in the bridegroom's hands, who returned them. In this fashion they gave and returned them as many as three times. Lastly, after the third time, the catechist poured some water into the hands of the bridegroom, over the rice and the coconut.

Next the bride and bridegroom rose from their seat, and a sort of procession round the altar began, in which one of the women relations took the lead with a lantern in her hand, and another followed with a water-vessel, sprinkling water little by little round the altar. A barber came next to show them the road, as is requisite in this ceremonial, then after him the newly-married couple, the bridegroom holding the bride's little finger in his closed hand. The line was closed by four or five of the relations [67].

In this order they passed round the altar three times, and the last time the newly-married couple made a profound obeisance with joined hands, having turned their backs to the altar and their faces towards the door. The catechist then took the water-vessel and poured the rest of its contents on them, and at the same time they ran to the door of the house and entered. After that one could not find out what went on inside.[1]

By everything relating to this marriage that I have just recounted, you can see to what point complaisance for these Christians is carried by the reverend Jesuit fathers, for I can

1. A parallel account of these wedding ceremonies will be found in Norbert, 'Mémoires Historiques,' ii. 233-241, in a comparative statement between Hindu and Christian usages drawn up by the Capuchins in 1711. We have: (1) Planting of the sacred tree; (2) erection of the *pandal*; (3) the altar with crucifix or Holy Virgin; (4) the copper vessels; (5) holy water in same; (6) offering of cooked rice; (7) removal of this rice by barber and washerman; (8) use of the medallion or *tali*; (9) gift of uncooked rice to the catechist; (10) recital of Litany of the Holy Virgin; (11) aspersion of bridal couple with holy water; (12) breaking of coconuts; (13) throwing of rice; (14) placing of five pots holding sprouting rice dedicated to Bhuma Devi and the other gods; (15) use of two other larger pots holding water dedicated to two river goddesses, Ganga and another.

assure you it is everywhere the same. The judicious Christian reader can pass judgment better than I can on this indulgent attitude, and decide what harm it must have done to our holy religion. I have not proposed to myself anything beyond a statement of the bare facts, and on these each man can make his own reflections. Let those who can and ought to apply a remedy do so according as they may judge best, but I pass on to other things which will not be found any less strange.

Since first the Christian religion was established in the world, it has till now been a thing unheard of to have nocturnal processions. But the reverend fathers have begun this novelty, making no scruple, from their first occupation of the cure of Pondicherry, to imitate the Hindus in this matter; I give here a description of one held in the night between the 14th and the 15th of the month of August [1701] on the Feast of the Assumption of the Holy Virgin.[1]

It began a little after nine o'clock in the evening without any preceding form of devotion. It had more the style of a play, as have all the processions and marriages of the Hindus and Mahomedans, and was not at all like a devout Christian function. A new spectacle was afforded us: Christian piety changed into cries, into torch illuminations, into rockets and other firewords made with powder of sulphur and 'chanffre.'[2] It is true that the cross was in the first place, but so smothered in flowers that it was impossible to see it. To this I must add that in the previous year it did not appear at all, probably not to shock these recent Christians of new manufacture. The statue of the Virgin was in the procession, but surrounded by parasols, while several persons fanned it, and drove off the flies with handkerchiefs. A number of Christians and Hindus followed, just as you see them follow in a marriage, and in no order. The former (the Christians) joined because they had no real devoutness; the latter (the Hindus), because they held the image to be that of Bagavaty (Bhagavati) and of Ram. As to

1. Norbert assigns it to the year 1700 (see his description of it in 'Mémoires Historiques,' 1747, i. 62).
2. I take this word to be meant for *canfre* (camphor). Compare Thevenot, 'Voyage,' v, 69; 'On y meloit beaucoup de lances à feu où on avail fait entrer quantité de canfre, ce qui faisait une flame blanche qui eblouissoit.'

the history of these gods, the reader will be pleased to learn something, however ridiculous it may be.

Bhagavati[1] was the daughter of a queen who, after she had lost her husband and her children [68], had communication with a young girl, and, conceiving, bore Bhagavati. She bears various names, such as Bangavaty (? Bhanumati), Dessarota (? Durga),[2] and others. But the most remarkable is Parmansuer (Paramesvari), which is special to her; just as that of Permansuer (Paramesvara) is to the Supreme Being. Thus just as 'Paramesvara' means 'god,' so does 'Paramesvar[i]' mean 'goddess.'

The history of this goddess is such a tangle, and so strongly opposed to common-sense, that it is a difficult matter to put it clearly and into such order as would be desirable. For they relate that she married, that she became with child by a shower of gold, and that she brought forth Ram. Some say Vishnu came down from heaven in the shape of this shower, then changed himself into an infant, and entered her womb. In short, somehow or other this child when born was named Ram, and these idolaters have such respect for him that his name is oftener on their lips than that of Jesus upon those of the devoutest of Christians. Their usual salutation on meeting is 'Ram, Ram.'

They depict this pretended goddess with a child in her arms; they celebrate a festival, and hold a procession in her honour. It takes place wherever her idols are worshipped in the month of Baderca [Bhadraka],[3] which corresponds to the moon of September, the date on which the Assumption Festival is celebrated, as everyone knows. This is the reason that these Hindus, seeing this image carried at night in procession with the same ceremonial as they observed themselves, concluded readily enough that it was that of their Bhagavati, and turned out to take part and do her honour.

The reverend fathers, to whom I return, are not satisfied with imitating these idolaters in their processions; they have gone farther, for they have forced the Christians to make use

1. Bhagavati, a name of the goddess Durga or Devi.
2. If this is to be taken as Dasarath, then that is the name of a male, and not of a female; he was the King of Ajudhya, and father of Ram.
3. Bhadra, Bhadon, the fifth month of the Hindus, corresponding to a period from about the middle of August to the middle of September.

of certain ashes made of cow-dung.[1] This product is much revered by Hindus, and for this reason they call it 'holy ashes.' They attribute to it various virtues which I will not detail, since I have spoken of them before (III. 114; IV. 66). Suffice it to say that their reverences not only approve of, but insist upon, their disciples making use of these ashes just as the idolaters do. All the same, it is necessary for me to add that these holy men observe great precautions against any accusation of indifference or weakness they might be reproached with in regard to Hindu superstitions. The fathers see that when the Christians go to the market to buy the ashes (where they are ordinarily on sale) their blessing is said over them before the converts use them. To this may be added that when anyone is to use the ashes, the fathers take the express precaution of forbidding the invocation of any false god, as is done) by Hindus [69]. Still, that does not hinder the Hindus from seeing these Christians displaying these ashes just in the way they do themselves, and thus they really believe them to be of their religion and to hold the same opinions as themselves.

The ashes of which I speak are something extraordinary, and in spite of what I have just been saying, I will not set out all their virtues according to the belief of the Hindus. Yet I find some points so singular that I believe they will interest my readers.

First of all, you must know that the Hindus in this country are divided into several sects, and that each sect has its sign or mark to distinguish it from the others. In short, this mark is applied on the forehead, on the arms, and on the abdomen, *et cetera*. They are just like, in that respect, to anti-Christ, of whom there is mention in the Apocalypse as bearing the mark of the Beast. In the same way these idolaters bear according to their different sects the mark of their beast, which is the cow,

1. The permission given to converts to continue the use of sect marks is one of the heads of accusation against the Jesuits in the so-called Malabar rites dispute, or dispute over concessions to Hindu converts. The papal legate, Cardinal de Tournon, condemned it, among other practices, in his edict of June 23, 1704. The struggle was long-continued, until the said edict was finally upheld by Pope Benedict XIV. in his constitution, dated September 12, 1744, 'Omnium sollicitudinum' (Norbert, Mémoires Historiques,' third edition, Besançon, 1747, and London, 1751, 4to., i. 131; iii. 553-621).

an animal which they venerate so deeply that they believe the dung, the urine, the milk, the buttermilk, and the butter produced by it, when mixed together and drunk, to be sufficient to wipe away all sin. Thus it is on the pretended virtues and merits of this beast that they place all their reliance and confidence. This is the reason that they call the ashes which they obtain from its burnt dung 'holy ashes.' They use them in different ways, but here are the different devices and their names. These are impressed or marked upon them with the said ashes:[1]

Lalati	Ordepound	Tripound	Bandouki
[Lalat]	[Urdhpund]	[Tripund]	[Binduka]
I	**V**	≣	**0**

Lalati (*Lalat*), i, is the distinctive sign of those who worship Roudra (Rudra) and his son Seti (Sati).[2] This Rudra is, these madmen say, the God of life and death; thus he subjects everyone to either whenever he wishes, and creates or kills whom he will. He is the third person of their false Trinity, according to some. But others say that it is Siva. This mark is imprinted or placed on the forehead, arms, breast, elbow, abdomen, thighs, and knees, invoking each time the name of Rudra and Sety (Sati).

Ordepound (*Urdhpund*), **V**, is the distinctive mark of the worshippers of Vishenou, or Visnu (Vishnu). They profess to represent thereby a very disgraceful thing, to name which modesty forbids. It is impressed on their foreheads while they invoke Vishnu. Sometimes they insert a red dot in the middle.

The Tripound (*Tripund*), ≣ ,is the distinctive sign of those who worship equally all the false gods. They rub the ashes on their hands [70], and then apply them to their heads. One

1. *Lalat* or *Lilat* (forehead), a coloured sectarial mark on the forehead (Platts, 'Dictionary,' 963). *Urdhapund,* a perpendicular line made with sandal on the forehead by Vaishnavas (*ibid.,* 104). *Tripund,* or *Tripundra,* three curved horizontal marks on the forehead made with the ashes of burnt cow-dung, sandal, etc., by the followers of Siva and Sakti. Their application is indispensable before beginning to worship (*ibid.,* 316). As the name denotes, there should only be three lines instead of the four given by Manucci. *Bindu* or *Binduka,* a drop, point, dot, spot, or mark (*ibid.,* 169). There is an elaborate account of these sect marks in 'Madras Manual of Administration,' i. 85, note.
2. Sati is a name of Uma, the *wife,* and not the *son,* of Rudra J. Garrett, 'Classical Dictionary of India,' 565).

hand has the three middle fingers bent with the thumb and the little finger extended; the other hand is held open. They repeat the words *Naroutchi hersu*,[1] which means [blank in text]. They join their hands, and make the *tripund* with either three or four fingers, as they please, saying *Nettrichada Chivon* (Netti + Chutti + Sivam)[2] — that is, 'To the head come Chiva or Siva.' This is one of the gods of their pretended Trinity. According to some accounts they next apply the ashes to their breast, saying *Marphou majesserent*[3] —that is to say, 'Let Rudra be on my breast.' This, too, is, as some state, another person of their false trinity, the one who presided over death. Afterwards the ashes are rubbed on the arms while they say, *Tolbairevem* (Tol Bhairavam)—that is, 'I invoke the god Bayrevu (Bhairava).[4] He is depicted with a very black face, and he is also feared beyond measure, because they hold that when he enters anyone's body he cannot be ejected again. For this reason he is accepted as the god of Force.

When they put the ashes on their elbows they say, *Tandon manicanken ranacancan*[5]—that is, 'On my wrists and elbows be Rancancan.' But it would take too long to tell tire story of this false god. It is enough to state that they consider he was engendered by their supreme god who dwelt with Vishnu disguised as a woman. From this union issued the beautiful divinity invoked in marking the wrists and elbows, their object being to obtain promptly what they desire.

They also put some of the ashes on the stomach and say, 'Mailastaren benarem' (*Mulasthanam Subrahmanya*)[6]—that is, 'May Subrahmanya be on my stomach.' This so-called divinity

1. Dr. Barnett proposes to read *herou* for *hersu*; then we can make out the words to be *ner* (*ukku*) + *sir* + *kuru* ('proper' + 'order' + 'do thou'). But the interpretation is very doubtful.
2. Dr. Barnett identifies this as *Netti-chutti-Sivan*, meaning literally 'forehead + ornament + Siva.'
3. Dr. Barnett suggests *marpu* (breast) + *mayesuran* (Maya and Iswara), or *marp' umaiyisuran*, '*breast*' + 'Uma and Iswara.'
4. Dr. Barnett says this may be *tolu* (or toru), 'worship' (in the imperative)—that is, 'Worship Bhairava'; or, perhaps, better, *tol* (shoulder) + Bhairava.
5. *Tandon* may be for *Tandavan* (Siva), or we may correct it to *Candon*. Then we could interpret thus: *Skanda* (the god)+*mani-kanagal* (Wrist-joints) + *kona-kanagal* (elbow-joints).
6. *Mulasthanam*, 'lower part of abdomen'; *benarem*, 'Subrahmanya.

is surnamed Aremocouet (*aru-mukham*),[1] and has one face in front and two on each side, making altogether five, and a sixth one on his stomach, as they assert, with which he governs the five other [faces], and he is made all of fire. They place some of these ashes on their loins while invoking Vishnu in his capacity of god of procreation. Farther on will be found the infamous things, the crimes, and the tergiversations that they attribute to this so-called god. While applying some of the ashes to the knees, they utter the same invocation, wet their hands a little, and take a taste of some of this unction on their tongue.[2]

The Bandouki (*Binduka*) is the sign and mark of the Zaina (Jain) sect, people who reject the ablutions and bathings in rivers affected by the Brahmans. As the bases of salvation they adopt charity and penance, but these they expound very imperfectly, for those virtues are applied to none but insects. They accept, however, all the books and fables of the other Hindus. Out of all the idols they worship only Dadinata (*Adinatha*)[3] and a certain Pitamber (*Pitambara*),[4] whom they hold to be a divinity apart. He was the founder of this sect nearly thirteen hundred years ago. These people also mark themselves very often [71] with the tripound (*tripund*) above the other sign, as a testimony that although they are of this caste (Jains), they still believe in all the other false gods, having even a special reliance upon Amahedou (*Mahadeva*).[5]

After enumerating all these characters, with all these ill-understood enigmas and peculiarities, may I not designate them the signs of the beast? For the Scripture tells us there are three kinds of beast. That is to say, one is really a beast, just as is the cow. Secondly, the devil is represented as a beast, and,

1. Subrahmanya, younger son of Siva ('Madras Manual of Administration, iii. 846, top line). *Aru-mukhavan*, 'the six-faced,' is one of his names (Ziegenbalg, English edition, p. 64).
2. The above invocations, with one or two others, are also given with verbal differences in Norbert, 'Mémoires Historiques,' 1747, ii. 242, 243. This other version has been referred to in attempting the above interpretations.
3. As Dr. L. D. Barnett points out, Dadinata must be meant for Adinatha, the legendary saint who was the first of the Jain apostles.
4. Dr. Barnett says Pitambar (clothed in yellow) is evidently Mahavira or Vardhamana, the last of the saints (*Arhat*), who was contemporary with Buddha.
5. Dr. Barnett says this may be meant for either Mahadeva or Mahendra; the former seems most likely.

finally, the same name is given to Antichrist. These characteristics, as it seems to me, agree admirably well with those marks I speak of. They who use them worship idols, and are the enemies of Jesus Christ; again, they are the sign of the demon, for by it he recognises those who are his. And, lastly, they are the sign of the beast, since they are, purely and simply, the excrement of a cow.

Superius quae; vernacula lingua explicare non libuit, ne rudes scandalizarentur, docti viri mihi auctores fuerunt ut latina apud doctos explicarem, quippe qui videant et judicent quantaes hæc signa sint abominationis. Dicam igitur quod illi qui talem sectam sequuntur, hoc signum deferunt in memoriam dei Yisenou qui nullibi poterat relinquere suam uxorem neque domi, neque stantem, neque sedentem in terra, sed multum diffidebat de illa, sive ob suam ipsius zelotypiam, sive ob mulieris inconstantiam, quare coactus erat illam in capite sedentem gestare, ita ut verenda caput tangerent quod **V** caractere representatur. Quando vero menstruum tempus aderat, ex isto infami loco spurcitiae sanguineae in caput et frontem Vishenou defluebant, quod per medianum punctum significatur, bestialis certe devotio et caracter. Quibus addam quod Dea ilia versa est in ventum, et sedit in arbore pipli, cuius folia ut dicunt re presentant membrum genitale muliebre, et est quasi populus nostra, et quam dicatam habent Deo Vishenou, quem dicunt in ea esse, et haec causa propter quam tam gentiles quam Christiani Jesuitici illam pro ceremoniis matrimonii praecipuis admittant, id est quia figuram matrimonii representat, in ea enim adstant Vishenou et eius uxor Savatri, Savatri quidem fertilis, et Vishenou generis humani conservator et auctor. Quae supradicta omnia apud Christianos penitus exstinxerant qui illos antea regebant Capucini in Pondicherry: nunc autem ut novos sibi discipulos et proselitas concilient, alia incedunt via et gentilizare a Deo cogunt, ut eos qui ad Ecclesiam sine predicto caractere veniunt, illis in ipsa ecclesia supra frontem adhi- [72] beant; unde schisma oritur inter antiquos et novos eorum Christianos, quorum primi folia abhorrent, alii approbant: primi [signum] abhorrent, et tamen per vim eo insigniri coguntur; alii approbant et coeteros missionarios tamquam minius peritos despiciunt. Gentiles vero ex hoc superbientes criminantur quod precedentes patres qui hanc rexerunt ecclesiam, non erant docti sed omnino rudes, et propterea superstitionis suse ritus gentilicios despiciebant, nunc autem quando venerunt docti illorum patres Jesuitae, iam ut sanctos et venerabiles recipiunt, et exercent ita ut iam sperent fore ut non multum post tempus religionem suam tamquam veram et ad salutem necessariam profiteantur.

As I have already spoken of Vishnu, it will not be out of place to describe him more minutely. They say he came from the belly of their [blank in text], and make of him the second person of their false trinity and the preserver of the human race. They add that to work unceasingly at this preservation he married Savati (Savitri) or Parvati (Parvati); that he metamorphosed himself several times into a woman, once into a whale, once into a tortoise; that at another time he assumed the shape of boar; that he made himself into a half lion half man. then became a dwarf, then a man taking the name Ram. They relate that in heaven he poisoned himself, that he returned to human shape to rest from his labours and to amuse himself. They also call him Crochenou (Krishna), a barbarous word to which these poor people themselves can hardly give a meaning, since they interpret it in many ways. He is addicted to every sort of vice; he is a parricide, an adulterer, raises quarrels and dissension everywhere, and is a great thief. Finally, this so-called god fled into a river to hide, and there changed himself into a fish and was caught by a fisherman. What strange blindness of the human mind! Of what is it not capable when it is blinded, or, rather, has been left to itself unenlightened by the Light from on high! But I must go on with my story.

Now I come to the burials of these idolatrous Christians, which are not less full of superstitious observances than are all their other ceremonials. As soon as anyone has passed away, some *betel* is put into his mouth, and his teeth are smeared with some juice of that leaf. The body is washed from head to foot with a solution of cow-dung, and the tripound (*tripund*) sect mark is made. Following the custom of the Sajuas (Saivas),[1] they make for the dead man a throne, called in the Malabar

1. The context requires some caste which buries its dead. The word might be read *Saivas* (Saivas), or, perhaps, taking it loosely, as *Sanyasis*. Now both the Saiva sect of Lingadharis and the Sanyasis of every sect bury their dead (Padfield, 'Hindu at Home,' p. 245). The body is decked out, the face exposed, and the sect marks made. It is then placed in a sitting posture in a sort of sedan-chair. There is always music with the procession (*ibid*., pp. 246, 247).

tongue a *pare* (*padai*).[1] It is constructed out of the canes of a wood they call *paxarambou* (*par-karumbu*),[2] which is nothing more nor less than the sugar-cane. The body is wrapped in the best cloth of cotton or of silk that they can procure; and the throne is decorated on the outside with many mirrors, to which are added cut cucumbers attached by little pieces of *betel*, some stalks of rice in the ear,[3] and at the four corners some banana plants. The corpse is [73] placed in this sort of shrine seated as in a chair, and in this equipment is carried in triumph on men's shoulders to the sound of trumpets, just as one might do to some holy man's relics.

With regard to these ridiculous interments. I knew a Malabar *macou* (*mukkava*),[4] boatman, who, in terror of being buried in this way, sent, when at the point of death, to have the measure taken of the Capuchin tombs, in order to be buried like a Christian. To this the Jesuits were opposed, and the poor man died eight or ten days afterwards, still claiming to be buried as a Christian. In the end the Jesuits granted the request, but consent was forced from them.

Some time afterwards a man named André, broker to the French Company, died.[5] His relations and Monsieur le Gouverneur (F. Martin) pressed for his burial in the fortress. To this the Jesuits would never consent, because they wanted liberty to bury him like a Hindu. I know not if they carried out all the ceremonial above described, but they had a night procession. In this the body was carried; there were drums and trumpets, followed by a number of matchlock-men, who from time to time fired off their pieces. After them came a throne like that described above, fashioned like a pagoda, and adorned with

1. *Padai* (Tamil), 'a bier.'
2. *Par-karumbu* (Tamil), 'wild sugar-cane' ('Madras Manual of Administration,' iii. 569).
3. The text has *apes*, which I take to be for *épis*, 'ears of corn'; or it might be for *hampes*,one meaning of which is 'stalk,' 'stem.'
4. *Mukkava*, a pearl-diver ('Madras Manual of Administration,' iii. 510).
5. This man André, a native Christian from Madras, is referred to in the Capuchin memorial drawn up by Father Thomas in 1733 (see Norbert, 'Mémoires Historiques,' ii. 273). He had given the land and the money to build the Capuchin church. The same funeral, or a similar one, is described by an eye-witness in Norbert, the same work, ii. 244. Father Dolu was the officiating priest.

XXXIV, The 'Adil Shahi Kings of Bijapur: (1) Yusuf; (2) Ashraf; (3) Ibrahim; (4) Muhammad; (5) 'Ali; (6) Muhammad; (7) 'Ali; (8) Sikandar

mirrors, *et cetera*. Next came the cross, along with the Jesuit fathers and Monsieur Appiany. The body was in a palanquin, preceded by several persons driving away the night flies (? mosquitoes) with handkerchiefs and cloths; others walked beside the palanquin and fanned the deceased. This funeral pomp struck one as rather more of a nuptial display than anything else.

On the thirtieth day after this interment there was another procession conducted with the same solemnity as the first. A hand-barrow (*cherolle*) or throne came first, decked with mirrors, *et cetera*. Placed above the portable throne was a cross, and inside it a large copper platter filled with rice flour. In the centre of the rice stood the half of a broken coconut, having its pulp still in it, but filled with cow's butter, in the midst of which stood a large burning wick. The Hindus call this the 'Fire of Heaven,' and therefore pay it great veneration, placing men round and in front of it, who fan it. The Jesuit fathers and the cross followed the moving throne. The drums and trumpets went before it, while the fireworks and the cattle (*bestes*) made a fine show.

The procession with the cross and the fathers stopped some time in front of the Hindu pagoda, a sort of polite attention that these idolaters never fail to show themselves at these places where they worship their false divinities. This observance their reverences were anxious not to omit [74].

They carried out the same etiquette at the house of the defunct, and then finally went to the place of burial. I am unable to express how much these ceremonies scandalized the French of the fortress; more especially the form of the *cherolle* or portable throne offended them very much, as also a sort of chapel in shape like a pagoda, which had been erected at the grave. In addition, there was an altar inside this chapel on its northern side, but made quite differently from our altars, and quite low, without crucifix or candlesticks, merely with a statue of the virgin. Around the grave there were four candlesticks, and in the middle a huge ball of rice-flour moistened with cow's butter. At the four corners were four other rice-balls of the same size, each having a lighted wick in its centre. From time to time these were fed with butter. There were also, all round, upon small stands, some one hundred and thirty-two other smaller balls with their wicks, and these, too, were from time to time sprinkled with butter. Lastly, when they had entered the tomb, the son of the deceased, and, still a child, with the aid of some of those present took the platter of which I have spoken, and carried it on his head to the centre of the tomb, and there the *Libera*[1] was sung, holy water was distributed, and the rice-balls were divided among those present.

From the whole of what is given above, one may decide what sort of Christianity it is that their reverences are founding in India. I will add the description of a Hindu procession, so that by comparing it with what the Jesuits allow to, or rather enforce on, their Christians, a saner judgment on the whole case may be arrived at.

On January 11 of this year 1702, there fell the Feast of Pongol,[2] or, in other words, Festival of the Cow, called by the Malabars perempomquen (par-pongalam)[3]—that is, 'she who gives everything.' In other parts of India it is celebrated about the summer, and at Pondicherry about the winter solstice. It is the festival, taken generally, of all cows. The hour of noon is chosen as the most auspicious for beginning the ceremonies. Those among the Hindus who own many of these cattle are special observers of the feast; those who possess only few unite and collect the cows of several households.

When the hour has come the cows are decorated, their horns are painted red, vermilion is applied to their heads just as is done to men. They are then sacrificed to, as if they were idols. The gifts consist of figs (bananas), coconuts, *jagri* (coarse sugar), ginger, and rice cooked in milk. Round their necks are thrown necklaces of flowers; they are bathed with saffron water, and a certain herb called *argounpoulou* (arghyam-polon).[4] Lastly,

1. 'The Libera,' the passage, near the middle of the service, beginning: Libera me, Domine, de morte aeterna, in die ilia tremenda: Quando coeli movendi sunt et terra' (see 'Rituale Romanum Pauli V. Pontificis Maximi jussu editum . . .,' Mechlin, 1872, p. 194). Mr. W. R. Philipps, to whom I am indebted for the reference, conjectures that this was the form in use among the Jesuits in India.
2. Pongal, from *pongu* (Tamil), 'to boil,' because new rice is boiled in milk with sugar and then distributed. The feast is celebrated when the sun enters Capricorn, about January 11, and it lasts three days ('Madras Manual of Administration,' iii. 695).
3. *Par-pongalam* (Tamil), 'the rite of boiling rice in milk.' As the use of milk is obligatory, the word is connected, though only indirectly, with the cow.
4. *Arghyam* (oblation), *polon* or puvulu (flower); an offering of *darbha* (*kusa*), grass.

they are incensed with the smoke of black raisins, an incense which [75] these misguided people employ in regard to their idols.[1] When this ceremonial is over, all the things included in the offerings are hung round the cow's necks, and thus decked out, they are paraded through the town in procession to the sound of drums and trumpets. The owners allow the devout to take each a little of the offerings and eat it; this is considered correct; or you may even keep some as a relic during the coming year, until another festival supervenes. Whatever of these offerings is left they convey by groups and throw into the ponds. After this is done the superstitious throw over each other the would-be sanctified and holy water. They consider it to have been sanctified by those plants, *et cetera*, which had touched the cow. Particular care is taken that these plants shall not touch the ground for fear of their being thereby contaminated. Finally, as the last stage, several women follow the procession and carefully gather up the cow-dung to be made into the ashes of which I have spoken; it is from this cow-dung that it must be made. Thus finishes the ceremony.

The truth is that the Malabar Christians do not follow out all these details. Only, on the previous day, they deliver their cows to an ordinary cowherd, making him some small payment, in return for which he charges himself with the performance of the rites in the mode he thinks best. Others content themselves with reddening the cows' horns and heads and wetting them with saffron water. Then they are loosed, and take part in the procession.

It is in honour of the solemn functions of this great festival that the Brahmans may be seen erecting an altar. Upon it they exhibit several idols; beneath it they place grain, vegetables, different sorts of merchandise, and some jewels. Before it they pass the whole night in prayer and chanting; then they inspect the things previously placed below the altar, and should any be missing or spoiled, it is an indication that in that year such article will be scarce and dear. It is also upon this day that they prognosticate whether there will be a murrain among cattle

1. Perhaps the brown seeds of wild rue are intended. They are burnt as incense to drive away evil spirits (see 'Madras Manual of Administration,' iii. 340). What Manucci means by 'black raisin' is not obvious.

or a pestilence among men. On all these points Christians as well as Hindus visit and consult them in the morning.

Finally, at the approach of evening, a solemn procession is formed, in which is prominent the idol Parmansouery (Parameswari)[1] with two of her children, Armogon (Arumukham)[1] and Comra (Kumara),[1] at her side. These two are also among their false gods. She is seated on a sort of hand-barrow or stretcher of enormous size. Isparou (Iswara)[1] followed seated in a hair placed on a kind of throne. You could also see the idol Benaerem (Vinayakam)[1] sitting on a big rat the size of a sucking-pig; and Bayraou (Bhairava),[1] so feared by the Hindus that they pay him greater honour than to the others. They came forth carried on platforms unescorted, while he was largely accompanied. When he was first placed on his wooden horse, all the idolaters then present [76] advanced one after another and prostrated themselves with their faces on the ground and kissed his feet.

But what was most remarkable in the last procession at Pondicherry was the travelling throne of their great idol. For that in which the Jesuit fathers paraded the statue of the Virgin Mary is exactly the same. This fact caused much scandal to many pious souls; more so from knowing that the Jesuits took the design and the dimensions from that used tor the idol. The procession was closed by several matchlockmen and some umbrella-holders. These latter protected all these divinities, particularly those whose names are given above. My beloved reader! How alike are the ceremonies observed in this procession and those observed at the festival of the Blessed Virgin! This is so much the case that Hindus and Malabar Christians attend, without distinction and without scruple, both the one and the other,[2] particularly as they [the

1. Parameswari, 'supreme goddess,' the consort of Siva; Arumukham, 'the six-faced,' a name for Subrahmanya, the younger son of Siva; Kumara, another name of the same god; Iswara, a name for Siva; Subrahmanya, son of Siva, and already mentioned as the 'six-faced,' but it is Ganesa or Pillaiyar whose vehicle is a large rat (Ziegenbalg, p. 161); Bhairava, 'the terrible,' is one of the manifestations of Siva.
2. The fact of the Hindu attendance is admitted by Pére Dolu himself; the difference lies in his inferences as to the reason. Quoting a letter from Père Laynes at Madura, he says: 'Dans la dernière solem nitè du jour de l'Assomption vous eussiez été charmé de voir les Gentils même à unir a nous pour contribuer aussi à honorer la reine du ciel' ('Lettres Edifiantes,' edition 1841, Panthéon Littéraire, ii. 284).

Hindus] look on the Blessed Virgin as their Bangavaty (Bhagavati) and the Infant Jesus as their false god, Ram.

These are the ceremonies that I have witnessed in the space of fifty years passed by me in this great empire. In it I have seen all these customs, which are not only evil, but hateful and abominable. For all those [sect] marks are meant only to distinguish one set of men from another, things that they connect with diabolical and sacrilegious invocations. Yet these are also employed by all the Christians of this region (? Pondicherry), who mark themselves with the said ashes and are under the guidance of the Jesuit fathers. As for the other Christians, those who live in the countries in submission to the King of Portugal, they have been absolutely forbidden by the Holy Inquisition to affix such marks. Nor have the Capuchin fathers, who for twenty-four years[1] directed the congregation of Malabar Christians at Pondicherry, ever allowed the use of these abominable ashes or any equivalent marks; with which deprivation these Christians were quite content, because they saw themselves made equal to, and put on the same footing as, the ancient Christians. But for the last three years, since the Jesuit fathers wrested from the Capuchins, by force and contrary to all right, the control of the said Malabar Christians, they have been obliged to make use of the said signs and marks. By this an opening has been given to the Brahmans and Hindus of Pondicherry and other places to say that their accursed religion is superior to ours. The earliest missionaries forbade Hindu ashes, processions, and other ceremonials, but at present the Jesuit fathers approve them all, and the Hindus say they hope that in the end the same will be the case with all their abominations. All this they say simply because these fathers imitate and conform to their (Hindu) ceremonies.

[77] But let us now come back to the persecutions at Tanjor, of which I have already spoken at some length. It is my duty, dear reader, to tell you what has since taken place. At the beginning of December (? 1701) the Reverend Father Martin,[2]

1. That is, from 1675 to 1699, when the charge was taken from them and given to the Jesuits.
2. Pierre Martin, born at Limoges February 5, 1665; left for India in 1694; died at Rome June 28, 1716. There are seven letters by him in 'Lettres Edifiantes et Curieuses' (C. Sommervogel, Bibliographie,' v. 624).

Jesuit, appeared at my house. After a good deal of ceremony and compliments, he produced a letter from Monsieur Martin, governor of Pondicherry, in which he begged me as a Christian to be so good as to interest myself in the protection of these oppressed believers, and procure for them some respite, they and their imprisoned pastors. He represented to me that their misfortunes arose from nothing but certain acts and importunities of this, that, and the other person in the king's entourage, whereby from being their friend he had been turned into their enemy.

The reverend father (Martin) had brought with him a large present made up of European curiosities, a mirror of crystal, and a poignard mounted with jewels in the style of this country. He expected by means of these presents to procure some letters of recommendation from the Governor-General Daoutan (Da,ud Khan), who has taken the place of Jufacarcan (Zu,lfiqar Khan).[1] He has been sent into this kingdom of the Karnatik by orders of Aurangzeb, whose domination extends over all the petty Hindu kings and governors of these countries, all of them being tributary to him, as I have (I think) already explained.

I took into consideration in a Christian spirit the misfortunes to which this new Christian community was exposed. I was also of opinion that all these presents would be useless and in vain; for this reason I did not think it advisable to present them, because these Mahomedans are very touchy, and I feared that the general might conceive some idea quite opposed to the facts. Neither did I desire the father to go to him, though this was his intention; and he meant to take me with him, he meeting the necessary expenses of the journey. I made up my mind to avoid all this labour and expenditure by writing a letter on the subject to this nobleman. In it I besought him as a friend, and by reason of the obligation that he had always professed to

1. After the Qutb Shahi kingdom of Gulkandah (Haidarabad) fell in 1687, Aurangzeb succeeded to all the claims made by that kingdom to the overlordship of the Karnatik. The *qaulnamah*, or agreement given by Shah Ji to Zu,lfiqar Khan, dated May 9, 1694, shows that Tanjor became a vassal State paying tribute to the Mogul (see Bernouilli, 'Recherches,' 1787, ii. 151, 161, essay by Anquetil Duperron). Da,ud Khan was Zu,lfiqar Khan's *naib*, or deputy.

be under to me, to look with a favourable eye upon the Christians of Tanjor. They had been cruelly persecuted by their king, who had unjustly imprisoned two Jesuit fathers, my near relations. Would he have the goodness to interpose with his authority to protect the said Christians and get those fathers out of prison, where they were so unjustly and so narrowly detained, and also procure the restitution to the former (the Christians) of the goods so unjustly forfeited? I wrote other letters on the same subject to the first minister of the Karnatik province [? the Diwan], who is always in attendance on the above general; also to other officers of the army with whom I was acquainted and who were great friends of mine. I sent all this correspondence to the camp by one of my servants.

After these dispatches had started, Père Martin proposed to leave for his college at Pondicherry, which is part of the same mission, and by his hands I sent [78] a letter in reply to that of Governor Martin, detailing what I had done for the relief of the Christians at his solicitation and as a response to the friendship with which he honoured me.

As soon as my man arrived at the army, he presented my letters to the general commanding, Da,ud Khan, along with some presents that I sent him on my own behalf. He also delivered the other letters to the first minister and the other officers to whom I had the honour of writing. These men, having read them and learnt that the captive fathers were my near relations, were extremely incensed against the King of Tanjor. The commanding general, in particular, and the first minister displayed much resentment on the subject; on the spot they sent for the envoy of that prince, who is always present in the army of the general to secure the interests of the king, his master. They blamed the king loudly for his hardihood in imprisoning the poor European Brahmans from Rome (that is the name they give the priests). To this they added some harsh and severe language, and told him they were amazed still more at the acts of the king, his master, when he knew that these fathers were near relations of the doctor Nicolas Manuchy, physician to the Mogul Emperor, his suzerain. To this Da,ud Khan added the words: 'He is also my physician and my father.' These last words were said by the general because from his early youth, when I still lived in the Mogul country, he had called me 'father.' Falling into a great rage, he ordered the agent to put such pressure on his master that the captive fathers, the Roman Brahmans, should be set at liberty and the Christians allowed to live according to their religion. He added: 'If you do not obey my commands I will have you put to death, and wage continual war against your master. Do not fail thus to write to him. I also require him to restore all the property that has been confiscated from the Christians.'

The envoy upon receiving these orders wrote in the above sense to his prince, and described the manner in which he had been treated by Da,ud Khan. The cause of this harshness was the persecution he had commenced against the Christians, and the confiscation of their goods. He prayed, therefore, first of all for the release of the Jesuit fathers, known as the Roman Brahmans, the cessation of all persecution of his Christian subjects, and the rebuilding of the ruined churches. As a consequence of these acts, he stood in danger of his life, and his majesty ran the risk of a war if these demands were not conceded.

[79] While this correspondence was in progress, Da,ud Khan, the first minister, and all the other officers, gave indications of taking the matter very much to heart, and swore with most terrible strength at the malignity of those deeds at Tanjor. The crime was so much the greater for being perpetrated upon poor people living peaceably, who had never given their king any cause of complaint.

Thus, no sooner had he received the letter of his envoy than the king sent forth edicts, whereby he permitted his fugitive Christian subjects to return unmolested to their houses, and there enjoy their possessions as heretofore. He ordered the release of those who were in prison, and all Christians were free to follow their religion. The two European fathers, the Roman Brahmans, were taken out of prison. But as the remedy came somewhat late, through the fault of the Jesuit fathers of Pondicherry, it appeared that one of them, attacked by fever and dysentery, had succumbed. He was a Portuguese, and his name was Simon Carvalho; but the other, a French father, was released, as well as all the other Christians.[1]

---

1. See note, *ante*, TV., fol. 60. Father Martin calls the Father Who died *Joseph* Carvalho. The other prisoner was probably Father Bertholdi. But

I also received, in connection with this affair, a letter from Da,ud Khan, addressed to the King of Tanjor. It was full both of menaces and compliments; its purpose was the securing to these poor persecuted men the liberty they had lost. I caused it to be conveyed to its destination, and by way of reply he (the king) announced that on the receipt of his envoy's letter he had complied with everything—the Christians were at rest, the Roman Brahmans at liberty—though it was known that they were not Brahmans, as they asserted, but of the same profession as those who dwelt at Pondicherry.

In spite of this, the prince was terribly enraged against the Christians, even going so far as to write to all the kings, his neighbours, asking them to destroy everyone of that faith found within their states. But the letters and the menaces of Da,ud Khan put an end to all these disorders, and not a single prince was found willing to follow the king's suggestion.

Upon the departure of the Reverend Father Martin for Pondicherry. I determined to visit that place myself, and send some of my most trusted servants to Tanjor. The latter were to make inquiries as precise as possible into the truth of the reports about the persecution. My object was to satisfy myself whether what was said about the reverend French Jesuit fathers in regard to the Hindu ceremonies they practised was true or false. On this head [80] I assure you that the whole is quite true, following the report of my servants and the statements of certain merchants I know. In addition, there is also what I learnt about it from several French clerics and secular priests, who had seen the reports and found them to be quite consistent and in accordance with the truth.

From what I have just said, and from what I said earlier, about the persecution, it will be clearly seen what were its causes, its commencement, its results, and its termination. In dealing with this matter, I took my part so far as my duty and my insufficient zeal impelled me. In order that the reader may be still better assured of the truth of all that I have advanced,

elsewhere in his letter of 1701 from Aour, he speaks of a Father *Simon* de Carvalho (J. Bertrand, 'Mission du Madurè,' iv. 124). The latter was transferred from Counampatty, where he had been three years, first to Aour as assistant to Father Bouchet, and then to a new mission at Totiam and Tourcour on the Maisur border.

here is the translation of a letter of thanks received from the Reverend Father Superior of the Mission upon the subject:

Sir,

I have received the letter that you did me the honour of writing to me, accompanied by *farmans* from the Mogul—*farmans* which were anxiously awaited by this Christian community. For, being the goal of their hopes, they contained the only remedy awaited by us all, to obtain which we have made so many efforts. But, to speak the truth, they depend entirely on the favour you have shown us—a favour, as cannot be gainsaid, worthy of eternal gratitude. This I yield to you with all my heart for all the effort, the expedition, and the charity that you have been so good as to display on this occasion towards this afflicted community. By this course we have been spared the sight, as we had feared, of the total failure of all that had caused us so much labour and exertion through so many years.

This mission expected no less from the ardent zeal which we all venerate in your person, and from the fervent love which you have exhibited all these years towards the members of this small company, and have also displayed to us in person on many occasions. The nature, sir, of this favour is so great, as well as the degree in which I esteem it, that words fail me to explain with the pen the feelings of my heart. Accept of them, I pray you, since the sincerer they are the more they are worthy of belief. I assure you that we recognise you, and will recognise you for ever, as the great benefactor and protector of this Mission. It is for this reason that it (the Mission) acknowledges itself under such a great obligation to return you eternal thanks from the depths of its heart.

You assure me that the said *farmans* contain nothing which could injure us [81], but, on the contrary, what will be of very great service. It is upon certainty in this respect that depends their successful working. This is why the Reverend Father Martin and all of us feared greatly we might find the ruin of this Christian community in what we had sought as a means of saving it. Our fear was increased, as you know, by the effort and subterfuge by which you obtained the said *farmans*. You assured us they would be favourable to us, and we have found them such. For on reading the *farman* of the *diwan* surreptitiously (*par finesse*),we have found in it all that we desired.

We assume that the others contain the same thing and the same conditions.

We have made up our minds to produce the said *farmans*, and for this reason we shall be greatly in need of the Mahomedan who brought them. He did not appear with them himself, but sent them by the hands of a servant. But we intend to remedy this defect, and we are on the look-out for some noble at Tanjor who will be good enough to introduce this servant to the king's presence, and support the letters by a statement to the same purport. In this way the king may not be vexed at our applying to his enemy to get deliverance from his tyranny. With such a protector we shall get the said letters delivered as soon as possible, praying the Lord our God to grant us success. It will be he who will amply recompense you. For it is to you that we owe everything, and are thereby eternally indebted to you. In that respect I offer myself most sincerely and with all my heart as always ready for your orders. I also ask, although you do not know me, for you to be assured that already for many years past I have desired to be counted among the number of your friends, for I admit myself to be under an obligation for all that, and even more in regard to you.

I am, etc.

[Here two unnumbered pages are inserted, giving the following letter:]

Here is another letter received by me from Father Martin on this subject; it will be of use as showing the intentions and the methods of the reverend fathers of the Society in this affair.

MONSIEUR NICOLAS MANOUCHY,

It is about two or three days ago that I arrived from the Mission, where I went to obtain more exact information of all that had passed in regard to the Nawab's letter which you so kindly procured on behalf of that afflicted Christian community. I write you this in order to give an account, as is my duty, of all the benefit that you have secured for us.

First of all, it is certain that the letters of the *nawab* and the *diwan* were written with all the force that could be desired, and the style in which they are worded proves plainly enough the great credit you possess at that court. Secondly, although Charnaomet (Shah Muhammad) did not fulfil the promise he had given you of sending us a *chobdar* to take the said letters to

Tanjor, no harm has ensued. For François Sobral, the young man who brought them, has done all that a chobdar could have done; indeed, I believe he could hardly have done as much. It is notorious, and all the world is witness, that the abovenamed Sobral spoke to the minister of the Tanjor king with extraordinary firmness and courage, and carried out the business with great prudence and dexterity. Thirdly, the news written from the mission here by the reverend fathers, that the said Sobral was a prisoner in the fortress of Tanjor was sent a little too precipitately. For the said fathers gave too much credit to a few silly Christians who had started such an irrelevant report. During the whole affair the authorities at Tanjor have not even threatened the said Sobral with anything of the sort. You were entirely justified in saying that you could not persuade yourself to belief in a report of that sort. It is a great drawback that we have only natives to give us information; and if the accounts of the persecution were not more trustworthy than those about Sobral being in prison, this community would be still as peaceful as ever it was. Fourthly, the sole hindrance there has been in the affair, and the only reason why the *nawab's* letter has not succeeded so entirely as we had wished, is that his [Da,ud Khan's] resident at the court of Tanjor, to whom the *diwan's* letter was addressed, is absent from this court, having gone away several months ago; for if he had been here, what doubt can there be that the letter of the *nawab*, when presented by him, would have produced its complete effect. But there was no one but his [the *wakil's*] son, who is still a child. Thus the king and his minister, who is our chief enemy, pay little regard to him and did with him as they pleased, and persuaded him of whatever they wished. Fifthly, in spite of the King of Tanjor's not having yielded to a letter of recommendation in such strong terms as that sent by the *nawab*, still, it has not failed to make a deep impression on his mind; for the queen pointed out to him that his minister had deceived him, and he ought to have continued his protection of the Christians. In addition to this the king was greatly irritated with Vagogipandidem (Venko Ji Panditam),[1] and said to him that his hatred to Christians had

1. The chief minister Bala Ji, 'or, as others call him, Vagoji-Pandiden' (Pére Martin's letter of 1701 in J. Bertrand, 'Mission da Maduré,' 1854, iv. 121).

brought him into the plight in which he now found himself. Vangogi (Venko Ji) aforesaid, ever an enemy of our holy religion, inspired the king with the idea that he could bring all to a conclusion, and that there was no necessity for displaying so much agitation. Sixthly, Sobral having demanded a reply to the *nawab's* letter, the minister told him that, being merely recommendatory, it required no answer. Besides, said he, the nowab is king in that country, but not in Tanjor; consequently, he had no business to interfere in the affair. He added that if the *nawab* gave sanction to the rebuilding of the pagoda of Canjivaron (Kanchi-varam, Canjevaram), as had been demanded of him, he (the rajah) would permit the restoration of the Christians' church. In fine, this minister betrayed a great deal of pride and much self-confidence, telling us or letting us understand that although the protector that we had sought out, and the person who had procured us the recommendation, had great credit, he had no fear of them whatever might happen. Thus he dismissed Sobral without any reply for the *nawab*, in spite of one having been prepared which Sobral actually saw. After its preparation the Brahmans, who are the counsellors of the king, and his chief minister came to the conclusion that it was not necessary to write, or, if it were, the answer should be sent through another channel. They tell us that this has been done, and we have not the least doubt that, to cover his tyranny, he has written many things opposed to God's law, and injurious to those who preach it and to the whole body of Christians.

But whatever they may have written, we feel we are safe. We are the more so, for we know that your charity having commenced so holy a work, that having laboured so hard and taken so much trouble, you will continue to show the same bowels of mercy and compassion as before; that you will not throw up an affair on which depends the peace of so many feeble Christians. Had they only the same strength and courage as those of the primitive Church, it would be unnecessary for us to make such efforts of solicitation on their behalf. But their natural timidity obliges us to afford them special help. This is the reason that the fathers of the Mission have given me fresh orders to report everything to you, and to urge you, by the wounded side of Jesus Christ, our common Redeemer, to kindly take up our cause, forgetting past disappointments and fatigues, but fixing your eyes only upon the glory of God and the salvation of these feeble and afflicted Christians. These latter centre all their hopes upon the credit you enjoy, your piety, and your generosity.

I should ere this have started to fling myself at your feet and pray the grant of this favour. But it is necessary to prepare some rarities to be presented to the *nawab*, to whom we are bound to show our gratitude for his first letter of recommendation. I do not mean to take a single step in this matter without your advice. For this reason I beg the favour of your writing me two lines of reply, and pointing out to me what I ought to do. My design would be to travel as far as Big Mount by land dressed as a Pandaran (*pandaram*[1]), and there await your directions for visiting the *nawab*. For you are acquainted with the case, and have already obtained so favourable and honourable a reception for our ambassador. It is thus certain that the glory of God will be a still stronger motive for procuring a missive as favourable to us as we could wish. Briefly, all is in your hands, and I await with impatience what it may please you to require of me in this affair. Meanwhile, I offer myself for anything that would be of service to you, et cetera. (From the Mission of Madura, February 6, 1702).

This, then, is the condition of things at Tanjor by the very statement of a father of the Society. In regard to this, let the reader notice that after the receipt of the letters from Da,ud Khan and the *diwan* the penalties inflicted upon the Christians ceased altogether. The ground, then, of the complaints and tears of the reverend fathers is that they wanted the king to order a church to be built for them at his expense. Unable to obtain this concession, they keep up continual sobbing and tears over the *débris* and ruins of that New Jerusalem, although, strictly speaking, this ought to be the least of their troubles. When occasionally the misfortunes of others afflict them, it is only through their bearing upon their own interests. When these are present in the most trifling affair, they do not hesitate to stir up the whole world to obtain redress for the wrong that they assert

1. A Hindu ascetic mendicant of the (so-called) Sudra, or even of a lower caste. A priest of the lower Hindu castes of South India and Ceylon (Yule, 666).

has been inflicted. As their grievances are frequently far from being the best-founded, they are skilful enough to bring God and religion to their side in order to obtain success in their design. To hear them talk about the persecution at Tanjor you would think it the most deplorable catastrophe that ever had been in the world, and willingly would they exclaim with the prophet Jeremiah: 'Behold, is there any grief like unto my grief that the eternal has done unto me ? He has made me cry aloud in the day of the burning of his wrath.'[1] In spite of this, to the shame of that Society be it said, they are governed by nothing but the desire of a small gain; they want a church that shall cost them nothing. Thereby they would like to prove that they have influence everywhere, that the will of kings is bent at their pleasure, and whenever they so desire. These are the reasons, making them move heaven and earth to induce Da,ud Khan to take action against the King of Tanjor, and compel him to build the church they hanker after.

Since I have spoken of the King of Tanjor, it will not be out of place to mention what happened at Tranquebar,[2] a place belonging to the Danes, lying close to the sea, and within the territories of the same prince upon the Choromandal coast. In the year 1699 it happened that a vassal of the king died; he held charge of the territories adjacent to Tranquebar. Upon his decease the Danes claimed the right to put into his place one of his bastard sons. The dead man's widow objected, seeing what manifest injustice was being done to her own son, the legitimate heir. But the Danes paid no heed to this objection, and proceeded to the carrying out of their project. The widow was forced to carry her complaint to the king [82]. The king pointed out to the Danes the wrong they

1. Perhaps a reference to chapter xlv. 3: 'Woe is me now! for the Lord hath added grief to my sorrow; I fainted in my sighing, and I find no rest.'
2. On Wednesday, March 1, 1699, a letter reached Madras from the Governor and Council of Tranquebar informing the English of their being 'straightly besieged by the King of Tanjor upon unjust pretences occasion'd by the death of the Vizidore Vannaque' (Wheeler, 'Madras in the Olden Time,' i. 341, and 'Public Consultations, Fort St. George,' xxviii. 39, 40). The ship *Sidgwick* was sent. The invader was defeated on March 30, and on April 24, 1699, terms were being negotiated. Thanks were received from Tranquebar on May 29; the forces lent had returned to Madras on May 22. Tranquebar lies fifty-one miles east from Tanjor; it was bought by the Danes from the Nayak of Tanjor in 1612, and sold to the English in 1845.

were committing in transferring the rights of the legitimate son to a bastard.

On their side the Danes paid no attention to this remonstrance or to any of the king's words. They replied that they were the masters, and were lords paramount over the country that they held, which had been ceded to them by the ancient kings of Tanjor.[1] Their domination extended as far as cannon shot, and the matter was no concern of his. Irritated at such arrogant pretentions, the king sent six thousand men against them to punish them—that is to say, three thousand horsemen and as many infantry. This force was joined by four thousand more men collected by the relations of the deceased from all directions. Tranquebar was besieged.

First of all, they began by stopping the entry of all provisions; next, they captured an earthen bastion outside the line of fortification, having in it four pieces of cannon. From this point of vantage they stopped the flow of water into the fortress. Finally, they advanced their entrenchments so close that there was only the length of a pistol-shot left between the combatants; in fact, they often at night talked to each other.

In this difficulty the Danes, not having enough men to garrison their town, which is of considerable extent, applied for aid to Mr. Thomas Pitt, governor of Madras. This gentleman sent them fifty soldiers and some provisions and ammunition with all possible expedition. On the arrival of these reinforcements the Danes regained their courage, and made repeated sorties, in which they lost several men. In the end they decided on a general attack upon all the enemy's entrenchments. They carried this out with such valour, their musketry fire was so heavy, and the number of grenades thrown so great, that the enemy was forced to retire. Following upon this success, the bastion that had been lost was retaken. But the investment continuing, provisions once more became scarce. Their wants were again supplied by Governor Pitt, who also sent them more ammunition. The hostilities lasted

1. The Mahrattah dynasty reigning at Tanjor in 1699 had only obtained the country in 1674. The Danes bought the land of their settlement in 1620.

about six months,[1] and peace was not secured until a compromise was made with the relations of the deceased, to whom the Danes paid over one hundred thousand rupees, at which price they granted their consent to the bastard's succession.

The Danes had sufficiently strong reasons for upholding and maintaining this bastard against the legitimate son. The father himself on his deathbed had made him over to the Danish commandant, knowing this son to be a man of intelligence, while his other son was incapable of governing or of supporting the Danes in their business. They dealt in several classes of goods which reached them from the interior, and during the father's government a practice had sprung up of paying no customs duty. They hoped to secure the same thing under the bastard [83], a great advantage for the company. It is for this and other similar reasons of interest that they protected him, and backed him up in his pretensions.

Should the account of the war against Tranquebar have proved not unpleasing to the reader, I flatter myself that the following will not be disagreeable. It is the war of the Mahomedans against the English at Cudeloure (Kudalur).[2] I begin with describing the situation of Fort St. David and Cuddalore, both belonging to the aforesaid English. They purchased them for the sum of sixty thousand *patacas* from Ram Rajah, [son of] Shiva Ji. In ancient times they belonged to the Kings of Bijapur, along with another town, also a dependency upon the said fort. Both places are strong, and surrounded by water supplied by a river which is near the sea.

1. An exaggeration (see the dates from the official records quoted in a previous note). The whole affair was over in about two months.
2. Cuddalore—from *Kudal* (Tamil), 'junction,' and *ur* (Tamil), Village'—a town close to the sea in the south Arkat district, ninety-nine miles south-south-west of Madras. It was obtained by the English from the Mahomedan Governor of Jinji in 1682. It gets its name from being at the junction of two small rivers. Fort St. David (also called Tegnapatam), two miles north-north-east of the native town of Cuddalore, was built by the English in 1690 on ground purchased from Ram Raja (son of Shiva Ji, Mahrattah), the then holder of Jinji, Tegnapatam is a popular corruption of Manucci's 'Tevanapatam' ('God + town'). It is now one of the subdivisions of the Cuddalore municipality.

The town of Tevenapatam is about three hundred paces from the fort, towards the north. The Dutch have a factory in the place, and pay the English two and a half per cent, upon all merchandise imported or exported. The place is inhabited by many weavers and cloth-printers, and there is a considerable trade in cloth.

Cuddalore is situated to the south of the said fort, having as inhabitants many merchants, weavers, and cloth-printers, like those above referred to. Dependent upon it there are six villages, which pay twelve thousand *patacas* of rent [*i.e.*, Rs. 24,000] to the company in return for all the grain, *et cetera*, which their lands produce. This is the place where, in 1698, the English had to defend themselves in war against the Mahomedans. The cause of dispute was as follows:

About two years earlier [*i.e.*, in 1696] an officer under Chilmancan (Sulaiman Khan),[1] governor of Porto Novo[2] and the neighbouring country, was passing through the territory of the English Company. He was stopped by a sergeant at an advanced post in the village of Tripapoulour (Tiruppappuliyur),[3] the reason assigned being that he could not be allowed a passage without a permit from the governor of Cuddalore. At this hindrance the officer grew angry, and began to abuse the sergeant and the sentry. Finding they would not allow him to pass peacefully, he determined to force his way. Thereupon the sergeant placed all the obstacles in his way that he could, even going the length of threatening to fire if he was violent. The other man would not listen, and tried to carry his point. The sergeant was at length forced to fire. The officer was greatly astonished, for

1. Sulaiman Khan, Panni, was the youngest brother of Da,ud Khan, Panni, the *naib*, or deputy, of Zu,lfiqar Khan, *subahdar* of the Dakhin. He lost his life at Lahor on March 17, 1712, fighting bravely on the side of Prince 'Azim-ush-shan, in the contest between the sons of Shah 'Alam, Bahadur Shah. These Pannis established themselves as hereditary Nawabs of Qamarnagar Karnul, and only became extinct so recently as 1848 ('Ma,asir-ul-Umara,' ii. 63), It was Sulaiman Khan's grand-nephew who shot Nawab Nasir Jang of Haidarabad on December 15, 1750.
2. Porto Novo, a town on the seacoast, fifteen miles south of Cuddalore.
3. Tiruppappuliyur (Tamil), 'holy + trumpet-flower-tree + tiger + town + a village in the Cuddalore district, three miles north-west of Cuddalore town ('Madras Manual of Administration,' iii. 242).

the shot killed an extremely fine horse that he was riding, valued by him at two thousand crowns. However, having a little recovered himself, he laid a complaint before Mr. Hatsell,[1] governor of that fort (St. David), who, by means of a few trifling presents, moderated the wrath into which the sergeant's bold act had thrown the Mahomedan.

However, in 1698, two years after the event I have just recounted, Sulaiman Khan passed near to Cuddalore, and was visited by the second in the council [at Fort St. David], who came out to greet him and congratulated him on his safe return from Jinji. This [84] governor thanked him very politely, and told him that in a few days he would come back to pay the English gentlemen a visit as he went by. With that idea he withdrew to his government of Chelembron (Chidambaram),[2] whence four days after his arrival he sent presents of sweetmeats to the governor and second-in-council at Cuddalore. These things they received graciously, in opposition to the ideas of the officer commanding the local garrison. He knew the Mahomedans, and warned the

1. William Hatsell, 'a man of true Piety and Sincerity,' was appointed youngest of Council at Fort St. George, and chief of the factory at Vizagapatam, by a letter from the Court to Fort St. George dated February 15, 1689. He was to come from China to 'the Coast' ('Letter Books,' ix. 8; 9). On October 3, 1690, the Court wrote that they 'intended' Mr. Hatsell for a 'considerable place' in the Bay [of Bengal] (*ibid.*, p. 116). On February 18, 1691, Hatsell was ordered to continue chief at Vizagapatam (*ibid.*, p. 145). On February 29, 1692, the Court wrote of Hatsell as 'our very good Governour of Tevenapatam' [*i.e.*, Fort St. David] (*bid.*, p. 191). On April 10, 1693, the Court commend the fidelity and prudent conduct of Hatsell, Governor of Tevenapatam, and desire his continuance there (*ibid.*, p. 250). On January 3, 1693-94, the Court again express their satisfaction (*ibid.*, p. 310). On March 6, 1694-95, Nathaniel Higginson was appointed Lieutenant-General of India, and Hatsell was made President of Fort St. George and Governor of Fort St. David (*ibid.*, p. 388). He continued to reside at Fort St. David until 1698. He resigned in March, 1699, and left for England, being succeeded by Mr. Frazer ('Public Consultations, March 23, 1699, Fort St. George,' xxviii. 52-54). He died before May, 1700, either on his voyage home or shortly afterwards ('Court Book,' vol. xxxviii.).
2. Chidambaram, a town eight miles from the sea, and twenty-one miles south-south-west of Cuddalore. It is the site of a large and celebrated Saivite temple. The Moguls made it their head-quarters in place of Jinji.

governor to put no trust in them; for probably he would find these sweets difficult of digestion.

Accordingly, some eight days afterwards, there arrived at Cuddalore some sixty horsemen,[1] who appeared at one of the gates and asked for entrance. The sergeant on guard refused to let them pass; they must wait for his captain's orders. Thereupon the officer in command used much bad language to the sentry, and made dispositions to force an entrance. As soon as the captain learnt what was going on, he sent word to the governor, then residing at Fort St. David. Thinking the matter one of little importance, the governor sent a note giving the order to let the men pass. He thought they were friendly, and their only object in coming to Cuddalore was to act as convoy to their king's treasure remittance, then on its way from his army.

Upon receiving the governor's note the captain ordered them to be admitted. Yet they had only come to seize the town by treachery, and cut the throats of all the English. This came out subsequently. Their pretended treasure was nothing more than some bags filled with gravel. But up to this point the governor had no suspicion of any sort. However, these treacherous men were no sooner inside than a number of others appeared, and these, too, were allowed to enter with the same facility. Again more of them came in. In the end there were as many as six hundred—namely, two hundred horsemen and four hundred foot soldiers.

When it was about midnight the brother-in-law of Sulaiman Khan arrived at one of the gates and wanted to go out. At this gate he met with a refusal, unless he obtained leave from the second-in-council for that purpose. In the end the leave was given, to him and all his retinue, for any hour of the night that they might desire. However, these gentlemen were far from going to sleep, for there were still five hundred men outside, with orders to reinforce those inside at the slightest signal given by the earlier arrivals. The agreed signal was that as soon as possible they should hoist their white flag upon one of the bastions.

Before this could be carried out, a native came and warned a

1. J. T. Wheeler ('Madras in the Olden Time,' i. 325) reports this incident as occurring on February 17, 1698; but, as the official records show, the 18th is the correct date. I give extracts from the Madras correspondence at the end of Manucci's narrative of the events.

man at the guard-house that these five hundred men were outside hidden among some palm-trees. At first the second-in-coundl refused credence to the report, asserting that these people were too much their friends; it was a mere invention, and he was assured they were incapable of playing them such a masty trick [85]. Oh! the simplicity of mankind, who remain undisturbed at the very moment when being betrayed in the blackest manner! Thus, even while he was speaking, the brother-in-law of Sulaiman Khan returned, followed by a body of cavalry. Asking for the officer on guard, the corporal appeared and said he was in command. Thereupon the treacherous man, without another word, drew his sword and delivered three blows on the corporal's head. Feeling himself wounded, the latter fired upon his assailant. But tire aim was spoiled by another horseman throwing himself between them, so that only the assailant's quiver was shot off.

At the same moment the sentry fired his piece and killed his man. But as the Mahomedans were in overpowering numbers, they advanced on him without giving him time to reload, and receiving forty-two sword-cuts, he was hewn to pieces. Next came the captain of the guard out of the second-in-council's house, and hearing the alarm given, thought at first he could redeem the position. But he could not do so quickly enough to prevent the brother-in-law of Sulaiman Khan having time to plant his flag upon the bastion at this gateway. Acting on the signal which they had agreed upon, the men in ambush rushed upon another gate; having him at their head, they hoped to find it open. In this expectation, however, they were disappointed; for the sergeant who was on guard had heard the alarm, and opened fire upon him, obliging him to take shelter from the balls below the town wall. His refuge was discovered by a soldier, who fired upon him through a port-hole and scattered his brains upon his horse's saddle.

As soon as Sulaiman Khan learnt the death of his brother-in-law, he lost heart in his enterprise,, particularly as he reposed great trust in the deceased. He was a man of good understanding, and greatly experienced in the practice of war. Then, while this was happening, the captain came up with reinforcements from the fortress and drove out all these traitors. They were forced to evacuate the two bastions they had occupied. A number of their men were left behind dead, but they subsequently removed the bodies. Including dead and wounded, they lost seventy men in their retreat.

The cowardice of this rabble upon this occasion seems most extraordinary, for they numbered over eleven hundred, while, in addition, they were masters of two bastions and of all the streets. In spite of these advantages, seventeen men repelled them to a great extent, and a reinforcement of forty men coming from the fortress [Fort St. David] completed their rout and ejected them completely, after a considerable loss, if we consider how few were the men on the English side. The latter lost two men, and had twenty-two wounded. Nevertheless, as soon as the Mahomedan was back within his district, he contemplated massing a still larger force, meaning to return to the charge. The next time he succeeded no better, and was repulsed every time he made an attempt; though it is true that he burnt four large villages belonging to the company.

[86] In the end this man came a third time with a still more formidable force than on the two former occasions, but he did no more harm than before, unless it were that the English were forced to bleed through their purse; for the governor of Madras, wearied by these continual squabbles, wrote to Julfacarkan (Zu,lfiqar Khan), governor of the province, and for a payment of the sum of thirty thousand crowns the troubles were set at rest, and without this action they would no doubt have lasted for a much longer time.

EVENTS AT CUDDALORE AND FORT ST. DAVID, FEBRUARY, 1697/8

From factory records, fort St. David, vol. I., pp. 24 FF.

Att a Consultation, Thursday, 17th February, Anno. 1697/8

Selimon Cawn writeing a very curious letter to the President last night, adviceing that the Kings treasure was going from thence to the Camp, under the conduct of 50 Horse, and desiring they might continue in Cuddalore this night, and as it was a festival with him, he sent 8 potts of Sweetmeats, with the King's Wacanavoo's brother. On considering tis requisite to keep a good correspondence with him, tis ordered, that some sweetmeats, fruit and China ware, to amount of 33 *pagados* (provided by Grupah, the expence Braminy) be sent him.

Diary. Friday, 18th February, 1697/8.

This morning about 6 a'Clock, hearing an alarm from Cuddalore, we answered it from the Fort Immediately, and hearing some small arms and some of their Guns go off, the Governor immediately sent Serjeant Smith with 20 men to Cuddalore with verball orders (not haveing time to write any) to follow the orders of the Councill and Capt. Hugonin there.

The Wind being southerly, we continued to hear their firing small arms, and some of their great Guns at Cuddalore, wherefore, the Presidt., Messrs. Ingram and Farmer order'd Ensign Kerr, with 30 men and a Drummer, to march immediattly thither with the best of our arms, and good store of ammunition, and that Mr. Berlu and Gratia Mentt, doe goe on horseback well armed; At same time the Govr. &ca. ordered all the out guards to joyn the guard of Trepopolore [three miles N.W. of Cuddalore], and upon advices of our people being engaged with the Moors, orders were sent to the Chief Officer to march directly to Cuddalore, and to kill, wound, and destroy all Moor men that came to oppose them. We discovered with our prospectives, some Moors Horsemen rideing between the houses and the river, with drawn swords in their hands.

About 7 this morning a Peon came from Cuddalore, adviseing that Selimon Cawns people had surprized our guard of Porto Novo gate, and killed and wounded some of our Souldiers; That Mr. Haynes, Capt. Hugonin and Serjeant Smith were engaged with the Moors.

About 9 Clock received a Note from Mr. Games that Captain Tracy was killed and one Benson a Souldier dyed of his wounds at Porto Novo gate, that the Corporall was despirately wounded in severall places, but likewise mentions that the Moors were beaten out of the Town, and that we had killed severall of them.

This afternoon the Presidt. went to Cuddalore, and orderd the Moor men there to interr the Corps of the Moor men that were killed, and consulted of what necessary to be done for security of the place.

This night sent a generall letter to Madrass, wherein advised that the Moors surprized our guard at Porto Novo gate and after wounding the Souldiers, a party of their horse appeard without the gate, who finding they had the command of the gate, enter'd the town, but this caused an alarm and Capt. Hugonin with about 18 men, marching towards them, was overpowered with their numbers, and the enimie made themselves masters of Chellumbrum Point, but after Serjeant Smith with his men engag'd them, and they perceived more Souldiers to come from the Fort, upon the approach of Ensign Kerr with his men, and after the Ensign fired some vollies, the Moors quitted the town in much disorder, but comeing upon a roguish designd (*sic*) they seized upon three of Mollem's Eliphants, value about 3000 pags. as soon as they had surprized the gate, and carried them away; they likewise robbed the shops in the bazar and severall houses; and Capt. Tracy who came hither lately in a sloop from Mallacca, going out Volunteer with Capt. Hugonin, was killed, and one Benson a Souldier; the Corporall at the gate mortally wounded, and about 5 or 6 of our English and Portuguez have slight wounds which we hope are cureable; Eight of the enimy remain, dead at Cuddalore, and they carried off severall that was kill'd, and no doubt but many of them was wounded; We have taken 6 horses, 3 of which are wounded; We likewise took two Bhylees [? Bhils] and 3 horsemen Prisoners.

Att a Consultation extraordinary, Saturday, 19th February.

This day the Councill mett upon consideration of yesterday's transactions, and tis ordered that the Presidt. write a Letter to the Nabob, and to Amer John, Abdall Labby,[1] and Ebrahim Cawn Gurry [? Ghori] about Selimon Cawns Villiany, because Ebrahim Cawn Gurry [Ghori] sent a message to the Governor, by a Mauldar [? amal-dar, a factor, a manager] belonging to Pullaverta Cheercon [? karkun, a clerk].

Capt. Calib Tracy ... yesterday was killed ...

Finding. by this action of Selimon Cawn that most of the moors are of a Base Treacherous and Perfidious temper It is thought requisite for future, that not above ten horsemen at a time, be permitted to come into the town, and that all of them leave their arms at the gate with the Centry, except 2 or 3 that may appear to be the Chiefest of them.

And haveing certain advices that Selimon Cawn arrived at Porto Novo yesterday about 4 a clock afternoon, tis thought requisite that the town of Trepopolore be preserved if possible, and tis ordered that Serjeant Smith with 12 English and 17 Portuguez Souldiers, doe repair to Trepopolore, where the Choultry they use to keep watch, being now entrench'd, that he remain there with his men and 30 peons, which we hope will be a means to prevent Collebeage [? Kali Beg] from trying up leaves, and the orders be given to Serjeant Smith with refference to the difference of yesterdays business.

Diary. Saturday, 19th February.

Messrs. Haynes and Mountague continued at Cuddalore. Orders were given to cutt down all trees and hedges that are near Cuddalore.

Sunday, 20th February, 1697/18.

About 12 clock this day, we had an account that Selimon Cawn designd an other attempt upon us; that he had gott 1000 Peons and 300 horse; that their resolutions were to fight and not to plunder; that Selimon Cawn has writt to the Worriar [? the chief of Udayarpallaiyam] for 2000 Peons, which were promist him. This afternoon about 2 clock the Govr. &ca. sent 20 Souldiers to Cuddalore, and about 4 clock an alarm was given at Cuddalore, which was immediatly answerd from the Fort, and thereupon the Honble. Presidt. &ca. sent 21 Souldiers more to Cuddalore, and ordered all the outguards to come to the Fort.

1. This name is meant, probably, for 'Abd-un-nabi; he was *faujdar* of Porto Novo. Mir Jan seems to have been the Company's agent at Court. Perhaps 'Labby' shows that Abdall Labby belonged to the local Mahomedan clan of that name.

This evening dispatched a generall letter to Madrass, adviseing that we had but 42 Souldiers in the Fort, 6 at the Barrs mouth and all the rest were at Cuddalore, that all our out-guards were withdrawn, so that all our out-towns were exposed to the Enimys fury; and thatt was impossible for us to avoid it; that we heard Mr. Jones the Dutch Chief at Porto Novo, did supply the Moors with powder and shott, upon their expedition hither. This day many thousands of the inhabitants left the Companys bounds.

Monday, 21th February, 1697/8.

This morning about 8 a clock, Selimon Cawn with his horse and foot enter'd the Right Honble. Companys bounds; They marcht under covert of the Gardens behind Cuddalore, and sett fire to all the houses in their way; the Guns from the Points there played upon them, which kept them from approaching very near. Nine a clock this morning, seeing a party of horse near Trepopolore, we fired a Gun from the Fort upon them. This Day we discovered the Enimy to burn the Houses in the out-towns as they came along.

A Sally was considered of to be made at night, which whilst the Governr. &ca. here were thinking of, Messrs. Haynes and Mountago: advised from Cuddalore, that they thought such a thing proper; wherefore the Govr., Messrs. Ingram, Farmer and Games agreed to send Mr. John Berlu and Ensign Henry Kerr, with 70 Souldiers and 200 Peons to fall upon the Enimy in the night, which we had discovered to lye upon the bank of the river, between Chummundulum and Trepopolore, twas agreed that 30 men should come from Cuddalore; Mr. Berlu was acquainted with the design, but the orders to him and the Ensign were sealed up and not to be opened till two a clock in the morning and they to march about 3 a clock. This day many thousand Inhabitants left the bounds, and the rest came as near the Fort as they could.

This night about 11 a clock, received a note from Messrs. Haynes and Mountague, signifying that they had advised Capt, Hugonin, who diswaded from sallying this night, saying that our men were weary; twas therefore laid aside.

Tuesday, 22th February, 1697/8

This morning Selimon Cawn marcht towards Mange Copang [a village near Cuddalore] and as we believed he intended to goe to the Sea side, and that way to come on the back of Tevenapatnam; to prevent which the Governr., Messrs. Ingram, Farmer and Games, sent out Mr. John Berlu and Ensign Henry Kerr, with 50 Souldiers, with which party Mr. Edmund Bugden went Volunteer; The Enimy marcht boldly towards them, haveing the advantage in numbers; the Horse took particular care to be out of Gun-shott, and rather appeared only to force on their foot, who spent great numbers of shott in vain, for their powder being weak, did not wound one of our men; Our people killed 4 or 5 of theirs, besides what wounded, and one of their footmen bad bis leg shott off by a field peice, which was sent upon the plain from Tevenapatnam gate, but notwithstanding all that we could doe, their flying partys continued to burn all our out-towns and great part of Mangee Copang, and perceiveing them to goe towards the water side, on the back of Tevenapatnam, we ordered our men to withdraw att 12 a' Clock at noon; They were much wearied in being engaged and continuing in open field till this time.

About one o'clock this afternoon, we perceived the Enimy to begin to return to the same quarters as they were at last night. This afternoon the Governr. and Councill ordered all the horse to be gott ready, and to borrow as many as to be had. This evening received a letter from Abdall Labby, in answer to the Presidts. sent the 19th Inst. disapproveing of Selimon Cawns actions, and adviseing of our opposeing him in all his ill designs.

This night dispatch't a generall letter to Madrass, adviseing the necessary, as also sending to Porto Novo to take the Ships there, but that we should be glad if there may not be a necessity for it, being senceable nothing but necessity should cause us to carry on a quarrell with the Mogulls subjects.

Wednesday, 23d February, 1697/8

This morning Selimon Cawn raised his Camp, which was upon the bank of Trepopolore river, marcht at the utmost extent of our bounds, and his people sett fire to all the houses at Trepopolore, Bandypollam, &ca. and severall places behind Cuddalore, where his footmen sculkt behind the gardens. He pitcht his tents upon the Hills, a little beyond our random; We fired about four eighteen pounders (the Gun being extraordinarily good) flung the shott amongst them, and by that means they were keept at a greater distance; the Battarys at Cuddalore played upon such as they could discover to come near to burn houses, and some of our Talliars [chief watchmen] being abroad shott a Bhylee [? Bhilah] in the legg.

This day we perceived the numbers of the Moors very plain as they marcht, and we hear consists of 200 horse and about 1200 foot. This evening an ordinary Moorman came from Selimon Cawn, who pretends to be an Amein; He says Selimon Cawn is very desirous of the body of his brother in law who was one of the horsemen that was kild near Chingie [? Jinji] Gate, at Cuddalore, the 18th Inst. we told the messenger that the body should be deliverd, if could be found. Mollem and the other Chuliars [a class of S. India Mahomedans], being in the fort, messengers were sent to Cuddalore to find out the body. And an other messenger comeing from Selimon Cawn this night about 8 a clock, twas agreed to deliver the body the next morning; and by this messenger we sent word that if Selimon Cawn would deliver Mollems 3 Eliphants we would deliver the Horses and Prisoeers.

Thursday, 24th February, 1697/8

'This morning the Presidt. received an answer from Ebrahim Cawn Gurry, expressing that Selimon Cawn had done a great deal of mischief without reason; that he would endeavour to perswade him to make restitution, and intended to come to Selimon Cawn's Camp for that Purpose.

About 12 a clock we discovered Ebrahim Cawn Gurry come to Selimon Cawns camp, which remains upon the Hills, just without our random; Upon his comeing into the bounds he sent a Mauldar [factor, manager] to the Presidt. to send our Egip Braminy to meet him at Selimon Cawns Camp, haveing desired the same in his letter; Our Egip [= *Dubash* or interpreter, apud Wheeler, 'Madras i. 364] did not return till about midnight when a Braminy from Ebrahim Cawn Gurry came with him, and finding by our Egip [interpreter] that his discourse to him was much different to what he writt in his letter, we thought fitt to hear what his Braminy had to say in the morning. This day Selimon Cawns people burnt what houses remaining, and cut what paddy they could come at, that was growing upon the ground.

Fryday, 25th February, 1697/8

Ebrahim Cawn Gurry remains encampt near Selimon Cawn, and this morning we discourst his Braminy, and then showed him Selimon Cawn [? read 'Ebrahim Cawn'] Gurry's two Letters, in both which he blamed Selimon Cawn; to which the Braminy answerd, that Selimon Cawn gave his Master a different representation of that matter; That his people came into Cuddalore with the Kings treasure, that our Souldiers were abusive to them, killd and wounded them, &ca. We told the Braminy that Ebrahim Cawn Gurry knew that it was quite otherwise, and himself knew so too, but he said that he must discourse as ordered, and that Ebrahim Cawn Gurry as Mediator to make Peace between Selimon Cawn and us, desired three things, vizt:

1st. Sending the body of Selimon Cawns brother in Law:

2d. The delivery of 5 Prisoners that were taken in the Skirmish at Cuddalore, who had their dependance on him, one a Faukeer, the other Horsekeepers and of as little account:

The 3d proposition was to give Selimon Cawn a sum of money; and then he would be gone:

We did not hesitate to grant the two first, but sent the 5 prisoners with his Braminy, and the Corps being found yesterday by Mollems people, we ordered to be sent to the Fort, and from thence they might receive it; the Braminy prest our sending of it, which we refused, and plainly told him, that no man had security in going near a man of Selimon Cawns temper.

As to his last proposition of giveing a Sum of money we told him that [we] did much admire Ebrahim Cawn Gurry should mention such a thing, when twas notoriously known Selimon Cawn had basely and wickedly robbed, plundered and damaged this place to a considerable amount; that we had represented the matter to Zulfauker Cawn, and did not question but he would order him to render satisfaction; That Ebrahim Cawn Gurry had in his letters exprest quite contrary as aforesaid, and we expected restitution for his wrongs; his Braminy did not propose the delivery of the four Horses, nor the other Prisoners that were servants to Selimon Cawn.

In discourse with the Braminy we are assured that Selimon Cawns people came into Cuddalore with some of the Kings treasure; Zulfauker Cawn had sent about 200 horsemen belonging to Ramsing for said treasure, which was about 25,000 Rups. Selimon Cawn was to send some horse as a Convoy with it towards the Camp, and haveing had evill designs against Cuddalore, took this opportunity, and there is reason to believe Ramsings people knew nothing of it till the morning, and then they hasted away with the treasure, tho' some of them were spectators of Selimon Cawns base attempt; and tis said that they have reported the same publickly at Zulfauker Cawns Camp to the dishonour of Selimon Cawn.

This evening our Mauldar [manager] returned from the Nabobs Camp [*i.e.*, Zu,lfiqar Khan's]; He brings no answer from Amer John to the Presidts. letter, nor from the Nabob; but a curtious letter from Abdall Labby ['Abd-un-nabi], who writes that he has represented Selimon Cawns base dealings to Zulfauker Cawn, and that we must make our application to the Nabob, that if we had done it sooner it might have prevented this vastly great loss.

Amer John told our Mauldar, that if we had killed Selimon Cawn in his base attempt upon us, Zulfauker would have been well pleased, and that an order was ready to be delivered him, requireing Collebcague not to give us any disturbance, but the same was not chopt [stamped with his seal], because Uttum-Chund had not received what he expected; and our Spye Braminy writes that Amer John told him we should upon no account give anything to Selimon, for it would be displeasing to Zulfauker, who would take care of our business more effectually when application was only made to himself; And Uttum Chund says, that Rama Rajah's[1] papers being in his custody, he observes the English gave much money to him for Tevenapatnam, &ca. but would give none to Zulfauker Cawn. Ebrahim Cawn Gurrys Egip [interpreter] and our Braminy went to their Camp, but did not return.

Yesterday and to-day, Selimon Cawn's and Ebrahim Cawn Gurry's people cut a great deal of Paddy in the bounds and carried great quantitys from Trepopolore and other out-towns, where the same was buried; The Pollygars [local chiefs] that were with them were chiefly concerned in carrying away plunder.

Saturday, 26th February, 1697/8

This morning our Egip [interpreter] and Ebrahim Cawn Gurrys Braminys returned, who were ordered to tell us, that with much difficulty he had perswaded Selimon Cawn to return to Chellumbrum, and desired the Corps might be sent, and the rest of the Prisoners and horses

1. That is, Ram Raj, Mahrattah, son of Shiva Ji, who held Jinji and its dependencies for a time.

delivered; Our Egip [interpreter] answered that he knew the Corps was ready, but he had no power to treat about the Prisoners and horses.

About 9 a clock in the morning Selimon Cawn took down his great Flags, and gave notice of his departure; about 11 they began to march under the hills without our bounds, towards Porto Novo; Ebrahim Cawn Gurry accompanyed him about 2 miles, and then returned at the extent of our bounds, where he desired Mr. Berlu might meet him, to treat about the delivery of the prisoners and horses; He had wholy waved the discourse of giving Selimon Cawn any money.

The Corps went so soon as to meet him, but his stay was so short, that he was gone before Mr. Berlu went three-fourths of the way; but his Braminy and two Mauldars [managers] being with Mr. Berlu, were ordered to acquaint him of his setting out to meet him. After Mr. Berlu's return, twas thought fitt to send a short letter to Ebrahim Cawn Gurry, adviseing him thereof, in which [we] did not mention any thing of the Prisoeers and horses.

If the Danes and the English have felt the ill-humour of the Mahomedans and of the Hindus in these regions, neither have the French been exempt. Here is what happened at Pondicherry, a place belonging to the royal company of that nation; it is situated upon the sea shore, and distant from Fort St. David about five leagues in a northern direction. The French re-established themselves here in 1698, after the conclusion of peace.[1] Many people rejoiced at their return, and a large number of merchants of the country hastened to the place to settle there under their protection. Nevertheless, it was not long before they were troubled by continual insults from a gang of robbers who fixed themselves in an adjacent place. Coming forth daily, they drove off all the cattle they could find; in this way there was almost continually some dispute to disentangle. Often the Frenchmen were forced to rise from table and take steps against them.

Among other instances, it came to pass once that some horsemen left the fortress on some such expedition. Two riders advanced further than was necessary, not considering what might happen to them. One of them, called Monsieur de Maisonneuve, having seen some men on foot driving off some cows, rode after

1. This restoration followed the Treaty of Ryswick concluded between the Dutch and French in 1697. Possession was taken about March 13 (New Style), 1699; not in 1698 (see congratulatory letter sent by Governor Pitt and Council to the Director-General and Council of Pondicherry on March 21, 1699, 'Letters from Fort St. George,' vol. ix., pp. 30, 31).

them with all possible speed, hoping to recover their prey from these robbers. But his horse being somewhat unmanageable, he could not carry out his purpose. While still in this unprepared state, there came forth from a neighbouring wood a considerable number of horsemen, who surrounded him.

Then that gentleman came to know that it is frequently a bad thing to trust to one's courage rather than one's judgment; for in spite of his defending himself with all imaginable courage, killing the captain of these rascals and unhorsing two of his band, their number was too great for one man. He also became wearied out with fighting, and at last succumbed to their blows, lost his life, and his body was cut to pieces. The second horseman, whose name was Monsieur de Liveman[1] when going to relieve his comrade, was shot through the arm by a ball from the enemy. Two foot soldiers following him were killed by some of the men in ambush. But soon, all the Frenchmen having reached the spot, the enemy retired. Yet after this skirmish they did not desist [87] from continuing the same insults as above referred to.

At length, in the month of October, 1701, Monsieur François Martin, governor of the fortress of Pondicherry, received a report that these insolent fellows meant to attack him. To this intent they had allied themselves with other robbers who hid in the woods and had constructed a small earthen fort in a village called Bamiapalam,[2] distant from Pondicherry about a league or more, and on the shore of the sea. At this place these wretches gave great trouble to travellers, and forced them to pay whatever they chose, and observed no limits of demand.

One night Monsieur Martin, to put an end to these excesses,

---

1. We are told by Dr. Jules Sottas ('Histoire,' p. 393) that after the Peace of Ryswick, *circa* 1700, 'M. de Livernan, un officier du Roi, commandait une petite garrison' at Pondicherry.
2. I cannot find this village. There was a Boomipollan, of which the Customs officer, or *Juncaneer*, obtained an annual present at Fort St. David (see Press List of Fort St. George Records, No. 8, entry 1551, of July 19, 1704). Under the form Bandipollan, it is mentioned in 'Madras Manual of Administration,' iii 242, as now one of the wards in Cuddalore town. There is a 'river of Bandupollum' on the map? of Fort St. David in R. Orme's 'Military Transactions,' vol. iii. It is shown as washing the north and east faces of Cuddalore; but, as it is sixteen miles from Pondicherry, a fort there would hardly be any threat to the French.

sent out one hundred French soldiers and two hundred natives with orders to attack this fort. They carried out this order in the morning of the next day, cut down the thorny scrub and the stakes[1] planted round it, and scrambled through the ditches. At once the blacks within the fort rose and fired several times, but harmed no one. On their part the French in good order fired on them, and threw several grenades into the fort. Others made for the gate, and having broken it in by beams and hatchets, entered most valiantly, cut several of the enemy into pieces, and made prisoners of the rest. Their captain, a black man, was seized while trying to escape, and was carried off as quickly as possible to Pondicherry, together with several wounded men. In this encounter there were some three hundred horsemen of Singy (? Jinji, the fort),[2] who wanted to come to their aid. But they took no action, because Monsieur Martin was ready to receive them with about four thousand men that he had placed in ambuscade in order to defend his people. Hearing of this, the enemy retired.

The wounded were brought, as I have said, to Pondicherry, where they were attended to and subsequently set at liberty. As for their leader, he was put on board the fleet leaving that year for Bengal, and I have never been able to ascertain what became of him. Since that time there have been no robberies, and the route past Bamiapalam has remained open. Thus nowadays, provided you can show a note from the said governor, you are no longer interfered with in the slightest. It is true that they do not pay the same respect to everybody, but he who can make himself feared is feared. The place is under the rule of the governor of Singy (Jinji), and is about fifteen leagues from Madras.

Up to this time this last town (Madras), where I have made my abode, had not been troubled by war on any considerable scale, and had enjoyed pleasant enough repose [88]. But now, in the midst of the troubles which have, agitated the other settlements on this coast, we have seen the appearance in the heavens, early in the year 1702, of a long tail, which at first led us to the belief that it was a comet, and yet no head to it was visible.

1. The word in the text is *flays*, which, in default of a better solution, I take to be *fla*, a Burgundian word for 'post,' 'stake.'
2. Or, perhaps, 'Singy' is meant for the name of some chief.

At length, after some days the two ends of this tail showed without any star. This celestial sign was visible from February 23 to March 6 following. The point was directed to the south, and it issued from the west; the head continued to advance towards the east. Such signs have ever been the harbingers of approaching calamity or some revolution among men. God only knows what may come of it, but we have already begun to feel the effects of a war, the details of which I will give. To be still more clear, it is necessary to begin somewhat farther back and tell you what brought it upon us.

I have already spoken of the general Da,ud Khan on several occasions. Here I must remark that he came to this province of the Karnatik in the month of January, 1701, and on his arrival he camped below the great fortress of Arcat (Arkat),[1] an ancient strong place of the Hindu kings, at a distance inland from Madras of about thirty-four leagues. Thence he did me the honour of addressing me a very civil letter, inviting me to pay him a visit. To do this I had not the slightest intention.

But the governor of this locality (Madras) and his council, having heard what was passing, made use of the occasion to send him a present, and congratulate him on his auspicious arrival. With this object they prayed me to render this service to their Company, and they associated with me in the task a Brahman clerk long in the service of the Company, whose name was Ramapa. At that time he was not in their service.[2]

I started and carried with me a fine present, consisting of

1. Arcot (Argadu) town is in the North Arcot district: it is sixty-six miles west of Madras. Da,ud Khan transferred the seat of the Karnatik government there from Jinji. Upon the fall of the Gulkandah kingdom in 1687, the Karnatik became a Mogul dependency; and when released from the long siege of Jinji, which fell in 1698, the Mogul officials became very active and troublesome. The Madras Records contain many entries from as early as May, 1699, showing Da,ud Khan to have been a source of constant apprehension both there and at Fort St. David.
2. The instructions to Manucci and Ramapa were dated January 16, 1701 ('Public Consultations,' xxx. 8-11). These were accompanied by three letters from Governor Pitt—two to Da,ud Khan and one to Muhammad Sa'id, the *Diwan*. Manucci and his companion returned unsuccessful on February 3 (*ibid.*, xxx. 29, 30). The documents can be read in Wheeler, 'Madras,' i 360-365. Wheeler states the cash present to have been. Rs. 3,000.

two cannon, several lengths of broad-cloth in scarlet and other colours, other pieces of gold cloth of Europe and China, and several rareties such as mirrors of all sizes, different kinds of crystal vases, and some weapons such as fusils, pistols, and sabres; also different kinds of wine; added to all of which was a sum of five thousand rupees. As soon as Da,ud Khan heard that I was coming, he desired to honour me so far as to send a captain with thirty horsemen and fifty musketeers to receive me at a distance of five leagues from his camp.

On the following day I gave myself the honour of going to visit him, when he displayed much tenderness and friendliness. Next I conveyed to him compliments on behalf of our governor; but he let me understand that he felt much resentment, and complaint that they had not already paid him a visit. They had not taken the same trouble as the Portuguese to pay him the usual compliments. My answer was [89] that when other governors had come to occupy the position he held, it was the custom to visit them at this very place where he now was. I could not run the risk of going any farther, on account of the great forests there were, filled with robbers, where I might possibly receive some injury and lose much of what I was bringing. The Portuguese could run a greater risk, for they brought nothing with them, and came only to demand favours.

He seemed satisfied with these reasons and others that I gave him on the subject, and after much discourse on divers matters, I laid before him a letter, and said to him that I had a present to offer on behalf of the governor and of the company; and I prayed most humbly that he would deign to accept it. His reply was that I need then only retire for repose to a tent which he had had erected for me close to his mansion. He would send word to me of the hour at which I could appear, as is the custom among the Mahomedans. Thereupon I took my leave of the general and retired to the tent, and it was impossible for me to get away from it to pay my respects to the first minister, Muhamad Sayd (Muhammad Sa'id, the *diwan*),[1] and all the other officers. For I expected from one moment to another to be called, nor did I wish to allow any opening for the complaint that I was not found in my lodgings.

With this thought in my mind I wanted to send the above-

1. Muhammad Sa'id was *Diwan* of the Karnatik.

mentioned Brahman to visit the chief minister, but he objected: that it was late, and he wanted to bathe his body according to their custom, which is to bathe everyday. Although he deceived me, I believed him all the same. However, not to neglect entirely my duty, according to the customs of the court, I sent a very honest youth, that I had brought with me from Madras, to make my compliments to the chief minister and intimate to him my arrival in the army. I sent him word that as it was late I was unable to acquit myself of what was due from me to him, but that in the morning I would do so without fail.

About half-past seven o'clock at night, Da,ud Khan sent me word that I might bring the present before him. This I did to a great extent, only keeping back in my custody the money and some of the trifling things. The reason for my so acting was that I could not then give him the money secretly, by reason of his being accompanied by many officers and other persons of consideration. Moreover, they look on it as a distinction and an honour to receive presents in public, but as regards money they never take it but in secret. I was thus obliged to beg him in a low voice to give me instructions to whom it should be delivered. He replied in the same way that I must keep it, that afterwards he would dispose of it as he judged most fitting. The Brahman, Ramapa, did not fail to notice the good reception given me, and all the honours showered on me, as also the friendliness displayed more and more by Da,ud Khan. Besides, the Nawab had fed me splendidly that evening, and had directed his major-domo to supply my table all the time I was with him just as if it were his own. For these reasons he (Ramapa), like a fool, proceeded to imagine that this would suffice, that the present had done all that was required [90], and thus it was of no use to give him (Da,ud Khan) anything more. It was advisable, Ramapa thought, to keep the money; and on this he imparted to me his idea.

He suggested that we should all the same enter it without fail in our account, and tell the governor that we had paid it over. To speak the truth, I was surprised at such a proposal, and to start with fell into such a violent rage with this Brahman that, in opposition to my nature, I spoke several sharp and harsh words to him, and went so far as to style him a thief and a traitor. For he knew very well that with the Mahomedans no present was better or more esteemed than money.

XXXV. Rajah Shiva Ji, Mahrattah

Vol. III *To face page 368*

The following day Da,ud Khan sent one of his servants to spy out the land, and discover from the Brahman how much money he had with him, and bring back a faithful report. He (Ramapa) quite forgot that the day before he had reported to another servant of this same Da,ud Khan that, in addition to the presents, we had brought some money, and this he had let out without first speaking to me. He told the second messenger that we had brought no money at all. At this information the general was so irritated that he sent back the present he had already accepted, and displayed extraordinary indignation against the Company. Yet with regard to me, he showed me still the same esteem, and did me always the same honour as before, in my quality of his sincere friend. As for the Brahman, he declined to see him again, and ordered the door of the house to be shut against him.

However, as soon as I saw the present come back, I went off to see Da,ud Khan, to whom in the sweetest and most flattering language I pointed out the injury that might be inflicted on me. I prayed him most humbly, even if he had no concern for the Company, at least to call to mind our ancient friendship. I was rather esteemed and liked by the English and the gentlemen of the Company. As they had heard of the friendship and respect that he (Da,ud Khan) had for me, that fact had induced them to send me to him to carry through their business with him. Furthermore, they knew my honesty and loyalty.

His reply was that, as for me, he would do anything I wanted, but that the English, settled within the country of the king, his master, possessed a strong place most useful and highly suitable for all sorts of merchandise and traffic. They had always been left undisturbed, and yet, without regard to the past, they now treated him in the most cavalier spirit, and gave him next to nothing. They failed to reflect that they had enriched themselves in his country to a most extraordinary degree. He believed they must have forgotten that he was general over the province of the Karnatik, and that since the fall of the Gulkandah kingdom they had rendered no account of their administration, good or bad, commencing with 1686. Nor had they accounted for the revenues from tobacco, *betel*, wine, *et cetera*, which reached a considerable sum every year. In his capacity of governor-general of the province he was forced to work for the progress and benefit of the king's interests. The English were very much mistaken if they thought by two thousand four hundred *patacas* [Rs. 4,800] to discharge the whole of their debt, and enjoy [91] freely all the revenues appertaining to the crown of his prince.

All this he said with the greatest imaginable fury and passion, which were increased by his hatred of the English for having killed his brother-in-law, who was slain in the fight at Cuddalore, as I have stated (IV. 85), while serving in the army of Sulaiman Khan, the general's brother. After his rage had cooled a little, he made me sit down beside him, and caused Ramapa to be sent for. To him he said in harsh words that he did not mean to accept the present; he might carry it back to his governor; for his part he did not accept presents of that sort. He would come himself with all promptitude possible to take what he anticipated would suit him better. As regards Manouchy, he would not allow of his return to Madras; he meant to retain him for himself, and still more so because he happened to want him for the treatment of some ailments.

At these words the Brahman withdrew and repaired to the tent and waited for me, so that we might concert what ought to be done at this conjuncture. But at the same moment the general called a captain known to me, named Mirmoin (? Mir Mu'in), an Uzbak by race, and ordered him to take two hundred horse and two thousand infantry, and proceed to Madras with all the haste he could. He was to invest that place, and prevent anything going into or coming out of it. He meant to follow in person very shortly. But the coming on of night hindered the execution of these orders with all the haste that he desired, for they are very slow in making a start.

Thus after supper I had the time to hold a conversation with Da,ud Khan at great length; and still more easy was it to do so that he was in high spirits, having drunk copiously of the European wines that I had brought for him. I began this talk by remarking to him that if he was so kind as to hold me in such great esteem, I must humbly supplicate him not to send either the captain or the soldiers. The matter was of the utmost importance for my reputation, which I placed entirely in his hands. If these soldiers proceeded to Madras, all the European nations, as well as the English, would attribute the fault to me; I should pass among them for a man void of either faith or fealty in any business confided to me.

I also prayed him to hinder the Brahman's departure, telling him the reasons I had for this course. In no shape or form was it advisable for him to leave except in my company; to do otherwise would be to put the fat in the fire. As concerned the revenues, I pointed out to him that at the time when the English came and occupied Madras it was nothing but one vast plain full of sand, uninhabited, and without any name or fame in India. On the other hand, it should be remembered that it was now highly populous, full of active merchants and other residents. It was the money of the English and their good government that had created all that prosperity, coupled with the justice they administered to everybody without fear or favour. If he intended to act with so much harshness and injustice, all the nations of Europe would abandon India. He must recollect the income and benefits which Aurangzeb had acquired; for from what entered and left Madras alone he collected more than one hundred thousand *patacas*.

In addition, there were many merchants, weavers, cloth-printers [92], and others, for all of whom the English provided a livelihood. Many subjects of the king of this realm and others knew very well that every year there were earned in Madras five *lakhs* of gold *pagodas* (equal to about one million of *patacas*, more or less) and over ten *lakhs* of silver rupees (which amounts to five hundred thousand *patacas*). The whole of this money remained in the country, and in exchange for all this the English carried off to Europe no more than some cotton cloth. Let him reflect, that if he objected to the residence of the English at Madras, and if he bothered his head about their gaining such considerable sums, it was requisite for Aurangzeb and his subjects to give them the time to withdraw to Europe. They (the English) set little store by the place; yet if they were forced to abandon it, they would also give up the other towns and factories they held in the Indies. In that case they would cease to be friends and become enemies. Upon their departure they would without fail seize every ship they came across, and thereby spread ruin and desolation throughout the Mogul empire.

I pointed out to him these things, not solely in respect of the English, but also as generally applicable to the other nations of Europe who were to be found in that empire. Da,ud Khan was favourably impressed by all these arguments, and gave me reasonable and satisfactory answers. In brief, he issued orders to stop the departure of the troops and the Brahman.

The next day I paid a visit to the chief minister and to all my other friends, and to them I related what had happened to me, although they knew it already. However, they felt my troubles acutely, and generously endeavoured to protect me. In this way, after a few days, I was given my dismissal, carrying a confirmation of all the *farmans* and favours accorded to the English, just in the manner that they desired.

Da,ud Khan now took the present again; and as he know that I had the money, it being only the Brahman who denied the fact, because he wished to embezzle it like the thief and the traitor he was, he (Da,ud Khan) accepted the present favourably and thought highly of it. He told me to retain the money until he sent someone to me to receive it. Upon this I took my leave of him.

Next day I sent on the present that I had for the chief minister, who took it with much politeness and many thanks. This lord is one of the most polished men to be found among the Mahomedans. He invited me to his table and entertained me magnificently, one of the greatest honours that these people can confer. However, the Brahman was jealous beyond measure of all the honours received by me from Da,ud Khan, from the chief minister, and all the other officers of the army, a feeling intensified by seeing himself despised and hated.

For this reason he designed covertly to make me lose the esteem and reputation that I had among the Mahomedans, and the property I held within the English jurisdiction. To this intent he tried to make use of the spies who were on the spot, men of his tribe, and wished to force them into writing to the Governor of Madras and his council that I was the sole cause of failure and the producer of all the disputes between the Mahomedans and the English. But the most intimate friends of the man knew that all he said was false, and all his inventions diabolic. They refused, but instead gave me warning of what was going On. They advised me not to put much trust in Ramapa. He, on the other hand, became more and more eager for my ruin and destruction, and had recourse to other methods. In pursuance of this idea, he sought the advice of another Brahman he knew, and then returned to our quarters. I asked him where he had been, and he told me he had come from the general's. The latter had given him an order to place the money in the hands of the servant of a Brahman called Longcarne (? Langkaran). Directly this servant came to us, we must obey the order forthwith and without objection. He added to this several words to persuade me that such was Da,ud Khan's wish.

When he had finished these words he went off on other business, and instantly those servants appeared and claimed the money. They told me they came on behalf of Da,ud Khan. There were several of them, and as soon as one had entered another put in an appearance. They solicited and importuned me to such an extent about this money, for which they said Da,ud Khan was waiting, that I remembered what the other Brahmans had said about not trusting Ramapa.

Then I recollected that Da,ud Khan had said he would inform me of the name of the person to whom he desired that I should count out this money. For these reasons, then, I would not deliver it to these servants; but to escape from their importunity, I said that they had only to wait a little while I went to fetch the money. However, instead of doing so, I made all the haste I could to get out and find Da,ud Khan. I discovered him in the midst of many officers conducting a review of his cavalry. In spite of this I went close to him, and twice over whispered into his ear, asking him to be gracious enough to send someone to receive the money.

To these words he replied by telling me to wait a little. When he had finished his inspection, I renewed my prayer that he would be good enough to relieve me of that burden, since he knew very well that I could not guard it securely. At last, to satisfy me, he sent for his treasurer, and after having had a good look, first one way and then the other, to see that no one was watching, he said to him privately, and to me also, that he must go to receive that money.

I returned to my quarters highly pleased, and there I found no trace of the lackeys I spoke of above, nor have I ever seen them since. In a little time the treasurer arrived, and I delivered the money to him in the presence of several of my friends and some servants of the company. He, too, was very joyful at receiving it, for there is no greater pleasure to these men than when they behold the store of their master on the increase.

Some little time afterwards the Brahman Ramapa returned, and although [94] he knew all that had happened, he made no sign; on the contrary, he asserted he knew nothing whatever. But I told him I had paid over the money to the general's treasurer, and not to the men of the Brahman, Langkaran. Upon this, in the humblest tone and his eyes swimming with tears, he began to make excuse, just as is their habit. For it may be truly said that these people are very much like crocodiles (*cocordilles*), whose skin changes at their will and pleasure.[1]

These difficulties occasioned me much trouble, and were all due to the Brahman; so great were they that I was not far from losing my life. The whole affair caused me the more vexation because this Brahman had many friends at Madras, and many relations among the merchants who were influential with the governor, *et cetera*. In spite of this, by Heaven's help I was delivered entirely, upholding my own honour and that of the company. Upon quitting the army I had the delight of hearing, mingled with other compliments, that all which had been gained was on account of me; I found myself also regaled by a very rich *sarapa* (set of robes), which I showed to the Brahman, who also received one for himself.

About fifteen days afterwards I returned to Madras, and rendered an account to the governor of all that I had done in regard to the interests of the company and to the matters he had committed to me. This generous man, having obtained full confirmation of my story, was very satisfied, and gave me many marks of his gratitude.[2] I did not tell him all that the Brahman had done to me, for he had besought me with tears in his eyes not to say anything. His tears compelled me to have compassion, and instead of telling, I made over to him two lengths of cloth, thereby rewarding his ingratitude and infamous conduct by a largesse. I let him see that a generous and Christian heart (be it said without boasting) never resents the wrongs or injustice done to it.

Here I must mention that while I was at the army there arrived from Pondicherry an envoy on behalf of Governor Martin. He came to negotiate about some business which concerned the Royal Company. The party brought some letters of recommendation on the subject addressed to me. But as I was just on the

1. Does he not mean to say 'chameleons'?
2. This statement is rather disingenuous, to say the least; for, according to the official resolution of February 3 (Wheeler, i. 365-367), Governor Pitt was the reverse of satisfied.

point of leaving, I declined to wait until all those difficulties were overcome; for it was of importance both to me and to the Noble Company of England that I should return with all possible speed to Madras. However, before I started I recommended the affairs of the Royal Company both to Da,ud Khan and to the chief minister, as well as to the other officials. All of them promised to be of use to me, and cause me to have satisfaction about those demands. As a matter of fact, I have reason to be satisfied with them; for Monsieur Martin afterwards wrote me letters of thanks and gratitude, notifying that my recommendations had been of great use to them, and enabled them to settle their business to their satisfaction and at a moderate cost. This assertion I believe all the more readily, since the Mahomedans act with the French in quite a different manner to that adopted with all other nations.

[95] Four months afterwards [1701] Da,ud Khan was passing from Arkat to Tanjor to receive the tribute paid by that king to the Mogul, as also the payments of other tributary kings. It is true that the envoy of that king and those of the other rulers, who are always present with Da,ud Khan, wished to pay the tribute at Arkat itself. Their object was to spare him the exertion of going so far; but he would not accept this excuse. He knew quite well what his travels might bring him in from these foreign states; for if he had received Aurangzeb's tribute at Arkat, there would have been no share for himself. The presents would come to more than the dues, whether he caused them to be given by threats or otherwise.

He started, then, for Tanjor, collected the tribute there, and obtained presents which satisfied him. On his way back he passed by Cuddalore, where the governor, Mr. Frazer, sent out men to salute him,[1] and presented him with an elephant, some pieces of scarlet cloth and other fine cloths of Europe and China, together with a sum of money and some European wines. All this was by way of compliment, for he (Frazer) feared this general, who was continually threatening him on account of the death of his brother-in-law. Neither he nor his sister could

1. Mr. Frazer was sent to take President Hatsell's place at Fort St. David on March 23, 1699 ('Fort St. George Public Consultations,' xxviii. 52-54). I cannot find a reference to these presents, but Da,ud Khan was in the neighbourhood of Fort St. David in May, 1701.

forget, and she cherished in her mind the belief that Cuddalore and the English were the cause of her husband's death.

However, all passed peaceably, for these people, through money and presents, can easily be made to forget the death of a relation, or any other thing. From that point the general (Da,ud Khan) moved close to Pondicherry, whence the governor sent out to salute him, and forwarded him a small present. Next he came to Sadraspatam,[1] where the Dutch did the same. These people (Mahomedans) have no hesitation in undertaking long journeys, provided that it suits their interests, as it always does happen to do on these occasions.

Lastly, he reached San Thome with all his army.[2] At this spot the Governor of Madras sent out to salute him Mr. Ellis, the second-in-council, accompanied by two other officials. They carried with them a present similar to the one I had given him when I applied for confirmation of the *farmans* to the company. Their orders were also to pay many compliments to the chief minister. Of all these duties the Englishmen acquitted themselves.

By chance I happened to be present when these gentlemen arrived at the camp, because I had gone there also to pay my respects to the general and the chief minister. The visitors were badly enough received; for Da,ud Khan declined to receive this 'ordinary present,' as he styled it. He told them plainly that these articles were not such as could be presented to a man of his rank. He felt astonished that the governor should send him presents of such small importance; he should remember that he was the first man in the province, and lieutenant-general for the Great Mogul. He also said to them that he was greatly amazed at the governor's sending a Brahman to Arkat in the company of Dr. Manouchy to take part in a discussion of their business. The matter [96] was fully important enough to demand quite another stamp of man than this Brahman, a nobody and of no

1. Sadras is forty miles south of Madras, and the Dutch factory there was established in 1647 ('Madras Manual of Administration,' iii. 775).
2. The particulars of this visit of Da,ud Khan to San Thome will be found in Wheeler, 'Madras in the Olden Time,' i. 369-380. He reached San Thome on July 2, and left for beyond Punamallai on July 17, 1701. The deputation on July 3 consisted of Mr. Ellis, Mr. Davenport, and Captain Lambert.

standing. His amazement was all the greater, since the man had tried to do harm to Dr. Manouchy, who had been brought up in the courts of Asia, more especially in that of the Great Mogul. He added some further words in my praise and to my honour, such as it is not meet for me to repeat.

In the end the Englishmen were given leave to depart, and they received some very fine cloth of gold and silver, of which he made them a present. He added many soft and sugared words, for he declared to them that he was a firm friend of their nation; they ought to repose entire confidence in him, for he would at all times be ready to do them a service in all matters. But along with these speeches he did not omit to tell them that presents sent to a minister of his standing ought to be large and proportionate to his rank and authority.

Those gentlemen wished to make excuses, but he declined to listen. Whatever efforts they made to persuade him that they were treating him exactly like all the other nawabs, his predecessors, and above all, Zu,lfiqar Khan, who is generalissimo at the court of the Mogul, he remained deaf to all their arguments. The English were much put out by this treatment, which was founded on nothing but cupidity. Therefore, foreseeing the inconveniences likely to be produced by his displeasure, they decided to employ some friends to plead their cause. They applied to the chief minister and others, who adjusted the quarrel.[1] The conditions were that the same presents should be sent again, adding five thousand rupees and some very rare European curiosities. After this they became friends.

Da,ud Khan subsequently [July 11] sent a message to the governor that he was desirous of visiting him, as he (Pitt) could not come to San Thome. The governor requested me to go to that place (San Thome) to receive him (Da,ud Khan) [July 12], and escort him to this fortress (Fort St. George), This I did. We left San Thome with fifty horsemen, as previously agreed on. On our way we met the councillors from Madras, accompanied by a part of the garrison. After reciprocal compliments between the two parties, we resumed our journey.

Upon reaching the gate of the town, we perceived all the soldiers—European and Indian—under arms, and drawn up in

1. For the Diwan's letter to Pitt of July 8, and Pitt's to the Diwan of July 9, 1701, see Wheeler, i. 374.

single rank on both sides from that spot up to the fort gate, while a number of armed men were on the town wall and the fort wall. These were arranged in excellent order, much to the astonishment of Da,ud Khan, who could not repress signs of admiration. Still greater was his amazement when, as they drew near the fort gateway, the soldiers and their officers, on catching sight of the governor, drew themselves up in line and went through divers movements which were quite unknown to him. They were only done in his honour and that of the governor. But being unaccustomed to all this military ceremonial, he was thrown into a state of confusion and apprehension. He believed himself to be already a prisoner. For this reason he spoke to me in a loud voice, requesting that all these men might be withdrawn. I reassured him, saying that [97] it was nothing but the usual ceremonial and method among these troops; he should not be in the least afraid, or suspect anything. At the same time, I took care to cry out to the soldiers that they must retire.

While I was speaking the governor arrived, accompanied by a large number of officials and servants. I told him (Pitt) he must embrace Da,ud Khan, who by this time had dismounted with all his retinue. This embrace was given, and then the chief minister and the *bakhshi* were received in the same fashion. Then we entered the fort, where the governor paid him innumerable tokens of respect and friendship, and conducted him to his rooms. These were magnificently furnished. The bed in his room was covered with a quilt of [blank].[1] He admired it in a way to show that he had never seen one like it before, and he begged me to ask the governor if he could give him a pattern of that coverlet, and this I did in a low voice.

The latter (Pitt), readier even to give than the other to ask, made him a present of two others. He even offered to give him the whole bed. Da,ud Khan would not accept this, contenting himself with the two bed-covers, these being of a wonderful, extraordinary, and strange workmanship. Upon entering the room, the governor presented to him a ball of ambergris mounted in gold, with a rich chain of the same metal. After this was done they sat down, and the conversation turned on various subjects with offers of service. When the talk was finished, the governor sent for wine, and drank to the health of King Aurangzeb to a salute of thirty-one guns.

1. 'Embroidered China quilts' are mentioned in Wheeler, p. 377.

Da,ud Khan responded to this politeness by drinking the health of the King of England, to the sound of as many cannon as before. Then they drank the health of the chief minister (*wazir*), Asad Khan, who is nowadays Mirolo Morao (*Amir-ul-umara*)—that is, 'Noble of Nobles.' This title was borne by Aurangzeb's uncle and father-in-law [*i.e.*, Shaistah Khan, died 1695]. A salute of twenty-one guns was fired. This was followed by a toast to Zu,lfiqar Khan, and one to Da,ud Khan himself, each with the same number of cannon. To end with, they drank to the *Diwan*, the chief minister of this general, and to his *bakhshi*, each time to the sound of fifteen cannon.

He was astonished at the rapidity and dexterity with which everything was carried out, and was highly gratified by it all. While these ceremonies were taking place, they made him a present of several cases of liqueurs, spirits, and wines of Europe of different sorts. All these he greatly prized. Next he was led into a large hall adorned with all kinds of arms. There he found a magnificent dinner prepared in European and in Indian fashion He admired the variety of the arms, for which, however, he had no envy, unless for the spears. Having asked the governor for one, two were given to him.

He then went to seek repose for an hour, and after that took his leave. The governor accompanied him as far as the fort gateway, the general protesting against his coming any farther. There they reiterated their compliments and polite speeches, and Mr. Pitt wished him a pleasant [98] journey. On his side the general put forward many offers of service, and assured him of a perpetual peace, wishing him every success in his enterprises and trading: and said he would ever remain his friend and protector so long as he ruled the province.

The governor did not withdraw until Da,ud Khan had mounted his horse—nay, wanted to hold the stirrup for him, but this Da,ud Khan would not allow. But to me he said in a low voice that he would like to be saluted with, some salvoes of artillery as he was leaving the town. This desire was carried out, the musketeers also accompanying him to the boundary of San Thome. I went with him half-way there, when he said that as it was already late I might go back to Madras. All this he said with many compliments and a thousand expressions of civility, ending by saying that he hoped to pass still two or three days in my house at the Big Mount,[1] and rest himself there. I consented with the greatest pleasure, as may be imagined. I went there to see him before he started for Arkat, when he gave me a valuable set of robes, and repeated his offer of serving me just as he was used to do on previous occasions.

The above is the mode in which things happened, and an arrangement was arrived at; the Mahomedans making profuse protestations to the English of service and friendship. We shall see next how these perfidious men acquitted themselves of such promises. At the end of December, 1701, I was at Pondichery on business connected with the Tanjor persecutions, of which I have spoken already (IV. 43-81). At the end of January in the next year [1702] I had trustworthy information that Da,ud Khan and the *diwan* with their whole army were about to leave Arkat again for Madras. This fact I learnt from different sources through various friends and officials known to me, some of whom sent a warning to me that during this march some harm was intended to Madras. He had received peremptory orders from the court to deal rigorously with the English.

This news forced me to forsake the pleasant company of the French, in order to return with all possible haste to Madras. I arrived there on February 2 of the same year [1702]. On my taking leave of them the governor, François Martin, and the other officials of the Royal Company, strongly enjoined me to let them know what happened between the English and the Mahomedans, sending off immediately express messengers (*pions*). This requisition I executed without fail.

A few days afterwards I warned Governor Pitt of Da,ud Khan's approach. In fact, he arrived at San Thome two days afterwards.[2] On my advice they sent to him a Mahomedan

1. St. Thomas's Mount, or Big Mount, is eight miles south-west of Madras. Manucci tells us elsewhere that he had a house and garden there; this was in addition to his house outside Tom Clarke's gate, between the Fort and the old Black Town. The latter house must have been destroyed in 1746, when the French cleared the ground to form a *glacis*.
2. According to the Madras records in Wheeler, i. 382, Da,ud Khan reached San Thome on the night of January 29, O.S. (February 9, N.S.). This accords fairly closely with Manucci's dates. Khwajah Ahmad must be the man styled 'Moollah' in the Records, and Narapa is there 'Narrain' or

servant of and trader under the Company, named Coja Ammad (Khwajah Ahmad), as also another merchant of the town named Narapa. But the second man fell ill, and only the first-named went; I went also.

There I found the general, the *diwan*, the *bakhshi*, and all the officers assembled. They received me most cordially, showing many signs of joy and embracing me. They sent without delay [99] for Khwajah Ahmad, who appeared at once. They directed him to inform the governor of Madras that they desired his presence at San Thome. They had important matters to communicate to him. If he could not come himself, would be send the second and third in council [February 4 or 15]. Then Da,ud Khan and the *diwan* turned towards me, and said I must confirm to those gentlemen (the English) whatever Khwajah Ahmad had been ordered to report to them. Then, taking me aside privately, they told me to be sure and tell the said governor to come himself without fail, or send the two others of his council. They said we must both of us return to San Thome, showing thereby that they had no confidence in Khwajah Ahmad, and had no belief in his truthfulness.

When we arrived at Madras we went together to see the governor, and told him what the Mahomedans had charged us to say to him. To this he replied that he neither meant to go himself nor send any of his council. He declined to do so on several grounds, principally because neither the second nor the third, nor anyone else, could speak 'Maure' [the language spoken by Mahomedans]. But he urged me earnestly to return to the general [Da,ud Khan] along with Khwajah Ahmad, and explain the reasons which hindered him from complying with his request. If he had any negotiations to make with him and his council, he could conduct them safely through Khwajah Ahmad as their qualified procurator.

The real reason why the governor declined to send anyone is that he feared the Mahomedans might oblige them by force to execute some writing, by which they undertook to be responsible for all piracies throughout the seas and on all the coasts of India. This is what they (the Mahomedans) had done at Surat to the other directors of the companies of France, Holland, and

'Paupa' (see Wheeler, p. 382, entry of January 28, and p. 384, entry of January 30). Manucci is not mentioned.

England.[1] Or he feared they might be seized and constrained to pay considerable sums to recover their liberty. This was a customary enough act among the Mahomedans, and yet it would greatly injure their Company.

However, Khwajah Ahmad and I returned to San Thome. I repeated to Da,ud Khan and the *diwan* all that the governor had said to me. As I was about to leave I perceived that things were approaching a rupture, whereupon I humbly besought them not to employ me in such thorny affairs. The intention of the two Mahomedans was to make use of me as mediator between the two parties. They had great faith in me because I spoke the language fairly well, and they imagined that without harming much the one or the other, I should deal with things to their advantage, and that in some degree I should adopt their side rather than the other.

Thus they laid before my eyes the great danger the English stood in of losing Madras. In so doing they somehow forgot that I, too, had been suckled in Europe as much as the English; that for the honour of my country and of all the other European nations, I was under greater obligation to them [the English] than I could possibly be to the Mahomedans. Under these circumstances I parted from them as civilly as I could, and on sufficiently good terms, in order to be able to advise the governor of what; I thought best for his reputation and the defence of the town.

Khwajah Ahmad remained behind at San Thome as agent, although to all appearance the Mahomedans [100] had little confidence in him. They said loudly that they must have Englishmen of the Council with whom to treat. To this demand they joined a good deal of invective, launched at that nation. Furthermore, they asserted they had a letter from Aurangzeb,[2] which could be communicated to no one but those gentlemen [the English council]. The affairs referred to in it were of such importance

1. This reason appears in the official Consultation (see Wheeler, i. 385, entry of February 4, 1702).
2. This was a *Hasb-ul-hukm*, or *wazir's* order, from Asad Khan, *wazir*, dated in the forty-fifth year (November 17, 1701). It interdicted trade with all Europeans on account of piracies committed by them contrary to written agreements. Their goods were to be seized and their persons confined (see Wheeler, i. 386). There was also a demand for 700,000 *pagodas*, the value of goods recovered from the wreck of the *Advice*, Aurangzeb claiming all such salvage as droits of the Crown.

that it was absolutely imperative for them and the English to confer on them. They added that the agent sent to them was a low and contemptible man—a personage, in one word, quite unsuited for the business in hand.

Khwajah Ahmad conveyed to the governor all that had been done and said, together with the menaces and ridiculous pretensions of Da,ud Khan. But the latter [Mr. Pitt], without putting himself otherwise to any particular trouble, began all the same his preparations to receive him, should he take it into his head to pay him a visit. With dauntless courage he went in person to inspect the fortifications of the town, caused the gates to be strengthened, and doubled the sentries. Every night he saw that the rounds were constantly on the move, and kept the sentries on the alert.

When this was reported to the general [Da,ud Khan], he grew still more angry with the governor. His resolve was that in every particular the English must submit to him, or he would besiege their town. Thus that very night it chanced that some thirty loads of fine cloth passed close to San Thome. The goods had been dispatched by the merchants of the company. He caused these to be stopped [February 6 or 17]; and although the total value did not exceed six thousand *patacas* [Rs. 12,000], the loss was felt all the same. The next day he sent some horsemen with some men on foot, who took possession of three villages dependent on this town.[1] Next he stopped the entry of all articles into the suburbs, and prevented the receipt of all supplies.

Pushed to an extremity, the English sent to ask under what orders he had resorted to these severities, by what authority he had occupied those villages, confiscated the cloth belonging to the Company, and was proceeding daily to further seizures. They asked also why he had made prisoners of the native merchants of the Company residing up-country, why he had seized the money and goods appertaining to the said Company.

To the whole of this the general replied that he had a letter

1. The three villages were Egmore, Pursewaukum, and Triplicane (Wheeler, i. 389). Egmore (seven + villages) is two miles west of the Fort; Pursewaukum (Palas-tree + village), the same distance in the same general direction; Triplicane (Holy + white lotus + tank) is one and three-quarter miles south-south-west of the Fort ('Madras Manual of Administration,' iii. 446, 448, 449).

from the king ordering him to stop the trade of all European nations, more especially that of the English. He was directed to restrict their movements and treat them somewhat rigorously Now these people call a little rigour' what would be looked on in Europe as the severest repression. He sent the governor a copy of the letter [February 6 or 17].

The reason for this order is that which I have already recorded (IV. 33)—namely, that the European pirates had in the previous year taken several Mahomedan ships belonging to surat merchants, causing them very heavy loss; so much so that they had closed the doors of their warehouses and stopped their entire trade. This did great harm to Aurangzeb, who lost greatly by the stoppage of trade. The complaints and lamentations raised had come to his majesty's ears, and he had resolved to set matters right by forcing all the European nations to free the seas, and make them safe by hunting down the said pirates. He also required them to give compensation for the plundered merchandise. His majesty's will was that, after all possible efforts had been made to find out which nation the pirates belonged to, they [? the money compensations] should be divided among the merchants who had been robbed.

However, Da,ud Khan and the *diwan*, having come to the conclusion that the English were quite resolved on resistance, that the town was fairly strong and very well [101] provided with artillery, and had a garrison of eight hundred seasoned soldiers, decided to send a message asking the governor to send me to San Thome. They were ready to discuss matters with me and settle the dispute to the advantage of the Company. In spite of some time having elapsed without my having seen the one or the other of the parties, the governor lost no time in sending me.

After an exchange of the usual compliments, Da,ud Khan began his reproaches about the English, whom he designated as over-proud and defers of his king's orders. In reply, I laid before him several arguments, which I will not set forth, to avoid wearying my readers. All I will mention is that I showed to him the great harm being done to the king's interests by the way he was acting. For these nations, worn out by such continuous ill-treatment, must inevitably in the end leave the country and close their trade. But as soon as ever they got out to sea, they would capture every merchant vessel they came across.

They would make descents on the ports upon the sea-shore, would carry off all they could find, would give quarter neither to rich nor poor, and wherever they landed would spread fire and desolation.

To all this I added that if they declined to listen To these arguments, so important in the interest of their king, I would, being his (the king's) servant, go to the court myself and prove to him the innocence of the English and the injustice being done to all Europeans. No consideration was being paid to the fact that these merchants were neither the defenders nor the protectors of these pirates, from whom they also suffered, and it was this very cause that made it impossible for any of the European nations to suppress them, or give the king the undertaking that he demanded.

In spite of this, Da,ud Khan wrote to the French at Pondicherry, the Dutch at Negapatam, and the Danes at Tranquebar, calling on them to send men and ships to help him against the English at Madras. These people, all of them, made excuses. While this was in progress attempts were made to appease the Mahomedans by pleasant words and making them limited promises. They were not thereby deterred from continuing their investment [of Madras], although carrying it out less rigorously than at first. In fact, four Englishmen who had been made prisoners at San Thome by Da,ud Khan's orders, when on their way from Cuddalore, were now released and sent here (Madras), each being presented with a *chaal* (shawl).[1]

I communicated to Monsieur Martin, governor of Pondicherry, all that happened between the Mahomedans and the English. I told him it would be a good thing to send some men to Da,ud Khan and the *diwan*, so as to turn their minds from doing at Pondicherry what they were doing at Madras. Thus that governor (Martin), who is extremely prudent and well versed in the Mahomedan ways of governing, decided to send one person with some presents for Da,ud Khan, the *diwan*, and some other officials. Consequently, on the 15th of the month of March of this year [1702], Monsieur Desprez,[2] a merchant

1. These were sailors from the wrecked vessel, the *Advice* (see Wheeler, i. 392).
2. Desprez was a son-in-law of Governor Martin. He is mentioned as secretary at Pondicherry in September, 1699, in A. Launay, 'Histoire des

of the Royal Company, arrived at San Thome, and at once informed me of his presence, sending me a letter from the governor. In it Monsieur Martin recommended to me this gentleman, and prayed me to aid and assist him in his negotiations with Da,ud Khan [102] and the other officials.

As soon as I heard this news I threw up all the business I had at Madras, and transferred myself in all haste to San Thome, wishing to be of use to the French to the utmost of my powers. This desire was increased by the fact that I have always esteemed, and shall continue to esteem, them by reason of their fine qualities, and the honourable attentions with which they have overwhelmed me.

After I had arrived at San Thome I had a conversation with the said Monsieur Desprez. I found him very much troubled; for never before, all his life long, had he been concerned in a similar business, and had never paid a visit to a Mahomedan of this rank. I gave him encouragement, and told him I would do all that was necessary to carry through the affairs of the Royal Company. I would accompany him on his visit to Da,ud Khan, the *diwan*, and the *bukhshi*, each one separately. This I did, and he was well received by these lords, who gave him many testimonies of the regard in which they held the French, and betrayed to him their pleasure at the French having sent to compliment them so very politely.

Monsieur Desprez had brought a present for Da,ud Khan and one for the *diwan*, and never dreamt that the *bakhshi* would also require to be remembered. But I adjusted all that. I observed that there was enough in what he had brought to bear division into three parts. This I did. In this way they were highly contented, and he obtained his leave to depart after a very short delay. It took him only eight days to get through the business. When he said good-bye, the *nawab* and all the other principal officials requested him to assure his governor of their friendship. He might live unconcerned, nor need he have

---

Missions de I'Inde (Société des Missions Etrangères).' i. 9. Mademoiselle Desprez was married at Pondicherry on February 22, 1705, to Claude Boyuin, Chevalier d'Hardancourt, an official of the French Company (see Part V., fol. 36). In the Madras Records the arrival of 'the French Secretary from Pollicherry with presents' is noted under March 5 (March 16, N.S.), 1702.

the slightest doubt about the respect they had for him personally; and in all that lay in their power, they would be always ready to help the French of the Royal Company. It sufficed that Monsieur Manouchy was the governor's friend to ensure their giving all the help that lay in their power, for was not he (Manucci) loved and respected by all the ministers of Aurangzeb?

Da,ud Khan sent to Monsieur Martin a very fine horse, valued at one thousand rupees, along with a costly set of robes; another set was given to the said Monsieur Desprez. The *diwan* and *bakhshi* also gave him a very good set each, and sent him off in a satisfactory manner. He bore with him a complimentary letter to the governor, and the latter was highly satisfied, being hardly able to contain himself for joy at being thus delivered from such rascals.

On the 22nd of the same month of March [1702] two Dutchmen appeared at San Thome;[1] they had been sent by the governor of Negapatam, being accompanied by ten half-castes and thirty armed messengers (*pions*), and bringing a considerable present. The head of this embassy was Monsieur Van derburg, the same who made over Pondicherry to the French on the conclusion of peace. He delivered it to Messieurs Des Augers and Martin.[2]

1. March 6, 1702: 'Receipt of advice from the spy Braminy from St. Thoma of the arrival there of the Dutch from Policat with a present for the Nabob'; March 13, 1702: 'Note of the advice from the Mulla at St. Thoma that the Dutch attended the Nabob with their Present' ('Fort St. George Public Consultations,' xxxi. 70, 73, 74). No entry of this business has been found in the Archives at the Hague.
2. The commander of the fleet sent off in 1698 to receive possession of Pondicherry was named Des Augiers. Martin arrived there from Bengal in the *Gaillard* on March 16, 1699 (Dr. Jules Sottas, 'Histoire,' 404, 408). Difficulties arose about the terms of restitution, and these were not adjusted until an agreement was drawn up on September 13, 1699. Of this writing a copy in French is attached to the General Letter from Batavia of January 20, 1700, now in the Archives at the Hague. It is executed by Martin, De Chalonge, and Cordier (Desprez, secretary), on behalf of the Royal Company of France; and on the other side by Johan Jacob Weitnaems and Pieter van der Burg (Steven Vimont, clerk), on behalf of the Dutch authorities at Negapatam; Dirck Comans, Governor and Director on the Choromandal Coast; Laurens Pit, Extraordinary Councillor and late Governor; and the other members of Council. A sum of 16,000 *pagodas* was

Da,ud Khan received these Dutchmen fairly well, and offered them many delicate attentions. Yet he went on as before with the investment of Madras, persisting in his attempt to rob the English of much money. On the other hand, the governor, still more obstinate than he, refused absolutely to give him anything. He was the more of this view that the investment was not carried out rigorously.

However, the English had great suspicions that those four wretched Portuguese traders at San Thome might do them harm with the Mahomedans, and might envenom their minds and stimulate their acts by [103] evil reports. All this was quite unfounded; for the inhabitants of San Thome are under a thousand obligations to the English of Madras, who have always protected them, and frequently furnished them with the means of support. Their suspicions were increased because the Lord Bishop of the place, called Dom Gaspar Alfonso, a member of the Society of Jesus, was the intimate friend of Da,ud Khan and of the *diwan*. The English were afraid he might speak evil of them. Furthermore, he had forwarded a protest to the governor of Madras under cover of a letter, doing this without any sort of grounds or reason.

LETTER OF THE BISHOP OF SAN THOME TO THE GOVERNOR OF MADRAS.[1]

Sir,

As I have received precise information that your lordship is resolved to send two ships to this port to bombard the town

---

to be paid down, and a further 8,000 *pagodas* in two equal instalments at the end of six and twelve months, with interest at 6 per cent, per annum. The Dutch evacuation was to be entirely completed on October 8, 1699. P. van der Burg is described as 'merchant and treasurer at the castle of Nega patam.' Apparently he is the man named by D. Havart, 'Op en Onder-gang,' Deel I, pp. 43, 55, as being head of Porto Novo in 1691, and previously at Tegenapatam (Cuddalore).

1. A contemporary translation is printed in Wheeler, i. 394. The date as there given is February 12, 1702, which is correct, and not the 22nd. The preposterous claim to San Thome as a Portuguese town should be noticed. It had been taken from them by the Qutb Shahi king in 1662, and never restored in sovereignty. They only returned there on sufferance about 1686.

and destroy it, I have decided to prepare the present letter and send it to your lordship with the enclosed protest.

I demand first of all most humbly of your lordship that you may be pleased to desist from this intention, because the traders of this place do not deserve such treatment. They have behaved on all occasions as trusty friends, and have always displayed marks of gratitude for the kind acts done to them by your lordship.

Furthermore, if your lordship will not desist, I deliver to him the enclosed protest in the name of the King of Portugal, to whom this town belongs. Your lordship must not be offended at this protest, for it is founded on justice and on our rights, and not intended to break off the friendship and regard owing by me to your lordship. For this reason I hope that you will receive it with the same civility with which I present it to your lordship, whom God have in His holy keeping.

At San Thome this 22nd of February, 1702.

Your most humble servant and friend.

The Bishop of Meliapur.

Protest of the Bishop of San Thome to the Governor of Madras

To the Governor of Madras:

I, Dom Gaspar Alfonso, bishop of the town of San Thome of Beliapur, member of his majesty's council, in the absence of Lucas Luiz da Oliveira,[1] chief captain, deceased.

We have learnt by a trustworthy report coming from the said fortress of Madraspatam that your lordship, upon the advice of his council, has made ready one or two ships fitted up with warlike instruments of destruction, intending to send them to this port to destroy the town of San Thome.

We are willing to believe that this is no more than a rumour, and that your lordship will not carry out what is talked about; for this town belongs to the King of Portugal; it is under his flag, it has a bishop, a chief captain, a judge, and all the other officials usually found in a town governed by him. We trust

1. There is a story about this Lucas Luiz da Oliveira given farther on (see fol. 207). He was in office on June 10, 1698 (Wheeler, i. 327), but I have not traced when he died. This protest is even in Wheeler, p. 395.

your lordship will not break the peace existing for so many years between the crowns of the most exalted Kings of Great Britain and of Portugal, nor act contrary thereto. Principally we do so because the inhabitants of this town have given no occasion, but have conducted themselves [104] under every circumstance that has arisen as trusty friends. However, if your lordship comes to the determination to act contrary to all these arguments, and break off the friendship between the two crowns and between us, we protest not once only, but several times, as is required by law, on behalf of the King of Portugal and on the part of the town, against all the injury and damage that may thereby result. Your lordship will have to render a full account thereof to the most exalted King of Great Britain, before whom our complaint will be carried, if your lordship acts to the prejudice of the King of Portugal and of this town. We ask him in all earnestness that he be pleased to accept this protest which we offer to him in all good faith, to the end of securing justice and our rights.

At San Thome, this 22nd of February, 1702.

DOM GASPER ALFONSO,
Bishop of Meliapur.

On April 3 [1702] Da,ud Khan sent away the Dutch envoy, having treated him rather coldly and granted him none of the things he demanded. This gentleman had asked for some villages. The general gave an absolute refusal, causing them to part far from satisfied with each other.

The investment of Madras continues, but in a very sluggish manner. However, Da,ud Khan gives out that he has no intention of abandoning it until he receives his king's orders to that effect.

With regard to the protest of the Bishop of San Thome entered above, I feel bound to remark that the said town belongs rightly to the Mahomedans, let Monsieur de Meliapur say what he pleases. But to set forth the matter properly and the present condition of the town, it is necessary to know that it is of very great extent, that the Mahomedans occupy the most important and far the larger part of it; and that they wield the government, while the Portuguese hold but a narrow space, which, taking it at its best, would not be large enough for one notable parish in European towns.

It is quite true that their (the Portuguese) houses are built right in the centre of the town; all the same, they are no longer its masters; on the contrary, it may be said that they are besieged within it from all sides. They are unable to issue an order there of the most insignificant, sort. Further, the Mogul and those who govern the Karnatik on his behalf do not regard it (San Thome) as belonging to the Portuguese any more than to the other European nations in India. This is clear from the Portuguese exercising no authority within it, their principal, not to say their sole, privilege being to fly their standard upon feast-days and Sundays. Hardly need we add that they are often interfered with even in this shadow of power, as I have already recorded (IV. 27, 28).

There can, then, be nothing more unfounded than the pretensions of this bishop, who wants through his protest to hinder the English, when they find themselves unjustly oppressed by the Mahomedans, from attacking those infidels in their own territory. Thus no very great attention was paid to him; and if there had been the power, as there was the will, there can be no doubt that before this time the English would have forced them (the Mahomedans) by a counter-attack to raise the siege of this town (Madras).

On April 20, 1702, Da,ud Khan received a letter from the Queen of Terchenepali (Trichinopoly), tributary to the Mogul, wherein this ruler begged him to undertake in person to assist her in the war she was obliged to wage against the Prince of Aurapaliam (Udayar-palaiyam),[1] another tributary of the Mughal. This man had already seized some of her towns. The letter stated with much exaggeration the iniquity of the rajah's proceedings, and was filled [105] with humble words and prayers intended to influence the general to come to her aid. With it came some very fine presents to be sent on to Aurangzeb, some for Da,ud Khan and some for the *diwan*. They consisted in a number of valuable trinkets and precious stones for the king, twenty thousand rupees in silver coin for the general, and ten thousand for the *diwan*—a metal with more virtues in the eyes

1. This rajah and the Queen of Trichinopoly and Madura have been already named on IV., fol. 63.

of these gentry than the most polished orations or the most loquacious tongues.

Still, the present did not work all the effects that the queen might have anticipated. Maybe this was not from want of will, for Da,ud Khan at the time was involved in this siege of Madras, so he confined himself to sending her a few troops. In his reply he notified to her how grieved he was at not being able to do more for her relief.

After the general had sat some two months in front of Madras, he recognised that all his efforts and all his trouble did not advance very much his business or his designs, that the English troubled their heads very little about the exertions he was making to annoy them. All this forced upon him the secret thought that he must withdraw. But before taking any overt step he intimated to Governor Pitt through me that the orders about the English received from the court were very severe and very precise. In fact, the king had given him a distinct command to allow them no rest until they had made complete reparation for the damage done by the pirates to the Mahomedans. Still, he saw plainly for his own part that it was most unfair, and that they had neither art nor part in the thefts of these scourers of the ocean. As a consequence he felt constrained to secure them terms. If they would make him a substantial payment, he undertook to demonstrate their innocence in such a way to his majesty that inevitably they must be restored to his good graces. 'But,' added he, 'I cannot carry this out without a reward proportionate to the service which I undertake to render, for both my honour and my interests require that the thing take place in this way.'

To speak the truth, he was not far wrong in what he said, for nothing is more disastrous to the general of an army among the Mahomedans than to appear before a fortress for a siege and yet draw no profit therefrom. Still more is this the case when the siege has been actually begun and persevered in for some time. For it does not matter specially whether they succeed in taking the place or not; on the contrary, they do all they can to prolong a siege as much as possible. Provided it suits their own interests, they trouble themselves little about those of the king or the honour of his arms. Thus what would be held in Europe as cowardice and open treason counts among them, if not for an act of high policy and the conduct of an able man, at any rate for a venial fault, and a proof that a man is acute enough to work things to his own advantage.

The amount asked by the general, to start with, was exorbitant, coming to nothing under five *lakhs* of rupees, which amounts to about two hundred and fifty thousand crowns (*écus*) [106]. The English rejected this proposal, as one may suppose, with a great deal of heat, and showed its injustice in emphatic terms. In the end, after other negotiations and much going back and fore between the two sides, it was agreed that they should pay twenty-five thousand rupees.[1]

Governor Pitt was brought with difficulty to give his consent. He said it was money thrown away. Only six months ago he made these gentlemen a very fine present. They had then assured him of their friendship and their protection. If they had paid no heed to their first engagement, they would pay as little to the second they now proffered. It would be seen that time after time they would return to the charge, whenever they took it into their heads that they wanted some money. He thought it more in accordance with the honour and the interest of the company to let the siege go on until reinforcements arrived from Europe. When that happened, they could by force of arms compel these infidels to confine themselves within the conditions of any treaty then made with them.

But at last the pressing solicitations of certain traders, European and Hindu, setting forth the misery endured by the smaller people and the poor of the place, compelled the governor to countersign an agreement to pay the above-named sum. On their side, the Mahomedans promised to raise the blockade and secure the return of the cloth and money they had seized. All these negotiations occupied nearly one month, and they were not completely finished until May 17.[2] On that day the

1. Sunday, May 3, 1702: 'Twenty thousand Rupees are to be paid by the English to the Nabob, and five thousand privately to the Dewan' (Wheeler, i. 405).
2. May 5, 1702, in the official records (Wheeler, i. 406). By the New Style it would be May 16. On May 11 (O.S.) Mr. Bugden, secretary, and Narrain were sent with the presents. On their way they were informed that the Nawab had left, but the *Diwan* would conclude the business ('Public Consultations, Fort St. George,' xxxi. 104-106).

blockade was raised, and the English on their side made ready to carry out what they had promised.

To this intent they sent on the twenty-fifth of the said month an official of the Company to San Thome to carry out the business. But when he arrived at a village called Triblicani (Triplicane),[1] half way to that town, he learnt that the general and all his troops had departed, whereby he was forced to retrace his steps before anything had been done. The next day I visited Big Mount, where I found the *nawab* and the *diwan* in my house. I expressed my joy at the termination of the dispute. On their side they gave me a thousand marks of kindness and favour. I entertained and regaled them to such extent as was in my power. They told me it was the fault of the English that things had not been settled much earlier, and their procrastination was the cause of it. Soon I took my leave, and we separated with numerous expressions on both sides of esteem and friendship. They informed me that they left behind their procurator (? *wakil*) to carry out the conditions they had agreed on with the English and receive the promised money.

Some time back we left Aurangzeb engaged in besieging the fortress of Khelna (IV. 33). The prince still persists though with small success. On his side the Shiva Ji (Mahrattahs) exerts himself to frustrate him and cause him as much injury as possible. He selects the spots that he deems the most unprotected, and he has recently fallen upon the town of Borampar (Burhanpur), and after making of it a scene of desolation, has captured and carried off the governor. His prisoner could only secure release by force of paying money.

The rajah turned his arms next [107] in the direction of Gulkandah. After appearing before that town, he entered it as into a conquered country, menaced it with fire and sword, and in the end forced the governor to pay him a considerable sum to save it from pillage.

The aged monarch heard of all these disasters, and felt them to the quick. He revolved in his mind all sorts of plans for preventing in the future such losses and disorders. They injure

1. Tiruvallikkéni, *tiru*, 'holy' + *alii*. 'white lotus' + *kéni*, 'tank.' Triplicane is now part of Madras, one and three-quarter miles south-south-west of the Fort. The land is all built over ('Madras Manual of Administration,' iii. 449).

him both in his honour and his interests. He has observed that all these things are principally due to the great agility of the Shiva Ji cavalry in carrying out their master's orders; he has, therefore, decided—and he could not do otherwise—to equip for war some fifteen thousand camels, and mount as many men on them, fitted out with all the arms and necessary *matériel* for making a good defence while on the march. He has no doubt that this device will prove most efficacious for forestalling and stopping the endless ravages of this rajah. The reason is that these animals can easily, without being much distressed, cover forty or fifty leagues every day. Such a journey cannot be accomplished by the smartest cavalry. If this corps can be formed, it will infallibly answer his purpose. But, while it is easy to procure camels, it is almost impossible to find enough men able to stand the tossing motion of these beasts. The men trained to ride them in this fashion are extremely few.

In the month of May in the same year [1702] Aurangzeb, knowing the rainy season would soon arrive, and aware of the impossiblity of undertaking anything until it was completely over, found it advisable to make a last effort to take the fort of Khelna. For this purpose he invested it still more strictly, having now some better troops. All his attempts were useless— nay, the enemy cut into pieces for him nearly six thousand *mansabdars* (officers). They were killed among the hills where that fort is situated. From this cause he was forced to abandon the enterprise, putting it off to a season and occasion more favourable to his designs.[1]

Everybody in India knows that Agrah is the place where the Mogul collects all his treasure, and thence withdraws subsequently such money as is required for the payment of his troops, even when the army is on the march. This money arrives only at intervals, and is used to pay those troops who serve directly under his orders. By this procedure he now and again suffers loss; for in spite of these remittances being furnished with a strong escort, there are some of his children who do not invariably maintain the respect and loyalty due to their king and their father.

Not long ago A'zam-tara [*i.e.*, A'zam Shah] did something

1. The subject of Khelna siege is resumed on IV., fol. 116.

to prove the above to be true. There was on its way to Aurangzeb's army [108] a considerable sum of money destined for the payment of his soldiers. He [A'zam Shah] stopped the convoy and took the money. It must be admitted that the prince wrote at the same time a most respectful letter to his father, attempting excuses for the act by stating the straits he was in for money. This was the reason forcing him to take what had been meant for his father's use. Furthermore, his majesty knew well where to find more. However, in spite of all this submissive language and excuses, the old man resented this trick most acutely, without making any outward sign. Seeing there was no remedy, he was content to hide his displeasure for fear of making matters worse.

In the course of my history I have often spoken of the general Ja'far Khan. He was the man of all those at court who made the greatest show, and was the most judicious in dealing with all sorts of people. What I have already said will be sufficient proof of that; but as I had forgotten some of his doings, which have since come to mind, I think it right not to deprive the attentive reader of the pleasure of hearing about them. Besides, what is done in India is so different from the habits and customs of Europe, that I imagine the smallest things happening there are worth communicating to Europeans.

The justice meted out by this lord to a man, who supplied his household with herbs and vegetables during his journey to Kashmir, marks equally his uprightness of mind and the profuseness of his expenditure. This man, then, of whom I speak, brought his accounts at the end of the year to the treasurer of this general's household, wishing to be paid for the supplies he had sent in. Having examined the accounts, this official found the amount so enormous that he decided to strike off the sum of eighty thousand rupees. The tradesman could not, and would not, allow this, and carried his grievance before the master of the house, and he on the instant ordered the payment of the whole demand, and forbad all further discussion.

Everybody in India knows how dear and scarce essence of roses is; though in some years it is less scarce than in others. Yet neither scarcity nor high cost deterred this general from having his horses rubbed with this liquid as a matter of course.

However, a year came in which he was forced to do without this luxury, for none could be found at any price. One of Ja'far Khan's grooms made a profit out of this dearth, for during the years of its abundance he had taken the trouble to accumulate, drop by drop, some twenty-five ounces from the drippings off the horses when he washed them. This poor man sold that quantity at fifty rupees the ounce, which placed him in easy circumstances, to the astonishment of those who heard the story.

While this noble was just and liberal, he had also a great and generous mind, and no occasion escaped him of giving proof of it. That was shown [109] more especially on an occasion, of which these are the details. The king took it into his head to fix the costume of the women in his harem, dividing them into groups or companies—that is, so many got up in such a manner and in such colours, another company in another colour, and so on for the whole of them. He was also anxious that these clothes should all be of the finest materials procurable. But when he set to work on this fantastic idea, he found there were three pieces of stuff deficient in the quantity required for one of the divisions. He had these pieces searched for everywhere, but nowhere could they be found. Finally, they told him that he might perhaps find some pieces at Ja'far Khan's, for he was always provided with whatever was most scarce and curious.

The king sent at once and requested him, if he had any pieces of this kind, to be good enough to send him the three of which he was in want. The noble was overjoyed at the chance of showing his eagerness to contribute to his majesty's gratification. However, giving no manifestation of his feelings, he sent for his first chamberlain, and ordered him to see if there were any similar pieces of stuff in his wardrobe. The man, having searched, came back and reported to him that there were close on one thousand pieces. 'Let there be sent,' answered he, 'one hundred to his majesty;' but the words were said with such a liberal and satisfied air, that the joy he felt in adding to the gratification of his king was evident in his eyes and countenance.

But these were not the only good qualities with which this noble was endowed. It can be said that if those I have just recorded made him loved and respected by man, there were others that would have recommended him highly in the sight of

God had he been a faithful Christian. In particular, he was extremely charitable, and his whole life was full of actions instigated by this virtue.

The trick he played upon his wife, wishing to test her, forms a most remarkable anecdote. One night he was coming back from the court and was about to enter his house, when near his door he met a poor Persian, who asked alms of him in humble tones. 'Draw nearer to the door,' replied he, 'and wait a moment for me; I will be sure and come back to you at once.' Then he entered and went straight to his wife's room, and asked her to be good enough to lend him ten thousand rupees. The lady answered somewhat coldly that she had no money by her. He said nothing. She was already in bed, so he thrust his foot quietly under the bedstead without being perceived by her or any of those present in the room, and got hold of one of her slippers, which he carried off and sent out to the beggar. This was a most extraordinary piece of almsgiving, for it was worth more than fifty thousand rupees. However, the princess, on awaking, wanted to get up but could not find her slipper. She began an unheard-of outcry, scolded one woman and had another beaten, but without finding what she was searching for.

While this hullabaloo was going on, Ja'far Khan came in, and put her partially out of pain by telling her that it was no use her looking any more for her slipper, for he had taken it and given it in alms to a beggar, she having no money to lend to him for the purpose. The princess was much grieved at the loss of her slipper. However, she did not lose her head, but forthwith sent for the beggar, having first obtained her husband's permission. The condition he imposed was that she should give the man ten thousand rupees before taking back what had been given to him. This plan was carried out. The beggar was found, and he gave back the slipper in return for a payment of ten thousand rupees—an alms which savoured of extravagance, even for a man as rich as Ja'far Khan possibly was. This fact the princess told the beggar pretty plainly, but she had to obey, as it was the general's wish.

[Omitted, a story of the King of Babylon, a merchant, and a jewel, it being neither Indian nor historical (fols. 110-113).]

[Omitted, for the same reason, another story of an Indian merchant who takes jewels for sale to Babylon (fols. 113-116).]

[116J Although Aurangzeb had lost six thousand *mansabdars* (officers) in besieging the fort of Khelna,[1] he still persisted. Finding that by force his designs were not advanced, he had recourse to the metal that possesses so much power over man, and by its means he won over the officer holding the gates. This man, like a coward, allowed the imperialists to enter, and they became masters of the place during the night of June 28 [1702].[2] This campaign was carried through by the care and exertions of the grand *wazir*, Asad Khan. The king was so well pleased that he accorded him the right of seating himself in the hall of audience during the sovereign's administration of justice. This distinction and mark of honour is so great that no king for many a year had granted it to any subject.

The Prince Shah 'Alam has also greatly distinguished himself in the wars, and has greatly contributed by his valour and conduct to the success of his father the emperor's arms. He has thereby acquired renown in the army and among the people. This result has not slightly inquieted the old man; however, he always has his wits about him, and whatever affair arises never fails to obviate anything likely to produce a diminution of his own power, or be prejudicial to his own acquired fame. He therefore decided to write a letter to the prince, his son, full of every mark of tenderness and love that a good father could show to a passionately adored child. The letter ran something in this way:

'My Dear Son,

'You can believe that I could have no greater joy than learning all the happy results gained by my arms under your orders. Renown trumpets everywhere the glory that you are continually adding to. Be assured that the interest I take in this is as great as if I had myself done all these fine things. Nor am I wrong in so doing, for what greater pleasure is there for an old man like me, whose only thought must be his departare

1. The subject of Khelna is continued here from IV., fols. 33 and 107.
2. If this date is Old Style, it agrees with the Mahomedan date in the 'Ma,asir-i-'Alamgiri,' p. 457 (see *ante*, note 43 to fol. 33).

from this world, than to have a son worthy of taking his place and ascending the throne of Taimur-i-lang. I am confident also that you have for me not only the feelings that Nature inspires, but in addition those that a great prince ought to have towards his king. For, in spite of some rumours being spread abroad that you contemplate assuming power as King of the World, for which you possess the qualifications, I have always considered it was your enemies who published such assertions with a view to harming you. Since I am aware of your moderation, I believe you will never dream of exercising such a power, except after the death of him to whom you owe your days. Meanwhile, until it please Heaven to withdraw me, I press you to accept the title of Merasha (Miran Shah), which is [117] that, as you know, given by Taimur-i-lang to his son. Furthermore, I pray you to remember me after my death. As a token of the memory that you would wish to perpetuate of a good father, and that your people may have ever before their eyes the acts of Aurangzeb, I ask you to make use after my death of the following inscriptions upon the money you will order to be coined:

' "I stamp my coin on the seven planets;
I sound my drums up to the clear moon;
I, Miran Shah, king all-powerful, without rival."

In addition I wish you every kind of happiness, and am, etc.'

This is the manner in which this old man expressed himself, adding several phrases common in their language, intimating that all things belonged to him (Shah 'Alam), and that, properly speaking, all the fruit he (Aurangzeb) would reap for his labour and trouble would be the thought of leaving after his death a wise and understanding son to occupy his place.

It was upon August 14 in the same year (1702) that Da,ud Khan, deputy governor of the Karnatik, made himself master of the fortress of Velours (Vellore, Vellur).[1] The same means were

1. Vel, 'acacia arabica' + *ūr*, 'village,' a town in the North Arcot district, seventy-eight miles west of Madras ('Madras Manual of Administration,' 975), Grant-Duff ('Mahrattas,' 180) assigns the surrender of Vellur to 1704. Sa'adatullah Khan was placed in charge. On fol. 152 we are told that the commandant who gave up this Fort was Ghulam 'Ali Khan,

XXXVI. Sharzah Khan, General of Bijapur

used as already indicated in the case of Khelna, money being the great moving force employed by these gentry to carry out their designs. In fine, by one method or another, they have hunted the Shiva Ji (*i.e.*, the Mahrattahs) out of the Karnatik, where he now possesses no single post, small or great.

After the fall of this fortress the deputy governor [Da,ud Khan] wrote a fine letter to the Mogul and sent him the keys of the place made in gold. In the letter he said how great was his joy in contributing to the glory of so great a monarch. He knew very well, it is true, that nothing in his person or efforts could possibly augment in the slightest degree what Renown had already proclaimed in his majesty's honour. But he felt some secret pleasure in seeing that what he had accomplished contributed to his majesty's satisfaction by bringing new places of strength into subjection under him. 'Thus I am persuaded,' added he, 'that your majesty will hear this news with pleasure, and will receive with the same feeling the golden keys of Vellur which I herewith send. In conclusion, I wish to your exalted person a perfect state of health and many happy and prosperous days.'

I spoke a great deal formerly of the general Bahadur Khan, who was highly esteemed by the king on account of his bravery, also because he was the son of his wet-nurse, and thus his fosterbrother. In addition, he had taken a leading part in the warlike conquests of this king, acquiring thereby a high degree of pride and a boldness of speech rare among orientals.

This line of behaviour was displeasing to the monarch, and he thought of a means of mortifying him somewhat. With this object he directed that this general's palanquin should be placed behind that of Asad Khan, the first minister of state. But having been warned of the affront to be shown him, Bahadur Khan refrained that day from attending the audience. All he did was to order some of his men to appear there, and should they try to place Asad Khan's palanquin in his place, they should offer opposition.

His orders were only too well executed. For when it was attempted to put the other palanquin in the general's place, his soldiers resisted and raised a hot quarrel with the first minister's men. It proceeded to such lengths that blood was spilt [118]. In the end the king was forced to intervene with his authority before the fight ceased.

In spite of his having been the principal instigator, he (Aurangzeb) concealed the fact as much as ever he could. He feared the power and ability of Bahadur Khan, and he knew him to be an intimate friend of Shah 'Alam. The king feared that if Bahadur Khan learnt that the affront had been given by his orders, he might ally himself with the prince and raise a rebellion. For this reason he went a few days afterwards to visit the general, and told him he must think no more of the affair. It had occurred without his (Aurangzeb's) knowledge, and solely through the captious temper of the minister's servants. For the future, he would issue an order preventing the raising of similar disputes in regard to his rank. He should experience nothing but the gratifications which he might look for as due to his merits and his services, of which he (Aurangzeb) would cherish an eternal remembrance. Bahadur Khan appeared satisfied with this sort of excuse, and upon this the quarrel was dropped.

When Khelna was ceded Aurangzeb felt no little satisfaction, and he gave the necessary orders for garrisoning it. That done, his next move was to effect his retirement. In that matter the Mahrattahs were far from idle, and discovering that the old man's only anxiety was to beat a retreat, they invaded the province of Barar. The officer in charge as governor there was the 'Ali Mardan Khan, of whom I have spoken before (IV. 16).[1]

They devastated every place that they found upon their route; whereupon the above officer, having gathered together all the troops he had, came against the said Mahrattahs. They thrashed him neck and crop, cut his troops to pieces, and took him prisoner. Out of their clutches he is hardly likely to come without the payment of a considerable sum by way of ransom, just as he had to do the first time he was captured in the way I have already recorded (IV. 16).

Although it might be said in a general way that since this prince ascended the throne his reign has been a continued series

1. On this man, see *ante* note 14 to Part IV., fol. 16.

of victories, still, he has not been exempt from misfortunes. Now and again accidents befall him, which inflict terrible mortification upon him without lessening in the least his courage or his ambition. Neither do they diminish his dissimulation, his unfailing resource in prosperity as in adversity.

The taking of Khelna has been followed by very disagreeable incidents, caused by the heavy rains and bad weather which overtook the army on its march. The rains have been so prodigious that they have washed away all the roads, devastated the country, and ruined the inhabitants. These latter place all their hopes upon a good harvest, and this has been entirely lost to them by the tempests destroying all the grain. A famine has been produced in the royal army.

This famine, joined to the difficulty, not to say the impossibility, there was of advancing by reason of those disorders [119] and the occurrence of a most terrible pestilence, caused the loss on this occasion of more than half of the army. The distress has been so great that there were men who, unable to carry their wives with them without exposing them to public view, have been so inhuman as to prefer killing them to enduring that affront. Even the king's own household felt the sad effects of this tempest, and several ladies held very dear by the king perished, the king himself having some difficulty in escaping.

Aurangzeb had no sooner heard the news that Da,ud Khan had cleared the Karnatik of the Mahrattahs than he forwarded orders to that general to force payment from the Rajah of Tanjor, the Queen of Trichinopoly, and some other neighbouring princes of the tribute they had hitherto paid to the Mahrattahs. These sums were to be in addition to the existing tribute previously collected by him from these princes. In these orders he set forth his reasons for making such a demand. Of these, the principal was that he had disbursed enormous sums in carrying on the war against this prince (*i.e.*, Shiva Ji, or the Mahrattahs). The Mahrattahs had continuously harassed these (local) princes by their raids and never-ending pillage. At present they had been delivered from those plunderers, and were enjoying the fruit of the Mogul victories. It was only fair that they should undertake a share of the expense that all these things had put him to. He also enjoined on Da,ud Khan in express terms that he must declare war against these princes, and constrain them to comply by force of arms.

In conformity with these orders Da,ud Khan sent to demand this tribute from the king and the queen above mentioned. He also asked for three hundred elephants, two hundred from the former and one hundred from the latter. He pointed out to them that the king was in urgent need of this number of these enormous beasts, to replace those that he had lost during the war, chiefly at the siege of Khelna. It should be noted that this is no more than the beginning of a quarrel about nothing (*querelled' allemands*), which the Mogul means to force upon these poor rulers, with the object of despoiling them and becoming absolute master of all their territories and all their treasures.

For it is an almost impossible thing for them to furnish him with the number of elephants he has requisitioned. The difficulty is increased by their never having maintained a quarter of these numbers in their service. But this king strives to be master of everything, and what matters it to him by what means he secures his end? These poor rajahs asked a month's time before replying to the demand. We shall see hereafter the result of their deliberations and what will come to pass.

In the end the above king and queen, of whom I have just spoken, have complied with the Mogul demands. Rather than have a war, of which the consequences could be no less than fatal to them, they have consented to furnish to the general, not the number of elephants he claimed, but as many as could be found in their states and belonging to their subjects.

I have spoken already of Bahadur Khan, Aurangzeb's forter-brother, but I overlooked a rather curious adventure which took place at his death.[1] When he fell ill [120], he grew so much worse that in a few days all hope was gone. Thus his doctor considered it advisable to warn the king of his dangerous condition. Instantly the king went off to visit him. The patient was warned of the king's intended visit, and at once ordered the preparation of a sort of throne, most gorgeous, all adorned with precious stones, and estimated as worth nearly five millions of

1. Bahadur Khan died on the 19th Muharram, 1109 H. (August 6, 1697), aged eighty-four ('Tarikh-i-Muhammadi,' relying on 'Ma,asir-i-'Alamgiri' and the 'Diwan-i-'Abid').

rupees. Subsequently to the prince taking his seat, there were brought several trays filled with precious stones of inestimable value, some weapons, also some horses and elephants.

The king accepted all the gifts, and intimated to him his sorrow at his illness. Then that noble began complimentary speeches, thanking his majesty for all his gracious favours, for all the benefits he had conferred, and imploring pardon for all his shortcomings, and the scanty gratitude he had shown for such signal condescension; for all this kindness he now felt deeply touched, and if he survived longer on earth he would give evidence by his conduct how deeply repentant he was for his faults. But since in all probability he was about to quit this world, he had no other medium for showing his sorrow except a flood of tears.

Aurangzeb replied that with all his heart he pardoned him, but there was one act for which there was no pardon possible, and he well knew what it was. With these words he withdrew, giving orders for the throne on which he had been seated to be removed to his own quarters. In spite of all the investigations made to find out this fault of Bahadur Khan's, which Aurangzeb would not pardon even on an occasion when nothing is refused, either among Mahomedans or among Hindus, no one ever succeeded in knowing what it was exactly. Only it was suspected that it was something involving the honour of the royal family.

However, people murmured at this hard-heartedness of Aurangzeb, and the number of those who talked about it was so great that he was forced to conceal the displeasure which he felt. One man paid for all; and he was the brother-in-law of Sambha Ji, Madou Ji (Madhu Ji) by name. This man's free remarks about the prince's harshness were reported. As he had a large following the king was afraid to chastise him; but, pretending a wish to do him higher honour, Aurangzeb changed his employment, and sent him to command the fortress of Gwaliyar. That place having a full number of troops, the king told him it was unnecessary to take his own men with him. This noble, delighted at the honour that he believed was being done to him in confiding to his charge the chief fortress in Hindustan, obeyed blindly; but as soon as he had entered the place he was decapitated by his majesty's orders.

[121] After the taking of Khelna, of which I spoke above (IV. 116), and the disasters following upon it during Aurangzeb's withdrawal, the Shiva Ji (*i.e.*, the Mahrattahs) threw himself once more upon the Mogul, and captured five of his officers. These men were of such importance that the king paid one hundred thousand rupees for the ransom of each of these gentlemen. After that, Aurangzeb made an attack on the fortress of Kondena (Kandanah),[1] where he is at present, and pressing the siege. Nevertheless, the Mahrattahs, without putting themselves out about that, have gone across the Narbada with fifty thousand horse. They have been formed into two divisions, and these have robbed and ravaged several provinces, among other places the town of Ceronge (Sironj), which they have plundered most fearfully.

I have spoken several times of Qasim Khan,[2] who was governor over the Pathans, as may be seen in my Second Part (II. 172). He was the man who betrayed them through the cutting up of a melon. Subsequently he governed in the country of Adouni (Aduni) in the kingdom of Visiapour (Bijapur) where an adventure happened to him which is rather curious.

There were two twin brothers, young and well grown, sons of a Hindu prince called Darumdas (Dharm Das). The mother of the youths died, and their father subsequently married again. As they did not get on with their step-mother, they quitted their father's house and went elsewhere in search of fortune. Fate decreed that they should enter the service of Qasim Khan, and they served him for a year and a half without receiving anything. At the end of

1. Kandanah, called by Shiva Ji Singhgarh, lies eleven miles south-west of Puna. It fell on the 2nd Zu,l Hijjah, 1114 H. (April 19, 1703), and was renamed by Aurangzeb 'Bakhshindah-bakhsh,' or 'Gift of the Giver' (Ma,asir-i-'Alamgiri,' 474; Thornton, 'Gazetteer,' 906; Grant-Duff, 59, 181).
2. I think that here Manucci must be confounding different men who held the same title; in fact, I have identified the man in the previous passage as Fida,e Khan (A'zam Khan). I think the man here intended is Qasim Khan, Kirmani, who late in the reign was governor of Sara, or the Bijapur Karnatik. In 1107 H. (1695-96) he marched from Aduni to join Khanahzad Khan and others. He was attacked by Santa Ji, Mahrattah, and forced to retire into a fortalice called Danderi, where he died of privation, or, as some say, poisoned himself ('Ma.asir-ul-Umara,' iii. 143; Khafi Khan, ii. 428, in 1105 H.; 'Ma,asir-i-'Alamgiri,' 374-378; Grant-Duff, 170). I can find nothing to confirm Manucci's story of Qasim Khan's death.

that time they presented a petition, begging him to order them to be paid. But, disregarding this application, he put them off with pleasant words for another six months.

At last they could endure it no longer; neither they nor their horses could last any further time. They seized the opportunity one day when he was reading the *Quran*; they entered his *darbar*, and prayed him most humbly to take compassion upon them. But instead of doing that, he replied: 'Get out of my sight, *kafirs*!' (that is, 'infidels.') But one of them pricked up courage and, drawing his sword, fell upon him and cut him to pieces.

The servants and other bystanders attempted to lay hold of the young man, and punish him for the crime that he had committed. The brother then drew his sword. Both of them turned and faced their assailants with such desperate courage that they slew twenty-five of them. At this point several persons came, and seeing what was going on, lost no time in closing the door; those who were still outside did the same, and then mounted on the wall and shot at the two Hindus with arrows and musket bullets. On seeing this, and feeling sure they could never escape alive, the young men preferred to take their own lives rather than suffer at the hands of others. Exclaiming, 'Let us die, as we were born, together,' and embracing, they plunged their daggers [122] each into the other's breast, and thus ended their existence. A similar occurrence took place in the previous year, when one Attach Kan (Atash Khan) was killed in exactly the same manner because he refused to pay his men.

[Pages 123 and 124 are blank.]

[125] I have often spoken in the preceding parts of this history of the bad conduct of the Portuguese in India, and the disorder thereby occasioned. In the present Part (IV.) I have already set forth to what lengths the passion for enriching themselves has carried the reverend Jesuit fathers. I have also stated somewhere or other (III. 229) that the tribunal of the Inquisition, ordered and established by the Church for good ends, was at Goa a perpetual source of injustice. They made use of it chiefly to overwhelm and min the innocent who had the misfortune to fall into its hands. Among several instances I had chosen that

of the reverend Father Ephraim, Capuchin, meaning to give an account of it to the public just as I learnt it from the father himself. But the haste with which I finished off my first three parts preluded me from so doing. I therefore insert it here.

This good father was a native of Nevers, of a distinguished family. Having embraced the religious life, he entered the Order of St. Francis, and was sent by his superiors to preach the Gospel in India. Passing through Madras, he was stopped there by the agent of the English Company for the purpose of affording spiritual food to the Christians inhabiting that place.[1] There he had continued to live in all innocence, having acquired a high reputation, not only as an honest man, but as a most zealous priest. He was a most rigid observer of the rules of his order. Thus things remained till 1649, when he had the misfortune to fall into the hands of the commissaries of the Inquisition established at San Thome. First of all, it must be explained what were the real reasons for his arrest, for what appeared on the surface was a mere pretext. The true reason was always concealed; it was, as one will see later on, nothing but an irreconcilable hatred and an excessive envy entertained against him by some persons of that place, the cause thereof being his virtues, his strict conduct, and the office that he held.

The first reason, then, for the detention of this excellent friar was, as admitted by the Grand Inquisitor of Goa himself on St. Mark's Day, 1651, a letter that Father Ephraim had written to Manuel Mascaregna (Mascarenhas),[2] Governor of San Thome, in which he objected to certain abuses then practised there and tolerated by him. The reason for this toleration was that the Portuguese took them for so many saintly acts, and consequently held Father Ephraim's condemnation

1. The request of the inhabitants and the Government order, both dated June 8, 1642, are given in Norbert, 'Mémoires Utiles et Nécessaires . . .' (Lucca, 1742), pp. 93-95, The matter is also referred to by Tavernier, 'Travels' (edition Ball), ii. 220. Father Ephraim died at Madras some time in 1694, his companion, Father Zenon, having passed away in 1687, aged eighty-five. Ephraim was succeeded by another French Capuchin, Father Michel Ange (in English records styled 'Michael Angelo') (Penny, 'Church in Madras,' 220, 223).
2. Manuel Mascharenhas de Almeda is referred to in the Fort St. George Record of October 27, 1646 (see *post* note 229 to Part IV., fol. 147).

to be a great liberty—nay, an attack upon religion. The reasons he alleged in his letter, hoping to bring them back to the true views of the Church, they looked on as so much damnable heresy. So fully persuaded were they of the orthodoxy of their belief in the disputed matter, and of the father's error, that the above inquisitor said to him that by Divine permission he had been allowed to sign that letter, affording thus an authentic proof that it proceeded from him. 'What it contains,' he went on, 'has been condemned not only by bachelors of law, but also by five doctors. The whole of them unanimously hold that it proceeded from a spirit tainted with the errors of Luther.'

The reason for this opinion was that at every line the father cited the Holy Scriptures, but said nothing about Saint Augustin or Saint Ambrose. The inquisitor added that, had the cardinals of the Holy Office read but once the propositions contained in the letter, they could never refrain from forthwith condemning the author to be, at the very least, stripped of his habit. 'This is why I must examine you strictly upon the doctrine and opinions of Luther.' This he said, and carried out his word most scrupulously in the first interrogatory to which the father was subjected. This was in the month of May, 1650, and they call it the general examination.

In this, after having badgered him this way and that upon his letter, and telling him that under the cloak and semblance of zeal it was crammed full of venom from the doctrines of Luther, the inquisitor added: 'It is not I who condemn you, as I have already told you, but the learned men of this town, for neither I nor these other secular priests have ever studied theology, all our knowledge being confined to the subject of canon law.'

The questions put to him upon this letter were derived from certain papers written at San Thome, being nothing but unfair commentary upon, and wrongly derived consequences [126] from, that letter. Having noticed this, Father Ephraim was unable to refrain from remarking to his judges: 'Would to God that those who drew up these writings against me were here in person, that I might answer them!' But the inquisitor, vexed that his ignorance had been noticed, interrupted him and reproved him with some temper, saying that the questions were made up in his own head without taking them from the writings of others. All the same, his assertion was obviously untrue. For the father was so close to him that he saw distinctly all that he did when drawing up his questions. Several times he addressed to him long admonitions, and introduced stories invented about him. Among others was one which concerned James I. of England, which he could have read nowhere except in the documents then lying before him.

The second cause [of the accusation] arose from two plays performed at this same San Thome at the cathedral church by order of the priest administering the bishopric. The occasion was the festival of the Assumption of the Virgin. These plays were so profane that some English, who attended at the request of the ecclesiastics themselves, made a mockery of them. They said to Father Ephraim that the Roman Catholics were profane persons, devoid of all respect for their religion. The good priest could not hear this without grief, and moved by zeal for God's house, he reproved in vigorous terms the authors of these profanations.

These were the two principal causes of his being put into prison. For if, in the statement of facts (*procès-verbal*) drawn up, there be other accusations, they were only frivolous items, manufactured after he had written the letter above referred to. This letter had so offended Hyerome (Geronimo) de Saa, the priest administering the bishopric,[1] that he assembled his friends and all of his faction to discuss whether they could find anything against the father. On the other hand, those to whom he had addressed a remonstrance, when they had so well earned it, saw now the opening for satisfying their anger. They did not allow it to slip by unused. But their accusations were so frivolous that the very inquisitor spoken of above said once to him (Father Ephraim) that no doubt all those who had sworn against him were malicious people; still, as what they had sworn concerned the Faith, their zeal was a good thing, and worthy of praise. Let the reader analyze a little the correctness of this proposition: 'They are malicious persons, but their zeal is good!' It must also be pointed out that all the accusations came from a single person, and there were no witnesses.

1. 'O Create (The believer)' of Goa, published on October 27, 1887, a document, dated Goa, August, 1636, which has an entry of the Rev. Hieronymo de Sa, theologian, archdeacon, and ecclesiastical 'Desembargador.' This is probably the person who, in 1649, was administering the Diocese of San Thome (W. R. P.).

They had to find means of executing the order [of arrest] passed against him, for he lived in a territory where the inquisitors had no jurisdiction. So the governor, Artus de Saa, on June 27, 1649, sent a Portuguese expressly to him praying him to come to San Thome. He was told that means were to be devised for reconciling him and the English Agent, with whom he was not on good terms owing to some differences between them that had arisen shortly before. The reverend father had often had recourse previously to the Portuguese, during the period of his stay at Madras, in regard to other disputes.

At this time (1649), and up to 1662, San Thome was a Portuguese possession, while Father Ephraim lived in Madras under the English flag. Tavernier's account of the proceedings against Father Ephraim should be compared ('Travels,' Ball's edition, i. 220 to 233). The English records of the period are very imperfect, but the following interesting fragments have been found with considerable difficulty by Miss M. Anstey.

I.
EXTRACT FROM SURAT GENERAL LETTER TO THE COURT OF DIRECTORS, JANUARY 10, 165½

'The Portugalls... In the time of the Late V. Roy Don Phillippo Masqurino [1646-1651] and since the Alteration of Government [at Goa][1] wee had some contending with them touching Injuries and affrounts done to your Agencie of Madraspatam occasioned by the Insolency and trechery of the friars of Santomay, who seazed, kept prisoner a long time, and after and afterwards sent him to the Inquisition of Goa, where hee was also detayned prisoner, one Friar Ephraim who was pastor or Curate unto the Mostezaes of Madraspatam; this unjust seazure and imprisonment (at the request of your Agent Ettca) wee often times complained of to the late V. Roy in espetiall, and to the now Governors at their first enterance into Authority and solicited his enfranchisement but being long delayed, the Agent Etts. seazed on the Padree Governor or cheife of their Convent of Friars at Santomay after which wee treated with them in more earnest manner, for preventing of a breach betweene them and us, argueing things with them as if wee then stood on

1. The Government was put into commission on the departure of Mascarenhas, May 31, 1651 (see Danvers, ii. 302).

equall Basis (as you may reade in one letter of ours, amongst others in the Copies of letters written in English and translated into Latine, directed unto the now Governors, dated the 25th and 28th of July last) aboute which time the friar of Santomay made his escape and soe wee were almost in despare of Friar Ephraims infranchisement though nevertheless, some few weekes after their receipt of our letters and after they had the knowledge of our prisoners escape, they sett the other at liberty, and advertized us thereof as an extraordinary favor, and out of their due respect unto the conservation of peace, unto which they pretend to stand sincerely affected, this breife story wee are confident you will have more largely from the Coast, as a business wherein they were most interessed, and therefore wee have toucht it but in breife and have advised the Agent rather to sufferance then the attempting of any Action whereby the peace betwixt us may be broaken, for they are too strong for us in India.' [O.C. No. 2228, pp. 29, 30.]

II.
TREATY BETWEEN HENRY GREENHILL, AGENT AT MADRAS, AND GOMEZ FRERA ANDRADA, CAPTAIN-GENERAL OF ST. THOME, DATED FORT ST. GEORGE, DECEMBER 30, 1651.

The preface to the treaty states that St. Thome and Fort St. George had been 'at odds by reason of preceeding disagreements Caused by the imprizonment of the Reverend father Ephraim as also the imprizonment of the Reverend Padre Governor both which at this present freely enjoy their liberty.' It is further stated that the treaty was agreed upon after 'discourse' between Agent Greenhill and Franciscus Vera de Figueredo. [O.C., No. 2238.]

III.
ERTRACT FROM FORT ST. GEORGE GENERAL LETTER TO THE COURT OF DIRECTORS, JANUARY 14, 165$\frac{1}{2}$.

'To requite the Portugalls affront in betraying the French Fryer to their bloody inquisition, wee, in Februarie last[1651], made seizure of their Padree Governor resolveing to detain him untill the other were sett at liberty but about 4 mos. after Vizt. the 11th of June [1651] in the dead of a darke night hee was conveyed over our walls with the laceing of a cott and treachery of one Richard Bradbury our Drummer who for that present had the round and charge of the watch, and soe they escaped both to St. Thomey, noe oppertunity since presenting [of] a reprisall keepeing themselves close within their walls, however our pursuance in vindication of this injury supported with the assistance of the President and Councell in Surrat and approved of by the other President and Councell in Bantam, hath effected the said Fryers liberty, as wee have bin lately advised by letters under his owne hand, brought hither by one Sigr. Fransisco Vera, an eminent Fidalgoe of that Nation and knowne freind to ors in the South Seas on whose ernest mediation for renewing a correspondencie with our Neighbours of St. Thomey, wee have condiscended to some Articles of Agreement (relateing to the Generall peace) that if possible wee may leive the more quietly with such insolent people, wee shall observe the caution touching Fryers and Jesuits whose smooth oratory cannot seduce us though beleeve now againe wee shall be too much troubled with their frequat Vissits.' [O.C. No. 2246.]

IV.

There is no previous reference to the handing over of Father Ephraim to the Inquisition at Goa, except the following remark in a General Letter from Fort St. George to the Court of Directors, dated January 18, 1650/1 (O.C. No. 2200): 'The Portugalls S. tomey have lately by order from the V. Roy tendered us much amyty for the time to come, but never a word of reparation for passed Injuries. . . .'

The priest administering the diocese also sent a letter asking the father to visit him on some important but secret business that had to be communicated to him. Upon this the worthy priest set out, but no sooner was he arrived near San Thome, although there he was still in Mahomedan territory, than he was seized, taken into the town, and carried to the Jesuit convent, being subjected on the way there to much abusive language from one of those who had seized him. There he found the priest administering the diocese seated on a chair. As soon as he appeared orders were given to put irons on his legs. This was done, but the irons were so small, so heavy, and so inconvenient, that at each step he fell like one dead. Noticing this, they were obliged to change them on the following day for others. In these he remained, at sea as on land, until November 10 (1649). Then, if it had not been for the reverend father Manuel de St. Joseph, Cordelier[1] who became surety to answer for him in his own person, and of his own authority removed these irons, he would have borne them until reaching Goa.

At this house of the Jesuits the father [Ephraim] was compelled to show that he was not exempt from the weaknesses of humanity. For, finding himself dealt with so harshly within a religious house, where charity is flaunted as motto, he was much affected. Still more was he so because these worthy fathers had on former occasions been most kind to him, showing him much [127] affection and civility. But what cut him to the heart was to find that he was refused confession and the Communion. The poor man grew so weak that he believed his end was approaching—so much so that he felt compelled to prepare for death, and to ask for a confessor with all the insistence that such a condition arouses in the heart of a good Christian. But they answered that there was no order to find him a confessor. At the sound of these words the worthy friar lost all heart and dissolved into tears. He said to himself: 'What! can it be that in a house of religion they refuse confession and Communion to a priest so near death?'

But if the harshness of the Jesuits went as far as this, he had afterwards ample cause, on the other hand, to thank for their gentle treatment the Cordelier fathers of the order of St. Francis and the Capuchins. Their tenderness to him was so great that he could never refrain, when on the subject, from according them a thousand praises, and even these, according to him, were far less than they deserved.

On January 15, 1650, the worthy father arrived in the roadstead of Goa; he was at once landed and taken to the house of the Inquisition. He reached it as the sun was setting. First of all he was taken into the gatekeeper's room; his hood was removed and his waist-cord. They also wanted to take off his gown, but he noticed there was present a child of twelve, and ho could not suppress the remark: 'Is it possible that you wish to strip me before this child?' This forced them to send the child away. Then the priest, who wrote down his name and the day of his being locked up, said it was not necessary to take off his clothes; they need only take away his crucifix, his breviary, and

1. *Cordelier*, a Franciscan friar, so named from the knotted cord worn as a girdle.

some papers wrapped in a covering that he had with him. This was done accordingly, and then he was taken inside the prison.

It is built like a cloister with two stories; each gallery is about fifty paces in length. The father measured it many a time going from his cell to the table of judgment. The room that he was first put into was very dark. On the Sunday he asked for his breviary, to which they replied that he was not in his convent, that he must have first the permission of the Archbishop. However, at two in the afternoon it was brought to him.

On Monday, January 17 [1650], the inquisitor sent for him, gave him his crucifix, and his name was recorded. On the Tuesday they changed his cell, telling him they wished to give him one with more light, where he could read his prayers. On March 21 he was once more removed, and again on April 1. All these rooms had the same length, breadth, and height; the last three had each a window barred with iron bars eleven feet long. The windows were at the height of two men from the floor, one and a half cubits in length, and one cubit in width. The embrasure was of about twelve feet. In the first cell there was no window, nothing but a small hole. The father [Ephraim] remained in the last cell given him until May 9, 1650. The inquisitor then saw that he was so weak that he could not hold himself up, so much so that he fell down two or three times in his presence. Moved with compassion, he sent him to another cell fifteen feet one way and eighteen feet the other, situated below the great hall of the Inquisition. It was dark but cool, and the fresher air gave him acute gouty pains in the feet and hands.

On the eve of Pentecost[1] the new inquisitor came to inspect the prison in the company of his predecessor. He ordered that he [Ephraim] should be given a companion to look after him. For on the previous day the turnkey had said that infallibly one day or the other he would be found dead. This companion remained with him from June 4, 1650, until November 5, 1651; it was, however, a privilege accorded to all the prisoners. The food was the same for everybody. Those who wanted it had a breakfast at six in the morning, dinner was at ten o'clock, and supper at four o'clock in the evening. The quality was decent, and the quantity sufficient for one person.

1. For the year 1650 this would, by the Roman Breviary, be June 4, New Style.

But let us now come to the beginning of proceedings. On March 14, 1650, the inquisitor sent for the father to the table, formally asked his name, his parentage, his position in life, his journeys, his studies, and his native land. He was then sent back. On Ash Wednesday,[1] a day [128] on which it is the inquisitor's habit to visit the prison, he said to the Father that he would not allow him to be confessed or to communicate, for certain reasons. Can those be called reasons—things which for their honour's sake it is inadvisable to enter here? But during all the time that he remained a prisoner he could never obtain a permission to be confessed or to communicate. Not even was he allowed to hear the saying of Mass throughout Holy Week. He asked that at least, as a favour, they would let him have a missal or the Holy Scriptures, that he might read there the story of our Lord Jesus Christ's passion. But the answer he got was that they could not accede to his demand, and yet they gave permission to his companion to be confessed and to communicate at the Easter feast.

In the month of May he was sent for to begin the general interrogatory. First of all he was questioned on the errors of Calvin and Luther. They obtained all their questions from a big printed book they had in their hands. After that was finished, the letter that I have spoken of was pulled out from a bundle of written papers, being the statement (*procés-verbal*) of the accusations brought against him. This statement was subsequently handed to him; and shortly I will present a translation of it, where can be discovered most of the things objected to in the letter.

On September 21 [1650] he was brought up for the special examination, when he was questioned upon the accusations that may be seen in the said procès. On November 4 following he was again summoned, and the recorder read out to him the statement of accusations (*procès-verbal*). This recorder was a Jesuit. When the Father (Ephraim) asked the inquisitor if this ecclesiastic were not of the Society of Jesus, he answered him, 'Yes.' Thereupon he replied that he would rather have had those people

1. The Ash Wednesday of 1650 fell on March 2, New Style; yet the course of the narrative seems to place it after March 14 (W. R. P.). I cannot explain the discrepancy; perhaps we ought to read *February* 14 above for *March* 14.

for his accusers than his judges. To this the inquisitor rejoined: 'What is this man's fault? It is we who do everything.'

Next they asked if the desired them to assign him an attorney to reply to the process, and the same inquisitor nominated the Reverend Father Commissary of the Order of St. Francis. The statement (*procès*) referred to was sent to him in his prison, with two sheets of paper, some pens, and some ink. Without delay Father Ephraim set to work to copy the statement word for word on the scraps of paper in which some powders sent to his comrade were wrapped,[1] for in no other way could he have concealed it After that he wrote brief replies to the accusations, and had them fair copied by his attorney when he came to see him.

It is the practice of the Inquisition to send for the attorney and administer an oath to him on the Holy Gospels that he will divulge all that passes between him and the prisoner, and that he will not supply to him any argument for his defence even if he were desired to do so. Nothing can be kept secret that passes between them, for when they are talking together there is always present in the room an officer of the Inquisition, sword at side. Thus the attorney is of no other use than for writing out the arguments and replies that the prisoner dictates to him, or hands over to him to be copied. Here follows the statement (procès), with the replies to the accusations contained in it.[2]

PROCESS OR SUMMARY OF THE ACCUSATIONS RAISED AGAINST FATHER EPHRAIM

The prosecution in a complaint against Father Ephraim of Nevers, a Frenchman by nationality, a Capuchin friar, and an apostolic missionary, living at Madras at the time of his imprisonment, and at present a prisoner in the prison of the Holy Office of this Inquisition, states:

THE FIRST ARTICLE

1. That the defendant, being a baptized Christian [129], and furthermore member of an order, and being consequently vowed to a still greater perfection of life, belief, and teaching,

1. Compare Tavernier (Ball's edition, i. 230) as to how some lead-pencils which had escaped seizure were used; the pieces of paper are there said to have contained tobacco in powder.
2. In the original the accusations and answers are placed side by side in parallel columns. For the sake of clearness, I write first the accusation and then the answer.

in accordance with the ordinances of the Holy Catholic Church, Apostolic and Roman, Our Mother, should not profess evil sentiments in regard to its traditions and decrees by perniciously interpreting its Councils, ceremonies, and customs. Nevertheless, he has acted exactly to the contrary, and forgetting his obligations, having neither fear of God nor of the sanctions of this tribunal, has asserted at a certain time and place indecorous and scandalous propositions, teaching new doctrines, denying the duty of adoring holy images, blaming the public use of them prevailing among Christians, forbidding or condemning the veneration paid to the holy relics of the saints, communicating several of these opinions to persons newly converted, ignorant and feeble in the Faith; conversing scandalously with heretics, Lutherans, Calvinists, and Protestants; approving by his intercourse their damnable heresy; reading their books and many others forbidden by the Holy Councils and the Bull *In Caena* [*Domini*].[1]

Since the defendant has transgressed in all these things to the great prejudice of his own soul and the scandal of the faithful, and has sinned against our Holy Faith, Catholic, Apostolic, and Roman, the prosecution demands that he be chastised according to his deserts.

ANSWER OF FATHERS EPHRAIM TO THE FIRST ACCUSATION.

[128] 'Gratis dictum jure negatur et absolute.'[2]

This article is a sort of prologue, where the accuser says as much ill as he can against the defendant. Being nothing but formalities, the attorney, as is the custom, retorts by setting forth numerous praises of his client. He says (*verbi gratia*) that he had been chosen by his bishops, and sent to the [129]

1. This Bull is so called, not, as usually, from the opening words, but because it was promulgated on a Maundy Thursday (*Feria quinta in Caena Domini*). It relates to the excommunication of heretics and contumacious persons, and was issued first by Pope Paul III. on April 13, 1536 (see 'Bullarium,' i. 718). It was read aloud at Rome every Maundy Thursday until the time of Clement XIV. (1769-1774). Paul V. gave the Bull its final form in 1610, and it was republished by Urban VIII. in 1627 (J. C. Earle, 'Manual of the Lives of the Popes,' p. 195; London. 1866) (W. R. P.).
2. These words and those at the end of the defence are evidently legal formulas, Literally, the, words mean, 'It is spoken free of cost by law, and a complete denial is given to the charge,' equivalent to, 'I claim a free trial, and entirely deny the charges.'

Indies to preach the faith, being fully known as a true Catholic, *et cetera*.

THE SECOND ARTICLE

[129] What is above stated is so true that the accused has confessed at this table during previous sittings that he has put forward certain propositions. Among such are: that the Holy Trinity ought not to be represented in the manner done in the Church; that an Anglican clergyman is a true priest; that the adoration of *Latria*[1] is not due to the Cross; that there should be no graven images, he saying that it was desirable to use paintings by reason of the fragile faith of ignorant Christians, this being a custom followed in his convents in France, and in the other churches of that kingdom, and for this reason he had declined to permit the [130] placing of the statue of Saint Anthony upon the altar at his church in Madras when his permission was sought. He has, moreover, confessed at this table that he had written a certain letter to a certain person, governor of a certain fortress held by Christians, the said letter having been shown to him at this table. In it he defends not merely the above propositions, but several others like unto them. This he has acknowledged in the examination conducted at this table. He has also confessed the possession of many heretical and schismatical books prohibited and condemned by the Church. Furthermore, he has read the Bible in Portuguese, and has taught it to children. The prosecution admits the confession of all these things, in so far as they make against the accused.

1. *Latria* is worship given to God alone, in opposition to the respect and honour given to saints, which is *Dulia*. The word is from the Greek *Latreia*, 'service for salary,' and by extension, 'worship' (*Littré*). In the 1900 edition of Annandale's Ogilvie's 'English Dictionary,' *Latria* is defined as 'the highest kind of worship or that paid to God, distinguished by Roman Catholics from *Dulia*, or the inferior worship paid to saints.' The use of the word goes back to the Third Session of the Council of Nicaea on September 26, 787. Tarasius, Patriarch of Constantinople, accepted the veneration of images, and said: 'We reverence them with relative regard, since they are made in the name of Christ and of His inviolate Mother, of the holy angels and the saints. Our *Latreia and pistis*, however, we evidently dedicate to God alone.' Whereupon all exclaimed: 'Thus believes the whole Synod' (C. J. Hefele, 'History of the Councils of the Church,' English translation, v. 365). Again, on p. 399, we are referred to the Tridentine Decrees, Sessio XXV., 'De Invocatione Sanctorum.'

[129] As regards the image of the most Holy Trinity, let them read Peruyuer,[1] Tostatus,[2] *et cetera*, and it will be seen that I need not reply to this article. With respect to the English cleryman the prosecution accuses me falsely, for I never said he was a true priest; but to make the matter more of a crime he has imagined that detail. It is quite true that I once said that, assuming that the clergyman had been consecrated by a bishop with the ceremonial followed in the Church, then in my belief he possessed the quality of priesthood; that I had read in certain books that the English had preserved those ceremonies when consecrating their bishops and priests. That consequently it could not be said of one of their clergy that he was a mere layman, for he might have the attributes of a priest. This is what I said, and not what that prosecution avers. Upon this head the reader will notice that Father Francis de Fonseca,[3] a famous and very learned preacher in India, and the inquisitor himself, contradicted me; that is, they said, heretic bishops consecrated according to the requisite ceremonial cannot confer any attributes, for they have not been thereto authorized by the Sovereign Pontiff. My reply to that can be consulted in the writings that I have forwarded to the Sorbonne.

In respect to the adoration of the Cross, I replied that the prosecutor need only read the decree of the Council of Nicaea,

1. Probably meant for Benedictus Pererus, S. J. (Perera or Pereyra), an expositor of the Scriptures, who died March 6, 1610, aged seventy-five. Probably the passages meant are those at pp. 81, 82, 155-159 of his work, 'Commentariorum in Danielem Prophetam Libri Sexdecim' ('Romae, in aedibus Populi Romani, Apud Georgium Ferrarium,' 1587), where the worship of images is spoken of.
2. Tostatus is Alphonsus Tostatus (Alfonso Tostado), Episcopus Abulensis (Bishop of Avila), died 1455. One edition of his 'Opera Omnia' is in twenty-seven volumes, folio (Venice, 1728). The passage required is, perhaps, Quaestio XXXIX., 'Quare in veteri testamento non fuerunt statuae vel imagines?' in his 'Commentaria in Primam Partem Exord. . . .' pp. 315 and 316 of 'Tostati Operum Tomus Secundus' (Venetis, N. Pezzana, 1728); or, better still, Quaestio V., 'Quare Christianis imagines et statuae permissae sfat ?' in 'Commentaria in Deuteronomium,' same edition of his works, vol. vii., p. 32. Tostatus is mentioned again on fol. 136.
3. In A. Franco's 'Synopsis,' 1726, there are three Fonsecas entered between 1617 and 1647 as having gone to the East, but none with this Christian name.

recognised by him in his third article of charge as a universal Council. There he will see who is the best Catholic of us two. With respect to graven images, it is untrue that I condemn or reject them as asserted by the prosecution. Let my letter be read, and if what I say means [130] the rejection of images, I shall say that by the same reasoning the Portuguese fathers reject the Holy Communion, since they refuse to administer it to the greater number of Indians as being unworthy; while Jesus Christ our Lord says, 'Nolite santum dare canibus' ['Give not that which is holy unto the dogs', Matt. vii. 6], which might be construed by saying that he rejected holy things.

In regard to what it is alleged that I said upon the customs of our convents, the prosecution does not repeat it in the sense used by me, for I said nothing more than that our altar [at Madras], being arranged like those of our convents in France, I was not obliged to conform to the fancies of certain Indians. They wished me to place the image of St. Anthony in the manner stated at the end of my letter. Were it true that I had rejected graven images, why should I have always worn the image of a crucifix in bronze?

As far as regards the letter written by me to the governor, my motives are detailed in the letter itself. In the interrogatories put to me on this subject, no error or rash expression has been pointed out to me. If this be done, I am ready to retract and renounce it.

In respect of forbidden books, everybody knows that I am a missionary, and that we are privileged to have printed books. The inquisitor once said to me that such privileges did not extend to India. To this I replied that, even granting that point to him, I had not transgressed in what I had done. For in 1640 his lordship the Primate of Goa[1] had inspected them, and given permission to use them within his archbishopric. In 1642 the reverend father, Maitre François de la Croix, Dominican,[2] commissary of the Holy Office, read them through twice, and made

1. In 1640 the Archbishopric of Goa was held by Francisco dos Martyres, a Fransiscan, born at Lisbon. He arrived at Goa on October 4, 1636, and died there on November 25, 1652 (C. C. Nazareth, 'Mitras Lusitanas,' i. 94-97).
2. This is in all probability the same person as the *Lucas* de la Croix spoken of on fols. 133 and 137 (see note to the first of these two passages).

a minute examination of them [131] without discovering anything worthy of censure. Again, in 1646, the priest administering the diocese of San Thome,[1] my accuser, gave me a writing under his hand, whereby he permitted me to make use of the privileges referred to within his bishopric. Hence I draw this inference (arguing thus to prove he was acting from passion): either he had seen my privileges or he had not seen them. If he saw and approved them, why at the present day does he accuse me because I used them? If he has not seen the books, how came he to give me a writing under his hand by which he certifies that he had seen and approved them?

As for the Bible in Portuguese, this is again a falsehood. It is true I have confessed to having translated the New Testament into Portuguese, but not the whole Bible, as asserted. The reasons that impelled me to do it were submitted by me to the persons to whom I was under an obligation to report my acts.

THE THIRD ARTICLE

[130] The defendant further accused of not making complete and true confession of his faults, but having, on the contrary, minimized them, prevaricated and used concealment. He has endeavoured by arguments, subterfuges, superficial signs, and sophistical twistings to hide and palliate the damnable purpose he had in making use of the propositions he put forward, the things done by him in regard to the Faith, and the contempt that he has displayed when speaking of sacred things that have been received and approved by the Church from the apostolic ages up to the present day. He has hid under the cloak of zeal the secret poison contained in the opinions he defends. He has shown visibly his vainglorious intention and his heretical determination not to conform to the belief of the whole Church universal. He confirms by his avowals the errors that he has taught and practised. On this head we have been instructed at this table, and it has, in addition, been confirmed by the interrogatories administered to him in person, whence it has been proved by the fullest evidence that he is infected with the heresy of those heretics—the Lutherans, Calvinists, and Protestants—hot only in the matter of invocation of saints, but in the worship relics and veneration of holy images. He has also tried

1. For Hieronymo de Sa, see *ante*, note 183 to fol. 126.

falsely and ignorantly to teach the said heresy by plausible reasoning, quite foreign to and far off from all truth. He has wished thereby to spread this heresy in India [131], seeing therein nothing worthy of censure.

Not only has the accused fallen into these heresies—that is to say, the one against the honour and veneration due to holy images of the saints, and the other against their blessed relics—but also into several other errors. He has said that abstinence[1] on Saturday is not an act of devotion, but a deception; *novenas*[2] to saints are inventions of the devil, and a mere sorcercer's rite. He has rejected graven images, it being more fitting, he says, to make use of paintings; he has read forbidden books, and has translated the Holy Bible into the vulgar tongue. By this erroneous doctrine he has contravened the rulings of several Councils, the decrees of the Pontiffs, and the ordinary usage of the Church Catholic, Apostolic, and Roman. Further, he has conversed and kept up friendship with heretics, not in civil business only, but also in matters of the Faith and of religion.

As he is an apostolic missionary known to the public, it was a part of his duty not to vary in the least from what is practised by other friars and apostolic missionaries. On the contrary, he has given occasion for the belief, through a certain letter that he addressed to a certain governor, that he not only teaches the propositions and errors contained therein, but affirms and defends them in that same letter, which is in his handwriting. He is not excused by saying that in France it is not the custom to place in churches cast-metal images, nor by resorting to other similar subterfuges. For, in spite of their not acknowledging in that kingdom (France) the Council of Trent,[3]

1. 'Abstinence' is the taking of no flesh meat; 'fasting' means taking only one full meal during the day, and no food at allbefore noon. Abstinence on Fridays and Saturdays throughout the year was a common rule in Catholic countries, and still is in Southern India it was the rule until quite recent times (W.R.P).
2. *Novena,* a nine days' prayer, made in preparation for a feast or at other times. It is a following of the example of the Apostles, who remained in prayer from Ascension Day to Pentecost. That is the idea (W.R.P.).
3. 'Suffice to say that, as regards the articles of faith promulgated by the Council, there never was any opposition offered by the Gallican Church to their complete and full recognition, (J. Waterworth, 'The Canons and

the use of images is all the same accepted by the whole Church universal. That Church used holy images many ages before the holding of the said Council or the publication of its decrees, that point having been defined by the Council of Nicaea, which is received and approved by all Christendom. From the whole of the foregoing it results that he [132] is infected by several heresies; that he denies and conceals his veritable intention, which is not to observe the ceremonies of the Roman Church so as to maintain them, but to continue in the same (the heresies), as may be noted from the boldness and impertinence with which he defends them.

ANSWER TO THE THIRD ARTICLE

[131] At the time when this Article was read to me, the inquisitor said to me that it raised the presumptions and conclusions that they drew about me. For this reason I replied by an absolute denial and condemnation of the rash conclusion they had made in regard to me. I ask the reader to peruse this article with great attention, and to ponder well the repetitions in these proceedings, and the sort of evidence they produce against me about all the calumnies they have invented. The letter was written to the governor; let it be read—let it be placed along side the accusations, then you will see at once the sophistry that they resort to against me. *A dicto secundum quid ad dictum simpliciter* ('Proceeding from a conditional statement, they turn it into an absolute one'). For I was never accused of all they have accumulated in this writing. The whole thing proceeds solely from the disapproval of, and the criticism by, Goa learned men upon my letter. Yet they pass over therein one of the chief crimes of which I am accused—that is, that I was [132] the enemy of the Rosary, and that I had repelled the proposition of certain humble Catholics, who said that we could ask nothing direct from God, but that all demands must be made to the Virgin. To this I made in the interrogatory the necessary answer. I do not desire to put my reply into this article, which is about inferences. As for the other accusations that follow, my reply was that they were accusations by drunkards,

Decrees of the Council of Trent,' Introduction, p. cclxiv; London, 1848). But the disciplinary provisions were never accepted by the Government of France.

known as such, and drawn up *ipso facto bibendi* ('in the very act of drinking'). Consequently they did not merit to be listened to, much less to be refuted.

THE FOURTH ARTICLE

[132] That the defendant was present in a certain place in company with some men, both heretics and Roman Catholics. There it chanced that a certain Catholic present in the company said that he was treasurer of the Bull of the Crusade, and that he intended in a few days to organize the procession.[1] The defendant began to speak about it with great contempt, saying that the said Bull was a fraud pure and simple, only meant for the making of money. Thereupon the said Catholic who had begun the conversation was very much shocked, and conceived a very bad opinion of the defendant.

ANSWER TO THE FOURTH ARTICLE

[132] This drunkard may perhaps have said to some Englishmen what is reported in this article, and the fumes of wine may have made him imagine that I said what issued from the mouth of some other person.

THE FIFTH ARTICLE

[132] That the defendant being at a certain place at a certain time, in company with certain persons, both heretics and Catholics, among other conversation that took place they came to talk of the Pope and the tribunal of the Holy Office. The defendant began to say: 'What is the Pope? What is the Inquisition?' In his country they had not, nor did they know

1. In the time of the Crusades certain spiritual favours were granted by the Popes to those giving alms towards their expenses. These favours have continued in Spain and the countries once subject to the Spanish Crown, including Portugal and its dependencies. The money is now devoted in Spain to the upkeep of churches. The name, 'Bull of the Crusade' is still in use in Spain, Portugal, and Italy. In Spain the administrator is now always the Archbishop of Toledo; in 1892 that office was held in Portugal by Antonio Ayres de Gouvea, titular Bishop of Bethsaida. See also two articles in the *Month* in February and March, 1904, by the Rev. Sydney F. Smith, S. J. (W. R. P.). Mr. Fhillipps sends me a curious printed 'Summary' now in use in Portugal, and to 'take the Bull' is to pay 40 *reis* and receive this printed leaflet in exchange. The latest repetition of the Bull is quoted therein as having been made on April 13, 1898.

of, any such Holy Office, but every one was let live as he chose, in accordance with his conscience. On hearing this a certain Catholic was very much scandalized, and left the company.

ANSWER TO THE FIFTH ARTICLE

[132] This drunkard, drinking once with some Englishmen, said that the Pope was the successor of our Lord Jesus Christ. On hearing these words those Englishmen began to laugh and make fun of him. For my part I reproved him for attempting to talk about religion, seeing he was so ignorant. I handed to him a paper written in Latin, in which I stated that Roman Catholics acknowledged the Pope as vicegerent of our Lord Jesus Christ, and St. Peter's successor. I recommended him to show this [paper] to the learned men at San Thome. Why has not this paper been sent on to the Holy Office? The inferences, are the inferences of a drunkard.

THE SIXTH ARTICLE

[132] That the defendant being in a certain place at a certain time, in the company of certain persons, a certain person sent to him a writing. In it the writer complained, and found it very ill, that under his very eyes he, a priest with charge of souls, permitted the English clergyman, a layman and a heretic, to baptize publicly in his congregation [133] the children of Catholic mothers. Having read this writing, the defendant grew very angry, and said that the clergyman was as good a priest as himself. This he repeated three or four times. At this a certain person present was extremely scandalized at hearing such comparisons instituted. It was judged by this and other talks he had with the defendant that the latter is not a Catholic, and from that time forth he had no good opinion of him.

ANSWER TO THE SIXTH ARTICLE

[132] This drunkard brought me a letter, and I told him the man who wrote it was mad if he believed I was able to hinder the English clergyman from baptizing the child of one of the principal Englishmen within his own country. I knew that the writer [133] was the Father Governor of San Thome, Hyeronimo de Saa, who toasted he had studied theology, and asserted with unexampled audacity that the English clergyman was a layman. I said that for my part I would not venture to affirm such a thing; it might well be the case that he had the qualification of

priest, as I have already said. But this witness was such an honest man as to be well known in this country as a liar, a pimp, a gross liver, a drunkard, and a manslayer. But if the three governors that I had seen at San Thome, or the Reverend Lucas de la Croix,[1] inquisitor, or the Reverend Father Emmanuel de Saint Joseph,[203] said that his testimony was worthy of credence, I too was satisfied to let it be received. It should be noticed that these three charges above given all proceed from this man of worth.

THE SEVENTH ARTICLE

[133] That the defendant being at a certain time in company of certain persons, both Catholics and heretics, among other conversation they came to talk of the collect in the Mass where they pray to God for the Pope. The defendant said that in the collect referred to he did not pray to God for the Pope first, but first of all for the Agent of the English within whose territory he dwelt, and in the second place for the King of France. Thereupon a certain Catholic then present told him to be careful ol what he said, that first of all we ought to pray to God for the Pope, because he was the Sovereign Pontiff and the Head of the Church. The defendant said once more that he did not name the Pope first, but the ruler of the place where he lived, and after him the King of France. By this the said person was much scandalized, and had no good opinion of the defendant.

---

1. Father Emmanuel de St. Joseph is the Franciscan Vice-Commissary whose certificate, dated September 23, 1650, appears further on (fols. 142-147). As for Lucas da Cruz, Dominican, mentioned already on fol. 130 and again on fol. 137, he began life as a soldier, but entered the Order at Cochin, acquired the degree of Doctor, was made head of the Dominican College at Goa, and then sent (*circa* 1634) as Visitor to Ceylon and Manar. He is said to have secured (*circa* 1640), when Vicar-General in Solor and Timor, a combination of the local Christian kings in the Indian Archipelago against the Dutch, and himself received a lance-wound at Malacca. He was, lastly, appointed Vicar-General of the Dominicans in India, also Inquisitor and Commissary of the Holy Office. He died in September, 1663. The above is condensed from the *Annuaire Dominicaine* for September, 1906, pp. 33 and 34, for an extract from which I am indebted to the Very Rev. Father Shapcote, O. P. English Provincial, through the good offices of Mr. W. R. Phillipps. Father Lucas da Cruz is also mentioned in C. C. Nazareth, 'Mitras Lusitanas,' i. 89, 123.

ANSWER TO THE SEVENTH ARTICLE

[133] In the book of Esdras can be read what are the effects of wine-bibbing.[1] These are accusations by a drunken man.

THE EIGHTH ARTICLE

[133] That the defendant being present in a certain place at a certain time in company of persons, both Catholics and heretics, a certain person went to speak to the English Agent about two women who had fled from Madras to San Thome. The governor of the said San Thome demanded them from the said person. He replied that the said women were white women, and Catholics; they could not be slaves of the [English] Company. Having sought asylum in the church, the governor [of San Thome] possessed no right of interference, still less so if the said women had been mixed up [134] in anything concerning the Holy Office (*i.e.*, the Inquisition). To that the Agent answered that the tribunal of the Holy Office took nobody but the rich. This reply so angered the said person that he made retort by applying his hand to his sword-hilt and saying: 'That is done only in the sect of Luther and of Calvin, and he might defend it, but in the tribunal of the Holy Office the Holy Ghost was present; there alone could truth be found, as was well known to Father Ephraim' (who was then present). To this the defendant replied in favour of the heretics by saying that in France, his native country, there was no Holy Office. To this the person referred to replied that from this cause his reverence's country was full of heretics. He found it wrong for the defendant not to confirm his words when he was disputing with a heretic.

ANSWER TO THE EIGHTH ARTICLE

[133] This drunkard has an imperfect recollection of both his own statement and mine. Mine was, seeing he was already somewhat heated with wine, that I asked him if the governor had sent him to talk about the Holy Office or about the business mentioned in his letter; but that there being an Inquisition in his country and none in mine, we both remained as we were before.

THE NINTH ARTICLE

[134] That the defendant being at a certain place at a certain time in company of persons both Catholic and heretic, they permitted

1. I Esdras iii. 17-24, beginning, 'O ye men, how exceeding strong is wine! It causeth all men to err who drink it.'

themselves certain words against the Sovereign Pontiff and the tribunal of the Holy Office. A certain person, a Catholic, argued to the contrary, but the defendant held his tongue, said not a word, and began to laugh. It was just as if he wished to side with the heretics and favour their views, demonstrating how little he had at heart the defence of the Church and of the Portuguese Christians.

ANSWER TO THE NINTH ARTICLE

[134] The poor drunkard saw me laughing at the absurdities he was guilty of, and at his state of intoxication. He imagined I was laughing at something else. Who could help laughing at the sight of a drunken man discoursing upon such subjects?

THE TENTH ARTICLE

[134] That the defendant being in a certain place at a certain time in the company of certain persons, among other talk they mentioned the tribunal of the Inquisition. The defendant stated that there was none in his country. He added that the tribunal was very severe, and did not seem to act conformably to justice in its proceedings. It did not discover the names of the witnesses to the defendants. To this the said person replied that it would, be very inconvenient to do so, as the defendants might tamper with the said witnesses.

ANSWER TO THE TENTH ARTICLE

[134] Some of the Portuguese told me they trembled when they heard the name of the Holy Office, where men were imprisoned without knowing why or wherefore, nor the name of the accusers or of the witnesses. For my part, I said that there were no things like that in our country, and that it seemed to me a harsh procedure. This is what I believe has been sent on; *ut me caperet in sermone.*[1]

THE ELEVENTH ARTICLE

[135] That the defendant being in a certain place at a certain time, and consorting in close friendship with heretics, there was a certain occasion on which it was necessary to have his consent

1. An allusion to Matt. xxii. 15 and Luke xx. 20, 'Ut caperent eum in sermone'; also found in Mark xii. 13, 'Ut eum caperent in verbo' (W.R.P.).

for the flight of several Catholic married women and girls to the homes of heretics, where they ran evident risk of perversion. He took no steps to hinder this.

ANSWER TO THE ELEVENTH ARTICLE

[135] If the four governors of San Thome who have lived there during the time I was at Madras, or the prelates and priests who have known me, make this accusation against me, I agree to be punished as a guilty person. Upon this subject is it possible that so many honest men who have known me should not display enough zeal to lodge a complaint, and that it must proceed from no one but an imprudent and passionate drunkard?

THE TWELFTH ARTICLE

[135] That the defendant being in the company of certain persons, one of them happened to speak of several men who dwelt in a certain fort of the heretics, living like men lost and attending their worship. The defendant then said a number of them were Catholics who confessed themselves to him in Lent. To this the person above referred to said that those who went to those services were not fit to confess, unless they made a solemn resolution to remain away from such places. For they sinned by this external act whereby they made show of professing that schism. To this the defendant replied that they might attend that worship with the idea of imploring God in their own way, and that he (defendant) went sometimes to the English meetings and said his prayers from his breviary while they recited their psalms.

ANSWER TO THE TWELFTH ARTICLE

[135] When I said this, I had drunk two or three glasses of strong Spanish wine; and that being the case, I am not astonished if I was not so very careful. For I have never been present at the prayers of the English gentlemen. They themselves can surely prove this, as also the Roman Catholics living at Madras. How possibly could I say that I went to their meetings and that I read there in my breviary? For what I did say referred to those who attended the services of the Dutch (for it was of them we were talking). These, though known to be Roman Catholics, were nevertheless obliged under heavy fines to be present at some of the Dutch devotional exercises. As I knew the facts, I said

they could not be condemned so severely as the priest who accuses me wished to lay down. This is what happened, and Mr. Sperrely was present at the discussion.

THE THIRTEENTH ARTICLE

[135] That the defendant being in a certain place in the company of certain persons, one of them began to talk about the English preacher. The defendant said he was a true priest ordained by their bishops, clothed with that dignity by due succession. On another occasion being with the same person, with whom he had held the above conversation in that company, he repeated the same thing, adding that the said English minister, when giving the Communion to his parishioners, consecrated [the elements] with the same words that we use. He praised the minister for his learning, stating that he had listened to him preaching to his congregation, the sermon being on the subject of the Communion, very well done and most devout.

ANSWER TO THE THIRTEENTH ARTICLE

[135] The worst of the matter is that this gentleman boasted of his own great learning. He contended that none but Saint Peter had made bishops. On my side I pointed out to him the contrary from Holy Scripture. Subsequently he declared that nobody had ever been made a bishop except by order of the Supreme Pontiff at Rome. I pointed out to him the contrary in the abridgment of [136] the Councils by Coriolanus,[1] and also, *Omnis potestas ordinis et jurisdictionis erat penes Pontificem Romanorum.* [All the power of ordination and the power of jurisdiction lay with the Roman Pontiff.] In spite of this, he affirmed that without the Pope's permission there could be no bishops having the proper qualifications. But what angered him above all was that he could find nothing as an answer to what I said. It is this, no doubt, that has made him invent

1. Franciscus a Coriolano, surnamed Longus, Capuchin, died 1625, aged sixty-three; author of 'Breviarium Chronologicum Pontificum et Conciliorum Omnium,' 7 vols., folio; Rome, 1622, or Lugduni, 1633 (see H. Hurter, 'Nomenclator,' i. 258). Or the work intended might be his 'Summa Conciliorum Omnium (a S. Petro usque ad Gregorium XV.),' Antwerpiae, 1623, 2 vols.; another edition is Parisiis, 1639. I have not seen either of the above works; but Louis Bail, in the preface to his 'Summa Conciliorum Omnium,' 1701, p. 8, mentions the abridgment of Coriolanus as one of his sources.

these accusations against me—namely, that I had listened to a sermon by the English clergyman—because he asked me in what way the said minister gave the communion to his flock, and I stated in reply, in simple terms, what I knew about it. He now wishes to make that a crime on my part; also my saying that he (the clergyman) was learned, and there was little doubt that the said minister spoke better Latin than my accuser.

THE FOURTEENTH ARTICLE

[136] That from all these faults, these words and propositions given forth by the defendant and defended by him, and from other things done by him in regard to religion, intimated to him at this table and confessed to by him, it results by a just, direct, and safe presumption that therefrom should be derived the accusation against the defendant that he has departed from the Faith—Catholic, Apostolic, and Roman—and has entertained erroneous ideas about its infallible doctrine drawn from Holy Scripture and the commentaries of the Holy Fathers received by the Universal Church and confirmed by the decrees of all the Pontiffs and Councils. He has followed and approved the errors of the Calvinist and Lutheran heresies or those of the Protestants rejected by the Church.

ANSWER TO THE FOURTEENTH ARTICLE

[136] Persons, in a passion and the learned men of Goa may draw such presumptions, founded upon their anger and their ignorance.

FIFTEENTH ARTICLE

[136] That the defendant has been several times exhorted at this table with abundant love to make a confession of his faults and declare the truth as to all that he has done, the intention and mind with which he has advanced these propositions in regard to the Faith, which by him have been expressed, published, and defended, and also all the other things he has done contrary to the Catholic, Apostolic, and Roman religion. This confession he has never been willing to make, but on the contrary he has obstinately, erroneously, and hypocritically maintained these errors by the sophistical and tortuous nature of his replies on this subject.

ANSWER TO THE FIFTEENTH ARTICLE

[136] Let the reader ponder on this fine conclusion, and say whether there is any answer to be made to conclusions thus made 'in the air.'

XXXVII. Madana, Brahman, Chief Minister of Gulkandah

Vol. III *To face page 432*

THE SIXTEENTH ARTICLE

[136] I demand the admission of these Articles, that the Court be fully constituted, and that the defendant, Father Ephraim of Nevers, as a heretic and an apostate from our holy Faith, a forger, a hypocrite, *et cetera*, be punished, as his faults deserve, with all the rigour of the law, in accordance with the regular procedure and the formulas of the Holy Office.

'Cum protestatione juris et expensis' [With protestation of (my) legal rights, and claiming costs].

Here you have, then, the charitable and merciful conclusions of these gentlemen. To them the father's procurator replied orally; and these replies having been signed by both parties, they were made over to the gaoler for delivery to the inquisitor. In the following January [1651] the accused was sent for to hear the public reading of the witnesses' depositions about all the impertinent things they imputed to him. To these statements the procurator replied by an absolute denial of everything that was said against the defendant. He repelled the said depositions as the testimony of persons incapable in law of giving evidence in a court of justice.

On May 25, 1651, Father Ephraim was once more sent for, and he was asked what books he required for the preparation of his defence, and they gave him Tostatus 'In Deu.'; Baronius 'An.,' 9; Bellarmino, 'Con.', tom. i.; 'O Catechismo de Pio Quinto' in Portuguese; Joseph Angles; Durandus, 'In Senten.'[1] On June

1. The books and authors intended seem to be:
   1. Bishop Alphonsus Tostatus (Tostado), Abulensis, died 1455 (see *ante*, note 194 to fol. 129). The reference 'In Deu.' is most probably intended for his commentary on Deuteronomy, vol. vii. of his works, Question V., p. 32, as already mentioned.
   2. Cardinal Cesare Baronius, Oratarian (1538-1607), 'Annales Ecclesiastici' (Venetiis, apud Haeredem Hieronymi Scotti, 1602). 12 vols., folio. See in vol. ix. on the Adoration of the Cross, pp. 75 A, 158 E to 159 A, 173 D and E, 436 C to E; and for the decisions of the Council of Nice thereon, see p. 420 B, section 53.
   3. Cardinal Roberto F. R. Bellarmino, Jesuit (1542-1621), T) 'Disputationes de Controversiis Christianae fidei adversus Haereticos,' tom. i. There is a Roman edition of 1832 in four volumes. Vol. i. contains the tract 'Appendix Tractatum de Cultu Imaginum,' and the passage on p. 986 quotes the finding of the Council of Nicaea: 'Neque eos cultu latriae qui Deo est proprius, adorandos.' Or the edition Venetiis, apud Societatem Minimam, 1599, may be consulted. In tomus secundus, cols, 841-856, in the second book of the 'Quarta Controversia Generalis, De Ecclesia

Triumphante,' there are the following chapters on the Adoration of the Cross: XXVI., De Adoratione Crucis; XXVIL, De Cruce vera Domini; XXVIII., De Imagine Crucis; XXIX., De Signo Crucis; XXX., Solvuntur Obiectiones Haereticorum. The reference 'Con. I.' must be intended for this work, 'De Controversiis . . . .'

4. 'O Catechismo,' the Catechism of the Council of Trent, first published in Latin by Pius V., and since translated into various languages. The Council decreed that such a book should be prepared. There are English editions by T. A. Buckley, B.A., 1852, and Jeremiah Donovan, D.D., 1854. I quote from the latter version: 'Question XX. This precept [Thou shalt not make to thyself a graven image] they do not violate who represent the Persons of the Trinity. . . for no one is so ignorant as to believe that by that image is expressed the Divinity' (p. 36). 'Question XXIV. But the pastor will show that it is not only lawful to have images in a church, and to pay them honour and respect, as the honour which is paid them is referred to their prototypes.' The Portuguese version referred to in the text is probably that by Dom Barth, dos Martyres (Lisboa, 1610, small 4to.), quoted by Migne in 'Dictionnaire de Bibliographic Catholique' (Paris, 1867), vol. ii., col. 883 ('Encyclopédie Theologique,' série iii., vol. xl.).
5. Josephus Angles Valentinus, a Franciscan Observantine, died *circa* 1587 (H. Hurter, 'Nomenclator,' i. 44), 'Flores Theologicarum Questionum in Quartum Librum "Sententiarum" [of Petrus Lombardus] Collecti,' 8vo.; Lugduni, 1587. I have not succeeded in identifying any passage bearing on Father Ephraim's case.
6. Since further on the Durandus referred to is said to have been condemned, it must be Gulielmus Durandus a S. Porciano, Dominican, died 1334; author of 'In Sententias Theologicas Petri Lombardi Commentarioram libri quatuor,' of which there were several editions in the sixteenth century (see H. Hurter, 'Nomenclator,' iv. 431-435). On p. 433 Hurter says: 'Non solum recessit [Durandus] a doctrina S. Thomae sed a pluribus placitis communis scholae consensu defensis opinionum singularium patronus: unde controversiis et oppugnationlbus praebent occasionem.' The passages on Images (quoted by G. Vazquez, p. 987) are in the Leyden edition of 1556, to be found on p. 198, ninth 'Distinction second 'Quaestio,' 'Utrum latria sit soli Deo exhibenda' (para. 4), and the third 'Questio,' 'Utrum dulia distinguatur a latria'—'whether *douleia* is to be distinguished from *latreia*—*i.e.* the, enforced from the free service of God. There is another Gulielmus Durandus, Bishop of Mende, died 1333, the author of 'Rationale Divinorum Officiorum.' The first edition was of 1459, and there were twenty-eight editions in the fifteenth and sixteenth centuries (see the English translation, 'The Symbolism of Churches and Church Ornaments,' by J. M. Neale and Benjamin Webb; Leeds, 1843). The portions affecting the charges against Father Ephraim seem to be chapter i. section 41, Of the Crosses: 'But the Cross is exalted on high to signify the victory of Christ'; and chapter iii., Of Pictures and Images; sections 2, 3, and

27 and 28 he was again sent for, and they enquired [137] if he had found references for what he had advanced. In the end the whole case was reduced to three articles. Firstly, about the image of the most holy Trinity; secondly, touching the priests' orders in the English Church; thirdly, about the adoration of *Latria*[1] to be paid to the Cross.

The inquisitor read to him the adverse opinion of the three learned men, who held him up as a Calvinist because he refused to give to the blessed Cross the adoration of Latria;[2] as overbold in condemning the display of the most Holy Trinity; and as *sapiens heresim* (savouring of heresy) in saying that the English clergyman might perhaps possess the character of priesthood. The writers that he adduced in his defence were described as rash and untrustworthy persons. The inquisitor said to him that Durandus had been condemned in a certain book called 'Expurgatorium.' He replied that they could hardly charge him with rashness, for he followed Catholic authors and men of great authority, such as are those named above. But to that remark he (the inquisitor) retorted that there were fourteen Jesuits who approved the representation of the most Holy Trinity. To that he (Father Ephraim) answered that the matter was not an article of faith, and that he would willingly follow the doctrine laid down by the authors now appealed to, but he had not been rash in following the contrary opinion.

As regards the qualification of the English clergyman, he had said from the first that if they pointed out to him a Catholic doctor who says that the English do not observe the required ceremonies, he would follow that doctor's opinion. They produced to him Suarez,[3] who, while allowing that they (the English

4, Objections against the Use of Pictures and Curtains Answered; section 5, The Place of Pictures; sections 6, 7, and 12, The Saviour: How Represented.

7. The work entitled 'Expurgatoriun' I have failed to identify.

1. See note to fol. 129. The three Articles left had formed—(1) The Third Article; (2) the Sixth Article; (3) part of the Second Article of Charge.
2. Compare the Vulgate of Matt. xvi. 23; Mark viii. 23; Rom. xi.20, xii. 16 (W.R.P.).
3. Franciscus Suarez, S.J., born at Granada January 5, 1548; died September 25, 1617. The work meant is 'Defensio fidei Catholicae adversus Anglicanae Sectae Errores published in 1613. In the edition of his 'Opera,' 26 vols., 1856-61, it is found in vol. xxiv., and the passages specially

Church) observe the ceremonial, affirms at the same time that they have not the intention of consecration when they admit a man to their orders. The father (Ephraim) replied that he would follow that opinion with all his heart.

In regard to the adoration of *Latria*,[1] he said he would never retract, because his opinion was a matter of faith, and in this matter he followed Baronius and Bellarmino. He begged that the doctors be produced, so that he might discuss this article with them.

On July 3 [1651] they brought to him a Jesuit named Gregoire de Mayeu,[2] and at once he was invited to send for the ninth volume of Baronius, and for Bellarmino. But this father was in such a rage that he said to the defendant, although actually reading Baronius at the time, that this author said nothing in his favour. 'Let your reverence read well,' was the reply, 'the passage quoted and the decree of the second Council of Nicaea.' Subsequently on reading Bellarmino he (the Jesuit) said to him (Ephraim) that he was right, and that the dispute between them was only one of names. Thereupon he went away.

On July 5 the inquisitors sent for the defendant again, and cited to him over again Bellarmino, and wrote out what this author said. After that he did not see this inquisitor again, for he died on the 17th of that month.

Upon November 4, 1651, one hour after mid-day, he was once more brought out of prison and placed before the table. There he found the Archbishop, the grand inquisitor, the second inquisitor, who was a Dominican named Father Lucas de la Croix, one Observantist father,[3] two or three more Dominicans, and one or two Jesuits, as he believes. The hall was decorated with

---

bearing on Anglican Orders are book i., chapters ii., xiv. (sections 8, 9, and 10), xvii., and xxii.

1. See note to fol 129.
2. 'Pas trace de Grégoire Mayea ou Mayer. II y bien un Gregorius Magalhaes né en 1614, recteur à Damao en 1656' (Father Alexander Brou, S.J., of Canterbury, to W. R. Philipps, December 30, 1906), think that probably this Gregorius Magalhaes is the person intended. There was a Mathias de Maya, who went to India in 1640 (see A. Franco, 'Synopsis,' 1726).
3. Observantist, of the Observance of St. Francis, a name given specially to the Cordeliers, who also call themselves Observantins (Littré). For Father Lucas de la Croix (or da Cruz), see note 203 to fol. 132, on the Sixth Article.

pieces of silk. The archbishop sat at the upper end of the table, his mitre in his hand. On his right was the grand inquisitor, at his left the second—that is, Father Lucas de la Croix, Dominican.

When Father Ephraim arrived close to the table the inquisitor said to him that they had seen once, and then reconsidered, the record of his case; that they were there assembled to pass judgment; that if he wished to say anything farther in justification he had but to speak. To that he replied that those who had censured his discourses and his writings had employed [138] sophisms, and had not acted uprightly with him. For he had advanced as the major premiss of an argument that a man consecrated by a heretic bishop (*servatis servandis*) [with the necessary reservations] received the attribute [of priesthood]. This they had treated as if he had brought forward instances and reasons for providing the minor premiss: 'This man has been consecrated by a heretic bishop, therefore he has the attributes [of priest],' and that he had, brought forward, as proof of this conclusion, the history that he told them. This was contrary to right reason, for, since this history was only of human authority, the conclusion could not be otherwise than of the same genus. Suarez affirms that the English clergy have not the [priestly] attributes. But this is a point in defendant's favour, showing that he made no invention out of his own head when he said that they (the English) followed the ancient ritual. For although he (Suarez) denies them the [priestly] attribute, because, as he says, they have not the intention of doing what is done by the church, nevertheless, from the whole of the passage referred to it can be gathered that the father (defendant) had not been rash, for he had invented nothing out of his own head. The inquisitor replied to him that his [the inquisitor's] predecessor was not obliged to show him the censures and criticism made against him.

The father (defendant) continued that, as regards the painting of the most Blessed Trinity, they had alleged against him that there were fourteen doctors teaching the contrary of the views he held. In spite of this assertion, they had only referred him to three Jesuits—namely, Tanerus, Vasques, and Layman,[1]

1. These three Jesuits are probably the following:
   1. Adam Tanner, born at Innsbruck 1571, admitted 1590; taught twenty-two years at Munich, Ingolstadt, and Vienna; he died May 25, 1632. He published fifty-one works between 1595 and 1613 (Sommervogel, vii., col. 1843). Probably the work referred to was 'Disputatio de

and these three Jesuits condemned the negative belief as a rash opinion. 'In addition,' said he, 'these three Jesuits are not well enough known in France to enter into comparison with Abulensis Tostatus and Durandus.[1] Perhaps the other doctors who affirm that this representation is legitimate are all Jesuits!

After that the inquisitor asked if he had anything farther to say. He replied that, if they found him guilty, would they be so good as to set before him what they considered worthy of reprehension in his writings. He was ready to reply. Then the inquisitor, speaking in a louder voice, with the tone of a half-angry man, said that the Holy Office had been long enough examining him for him to be fully instructed about what there was he had to answer. Forthwith he rang his hand-bell to summon the warder and have the defendant removed again to his prison.

Upon November 5 [1651], at eight o'clock in the morning, he was recalled to the same hall, where he found seated none but the two inquisitors. As soon as he reached the table the secretary read to him the sentence passed against him by the Holy Office. It condemned him to appear and read a paper from the pulpit of the cathedral church while Mass was being sung. The paper began as follows:

'I, Father Ephraim of Nevers, when living at Madras, said

SS. Trinitatis Mysterio . . . Anno MDCXIII.,' at pp. 136-190 of 'Disputationum Theologicarum A Tanner . . . Libri Quatuor,' Ingolstadi, 1618, 2 vols.

2. Gabriele Vazquez, born 1551, died September 23, 1604. His works, in nine volumes, appeared in 1631 (Hugo Hurter, 'Nomenclator,' i 142). He writes about images in 'Disputationes CI-CIC of his 'Commentariorum, ac Disputationum in Tertiam Partem Sanct. Thomae' (Lugduni, Sumptibus Jacobi Cardon, 1631), vol. i., pp. 638-739. The image of the Trinity is dealt with in section 28 of 'Disputatio CIII.,' p. 676. In the Ingoldstadt edition of this work (1610), 'Disputatio CIII.' begins on p. 978.

3. Paul Layman, born at Innsbruck 1574, admitted 1594; died at Constance November 13, 1635. He was the author of thirty-five printed works, the latest, appearing in 1634 (Sommervogel, iv., col. 1582; H. Hurter, 'Nomenclator,' i. 363). I have failed to fix the work in which he discusses the question of representing the Holy Trinity.

1. Abulensis and Tostatus are one man 'see notes to fol. 129, Answer to Second Article, and to fol. 136, also H. Hurter, 'Nomenclator,' iv. 763: 'Factus est [Alph. Tostatus] episcopus abulensis . . . hinc saepe dictus est simpliciter Abulensis'). For Durandus, see the note to fol. 136.

it was not necessary to adore the Cross with the worship of *Latria*, that the image of the most Blessed Trinity should not be depicted, that the clergyman of the English was a priest, and that it was not advisable to have in churches in this country molten images—propositions which are rash, erroneous, and of evil repute in the Faith. All these I disavow, and affirm that the adoration of *Latria* should be paid to the Cross, that paintings of the image of the most Blessed Trinity may be made, that the clergyman of the English is not a priest, and that molten images should be maintained in churches.'

This is the substance of the sentence. To this the father answered that he could not conscientiously disavow the matter regarding the adoration of the Cross, for that had been defined by the Second Council of Nicaea, and that he would never say anything contrary to the decree of the said Council. If they would insert in their sentence the expression of Bellarmino—'improper and relative adoration'—then he (Ephraim) would say the same as that writer did; he had never departed from that manner of speaking relatively. Upon this the two inquisitors looked at each other, and after that directed the entry as an interlineation of the words '*adoratio respective*'[1] [139].

As for the sacerdotal character of the English clergyman, he answered that he had never affirmed it in that absolute manner, and they ought to consider the mode and the occasion of his saying what he had asserted. But the first inquisitor answered him angrily that it had been proved against him, and that he should speak no more. On perceiving this, and that these gentlemen were determined to deal with him in this manner, the poor culprit held his tongue, so as to escape from their hands, his statements serving no other end than to irritate them against him.

Lastly, the warder, two other Portuguese, and the secretary of the Holy Office conducted him to the cathedral church, where he read the paper, with the modification about the adoration of

1. 'I take "improper adoration" to mean such as is not proper to the material cross itself, and "relative adoration" to mean having respect to Our Lord who suffered on the cross, but not to the cross itself. The inquisitors rejected the word "improper," but accepted "relative," though it is not clear to me where the interlineation was made' (W. R. P.). See Hefere's 'History of the Councils of the Church,' English translation, vol. v., pp. 260-394, on the Council of Nicaea, A.D. 787.

the Cross. The reading of it ended, they brought him back to the hall, where they went over the subject with him. The second inquisitor said to him it was incumbent on him to preach unconditionally that the Cross should be adored, with the absolute adoration of *Latria,* and not relative adoration. To wind up they embraced him, paid him a thousand compliments, and strongly urged him not to return to Madras. He would thus evade the hatred of the secular priests, who would, no doubt, continue to persecute him. He was then carried in a palanquin to the convent of St. Francis, and word was sent to the reverend father, the gaoler, that he (Ephraim) was free, and might go where he chose.

Just let the reader reflect now how those gentlemen condemned the decree of the second Council of Nicaea as 'rash,' that word appearing in their sentence! With reference to what concerns the priesthood of the English clergyman, the charge was never proved against him (Ephraim). It was nothing more than the invention of a drunken man. The other two disputed opinions were submitted to the Sorbonne, which approved what the father had said on those heads. Thus you have in a few words how he was released from prison.

On obtaining his freedom he went to the convent of St. Francis and celebrated Holy Mass, which he had not done since December 28, 1649, up to that day, December 5, 1651;[1] nor had he heard it said. After the Mass, the reverend father provincial and all the others of the community gave him many congratulations on his discharge. Upon the same day they conducted him to the Capuchin convent, where he was met by a procession at the gate of the cloister, which, singing the *Te Deum Laudamus,* escorted him into their church. The kindness they showed him was such that it is not easy to express it. He remained with them up to January 25 [1652], and they treated him so kindly that he regained sufficient strength to make by

1. These dates are in apparent contradiction with those on fols. 126 and 138, which give November 10, 1649, for the commencement of his imprisonment, and November 5, 1651, for his release. A little further on there is an impossible statement of dates, which would be removed if we read for the second date January 31 instead of January 21. The Franciscan convent is near the ruins of the Palace of the Inquisition (Fonseca, 'Goa,' p. 220). I cannot find that there was any convent of Capuchins at Goa.

land the journey of three hundred leagues required to reach Madras. For when he first came out of prison he was so weak that he fell at every step.

He remained at Goa until January 21 [1652], on which day he started for Madras, as said before in opposition to the wishes of the archbishop and the inquisitors. After his release they pressed him a great deal to return no more to that place, alleging as reason the hate of the secular priests at San Thome. Their hatred was so envenomed that they would persecute him to the last day of his life. However, they left him at liberty to go where he pleased, for they could not hinder him; but they entreated him to make them that concession. But the reverend fathers of the Observance and the Capuchins were so greatly shocked at that request that they advised him, in spite of it, to return to Madras If he did not act thus, his enemies would without fail publish all over the coast that his non-return was due to his being a heretic. This would be a great dishonour to the order of St. Francis. F. this reason the whole community begged him to make all possible haste to rejoin his mission.

This he did, and arrived there on April 3 of the same year [1652]. After his arrival they deprived him [140] of the ew Testament he had translated info Portuguese. It was stolen from him at the bidding of a Dominican, who styled himself Commissary of the Holy Office of San Thome, and one of the men who had sworn against him on the last and last but one articles of the above-related accusation. By this [the theft] it is clear that they still sought openings to get him into trouble. But his confidence in God delivered him from their persecutions until his death, which happened at Madras in 1694 at a very advanced age. He left behind so great a reputation that it will endure far into the centuries to come; and to perpetuate it m Europe, I add a translation of some certificates issued in his favour on the subject of his conduct.[1]

Certificate of the very reverend father anthoind de christ, vicar and provincial of the reverend augustinian fathers of the congregation of the east indies—[may 18, 1650].

I, Anthoine de Christ, Vicar and Provincial of the Hermits of our Father St. Augustin, of the Congregation of the East

1. Father Ephraim was alive in September, 1693 (see Wheeler, Madras,' i. 278; Penny, 'Church in Madras,' p. 223).

Indies, certify it to be entirely true that I have been several times on different occasions in the town of Meliapour (Mailapur), called San Thome, and thence have gone several times to the town and fort of the English called Madraspatam or Chinipatnam, which is close to Meliapour. My only inducement was the good fame and great reputation of the reverend father Ephraim of Nevers, a Capuchin of the order of the Seraphic Father St. Francis, a Frenchman by nation. This glorious reputation was so well established that it had spread itself all over the coasts of Gingerly and Choromandal,[1] and had passed into the kingdom of Gulkandah, where the Portuguese and the Indian Christians, even the Mahomedans and Hindus, failed not to praise him and to say a thousand good things of his virtues, exalting much his humility, his poverty, and his chastity; also saying that he was polite to everybody and very charitable. All the Christians who had any business at the said Fort and applied to him came away always very well satisfied. He helped them, and served them with the English gentlemen to the utmost of his power, a fact that I have seen with my own eyes.

He assisted the poor, gathered the wandering sheep who put themselves under his care, and displayed great zeal for the progress of that Christian community. He taught in his school Catholic doctrine to all the children, as well Catholics as heretics, to the great satisfaction of serious men and the confusion of those who by their office were under obligation to do it and did it not. He disputed with the heretics and convinced them out of their own Bible, whereby he gave authentic testimony of his great capacity. As he was well versed in these controversies, he confounded all who argued with him. He showed in the conversations he held with all sorts of men of different nations that he understood well foreign languages. He was also very learned, and known to all learned persons throughout India. His memory was a very happy one; he had ranged in it all the heresies and all the errors that have arisen touching our Holy Faith. He confounded them, by the promptness of his answers, in a way that it was impossible not to admire.

For this reason it was evident that it was very useful, necessary, and glorious for Christianity that he should remain at

1. That is, the whole east coast up to Jagannath in Orissah, Gingerli beginning where Choromandal ends.

Madras. He could there defend our holy Faith against different heretics who land there from all parts of the world. Furthermore, it is certain that Father Ephraim was of the greatest use to the Christians of Madras in particular, for he taught in his school the mysteries of our holy religion with a zeal and a fervour that were most noticeable. He also taught the children to read not only in Portuguese, but in Latin, which they pronounced as [141] if they knew those languages perfectly. He had also trained his scholars to sing the Mass after the mode of the Capuchins. They sang it every Sunday and on the principal festivals, the father standing at the altar and they in the choir. The whole was done with exemplary modesty.

The father preached on festivals and Sundays after the Gospel in the Mass with great zeal and much fervour of mind, teaching good life, good thoughts, and good deeds; this not only by words but still more by his good life, his good example, and the practice of all virtues, monastic and evangelical. To give greater weight to all this, he abstracted from the Holy Gospel the mysteries of our salvation, and drew them up in the form of a catechism by question and answer. All that was in Portuguese; he made all his scholars read it and learn it by heart. It is a work from which those of greater age have derived much profit, to the good of their souls, whence it results that it was of benefit to everybody. In addition, this friar built a neat devotional church,[1] well provided with ornaments, and in it divine service is celebrated with great propriety and devotion, a thing which raises our minds to God.

When the Reverend Father Ambroise of Rennes, visitor of the Capuchin missions, arrived, he came to see me. After several conversations we had over the proceedings of Father Ephraim, he told me that he went away much consoled at seeing so religiously appropriate and well-adorned a church, still more at the great and edifying zeal with which Father Ephraim's life was filled. I also certify it to be entirely true that I have heard the Father Governor of San Thome, named Hierome de Saa, always speak evil of the said Reverend Father Ephraim. He let it be known that he was

1. The French epithet is *dévote* in the second meaning given by' Littré, who quotes Chateaubriand in support: 'Rien n'est plus agréable et plus *dévote* que cette église souterraine.' Mr. Philipps says he often hears the phrase, 'a devotional church,' applied to one which disposes the mind to piety and devotion.

very angry because he (Ephraim) lived at Madras without his orders, and had founded a church without his permission. For he had intended to establish there one of his own priests. To this I replied that his secular priests would give very poor answers to the difficulties and doubts propounded to them by the heretics in regard to our Holy Faith. For not one of them was learned; all were ignorant and illiterate.

In testimony of what is above stated either as eye-witness or as having heard the same from persons worthy of belief, and because two Capuchin fathers—that is to say, the Reverend Father Ambroise of Preuilly[1] and the reverend Father Giles of Dijon—come from Persia to this town of Goa—have asked me to do so, I have drawn up the present certificate, and attest it by an oath on my sacred orders and my religious profession.

Done at the convent of the Seraphic Father St. Francis in the town of Goa, this 18th of May, 1650, signed by my hand, attested and sealed with the petty seal of my office.

F^{r}. ANT^{e}. DE CHRISTO, Vig^{re}.

Provincial, ut supra.

[ATTESTATION OF THE PROVINCIAL OF THE CAPUCHINS, DATED SEPTEMBER 5, 1650.]

I, François Hyacinthe de Dieu, privileged reader in Sacred Theology, Provincial Vicar of the holy Province of the Mother of God of the Capuchins of our Father Saint Francis in the East Indies, testify that the present Certificate agrees with the original, from which it has been drawn and copied, the same having been drawn up by the Reverend Father Anthoine de Christ, Provincial of the Hermits of Saint Augustin. I have read the said original, and had it in my hands; I have collated it with this copy, which entirely agrees with it. In testimony thereof I have issued the present attestation, written and signed with my own hand, and have caused to be affixed to it the small seal of Our Office.

Done within our convent of the Mother of God at Goa, the 5th September, 1650.

(Signed) FR. HYACINTHE DE DIEU.

1. Preuilly, a town and commune in Indre et Loire, nineteen milessouth-west Loches (A. Keith Johnston, 'General Dictionary of Geography,' 1877, p. 1128).

Certificate by the reverend father manuel, vice-commissary-general of the order of our seraphic father saint francis, set over all the friars of that observance upon the coast of choromandal [142]. [september 23, 1650.]

I, the undersigned, Father Manuel de St. Joseph, a professed religious of Our Seraphic Father St. Francis in the Province of the Apostle St. Thomas in the East Indies, hereby certify as follows:

When I was rector of the church and parish of Our Lady or the Light[1] at San Thome, and Commissary throughout the Choromandal coast set over the friars and Province of the said order, there came to Madras, a fortress of the English, a Capuchin monk, French by nation, named Father Ephraim of Nevers. He was in search of a passage to Pegu upon some English vessel; and his object was to assist there as a missionary sanctioned by His Holiness to aid in the work of one of our fathers then working in that Mission (Pegu).

But the English governor, who is the head of that fort, begged him with great urgency and warmth to remain where he was, and to found there a church for the consolation of all the French—I mean to say, the Roman Catholic Christians living there. These Christians could not enter the jurisdiction of the Portuguese on account of their criminal courts or for other reasons, when they wanted either to get married or to partake of the other sacraments. In addition, those living at Pallacatta,[2] belonging

1. This church still exists; it is shown as Lux Church, outside, and slightly to the north-west, of San Thome, in Constable's 'Hand Atlas,' Plate XLI. Mr. Philipps, referring to the 'Annuario do Arcebispado de Goa . . .' (Nova Goa, 1885), p. 128, finds, under 'Vicariate-General of Meliapur,' the entry: 'Missao da Luz, orago (*i.e.*, dedication) Nossa Senhora da Luz, fundada em 1516.' This makes it the oldest Portuguese church near Madras. The story goes that when they first landed, they were guided to this spot by a light, and accepting this as a good omen, built a chapel. But the tale is a doubtful one, as this dedication is not unknown elsewhere—for instance, at Goa (see Fonseca, pp. 245, 275, 277). A more recent record, the 'Madras Catholic Directory of 1906,' calls it the Church of Our Lady of the Snows, the 'Luz,' and assigns the foundation to 1510.
2. Pulicat (*Pala-kadu*, 'Old Forest'), a town in the Chingleput district, twenty-four miles north of Madras. The earliest Dutch fort, called Geldria, was established here in 1609. Taken and restored several times,

to the Dutch, and about seven leagues from San Thome, could not go there owing to the war between the Dutch and the Portuguese.

If Father Ephraim settled in Madras, all these grievances would be remedied. He would render a great service to our Church, and give exceptional succour to forsaken souls. For if his zeal constrained him to undertake such perilous voyages to search for lost souls, and forward the conversion of others already beginning to doubt, right reasoning required that he should still more eagerly seek to gain over souls already converted, who were straying in the paths of perdition, merely from want of a shepherd to gather them within the fold of Holy Church. They needed spiritual pasturage by means of the sacraments, of which they had been so long deprived, to the danger of their salvation. Thus they lived excommunicated, sunk in grossness, and dying in evil state, forfeited both soul and heaven.

Father Ephraim, moved by these reasons, and out of zeal for the salvation of these poor people, also because he was glad to be able to establish a public church within the country of the English and in sight of their fort, decided to take up his abode at Madras. He built a church dedicated to the Apostle St. Andrew,[1] and in it celebrated publicly divine service, carried out the procession of the Blessed Sacrament in the streets, accompanied by many people. There was great reverence and much devotion, not solely by the Catholics of Madras, but by those of San Thome. The latter went to Madras out of devotion, in order to assist in celebrating the festivals with greater solemnity. Even the English fired their cannon when the procession passed in front of the Fort.

During Lent the father preached publicly on the Passion of Our Lord Jesus Christ, and set forth the mysteries of our Faith with a singular devotion. Thus there were to be seen a crowd of persons from Madras, San Thome, and Puliacat; even the English and their clergyman were present at these representations. In Holy Week he conducted all the offices in his church, sang Matins

---

it was finally ceded to the English in 1825 ('Madras Manual of Administration,' iii.' 671). Mr. Philipps thinks the quotations in Yule, 736, suggest *Palaiya-kottai*, 'Old Fort,' as the true derivation.

1. This dedication is confirmed by an incidental mention in a Government Consultation of November 1, 1694 (Penny, 'Church in Madras,' p. 224).

and *Tenebrae* with his scholars, the whole after the manner of the Capuchins [143]. On Holy Thursday he decorated the sepulchre and the oratory, where the most Blessed Sacrament was laid. On Good Friday he represented the Passion and preached on it, having displayed an image of Our Lord's body being brought down dead from the cross. We other friars went to help him at the solemn festivals, since the father did hot begin until we had finished at San Thome.

At the Christmas festival he represented the mystery of the birth of the Infant Jesus laid in a cradle. He thus excited the devotion of the people, while many Mahomedans and Hindus came during the most solemn festivals to see this father's church. The English gave him every year what he demanded for his decorations. He took no alms for Masses nor for burials; but imitating the example of Tobias, he buried them without fee for the love of God. This he did even when they were poor, and if there were not enough men to carry the dead body he helped in the task. He has never received any gifts for administering Baptism or Marriages, and all the other sacraments were performed gratis.

Neither did he receive pecuniary gifts for the support of his own person; but he took the gifts made to him of a little rice or other things necessary to sustain life. This conduct provoked the admiration of the Catholics, the English, and even of the Mahomedans and Hindus. They saw him acting contrary to other ecclesiastics and the secular priests. He kept up in his dwelling a public school for children, several of whom were English. These children were taught the doctrines of Christianity. At all times he argued against heretics, and convinced them out of other own Bible. By this he showed that he was extremely well read in controversial books, and understood all the errors of these heresies, and could refute them. He did this not only with the English, but the Dutch—an obvious proof that he knew the sacred writings very well and also foreign tongues.

He was learned and well read, which was the motive—nay, one of the principal reasons—and the occasion of the troubles and disagreeables which he suffered, and at this moment suffers in the dungeons of the Holy Office. The cause was the extraordinary envy and hatred entertained against him by the Jesuits and the secular priests of San Thome. This was due to the fruits reaped by the labours of this truly apostolic missionary, and the esteem, respect, and veneration felt for him by the Catholics, the heretics, the Hindus, and the Mahomedans. These all applied to him the name of Apostle, a holy and perfect man, not only by reason of his exemplary life and his practising the evangelical virtues, but also for his eminent doctrine. For it seemed as if Our Lord had led him to this country and these unbelieving kingdoms among Hindus, Mahomedans, and enemies of our Holy Faith, in order that by the saintliness of his life and the excellence of his teaching, he should increase the glory of the Gospel and work for the conversion of souls. He had a special gift for all languages, for in addition to the dead languages which all the learned know, he understood Arabic, Persian, Turkish, Mosarabic,[1] and English. For the greater profit of his people he extracted from the Holy Gospels the mysteries of our faith and salvation, and translated them into Portuguese in the form of a catechism. This he gave to his pupils to read, and made them learn it by heart, so that our holy religion might be imprinted better on their memory. This work was useful not only to children, but to old people.

I also certify that I have always heard evil words about Father Ephraim from the Priest Governor of the San Thome bishopric; his name is Hyeronime de Saa. He showed himself [144] openly the Father's deadly enemy, proclaiming at every turn the ill-will he bore to him for having founded a church without his orders and without his consent. He had wished to

1. Mosarabic is, perhaps, meant for the special liturgy in Greak character, but the words mostly Latin, used by the *Mozarabiques*, or Christians in Spain living under Mahomedan rule. The word is said to be derived from *musta'ribah* (Arabic), a stranger (Littré). The language was 'the peculiar dialect of Latin that the Romanized Spaniards of Cordova had spoken, greatly modified by two or three centuries of Arabic intercourse' (Martin Hume, 'Spanish Influence on English Literature,' p. 17). Mr. Philipps doubts the propriety of this identification for the word in the text; he also questions Littrés assertion that the Greek character was used. He relies on R. Biron's translation of S. Bäumer's 'Histoire du Bréviaire' (Paris, 1905), i. 349, 350, and L. Duchesne, 'Christian Worship' (English translation, London, 1903), p. 119. His other point is that the Hindustani spoken at Madras is called in Tamil *aravi*; thus the word *mosarabic* might be meant for that tongue, or perhaps for 'colloquial Arabic.' The only surviving specimen of the Mozarabic liturgy is a Missal recovered by Cardinal Ximenes; it is printed in Migne's 'Patrologia Latina,' vol. Ixxxv., edited by A. Leslie, S.J.

establish there one of his priests and eject Father Ephraim, to which he would willingly have consented. But the English would never consent, on account of the scandalous lives of the San Thome fathers. They knew well they were all licentious—a fact quite scandalous and public, each one keeping a mistress in his house. In this accusation was also included this same administrator of the diocese, according to the public voice in the town of San Thome.

Since the women they lived with were poor and subsisted by infamous prostitution of their bodies, they sometimes visited Englishmen in the town [of Madras] and submitted themselves to them. They confided to these men all that passed between them and the fathers of San Thome. This is the reason that the English refused to look at the Portuguese fathers, and in their talk spoke of their evil lives. I have often heard Father Ephraim say that his hardest task was to defend the priests of San Thome against the tongues of the English, and reply to the scandalous accusations made against and stories told about them. These stories were founded on the statements of the public women. It was also the case that they (the priests) went themselves to Madras to collect alms, and there drank with the English to such excess that they always came away drunk; in fact, so drunk that, unable to walk, it was requisite to carry them home. This happened to that same priest-administrator of the diocese and three other of his priests, greatly to the scandal of the public.

Furthermore, in several other conversations that I have had with the said priest-administrator I have heard him make great complaint that Father Ephraim unjustly occupied the post of one of his priests, and that the place was one subject to his jurisdiction. To which I replied that Madras was not within his jurisdiction, it being a country owned by a Hindu king who had given it to the English, and they had built a fort and established a government. For this reason neither the King of Portugal nor the Bishop of Meliapur (Mailapur) had any jurisdiction in that territory, and still less could make any claim thereto. Further, I told him several times that there Was not a single priest at San Thome fit to live among heretics and convert them by an exemplary life. Still less was there any who could by his knowledge refute errors and heresies as Father Ephraim did. Not one of them was able even to read his breviary properly, or to say a Mass as it ought to be done. In this way, if any one of them occupied the said church [at Madras] he would create a great confusion, he would be a great dishonour, and would commit great affront to our Holy Catholic faith.

It was from these differences that arose so much animosity and ill-will against the father. Not only did the secular priests enter into the quarrel, but the fathers of the Society of Jesus took a leading part. They incited the priests against the poor father. Neither the one nor the other group could, however, revenge themselves or deprive him of his employment. Thus they made a malicious accusation against him to the Holy Office that he was the author of certain false assertions and of other statements they only partly understood. For, not being learned, but, on the contrary, very ignorant, they caused by their depositions and accusations the issue of an order from the Holy Office. It was directed to the said priest administering the diocese of San Thome, and required him to cause Father Ephraim to be arrested, and sent to Goa to the Holy Office.

The order was carried out with such harshness as to make it quite manifest that passion was the moving force with the said administrator, his priests, and the Jesuits. For, first of all, this capture and this [145] imprisonment were entirely opposed to the rules followed by the officials of the Inquisition—at least, were opposed to the rules of the Holy Office in similar affairs. What is meant is that the law of the Inquisition enjoins that a capture be made secretly, while this one was so public that it resembled rather (if I may be permitted the comparison) the seizure of our Lord Jesus Christ than a hidden arrest. It was such that, since the Holy Office was established in the East Indies, never has an arrest been seen so public or so degrading.

The practice of the inquisitors when they order the taking of some Jew or some new Christian layman,[1] is to capture the man by means of a familiar, with a great deal of secrecy, conveying him in a palanquin securely closed. But the priest-administrator of the diocese of San Thome sent a company of soldiers and armed satellites to seize Father Ephraim. Two of them dragged, him along bound: one went in front hauling at the rope round his gown, while the other followed, holding another rope, which he had tied round the prisoner. In this scandalous manner they

1. Mr. Philipps suggests that 'new Christian' may be used here in the peculiar Spanish and Portuguese sense of a descendant from a Jewish convert.

took him publicly through the whole town of San Thome. Thereby they affronted the poor father and greatly dishonoured the habit of Saint Francis.

Many people—Christians, Mahomedans, and Hindus—followed weeping and wailing over his lamentable state. They detested what was being done, and invoked Heaven against the cruelty practised on a man they held to be a saint. The administrator of the diocese preceded his captive, lying at full length in his palanquin, borne by six to eight coolies, just as if he were a conqueror leading his enemy in triumph. In this manner, as cruel as it was to be deplored, he conducted Father Ephraim, his prisoner, in the midst of his satellites, to the college of the fathers of the Society of Jesus. There they put fetters on his feet so heavy that the father fell three times and fainted as one dead, owing to the weight of the irons, he being a man of feeble and delicate constitution. He was also overcome at finding himself in such a degraded and disgraced position.

In this condition the priest-administrator sent the imprisoned father to a cell so narrow that he could hardly move in it, and so dark that there was only light to see his sufferings and the cruelty of his brethren. The Jesuits, on seeing the good friar in such a pitiable condition, and for three days unable to eat, grew afraid that he might die in their house and college. They went to the administrator and warned him to be careful. On their solicitation he changed the heavy irons then on the prisoner's legs for ones smaller and more humane. Nevertheless, he was left in his dark dungeon, where he could speak to no one.

In time he grew so weak that it was thought he was dying. He was attacked by diarrhoea, which lasted eighteen days, and he was unable to eat. As he really believed that death was at hand, he prayed the fathers that one of them might have the kindness to confess him. This they would never consent to do, in spite of their being under obligation as ecclesiastics to administer to him the Sacrament of Penitence, since he asked for it and was in peril of death. They should not have listened to the administrator's opposition, for the tribunal of the Holy Office grants to prisoners sacramental confession whenever asked, and prisoners are even exhorted to confess.

Furthermore, the Jesuits ought not to have allowed the administrator of the diocese to put irons upon the father when he placed him under guard in their college, for they knew quite well that such was not the order of the Inquisition nor of the inquisitors. What is more, if the father had so wished, he need never have fallen into their hands. For the Agent of the English had warned him [146] not to go to San Thome, because he knew that the governor there had an order from the Holy Office to arrest him. The said governor [of San Thome] made so little of a secret of the subject that before Father Ephraim was seized everybody was aware of the order he had received to that effect. He had read his commission and the warrant of arrest sent him by the inquisitors to a Dominican named Father François de Fonseca, and to another father named Thomas Mexia.

The latter published the fact everywhere, so that even the English knew it and warned the father. But he was so confident in his innocence that he paid no heed to this advice, and went to Our Lady of the Light,[1] a [Capuchin] church within our jurisdiction. He had been invited there by a letter from the said administrator saying that he wanted to communicate with him on certain business. There the administrator also went himself in order to seize the father's person in the way' already indicated.

Subsequently he caused the father to be put publicly on board a ship with the irons on his legs. He was taken to Negapatam, and there sent ashore in the above condition in the sight of the whole town, greatly to the disgrace and dishonour of the habit of St. Francis. He was sent on board again in the same way, and carried to Manaar. I heard of this when I was for a time in the country of Jafnapatam, near Manaar.[2] I was then inspecting the convents of our order under a commission from the reverend father our Commissary-General. My duty was to collect our brethren for a Provincial Chapter that was about to be held.

I threw up my inspection and all my other work in order to reach Manaar. There I found the said Father Ephraim with the

1. That is to say, the Lux or Luz Church, between Madras and San Thome (see note 222 to fol. 142).
2. Manar, a town on an island of the same name off the coast of Ceylon, lat. 9° 3′, long. 80° The Jafna Peninsula is at the north end of Ceylon, some fifty or sixty miles from Manar. Mr. Philipps, who has visited the spot several times, says that in Portuguese days the only passage was between Manar Island and Ceylon; now all ships use the Pamban Channel between the Indian mainland and Ramesvaram. This channel was made in the nineteenth century by the sea breaking through; it has since been enlarged by blasting.

same irons upon him as above described. On beholding this, I promptly sent for the captain of the ship to whom he had been made over. I gave an undertaking in writing to produce him before the tribunal of the Holy Office; and in case of default I agreed to answer with my own person. The captain transferred his responsibility on to my shoulders, and made over the father to me. Forthwith I had his leg-irons removed. This I did not only to remove the opprobrium thereby cast upon our religion and our habit, but because I knew his virtue and holiness, having been for five years and a half his confessor, and we had been on very familiar terms of intercourse. I knew, in addition, that all the things imputed to him proceeded from the malignity of his accusers. It was nothing, all of it, but envy, mere hatred, and falsehood.

I also certify it to be true that if this good friar had wished to take to flight after his irons had been removed, he could easily have done so. He could have gone away to Tuticorin, which is a country of the Hindus, or to Cochin; for he was always in freedom, and went by himself wherever he pleased without my paying any heed. I knew his innocence, of which he has given sufficient proof; for although able to deliver himself from the prisons of the Holy Office, he has disdained to do so.

I say, further, that the said father was of the greatest service to the Portuguese of San Thome; and in all the disputes they had with the English, whether important or not, they obtained a favourable issue by the mediation of this father, for the English respected him greatly. As a proof thereof, take the case of a Portuguese who killed an Englishman in their fort of Madras, and the English intended to execute the murderer on the, spot, not even leaving him time to confess himself. The Père Ephraim succeeded in obtaining from the Agent, in teeth of his council's opposition, a respite of three days in order that the man might prepare himself worthily for confession, and set his conscience at rest. During these three days the father lived continuously in the prison, consoling the guilty man both day and night. He accompanied him to his execution with a crucifix in his hand, and never abandoned; the man until his last sigh, and this he did against the will of the English.

NOTE FROM THE ENGLISH RECORDS

[Although Father Ephraim is not mentioned, there can be little doubt that the incident referred to is file one given in a supplement to a general letter from Fort St. George dated September 20, 1642 (Original Correspondence, No. 1791), under the heading, 'Passages on this Coast from ye pr^{o} 7^{br} 1641 to ye p^{ro} 7^{ber} 1642. The account runs as follows:

'The 11" of August [1642] 3 Portugall Soldiers belonging to the Armada: 11 small Frigotts sent for the Reliefe of St Thoma, with 270 Soldiers came to our Towne, and in a base Arack house, fell to drincking with a Dane, and at length together by the ears, in fine the 3 Portugalls with their rapiers made uppon him and wounded him in 7 places, notice of which being given us, wee sent two Soldiers to part them, who no sooner entred within the Yard, and Commanded them to desist, but on of the three aforesaid soldiers by name Anthony Myrando, ran the one of our 2 soldiers into the right Pappe that instantly he dyed without speaking one word; so soone as they perceived what they had done, they all 3 fledd, but within lesse than halfe an hower, were all thre taken, and being truly informed which was the Homicide, wee kept him and suffered the others to depart for S^{+} Thoma, from whence wee received many Letters to release him for that he was a phydalgo, but what thorough our Naiques importunitie, together with our owne people, wee cold not reprieve him till advized to Surrat, but were even forced to execute him the 13th d° [? ditto] the morning, and because he pretended to be a Gentleman as aforesaid, wee shott him to death before our Corps du guards; Since when wee have byn wonderful! at ease in respect of the Portugalls, for till then wee were dayly troubled with one or other, And now in this place it will not be imperninent [? impertinent] before wee conclude to say Some what of St Thoma, where from the time the Armado arrived, which was in May last, to the time they parted, which was the 20th of August it is not to be spoken what a many murthers and other crimes which in any part of Christendome deserved death, were committed by the Soldiers, yet no one man suffered for it among them; this Homicide Myrando about the prime of August kild a man in St Thoma and rann hither for sanctuary, and being wee would not protect him he not having made his peace, he vou'd in some of our hearing to be the death of some English man ere he left the Coast, the said Myrando further confessed ere he Suffered, that this was the 7th Murther he had Committed, but now say the Portugalls of St Thoma or rather the Capt. More [Chief Captain] (for all the Citizens rejoice at what wee did), the peace is broke and they expect order from the Viceroy to fall on us, which were it so (or wee faile much in our Judgements) S[t] Thoma woold not Continue a month more in the hands of the Portugalls.'

In another account of the murder in Original Correspondence, No. 1792, the name of the murdered soldier is given as James Jaques, and it is also stated that the *naique* [the native ruler of the country] sent a large body of soldiers into the town, and insisted on the summary execution of the murderer. Father Ephraim, having been appointed chaplain on June 8, 1642, must have been in Fort St. George in August of that year.]

If on this occasion and on others the father had not been living at Madras, the English would have broken with us. Indeed, this happened once when he was away. It was the [147] occasion when the general Dom Louis de Mello carried away a ship from their port, and took possession thereof against all reason and justice. For the viceroy caused it afterwards to be restored, and removed the general from his appointment at San Thome.[1]

The father found a remedy for all these differences, and by his prudence moderated the passions on both sides. To this he was impelled by his zeal for public peace and welfare, and in this he rendered great service to God, to the king, and to the Portuguese of Mailapur.

Furthermore, two Capuchin fathers, who came from Persia as assistants to Father Ephraim—that is to say, Father Friar Ambrose of Preuilly and Father Friar Gilles of Dijon—have asked

1. Manuel Mascarenhas has been already mentioned in IV., fol 125. The only trace of the incident in the text to be found in the English records is in Original Correspondence, 2006, under date of October 27, 1646: 'The Demands of the Worpll. Agent Esq[re] Councell of Coast Choromandel' (Sir Thomas Ivie) 'in the behalf of the Honble. English East India Company to the Generall of St. Thome, Manuel Mascharinhas de Almeda Vizt, Wee demand plenary Satisfaction of Don Lewis de Mello, the quondam Generali of St. Thome, for what injuries committed by him to the Honble. Compa. which were Specifyed in a list sent to the V. Roy,' The man referred to is, no doubt, the Augustinian friar Luiz de Mello, Vicar-General and Governor of San Thome in 1639, subsequently elected Bishop of that place, but died before his confirmation (C. C. de Nazareth, 'Mitras Lusitanas no Oriente,' part iii., p. 99; Bombay, 1888).

me for the present certificate as a justification of the said father, their brother, and to prove his innocence. I have drawn it up strictly according to truth as an eye-witness of almost all the things that I record and affirm, for I have been his confessor five years and a half, and have conversed with him with all imaginable familiarity. During most of this time we were together, either I in his hospice and church, or he in ours. If I tried to record here all that I know of the said father—of his virtues, of the service he rendered to Christianity in general and to his mission in particular, or did for the welfare and salvation of souls, I should never be finished.

All that I have entered in the present certificate I confirm by an oath on my religious profession and on my holy orders as being absolutely true.

Done at Goa in the convent of the Mother of God of the Capuchin Fathers this 23rd September, 1650.

(Signed) F. MANUEL DE ST. JOSEPH.

We, the undersigned. Friar Anthoine de Santiago and Friar Martin de St. Jean, professed religious in the Province of Mère de Dieu of the reformed discalced[1] order of the Capuchins of Our Father St. Francis in the East Indies, the one Guardian of the Convent of the Mère de Dieu at Goa, and the other Assistant Commissary to the Reverend Father Provincial, Friar Hyacinthe de Dieu.

Hereby certify that the present certificate above written of the Reverend Father Friar Manuel de St. Joseph, preacher, who has been very frequently Superior of the Province of the Apostle St. Thomas, and Definitor[2] in that of the Mother of God, is written and signed by his own hand, for we know thoroughly well his handwriting and signature; and we therefore certify and swear to the above each by his religious profession and *in verbo sacerdotis*, and in attestation thereof have both of us signed these presents with our sign manual. I, Friar Anthoine de Santiago, have written the present attestation with my hand, and jointly with me has

1. I had written 'bare-footed' as better English, but Mr. Philipps tells me that 'discalced' is the recognised word among English Catholics.
2. This word, for which there is no English equivalent, means practically 'Assistant to the Provincial' (W. R. P.).

signed Friar Martin de St. Jean, Provincial Commissary, and we have appended the seal of our Convent of the Mère de Dieu.

Done at Goa this 19th October, 1650.

(Signed) FR. ANTHOINE DE SANTIAGO, *ut supra.*
(Signed) FR. MARTIN DE ST. JEAN, *ut supra.*

[Folio 148 is blank.][1]

[149] When the Great Mogul placed the government of the Karnatik in the hands of Da,ud Khan, he gave him secret orders to put to death certain powerful princes. These orders the other generals, his predecessors, had found impossible of execution; but this one, aware that his strength was not sufficient to execute his purpose, had recourse to stratagem. He made abundant promises to these princes, and thereby induced them to pay him a visit. However, they did not put much trust in him, more especially as they knew Mahomedan ways; they usually promise a great deal, and afterwards perform the very least they can. Therefore those princes came to visit him at the head of an army of one hundred thousand soldiers.

But Da,ud Khan feared neither them nor their army. He did not forego his design. When they came to bid him good-bye, he engaged them in conversation. He was seated in the middle. Seizing a poignard, he killed one on the spot, and with the other hand grasped the second one's beard. This man was made a prisoner, and a few hours afterwards his life was taken. When this event reached the ears of the army of these two unfortunate princes, this immense multitude, instead of avenging their masters, took to flight, for it is the ordinary custom of this country that on the death of a commander his soldiers forthwith take to flight. The name of the leader killed with the poignard was Mattalava, and that of the other Sevagy (Shiva Ji).

There can be no doubt that this Da,ud Khan is valiant and bold, but sometimes cruel, as I know from experience. His legitimate wife having at two different times brought forth daughters, when report of their birth was made to him he entered his seraglio, or *mahal*, took the infants and tyrannically cut them into pieces.

1. Père Norbert has a strange version of the Father Ephraim episode (see 'Mèmoires Historiques,' vol. iii., p. 56; London, 1752). Ephraim's seizure he wrongly attributes to a Jesuit intrigue, and tells a romance about his forcible release at Goa by a landing party from an English man-of-war.

He said that those men should not be praised who were proud of having offspring. However, the wife, cast down at finding herself in the hands of such a tyrant, left him and went to live with her parents.

In the year 1702 it chanced that one of this general's concubines became pregnant, and, to conceal the fact from him, she gave out that she was ill. She was delivered secretly of a boy, at which she was extremely rejoiced, imagining that Da,ud Khan would not be so cruel to this child as he had been to the others, more especially as it was his only heir. However, fearing that this tyrant might do some cruel deed to this innocent creature, she told his brother Bedercan (Bahadur Khan) about it, with the object that he should speak to Da,ud Khan, and so arrange matters that he should not deal with this child as he had done with his daughters by taking their lives. For this purpose Bahadur Khan presented the cruel wretch with a tray filled with gold coins. Da,ud Khan asked him what this novel act meant. He replied: 'My lord, it is to congratulate you upon the new heir that Heaven has given you. As it is [150] a male child, I pray you to give it the name of our father.'

Without listening to any arguments, Da,ud Khan rose up in a state of fury, gave a kick to the tray, and pursued his brother with torrents of abuse, then, turning angrily, went to the door of the seraglio. He found it shut. He wanted to open it with force by axes and hammers. Unable to manage this, he had it taken from its hinges. Entering, he sought on all sides for the infant, which had been hidden. At length he found it held to her bosom by one of his female relations. Showing neither compassion nor remorse, he wrenched it from her, threw it on the ground, took its life, and spurned it with his feet. No one had the hardihood to interfere. At once he came forth somewhat pacified, and began to give audience to his captains, who had hurried there in the hope of stopping this outrage. They had arrived too late, but there they stood in dejection, their heads sunk on their chests. He asked what their silence betokened, and their sadness. They answered that it was from seeing the tyranny he had displayed to his own flesh and blood, and how little they had expected such a manner of acting. He retorted that the mother was low born and not of his race, that such offspring could never be courageous, and would only have lived on to disgrace him.

In the year 1703 I received a letter from this Da,ud Khan, and another from the *diwan* Chaadetulacan (Sa'adatullah Khan),[1] and several others from other lords. By these letters they entreated me to visit them, especially as they had much need of me. I began my journey on February 27 of the same year (1703), and found the said general at the town of Carpa (Cuddapah, Karapa)[2] distant one hundred and twenty leagues from Madras. I was very well received by these gentlemen according to their customs. They asked me to be so good as to treat a captain named Mohamed Jafar (Muhammad Ja'far), a Persian by race. I would not undertake the case, for he was already moribund; in fact, he died a few days afterwards. During the short time I was with their army I got no time to rest, for everybody pestered me, as their way is, for medicines, even those who had no need of them. They would say as a reason, 'I have no appetite; give me some medicine to make me eat like an elephant, or like a camel, or at any rate like a horse.' And all these brute-like demands simply to have strength to slake their sensuality! For their minds are filled with, and they have no other diversion than, the desire to steal all they can, for no other object than the accomplishment of their carnal desires.

At the end of fifteen days they gaveme leave to go, in an honourable manner, conferring on me a *sarapa* (set of robes) and enough money to pay the cost of my journey. These gentlemen gave me a letter for the governor of this place (Madras) conveying many thanks for having sent me, and they told him other details [151] of my journey. Verbally they directed me to say to the said governor that he must give back three villages, those that Zu,lfiqar Khan had presented to the Honorable Company of England in the days of his being governor; since then fresh orders had been received to take possession of them again.[3]

1. This man must be the Sa'adatullah Khan, Nawayat, who died on the 19th Rabi' II, 1145 H. (October 8, 1732), aged about eighty (lunar) years ('Ma,asir-ul-Umara,' ii. 513; Wilks, 'South of India,' i. 248; and 'Tarikh-i-Muhammadi'). His nephew, Dost 'Ali Khan, and his son-in-law, Husain Dost Khan (Chanda Sahib), figure largely in the contests following the death of Nizam-ul-Mulk Asaf Jah, in which the English and the French took different sides.
2. Cuddapah, 137 miles north-west of Madras ('Madras Manual of Administration,' iii. 244).
3. I cannot find this transaction, but possibly these villages were granted by the *parwanaks* received from Zu,lfiqar Khan on September 10, 1698 (Wheeler, 'Madras,' i. 339). Judging by what Wheeler says (ii. 14) in

I arrived at Madras and carried out the orders that had been given to me. But the governor, Thomas Pitt, paid no heed to the message; for, having much experience, he knows perfectly the manners and customs of this kind of people. They seek continually fresh methods of capturing some money. His reply to them was that he was the owner of the three villages, and that he meant to keep them, so much so that to this day he remains in possession. On this reply there came certain menaces, but in the end the thing blew over without further disturbance.

The said *diwan* gave me another letter for the Governor of Pondicherry, François Martin, which contained nothing but some compliments and friendly expressions. But the said *diwan* or governor directed me verbally to say to the said Sieur Martin that he had received orders from the king (Aurangzeb) to obtain the lands controlled by Pondicherry. The answer given [by the French] was that they had been bought from the hands of Roma Raja (Ram Raja), son of Shiva Ji; that afterwards they had received them back at the hands of the Dutch;[1] that the lands were in their possession, and they meant to keep them to all eternity. After this reply they sent him a few presents, and since then nothing more has been said about the matter. It is the fashion of these Moguls to make a display of power [in this way], and proclaim themselves all-powerful and masters of everything. Subsequently, when they discover that they cannot overcome either by force or artifice, they dissemble; but if at a future time an occasion presents itself, they keep neither their word nor the friendship that they had promised.

I noticed in this little journey that the country is full of hills, and that the roads are very narrow. Thus, had the inhabitants displayed any courage or valour, it would never have been possible

---

regard to an attempt to take possession in March 1703, the three villages were Egmore, Pursewaukum, and Triplicane, all now included in Madras city.

1. Ram Raja held Tanjor and lived in Jinji from 1690 to 1697 (see Grant Duff, pp. 163 and 171). The Dutch restored Pondicherry in 1699 under the Treaty of Ryswick of 1697. This occasion when the French employed Manucci's good offices is probably that mentioned in the Chevalier Martin's letter of February 5, 1703, when he transmitted do France a copy of the instructions given (C^2 67, fol. 11).

for the Moguls, with all the forces at their command, to make themselves masters of it. I also beheld several ancient fortresses built by the Hindu princes of the Karnatik; for those who are nowadays in command on behalf of the Mogul had been warned of my approach, and invited me to visit them. Each one made me a present, such as some pieces of silk, some shawls,[1] *et cetera*, and treated me most splendidly according to their fashion. It is true that they did not present these things to me for nothing, for in return I gave them such medicines as they wanted.

I noticed that these fortresses had not been designed by good architects or engineers. The works are [? weak][2] in spite of their walls being built of great hewn stones fixed in cement, and their being provided with hollows or ditches right round them. In some ditches there is a water-supply, in others none. The forts have also some pieces of artillery twenty to twenty-five feet long, of which the calibre is so extremely large that a big [152] fat man can easily get inside. The greater number of these guns lie on the ground outside the fort gates. There are, in addition, a few inside in different positions. I also noticed some small pieces on the walls and bastions, carrying a ball of from one half pound to three pounds' weight. They were mounted on heavy blocks of wood, without carriages or wheels, and their muzzles pointed into the air. Their only use is to make a noise and smoke on the days when a new moon appears, or when it is intended to frighten someone; for to go through any drill with them, or to teach how to aim them in one direction or another, that is an impossible thing. Nevertheless, the Mogul never omits to sanction the money necessary for efficiently providing all these fortresses, and sees that there are faithful officers in charge, as Darroges (*daroghah*), Ammy (*amin*), and Morseg (*mushrif*)—that is to say [blank in original].[3] In addition there is commandant at each fortified place. But the whole lot are thieves, and the places are kept like cowsheds.

During this journey I also received an invitation from Gulla Maly Can (Ghulam 'Ali Khan), governor of the fortress of

1. The text has *chalet*, which I take to be a copyist's error for *chāles*—that is, 'shawls.'
2. The word is wanting in the text.
3. These three words might be translated by 'superintendent,' 'accountant,' and 'storekeeper,' The vernacular name of the commandant would be *qila'hdar*.

Velours (Velur, Vellore),[1] my ancient friend who gave himself up to Da,ud Khan, as I have related (IV. 117). This lord received me with great joy, the more so that at the moment they were in the midst of feasts and banquets in honour of the birth of some grandson of his. This event he had looked forward to for several years past, and now attributed to the virtues of my medicine the appearance in the world of this new heir to his wealth. For this reason he gave me several things and uttered many expressions of gratitude; in addition, he sent with me as an escort twenty-five horsemen and five match-lockmen.

The fortress of Vellore is large and well built. It has lateral supporting walls,[2] and the ditch is large, about fifty cubits in width, and filled by springs rising in it. The water is full of crocodiles, and if by misfortune anyone falls in, he is at once torn to pieces and eaten up by them. Out of curiosity I went quite close to the ditch; these animals, seeing on the water the shadow of human beings, opened their jaws. I threw them a goat, which they tore to pieces at once and ate, snatching the pieces out of each other's jaws. I observed that at the noise these made other crocodiles rushed from different parts of the ditch. They were in such great numbers, and there was such great confusion, that they could not be counted. They kept their heads out of the water and their jaws wide open. As a pastime I threw them several goats in pieces; they fell upon the pieces, and without any chewing swallowed them at one mouthful. At another place I made the men throw in some heads of goats with large horns. But no sooner had they been thrown in than the crocodiles with a toss of the head had at once swallowed them, for these animals are monstrous. It can also be said that they render the fortress stronger, and defend it from any assault that might be delivered. But what protection [153] are they against the high hills surrounding the place, from the summit of which the walls could be knocked down by pieces of artillery?

According to the custom of the country there come at times strange men who, as a sacrifice for their sins, throw themselves

---

1. Vellur (Vellore), a town in the North Arcot district, seventy-eight miles west of Madras; it has an ancient fortress ('Madras Manual of Administration,' iii. 975).
2. *Contremurs*: small walls built laterally to another to hold it up and strengthen it (Littré).

into this ditch. The Mahomedans often sacrifice buffaloes, cows, goats, *et cetera*, and all this forms the food of the crocodiles. Da,ud Khan, when he mastered this fortress, had all the thieves caught in the army thrown to these crocodiles. This he did by way of a thanksgiving sacrifice for the reduction of a place of such fame. This is what they ordinarily do to secure good success in their designs.

In the year 1703 it happened that a Mogul ship coming from Mecca, full of pious Muslims returning home after a pilgrimage to the tomb of their false prophet, was taken by pirates off the port of Surat. In it there was more than a million of rupees' worth of *patacas* and *sequins* in addition to the merchandise. On seeing this vessel the pirates boarded it in silence, sword in hand. But they did not succeed in surprising it as they had hoped, for some Pures[1] came forward to resist along with some Persians, Pathans, and Arabs armed with scimitars. The pirates lost more than twenty men, and thus the captain of the corsair was forced into a prompt recourse to firearms. By these he made himself master of the ship, carried off the richest of the passengers, and released the rest.

The governor of the place (Surat), being informed of what had taken place, ordered the arrest of the English and Dutch presidents then at Surat, threw them into prison, and subjected them to severities. He obtained from the Dutch five hundred thousand rupees and from the English another sum of money, and in addition they were subjected to great hardships in the matter of food and drink. The Dutch governor of Colhin, (Cochin) having heard of the occurrence, sent at once seven ships of war to blockade the port of Surat, and the English governor of Bombay also sent three.

Upon the arrival of all these men-of-war they seized all the Mahomedan vessels found there. They dealt out the same rigour to the Mahomedan crews as had been shown to the Europeans on land. They demanded a return of the sum of money that had been forcibly taken, and, in addition, another amount that had been taken some years before in a most unjust manner. They claimed also the interest on this second sum. In addition to the

1. For this word 'Pures,' all I can suggest is that it is intended for 'Parsi' or 'Purbiyah' (native of Bengal or Bihar).

release of the prisoners, it was intended that the Moguls should be forced to make peace and restore the conditions prevailing in the time of Shahjahan. Seeing the resolution of the Europeans, and the great loss they would cause to his seaport, the king dismissed the governor and all the principal officers, and issued fresh orders that the European demands must be satisfied. In this way peace was made.[1]

NOTE ON SURAT AND THE PIRACY TROUBLES.

[The complaints of the Mogul emperor about European piracy on the high seas between Jeddah and Surat go back to 1693, or even to 1689 (Khafi Khan, ii. 421; Elliot and Dowson, 'Mahomedan Historians,' vii. 350; Hunter, 'British India,' ii. 265). The merchant 'Abd-ul-ghaffur, of Surat, who figures in the earlier dispute of 1693-94, is again prominent in that of 1703. The later trouble is to be traced more immediately to the so-called Muchalkahs (agreements) which Amanat Khan, the then *faujdar* of Surat, forced the Dutch, English, and French, to sign in February 1699. By these a guarantee was given to protect and convoy the Mogul ships, and to make good all losses from piracy.

In the Dutch agreement a money payment was also stipulated for, but this clause was rejected by the Batavia Council. Their obligation to convoy the pilgrim ships to Mecca was, however, carried out for two or three years to the great injury of the Dutch Company, which lost three or four of its ships. Moreover, payment of the money was insisted on. Ketting, who had signed the bond, died on December 16, 1699 and was succeeded by Henry Zwaardekron, who tried hard for several years to secure its annulment. He, too, was imprisoned, and was not set at liberty till 1703, when his successor, Pieter de Vos, arrived with a fleet. Directly these ships had sailed, the violence recommenced against the new Director and the other officials (Dubois, 'Vies,' pp. 263 and 264, founded on Valentyn, iv. part ii., 270, 271).

On August 9, 1703, nine ships, belonging to Surat, arrived safely at that port from Jeddah and Makhah (Mocha), bringing a 'vast treasure.' Five ships, not then ready to sail, had been left at Mocha. On August 27, 1703, these laggards were 'off the island of St. John's,[2] bending their course to Surat,' when two

1. The subject is resumed on fol. 185, Part IV.
2. In lat. 20° 12′, eighty-eight miles north of Bombay, properly Sanjan (Yule, 782).

XXXVIII. Muhammad Ibrahim, a Glkandah General

Vol. III *To face page 364*

pirates bore down on them. Next day one ship, owned by 'Abd-ul-ghaffur, was taken near Surat. The smaller pirate stood after two merchantmen 'that had gone to the southward, and took one of them belonging to Cossim Chy (? Qasim Bhai).' The other, owned by 'Abd-ul-ghaffur, got safely into Bombay, though closely pursued as far as Old Woman's Island.

On August 31 (1703), when the news reached Surat, the governor seized all the brokers of the European companies 'with your Honour's old brokers Vittul (? Baital) and Kyssa Parrack (? Kishna Parakh).' Gayer, the English agent, attempted unsuccessfully to provision their factory. But it was surrounded by soldiers, 'so that neither victuals, water, servants, nor anything else, might come near us, nor the least scrap of paper come in or go out.' The Mahomedans believed that the culprits were the English ship *Regard* and a smaller vessel from Bombay.

The Dutch were dealt with like the English, but they were 'well stored with provisions.' The native brokers of the French Company and of the New (English) Company were released, but those of the Dutch and English were 'barbarously tortured.' Three lakhs of rupees were extorted from the 'Parakhs,' and three from the Dutch brokers. After thirteen days a small daily portion of provisions was admitted to the English and Dutch factories, and on October 13 three servants were allowed entrance. On November 26 matters were still in the same position. Up to February 16, 1704, the two factories were still guarded, but by a smaller number of men; also provisions and servants were more freely admitted, and all of the Europeans might walk about the city, 'except John Gayer and Stephen Colt.' On March 15, 1704, the guards were removed.

At the request of Gayer, Nicholas Waite, the New Company's official at Bombay, sent the ships *Samuel* and *Mary*, and the sloop *Beatrix*, to 'lay before the bar' and go in search of the pirates. This was in September, 1703. In the same month seven Dutch ships arrived from Batavia and 'stopped the port' until, in February, 1704, 'matters were accommodated.'

The Dutch narrative of the same events exists in the Hague Archives, in three long covering letters from Pieter de Vos, Directeur, and six others of the Surat Council—two to headquarters at Batavia, dated February 27 and March 9, 1704, and one to their High Mightinesses at Amsterdam, dated April 17,

1704. There are thirty-four enclosures—eleven letters from Pieter de Vos to commanders of ships off Surat, dated between September 22, 1703, and February, 1704; two to Simon Langendan of the *Zuiddorp*; one from Adrian de Palensteyn of the *Beverwyk* to P. de Vos; five *ruqqa'hs* (notes) from P. de Vos to I'tibar Khan, the governor, and four replies from I'tibar Khan; one *ruqqa'h* to Qazi Muhammad Sa'id; one *ruqqa'h* from A. de Palensteyn to I'tibar Khan, and the reply; an 'arzdasht, or dispatch, from Ttibar Khan to the Mogul Court, dated November 24, 1703 (the addressee is 'Inayatullah Khan, chief *Diwan*); *ruqqa'hs* from de Vos and Palensteyn to the new governor, Najabat Khan, and three *ruqqa'hs* from Najabat Khan to them, giving cover to a Hasb-ol-hukm (order by *wazir* in the emperor's name), dated 8 Shawwal, year 48, 1115 H. (February 13, 1704); and, finally, a bond by the native merchants of Surat, executed on March 19, 1704.

In brief the story is this: When the news of the piracy reached Surat, I'tibar Khan proceeded to enforce the provisions of a *muchalkah* (a bond or agreement) extorted from the Europeans in February, 1669, by the then governor, Amanat Khan, On September 20, 1703, the Dutch ship *Zuiddorp* arrived, and on October 24 she was followed by the *Beverwyk* and five others. The port was blockaded, and a correspondence ensued. Finally, on November 24, 1703, I'tibar Khan made a report to court, his action was disapproved, and he was superseded by Najabat Khan. An imperial order was received on March 8, 1704, setting aside the agreement of February, 1699, and withdrawing all demands. A document was taken from the Surat merchants on March 19, 1704, to the effect that they had no further claims.

From the English records we get the statement that, so early as September 23, 1703, the Mogul Court had become alarmed, and had called upon I'tibar Khan to report 'why he exacted money from the Hatmen on account of the late Pyracy.' On December 20 the English heard he was superseded by the *faujdar* of Malkher. This man was Najabat Khan, son of the Najabat Khan of Shahjahan's time and the first years of Aurangzeb. They then refer to the *Hasb-ul-hukm* of February 13, by which the dispute was closed for the time being (Factory. Records Surat, vols. xiii., c., and ci.; Original Correspondence, vol. lii.)]

A few days before the arrival of the European [ships] at this port (Surat), as I have stated above, the town was surrounded by the Shiva Ji [the Mahrattahs] with a force of 20,000 horsemen. They made considerable efforts to take the place, but they did not succeed, being driven away by the Europeans residing there. The Shiva Ji [Mahrattahs] returned, after having pillaged the suburbs and burnt [154] all that they could, to such an extent that they ruined the province and killed in it over three millions of people.[1]

At this period there appeared five Arab vessels from Mosquat (Masqat), and they went about ravaging and pillaging everywhere in the territory of Dumar (Daman), as they had done previously in the island of Salsetta (Salseite), between the town of Bassahim (Bassain) and the island of Bombay. They stayed seven days, and stole all they could find, and with their plunder loaded fifteen ships. The more valuable part of the merchandise belonged to the Jesuits. Along with the goods they carried off all the best-looking among the natives of the country. This they did by reason of the violent resistance that had been offered to them.

The Viceroy of Goa, named Guaytana de Mello de Castrol[2] (son of the Anthoine de Mello de Castro of whom I have spoken in my First and Second Parts) (II. 129), sent in pursuit of these Arabs the general of the Portuguese forces, named Dom Anthoine de Menezes. On January 23, 1704, he attacked them with seven

1. The burning and pillaging at this time are referred to in a Bombay letter received at Madras on May 1,1703 ('Public Consultations,' vol. xxxii., p. 68). Again, on September 30, 1703, we find the remarks: 'This two or three days past wee have been informed 10,000 men ('tis said the Savagee) with 30,000 pair of oxen has bin upp and downe the Country getting corne.' Again, on October 27, 1703, 'an allarum of the Sevajees being with 85,000 men at Nunderaband [Nazarbar in Baglanah] but sixty course (*kos*) from this town.' On October 29 1703, they speak of information of 'the Sevajees designe—vissitting Suratt this Season.' Two thousand men were sent to Surat under 'Sultan Osman Shaw [? A'zam Shah]; no signs of the Enemy's approach.' On December 9, 1703, the order to the Prince's forces to proceed to Ahmadavad (Ahmadabad) was counter-manded, and the troops were ordered to 'tarry about this place in case the Savajee should vissitt it' (Factory Records, Surat, vol. xiii.).
2. No. 69, Caetano de Mello de Castro, Viceroy, 1703-07 (F. C. Danvers, ii. 489).

ships at three o'clock in the afternoon. The combat was a terrible one, continuing until the going down of the sun; but at last the Portuguese took two Arab vessels, and two others stood out to sea in a very damaged condition. It is not known whether they founded or made for Masqat. One more of their ships was reduced to such straits that it retreated into the Surat river in company with six Arab merchantmen. He (Menezes) remained off the bar of Surat, so as to prevent the issue of the said vessels from that port.[1]

In the year 1702 Shah 'Alam being in the province of Kabul, one of his captains, named Pordelacam (Purdil Khan), son of Dalilcan (Diler Khan), of the Pathan race,[2] wished to traverse with his cavalry a route by which Mogul armies were not accustomed to pass. Upon this the lord of the country, also of Pathan race, protested against his marching, and prayed him to adopt the usual route. He added that he would not allow the setting up of new usages affecting him and his people, and, if he acted to the contrary, he would experience exactly what had happened to Akbar's troops.

However, no account was taken of this protest, and relying on his own valour and exceptional courage, he (Purdil Khan) entered the other's country. As soon as he had done so he was surrounded in the midst of mountains by a number of men who barred the road. It ended in all his men being killed without a single one escaping. Moreover, all the chiefs of the same race (Pathans) assembled and closed all the routes. Shah 'Alam, on hearing what had happened, grieved much over the loss of a leader so valiant, though wanting in prudence. He was obliged to send presents to allay the fury of this barbarous people, in order that they might leave the routes open, that the great caravans might be allowed to pass, and that he himself might find his road open for his annual journey to and fro [*i.e.*, from Kabul to Peshawar]. When princes pass through this land of mountains they are never without fear of something happening to them, as has formerly been

1. The subject of these Arab incursions is returned to on fol. 203.
2. In all probability this is the Kamal-ud-din, son of Diler Khan, Daudzai, who was killed by a bullet when trying to force a pass between Khost and Kabul in 1113 H. (1701-1702) (see H. G. Raverty's 'Notes on Afghanistan,' 1880-83, p. 376, relying on Afzal Khan, Khatak, Tarikh-i-murassa").

the case with others, as can be ascertained from my First and Second Parts (I. 123; II. 148, 153).

[155] in the year 1703 Aurangzeb, having taken the fortress of Shiva Ji (the Mahrattahs) named Condena (Kandanah),[1] he marched off and pitched his camp close to a place called Punia (Puna). It was here that he (Shiva Ji) killed the son of Shaistah Khan and that noble was himself wounded, as may have been seen in my First and Second Parts (II. 77).

During the monarch's march to this place it happened that an officer named Mira Baffa (Mir Wafa), who had risen at the court by the favour and the support of the *wazir*, Asad Khan, forgetting all the benefits he had received, erected his tents in the *wazir's* quarters. The *wazir's* servants, observing this unaccustomed boldness, never resorted to by anyone else, protested in a modest manner. But since the noble would not listen to reason, the servants of Asad Khan cut the intruder's tent-ropes and put his men to flight by a hearty use of their staves. When the king heard of the affair he seemed put out, and sent a message to the *wazir* directing him to visit the quarters of Mirza Wafa and make him excuses. The *wazir* pretended he did not understand; but the king did not desist from sending order after order. Thus the *wazir* was forced to obey, to his great chagrin and much against his will.[2]

Zu,lfiqar Khan, who was then on duty against the Shiva Ji (the Mahrattahs) in the direction of Surat, on learning of this dispute, resented very much the affront put upon his father. After the enemy had retreated, this general started for the court. On the way he received orders from His Majesty to proceed to the aid of the province of Bartar (? Bidar or Barar), where other bodies of Mahrattahs were ruining and ravaging the country. But

1. Kandanah was taken on the 2nd Zu,l Hijjah, 1114 H. (April 19, 1703), and renamed Bakhshindah Bakhsh. It is Shiva Ji's 'Singhgarh,' and lies eleven miles south-west of Puna ('Ma,asir-i-'Alamgiri,' 474; Thornton, 'Gazetteer,' 906; Grant-Duff, p. 27).
2. In the 'Ma,asir-ul-Umara,' i. 319, under Asad Khan, forty-seventh year, January, 1703, to January, 1704, this story is told differently. The squabble was with 'Inayatullah Khan. The *wazir's* tents had been pitched in a hollow, and this place was swamped during some rain. The *wazir's* servants wanted 'Inayatullah Khan to vacate his position, which was on a high and dry site. Perhaps Inayatullah Khan's original name may have been Mir Wafa.

the general made humble supplication to His Majesty that he might be permitted to come to court, for he had a communication to make.

He received the answer that he must march to the point given in his orders with all possible haste, and that such was the king's pleasure. He sent back word that he could not march, without having seen His Majesty in person. On finding him so determined, the king consented that he should come. As soon as he arrived he made the first complimentary speeches as usual, then took off his sword, laid it on the ground, and spoke to the king as follows: 'Your Majesty knows that my ancestors have served the emperors Humayun, Akbar, Jahangir, and Shahjahan, and your Majesty, too, with all possible fidelity, that we have never been deprived of our privileges, that all the kings just named maintained them, and even gloried in our splendid mode of living, the honours rendered to us, and all the respect paid to our dignity. But your Greatness has not thought it well to uphold these privileges, now so ancient; for you have obliged the chief *wazir* to beg pardon from a person that he had displeased. Since your Majesty has changed so much as well as the times, you [156] can provide yourself with some other general. As for me, I can no longer serve your Majesty.'

Having heard this speech, the king could not fail to become despondent, but, dissembling, he pacified the general and consoled him, saying that no one could withdraw from him his ancient privileges, that he merited their continuance by reason of his merit and his services as much as by his birth. He had been wrongly informed, and he would soon set the matter right. At the same time he commanded him to resume his sword. However, Zu,lfiqar Khan declined to take up his sword and bind it on, giving several reasons that hindered him. Thus the king's soft words went for nothing. In this way three times over the king told him to fasten on his sword, and yet he remained firm to his text, and would not obey. Seeing this, the king told his son, Kaembath (Kam Bakhsh), who was present, to come forward and attach the weapon with his own bands. The prince did as he was told, and the other could hardly refuse, seeing that it was the king's own son who was conferring on him this honour.

After this the king made him draw closer to his person, put a hand upon his head, and said he esteemed him equal to his own son. As a still further consolation the king took the dagger from his own waist-belt, and with own hands stuck it into Zu,lfiqar Khan's, invested him with a set of costly robes, gave him a horse bearing a saddle covered with precious stones, along with twelve other horses and two elephants very richly caparisoned. In this way he sent him off, telling him to go now and chastise the enemy.

From want of wisdom and honour many people in India are unworthy of any respect—just as little as some Europeans under similar circumstances. Finding themselves raised in fortune and provided with wealth that Nature had originally refused them, they decline, nevertheless, to admit what God and Nature have done for them. An instance of what I allude to happened at Goa in the year 1666, under the government of the then Viceroy, Anthoine de Mello de Castro, when I was living in that town.

There was a Portuguese gentleman, called Dom Anthoine Franco de Amiral, a rich and powerful man much loved by the Viceroy. This man, while still a youth, had come as a soldier from Portugal to India. When he had passed the Cape of Good Hope he changed his Christian name and surname, and as soon as he reached Goa he married a rich girl, who owned a great deal of real property.

The father of this gentleman learnt that his son had become very rich, and this induced him to write several letters reminding him that he ought to be good enough to remember his father, who was in great want. But the young man paid no heed to all these letters, and sent no answer. Not knowing the cause of this silence, the good old man imagined that perhaps his letters had not been received. He embarked on a voyage to the Indies. On arriving, though Very badly clad, he made straight for his son's house [157] and entered. The Kaffirs and the servants stopped him from going farther, saying he could not go in until they had warned their master. The good old man said innocently: 'Let me in; I am the father of this gentleman.' In spite of this they would not allow him to pass.

The master of the house, on learning what was going on, put his head out of the window and ordered his Kaffirs and his servants to put his father out. He accompanied the order with much abusive language, calling his father a brute, a peasant, a man out of his mind; he was not the son of any such low-born man. By this talk the good old man was forced to withdraw as best he could, hanging his head for shame, and his only resource was to beg alms from door to door to obtain necessary food.

One day when the viceroy was walking in his garden the old man found an occasion to approach, and he said somewhat innocently that he had to communicate to his Excellency a matter of great importance. The viceroy, who was in a fairly good humour, called him near and asked his wishes. He used the opportunity to tell the story of all that had passed, showed the governor the certificates from the parish where his son was born, and specified the trade he followed when in Portugal, which was the making of saddles and boots. The viceroy consoled the old man, and assured him that he should be satisfied and sent back to Portugal.

The sharp-witted viceroy, in order to force the son to admit his origin, sent for a hide, and set to work to cut out boots as worn in Portugal. He was unable to carry out his intention after many attempts. While thus occupied the gentleman came in and noticed that his Excellency was not even near succeeding in what he wanted to do. This forced him into saying: 'What is it your Excellency wants to do? Why are you taking all that trouble?' He answered that the leather was for a pair of boots after the pattern of their country. The gentleman, without guessing the viceroy's object, put himself at once into the proper attitude for cutting them out, saying that from infancy he had been used to wearing boots and riding on horseback.

By this trick the quick-witted viceroy learnt what the man had been, but allowed no sign of it to escape him; and after a longish conversation on different subjects, he told him that he was in need of a loan of 50,000 *scraphins* (? *ashrafi*)[1], which he would return on the following day. The young man forwarded the money at once. Next day the viceroy sent for the good old man, and made him hide in the room where the money was placed. He then sent for the young gentleman, and, taking his hand, led him into that room, saying to him: 'Behold your father, to whom you are under great obligations; make up your mind to give him all that is necessary to travel home again. Indeed, he must be allowed to carry away the 50,000 *seraphins*, and by that payment I shall have acquitted myself towards you in regard to my debt'. He added some severe words of reproof, and sent him away. Thus the old man went back to Portugal well provided.

1. According to Yule, 874, a silver coin current at Goa, and Worth 1s. 6d.

This story shows how the wisdom of men in power may remedy many things, and how much greater is the success obtained by such means than by violence.

There was in the Mogul country an officer named Fatulacan (Fathullah Khan), an Uzbak or Tartar by race. He started from Hindustan at the head of a large body of troops, convoying a large sum in gold and silver coin for the disbursements of the royal army. When they arrived at the town of Aurangabad, the insolent Mogul soldiers began to rob many of the shops [158] and beat men in different quarters of the town. The governor of the place was 'Ali Mardan Khan, the same who had been captured twice by the Mahrattahs.[1] He sent some troops to suppress this unexpected disorder. But when the soldiers arrived the mutinous Moguls declined to pay any attention to them; thus a fight arose between the two sides, and several dead were left on the field. Fathullah Khan was much incensed by this, ordered his drums to beat, assembled his cavalry, and marched against the governor of the town.

The latter, when he received this report, sent out messengers to stop the advance, requesting the commander to retire and resume his journey. Fathullah Khan declined to listen, an engagement took place, and three hundred horsemen were slain and four hundred wounded. Fathullah Khan was obliged to withdraw. When the matter was brought before the king, he deprived Fathullah Khan of his rank and pay, called him a thief, and said the only thing he knew was how to rob the king's domain, which even the Mahrattahs themselves were not guilty of. As for 'Ali Mardan Khan, he was promoted, and praised for protecting the towns and country belonging to Mogul Empire.[2]

This great king (Aurangzeb), finding himself so advanced in years, with little hope of living much longer, tried to invent some means of taking the fortresses and lands held by the Mahrattahs. He thought of a deception by which he hoped to raise discord among the Mahrattah leaders. There was in captivity

1. For 'Ali Mardan Khan, Haidarabadi see note 14, Part IV., fol. 16.
2. The man referred to in this story must be Fathullah Khan, Khosti (Muhammad Sadiq) (see 'Ma,asir-ul-Umara,' iii. 40, which says nothing, however, of this episode). He left the Dakhin for Kabul in 1706, and died shortly after 1707.

a son of Sambha Ji, whom he (Aurangzeb) had brought up from his infancy.[1] He summoned him to his presence, struck off his fetters, put on him a set of rich robes, and ordered his own son, Kam Bakhsh, to take charge of him. He was accorded his liberty, and the rank of a *haft hazari* (7,000) was conferred on him. He was given the right to receive one-fourth of the revenues of various provinces in the Dakhin and the two Karnatiks. As for the prince (Kam Bakhsh), he was made lord of the provinces of Bijapur and Gulkandah, as also of all the fortresses in the two Karnatiks. Aurangzeb told the prince he meant to leave him behind in the Dakhin to take his place, intending himself retire to the town of Dihli, there to live at his ease and seek God's favour during the few days of life that remained. This news spread abroad at once in all directions, and many persons rejoiced, hoping thereby to obtain employment. But one year has already gone by without to this day any steps being taken to put this plan into execution.

All these artifices were resorted to by Aurangzeb merely in the hope that the Mahrattah captains would flock in numbers to enter the service of the prince, his son, and that the union existing among them would in this way be broken up. However, they knew the tricks of this monarch, and took no heed of his orders, but found it much more worth their while to plunder and carry off treasure from the different parts of the empire. As for the Mahrattah prince, to whom he had given freedom, all that he gained was the repute of having a large allowance without other profit, for he continued to be strictly guarded by careful warders.

This prince (Aurangzeb), finding that his troops could inflict no harm on those of the Mahrattahs, started several subtle devices, according to his usual practice [159]. He wrote several' letters to a Brahman, Ram Chand Pandit,[2] who is bringing up

---

1. Grant-Duff, 179, relying on Khafi Khan and Scott's 'Dekkan,' says there was about this time a talk of releasing the youthful Sahu, son of Sambha Ji. The same fact is indicated by the young rajah's being made over to Zu,lfiqar Khan (see 'Ma,sir-i-'Alamgiri,' p. 511, entry of 16th Shawwal, fiftieth year, 1117 H. [January 31, 1706]).
2. Probably meant for Ram Chandar Pant, Burikar, who had been 'Pant Amat,' the second official in the Mahrattah State, in Shiva Ji's time (1676), but had been displaced. He was restored to office in 1698, and was still in power in 1711 (Grant-Duff, 118, 171, 188).

the son of Shiva Ji and rules over all his might, inviting him (the Pandit) to court. He promised him that he should be appointed grand *wazir* on account of his exceeding great wisdom. He had need of a man like him, one who possessed superior judgment. But on all those promises no hopes were built; they knew already by long experience the true nature of his faithless promisings.

It happened that in the kingdom of Bijapur other troops of the Mahrattahs encountered some captains of the Mogul: there was a fight, and the Mahrattahs were the conquerors. They killed the leader, Sequinazam (? Shekh Nizam), and his son; while Solimancan (Sulaiman Khan), brother of the Da,ud Khan of whom I spoke above, was made a prisoner and taken to the captain Gemsircan (Jamshid Khan).[1]

In the month of January, 1704, the Mahrattahs entered the kingdom of Bijapur, and collected from several of its provinces one-fourth of all the revenues (for he who did not pay willingly and at once was robbed of all that he had, and even the principal men of the villages were taken prisoners). In this way they were so successful that they reached their homes without any hindrance.

In the month of February of the same year (1704) there appeared another force of twelve thousand horse and ten thousand foot, which attacked a factory (*habitation*) called Policonde (Palakollu),[2] five leagues from Machhlipatanam (Masulipatam). This army took up its quarters at the above place, and thence dispatched troops in different directions, and exacted everywhere one-fourth of the revenues with great rigour. The deputies of the king, the governors and generals of the regions, could not prevent these extortions. As to the port of Masulipatam, it was fortified as well as could be managed; five earthen bastions surrounded by thorn hedges were erected, and twenty-five pieces of artillery were mounted. The English and the Dutch mounted

1. This may be the Jamshid Khan, Bijapuri, who was killed a bullet at the siege of Wakinkerah in Zi Hijjah, 1116 H. (April, 1705) ('Tarikh-i-Muhammadi' and 'Ma,asir-i-'Alamgiri,' 503).
2. This must be Palakollu (Palcole), in the Narsapur division of the Godaveri district, six miles north-north-east of Narsapur. It was the first settlement of the Dutch, who opened a factory there in 1652. It was finally ceded to the English on June 1, 1825 ('Madras Manual of Administration,' iii. 663). It lies about sixty miles north-east of Masulipatam. Palcondah, in the Vizagapatam district, is still farther off.

guard with great exactitude; but the Mahrattahs, having taken all they could get, retired.

One day the governor of Masulipatam left the fortress for a factory (*habitation*) near the said place; it is called [blank in original]. Thereupon the Dutch seized the occasion. They already had their eye on the fortress, and on the treasure stored there for safety by some people of the neighbourhood, who were afraid of being plundered by the enemy. The Dutch determined to take possession, and raised a dispute for that purpose.[1] They sent some of their people at the head of armed messengers (*peons*) with flags flying and drums beating, just as the governor did when he went out for recreation. When the governor knew of this attempt he broke up the drums and made a row, but the Dutch dissembled and went back to their house. Next day they seized the gates, fortified the bastions, and trained the guns upon the town. They sent infantry to the governor's house, and ordered the rest of his men to withdraw. The Mogul troops obeyed, and the Dutch took possession of the fortress with the money in it, but did no harm to the inhabitants.

On learning this event the governor sent to ask the reason of their taking the fortress and the treasure within it. To this

1. There are only traces of these events in the English records. For instance, on March 13, 1704, we read: 'Metchlipatam is fortifyed per the Dutch and us as well as the short time wee have will permitt, but 'tis feared the ffusdar [*faujdar*] of this place will make no opposition when the robbers come; the Dutch has already received 20 soldiers and officers from Negapatam, the Morattas being expected here in a few days.' And again (May 11, 1704): 'The Morattas are now gone from hence, therefore no occasion to send down any people upon their Account' (Factory Records, Fort St. George, vol. xxxv.). The Dutch account of these events can be seen in a letter of October 19, 1704, from Negapatam to Willem van Outshoorn, Governor-General, and the Council at Batavia, The assailant seems to have been the 'robber' Riza Khan. The twenty soldiers were dispatched from Negapatam on March 20 in the *Drakensteyn*, and placed under the command of Ensign Jeronimus Leek. A Portuguese sloop, manned by *topases* and Bengalis, had been hired on the spot in preparation for flight, and sixty local boatmen were also entertained. The *faujdar* and his brother, the *daroghah*, were suspected of collusion with the invader, and this was borne out by their subsequent flight when they found the Europeans were on the alert and too strong for them. Riza Khan, who had been encamped two and a half Dutch miles west of Euroepalem, finally made off by Way of Nagelwanse and Palewanse into another district.

they replied briefly that when the king asked the question they would give an answer. In this way the affair dropped.

Let us return once more to an enquiry into the doings of the Mahrattahs. In this year of 1704, in the month of [160] January, they crossed the Narbada river, penetrated the forests of Mandu, plundering and ravaging several provinces, as well as the town of Sironj. Not content even with this, they went farther, and going through the hill-passes of Narwar, they entered the province of Calabad (Kalpi),[1] close to the Gwaliyar fortress, a three days' journey from Agrah. They traversed other provinces, doing everywhere a great deal of damage. In this way they returned to their own country without anyone being able to interfere with them.

These forays are of great profit to Shiva Ji, in addition to his soldiers' booty. For as soon as they enter the Mogul's dominions, that sovereign's governors send men to offer them a large sum of money: if they think fit, they take it; if not, they burn and destroy in all directions. The Mahrattah ruler is at this time very powerful; he has under him over one hundred thousand horsemen. This is the reason he ventures to test the valour of and to defy the Mogul; and what this old man used to do formerly to other kings and princes the Mahrattah does nowadays to him.

In the raid above described, which he (*i.e.*, the Mahrattahs) carried out with such overwhelming strength, he came across a Hindu princess. She was a Rector (Rathor) by race, and was convoying a girl, the daughter of a Hindu prince, a Cachoux (Kachhwahah) by race, who was about to be married to her son. The latter was at the time serving in the royal army. She had in her train a thousand Rajput horsemen, and carried with her things of considerable value. These were required for celebrating the marriage with all possible pomp. But this princess met with disgrace; she was overtaken on her road by the enemy and all his army. He sent her word that she must deliver up all she had before he would release her.

The courageous Rajput princess, defying Death, went out to

1. Comparing this with another passage on fol. 163, where the reading is 'Calabay,' I think that Kalpi, on the Jamnah, is the place intended, although it is many miles from Gwaliyar. Could the word be meant for the Koolet of the Indian Atlas, Sheet No. 51, N.E., lying about six miles north-west of Gwaliyar?

face the enemy. She held it to be a dishonour to surrender the precious stones and ornaments that her daughter-in-law was to wear. The Rajputs fought valiantly until they were all killed. Having no more men with which to continue the fight; she drew a dagger and slew her daughter-in-law, saying it was better to die with honour than to drag on a miserable existence in the hands of Shiva Ji. She repeated the same thing as to herself, and thrust the dagger into her own heart. Thus did she end the sad tragedy, and the enemy took everything.

In the beginning of May in this present year of 1704 sixty thousand Mahrattah horsemen appeared in the Karnatak and in Bijapur. They were under the command of some good officers. Having entered the country, they took several forts; then a number of them encamped in front of a large fortified place called Sira (Sira).[1] After this they separated themselves into three divisions, which marched in different directions.

The first division turned towards the Karnatik, where the prince and lord of the country made a present to them of three millions of rupees. Thence they entered the country adjoining the territories of the Trichinapali (Trichinopoly) kingdom. There, too, they realized a very large sum as tribute. Next they went on to Tanjor,[2] where they were well received, particularly as they brought with them the son of Ram Chand, Pandit, chief minister of the Mahrattah ruler, for the celebration of his marriage to the princess of Tanjor. They meant thereby to preserve the friendship between them, and defend that country from the menaces of the Mogul.

However, Da,ud Khan was not without apprehension, for he felt great fear of not being able to resist these bold Mahrattahs. This fear compelled him to send an envoy, through whom he asked as a favour that nothing might be undertaken against him. As a return he would give the raiders a present of two hundred thousand rupees. The commanders sent the man away, having

1. Sira, a town, with a fort, in the Nandidrug district of Maisur, seventy-three miles north-west of Bangalore (Thornton 'Gazetteer,' 871). It was the headquarters of the Karnatik Bijapur *faujdar* from 1686.
2. Trichinopoly, lat. 10° 32′, long. 76° 16′, is some 300 miles south-east of Sira, in the Nandidrug district of Maisur. Tanjor, lat 10° 47′, long. 79° 12′, is thirty miles east of Trichinopoly (Thornton, 990, 957). The Tanjor princes at this time were Mahrattahs. For Ram Chand, see note 255, *ante*, fol. 159.

simply turned their backs on him, saying that Da,ud Khan need not concern himself about giving them money; it belonged to them [161] already, and they would take good care that they collected it. On hearing this depressing news Da,ud Khan was much cast down. It is for this reason that he quitted Arkat, and fortified himself in the upper part of the fortress of Velours (Vellur),[1] this being the strongest place to be found in the Karnatik of Gulkandah.

The second army made for the town of Gulkandah, which it invested, and there they are at the present moment in the prosecution of their enterprise. The third army is advancing into the rest of the country, conquering as much of it as it can, placing commandants in the forts and places that it captures.

The governor of the town of Adoni,[2] whose name was Cod Vandcan (Khudabandah Khan),[3] son of Sha,istah Khan, feared that some misfortune would befall him as had happened to others in previous years. He therefore sent a large sum of money to obviate their interfering with him. The Mahrattah leader sent him word that, as a son of Sha,istah Khan, a prince so high in degree and so liberal, he had no intention of doing him any harm. For the same reason he declined to touch his money. All he demanded was the surrender of [blank in original], chief minister and farmer of the revenues of these provinces. If he did not comply, the heads of both should be cut off. Khudabandah Khan, finding himself in such great peril, was forced to deliver the Mahrattahs the minister in question. He (Khudabandah Khan) received his own liberty and that of his family, but he had to depart unprovided and leave his baggage behind him.

It is a remarkable thing to see these leaders, so many in number, yet without any prince to direct them, make war on the Mogul. They perpetrate constant ravages first in one part, then in another of that empire. In the process they carry off much wealth, while by their foresight and valour they continue constantly victorious. The reason is, as it seems to me, because they keep

1. Arcot (Arkat), lat. 12° 54′, long. 79° 7′, sixty-five miles west of Madras; Vellur is fourteen miles west of Arkat.
2. Adoni, 261 miles north-west of Madras, in the Ballari district.
3. Khudabandah Khan, in the forty-sixth year (1703-1704), replaced Chin Qilich Khan as *faujdar* of the Karnatik (Bijapur). He married a daughter of Asad Khan, *wazir*. He died of wounds received at Jajau, 1119 H. (June, 1707) ('Ma,asir-ul-Umara,' i. 814).

ever before their eyes the lesson that Taimur-i-lang gave long ago to his generals a few days before his death. It is as follows:

This great prince, being ill and having no longer any hope of life, ordered his attendants to bring to him the quiver in which he carried his arrows. He sent for the principal captains in his army. He ordered one of them to draw out an arrow from the quiver and break it. He did so. Another was ordered to withdraw ten at once, and try to break them at one effort with both hands. He failed to break them. Thereupon Taimur-i-lang delivered the following speech to them:

'I feel, as if warned by God, that I cannot live much longer, and at my departure you lose a good friend and a great leader. Thus you will no longer have anyone to direct you. For I note that my son, Sultan Abujahid (Abu Sa'id), has not the ability required to lead you, or to exercise the command over such a numerous army. However, if you wish to be always victors and and never to be overcome, you must remain ever united, for as you have just seen by experiment, ten arrows joined together cannot be broken, but taken singly they can easily be broken. In the same way, if there is division among you, your enemies will soon succeed in undoing you. But if you remain united their efforts will be in vain, and turn only to their own shame.' This it is which leads me to believe that the union among the above leaders (the Mahrattahs), for so many years on end, is the cause of their mutual preservation.

These [Mahrattah] leaders and their troops move in these days with much confidence, because they have cowed the Mogul commanders and inspired them with fear. At the present time they possess [162] artillery, musketry, bows and arrows, with elephants and camels for all their baggage and tents. They carry these last to secure some repose from time to time as they find it convenient. In short, they are equipped and move about just like the armies of the Mogul. Under this head arises the reflection that only a few years ago they did not march about in this fashion. In those days their arms were only lances and long swords two inches wide. Armed thus, they prowled about on the frontiers, picking up here and there what they could; then they made off home again. But at the present time they move like conquerors, showing no fear of any Mogul troops.

At the commencement of June in the same year (1704) they (the Mahrattahs) attacked Gulkandah, and took possession of much property. Thereupon the governor of that place, seeing that he could not resist, was obliged to take refuge in the fortress of Badnagar (Bhagnagar),[1] where they left him no peace until by many threats they forced him into paying a large sum.

Da,ud Khan found that his arms and his forces would not justify resistance to the enemy; he therefore came to terms and paid five *lakhs* of rupees. Although the Mahrattahs took the money, that did not induce them to retire. They continued to pillage the country round Adoni and Sira. Up to this moment the Mogul has sent no reinforcements. The reason is that he is engaged with another of the Mahrattah armies which has surrounded him, and is robbing and stealing in every direction.

Perhaps the reader will not be displeased at learning what is passing in Siam since the death of the old king. Here is a brief account of the facts in a letter from a friend of mine in that country:

'Sir,

'It is a long time since I heard from you or our friends on the Choromandal Coast. I am not without concern for this, sir, and I feel this silence very much. It is true that the openings for sending letters here are at the present time very rare, and I feel sure you would not allow one to pass without giving me some sign of remembering me.

'I have found the kingdom of Siam in a very different condition from that I saw it in twenty years ago. In those days it was very flourishing, and there was considerable trade. Now it is in a miserable state, and abandoned by almost all the other nations. Nothing comes here but a few Chinese vessels, or some from Bengal and Surat, and these even, once they have been here, never come back a second time. Things were in this state in the reign of the old king, who died at the beginning of the year 1703.

'The chief prince, who has succeeded to him, appears to have the desire of treating traders better than his father did. He urges all foreign nations to come and establish themselves in his kingdom, and to induce them to come he makes very advantageous offers. He has declared to me more than once that he would have the greatest pleasure at seeing some Frenchmen in his country.

1. Bhagnagar, the ancient name of Haidarabad; Gulkandah, the fortress, is seven miles west of the city.

He would allow them to settle where they liked; he would protect them; he would give to them the same privileges as to the Dutch He insisted that I must write to this effect to France and to India. I have done so in order not to displease him, although I am fully persuaded that not very much heed will be paid to his offers.

'If he had pushed his generosity to the point of ceding Mergui,[1] they might have been more disposed to renew the intercourse between France and Siam. But it is not a thing they dream of here, and it would be deceiving oneself to look for anything of the sort.

"I do not know yet whether the words of this new king can be much relied on. When he was only prince [163] he gave no great grounds for being satisfied with his conduct; and one must not be easily persuaded that inclinations so evil as his could be changed all of a sudden. Monsieur le Chevalier Martin and the gentlemen who are directors at Surat and in Bengal, being so wise and prudent as they are, will think more than once before becoming involved in a business of which the results might be far from agreeable.

'The new king, having made all his arrangements beforehand (and that a long time ago), ascended the throne without hindrance.[2] His brother, a young prince of fourteen or fifteen years, to whom the crown belonged as of right, since he was born of a princess of ancient family, was in no position to resist. This unfortunate young prince was the first victim of his brother's jealousy and passion. Some mandarins who had espoused his cause shared his fate. All these tragical events were carried out with great shedding of blood. Following on these cruel executions

1. Mergui, a seaport town, now in the British district of Tenasserim, under the Government of Burma, lat. 12° 27′, long. 98° 42′. We took it from the Burmese in 1824 or 1825, but in the seventeenth century it belonged to the Siamese, and it was then the chief door of approach for Europeans to that kingdom. Louis XI. tried to obtain its cession, and at one time (*circa* 1688) it was intended to transfer to it from Pondicherry the chief seat of the French Compagnie Royale.
2. Colonel G. E. Gerini, whose acquaintance with Siamese history and topography is so profound, writes to me: The new king, who succeeded in 1703 or 1704, was popularly known as P'hra P'huttha-hao Sua, or "Tiger King," from his profligate habits. On succeeding to the throne after the death of his foster-father, P'hetha-racha, he rid himself of the two principal sons of his predecessor and of other possible pretenders.'

everybody bent beneath the tyrant's sway, except the governor of Lygor (Ligor),[1] He has refused to submit, and has resolved to avenge the death of the young prince who has been so unjustly made away with. As this governor belongs to one of the most ancient families of the kingdom, and has brought over to his side the kings of Singor (Singora)[1] and of Pattang (Patani),[1] he is causing terrible uneasiness to the new monarch.

'Things being in this position, you can easily judge, sir, that religion does not make here any great progress. The population, overwhelmed with labours and necessities, has not the time nor the frame of mind required for listening to such serious matters or of such grave consequences as a change of religion. We must wait in patience for the moment God has fixed and appointed, in the riches of His wisdom and foreknowledge, for the conversion of these poor idolaters. It is true that some are baptized, but they are few in number. As for infants at the point of death, many of these are baptized; and every year the number of these amounts to one thousand, sometimes to twelve hundred. There are also two missionaries who are constantly occupied in this labour of love.

''The college is almost as numerously attended as it was twenty years ago; there are forty students, who study with much zeal and emulation, and at the same time advance greatly in piety and virtue.

'I am (et cetera)'

I have already stated, in speaking of the past months, that the Mahrattas had gone as far as Calabay (? Kalpi),[2] close to the fortress of Gwaliyar. Aurangzeb, fearing they might go on and capture the town of Agrah, sent in pursuit his grandson, Bader Bact (Bedar Bakht), son of Azamtara (A'zam Tara). He gave him, however, a very small army, and the prince set out in

1. These three places—Ligor, Singora, and Patani—lie not far apart from each other in the north-east corner of the Malay Peninsula, and are still dependent on Siam. Colonel Gerini approves of my proposed identifications. The Malay Ligor (the Lugor of many European writers in Manucci's period) is the Siamese Lakhon or Nakhon (Nagara), Sri Dhammaraj. Reference may be made to Colonel Gerini's article in the *Journal of the Royal Asiatic Society*, 1904, pp. 720 and 721, and Fullarton's 'Gazetteer of the World,' vol. iv., p. 733, and vol. v., p. 808.
2. For this tentative identification with Kalpi, see *ante*, note 259, fol. 160.

obedience to his grandfather's order. However, he did not hurry, and went another road, simply that he might not come across the enemy. He made for the town of Ygen (Ujjain),[1] near the province of Gujarat, where his father was then governor. When the enemy had retreated, Aurangzeb sent for the prince, but he did not obey, excusing himself by asserting he was ill. When the princes are away [164] from the king's presence they take women (?), because then they have more liberty.

[The rest of folio 164 is blank.]

END OF VOL. III

1. Bedar Bakht was appointed to the province of Malwah, in which Ujjain is situated, in the forty-eighth year, 1115 H. (January to December, 1704) ('Ma,asir-i-'Alamgiri,' p. 483).

ADDITIONAL NOTES AND EMENDATIONS

Page 5, note 8.—In the last but one line after 'V.=3 and 4' insert 'VI.=7.'

Page 7, last line: *Written on the head*.—In the Orientalist, i. 230-233, is an article entitled *Iseketuvava*, 'Inscription on the Head,' by C. Alwis. Robert Knox, 'Historical Relation of Ceylon' (1681), p. 85, says the Cingalese have a proverb, *Oluve kotala tiyanava*, 'It is written on the head.' The Rev. H. Horsley, C.M.S., thus renders the Tamil:

'No man escapes the writing dread
Of Brahma, branded on the head.'

Page 9, note 16: *Incarnations of Vishnu*.—Dr. Grierson writes that the Bhagavata Purana, I., iii. (*cf*. II., vii.), gives twenty-two incarnations. But modern Vaishnavas have (since Nabha Dasa's time) a list of twenty-four. Dr. Grierson has worked the matter out on these lines in the translation of the 'Bhakta Mala,' upon which he is now engaged.

Page 16, line 2 from foot: *Atanary*.—The Italian text has *artanary*, which is nearer the true form.

Page 19, line 13: *Which some hang from their neck*.—'They [the Tschilamadakarer] carry also a *lingam* of christal about them' (J. T. Philipps, 'Account of the Religion . . .' [1717]).

Page 20, line 13: *A fruit*.—This fruit is (Tamil) *ai-virali*, 'Bryonia laciniosa' L.

Page 42, line 2 from foot: *Nostiguer*.—That *Nastika* is the word intended is shown by a passage in Father Pierre Martin's letter of November 8, 1709: 'There is a class of men who, so it seems, profess that they do not recognise any divinity; they are called *Nagastagher* (J. Bertrand, S.J., 'La Mission de Maduré,' iv. 193).

Page 53, line 18: A *pilgrimage*.—E. Thurston, 'Ethnographic Notes' (1906), p. 1, quotes this pretended flight to Banaras, known as *Kasiyatra*.

Page 54, line 4, and note 69: *Scuderis*.—Mr. Ferguson suggests the native word *gudri*, 'a quilt.' Compare p. 66, where we are told the bride is seated on a mat.

Page 63, last line: *Earthen figures*.—Here again Mr. Ferguson would, instead of passe, read paste (*i.e*., pâte, the text being here in French), 'figures made of a paste.'

Page 68, line 4: *Hindu burials*.—'They are buried in a sitting posture with their hands lifted up, as if they were in an act of devotion, which they call *T schimadu*' (J. T. Philipps, 'Religion, Manners, and Learning . . . of Malabar' [1717], p. 35).

Page 73, line 10: *Twelve 'covados*.'—Elephants were always measured in *covados*, a lineal measure of 16 Dutch inches or 1½ Rhenish feet. Johann Jacob Saar, in his account of Ceylon, 1647-57, said he had seen elephants 7 to 10 *covados* in height, and the largest 11 *covados* (see the *Journal of the Ceylon Branch, Royal Asiatic Society*, xi. 253, xv. 181,

194, quoting Saar's book and 'The Ceylon Elephant,' by Cornelis Taayvan Wezel [1713]). The second article gives incidentally the derivation of the curious French word *cornac*—viz., *kuru* (elephant), *nayaka* (chief); and see also Yule, p. 256. Sir J. Emerson Tennent, 'Wild Elephants,' p. 30, remarks on the extravagant estimates of elephants' height current in Ceylon even so late as 1806. Out of 1,100 measured, not one reached 11 feet.

Page 73, line 33; *A certain oil.*—Mr. Ferguson states that this assertion about a scented oil is a fiction.

Page 86: *Negotiations at Gulkandah.*—The first step in the employment of Manucci is recorded in a minute of March 7, 1687. Having had their letters sent back, the Council agreed to take 'the advice of Senor Manuche, an Italian doctor inhabitant of this Town, who was formerly in the Mogul's service.' His advice was to send a letter about their wrongs in the 'Bay' by his servant, accompanied by four Rajputs, this letter to be delivered to two Englishmen, Thomas and Richard Goodlad [? read 'Thomas Goodlad and Richard Cogan']. The Englishmen were to wait for the emperor's appearance in public, and hold up the letter so that it could be seen, when it would be received and read. Otherwise the great men through whose hands it passed would suppress the true contents.

Page 89, line 8: *Abnus.*—Mr. Ellis points out that 'Abnus' means 'John' through an intermediate form 'Avanus' (see Rieu, 'Persian Catalogue,' p. 5). 'Ibnus' and 'Avannes' are other forms met with. On December 8, 1685, it was reported that the English had seized some ships, one of them belonging to John de Marks. This must be the same man (A. T. Pringle, 'Diary and Consultations, 1685,' p. 161).

Page 92, note 101: *March* 1, 1639.—Colonel Love corrects this date; it should be August 22, 1639. The 'Madras Manual' is wrong.

Page 93, note 103: *Vijayanagar kingdom.*—The chronology of the Vijayanagar dynasties seems to be exceptionally uncertain. Probably that in R. Sewell, 'A Forgotten Empire' (1900), pp. 199, 214, 216, 404, founded on Dr. Hultsche's researches, should be preferred. According to those results, Ram Raya attained a king's status in 1542, and was killed in battle on January 26, 1565, at the age of ninety-six. The battle, though known as that of Talikot, was fought far from that place, probably about ten miles from Ram Raya's camp at Mudkal.

Page 94, line 16: *Head carpet-spreader.*—Both Mr. Ferguson and Mr. Philipps would read *estribeiro mor*, 'chief equerry.'

Page 95.—*Tevere* (Tevar) is the Tamil Devar (Tevar), the plural of Devan (Tevan), used honorifically. See Beschi, 'Dictionary of Common Tamil,' s.v.

Page 95, note 106, table.—*Kirhasu* must be corrected to 'Kizhava (=Kilava),' meaning 'the old man'; his name was Raghunath. The letter represented by '*l*' is said by Percival, 'Tamil-English Dictionary,' to be a mixture of 'r,' l,' and the French 'j.' This letter the Madras Government, in its transliteration scheme, chooses to represent by 'zh.'

Page 95, line 6: *Lands of Marava.*—'As the name of a country Marava would mean, in Manucci's time, the region covered by the present *zamindaris* of Ramnad and Shivaganga, then ruled by Maravar *polygars*. But the Maravar tribe was not confined to those boundaries; it extended into Tinnevelly, as may be seen, for instance, in the map of La Croze, 'Histoire du Christianisme,' 1758 (W. R. P.).

Page 95, line 6: *Utiar.*—As to this name, see additional notes to III., p. 224.

Page 95, line 7; *Rameshwaram.*—See J. Fergusson, 'History of Indian and Eastern Architecture' (1876), pp. 355-358. The temple was built between 1550 and 1700. On p. 356 there is a plan, and on p. 358 a view of the centre corridor.

Page 96, paragraph 1: *Tevar and Madura.*—Valentyn, 'Ceylon,' p. 234, says a good deal about the 'Land van den Teuver.' In 1675 the country from Adam's Bridge and Walemvekem had been for eighteen years divided into two parts: the northern under the Lord Tirewenapulle, and the southern under Razonade (Raghunath) Teuver. Both divisions paid tribute to the Naik of Madura. Tirewenapulle was supported by the Portuguese and the Naik of Tanjor; Teuver by the lord of Madura. The enmity of Teuver to the Portuguese passed on to the Dutch in 1658 on their taking Tuticorin, and was increased by their capture of Mannar. The story is continued at length on pp. 235, 236. According to J. H. Nelson, 'Madura' (part iii.), the history of Ramnad is in abstract as follows: (I.) Sadeika Tevan, Udeiyan, Sethupati, was restored to Ramnad by the Madura *naik* (c. 1605), and died c. 1621 (pp. 109. 110). He had various capitals: Rameshwaram, Tondi, Raghunathapura, and Virava Nallur (p. 114). (II.) His son and successor, Kuttan, the second Sethupati, died 1635 (p. 128). (III.) A son, Sadeika Tevan II., otherwise Dalavay Sethupati, succeeded him. About 1638 an illegitimate brother, known familiarly as Tambi, quarrelled with the Dalavay, fled to Madura, and was there appointed Sethupati. Ramnad was invaded by Madura troops, and on the capture of the capital by storm Dalavay fled to Pambam island, but in the eno he was made a prisoner, along with a nephew, Tanakka, and sent to Madura in chains. After a time he was restored, but (c. 1645), was murdered by Tambi. (IV.) Tambi, unable to master the whole country, consented to a division. Raghunath, the adopted son of No. II., obtained Ramnad, while Shivaganga was given to Tambi, and Tiruvadanei was assigned jointly to Tanakka and Narayana, younger brothers of Raghunath. In a few years the other assignees died, and the territory was reunited under (V.) Raghunath (c. 1659), who ruled for nearly thirty years (pp. 128, 130, 205), dying c. 1685. (VI.) A nephew, Raja Suria, succeeded, but six months afterwards was killed (pp. 205, 206). (VII). Raghunath, nicknamed Kilavan, or the 'Old Man,' an illegitimate son of Raghunath Sethupati, fought his way to the throne, and reigned for twenty-five years (d. 1710) (p. 244).

Page 96, note 110: *chinna*=small.—According to Beschi. *mudal* means 'the beginning,' hence the idea of pre-eminence. It is used as a title with the ending *yar,* in the form Mudaliyar, by various castes, respectable and otherwise; even the Chucklers (leather-dressers) use it.

Page 99, line 14: A daughter of rare beauty.—It was in 1674 that Achyuta Vijaya Raghava, King of Tanjor, refused to give his daughter to Chokka Nath, ruler of Madura. War was declared and Tanjor taken, the king, an old man of eighty, meeting death heroically in single combat after immolating his family (Nelson, 'Madura,' part iii., pp. 191, 192).

Page 99, note 113.—For *Chakka-nath,* read *Chokka-nath,* 'The beautiful lord' (Beschi, 'Dictionary').

Page 101, paragraph 3: The *pearl fishery.*—There are other accounts of this fishery about the same period. See Cardim, 'Relations des Missions de la Province de Malabar' (1645-1646), pp. 244-248, and Father Martin the Jesuit's description in 1700, reprinted in E. Thurston's 'Madras Government Museum Bulletin,' No. 1 (Madras, 1894), pp. 9-11. Neither of these speak of the *coita.* But Mr. Ferguson's guess was correct. See the 'Ceylon Official Glossary': *Coyta,* 'a Public Works Department tool, a bill-hook.' Also George F. d'Penha, 'Folklore in Salsette,' *Indian Antiquary,* xx. (1891), 234, *koitâ;* and H. H. Wilson, 'Glossary,' 296, *koyata* (corruptly, *koyt*), a Marathi word for a bill-hook.

Page 106, line 21: *Trivambur.*—For Trivettore, see Sir R. C. Temple's 'T. Bowrey,' p. 8, and the references there in his note 1; there is also a drawing of the pagoda. But Manucci may mean the 'Tirepoloer' of Havart, i., 102, and of Valentyn, 'Choromandel,' p. 12. See further on the additional note to 111., 352. Colonel Love suggests looking for the place south-west of San Thome, near Guindy, and refers me to an entry of January 1, 1759 (Madras Records, Public sundries, No. 13) : 'Trevembore, a village about two miles to the southward of San Thome.' But I think now that the Tirvaumyore of the 'Madras Manual,' iii. 865 (Tirevamoor on Pharaoh's Map), must be meant. It is an important Brahman settlement half a mile from the sea, and about nine miles south of Madras. It is the birthplace of Valmiki, and has a temple and tank.

Page 108, line 13 : J. P. *de Faria.*—This man is mentioned again on p. 195. See the additional note there.

Page 109, note 125: *Cochin.*—Mr. Ferguson writes that Cochin was never *taken* by the Portuguese; the rajah received them in a friendly manner from the first. It was visited by Cabral in 1500, a factory was started in 1502, and the fort built in 1507.

Page 112, note 127: F. *Mascarenhas.*—See *ante,* additional note, Vol. I., p. 223.

Page 113, line 31: *Father da Costa.*—In Franco's 'Synopsis' (1726) there are, between 1665 and 1680, seven Jesuits of this name who left for India. In the absence of a Christian name, it is impossible to identify the one referred to.

Page 118, line 8: *Para.*—Mr. Ferguson writes that the *parrah* is in Ceylon a measure for rice, equal to thirty heaped *seers,* the *seer* being 'a measure of capacity about equal to a quart' ('Ceylon Official Glossary'). In Tamil for *parai,* the first meaning is 'a drum' and the second 'a measure for lime, a para' (Percival,. 'Tamil-English Dictionary'). In Singhalese *biraya* is defined as 'a parrah containing 24 *neliyas,* or a quarter of a bushel' (Clough, 'Sinhalese-English Dictionary'). Colonel H.D. Love, R. E., tells me that to this day the *para* or *parrah* of lime figures constantly in Madras specifications for mortar.

Page 118, line 10, and note 131: *Cal.*—Mr. Ferguson says *cal,* 'lime,' is right.

Page 118, line 5 from foot and note 134: *Ydes.*—'The whole difficulty arises, as I now see, from a copyist's error, pardonable enough, in reading *hyde* and *yde* for *hycle* and *ycte*. See Monsenhor S. R. Dalgado's 'Dialecto Indo-Portuguese de Goa,' p. 19 : *'Icle,* s.m., stem of a coco-nut palm leaf, from the Malayalam.' The Tamil is *irkkil,* 'the feathers of an arrow' (Percival, p. 41). Mr. Ferguson says in Ceylon they call it an *eekle,* and speak of *eekle* brooms. This explanation also applies to Vol. I., p. 57.

Page 125, last line, and note 143.—F. Martin heard at Masulipatam in May, 1672, of 'Abdullah Qutb Shah's death. He makes the assertion, like Manucci, that Abu,l Hasan was 'descended from the ancient kings of Gulkandah.' Khafi Khan, vol. iii. (British Museum, Additional MS., No. 26,265, fol. 415*b*), says his Qutb Shahi descent was through his mother. He was the husband of 'Abdullah's third daughter. The eldest daughter married Sultan Muhammad, son of Aurangzeb, and the second girl's husband was known as 'Bara Mirza' (F. Martin, 'Memoires,' T* 1169, fol. 125). A full account of Abu,l Hassan's origin, marriage, and accession will be found in an appendix to J. Ovington, 'Voyage to Suratt' (1696), pp. 523-552. Here the second daughter's husband is called 'Meera Mamoed' (? Mir Ahmed), an Arab of high birth. He is possibly identical with the Sharif-ul-mulk mentioned by Manucci (Vol. II., p. 273), who surrendered to Shah 'Alam in 1685 ('Ma,asir-ul-umara,' ii. 688), and died Sha'ban 24, 1098 H., July 5, 1687.

Page 126, note 144, last line : 1660.—Negapatam was taken by the Dutch in 1658 (D.W.F.).

Page 129, line 26: *A. de Barro, S. J.*—Antonius Barros, S. J., a Portuguese, left for India in 1665 (A. Franco, 'Synopsis,' 1726).

Page 131, line 14 : *L. da Cunha.*—This man is probably the same as the one mentioned post, p. 150.

Page 133, line 11: *Long-armed Portuguese.*—For another mention of a long-armed man from San Thome, see Teixeira (Hakluyt Society), 205. Teixeira saw him in Cochin about 1590-1591. The Gentiles did him reverence, and he had orders not to travel in those lands without special permission. This may be the J. Carvalho of the text.

Page 137, line 4 from foot, and note 154: *Emperumalvedam.*—I am indebted to Dr. L. D. Barnett for the following note: 'The word *Emperumalvedam* strongly suggests a degraded form of the cult of Vishnu as expounded by Ramanuja. *Peru-mal,* "great Mai," is the title of Vishnu in Tamil, and thus the name would mean "The Veda [scripture] of our Great [God] Vishnu." We may also change *l* to *n,* and read Emperuman: this would mean "The Scripture of our Lord" (*viz.,* Vishnu, or his incarnation Ramanuja.' The Rev. F. Penny has also obtained the same explanation from another Tamil scholar. There is some evidence that branches of the Vaishnavas are of loose sexual morality. See *Chattadavar*, 'a class of Vaishnavas of a mixed kind, among whom, as report goes, there is community of wives' (J. P. Rottler, 'Tamil-English Dictionary,' i., part ii., p. 267, s.v.). I have since come across a form of the word in Jenkin T. Philipps's 'Account of the Religion ... of Malabar,' 1717, p. 36 : 'The sixth sect, *Nama-perumal-wedum*, does also carry upon their foreheads or arms the "dirunaman" (*tiru-namam*, or holy ashes), and worships Rischten or Wischtnu.' The puzzle remains as to why Manucci gave a Tamil name to a sect he found at Trimbak.

Page 139, line 2 from foot, and note 158: *Deltor.*—See 'T. Bowrey,' pp. 51, note 1; 64, note 1; 70, note 1; 257, note 6. He was French agent at Madras in 1673-74, when De la Haye was holding San Thome, and is mentioned in 1681 as chief of Pondicherry. Once, in August, 1685, the Fort St. George council received a letter from him from Pondicherry (A. T. Pringle, 'Diary and Consultations, 1685,' p. 121).

Page 142, note 159 : *Tabales.*—The form in the Portuguese dictionaries is *atabal*, pl. *atabales*, 'kettledrum,' from the Arabic *tabl*.

Page 147, line 21: *A miscarriage.*—The burial takes place in the house, so that the child may be reincarnated in some woman of the household See W. Crooke, 'Things Indian,' 128.

Page 150, line 19: *L. da Cunha.*—This is probably the man already mentioned in Vol. III., p. 131.

Page 151, line 3 from foot: *A Portuguese.*—Apparently he is identical with the Joao Carvalho referred to further on. See p. 209.

Page 152, line 17: *M. Corte Real.*—From Documents Nos. 706 and 723, dated Lisbon, April 13, 1665, and April 12, 1667, printed in Archivo da Relacao, de Goa,' it seems that Antonio de Mello de Castro, viceroy, caused Manoel Cortê Real de Sampaio to be imprisoned with fetters on his legs in the Aguada fortress, on account of the resistance offered in May, 1663, to the viceroy, the *fidalgos*, and the civil magistrate, Luiz Monteiro da Costa, by Sampaio's servants and caffres, at a time when the above officials went to the house to inquire into some matter (not specified). In this affray the viceroy was slightly wounded in one hand. The king ordered Sampaio's release, and appointed him to be judge of the knights.

Page 154, line 17: *Staves.*—The word used is *bocamartes* (*properly, bacamartes*), and it ought to have been translated 'blunderbusses.' See the definition of a *bacamarte* in L. Cordeiro, 'Como Se perdeu Ormuz,' p. 74: 'Firearms in use throughout India; they have a barrel three spans in length and a flint-lock. They throw a ball of two or three ounces, and at the end of a street against a crowd they are as effective as a swivel-gun.'

Page 155, paragraph 2: *Disorder in Goa.*—These statements are confirmed by documents in the 'Archivo da Relaçao de Goa.' No. 640 is an *atvard* (rescript) by D. Filippe Mascarenhas, dated Goa, January 9, 1645, referring to the many deaths caused by the general carrying of flint-locks, and forbidding the practice under severe penalties; also prohibiting the carrying by caffres or servants of 'cutlasses, broadswords, assegais, bows, arrows, daggers, either when alone or when in company of their lords and masters. They might carry umbrellas, of which the bamboo sticks were to be hollow and not to be iron-shod.' It also enacted that any caffre lifting his hand to a white man should suffer death. No. 648, of March 3, 1648, has reference to the discovery, on February 25, 26, on the public gallows at Mandovim, of an effigy with an inscription, purporting to be from the king, saying that he had ordered Dom Filippe to be hanged, and adding other calumnies. No. 656, of October 17, 1651; relates to an attack on Sunday, October 15, by twelve or fourteen caffres armed with bamboos on Dom Jorge de Amaral de Vasconcellos, general criminal magistrate, and his servants at his house. The party was joined by fifteen other caffres, all from the college of San Roque (one of the Jesuit institutions), having been sent by the padres thereof, who themselves, from their windows, jeered at the magistrate. The cause of all this was his having decided a civil suit against those padres.

Page 159, paragraph 2: *War of Bijapur against Goa.*—In the description in O.D. 45, *Réserve,* opposite the portrait of the 'Adil Shahi kings (Illustration No. XXXIV., at p. 334 of Vol. III.), we are told that it was in the reign of No. 7 ('Ali, 1656-73) that Luiz de Mendonça Furtado led a force against a Bijapur army commanded by Abdula Quin ('Abdullah Khan). This was also the reign in which Sharzah Khan repelled Jai Singh's invasion (c. 1666).

Page 159, line 32 : *Father Gonsallo Martins.*—Gonfalo Martins, 'procurator of the Society,' is named in a letter of Dom Filippe Mascarenhas, viceroy, dated January 8, 1646; and again he is spoken of by the Conde de Obidos, viceroy, on March 4, 1653, as a very practical and experienced person, whom he is sending to negotiate a peace [? with Bijapur]. (India Office, 'Portuguese Transcripts,' vols. xv., xvi., 'Books of the Monsoons').

Page 160, note 181: *Portraits.*—It is to be inferred from Fonseca, p. 100, and Burton, 'Goa,' 42, that the pictures are now in the new palace at Panjim, and have been there since 1764.

Page 170, line 21: *Maria de Taides.*—The name is spelt 'Ataides' in Part V. See Vol. IV., p. 188.

Page 171, last line, and note 194 : 1666.—As before, Mr. Ferguson thinks 1666 is correct. See note to Introduction, p. lvii.

Page 172, line 9: *Damiao Vieira.*—'This is the man already spoken of in Vol. II., p. 132.

Page 173, line 5 and note 197: *Paniāra.*—The note is wrong. The word is the Tamil *paniyāram, or panikaram,* 'sweet cakes, fritters, pastry' (Percival, 'Tamil-English Dictionary,' pp. 228, 234).

Page 173, line 3 from foot: *Butando*— As before, see additional note to Vol. II., p. 413, this is meant for Tibet.

Page 173, line 2 from foot: *Mirobolanos quebulos.*—Kabuli *myrobalans* are mentioned by Al Idrisi (see Elliot and Dowson, 'History,' i. 92).

These nuts are largely grown at one village in the north-east of the Kolaba district, the place of export being Chewal (Chaul), whence it is argued that the 'Chebula' in the botanical name is simply *chevali*, 'of or belonging to Chewal' ('Bombay Gazetteer,' xi. 25).

Page 174, paragraph 2 : *Missionaries for China.*—Their visit to Madras must have taken place in 1697 or 1698. We can trace most of these names in Norbert's 'Mémoires Historiques' (edition 1766), vol. vi. dealing with the China missions. (1) F. Antonio di Castr 'Ocaro, Italian Franciscan, Missionary of the Congregation and Bishop of Loriman, Vicar Apostolic of Kensi and Shansi; remained in China, p. 368, No. 3. (2) Luigi Andrea Appiani, Italian, interpreter of Cardinal de Tournon, put in prison first at Pekin, then at Canton, p. 365, No. 7. He died in Canton. There is more about L. A. Appiani in 'Mémoire Storiche' (8 vols., 1761), see part v., cols. 352, 353, giving a letter of 1728, written by him from Canton to his nephew. He was related to Cardinal de Tournon through the Cardinal's mother, and being then sixty-six, must have been born in 1662. He left Rome in 1696, passed through India, and reached China on October 14, 1699. From 1705 he was the Cardinal's interpreter, and in 1728 had been ten years and three-quarters in prison. (3) Giovanni Donato Mezzafalce, Italian, Vicar Apostolic of Le Kiang, Missionary of the Congregation, exiled from China, p. 365, No. 3. (4) Monseigneur Mullener, German, Bishop of Miriophitan, Vicar Apostolic of Succiven, remained in China at his own risk, p. 367, No. 1. (5) Monseigneur Alvaro de Benevent, Spaniard, Augustinian, Bishop of Ascalon, Vicar Apostolic of Kiangsi, sent to Macao, p. 367. No. 28. The other three priests are not named.

Page 176, line 4: *Lanha.*—As to this word, Monsenhor Dalgado ('Dialecto Indo-Portugues de Goa,' p. 19) has, '*Lanha*, unripe coco-nut.' and quotes Garcia : 'This nut, when green, the Malabaris call *elevi*, and here in Goa it is *lanha*.' The etymology is unknown. Mr. Ferguson suspects it is from Tamil *ilankay*, 'green, unripe fruit; fruit just formed' (Percival, 'Tamil-English Dictionary'). *Lanha* is not in Yule, but an allusion is made to it in a note on p. 874 (second edition), under 'Sura.'

Page 176, lines 12 and 16: *Cherata.*—Tamil, *chirattai*, 'the shell of the palmyra fruit.'

Page 177, line 21: *A sort of marmalade.*—The substance described is a favourite food of the Tamils in Jaffna, and is called *pinattu*, or *panattu*. It is described in Tennent's 'Ceylon,' fourth edition, ii. 525, as an orange-coloured pulp mixed with fibre; the juice is expressed and dried in squares in the sun, and then used for cakes, soup, or curry.

Page 181, line 20: *Zarvatane.*—For other accounts of this weapon see Teixeira (Hakluyt Society), pp. 6, 268, and the references in Pyrard (Hakluyt Society), ii. 165, note.

Page 181, line 3 from foot: *Serpali.*—Mr. Philipps proposes to identify this with Trichinopoly. In Tamil we have *Tirichchirappalli.* Dropping the prefix *Tiri* (holy), you have left Chirapalli or Sirapalli, the same letter serving in Tamil for 'ch' and 's.' On the maps we have

Trichirapali (La Croze, 1758), and *Tirushirapali* (D' Anville, 1751). Yule, p. 938, says the name is Sirapalli in the 'Tevaram.'

Page 184, note 213: *Brahmanpuri.*—This place is in the Sholapur district, sixteen miles east of Pandharpur ('Bombay Gazetteer,' xx., 411).

Page 191, line 21, and note 218: *Faracfal.*—Farrukh-fal (of happy omen, auspicious) was a younger son of Yamin-ud-daulah Asaf Jah, and therefore a younger brother of Shaistah Khan. On account of his corpulence and great weight Farrukh-fal retired into private life. He hoarded the presents and gifts obtained from the king at the '*Ids* and other festivals, and thus accumulated a great fortune. See 'Ma,asir-ul-umara,' iii. 707, s.v. Muhammad Yar Khan, who married his own cousin, Farrukh-fal's daughter. The marriage took place in 1082 H. (1671-1672), 'Ma,asir-i-'Alamgiri,' 110, line 7. Farrukh-fal has been mentioned once before, Vol. II. p. 365.

Page 194, line 35: *Pê-de-patta.*—Literally, 'goose-foot.'

Page 195, Note 221.—The Dutch took Negapatam in 1658, not 1660.

Page 195, line 9 : *J. P. de Faria.*—This man, already referred to on p. 108, was a person of note at this period. Mr. Ferguson, in his 'Captain Robert Knox,' quotes a letter from the Agent, etc., at Madras to the H.E.I. Company, dated July 20, 1663, stating that the ship *Anne* (renamed the *Hope*) had been sold to 'Signor Joan Perera da Faria and a Raccan Nocquedah [Arakan skipper].' There is also a letter from the King of Portugal to the Viceroy of India, dated March 17, 1674, in which da Faria is referred to; and a letter from him to the viceroy, reporting the capture of San Thome by the French. In Pringle's 'Selections from the Consultations of the Agent, etc., of Fort St. George, 1681,' Faria is referred to on pp. 4 and 15. In the latter place he is spoken of as the commander of the *James* bulwark of Madras. His son (of the same name), is mentioned on p 2. No reference to either appears in later volumes.

Page 209, line 18: J. *Carvalho.*—Apparently he is the person referred to in Vol. III., p. 152.

Page 208, lines 3 and 12, and note 227 on p. 207 : *Rey Freire.*— Here and throughout read 'Ruy Freire.' He did not command at Ormuz when it was surrendered in 1622; it was the fleet that he commanded. He surrendered to the English at Kishm February 1, 1622, while Ormuz held out until April 23 following. He had left Portugal April 1, 1619, with two *galleons* and three other vessels (see L. Cordeiro, 'Como se perdeu Ormuz,' p. 17). He was a native of the town of Beja; the son of Joao Freire de Andrada 'Desembargador.' He died at Masqat in September, 1633. See Paulo Craesbeeck, 'Commentarios' (1647), chap, i., and p. 179.

Page 209, paragraph 2: *Capture of Ruy Freire de Andrada.*—The capture and escape are both historical, but the English were the captors, and not the Arabs. According to the English records, Ruy Freire escaped from the *Lion*, lying off Surat, during the night of March 16, 1622, with two other Portuguese and a negro. A skiff had been negligently left alongside, and Beversham, the master, put the blame on the watch of six armed men, coupled with the carelessness of the boatswain about the skiff (see W. Foster, 'The English Factories in India, 1622-23,' pp. 60 and 83, and the documents quoted there). The Portuguese version of the story, as given by Paulo Craesbeeck, 'Commentarios' (1647), repeated in L. Cordeiro's modern work, is much more romantic. Ruy Freire asked for leave to keep Easter Day, and was allowed to send men to Portuguese territory for two pipes of wine. By his order one was drugged with *dhatura* and presented to the Englishmen. As soon as captain, officers, and crew were overpowered by sleep, Ruy Freire and his companions got into a boat. When fired on from other ships they jumped into the sea and swam to land. By dawn they had reached Daman; thence they moved to Bassain, where a small vessel was bought and armed. Some time in May, when in mid-ocean steering his course to Ormuz, he encountered Jorge de Souza, and learnt from him that the fortress had fallen. He returned to Chaul, and went thence to Goa. The starting-point of this story is defective, since in 1622 Easter Day fell on April 21, O.S., and the escape was made on March 16. The East India Company, in their court minute of August 6, 1623, state their belief that a bribe of £1,000 had been paid, but other of their remarks prove that Ruy Freire had already asserted that it was 'by the drunkenes of the master and the companie' that he escaped. Ruy Freire was posted to Masqat, and died there in September, 1633.

Page 210, line 2 from foot: *Lunna.*—Dr. Grierson points out that here Manucci must be recording stories he had heard about the mythical sorceress 'Lona, Chamarin.' In Hindu tradition she is the prototype of all great magicians, and is said to have lived in that home of sorcery, Kamrup, in Assam. Malik Muhammad, 'Padumawati,' 486, vi. (Ram Jasan's edition), speaking of the magician, Raghava Chetana, says: *Yah kar guru guru chamarin Lona/Sikha Kanwru pat hat tona*—'His guru is Lona Chamarin; when studying in Kamrupa he learnt the incantations.' For the legend of Lona, see W. Crooke, 'Tribes and Castes . . .,' ii. 170, 171, and his 'Introduction to the Popular Religion . . .,' p. 366, *cf.* p. 104 (where she is called Nona).

Page 212, paragraph 1: *Crocodile of the Oath.*—Jean Thevenot, who was in those regions about 1667, has the same story, but without the anecdote of the two bothers. Thevenot connects the story with a reservoir in the courtyard of a temple situated on the bank of a stream called by the Portuguese Rio Largo. There was said to be an underground communication between the tank and the river. In Thevenot's time there was no crocodile. See 'Voyages' (1727), v. 265. The same ruse, as that in Manucci's anecdote, was employed in a case tried by Sancho Panza, when Governor of Barataria. See 'Don Quixote,' part ii., chap. xlv.

Page 223, line 26, and note 10: *Granthaka.*—Among the Tamils this word is still popularly used for Sanskrit, so Mr. Philipps informs me, and when talking in English they will say, 'So-and-so knows *grantham*.'

Page 224, line 4: *J. de Britto.*—The place of Father de Britco's martyrdom is 'Woorioor' (*cf.* Pharaoh's 'Atlas' [1855]); it lies in the north-east corner of Ramnad zamindari, not far from the Tanjor district boundary, about 51 miles from Pamban point. It is not far from the coast road along which, between 1872 and 1875, Mr. Philipps found a constant stream of pilgrims passing to Rameshwaram.

Page 224, line 10; page 224, lines 16 and 24 : *Utiar.*—It is clear that there was some place known to Europeans by this name in the seventeenth and eighteenth centuries. In Tamil Udaiyar is a title, and is applied in Ceylon, Mr. Ferguson says, to a kind of headman. According to Nelson, 'Madura,' part iii., pp. 109, 110, it was used by the Ramnad Nayak, the Sethupati, and probably misapplied by Europeans, and turned into a place-name. In 1639 we hear of a fortress called Uthear in Pampa (Pamban) (Danvers, ii. 268). Possibly the Portuguese built it, and the Dutch had a small one at Pamban, which is still called the Dutch fort. In 1746 de Beauvais published a life of the Venerable J. de Brito, of which an English translation appeared in 1853 (? by Father Faber). On p. 381 it mentions a port called Ostiar, at which de Brito disembarked on his return from 'Topo,' near Cochin. The map in La Croze, edition of 1724, shows an 'Outiar' on the mainland just opposite Rameshwaram island. It will also be found in Orme's map of the Choromandal coast in his 'Military Transactions.' This is founded chiefly on D'Anville; upon the other map in Orme, the one by John Call, engineer, it does not appear. Most probably, then, Manucci's 'Utiar' was at modern Mandapam, on the mainland, the usual point of crossing to Pamban on the island; or it was at Tonitori ('boat ferry'), three miles further on, at the very point of the mainland, marked on map No. 41 in Pharaoh's 'Atlas' of 1855 by the word 'Pagoda.'

Page 224, line 12 and note 13: *Mannar.*—As Mr. Ferguson believes, Baldæus was the author of this false etymology (see chap, xliii. [or chap. xliv. of English translation] Churchill's 'Voyages,' vol. iii., p. 708). The derivation is uncertain; it was discussed in the 'Ceylon Literary Register,' iv. 303, 322.

Page 224, line 13: *Costa da Emsiada.*—Properly 'ensiada.' It was the name always applied by the Portuguese, and by the Dutch after them, to the coast forming the old southern boundary of the 'Teuver's country' (Ramnad) (see Valentyn, 'Ceylon,' p. 235). Mr. Philipps thinks it could be applied to the Indian coast-line of either Palk's Gulf or the Gulf of Mannar, or to both. From Point Calimere to Tuticorin you would get roughly Manucci's 80 leagues (say 240 miles).

Page 224, line 14: *Coniumeres.*—This is not Cape Comorin, but 'Calimere'; the Portuguese called in Canhameira. There seems to be some confusion about this name in Yule and Burnell, even in the second edition, p. 157. See Sanson's map of 1652, reprinted in Danvers, vol. i., 'Capa Conimeira' and 'Conhomeira' (town).

Page 224, paragraph 2: *Breadth of crossing.*—Mr. Philipps, who was several years in the neighbourhood, says that from Mandapam to Pamban it is about three miles, and from Tonitori to the same place a little under one mile. He does not see how obstructing the passage could prevent access to the Rameshwaram temple, it being open to attack from other directions. As to the blocks of marble, he says the sea having eaten off the top of the sandstone reef, the large flat blocks have something of an artificial look at low water. The double line of cut stones along the road from Pamban to Rameshwaram was intended, it is supposed, for the wheels of the idol-car, which is said to have been brought in old days across the reef to the mainland.

Page 225, paragraph 1: *A rough country.*—Mr. Philipps agrees that it is a 'rough country,' where the *babul* tree to this day predominates, though its spikes are not worse than elsewhere. But there is a banyan-tree avenue from Pamban to the temple eight miles long, and palmyra palms are numerous.

Page 225, line 17: *Surrjana.*—This word means 'Syriac,' the liturgical language of the Christians of St. Thomas, whether Nestorians, Jacobites, or Roman Catholics. See the expression, 'na lingua Suriana' in F. de Souza, 'Oriente Conquistado' (1710), ii. p. 71, as quoted by G. T. Mackenzie, 'Christianity in Travancore' (1901), p. 64.

Page 225, line 2 from foot: *Fine canes.*—I ought to have translated 'fine cinnamon which the inhabitants use in their cookery.'

Page 226, line 6 *et seq.* and line 21 *et seq.*: *The tooth relic or Dalada.* — Manucci's account is very incorrect; the best one is found in Couto, 'Da Asia,' Decada VII., livro 9, cap. ii., p. 316 (edition 1783), and cap. xvii., p. 428. See also a memoir by J. G. da Cunha (London, 1875), pp. 40, 44. The Portuguese believed the relic was handed, mounted in gold, to Dom Constantino de Bragança in 1560. D. de Couto and Faria y Souza say it was the tooth of an ape. An envoy from the King of Pegu arrived at Goa in 1561, and made an unlimited offer for its restoration. The Archbishop interfered; the relic was reduced to powder and burnt. See also Linschoten (Hakluyt Society), i., p. 292.

Page 227, paragraph 4 and page 228 paragraph 1: *The thunderbolt.* The statement about the thunderbolt is, Mr. Ferguson holds, both interesting and historical. The 'Mahavanso' (L. C. Wijesinha, Mudaliyar, editor, part ii., chaps, xxxix.-c., Columbo, 1889), p. 328, chap, xcv., after recording the birth at Mahiyasigana (Bintenna) of Raja Sinha II., says (vers. 14-17) that on the same night the leader of the enemy (the Portuguese) dreamed a terrible dream. A spark arose the size of a firefly and grew till it reached Columbo, where it set everything on fire. That day the enemy's host which was approaching Sirivaddhana [Kandy] fled in terror. The reference seems to be to what Bocarro, 'Decada 13' (1876), p. 45, calls the 'famosa retirada' of Dom Jeronymo de Azevedo from the fortress of Balane (near Kandy) in February, 1603, when he reached Malvana after great loss in killed and wounded. The only objection is that Raja Sinha's birth could not have taken place before 1606. Manucci is quite wrong in coupling the name of Constantino de Sá with that of D. J. de Azevedo; the latter was captain-General of Ceylon in 1594-1612, while the former was there in 1618-21. Dom Constantino returned in 1623, and in 1630 was killed with all his army in Uva. This is the event referred to in the second paragraph of the text.

Page 228, paragraph 2: Dutch in Ceylon.—There were several fleets sent to Ceylon before that under Rijkloff van Goens in 1658. 'Tuf de

Barbon' and 'Coquinto' are inexplicable. But 'Arriam de Vandermuis' is evidently Adriaan van der Meiden, who succeeded to the command on Hulft's death, and was the first Dutch Governor of Ceylon.

Page 228, note 22: *Portuguese commanders.*—A. de Sousa Coutinho had been sent to supersede F. de Mello de Castro, but the latter, being unable to leave owing to the siege of Columbo, acted as second-in-command. De Sousa's son had no part in the command.

Page 230, line 21, and note 28: *Trimanas.*—A better identification is proposed both by Mr. Ferguson and Mr. Philipps. It is Tiru-malaivasal, the Trimelavaas of English and Dutch writers. See Havart, i., p. 42; T. Bowrey, xxxiii.; Pringle, 'Consultations . . . 1681,' p. 70, note 89. It is a town in the Tanjor district, fifty-seven miles north-east by east of Tanjor (lat. 11° 13', long. 79° 56'). The map of 1652 in Danvers, and that in La Croze (1724), actually spelt it Triminavaz. It was probably once a place of some importance. The 'Madras Manual of Administration,' iii., p. 827, says it has an old Saiva temple.

Page 233, line 13: *Evantica.*—Mr. Crooke writes: 'Can this be a confusion with Avanti=Ujjain?'

Page 252, note 8: *Praying stones.*—Mr. Abu,l Hasan Khan, Wahid-ul-mulk, Kirmani, tells me that the idea is rather to obviate possible pollution by touching the ground. The practice is common in Persia, and the round disc of clay used there is called a *muhr*.

Page 262, paragraph 1 and note 17 on page 261: *Hiranyagar bha.*—Frazer, 'Golden Bough,' second edition, i., p. 307, refers to this practice in chap, i., 'Perils of the Soul,' Sections 1 to 3, 'Royal and Priestly Taboos.' His authority is 'Asiatick Researches,' quarto edition, vol. vi., p. 535 (article by Captain Francis Wilford). This was a case of two Hindus sent by the Mahrattah Raghunath Rao (Ragoba) to England. They only reached Suez; still, they were put out of caste on their return. Unable to pay for a gold image of a woman or a cow, they compounded by providing a gold *yoni* through which they were dragged. E. Thurston, 'Ethnographic Notes' (1906), gives a Tanjor Nayak's case, *c.* 1664-65, evidently taken at secondhand from J. H. Nelson, 'Madura,' part iii., p. 188. This king's name was Vijaya Raghava, and hence probably came Manucci's name (line 13), 'the Victorious,=*Vijaya*.

Page 262, note 18: *Conquest of San Thome.*—See further the authorities in T. Bowrey, xxxviii., note 4; xlv., note 1—viz., J. Thevenot, iii., p. 105; Schouten, i. 488; Fryer, 43; L'Estra, 173.

Page 263, line 1; *Raja Culy.*—I now identify this Riza Quli as the man holding the title of Neknam Khan. He seems to have come to the Karnatik as governor about 1661. J. Thevenot, who was through the country in 1666, speaks of him as still in power, and tells us that he was a eunuch named 'Raja Couli,' aged seventy, on whom the title of Neknam Khan had been conferred. He had conquered the country with extraordinary rapidity. It was from him apparently that Sir William Lang- home obtained in 1671 the 'cowle,' or grant, of the Madras customs at a fixed rent of Rs. 4,200 per annum. Neknam Khan died in April or May, 1672, and was succeeded by Muhammad Ibrahim. See J. Thevenot,

'Voyages' (1727), v., p. 273; Wheeler, 'Madras,' i., pp. 34, 81, 82, 85; C. R. Wilson, 'Surman Diary,' Appendix, p. 257; F. Martin, 'Mémoires,' fol. 121, *recto*.

Page 264, line 10: *Portuguese return to San Thome.*—In 1687 the Portuguese entered into negotiations for a lease of the town, but these were defeated by Elihu Yale. See Pringle, 'Diary . . . Fort St. George, 1684,' p. 171, note 27, quoting Wheeler, 'Madras,' i., p. 176 (edition ,1861).

Page 264, paragraph 2: *Settlement of loose women near Goa.*—There seem to have been two communities of this kind. The more celebrated is that of Seroda or Siridao on the coast, six miles south-west of Goa city, on Goa Island, between Bambooleem and Nazareth. We have the accounts of two visits to it—in 1833 by Walter Campbell, 'My Indian Journal,' p. 211, and in 1851 by R. F. Burton, 'Goa,' p. 117—the first as sentimental as the second is brutally unromantic. The face reproduced in Campbell's drawing is a lovely one. But the place intended by Manucci lies in another direction, probably at Narva on Piedade Island, about two and a half to three miles north-east of Goa city, identical most probably with Fryer's 'Norway,' edition 1698, p. 152. This must also be the village mentioned by Grose, 'Voyage to the East Indies' (edition 1766), i., p. 140.

Page 268, paragraph 2: *C. de Souza Coutinho.*—Christavaon de Souza Coutinho was in 1683 captain and governor of Bardes, close to Goa. 'His family have ruined India. His uncle, Manuel, weakly lost Malacca; his father, Antonio, lost Ceylon; and he himself lost the richest fleet in India of our time. Now (1683) he has lost Bardes' (India Office, 'Portuguese Transcripts,' Translations, 'Noticias,' vol. ii., p. 440). For Manuel, see Danvers, ii., pp. 26, 67, 78, 81, 82, and for Antonio, *ibid.*, 311, 317, 320.

Page 268, line 22: *Father F. Seraphino.*—These stories of priestly domination are confirmed by what happened at Chaul in 1683. On August 18 Sambha Ji assaulted Chaul and was repulsed. During the action the five guns on the walls were brought into play, but at the first discharge the carriages broke into pieces; the powder was also no more than a little charcoal, and the loaded cannon had not been discharged for fifteen years. The writer attributes the whole fault to the greed of the Jesuits, who were administrators for military stores. Not even the governor himself could fire a gun without their permission (India Office, 'Portuguese Transcripts,' Translations, 'Noticias,' pp. 366-447).

Page 269, line 31: *Renols.*—*Reinicola, Reinol* 'of the kingdom' (Portugal).

Page 270, paragraph 1, and note 33: *French loss of San Thome.*—Valentyn, 'Choromandel,' p. 12, gives a plan with wall and ditch, but says that in his time (?1675) it was only a heap of rubbish. More about the French at San Thome will be found in T. Bowrey, pp. 46, note 4, 64-66; Fryer, p. 41; Valentyn, 'Ceylon,' p. 246 (Rykloff's letter of 1675), De Lestra, pp. 34, 59.

Page 271, note 35, lines 22 to 31, should read thus: 'Between 1662 and 1664 he was Procurator of the province, and subsequently Rector of the College of the Holy Faith, and Rector of the Novitiate at Goa. He took his four vows at Goa on September 8, 1663. In 1667 he became Superior of the Canara mission, and afterwards *Socius* of the Father Provincial and visitor of the division of the Province styled the Northern (*regio Aquilonis*). He was sent to Rome in 1677 as Procurator. In 1679 he was serving as a parish priest in the Northern division, and subsequently was rector of the great college, of St. Paul at Goa, and *præpositius* of Goa province. In 1688 he was made *prapositus* of the Malabar province, and governed it until 1689, 'in all of which,' etc.

Page 279, paragraph 3: *The Mendoças.*—In the 'Archivo da Relacao dc Goa' the documents 674-681 refer to the Bassain murders. The dates are May 9, October 19, October 20, November 3, November 8, November 10, 1656, February 26, 1657. The last of the eight is unsigned and undated. The case was submitted to the Goa tribunal by Francisco de Melio Sampaio, captain of Bassain. First of all the general criminal magistrate, Dr. Jorge do Amaral e Vasconcellos, was sent from Goa with powers to investigate into the murders of Francisco Soares da Costa, magistrate (*ouvidor*), and of the brothers Luiz and Manuel de Mendonfa. Later, the chief justice, Joao Alvares Carrilho, was sent with full powers to deal with the matter, and, if necessary, to depose the captain of Bassain, Francisco de Mello Sampaio. He was to send this man a prisoner to Goa. His orders were also to proceed against Jorge do Amaral de Loureiro, whom Francisco de Mello had appointed magistrate. Both Dr. Jorge do Amaral e Vasconcellos and Joao Alvares Carrilho were murdered, the former by poison. Finally in 1657 another chief justice, Dr. Manoel Martins Madeira, was sent to investigate into the facts. The result is not on record. The murderers, who fled into Mogul territory, seem to have been the captain-general, F. de Mello de Sampaio, and his brother Diogo. See Document 698, dated Lisbon, April 1662.

Page 281, line 13: *Innundation at Masulipatam.*—Havart, i. 196-205, gives a graphic description by an eyewitness of this flood, which occurred not in 1680, but on October 23-25, 1679.

Page 281, line 16: *Comet.*—I think this must be the same comet as the one said on p. 365 to have appeared in 1702, for as it came in February or March, that would be 1701, Old Style, and 1702, New Style.

Page 284, note 44: The *Muchalkah.*—The document of February 24, 1699, does not contain these provisions. It binds the Dutch to capture pirates, and restore the goods plundered, or pay the value, under penalty of having to quit Mogul territory. The two undertakings in the note are given by Valentyn in two preceding paragraphs. The sum to be paid was Rs. 24,00,000, not Rs. 24,000 (as in my note). I followed Dubois, and was misled by him.

Page 285, paragraph 1: *W. Norris.*—The Mogul camp was near the Mahrattah stronghold of Panhala. See, *ante*, Vol. II., p. 293. The date was April 28, 1701. Beckles Wilson, 'Ledger and Sword' (ii. 9. note), gives a long list of persons making up the procession.

Page 293, line 25: *'Abd-ul-ghafur.*—This 'Abd-ul-ghafur was a Bohrah, and at his death (*c.* 1717-18) is said to have left a fortune of six *krors* of rupees (over six millions sterling) (Khafi Khan, ii. 942, *Tarikh-i-Muhammadi,* 1146 H.). The man's wealth may be guessed from Captain Hamilton's statement, 'New Account,' i 149, that he sent out yearly twenty sail of merchantmen. It was said that the Moguls extorted a million sterling from his heirs.

Page 295, last line: *Mandeli.*—Mr. Philipps would take this as meant for Mudali. There is evidence to show that the word Mudali is used in some districts as a caste name as well as a mere title—at any rate, by Roman Catholics: J. A. Dubois (ed. 1906), 15, 16; L. Renevier, 'Notice sur l'origine de la Chapelle ... a Villenour' (Pondicherry, 1877), 6, 9, 14; Letter from Father Mond, SJ. (Palemkottah, 1877, privately printed), and a MS. Census of Catholics in Marava, 1876. In this last document, out of twenty-two castes, the 'Moudelys' are placed next in order to the Vellalans, a highly respectable caste.

Page 298, line 4 from foot: *Third order.*—Mr. Philipps holds that this must be a stroke of malice on Manucci's part, for the Society of Jesus never had a third order, or similar lay body, attached to it.

Page 305, line 13 and note 62: *Romapuri.*—Mr. Philipps holds that

Romapuri is an adjective formed from Romapur (or Uromapur), the ordinary Tamil word for the city of Rome. It is placed by Beschi under *Puri* (town). But I still think the adoption of the form may have been influenced in the way stated in my note.

Page 315, note 72: *Father Bertholdi.*—In the Patriarch of Antioch's Decree of June 23, 1704, he is designated as Carlo Michaele Bertoldi (Norbert, 'Mémoires Historiques,' 1747, i. 116).

Page 316, line 23, and note 77: *Aurpaliam.*—The kingdom of Aura is mentioned in the 'Imperial Gazetteer of India,' first edition, iii. 131, under Dharampuri, which belonged to that kingdom up to 1688, when it was annexed by Maisur. This shows that the kingdom was of considerable extent, if the place in the note was the capital. The two places are 104 miles apart.

Page 317, note 78 : *Aour.*—This place is about thirteen miles and a half nearly due south of Trichinopoly. Out of deference to the Portuguese the Catholic Church here is still left in the diocese of Mailapur (San Thome). Other spellings are Aur, Avoor, Auvoor, Aghoor.

Page 318, paragraph 3: *A cross hidden in a bunch of flowers.*— from the 'Memorie Storiche' (1761), vol. v., p. 8, as quoted by R. C. Jenkins (The Jesuits in China,' p. 18), I find that on September 1, 1645, a reference was made to the Propaganda, one question being 'whether Christian magistrates may carry a cross hidden under the flowers which are presented at the heathen altars, and secretly worship that cross.' The reply was in the negative. The passage is also in Norbert (edition 1766), vol. vi., p. 5 (seventh question).

Page 321, line 18: *Arack.*—*Arasu, arasmaram,* s., a tree, the *Ficus religiosa; arasani,* a bough of this tree, which, together with one from the *Kaliyana murruku* [marriage lemon-tree], is fixed in the middle of the marriage *pandal,* called *arasanikkal,* and round which the parties go when performing particular ceremonies (Percival 'Tamil-English Dictionary').

Page 322, line 20: *Ramade.*—Mr. Ferguson says perhaps *ramade* represents *arai-madam,* Tamil for 'single roomed-house.' On the other hand, Mr. Philipps (I think with more probability) refers it to the Portuguese *Ramada,* (literally, 'boughs or leaves'), and finds that word used as equivalent to *pandal* in a letter from Father Hieronymo de Bellem, Provincial of 'Madre de Deos,' to the Goa viceroy, dated November 10, 1727. See J. H. da Cunha Rivara ('Ensaio Historico,' Goa, 1858, p. 332).

Page 326, paragraph 1 : *Procession of August,* 1701.—In a letter dated October 30, 1702, written to Friar François Marie de Tours at Rome, Father Paul de Vendôme comments on the heathen nature of this procession (Archives Nationales, K. 1374, Document No. 41).

Page 334, line 7, and note 114: *Apes.*—Could this be Castañeda's *apes* ? See Yule, s.v. 'Hopper,' p. 425, 'flat cakes of rice flour.' This is from Tamil *appan,* 'bread' (D. W. F.).

Page 335, line 2: *Monsieur Appiany.*—There was at San Thome in 1702-3 a Giovanni Appiani, priest of the Congregation missions. He attests a copy of the bishop's certificate in favour of the Jesuits (Archieves Nationales, Paris, K. 1374, Document No. 43). Possibly he was a relation of the better-known Luigi Andrea Appiani in China. See *ante,* additional note, to Vol. III., p. 174.

Page 349, line 7: *Jeremiah.*—The quotation is from Lamentations i., v. 12.

Page 350, note 131, last line.—It was on November 19, 1620 (not in 1612), that Tranquebar was conceded to the Danes. See Mr. Ferguson's letter in the *Journal* R.A.S. for 1898, pp. 625-7.

Page 352, line 19, and note 137 : *Tripapoulour.*—For 'Tirepopelier' see Baldaeus, 'Malabar en Choromandel,' chap, xxiii., and Valentyn, 'Choromandel,' p. 9.

Page 359, line 35 : *Mange Copang.*—Manji Kuppan, lying to the north, where the civil station is situated, is now known as Cuddalore New Town, while ancient Cuddalore is called 'Old Town.' The ruined fort St. David lies between the two. There are railway-stations at both towns, two miles apart.

Page 360, line 26: *Our random.*—A. T. Pringle ('Diary . . . of Fort St. George, 1685,' p. 170) speaks of the cession of 'two myles of ground, or y[e], *randome* of a shotte of a p[e] of ornance, next and round about the town.' On p. 198, note 109, there is another instance in the year 1695. Pringle also quotes a passage from Kenelm Digby, cited in Todd's Johnson, second edition.

Page 361, line 7: *Egip.*—H. H. Wilson, in his 'Glossary,' p. 206, suggests *Hejib,* and C. P. Brown has *hejib,* a clerk or writer. *Egib* may be a corruption of *hajib,* a door-keeper or chamberlain, applied to a confidential servant sent as a messenger. A. T. Pringle ('Selections from the Consultations . . . 1681,' P. 68, note 57).

Page 363, line 2 from foot : *Maisonneuve*. Governor F. Martin writes to Pontchartrain on February 15, 1700 ('Archives du Ministère des Colonies,' C^2 65, fols. 67, *verso*, to 68): 'A very unpleasant affair has happened, and we may yet feel further evil consequences from it, owing to that belief usual among Mahomedans that it is a sort of meritorious act to injure Christians, even when they themselves are entirely to blame. Round Pondicherry are several small fortified places governed by Mahomedans, who allow their garrisons to wander over the country, plundering it, and even intruding into other jurisdictions. By this conduct they hope to be free of having to provide their soldiers' pay.

'A party from one of these forts, situated about eight leagues from Pondicherry, after driving some cattle from various places, entered upon lands dependent on our fort, whence on November 17 [1699] they drove before them some two to three hundred head of cattle belonging to our townsmen. As soon as we learned this we mounted our horses.

'Monsieur de Livernan, naval lieutenant in the king's service and commanding our troops, was the first, followed by the Sieur de Maisonneuve, also an ensign of marine and lieutenant of a company in the fort. From one of the gates of the town the commandant saw the enemy enter a wood half a league off with their booty. Some of our *lascarins* (*lashkaris*)—that is, soldiers of the country—had followed and were engaged with the enemy in the wood. Monsieur de Saint-Mars and I (Martin) were at the head of a detachment on its march from the fort.

'Monsieur de Livernan, seeing that it would be some time before our men could be supported, and being full of ardour and courage, pushed on, followed by the Sieur de Maisonneuve. As they entered the wood they found twenty to thirty horsemen and some men on foot, who advanced against them and fired. While the commandant was taking aim, a musket-ball struck him and broke the small bone of his right arm, a little above the wrist. Put *hors de combat* by this wound, he was forced to retire.

'The Sieur de Maisonneuve was next attacked by the same horsemen, and being pressed by them, he shot their leader down. The men, excited by this loss, surrounded him; he warded off several blows with his sword, but in the end, overcome by numbers, he was cut down and left on the field.

'We and our detachment reached the wood as the fight ended. The enemy had retreated at the gallop, and were so far off that there was no hope of coming up with them. We returned to the fort, and wrote to the principal officials of the province, setting forth our complaints. The only satisfaction we have obtained is their censuring the governor of the fort from which the marauders had issued. Their leader died of his wound five or six days after receiving it. Monsieur de Livernan is out of all danger from his, but it will be a month more before his arm is restored to its ordinary condition.

'I cannot praise sufficiently, my lord, the zeal and energy of the commandant in carrying out the king's orders for the interests of the

Company, which he warmly enters into. Personally, I am thankful for his care to maintain the good terms on which we stand, so conducive to good public results. It were to be wished that the king's officers under him, the Sieurs de Saint-Mars and La Chenardière, who are naval ensigns acting as captains of the two companies, would also see their way to a similar understanding.'

The Sieur de Livernan tells the story himself in his letter of February 19, 1700 (C^2 65, fol. 95). In its main lines it is the same as Martin's account; but Maisonneuve's death is given somewhat differently. When wounded himself, de Livernan made over his musket to Maisonneuve. They resolved to rejoin Martin; then Maisonneuve turned to the left, and fell, no doubt, into an ambuscade, where he perished after wounding the enemy's leader.

De Livernan arrived in India in 1699 with Des Angiers, his instructions being dated November 30, 1697; he resigned and left for France in February, 1701. See Kaepplin, 547, 549.

In a memoir on the French Company, 'Bibliothèque Nationale MS. Français,' No. 6,231, fol. 25, *verso*, the combat is told to the same effect as in M. Martin's letter, the writer adding that Maisonneuve was 'haché en pieces.' He gives the date as November 27, 1699.

Page 364, line 25; *Bamiapalam.*—Mr. Philipps has found this place for me where I ought to have looked for it myself. It is on Indian Atlas Sheet, No. 80, and also on map No. 11 of Pharaoh's Atlas (1855). It appears as Bommaya-paleiyam, being just outside of and on the north edge of the French territory. It lies on the old sandy road along the seashore. The attack on Bamiapallam took place upon August 6, 1701; Kaepplin, 483, relying on an MS. 'Journal,' by F. Martin.

Page 374, line 4 from foot: *An envoy from Governor Martin.*—The resolution is dated February 6, 1701, and the bearers of the presents were two natives of India (P. Kaepplin, p. 482).

Page 380, note 158 : *Tom Clarke's gate.*—I beg a reference to the additional note to the Introduction, p. Lxiv, (Vol. I.), founded on Colonel Love's and Mr. Penny's information.

Page 385, last line, and note 164: *Desprez.*—He left Pondicherry March 12, 1702, and reached the Nawab's camp on the 16th. At his second audience on the 23rd, he was accompanied by Manucci, and at his leave-taking on the 25th, Da,ud Khan offered the French a cession of Madras on condition of ejecting the English (Kaepplin, p. 487, relying on F. Martin's MS. 'Journal').

Page 386, line 8: *Wishing to be of use to the French.*—A further instance of Manucci's employment by the French is found in a letter from Pondicherry to the Directors of the French Company, dated February 5, 1703, where it is said : 'We send a copy of the instructions, which we have given to the Sieur Manouchy, in order that he may take steps with the general of the "Mores" (Mahomedans) and the *diwan* in case of need' ('Ministère des Colonies,' C^2 67, fol. 11). Colonel H. D. I.ove has favoured me with a copy of the previous minute on the same subject, taken from the Pondicherry records. It is dated January 15,

1703. After reciting rumours of a declaration of war against France, the news brought by a Portuguese captain, Manuei Rodrigues, that he had seen five Dutch vessels assembled at Malacca, and the fact of Dutch preparations at Negapatam and in Ceylon, it assumes that Pondicherry is threatened. It was resolved to sell as far as possible the coin and ingots with the stock of cloth and coral, and that any unsold surplus should be deposited with the English at Madras and Fort St. David, as had been done in 1693, through the good offices of Monsieur Chardin. The same reasons led them to open negotiations with Nawab Da,ud Khan, and ask for his protection in case of need. 'To do this with the least publicity and expense, they had selected and appointed the Sieur Nicolas Manouchy, Venetian by birth, married and established at Madras for twenty years past, and an old friend of the French, known to and honoured by the highest noblemen at the Mogul court by reason of having there practised medicine with success for several years, and particularly esteemed by the Nawab Da,ud Khan and the *diwan*, or intendant of the army. The instructions necessary for this negotiation will be delivered to the said Sieur Manouchy, by which he shall be bound, and to which he shall conform most exactly.' The signatories are Martin, de Chalonge, D'hardancourt, Delebat, and Desprez. Again, when difficulties arose in 1712 with a new *Diwan*, the Chevalier Hébert sent Manucci to him with a present of 300 *pagodas* ('Bibliothèque Nationale,' Ariel Collection, No. 8,927, f. 153, quoted by P. Kaepplin, pp. 616, 617, note 1).

Page 387, note 166: *P. van der Burg*.—For this man see also Havart, iii. 18, 19 (1672-76), and Valentyn, 'Choromandel,' p. 16 (1672-74 and 1709-20).

Page 408, note 181: *French Capuchins at Madras*.—These Capuchins did not meet with unfailing good treatment. In 1668 Fathers Ephraim and Zeno were expelled by Sir Edward Winter, when they retired to San Thome. A court minute of December 16, 1668, ordered that they should be encouraged to return 'as they shall be found to deserve' (vol. xxv., fol. 180). Sir E. Winter was governor by right 1661-65, and by usurpation 1665-68 (Wheeler, 'Madras,' i. 33). Fathers Ephraim and Zenon were again turned out, along with Pierre Deltori, early in 1674, at the instigation of the Dutch, then engaged in hostilities with the French at San Thome. The party went *via* Jinji to Pondicherry, then a mere village, where they were sheltered by F. Martin and de Lespinay ('Mémoires,' T* 1169, fols. 241, 243, and 246).

Page 408, line 12: *A high reputation*.—Father Jean Baptiste de Saint Aignan in his report to Colbert, dated Easter, 1670, says the bishops of Beryte and of Heliopolis, styled the Madras Capuchins 'des véritables apôtres et enfants de Saint François.' See A. Rabbath, S. J., 'Documents Inédits' (Paris, 1907), i. 516.

Page 410, note 183: *Father de Sa*.—The name of Jeronymo de Sa, 'treasurer-in-chief of the see of Goa,' is given in the letter of the viceroy to the King of Portugal, dated December 28, 1651, when reporting on Father Ephraim's case (India Office, "Portuguese Transcripts.' Translations vol. xvii., 'Books of the Monsoons').

Page 411, at end of paragraph 1: *Le Gouz's account.*—At the end of February, 1650, Le Gouz and Father Zeno, who had been travelling together, arrived at Swally (off Surat). There they heard of Father Ephraim's arrest. His crime, they heard, was that he had denounced the Catholics, who had beaten and thrown into wells the images of St. Anthony and of the Blessed Virgin, and by so doing behaved worse than the Hindus, who at least respect what they hold to be holy. A Portuguese friar felt aggrieved, and Father Ephraim was sent for to San Thome, but maintained his opinion. They admonished him, that he, a thing of naught, a pedaço of a foreigner, should not utter such things. As the Franciscans somewhat favoured him, he was not arrested then; but shortly afterwards, while on Portuguese territory, the officials of the Holy Office laid hold of him. Father Zeno remarked to Le Gouz that it was no wonder, if the Portuguese fathers knew nothing of the decrees of councils, for mostly they came to India as soldiers, and there entered holy orders. He hoped the French would come to trade in India, as they would bring with them men of learning. Le Gouz had met Father Zeno at Surat in 1648, where he had then been ten years. They travelled down the coast as far as Goa, and thence back to Surat. In that year the Grand Inquisitor at Goa was, a *renol* (native of Portugal) and a secular priest, his colleague being a Dominican. Le Gouz left Swally on March 1, 1649/50, on board an English vessel, and Father Zeno started by land for Madras to take charge of the parish ('Les Voyages et Observations du Sieur de la Boullaye Le Gouz ...' [1653], pp. 126, 190, 193, 214, 222, 264).

Page 414, line 25, *Capuchin*: page 441, line 13, and footnote 217 on p. 440, *convent of Capuchins*; page 444, line 24, *province of the Mother of God of the Capuchins . . . in the East Indies*; page 452, line 15, a [*Capuchin*] *church.*—The Portuguese cause confusion, Mr. Philipps writes, by using the name *Capuchos* for those who were not Capuchins at all in the usually accepted sense. In Italy the 'minori cappuccini' are the members of the body finally approved as an independent order in 1619 by Paul V. These Capuchins never had any houses in Portugal or in the Portuguese dependencies in the East. The Capuchos at, Goa or Mailapur were 'Observantes Reformados.' The order founded by St. Francis, who died in 1226, divided itself into (A) Conventuals (*minori conventuali*), and (B) Observances (*minori osservanti*). The Franciscans who followed the Portuguese to India were Observantines, and in 1618 were formed into an independent Indian province, with the name of St. Thomas (see Rivara, 'Lingua Concani,' p. 23). In 1628, with the sanetion of Urban VIII., the Portuguese Observantines in India divided into (1) the original Observantines, (2) Observantes Reformados, popularly styled *Capuchos or Recolétos*: and the convents were divided. The latter body obtained those of Madre de Deus, of the Cabo, and of the Pilar. These Capuchos formed the 'Provincia Capucha da Madre de Deus.' These facts explain page 440, line 23, and line 28. First of all Father Ephraim said Mass at the Convent of St. Francis (of the

Obser vantes), and then at the Convent of the Mother of God (of the Obser- vantes Reformados). See Fonseca, 'Goa,' p. 220; and Archbishop Joao Chrystomo d'Amorim Pessoa, 'Noticia sobra o Estado do Real Padroado Portuguez das Indias Orientes no anno de 1779,' 'Obras,' iii., part i., p. 253.

Page 419, line 9, and note 192: *Latria.*—This word is also in the New Oxford Dictionary, but with no example between 1645 and 1845.

Page 444, line 11: *Ambroise of Preuilly.*—This must be the Capuchin that Manucci met at Surat in 1656 (see Vol. I., p. 61). François Martin, in his 'Mémoires, fol. 71, speaks of Father Ambroise acting as interpreter to Monsieur de Faye, French Director in March, 1669, when he paid a visit to the Mahomedan Governor of Surat. Carre, 'Voyage des Indes Orientales' (1699), p. 24, referring to 1669 or 1670, states that Father Ambroise was then head of the Capuchins at Surat.

Page 445, note 222: *Portuguese at San Thome.*—The first visit of the Portuguese to the tomb of St. Thomas seems to have been made in 1510. They heard of it from an Armenian called Sikandar, and they started from Pulicat to find the place (Barros, 'Decada III.,' livro vii, capitulo 11 [vol. iii., p. 222 in edition of 1777]).

Page 445, note 223: *Geldria.*—The Dutch fort Geldria, built in 1613-15, received its name from its founder, Wemmer van Berchem, a native of Gelders (see L. C. D. van Dijk, "Tes Jaren uit het leven van Wemmer van Berchem,' pp. 19, 20, 30 note; and Valentyn, 'Choromati- del,' p. 13). It was in 1610 that the Dutch obtained leave to found a settlement at Pulicat (see the agreement, dated April 24, 1610, between Captain Arent Maertszoom and Venkata Pati Raya, in Heeres, 'Corpus Diplomaticum Neerlando-Indicum' [1907], pp. 84, 85). As to the etymology of Pulicat, see Havart, i. 105; and Thomas Bowrey, p. 52, note. The oldest Portuguese form is Paleacate.

Page 448, note 225, line 13: *His other point.*—I find I have sadly mis-represented Mr. Philipps's meaning. This sentence should read: 'His other point is that in the Hindustani spoken at Madras, Tamil is called "Aravi" ' (H. H. Wilson, 'Glossary,' p. 31). Thus the text by 'Arabi' might mean the Tamil language, which is not otherwise mentioned. On the other hand, it is strange that if that language were intended it should not be called Malabar, Tamul, or Thamul, The two latter words were in use by the Portuguese in 1654 and 1656. See Rivara, 'Lingua Concani,' pp. 225, 226.

Page 455, note 229, line 11: *Governor.*—This should be read as 'governor of the bishopric'—*i.e.*, administering it during a vacancy of the 'See.

Page 456, line 18: *Friar Antonio.*—Antonio de Santiago, Capucho, is mentioned twice in letters from the Viceroy of Goa to the king, dated May 15 and August 23, 1658. He was then Commissary-General of the Franciscan Observantines of the Mother of God province, and a religious in that convent. For the meaning of 'Capucho,' see additional note to iii., p. 414.

Page 456, line 20, and note 230: *Discalced.*—This word is in the New Oxford Dictionary, but without an instance between 1700 and 1867.

Page 456, line 27: *Superior of the Province of the Apostle St. Thomas.*—Father Manuel must have been an Observantine and not an Observantine Reformado, because (1) the Luz Church at San Thome was the only one on the Choromandel coast held by the former body; (2) above his signature on p. 456, he says not *our* but *the* convent of the Capuchin fathers; (3) all Franciscan missioners in the south, with one exception, belonged to the Observantines. From 1619 the Indian province had not only a Minister Provincial, but a Commissary-General sent from Portugal ('Rivara,' p. 25). Apparently the Commissary ruled over both orders of the Franciscans.

Page 456, line 28, and note 231: *Definitor.*—This word is in the New Oxford Dictionary, but without any instance between 1745 and 1867.

Page 462, lines 11 and 12: *The fortress of Vellore . . . the ditch is large .*—Compare Leyden's 'Farewell Velura's moat-girt towers ('Poetical Remains' [1819], p. 159).

Page 463, line 15: *Pures.*—Mr. Philipps makes a very good suggestion. Why not 'Bohrahs,' who are Mahomedans, and likely to be on board a pilgrim ship? There is a form 'Bohari,' which comes very near Manucci's 'Pures' (H. H. Wilson, 'Glossary,' p. 91).

Page 464, line 11: *Even to* 1689.—According to Captain Hamilton, New Account,' i., pp. 202-219, 232, the trouble began at the end of 1687 with Governor Child's Paper of Grievances (thirty-five articles), to which Aurangzeb replied with a *farman* of the thirty-first year (July 11, 1687, to June 30, 1688).

Page 465, line 6: *Old Woman's Island.*—'Old Woman's Island is only separated from Bombay at flood-tide, and it can be easily reached on foot at the ebb' (J. H, Grose, 'Voyage to the East Indies,' edition of 1766, i. p. 57).

Page 466, line 5 from foot: *Najabat Khan.*—The new governor arrived in January, 1704. See Kaepplin, p. 532.

Page 467, line 1: *Attack on Surat.*—This event belongs to February, 1703. The Mahomedan officials did nothing, and left all defence to the foreign merchants. The Europeans fortified and defended their factories, and the Asiatics manned the walls. The environs were plundered, and after ten days the Mahrattahs retired with an immense booty (Kaepplin, p. 498, from French sources).

Page 467, second paragraph: *Arab raid.*—The Arabs of Masqat plundered Surat in September, 1703. See Kaepplin, p. 535.

Page 475, line 25, and note 257: *Palakollu.*—Palakollu was not the first settlement of the Dutch; there is a note on it in T. Bowrey, p. 105, note 2; and J. E. Heeres, 'Corpus Diplomaticum Neerlando-Indicum,' p. 232, note 2, corrects the erroneous date of 1652 in the 'Imperial Gazetteer,' p. 254. In Havart, iii. *et seq.*, is given the list of the Dutch chiefs of Palakollu from 1613 (D. W. F.).

Page 477, line 9; page 483, line 27: *Calabad, Calabay.*—Colonel D. G. Pitcher furnishes me with what must be accepted, I think, as a much better identification. He suggests Kalabagh, long. 77° 40′, lat. 24° 51′, a halting-place on the old Dakhin road, and over 100 miles south of Gwaliyar. See Indian Atlas, Sheet No. 52, south-east. In the 'Journal of John Jourdain' (Hakluyt Society, 1905), p. 151, it is spelt 'Collybaye,' and Tavernier (Ball's edition, i., pp. 57, 58) has it in the form of 'Callabas.' The place is certainly not very near to Gwaliyar, and south instead of north of Narwar, but in 1705 the Mahrattahs could hardly have penetrated much farther north than Kalabagh.

Page 483, line 21: The *college.*—This is possibly an allusion to the seminary established by the Société des Missions Etrangères of Paris, for the training of native priests. It was opened at Ayuthia (Juthia, Yuthia) in Siam about 1666, and there remained until 1767, when that town was destroyed. During 1767-69 it was at Hon Dôt, in Cambodia, and thence was transferred to Virampatnam, near Pondicherry. It was closed in 1782. In 1807, after the British had acquired the Straits Settlements, it was re-established at Penang, and there it still continues and flourishes. See 'Missiones Catholicæ . . . Descriptæ, Anno 1901,' Rome, 1901, p. 690.